Malcolm C. MacLeod

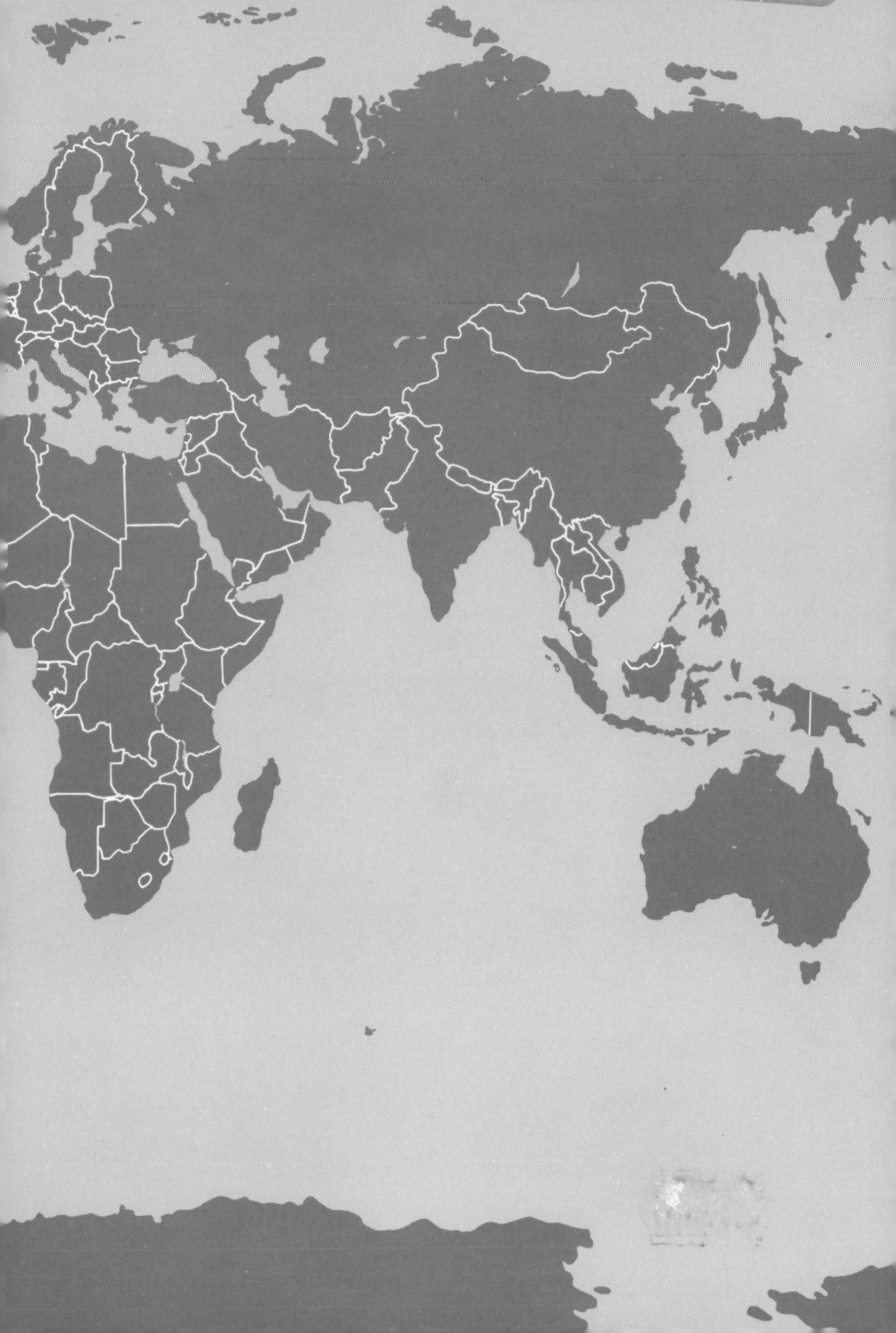

Iran
a country study

Foreign Area Studies
The American University
Edited by
Richard F. Nyrop
Research Completed
January 1978
DA Pam 550-68
Supersedes 1971 Edition

The winged lion on the cover

is part of a glazed brick
panel from Susa, on display
in the Tehran Archaeological
Museum

Library of Congress Cataloging in Publication Data

American University, Washington, D.C.   Foreign Area Studies.
   Iran, a country study.

   Supersedes the 1971 ed. prepared by H. H. Smith and others,
and issued under title: Area handbook for Iran.
   "Research completed January 1978."
   "DA pam 550–68."
   Bibliography: p. 455.
   Includes index.
   1. Iran.   I.   Nyrop, Richard F.   II.   Smith, Harvey Henry,
1892–   Area handbook for Iran. III Title.

DS254.5.A63   1978   955   78–11871

For sale by the Superintendent of Documents, U.S. Government Printing Office
Washington, D.C. 20402

Stock No. 008-020-00761-7

Foreword

This volume is one of a continuing series of books written by Foreign Area Studies, The American University, under the Area Handbook Program. Its title, format and substance reflect modifications introduced into the series in 1978. The last page of this book provides a listing of other country studies published. Each book in the series deals with a particular foreign country, describing and analyzing its economic, military, political, and social systems and institutions and examining the interrelationships of those systems and institutions and the ways that they are shaped by cultural factors. Each study is written by a multidisciplinary team of social scientists. The authors seek to provide a basic insight and understanding of the society under observation, striving for a dynamic rather than a static portrayal of it. The study focuses on historical antecedents and on the cultural, political, and socioeconomic characteristics that contribute to cohesion and cleavage within the society. Particular attention is given to the origins and traditions of the people who make up the society, their dominant beliefs and values, their community of interests and the issues on which they are divided, the nature and extent of their involvement with the national institutions, and their attitudes toward each other and toward the social system and political order within which they live.

The contents of the book represent the work of Foreign Area Studies and are not set forth as the official view of the United States government. The authors have sought to adhere to accepted standards of scholarly objectivity. Such corrections, additions, and suggestions for factual or other changes that readers may have will be welcomed for use in future revisions.

William Evans-Smith
Director, Foreign Area Studies
The American University
Washington, D.C. 20016

Acknowledgments

The authors are grateful to individuals in various agencies of the United States government who gave of their time, research materials, and special knowledge to provide data and perspective. Additionally a number of Iranian officials and private citizens resident in Washington, D.C., were most helpful.

The authors also wish to express their gratitude to members of the Foreign Area Studies staff who contributed directly to the preparation of the manuscript. These persons include Frederica M. Bunge, who, in her capacity as assistant director for research, reviewed all the textual material; Sheila Ross, who edited the manuscript; and Harriett R. Blood, who prepared the graphics. The team appreciates as well the assistance provided by Gilda V. Nimer, Librarian, and Ernest Will, Publications Manager.

Special thanks are owed to James R. Eschinger who is responsible for the typography and design of the new series of country studies (introduced in 1978) and for the concept for this cover, which shows a portion of a glazed brick panel from Susa. Execution of the concept was carried out by Maria Bach under the direction of Michael T. Graham, of The American University Department of Art. The inclusion of photographs in this study was made possible by the generosity of various individuals and public and private agencies. We acknowledge our indebtedness especially to those persons who contributed original work not previously published.

Preface

In early 1978 the government of Iran—which is to say the monarch, Shahanshah Mohammad Reza Pahlavi—was continuing its impressive and expensive industrial expansion, economic diversification, and military buildup. The unprecedented increases in world prices for petroleum in the early and mid-1970s vastly increased the government's revenues and enabled it to order massive quantities of sophisticated military equipment. Between 1971 and 1977 Iran placed approximately US$11.8 billion of orders with American aircraft and other weapons manufacturers and bought additional weapon systems elsewhere, particularly from Great Britain but also from France, the Federal Republic of Germany (West Germany), and the Soviet Union. The government also invested large sums in several industrial firms in Western Europe. Iran possessed one of the strongest military forces in the Middle East, and its foreign economic activities had significantly enhanced its regional and worldwide importance.

This study replaces the *Area Handbook for Iran* (1971), large sections of which were seriously outdated. The study results from the combined efforts of a Foreign Area Studies multidisciplinary team of researchers assisted by the organization's support staff. Sources of information included scholarly studies, official reports of governments and international organizations, foreign and domestic newspapers, and numerous periodicals. A bibliography of sources used appears at the end of the book; brief comments on some of the more valuable sources as possible further reading appear at the end of most chapters. Responsibility for the presentation of the data and perspective of course remains with the authors. Although notice is taken in chapter 12 of the riots that occurred in Tabriz in early March 1978, the research for this book was completed in January of that year.

Economic and demographic data ranged from excellent to questionable to not available. Except for data on oil production and revenues and on weapons procurement, which are relatively up-to-date and reliable, the data should be used with caution.

The transliteration of Farsi (Persian) words and phrases posed a particular problem. For words that are of direct Arabic origin—such as Muhammad (the Prophet), *mujtahid*, Muslim, Quran, and shariah—the authors followed a modified version of the system for Arabic adopted by the United States Board on Geographic Names and the Permanent Committee on Geographic Names for British Official Use, known as the BGN/PCGN system. (The modification is a significant one, entailing the deletion of all diacritical marks and hyphens.) The BGN/PCGN system was also used to transliterate Farsi, again without the diacritics. In numerous instances, however, place-names were so well known by another spelling that to have used the BGN/PCGN system might have caused confusion. For example, the reader will find Meshed rather than Mashhad and Isfahan rather than Esfahan.

An effort has been made to limit the use of foreign words and phrases. Those deemed essential to an understanding of the society have been briefly defined where they first appear in a chapter or reference has been made to the Glossary, included for the reader's convenience. Iran officially employs the metric system, which is also used by most large commercial and industrial firms. In the older bazaars of the cities and in the rural markets, however, an indigenous system continues in use (see weights and measures in the Glossary).

Although the Islamic hijra calendar, which has 354 days divided into twelve months, continues in use for religious purposes, official and private business are conducted according to the Iranian calendar, which like the Gregorian calendar has 365 days and a leap year. The Iranian New Year's Day (No Ruz) is on March 21 of the Gregorian calendar. The fiscal year is the same as the calendar year; fiscal year (FY) 1977, for example, began on March 21, 1977, and ended on March 20, 1978. The Gregorian calendar year 1977 corresponds roughly to the Iranian calendar year 2535, a variation of approximately 558 years. A comparison of the three calendars is provided for the reader's convenience (see fig. A). A chronology of important historical events is also included (see table A).

Richard F. Nyrop

*   *   *

On August 27, 1978—eight months after research and writing on this study were completed and only days before the book actually went to press—the shah appointed Jaafar Sharif-Emmami prime minister. Sharif-Emmami, who had served as prime minister for a brief period in 1960 and 1961 and who when appointed was the president of the Senate, replaced Jamshid Amuzegar, who had been in office only a year. All but five of the other twenty-four cabinet ministers were also replaced; General Reza Azimi, minister of war, and Mohammad Yeganeh, minister of economic affairs and finance, were two prominent ministers who retained their posts.

The cabinet changes came in the wake of eight months of increasingly violent demonstrations against the government in most major cities; hundreds of people had been killed, hundreds more wounded, and an unknown number imprisoned. By June 1978 most universities had been closed. Although the government blamed both the "red Marxists" and the "black conservatives" among the Islamic clergy (see Glossary), it was becoming more and more evident that students, bazaar merchants, and numerous other urban groups were joining the religious extremists in attacks on the government. On August 19 a theater in the oil refinery city of Abadan was set on fire, causing the deaths of nearly 400 people. The government arrested a number of schoolteachers and charged them with the crime, but on Friday, August 25, tens of thousands of people listened to inflammatory speeches in the city's mosques and then moved onto the streets in particularly violent demonstrations that were directed not against the schoolteachers or the government but specifically against the shah. During the disturbances senior religious leaders openly stated to foreign newspaper correspondents that "the shah must go."

The new prime minister, who reportedly has close personal relations with many of the more prominent religious leaders, announced a number of immediate concessions to the conservative religious groups. Among the concessions were the abolition of the cabinet post of minister of state for women's affairs and the banning of gambling. In addition the prime minister reinstituted the Muslim hijra calendar as the official calendar, replacing the imperial Iranian calendar that had been adopted in 1976 at the specific request of the shah. In an apparent attempt to underscore the regime's awareness of the need to become more tolerant and responsive, his new cabinet also reportedly removed the censorship of the privately owned press and took other steps designed to loosen many years of rigorous restraints on political life. Perhaps as a result, as many as thirty groups are said to have announced their intention to organize themselves into new political parties.

In June 1978 the shah announced the appointment of a new chief of the National Intelligence and Security Organization (Sazeman Ettelaat va Amniyat Kashvar—SAVAK), Lieutenant General Naser Moqaddam (see SAVAK, ch. 12). Observers noted that in the cabinet appointed on August 27 the new minister of interior was General Abbas Gharabaghi, until that time the commander of the Imperial Iranian Gendarmerie. Gharabaghi was reputed to be a tough, aggressive, law and order official. According to newspaper reports from Tehran, the concessions to the religious leaders were being accompanied by the quiet arrests of some of the more extreme and violence prone religious leaders and their detention in, or exile to, remote sections of the country.

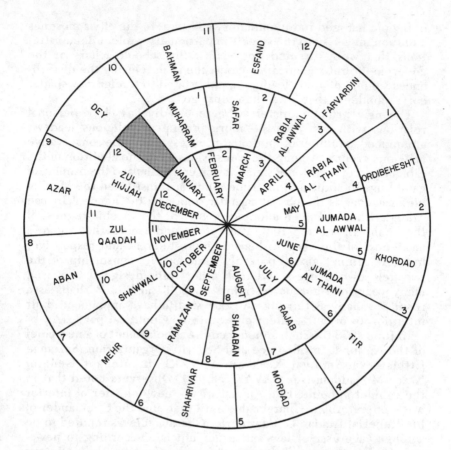

Note—The center circle represents the Gregorian calendar, the middle circle the Hijra (or Muslim) calendar, and the outer circle the Iranian calendar. Gregorian 1978 corresponds, approximately, to Hijra 1398 and to Iranian 2536. Six Iranian months—Farvardin, Ordibehesht, Khordad, Tir, Mordad, and Shahrivar—have thirty-one days and five—Mehr, Aban, Azar, Dey, and Bahman—have thirty days. The twelfth month, Esfand, has twenty-nine days except in leap years when it has thirty days. The first day of Farvardin, No Ruz or New Year's Day, is March 21. Shaded area represents eleven-day discrepancy between Hijra (lunar) calendar and solar calendar.

Figure A. *Comparison of Iranian, Hijra, and Gregorian Calendars*

Table A. Chronology of Important Events

Periods and Dates	Events
PRE-MEDEAN	
ca. 6000–2000 B.C.	Settled agriculture among indigenous peoples; brick dwellings; pottery; major settlements at Susa, Tepe Hisar, Sialk, Tepe Gujan, Zuriyeh, Hansanlu
ca. 1500 B.C.	Migratory invasions into region by Medes, Scythians, and Parsua (Persians)
MEDEAN EMPIRE (614 B.C.)	Medean chief, Cyaxeres (Uvakhstra), captured and leveled Assyrian capital, Nineveh; expansion of area under Medean control; the Parsua became vassals of Medes
ACHAEMENIDS (550–330 B.C.) .	Cambyses I, son of Cyrus I, married a daughter of Medean king; their son, Cyrus II, subjugated Medes and then established world empire; Zoroastrianism became most important religion
Cyrus II (559–529 B.C.)	Capture of Babylon in 539 B.C.; empire extended east to Hindu Kush
Cambyses II (529–522 B.C.) ..	Invaded and captured Egypt, Palestine, Syria, and parts of Asia Minor
Darius I (522–486 B.C.)	Crushed Egyptian revolt; Battle of Marathon in 490 B.C.; retreat of empire to Asia Minor
Xerxes (486–465 B.C.)	Period of military defeats in west
465–330 B.C.	Disintegration of Achaemenid power; last ruler in dynasty killed by his subjects
GREEK OCCUPATION	
331–323 B.C.	Alexander the Great invaded and conquered region; Hellenistic culture amalgamated with indigenous culture
311–150 B.C.	Descendants of Alexander's general, Seleucus, sought to maintain geographical integrity of empire in face of local rebellions and foreign incursions
PARTHIAN EMPIRE (129 B.C.–A.D. 226)	Parthian Arsacids expanded and eventually overcame Seleucids; assimilation of Greek governmental practices; old Persian title king of kings restored; country organized on feudal basis with vassal princes
SASSANIAN EMPIRE (A.D. 226–641)	First native dynasty since Achaemenids and was patterned after them; king relied on Zoroastrian clergy and nobility to operate highly centralized government; entrenched class system

ISLAMIC CONQUEST

ca. 642–ca. 800 .... Arab Muslim armies overcame and easily conquered region, which falls under rule of Arab caliphates; by ca. 800 bulk of inhabitants converted to Islam; country divided into provinces headed by military governors; most administrators Iranians

ca. 800–ca. 1050 .... Rise of minor and localized Iranian dynasties; Iranian nationalism expressed in growing adherence to Shiite (Shia) Islam; literature stressed pre-Islamic themes and language

SELJUQ EMPIRE

(1037–1157) .... Seljuq Turks conquered local kingdoms, incorporating them into Seljuq Empire; Seljuqs sought to reassert Sunni Islam; rise of the "Assasins," an Ismaili group committed to political resistance to Seljuq, Sunni rule

MONGOL INVASIONS .... In 1220 armies of Genghis Khan invaded and devastated much of Iran

Ilkhanid Dynasty .... Successors of Mongol invaders converted
(1256–ca. 1375) to Islam and adopted Iranian culture; excellent administration and extensive patronage of the arts

Timurid Dynasty .... Central Asian Turkic-speaking people led
(ca. 1375–1499) by Timur (Tamerlane) wrest control of Iran from Ilkhanids, whose administrative procedures were retained; flourishing of arts and sciences, period of famous poet Hafiz

SAFAVID DYNASTY (1502–1736) First native dynasty in eight centuries; traced its line to Seventh Shia Imam. Shia Islam proclaimed state religion; shah had virtually absolute rule; period of intense nationalism

Shah Abbas (1587–1628) .... Opened Iran to west; granted concessions to Dutch and British; public works at state expense; consolidation of power of the monarchy

AFSHAR DYNASTY (1736–50) ..... Nadir Shah, tribesman from north and military genius, proclaimed himself shah; numerous forays into India; Sunni Islam proclaimed state religion; overtaxation of land; poor administration

ZAND DYNASTY (1750–94) .... Muhammad Karim Khan Zand established dynasty with capital in Shiraz; many social and community improvements; struggle for supremacy among Turkish tribes

QAJAR DYNASTY (1796–1925)	Turkish Qajar tribe established itself as central power; landholders acquired greater power
Fath Ali Shah .... (1797–1834)	Army ill equipped; by Treaty of Gulistan, Georgia ceded to Czarist Russia; intense rivalry between Russia and Great Britain for Iranian interests
Nasir al Din Shah .... (1848–96)	Sought to create modern army; commercial concessions made to British to increase holdings of treasury; public agitation against foreign influence
1905–06	Shah forced to proclaim constitution and establish an elective assembly
1907	Iran divided into spheres of influence by Russia and Great Britain
1908–11	Shah's counterconstitutional coup overturned by tribal forces
1914–17	Iran declared itself neutral in World War I and was then occupied by Russian and British troops; central government emasculated
1921–25	Coup d'etat led by Reza Khan; tribal rebellions suppressed; 1924 end of Qajar Dynasty
PAHLAVI DYNASTY (1925–) .	Reza Khan founded Pahlavi dynasty and instituted numerous Westernizing reforms; oil royalties used to finance development
1941	Iran had declared itself netural in 1939; British, Russian, and American troops invaded and occupied Iran; Reza Shah abdicated in favor of son, Mohammad Reza Pahlavi, who succeeded to throne
1951–53	Prime Minister Mohammad Mossadeq nationalized oil industry, which provoked boycott by European powers; Mossadeq ousted; return of shah to position of central authority
1963	Proclamation by shah of White Revolution of the Shah and the People (Shah-People Revolution)
1965	Majlis conferred title Aryamehr (Light of the Aryans) on shah
1967	Formal coronation of Shah and Shahbanou; their eldest son, Reza Cyrus, named crown prince

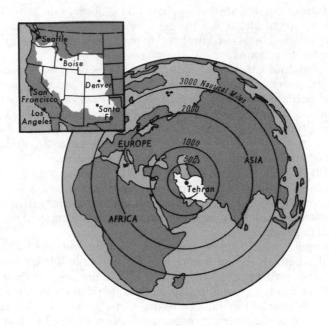

Country

Formal Name: Empire of Iran.
Short Form: Iran.
Term for Citizens: Iranian.
Capital: Tehran.

Geography

Size: Land area of about 636,000 square miles; sovereignty claimed over territorial waters up to twelve nautical miles.

Topography: Large central plateau surrounded on three sides by rugged mountain ranges. Highest peak is Mount Damavand, given as more than 18,000 feet; Caspian Sea listed as about ninety-two feet below sea level.

Climate: Annual rainfall is about fifty inches in the mountains of the west and southwest with heaviest concentrations from December to March; in the Central Plateau desert, less than two inches. Temperatures vary from −18°F in the mountainous northwest to 132°F in parts of the desert. In the northwest winters frequently exceed six months; summers are short and mild. In the desert freezing temperatures occur in winter, and some areas are without rain for years.

Society
Population: Estimated at well over 34 million in mid-1977, growing at a rate of about 2.7 percent per annum. Population almost evenly divided between rural and urban; nomands and seminomads estimated to account for less than 5 percent.

Education and Literacy: Education basically free at primary and secondary levels, and financial assistance provided at higher levels. Enrollments doubled between 1963 and 1973, and expansion was continuing in late 1970s. Despite growth and activities of Literacy Corps, literacy estimated at about 37 percent in 1977. Local universities had scores of thousands of students; an estimated 60,000 Iranians study abroad, mostly in the United States.

Health: Chief causes of mortality reported as infant diseases, gastrointestinal diseases, respiratory system diseases, and parasitic diseases. Modern medical services expanding rapidly in mid-1970s but estimated additional 22,000 doctors needed to augment services of 12,000 in practice.

Languages: Farsi (or Persian as it is known outside Iran), is the official language, is the native tongue of over half the population, and is spoken as a second language by the majority of the remainder. Turkic languages, Kurdish, and Arabic also important.

Ethnic Groups: Persians constitute the largest ethnic group (63 percent); other important groups are Kurds, Azarbaijanis, Lurs, Baktiaris, Qashqais, Baluchis, and Arabs.

Religion: Shiite Islam official religion with approximately 90 percent adherence; also Sunni Muslims, Jews, Armenian Christians, Assyrian Christians, Bahais, and Zoroastrians.

Government and Politics
Governmental Structure: Constitutional monarchy and highly centralized unitary state in which Shahanshah Mohammad Reza Pahlavi plays an active decisionmaking role in important affairs of state. The shah, who ascended the throne in 1941, is head of state and de facto head of government, although technically the head of government is the prime minister who is appointed by the shah to chair the cabinet of ministers. The governmental system rests on the constitutional system laid down in 1906 and 1907 and is divided into executive, bicameral legislature (the lower house Majlis and Senate), and judiciary.

Politics: One-party system under the Iran National Resurgence Party (Rastakhiz-e-Mellat-e-Iran or, more popularly, the Rastakhiz Party) since March 1975. The party serves as the political arm of the shah-centered system whose three supreme principles affirm the inviolability of the monarchy, the Constitution, and the Shah-People Revolution (known originally as the White Revolution—see Glossary). In 1977 all political and governmental efforts remained committed to the achievement of multifaceted goals set forth since 1963 under wide-ranging programs of national modernization known as the Shah-People Revolution. The armed forces continue to serve as the most—and the only—important power base for the shah. Political opposition is minor but vocal and potentially volatile, especially if the country's college students, intellectuals, and some religious leaders find a common organizational focus. Possibility of organized, effective dissidence remained slight, given the omnipresence of the shah's secret police, the National Intelligence and Security Organization (Sazeman Ettelaat va Amniyat Kashvar—SAVAK).

Administrative Divisions: Country divided into twenty-three provinces *(ostans)*, each under a governor general *(ostandar)*; a province subdivided into districts *(shahrestans)*, each under a governor *(farmandar)*; each district, into subdistricts *(bakhsh)* under lieutenant governors *(bakhshdar)* and into cities and towns; each subdistrict, into countries or townships *(dehistans)*, under sheriffs *(dehdar)*; each township, into villages *(deh)* under village headmen *(kadkhudas*—see Glossary). Except for village headmen, all local heads are appointive and are answerable to the central Ministry of Interior.

Judicial System: The judiciary consists of the Supreme Court (also called the Court of Cassation); the courts of appeal or high courts; district courts; and the houses of equity (for rural areas) and the councils of arbitration (for cities). Military courts also are integral part of judicial system with jurisdiction over broadly phrased political crimes.

International Affairs: Increasingly independent foreign policy posture, though allied with the West through mutual defense pacts—multilaterally through the Central Treaty Organization (CENTO) and bilaterally with the United States. No major sources of friction with any foreign state. Growing emphasis placed on the centrality of self-reliant defense capability to ensure the security and stability of the Persian Gulf and Indian Ocean regions. A member of the United Nations (UN); diplomatic ties with more than 120 nations.

Economy

Salient Features: A developing country using its oil revenues to establish an industrial base for self-sustaining growth in future. Gross national product (GNP) approximately US$57.5 billion in fiscal year (FY—see Glossary) 1976. GNP per year capita about US$2,200 in September 1977. GNP growth rate 29 percent a year in constant prices FY 1971–FY 1974. Economy ranked fifteenth in noncommunist world in 1977. Has extensive natural resources for development.

Oil Industry: Fourth largest producer and second largest exporter in world in 1976. (United States, Soviet Union, and Saudi Arabia largest producers, Saudi Arabia largest exporter.) Oil revenues about US$20 billion in FY 1976. Oil production expected to decline in mid-1980s unless there are large new finds. Very large natural gas deposits (perhaps largest in world) for future energy and petrochemical use.

Industry: Accounted for 18 percent of gross domestic product (GDP) including manufacturing, construction, water, and power in FY 1975 and largest source of employment. Extensive range of manufacturing from handicraft carpets to latest technological processes in steel and petrochemicals. Industry fast developing since 1960; will be economy's major source of income and employment in future.

Agriculture: Accounted for 9 percent of GDP in FY 1975 and employed about 30 percent of work force. Scarcity of water and use of traditional farming practices caused sector to grow more slowly than population in 1970s. Country hopes to become self-sufficient in grains by 1980s but will remain large importer of food for many years.

Foreign Trade: Exports about US$15 billion in FY 1976 of which 96 percent from oil. Imports nearly US$13 billion in FY 1976—52 percent intermediate goods, 30 percent machinery, and 18 percent consumer goods. Trade predominantly with industrialized countries.

International Finance: Fairly heavy foreign borrowing in FY 1976 and FY 1977 to finance budget and development. Some direct investment by foreign corporations. Had large foreign aid and investment program. Net exporter of capital in FY 1974–75.

Currency: Rial (see Glossary).

Transportation and Communications

Roads: In 1976 nearly 34,000 miles of roads, of which about 12,000 miles asphalt, about 11,000 miles of surfaced feeder roads, and 11,000 miles of improved earth. Main areas connected but lacked sufficient feeder roads. Some areas still lacked roads and modern transport.

Railroads: About 2,700 miles of standard-gauge track. Rail connections with Turkey and Soviet Union. Large capacity increase and additional international connections planned.

Pipelines: About 5,100 miles in 1976. Pipelines used for most movement of crude, petroleum products, and natural gas.

Airports: Eighteen major airports in 1976 of which two (Tehran and Abadan) were international.

Communications: Most advanced telecommunications in Middle East with high capacity network and good links to other parts of world. About 800,000 phones in 1976, far fewer than potential subscribers.

National Security

Armed Forces (1977): Army—220,000; navy—30,000; air force—100,000. Majority conscripted.

Combat Units and Major Equipment: 1977: Army—three armored divisions, four infantry divisions, four independent brigades, one surface-to-air missile (SAM) battalion. Army Aviation Command; over 3,000 tanks, over 600 combat helicopters (including those on order). Navy—about sixty combat vessels including destroyers, frigates, and hovercraft; three marine battalions; naval air with forty aircraft. Air force—twenty-two fighter squadrons, one reconnaissance squadron, three SAM battalions; 652 combat aircraft in inventory or on order.

Military Budget (1976): US$9.5 billion. About 30 percent of government expenditures; 17.4 percent of GDP.

Police Agencies (1977): Gendarmerie—75,000; National Police—40,000; SAVAK—10,000, estimated.

Foreign Military Treaties: Member of CENTO.

A 1959 executive agreement with the United States provides that "in case of aggression against Iran, the . . . United States . . . will take such appropriate action, including the use of armed forces, as may be mutually agreed upon . . ."

Contents

ANCIENT IRAN—Pre-Achaemenid Iran—Immigration of the Medes and Persians—Achaemenid Empire (550–330 B.C.)—Alexander the Great, the Seleucids, and the Parthians — Sassanian Empire (A.D. 226–641)— ISLAMIC CONQUEST — INVASIONS OF THE MONGOLS AND TAMERLANE—SAFAVID DYNASTY (1502–1736)—RISE OF THE QAJAR DYNASTY— Nationalism and Revolution— Foreign Influence and the World War I Period— REZA SHAH AND THE ESTABLISHMENT OF THE PAHLAVI DYNASTY —WORLD WAR II AND THE AZARBAIJAN CRISIS —MOHAMMAD MOSSADEQ AND OIL NATIONAL-IZATION—MOHAMMAD REZA PAHLAVI AND THE WHITE REVOLUTION

POPULATION STRUCTURE AND DYNAMICS— FAMILY PLANNING—SETTLEMENT PATTERNS— LABOR FORCE—DIET AND NUTRITION— HOUSING—CONSUMPTION PATTERNS — RECREATION — WELFARE — HEALTH—Medical Personnel and Facilities— Health Hazards and Preventive Medicine—Water Supply and Sanitation—Traditional Beliefs and Practices—EDUCATION

PRE-ISLAMIC RELIGIONS—The Cult of Mithra— Manichaeism and Mazdakism—ISLAMIC CONQUEST —BASIC ISLAMIC BELIEFS—SHIA BRANCH OF ISLAM—Shia Dogma—Religious Obligations of Shia Islam—Religious Institutions and Organizations— Organization of the Shiite Religion—Deviant Religious Movements—MINORITY RELIGIONS

National Iranian Oil Company—Consortium Agreement—Other Concessions—Sales and Purchase Agreement, 1973—Production and Revenues—Refineries and Terminals—Natural Gas— Domestic Consumption of Petroleum— OTHER INDUSTRY—Early Industrialization—Natural Resources—Electric Power Base—Industrialization Since World War II—The Legacy of Rapid Growth

List of Figures

List of Tables

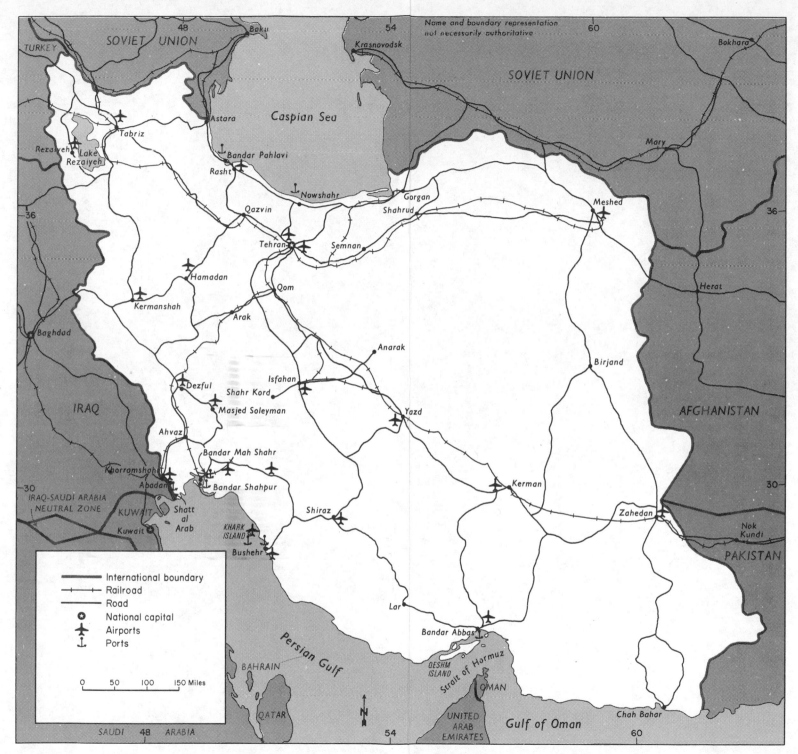

Figure 1. Iran

Chapter 1. General Character of the Society

TO THE MAJORITY of Iranians—the Western-educated elite as well as the great bulk of the population whose knowledge of secular and religious history is derived from legends and folk beliefs—the establishment and expansion of the Achaemenid Empire by Cyrus II and Darius I in the sixth century B.C. are surpassed in importance and reality only by the central role in Iranian life of Shiite Islam. The land that is now Iran was invaded numerous times in the twenty-five centuries between Cyrus II and the ruler in early 1978, Mohammad Reza Pahlavi, but the indigenous peoples assimilated the conquerors and their cultures and made them Iranian. This they did with Islam.

Islam was, and remains, a monotheistic religion centered on the message transmitted by the Prophet Muhammad (see Basic Islamic Beliefs, ch. 4). Muhammad began his ministry in A.D. 610, and by the time of his death in 632 he and his followers had secured control of all of Arabia and had begun the outward movement that would in a few centuries conquer and convert most of the Middle East, North Africa, Spain, and large parts of South Asia. By 650 the Sassanian Empire had been defeated by a small but efficient Arab force (see Islamic Conquest, ch. 2). Within a few years the first and the greatest schism in Islamic history occurred, and three deaths associated with that schism would be of lasting significance to Iran's civic and religious culture.

Muhammad had not designated a successor to his role as caliph (temporal ruler), and after his death there were disagreements and disputes on this matter among his followers. The first two caliphs, Abu Bakr and Umar, were nevertheless chosen unanimously. The election of Uthman as the third caliph was opposed, however, and later disputed. The opposition favored the candidacy of Ali, a cousin and close associate of the Prophet who had chosen Ali to marry Fatima, the Prophet's only child. When Uthman was murdered, Ali was elected the fourth caliph, but the cleavage between the Party of Ali (Shiat Ali) and other Muslims steadily worsened. Battles between Muslims broke out for the first time, and theological disputes became increasingly bitter.

In 661 Ali was killed while at prayer in a mosque in Kufa (present-day Karbala in Iraq). Shortly thereafter Hassan, his first son, died, reputedly poisoned by the new caliph. In 680 Husayn, Ali's second son, was killed with 200 male and female followers at Kufa. These three deaths set the pattern of martyrs, mysticism, and sainthood that has since distinguished Shiite (or Shia) Islam. The deaths of the Prophet's only son-in-law and his only grandsons have always struck a responsive chord in the Iranian psyche.

There are at least a few Shiites in all Muslim countries, and in a few Muslim states they form influential minorities. In Iran, however, between 85 and 90 percent of the population adhere to Shia

3

Islam. An Egyptian, or Syrian, or Pakistani Shiite reveres the twelve Shia Imams (see Glossary) as descendants of the Prophet and as saintly religious figures. An Iranian Shiite, however, venerates a figure such as Imam Reza, the Eighth Imam, not only as a martyr and a saintly intercessor for mortals in time of need but also as an authentically Iranian national hero (see Shia Branch of Islam, ch. 4).

A central article of faith concerns the Twelfth Imam, Muhammad al Muntazar, who went into hiding (known as occultation) in the ninth century to avoid assassination by the caliph, the fate of most of his predecessors. Shiites believe that this Imam (known as Imami Asr, the Imam of the Period, and Sahib al Zaman, the Lord of the Age) is not dead and will someday reveal himself, abolish all fake religions, punish the wicked, and reward the faithful. Iran's Constitution, which specifies Shiite Islam as the state religion, provides that pending the return of the Imami Asr, the shah rules in his stead as the caretaker of the nation and the people.

The Imamate began with Ali, and he remains the key figure. To be a Muslim an individual must, at least once in his or her lifetime, utter the fundamental articles of faith, the *shahada*, with unquestioning acceptance and belief. Sunnis, members of the majority branch of Islam, attest that "There is no God (Allah) but God and Muhammad is his Prophet." (*Allah* is the Arabic word for god, not the name of *a* god.) Shiites, to the dismay of the Sunnis, add the phrase "Muhammad is the Prophet of God and Ali is the Saint of God."

By the tenth century most Iranians were Shiites, and the religion at the popular and official level had incorporated many aspects of pre-Islamic religious and cultural beliefs and attitudes. This was most apparent with respect to the monarch, known as the shah. Ancient inscriptions frequently identify the shah as a god, as blessed by god or the gods, and as the interpreter of the will of the gods. Almost without interruption throughout its history, Iran has been ruled by a monarch, whose rule was generally accepted as one of divine right. At times the shah's rule was forceful and complete, reaching directly or indirectly to each corner of the realm. At other times the shah reigned as an incompetent voluptuary, almost inviting an internal coup or a foreign conqueror, and one or the other almost always came. But the concept of an absolute monarch was only rarely challenged and when challenged even more rarely successful.

In early 1978 the shah (Shahanshah Aryamehr—the King of Kings and the Light of the Aryans) faced no serious challenge. He almost lost the Peacock Throne in 1953, but with American encouragement and assistance he retained the loyalty of key senior military officers who crushed his opponents (see Mohammad Mossadeq and Oil Nationalization, ch. 2). In 1967 he crowned himself shahanshah and crowned his wife, Farah Diba, as the empress, or shahbanou (meaning wife of the shah). By the mid-

1970s the shah was firmly situated at the apex of a stratified, hierachical society and of a political system that possessed no effective legal checks on his official activities. All important economic, military, and political decisions either were made by him personally or were made by trusted aides who were keenly aware of the shah's wishes (see ch. 6; ch. 7; ch. 13).

To a marked degree he determined the composition of the small elite upper class, which included less than 1 percent of the population (see Structure of Society, ch. 5). The shah retained and exercised absolute control over the promotions and assignments of all middle and senior grade military, police, and security officers and civil service officials, and he possessed a virtual monopoly of political power. Because of the government's dominance in the economic sphere in terms of credit, import licenses, taxes, and contracts, the shah could reward or penalize industrialists and commercial entrepreneurs. The implementation of his 1963 land reform legislation had, by the mid-1970s, effectively destroyed the political power of the great, absentee landlords who theretofore had posed the most effective challenge to his rule (see Land Reform, ch. 11).

In addition to his control over the elite and his ability to reward or punish economically the members of the expanding middle class of skilled technicians, midlevel professionals and managers, bazaar merchants, and related occupations, the shah's government exercised considerable power to determine what the people heard and read about events in Iran and abroad. Radio and television were government owned and operated and were the most important channels for transmitting official versions of domestic and foreign news. Although there were some privately owned newspapers and journals, they were subject to direct and indirect censorship (see table 1, Appendix A). Nothing, for example, could be printed that was critical of the shah. Moreover newspaper publishers depended heavily on government advertising and on its supplies of newsprint. In sum, many observers asserted that the shah's dominance in such traditional areas as military power and political affairs and his influence over and manipulation of mass communications, the economy, and the society made his control of the state and the people more pervasive than any of his predecessors.

The shah's immediate predecessor was his father, Reza Shah Pahlavi, who founded the Pahlavi dynasty in 1925. Reza Shah had sought to remain neutral when World War II began in 1939. He retained close commercial ties with Nazi Germany, however, and after Germany attacked the Soviet Union, he refused to allow the transit of war matériel and supplies through Iran to the Soviets. British and Soviet forces. Fearing that the British and the Soviets might abolish the monarchy to get rid of him, Reza Shah abdicated in favor of his son, who was twenty-two when he assumed the throne on September 16, 1941.

By the mid-1960s Mohammad Reza Pahlavi had established his political control, which he has since refined and institutionalized. Also, he had intensified the efforts to industrialize the economy that his father had begun in the 1930s, and he had begun the process of modernizing and expanding the armed forces. Steadily increasing oil revenues enabled the shah in 1967 to be less dependent on aid and assistance from foreign governments, particularly from the United States, which had been providing extensive help for almost two decades.

Oil was discovered in Iran in 1908, the earliest discovery in the Middle East (see Appendix B). By the mid-1970s Iran was the fourth largest producer of oil in the world, and only neighboring Saudi Arabia exported more oil. Between 1955, by which time Iran's nationalization of its petroleum industry was complete, and 1974 crude oil production and oil revenues rose dramatically. In 1955 a daily average of 329,000 barrels per day (see Glossary) was produced, providing oil receipts for the year of slightly over US$90 million. By 1964 average daily production reached almost 1.7 million barrels, and the year's receipts were in excess of US$482 million. In 1973 the average daily production was over 5.9 million, and receipts were almost US$4.4 billion. By 1974 daily production averaged just over 6 million barrels, but because of sharp increases in oil prices, receipts jumped to more than US$21.4 billion. Production, and therefore receipts, decreased considerably in 1976 and 1977 as a result of reduced demand, probably temporary, by Iran's customers.

By the mid-1980s Iran's oil production will, unless new oil fields are discovered, begin a slow but steady decline. Observers predict that by about the mid-1990s Iran's decreasing reserves will be adequate to meet the economy's increasing demands but that Iran will cease to be a factor in the international oil business. The nation's proven reserves of natural gas are huge, however, and its exports of gas—in the late 1970s confined to the Soviet Union—may be expanded. The government's economic planners project a heavy use of gas as a fuel source and as a component in its constantly growing petrochemical industries (see Oil Industry, ch. 10).

As a result of the massive increases in oil revenues the shah was able to accelerate efforts to achieve his goal of making Iran one of the top five world powers by the year 2000. Huge sums of money were allocated to industry, irrigation projects, expansion and modernization of transportation systems, education, and various social services. The largest single category of expenditures by far, however, was devoted to modernizing and expanding the military and security services (see ch. 9).

By late 1977 the armed forces numbered about 350,000: the army had about 220,000; the navy, 30,000; and the air force, 100,000. This was nearly double the figures for 1967 when the army had about 164,000 officers and men; the navy, 6,000; and the air force, 10,000. The increase in equipment was equally impres-

Shahyadi Aryamehr Monument, Tehran

sive. In 1967, for example, the air force had two tactical fighter squadrons with F-5s; four interceptor squadrons with F-86s; and one tactical reconnaissance squadron with RT-33s. By mid-1977 the air force had in its inventory or on order 173 fighter bombers (F-4E and F-4D) equipped with air-to-air and air-to-surface missiles and 421 fighters (twelve F-5A; 141 F-5E; twenty-eight F-5F; eighty F-14A with Phoenix missiles; and 160 F-16 on order. In addition the air force possessed a large transport and tanker fleet and a large and expanding force of helicopters (see Organization, Size, and Equipment, ch. 13). The weapons systems of the army and navy were also undergoing a truly massive acquisition of sophisticated weapons.

The shah and his spokesmen justified the arms expenditures on a number of geopolitical factors. The most obvious of these factors, though not the decisive one, was Iran's long boundary with past enemies who were potential future adversaries (see fig. 1). In 1962 Iran stated that it would never serve as a site for foreign (American) nuclear weapons aimed at the Soviet Union, and since that time Iran and the Soviets have engaged in mutually advantageous commercial and diplomatic relations (see ch. 8; Oil Industry, ch. 10) Nevertheless Iran's leaders remember that during the nineteenth and early twentieth century, Czarist Russia frequently interfered in Iranian affairs and, with the United Kingdom, claimed a sphere of influence. In the aftermath of World War II the Soviet Union was instrumental in the creation of two short-lived secessionist republics in northwest Iran and desisted from those activities only under strong pressure from the United Nations and the United States (see Rise of the Qajar Dynasty, World War II and the Azarbaijan Crisis, ch. 2).

Iran's relations with Pakistan and Turkey, fellow members of the Central Treaty Organization (CENTO) and the Regional Cooperation for Development (RDC), have long been close, and relations with Afghanistan have at least been correct. Relations with Iraq, however, have at times been close to full-scale war. The Baath Party government in Iraq, which has governed since a violent military coup in 1958 that included the murder of the king and his chief officials, long served as a haven for anti-shah refugees from Iran. Beginning in the late 1960s Iran substantially increased its unofficial assistance to Kurdish rebels in Iraq. In 1975, however, the two states concluded an agreement that resolved several specific problems. Among other agreements Iran ended its aid to the Kurdish rebels, and Iraq accepted Iran's claim to a thalweg division of the Shaat al Arab, i.e., the center of the main navigable channel of the waterway was made the boundary line between the two states (see ch. 8).

The matter of greatest external concern to Iran centered on sea traffic through the Strait of Hormuz, which links the Persian Gulf—the locale of the oil-exporting ports of Iran and most of the Arabian Peninsula oil states—with the Gulf of Oman, the Indian

Ocean, and the sea-lanes of the world. The strait is one of the most heavily used waterways in the world, and Iran would undoubtedly resist any effort by an unfriendly power to gain control of the strait. Moreover the shah clearly views the stability of the conservative monarchical regimes of the Arabian Peninsula as vital to Iran's national interest. The shah also desires that at some time in the future the Indian Ocean will become subject to the protection and control of the expanding Imperial Iranian Navy.

Iran claims twelve nautical miles of territorial waters, and at one point this claim overlaps the territorial waters of the Sultanate of Oman, which also claims twelve nautical miles. The main sea channel is in Oman's territorial water (see fig. 2). In the mid-1970s

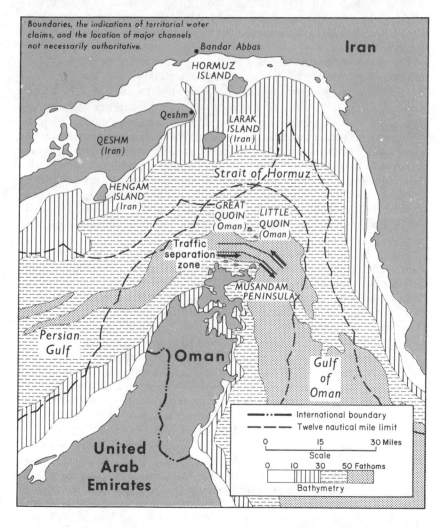

Figure 2. Strait of Hormuz

Iran provided extensive military support to the Omani government to assist it in suppressing a rebellion. Iran could be expected to react sharply to a threat to Oman's stability and its sovereignty vis-à-vis the strait.

Among the more formidable of the many obstacles to attaining world power status within a generation are the low rate of literacy and the generally grim state of agriculture. Of the population of approximately 34 million in 1977, only an estimated 37 percent were literate. Some observers believed that the literacy rate was inflated. In the mid-1970s, for example, approximately half of enlisted army personnel were either illiterate or only marginally literate. Because these individuals—mostly conscripts—were young enough to have benefited from the expansion of the educational system in the late 1960s and early 1970s one may reasonably conclude that the literacy rate for the population as a whole was below 37 percent.

The low rate poses several economic and military problems. The severe shortage of skilled laborers, technicians, medical services personnel, engineers, and others essential to an industrializing economy has led to the recruitment of a large number of foreigners. The lack of adequately trained personnel, for example, was cited as one of the contributing causes for Iran's prolonged power shortages, which in 1976 and again in 1977 resulted in several blackouts and the shutdown of manufacturing plants for long periods. Moreover the acute shortage of Iranian technicians available to the armed forces means that well into the 1980s or longer Iran will remain dependent on foreign, mostly American, personnel to maintain and in some instances to operate the military's highly sophisticated weapons systems.

Although in the early 1970s the government began to devote more attention and resources to the dismal agricultural situation, foreign observers doubted that Iran could, in the foreseeable future, achieve its goal of basic self-sufficiency in food. Not only was the population expanding at a rate of close to 3 percent per annum, but demand and consumption by the 47 percent of the population living in urban areas was also increasing rapidly.

The major agricultural problems, however, related directly to generally poor conditions for farming and livestock because of poor soil and an unfavorable climate. The data available in late 1977 were in some respects contradictory, but they indicated that of the country's 407.5 million acres, only about 30 percent were arable and only a little over 12 percent had ever been cultivated (see fig. on land use, ch. 11). In 1974, a fairly representative year, about 9.4 million acres were farmed under irrigation and about 11.8 million acres were under dry farming. The only hope of significant increases in food production lay in bringing more arable land under irrigation, and large sums of money were being invested in dam and irrigation projects in the mid- and late 1970s. The projects were very expensive and complex, however, and significant increases in food production were judged to be several years away (see Organization of Agriculture, ch. 11).

Geography and climate have played a direct role in shaping the country's settlement patterns. Scarcity and inaccessibility of water, a hostile terrain, and extremes of climate continue to restrict habitation largely to the northern areas, where precipitation and soils permit cultivation, and to the southwestern coastal areas, where commercial enterprises are located. Large sections of the Central Plateau remain virtually uninhabited.

Climate is characterized by wide ranges in precipitation and temperature. Seasonal changes are abrupt and clear cut; fall and spring are short. The prevailing winds and the mountains combine to produce adequate precipitation in the northwest and along the Caspian Sea but almost none in eastern deserts. The mountain country of the northwest, particularly the provinces of East Azarbaijan and West Azarbaijan, receives sufficient precipitation and mountain runoff to attract many people to the valleys, where they raise a variety of crops considerably in excess of their own needs (see fig. on administrative divisions, ch. 6). More than 50 percent of the inhabitants live in less than 30 percent of the country's area.

Winters in the mountains of the northwest frequently exceed six months, and summers are short and mild. In the eastern deserts freezing temperatures occur in winter, and the temperature often soars to over 132°F in summer. Snow never quite disappears from some northern slopes of the Elburz Mountains in the north, whereas about 400 miles to the southeast, at elevations of 2,000 feet, there are some of the hottest and driest areas of the world.

The country as a whole is located on a high triangular plateau. In general the plateau is part of a larger plateau that includes parts of Afghanistan and Pakistan. Geologists explain that the region was formed and shaped—and continues to be influenced—by the uplifiting and folding effect of three giant blocs or plates pressing against each other: the Arabian plate, the Eurasian plate, and the Indian plate. The squeezing and pressing resulted in considerable folding at the edges and some folding in the interior, thus forming the mountain ranges. Subterranean shifts produced numerous faults in the earth's crust, and it is along or near these faults that the country's frequent and devastating earthquakes occur (see fig. 3). Although the figures are rough estimates, Iranian government sources in 1976 stated that more than 60,000 people had been killed in earthquakes in the preceding fifteen years.

For centuries the level of the Caspian Sea, the worlds's largest landlocked body of water, declined irregularly, and the coastal plain represents former sea floor plus new top soil. In 1973 official elevation of the sea was ninety-two feet below sea level. The fall of the water level has been halted by the construction of a canal system connecting the Caspian and Black seas. Generally the coast is smooth and shallow, but two lagoons, requiring constant dredging, make possible the well-sheltered ports of Bandar Shah, on the eastern end of the shoreline, and Bandar Pahlavi, near the western end.

About half of the country is within the sparsely settled Central Plateau. Summer temperatures in the basin are extremely high, sometimes rising to more than 125°F, but winters can be bitterly cold. The deserts are among the driest and most barren in the world, and black, muddy salt marshes present dangers to the traveler. Settlement is confined to oases and to the flanks of small mountain chains; pastoralism is almost impossible.

The region, having no outward drainage, occupies a series of closed basins with elevations of 2,000 to 3,000 feet and is almost completely surrounded by mountains. Rain falls only in winter and never measures more than a few inches a year. The basins have central drainage areas that may remain dry for months or years. The lowest parts may have lakes a few inches deep that dry up and leave salt crests known as *kavirs*. As evaporation proceeds, the thick plates of crystallized salt increase in size, press against each other, break up, and give the appearance of glaciers; underneath the crusts lie marshes of black, slimy mud. Because of the danger of crossing the marshes, many are unexplored. The firm, hard gravel plains that may surround the salt flats are called *dashts*. The extensive Dasht-i-Kavir and Dasht-i-Lut deserts are located in the Central Plateau.

The broken and irregular ranges of the eastern mountains, extending from the Soviet Union in the north to Pakistan in the south, are barren, but the valleys that intersperse the area are fertile. Violent winds blow dust all summer and bring severe blizzards in the winter. The temperature runs to extremes, both hot and cold, and there is very little rain.

In the north, where the mountains reach 7,000 to 9,000 feet, cattle grazing and settlements can be found above 4,000 feet. Wheat, barley, vegetables, and fruit are common crops on irrigated lands. A few farmers grow dates and cereal crops, and farther south some people earn a living from fishing in Lake Helmand along the Afghanistan border. This lake region of the Sistan basin in the southeast usually has sufficient water for crops, but farming is handicapped by occasional drought years.

Throughout most of the country, water has been such a problem that all water resources were nationalized in October 1967. Less than 14 percent of the land receives over 52 percent of the precipitation. In some areas precipitation is lacking for long periods of time. Sudden storms with heavy rains a few times a year may provide the entire annual rainfall. Beyond the local damage that these storms bring about, the rapid runoff precludes the use of precipitation for agricultural purposes.

Where rivers and precipitation were insufficient, the solution was irrigation or storage; if these measures failed or were lacking, inhabitants moved away. In food production, water is regarded as more important than land itself. Where rainfall is inadequate, three sources of supplementary water for crops must be available —wells, rivers, and either springs, reservoirs, or *qanats*. A *qanat* consists of a line of shafts sunk to intercept a man-made underground conduit originating at a water collection point, ususally the base of a mountain. The shafts are used as wells at intermediate habitation points. In more arid areas, underground stone structures built with domed masonry roofs, known as *birkehs*, serve as storage pools; they are not wholly satisfactory, however, since their vulnerability to pollution is high.

Evaporation compounds the problem. Specialists estimate that 50 to 60 percent of the water evaporates in the intense summer heat. Ground absorption varies according to soil composition and structure, but it is considerable. Experts estimate that the rivers and streams carry only one-fourth of the precipitation the country receives. Absorption into the ground, however, gives promise of long-range advantages; government studies have been made to locate subsurface accumulation areas, and by the late 1970s several thousand producing wells had been sunk.

The major drainage basins are the Persian Gulf and Gulf of Oman in the south, the Central Plateau, Lake Rezaiyeh in the northwest, and the Caspian Sea, into which the Atrak and Gorgan rivers flow, northeast of Tehran. Because of the mountain drainage structure in the marginal regions, more than half of the country's surface loses its water to the interior. Scattered subbasins or sumps, which are low points in the larger inland basins, can be used to collect water, naturally or artificially, in sufficient amounts to support habitation. There is evidence that a more extensive network of rivers existed in earlier eras, but in modern times the drainage system by rivers and streams is abbreviated and, in some places, intermittent. The absence of any river with a substantial volume of flow emphasizes the extremely arid, segmented conditions of the terrain. There are only six rivers that drain the interior slopes, and these dwindle to brooks or dry up completely during the hot months.

Until well into the twentieth century, travel in most of the country was difficult and hazardous. The mountains and deserts made direct travel impractical, and they continue to make the maintenance of the country's road and railroad systems constant and expensive. This natural constraint on travel contributed to the continuation of the ethnic and linguistic diversity of the people and made Iran a highly regionalized country with localized loyalties and identities. Farsi (or Persian as it is commonly known outside Iran) has long been the most widely used language, and in the 1970s it remained the sole official language. But the centuries of migrations and invasions brought into the area numerous people speaking languages that are not, as are Farsi, Kurdish, and other tongues, Indo-European. Arabic, the language of the Quran and of the fairly large Arab minority, is a Semitic language. The mother

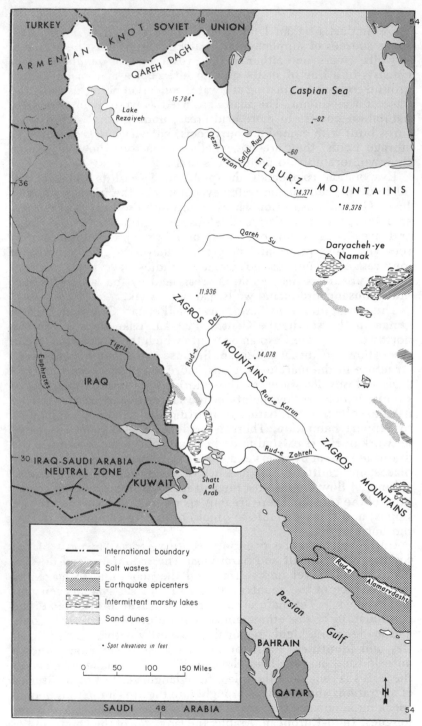

Figure 3. Topography and Drainage

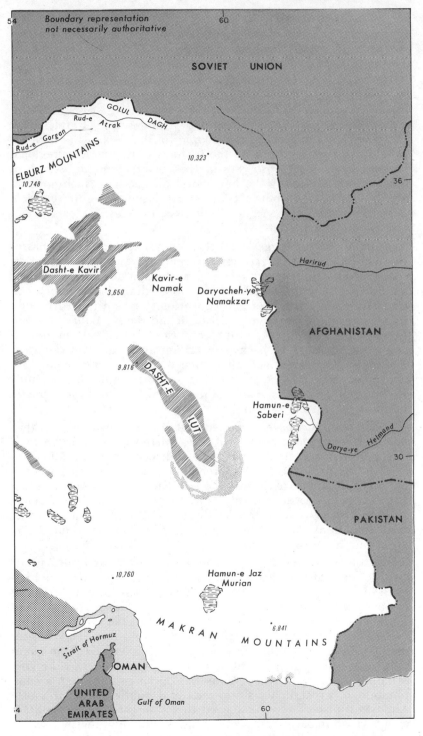

Boundary representation
not necessarily authoritative

SOVIET UNION

GOLUL DAGH
Rud-e Atrak
Rud-e Gorgan
ELBURZ MOUNTAINS
•10,748

•10,323

36

Dasht-e Kavir
•3,650

Kavir-e Namak

Daryacheh-ye Namakzar

Harirud

AFGHANISTAN

•9,816   DASHT-E LUT

Hamun-e Saberi

Darya-ye Helmand

30

PAKISTAN

•10,760

Hamun-e Jaz Murian

MAKRAN   MOUNTAINS
•6,841

Strait of Hormuz

OMAN

UNITED ARAB EMIRATES

Gulf of Oman

60

tongue of a majority of the populations of East and West Azarbaijan provinces and the northern part of Khorasan Province, is
Turkic, a Ural-Altaic language (see Lanuages, ch. 5).

The continuing loyalty of many Iranians to languages other than
Farsi and the persistence of regional as opposed to national patri-
otism have made difficult the development of a strong sense of
national identity. Nevertheless the strong sense of attachment
shared by the majority of the people to Shia Islam, the national
religion, serves to attenuate the feelings of linguistic or regional
parochialism. Most observers of the society tend to ascribe to
other levels of society the behavioral pattens that such political
analysts as Marvin Zonis set forth for the political elite: political
cynicism or passivity, personal mistrust, manifest insecurity, and
interpersonal exploitation.

Many observers suggest that the general attitude of the masses
toward individuals in authority creates a social and political
framework within which a strong authoritarian ruler is viewed
almost as a function of natural law. According to this interpretation, Iranians have, over the centuries, become inured to sub-
mitting to authority or to resisting it indirectly. Behavioral patterns sanctioned by long use condition individuals in power-
asserting positions to behave in an authoritarian way if only to
maintain the respect and allegiance of those under them. This
continues to be applied at all levels, from the father in the family
to the shah, and it has enabled the shah to implement his policies
without serious opposition.

Other observers have suggested that the resistance is more than
nominal, and they assert that the existence of a large, well-
financed, and powerful intelligence and security organization tes-
tifies to the presence of widespread oppostion to the shah's domination of all aspects of society (see Law Enforcement Agencies, ch.
12). These observers identify students, some of the traditional
religious leaders, and others in the growing middle class as those
most impatient with what they view as the shah's manipulation of
all segments of society (see ch. 7).

Still other observers believe that whereas most Iranians passively accept authoritarian behavior from their superiors and behave in like manner toward their inferiors, a small but increasing
minority is, unsuccessfully, seeking to challenge the system.
These observers point out, however, that the shah had been highly
successful in bringing most of his critics into line. This success
resulted in part from the efficiency and pervasiveness of the secret
police, but of perhaps equal or greater importance was the government's ability to co-opt potential opponents through a combination of great financial rewards and subtle social pressure.
Almost all observers were agreed that short of a violent military
coup, which in early 1978 seemed highly unlikely, the shah would
retain control of events in Iran for a long time to come.

Chapter 2. History Of The People

THE LONG-POSTPONED coronation of Mohammad Reza Pahlavi in October 1967 was accomplished with all the accoutrements and pomp associated with the ancient Iranian monarchy. The event firmly established the Pahlavi dynasty, which had been founded in 1925 by the shah's father, Reza Khan, in an atmosphere redolent with nationalistic hopes.

The institution of the monarchy in Iran had been degraded by the previous dynasty, the Qajars. Most Qajar shahs evinced an inability to cope or even to acknowledge the necessity for Iran to modernize or for the shahs to relinquish any of the perquisites of oriental despotism. As a result, Iran under the Qajars had been easy prey for Western industrialized powers, particularly Great Britain and Czarist Russia, for whom Iran was of great strategic and economic importance.

Both Russia and Great Britain were too firmly ensconced in Iran for their interests or influence to be eradicated during Reza Shah's rule. The exploitations and coastal colonizations by these powers had culminated in the ultimate humiliation of occupation during Reza Shah's reign in the early part of World War II. The Iranians were not unused to the rule of foreigners. The country's diverse ethnic blend is the legacy of scores of foreign invaders. The chief differences between the twentieth century invaders from those of earlier centuries was that former conquerors had come from less advanced civilizations and had become "Iranicized" during their rule in the country. Also, although they frequently devastated the country, they stimulated the culture.

Iran was enriched by these incursions because of its uncommon capacity to internalize all foreign influences and translate them into a native idiom. The Iranian historical reference point has always been their first local dynasty, the Achaemenids, who attained universal greatness under the brilliant leadership of Cyrus the Great (sixth century B. C.) and Darius the Great. Establishing an unbroken pattern for the historical process in Iran, the Achaemenids were eventually vanquished when their shahs proved weak and ineffectual. There is no romanticization in Iran of their first conqueror, Alexander the Great, who is remembered today as "that Hellenic alcoholic who burned Persepolis," despite the fact that he was a great admirer and imitator of Iranian culture.

The next great Iranian dynasty was the Sassanid whose rule was overthrown by the newly Muslim and enthusiastic Arab warriors from the Arabian Peninsula. The Iranians eventually accepted Islam but managed to imbue it with traditional Iranian values. Iran performed a great service for Islam in that it destroyed the then prevalent equation that "Islam equals Arab." Today 90 percent of the Iranian population is Shiite Muslim; Iran is the only country to have a Shiite majority. Shiism is particularly suited to pre-Islamic

Iranian traditions because of the idea, unique among Muslim sects, that there was a God-invested order of those who deserved to rule the Muslim world because of their descent from Ali, the Prophet Muhammad's son-in-law. These Muslim Imams, (see Glossary), as they are called, the third of whom married an Iranian princess, are glorified in the manner of the heroic secular figures from Iran's past. Iranians were the first Muslims to have used human figures in their art, and the celebrated Persian miniature painters often depicted great religious leaders just as their artistic ancestors had glorified the shahs in monumental bas-reliefs.

There has been a consistency in the manner of great Iranian monarchs that many specialists perceive as a conscious imitation. Unfortunately this imitation has not been confined to merely the symbols, devices, and cultivation of these shahs. It has also included their tendency to despotism and to certain savage eccentricities.

Ancient Iran
Pre-Achaemenid Iran

Iran's history as a nation of people speaking an Indo-European language did not begin until the middle of the second millennium B. C. Before then Iran was occupied by peoples with a variety of cultures. Written sources for the long and important pre-Achaemenid period are very scarce, however, and mostly from Assyria because the Iranians themselves were slow in developing a script. Information for this period must be pieced together from foreign inscriptions and the spectacular artifacts found in situ. Pre-Achaemenid archaeology is not nearly as advanced as Greek archaeology, for example, or archaeology from later Iranian periods. The chronology and provenance of the older cultures therefore is highly conjectural.

The geography of Iran—high mountains, forbidding deserts, and huge and uninhabitable salt marshes—discouraged the early formation of a centralized political or economic entity and postponed the growth of urban centers. Despite the continuing efforts of its monarchs, Iran has remained a highly regional society. There are numerous artifacts attesting to settled agriculture, permanent sun-dried brick dwellings, and pottery making from the sixth millennium. The most advanced area technologically was ancient Susiana, present-day Khuzestan Province. By the fourth millennium the inhabitants of Susiana, the Elamites, had developed semipictographic writing, the proto-Elamite script. Because of the proximity of the Elamites to the highly advanced and literate civilization of Sumer in Mesopotamia, to the west, archaeologists conjecture that the Elamites learned writing and other sophisticated cultural techniques from the Sumerians.

Sumerian influence became particularly strong when the Elamites were occupied or at least came under the domination of two Mesopotamian cultures, those of Akkad and Ur, during the middle of the third millennium. Mesopotamian art, literature, and religion made their debut at Susa, the Elamite capital, during this period (see fig. 4). By 2000 B. C. the Elamites had become unified enough to destroy the city of Ur. Elamite civilization developed rapidly from that point, and by the early 1300s its art was at its most impressive. A gigantic ziggurat at Dur Untashi and other religious temples on the Mesopotamian model appeared. Works in the round, including the largest metal statue (3,860 pounds) yet to be found in the Middle East, are part of the Elamite artistic legacy. Elamite bas-reliefs carved in rock provided the Achaemenids with a prototype for the bas-relief processional scenes, the most used medium of Achaemenid artistic expression.

Evidence of other major peoples in the area at this period is not as extensive, but six other groups have been identified. The Ellipi, longtime vassals of the Assyrians, were the Elamites' closest neighbors to the north, living on the plain of Kermanshahan and in the upper valley of the Rudkhaneh (stream or river) Karkheh. The Kassi, an Asiatic mountain people, lived in the area of present-day Lorestan. In the sixteenth century B. C. they moved across the Mesopotamian plain, overthrew the indigenous people, and founded a dynasty at Babylon. In the twelfth century they were driven back to Lorestan by the Elamite king, Shutruk Nahhunte. The famous Lorestan bronzes, highly elaborate and decorated pieces with animal heads and heroic motifs, date from the Kassite return to their homeland.

The Lullubi—living between the Mesopotamian plains and Kermanshahan—and the Guti—the Lullubi's neighbors to the north in the Kordestan (Kurdistan) Mountains—acting together or separately, periodically attacked the civilizations to the west. Little is known of the Mannai, inhabitants of the area between Kordestan and Azarbaijan southwest of Lake Rezaiyeh (Lake Urmia). It is assumed they were important because of the rich archaeological finds at Hasanlu and Zuriyeh. Artifacts from Hasanlu, many executed in gold and of a very high artistic quality, depict religious rituals, battle scenes, and most notably Mesopotamian theogonic and heroic myths.

The last non-Indo-European people to settle in Iran before the Achaemenids were the Urartu who came to the area around Lake Van (in present-day Turkey) in approximately 850 B. C. They ultimately extended their conquests from the south of Lake Rezaiyeh to the Black Sea and became sufficiently powerful to threaten the Assyrians. The Urartu distinguished themselves artistically by developing the protoma, or half-figure of animals, usually griffins or lions. Achaemenid artists amplified these early designs and made them symbols of the Persian king.

Immigration of the Medes and Persians

Small groups of nomadic, horseriding peoples speaking Indo-European languages began moving into the Iranian cultural area from Central Asia near the end of the second millennium. Population pressures, overgrazing in their home area, and hostile

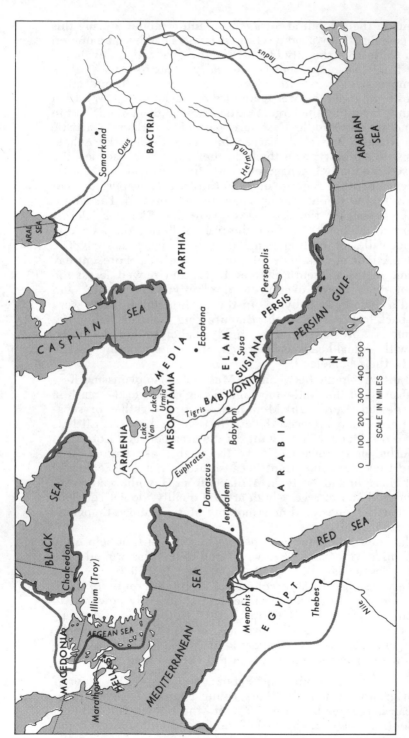

Source: Based on information from *Hammond World Atlas*, Maplewood, New Jersey, 1971; and Herbert H. Vreeland (ed.), *Iran*, New Haven, 1957.

Figure 4. Persian Empire, Ca. 500 B.C.

neighbors may have prompted these migrations. Some of the groups settled in eastern Iran but others, those who were to leave significant historical records, pushed further west toward the Zagros Mountains (see fig. on Topography and Drainage, ch. 1.).

Three major groups are identifiable—the Amadai or Mada (Medes), the Parsua or Parsa (Persians), and the Scythians. The Scythians established themselves in the northern Zagros Mountains and clung to a seminomadic existence where raiding was the chief form of economic enterprise. The Medes and Persians did not immediately displace the indigenous people since it was everyone's common aim to repel the Assyrians to the west. The Medes settled over a huge area, reaching as far as modern Tabriz in the north and Isfahan in the south. They had their capital at Ecbatana (Hamadan) and annually paid tribute to the Assyrians.

Written records of the Persians exist from Assyrian inscriptions of 844 B. C. The Persians at this time were established in three areas; to the south of Lake Rezaiyeh, on the northern border of the kingdom of the Elamites, and in the environs of modern Shiraz, which would be their eventual settling place and to which they would give the name Parsa (modern Fars Province). By the beginning of the eighth century B. C. the Persians had formed alliances with the Ellipi, the Elamites, and the people of Anshan, originally a settlement of the Elamites. A period of consolidation of Median and Persian power coincided with the weakened condition of the old kingdoms of the Urartu and the Mannai. In 614 B. C. the leader of the Medes, Cyaxeres (Uvakhshtra), with the aid of the Scythians and Babylonians, captured and leveled Nineveh, the Assyrian capital. When Cyaxeres returned home he extended his realm as far as modern Gorgan, near the eastern shore of the Caspian Sea (see fig. 1).

During the seventh century B. C. the Persians were led by Hakamanish (Achaemenes), eponymous ancestor of the Achaemenid dynasty. During the reign of his son, Chishpish (Teispes), the Persians became vassals of the Medes but nevertheless were able to expand their territory considerably. At Chishpish's death the lands of the Persians were divided between his sons. Ariyarumna (Ariarmnes) took Anshan and Parsa, and Kurush (Cyrus I) took the Elamite lands. Kurush's son, Cambyses I (Kambujiya) married the daughter of the Median king and their son, Cyrus II (also known as Cyrus the Great and Cyrus the Younger), led all the Persian tribes against his Median grandfather. Then, with the combined forces of the Medes and the Persians supporting him, Cyrus set about establishing the most extensive empire known in the ancient world.

The Achaemenid Empire (550–330 B. C.)

By 546 B. C. Cyrus had defeated Croesus, the Lydian king of fabled wealth, and had secured control of the Aegean coast of Asia Minor, Armenia, and the Greek colonies along the Levant. Moving east, he took Parthia, Chorasmia, and Bactria. He besieged and captured Babylon in 539 and released the Jews who had been held captive there, thus ensuring his immortality in the Book of Isaiah. By the time of his death in 529 Cyrus' kingdom extended as far east as the Hindu Kush in Afghanistan.

Cyrus' unstable son, Cambyses II, took Egypt and later committed suicide during a revolt led by a priest, Gaumata, who usurped the throne until overthrown in 522 by a member of a lateral branch of the Achaemenid family, Darius I (Darayarahush, known as Darius the Great). Darius spent the last years of his reign suppressing revolts throughout the empire and staving off repeated attempts at invasions by barbarians from the north. He unsuccessfully attacked the Greek mainland because of the support given by mainland Greek states to Greek colonies under his aegis and, as a result of the Battle of Marathon in 490, was forced to retract the limits of the empire to Asia Minor.

Marathon, although a celebrated event in Greek history, was of minimal importance to the Persians. The Achaemenids had paid the price of overexpansion and thereafter consolidated areas firmly under their control. It was Cyrus and Darius who, by sound and far-sighted administrative planning, brilliant military maneuvering, and a humanistic world view, established the greatness of the Achaemenids and in less than thirty years raised them from an obscure tribe to a world power. The quality of the Achaemenids as rulers began to disintegrate after the death of Cyrus in 486. His son and successor, Xerxes, was chiefly occupied with the suppression of revolts in Egypt and Babylon. Inflamed by the successes of his ancestors but lacking their genius, Xerxes attempted to conquer the Greek Peloponnesus. Reinforced by a victory at Thermopylae, he overextended his forces and suffered overwhelming defeats at Salamis and Plataea. By the time of the death of his successor, Artaxerxes I, in 424, the imperial court was beset by factionalism from among the lateral family branches, a condition that persisted until the death in 330 of the last of the Achaemenids, Darius III, at the hands of his own subjects.

Despotism, which was enlightened in the case of the early Achaemenids, was necessary to secure an extensive empire. The Achaemenids allowed a certain amount of regional autonomy in the form of the satrapy system. A satrapy was an administrative unit, usually organized on a geographical basis. A satrap (governor) administered the region and was responsible for informing the central government of the particular needs of the area and for maintaining federal institutions within it. Frequently a local leader was installed as satrap. In addition to the satrap, a general—who supervised military recruitment and ensured the pacification of an area—and a state secretary—who recorded official procedures—were also appointed to each region. Although the satrap was immediately responsible for the internal affairs of his satrapy, the general and the state secretary were not under his control but reported directly to the central government. Government inspectors were sent on surprise visits to the satrapies to ensure that the three officers were not in league against the empire in any way. Secession attempts or the defrauding of taxes were treated with equal severity by the central government.

The twenty satrapies were linked by a 1,500-mile highway, the most impressive stretch being the royal road from Susa to Sardis, built by command of Darius. Relays of mounted couriers could reach the most remote areas in fifteen days. The secret police, the "Eyes and Ears of the King," roamed throughout the empire and reported potential dissidents to the central authority. Additionally the king had a personal bodyguard, always kept exactly at 10,000 men, called the Immortals.

The language in greatest use in the empire was Aramaic. Old Persian was the "official language" of the empire but was only used for inscriptions and royal proclamations. An inscription commanded by Darius at Behistun near Kermanshah was in three languages, all in cuneiform—Old Persian, Akkadian, and Elamite. This particular inscription is of tremendous importance to archaeologists and linguists because it provided the key to transcribing cuneiform. Loan words from Old Persian to original Aramaic portions of the Old Testament give an indication of the extent of the cultural influence of the language of the Achaemenids. Peter Moorey cites as typical examples chief ministers, counselors, police chiefs, corporal punishment, written order, message, belt, trousers, furnishings, and ration.

The revenue for the Achaemenid Empire came from agriculture, tribute, and trade. The *qanat* system, an irrigation method by which underground water is tapped and fed into huge underground channels, developed during the Achaemenid period and continued to be a valuable water resource technique in the twentieth century. The *qanat* was also introduced in lands under Iranian occupation in the medieval period, and *qanat* systems built during that time in Oman, for example, continue to function in the 1970s.

Because of the vast reaches of the empire, trade or tribute in barter goods was inefficient. Coins had been in use in the ancient world only for a short time, but Darius was quick to see their advantages and revolutionized the economy of the empire by placing it on a silver and gold coinage system. Trade was extensive, and the efficient infrastructure facilitated the exchange of commodities between far reaches of the empire. Persian words for typical items of trade became prevalent throughout the Middle East and eventually entered the English language—bazaar, shawl, sash, turquoise, tiara, orange, lemon, melon, peach, spinach, and asparagus.

During his reign Darius codified the *data,* a universal legal system upon which much of later Iranian law would be based. Cyrus had chosen Ecbatana, the seat of the Median kingdom, for his capital. Later Pasargadae (camp of the Persians) was designed as the new capital of the Achaemenids. With the accumulation of new territories, however, it became too remote to serve as the administrative center of the empire and Susa, the old Elamite capital, was used; all Achaemenid kings continued to be crowned at Pasargadae. Darius chose to build a new capital at the very center of the empire, which would express in its archaeology and its art the tremendous achievements of his dynasty. Persepolis (city of the Persians) became the place where vassal states would offer their yearly tribute at the festival celebrating the spring equinox, No Ruz, a celebration that is continued in present-day Iran and marks the New Year.

The conception of Persepolis was intensely nationalistic; that is, Darius perceived himself not only as the conqueror of vast amounts of territory but also as the leader of conglomerates of people to whom he had given a new and single indentity. Achaemenid art and architecture is at once distinctive and also highly eclectic. The Achaemenids had taken the art forms and the cultural and religious traditions of many of the ancient Near Eastern peoples and crystallized them into a single form. Because Zoroastrianism (Mazdeanism), the prevailing religion of Iran at the time, forbade the use of religious temples, architecture and art were almost totally monarchical in subject content. The iconography of Persepolis celebrates the king and the office of the monarch. The king, not a god, becomes the symbol of all that is great and the instrument by which his people vicariously enjoy greatness.

The institution of monarchy as a central theme of Iranian history, and the apparent devotion of the Iranian people to it, certainly begins in this period. Achaemenid kings reverenced and showed gratitude to the gods but not in the way that was most common in the ancient world. Inscriptions make it clear that while the gods assist the king, they do so because the particular virtues the king possesses entitle him to the gods' good graces. The inscription of Darius at Behistun reads, "Ahura Mazda and the other gods helped me because I have been neither a liar, nor cruel, nor more of a tyrant towards the weak than towards the strong, and because I have acted with rectitude."

The religion of the early Achaemenid kings is conjectural. Inscriptions from the reigns of both Cyrus and Darius celebrate Ahura Mazda, god of the Zoroastrians, but the inscriptions also mention Babylonian gods. Because Zoroastrianism was a national religion, the Achaemenid kings were clearly drawn to it; later Achaemenid rulers were strong supporters. In 441 Artaxerxes I changed the civil calendar and named the months after leading figures in the Zoroastrian pantheon. Other Achaemenid kings appear to have adopted the highly recommended Zoroastrian practice of marriage with uterine siblings.

Later Achaemenid kings, though not comparable in leadership qualities with the early leaders, were able to enjoy and improve on

Bas-relief from the Hall of 100 Columns, Persepolis
U.S. Army photograph

the fruit of empire. At the beginning of the Achaemenid period Iran, although the center of empire, was underdeveloped compared with Babylon, Egypt, and other major centers of civilization. But by the beginning of the fourth century, although beset by political troubles at home and abroad, wealth had brought the luxury of civilized leisure to Iran. The famed "Persian garden," a major motif in Persian poetry, appeared. The Spartan Lysander was amazed when Cyrus showed him his garden, which Cyrus had planned and in which he worked every evening before dinner. The Persian word meaning the pleasure park of the king, *paradise,* is also a legacy of the Achaemenids.

The importance of the Achaemenids in ancient history is obvious, and the continued importance of this dynasty to the historical consciousness of contemporary Iranians can scarcely be overemphasized. Identification with the Achaemenids and constant repetition of the symbols of their rule rallied Iranian national pride during repeated periods of humiliating foreign occupation. A representative Iranian government publication of the mid-1970s noted "Though twenty-five centuries have passed since the days of Darius and Cyrus, the spirit and traditions of Achaemenid Iran still survive in almost every feature of the Iranian way of life . . . . including the monarchy."

Alexander the Great, the Seleucids, and the Parthians

The disintegration of the Achaemenid Empire was not solely the result of the weaknesses of the late rulers. After the devastating internecine wars of the Greek city-states, in which Iranian royal factions were actively involved, a strong Greek leader, Philip of Macedon—allied neither with strong Sparta nor enfeebled Athens—began the long task of uniting the Greek states. His charismatic and indefatigable son, Alexander, was accepted as leader by the fractious Greeks and by 334 B. C. had advanced to Asia Minor, an Iranian satrapy. In quick succession he took Egypt, Babylon, and then, over the course of two years, the heart of the Achaemenid Empire—Susa, Ecbatana, and Persepolis, which he burned. The death of Darius III in 330 merely meant that Alexander did not have to assassinate the king before assuming power.

The vast reaches of the empire fired Alexander's imagination in a way that Egypt and Babylon had not. Although he was determined to push further east to India, he envisioned a new world empire based on a fusion of Greek and Iranian culture and ideals. Alexander began to wear the dress of Iranian kings and to insist on the ceremonials of the Iranian court, including compulsory prostration before him, a conceit that was offensive to his egalitarian minded Macedonian soldiers. Alexander married Roxana (Roshanak), the daughter of the most powerful of the Bactrian chiefs and in 324 commanded his officers and 10,000 of his soldiers to marry Iranian women. The mass wedding, held at Susa, was more than symbolic; it was the literal articulation of Alexander's desire to consummate the union of the Greek and Iranian people. Alexander

then restructured his army because many of his men wanted to
return home and had become refractory and also because he
wished to place Iranian solders on an equal footing with the
Macedonians.

In Babylon in 323 Alexander was suddenly stricken with fever
and died, leaving no heir. His Macedonian officers had found
Alexander's universalistic notions too idealized and frankly viewed
as repugnant the idea of merging a "superior people" with "barbarians." The Iranians had similar feelings. Alexander's most important Macedonian generals became his *diadochi* (successors) and
for several years fought among themselves for his domains, while
local Iranian leaders, particularly those in areas only superficially
conquered by Alexander, led local uprisings. Gradually Alexander's empire became divided among four generals. Seleucus,
the only Macedonian general who had not abandoned his Iranian
wife, was ruler of Babylon by 312 B. C. and gradually reconquered
most of Iran. Seleucus' son, Antiochus I, succeeded him in 281,
and during his reign there was a numerous influx of Greeks into
Iranian territory. Most of the immigrants were involved in trade
and established colonies along with the trade routes from Greece
to India. Hellenistic motifs in art, architecture, and urban planning became prevalent throughout the area and for several centuries dominated artistic production in Iran. For the first time Iran
received cultural stimulation from the West, an orientation that
would diminish but would never be entirely displaced.

The Seleucids had continual problems with other dynasties of
diadochi, particularly the Ptolemys in Egypt. Nevertheless the
Seleucids were able to hold power, however tenuously, while a
new kingdom was gaining strength. The Parni, Iranian nomads
from the east, began to establish a powerful presence in a region
the Greeks called Parthia, the old Achaemenid province of Par-
thava. Arsaces (Arshak) was chosen as their first king. He is the
eponymous ancestor of their dynasty, the Arsacids, or Parthians,
as they are frequently called. In 247 B. C. Arsaces revolted against
the Seleucid governor and established the integrity of Arsacid
rule. Attempts to reconquer the area by the Seleucids proved
fruitless. Because of the military genius of King Mithridates I, the
Arsacids were able to extend their rule in the second century B. C.
to Bactria, Parsa, Babylon, Susiana, and Media.

In addition to the gradual encroachment of the Parthians, the
Seleucids were also faced with the growing power of Rome and the
extension of its empire and with independence revolts in Armenia
and Bactria. A Seleucid, Antiochus IV Epiphanes, managed to
retake the eastern dominions of Iran and to nurture Hellenism in
the area, but Parthian conquests reached from India to Armenia
under the rule of Mithridates II (123–87).

After the victories of Mithridates II, the Parthians began to
claim descent both from the Greeks and from the Achaemenids to
add an aura of respectability to their own meager cultural background, a practice common to later dynasties. Although the Par-

thians were Iranians, spoke a language similar to that of the Achaemenids, and used the Iranian Pahlavi script, they are not accepted by contemporary Iranians as true inheritors of Achaemenid glory, perhaps because they did not add anything of significance to Iranian civilization or, more probably, because too many adopted Greek names and identified with Greek culture. An Iranian government publication notes, "Though one cannot speak of any great Parthian king in the context of the Iranian people, the Parthians played the important role of preservers of Iranian civilization, which had suffered gravely at the hands of the occupying power [Alexander and the Seleucids] from Greece."

Sassanian Empire (A. D. 226–641)

During Iran's foreign occupation and the rule of the Parthians, the heritage of the Achaemenids had been preserved and even nurtured in the Achaemenid home province of Persis. Sassan, a legendary heroic figure there, had a descendant, Papuk, who was the chief priest at Istakhr, the capital built to replace ruined Persepolis. Because of his position his family possessed a considerable amount of secular authority and a member of it, Ardeshir, was chosen to be the Parthian representative with vassal status. Ardeshir overthrew the last Parthian king, Artabanus V, in A. D. 224, became the first Sassanian king, and founded a dynasty that lasted for four centuries. The Sassanians chose the Parthian winter capital at Ctesiphon in Mesopotamia as their administrative center because it was so well-equipped; however, they consciously strove to resuscitate Iranian traditions and to obliterate Greek cultural influence. Ambitious urban planning, agricultural projects, and technological improvements were systematically handled by an efficient and centralized administration.

Faced with the severe external threat of Rome, the Sassanians were determined to prevent any internal threats to their sovereignty, which seemed probable considering Iran's previous history. Although rigorous in the secular enforcement of their authority, the Sassanians were aided by the conventions of Zoroastrianism, which was declared the state religion by the Sassanians. The religious tolerance notable in previous dynasties, particularly under the Achaemenids, was replaced with a despotic fanaticism that prohibited the practice of other religions and insisted on careful observance of the minutiae of its rituals. The hereditary Zoroastrian priesthood became immensely powerful, and a caste system, believed to have been divided into four basic hereditary classes—priests, warriors, secretaries, and common people, in descending order—marked the social system. The first three classes were subdivided into further classifications. Although the exact social climate is difficult to ascertain, it is certain that there was a very small privileged class. There appears to have been virtually no social mobility; destiny was determined by birth. Only the kings and the *shahrdar* (minor kings) in provinces of the empire were superior to the priestly caste.

Early in the Sassanian period one of the king's sons was usually chosen as successor. Later, however, the king was elected by a triumvirate composed of the head of the priestly caste, the *morbadan mobad*, the military chief, the *iran spahbad*, and the chief of the bureaucracy, the *iran-diberbad*. Acting on evaluations written by the king before his death, a new king was chosen; the priestly caste made the final decision.

With internal affairs so securely managed by the various vested interest groups, the kings were relatively free to devote themselves to the triple task of fighting their external enemies to the west, securing their frontiers from the ever-increasing encroachments of the Huns in the east, and physically improving the nation. Rome had replaced Greece as Iran's traditional western enemy, and with the Roman capital situated at Constantinople, Rome concentrated on its eastern territories, many of which bordered on Sassanian ones. Hostilities, therefore, were frequent (see fig. 5).

Three Sassanian kings particularly distinguished themselves. Shapur I, son and successor of Ardeshir, was successful in his campaigns against Rome and even managed to capture the Roman emperor, Valerian. In Iran Shahpur I is often referred to as Shahpur the Shoulder Piercer, for the development of an innovative technique by which captives were brought back from battle with ropes threaded under their shoulder blades to keep them in file.

Xenophobia and nationalistic jingoism were at their height during Shahpur's reign. Sassanian soldiers of non-Iranian birth had the official name of *aniran*, that is, non-Iranian, although *aniran* was an adjective used pejoratively in many instances and seen frequently in inscriptions of the period. An inscription from Shahpur's reign is illuminating because it makes clear both that Zoroastrianism had become polytheistic and that the king considered himself to be one of the gods; "I, adorer of Mazda, the god Shahpur, king of kings of Iranians and non-Iranians, of the race of the gods, son of the adorer of Mazda, of the god Ardeshir . . . I am the ruler." Shahpur's inflated estimation of himself became the norm for Sassanian kings.

Khasrow I (also known as Anushirvan the Just, he of the Immortal Spirit) ruled between 531 and 589. He is regarded by historians and contemporary Iranians to be the most distinguished of his line. Legend has it that he will return at the end of the world and rescue Iran. Khasrow's rule was as autocratic as any of his predecessors or successors, but the Iranian people appeared to have become accustomed to a ruler having these characteristics, and it is possible that a ruler without them would not have garnered sufficient respect or authority. The severity of his rule, however, was tempered by justice, probity, and paternalistic benevolence. He initiated reforms on many levels, and the quality of life for most Iranians was clearly improved. The economy flourished, and

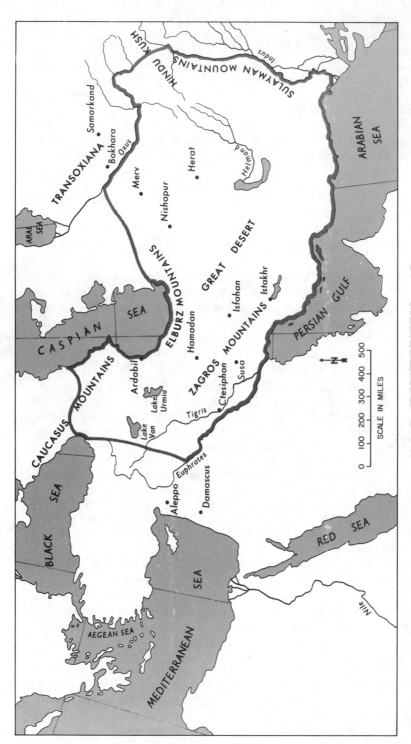

Source: Based on information from *Historical Atlas of the Muslim Peoples*, Amsterdam, 1957.

Figure 5. Sassanian Empire, Sixth Century

native artisans and poets were encouraged to experiment with local forms.

Khasrow II (591–628) was the last great Sassanian. Court splendor and artistic achievement matched his initial military successes. Iranian troops captured Damascus, seized the Holy Cross in Jerusalem, and marched close to Constantinople. The Byzantine emperor, Heraclius, counterattacked in a series of unusual maneuvers that brought forces far into Sassanian territory. A truce was eventually signed, but it was obvious that the Sassanians were in decline. Revolution could not come from within; social control was too absolute. But the rigidity that made the system immune from within spawned a passivity that made the country ripe for an invader who could sufficiently challenge the social system and had a force enthusiastic enough to attempt it.

Islamic Conquest

The power that toppled the Sassanians came from an unexpected source as far as the Iranians were concerned. Arabs and Iranians were known to each other because of their mutual trading activities and because for a brief period Yemen, in southern Arabia, was an Iranian satrapy. The Iranians also knew that Arabs, a tribally oriented people, had never been organized under the rule of a single power and were at a primitive level of military development.

Events in Arabia changed rapidly and dramatically in the sixth century when a member of the Hashimite clan of the powerful Quraysh tribe of Mecca claimed prophethood and began gathering adherents for the monotheistic religion, Islam, which had been revealed to him (see ch. 4). The conversion of Arabia proved to be the most difficult of the Islamic conquests because of the entrenched tribalism of the area. Within one year of the death of the Prophet Muhammad in A. D. 632, however, Arabia was secure enough for the Prophet's secular successor, Abu Bakr, the first caliph, to begin the campaign against the Byzantine and Sassanian empires.

The Byzantine army was defeated at Damascus in 635, and by 637 the Islamic army of nomadic warriors had occupied Ctesiphon, the capital of the Sassanians, and renamed it Madain. Although the Sassanian forces were vastly superior in techniques and numbers—a very conservative estimate places the proportion of Arabs to Iranians at one to three—the Sassanians were militarily exhausted after their unremitting campaigns with the Byzantines. Sassanian troops fought ineffectually, lacking sufficient reinforcement. More important, the Iranian people had been badgered into a state of passivity and offered little resistance.

The Islamic conquest was aided by the fact that both the Byzantine and Sassanian empires were culturally and socially bankrupt, and the native populations had little to lose by cooperating with the conquering power. Because Muslim warriors were at this time fighting a holy war (jihad)—as they perceived it—they were regulated by religious law, which strictly prohibited rape and the killing of women, children, religious leaders, or anyone who was not actually engaged in warfare. Further the Muslim warriors had come to conquer and settle a land under Islamic law. It was not in their economic interest to unnecessarily destroy or pillage.

The Arabs were well aware that although the conquered people might be religiously "benighted," they had long possessed urban institutions and civilized refinements, including administrative experience that the Arabs admired and wished to sustain. Conversions to Islam were fairly rapid in two castes. The lower castes were attracted by Quranic dictum that stressed piety and good works as opposed to birth or caste as the measure of a man: "Truly, the noblest among you before God is the most righteous among you" (Sura 49, Verse 3). The second largest caste that converted was the priestly caste, whose members wished to retain, if possible, their positions within their power structure. Conversion was certainly not discouraged, but neither was it forced on the population. Non-Muslims had to pay a poll tax, *jizya,* and this was an important source of revenue. Conversion to Islam was most rapid in cities and towns where an Arab garrison was settled. It was not until the ninth century that the majority of Iranians became Muslim. In the eastern provinces *Arab* became a synonym for *Muslim* in the local language. Early converts such as the Tajiks, most of whom live in Soviet Central Asia, are still called *Arab* although they are Iranian.

Umar, the second orthodox caliph, organized the administration of the conquered Iranian lands. Acting on the advice of an Iranian, Umar continued the Sassanian office of the divan, a register to control income and expenditure and an institution that would be used henceforth throughout the lands of the Islamic conquest. *Dihqans,* minor revenue collection officials under the Sassanians, retained their function of assessing and collecting taxes. Tax collectors in Iran had never enjoyed universal popularity, but the Arabs found them particularly noisome, "by reason of their nationality, their office, and their over-efficiency . . . . 'remembering even the husks of the rice'."

The Arabs adopted the Sassanian coinage system and thus, strangely enough, retained the iconography of a Zoroastrian fire altar with a priest on either side even when the coins were reminted. Eventually the priests and fire altar became stylized as three parallel lines. This kind of coin enjoyed great popularity and was used in Islamic lands as distant as southern Spain. Arabic replaced Persian as the official language. It was politically astute and also considered fashionable for Iranians to intersperse their Persian with Arabic words, and a slow Arabicization of Persian occurred. In the agricultural and less densely settled provinces in the east, however, there were few who learned Arabic, and Dari, the spoken language of the Sassanian convert, was used. Thus a form of the Persian language was spread by Arabs to areas where it was hitherto little known. Dari is spoken Persian without the later Arab embellishments, the antecedent to Farsi, the modern Persian language spoken today.

There was considerable culture shock in Iran during the first 150 years of the conquest. Desert Arabs were at first too amazed at the richness of Iranian culture to display arrogance over their more immediate connection with Islam. They intermarried with the Iranian population and adopted many Iranian customs. Gradually, however, the Iranians found that the Arab Muslims seemed to have a double standard when it came to the question of social standing. If submission to the will of God and the performance of good acts determined the nobility of man, why were the Iranians, who had many pious Muslims among them, consistently treated as inferiors, and why did Umayyad leaders proclaim themselves as the privileged elite? Resentment grew, and it became clear that while Iranians could be excellent Muslims, they had no intention of internalizing Arab values and mores at the expense of their own venerated traditions. This attitude proved to be significant in establishing Islam as a universal religion. It was the Iranians, as the distinguished scholar Richard Frye points out, who, by clinging to their own traditions, broke the equation Islam equals Arab.

A violent literary controversy between Arabs and Iranians, called the Shuubiyah controversy, became one outlet for the mutual antipathy that many Arabs and Iranians held for each other. The various *shuubis* (from the Arabic word for group, *shuub*) claimed equality with or superiority to the Arabs. Political aspirations, religious views, and, particularly, ethnic considerations formed the subject matter of the debate. Iranians accused Arabs of being lizard eaters. Arabs accused Iranians of being incestuous because of the previous Sassanian practice of marriage with sisters or mothers. Although the Shuubiyah was not an organized effort, it is of considerable importance in the consideration of the assimilation of diverse peoples under the Islamic aegis. A heated tone was the hallmark of the interchange, as in this typical reply to a *shuubi*, "[You] very ignorant apostate and depraved religious hypocrite . . . may your mother be bereft of you . . . true justice in answering you . . . would consist of stripping you of your skin and crucifying you on your gate."

By 650 Muslims had reached the Oxus River (Amu Darya) and had conquered all the Sassanian domains, though some were more strongly held than others. Shortly after, Arab expansion and conquest virtually ceased. The status quo was maintained by the groups in power; political and religious rebellion took place outside the major power structure. The ideologies of the rebellions were usually couched in religious terms. Frequently the interpretation of a point of doctrine was sufficient to spark armed warfare. More often religion was the rationalization for dissatisfactions that might more adequately be described as nationalistic or cultural in nature.

By the end of the seventh century there was already considerable factionalism within the Islamic community, ostensibly caused by differing views on the question of rightful succession to the office of caliph. The end result, after several assassinations and open warfare, was schism. Three core sects emerged. The Ahl al Sunna or Sunnis (from the Arabic word meaning tradition); the Kharajites (seceeders); and the Shiat Ali (Party of Ali), the Shiites or Shias, who maintain that only a descendant of the Prophet Muhammad can be the rightful leader of the Islamic community. The Prophet had only one living issue, a daughter Fatima who married her cousin, Ali, a man distinguished by his piety and empathy with the common people.

Ali's election to the caliphate was challenged by Muawiya in open warfare, and when Ali was assassinated by a Kharajite while praying in a mosque at Kufa in 661, Muawiya was declared caliph by the majority of the Islamic community. He became the first caliph of the Umayyad dynasty; its capital was at Damascus.

Ali's unnatural death ensured the future of the Shiite movement and quickened its momentum. With the single exception of the Prophet no man has had a greater impact on Islamic history, and no man has had a greater impact on Iranian history. The Shiite declaration of faith is, "There is no God but God; Muhammad is the Prophet of God and Ali is the Saint of God." Ali's oldest son Hassan received the title Lord of all Martyrs because it was popularly held that Muawiya had him poisoned.

Ali's youngest son Husayn refused to pay the homage commanded by Muawiya's son and successor Yazid I and fled to Mecca where he was asked to lead the Shiites—mostly Iraqis—in a revolt. The governor of Kufa discovered the plot and sent detachments to dissuade him. At Karbala, in Iraq, Husayn's band of 200 men and women followers, unwilling to surrender, were finally cut down by about 4,000 Umayyad troops. The Umayyad leader received Husayn's head, and Husayn's death in 680 on the tenth of Muharram continues to be observed as a day of mourning for all Shiites (see ch. 4).

Originally both Sunnis and Shias had approximately an equal number of adherents in Iran. With the deaths of Ali, Hassan, and Husayn, popular sympathy increased, and more Iranian groups became Shiites. Iranians had a national interest in the Shia cause because Husayn had married a daughter of the last Sassanian king—although they hardly needed an inducement to support any group that was opposed to the detested Umayyads. The idea of a leader who came from one special line was also more in accord with Iranian monarchical traditions.

Many minor and unsuccessful insurrections against the Umayyad caliphate were mounted from Iran. Large numbers of the defeated fled to Iran's easternmost province, Khorasan. There, at the city of Merv (present-day Mary in the Soviet Union), a faction that supported a descendant of the Prophet's uncle, Al Abbas, was able to organize the rebels under the battle cry "The House of Hashim." Hashim was ancestor of both the Shia line and the Al Abbas line, and the Shiites therefore actively supported the group leader, Abu Muslim. In 747 his army attacked the Umayyads and occupied Iraq. In 750 Abdul Abbas (not a Shiite) was established in Baghdad as the first caliph of the Abbasid dynasty.

The many Iranians who had supported the movement, some only covertly at first, gained prestige. The new dynasty was of Iranian origin and took many of the trappings of Iranian kingship to Baghdad. They secluded themselves from common view with veils and curtains. Before approaching the caliph visitors had to remove their shoes as though they were on sacred ground, and a huge contingent of bodyguards, including a chief executioner, kept petitioners at a respectful distance.

Nomadic, Turkic-speaking warriors had been moving out of Central Asia into Transoxiana (i.e., across the Oxus River), for more than a millennium. The Abbasid caliphs began enlisting these people as slave warriors as early as the ninth century. Shortly thereafter the real power of the Abbasid caliphs began to wane; eventually they became religious figureheads while the warrior slaves ruled. As the power of the Abbasid caliphs diminished, a series of independent dynasties rose in Iran, some with considerable influence and power. Among the most important were the Tahrids in Khorasan (820–872); the Saffarids in Seistan (867–903, present-day Sistan); and the Samanids, originally at Bokhara (in present-day Soviet Union). The Samanids eventually ruled an area from central Iran to India.

Like the Abbasids, many of the local Iranian dynasties used Turkish slaves in their armies and administration. As the Samanids declined, a Turkish line, the Ghaznavids, slowly developed. In 961 a Turkish slave governor of the Samanids, Alptigin, attacked Ghazni (in present-day Afghanistan) and established a dynasty that lasted to 1186.

Several of their cities had been lost to another Turkish group, the Seljuqs, in the previous century. The Seljuqs were the ruling clan of the Qiniq group of the Oghuz or Ghuzz Turks, who lived north of the Oxus River. Their leader, Tughril Beg, turned his warriors against the Ghaznavids in Khorasan. He moved south and then west, conquering but not wasting the cities in his path. In 1055 the caliph in Baghdad gave Tughril Beg robes, gifts, and the title King of the East.

There were several lines of Seljuqs; the main line controlled the Bosphorus to Chinese Turkestan for 100 years. The Seljuqs continued to expand their territories, but they were content to let Iranians administer and rule. One Seljuq, Malik Shah, extended Turkish rule to the Levant, Anatolia, and parts of Arabia. During his rule Iran enjoyed a cultural and scientific renaissance, largely attributed to his brillant Iranian vizier, Nizam al Mulk, one of the most skillful administrators in history. An astronomy observatory was established in which Umar (Omar) Khayyam did much of his experimentation for a new calendar, and religious schools were built in all the major towns. Abu Hamid Ghazali, one of the greatest Islamic theologians, and other eminent scholars were brought to the Seljuq capital at Baghdad and encouraged and supported in their work.

The only serious internal threat the Seljuqs experienced was that of another religious division. The Ismailis, a secret sect, had their headquarters at Alumut between Rasht and Tehran. They controlled the immediate area for more than 150 years and sporadically sent out adherents to murder important officials. In Syria they were known as the Hashishiyya because popular legend had it that they smoked hashish before their missions. The word *hashishiyya* became corrupted to *assassin* by the medeival Europeans.

Invasions of the Mongols and Tamerlane

After the death of Malik Shah, Iran once again reverted to petty dynasties. A powerful leader, Temujin, had brought together a majority of the Mongol tribes and led them on a devastating sweep through China. About this time he changed his name to Genghis (Chinghiz) Khan (world conqueror). In 1219 he turned his 700,000 forces west and quickly devastated Bokhara, Samarkand, Balkh, Merv, and Nishapur (present-day Neyshabur), where he slaughtered every living thing. Before his death in 1227 he had reached western Azarbaijan, pillaging and burning cities along the way.

The Mongol invasion was disastrous to the Iranians. As a result of the destruction of *qanat* systems, oasis cities were created in a land where they had previously been rare. A large proportion of the population, particularly male, was exterminated. Between 1220 and 1258 the population of Iran dropped to about one-fourth of what it had been.

After Genghis' death, Iran enjoyed a brief respite that ended with the arrival of Hulagu Khan, Genghis' grandson. In 1258 he seized Baghdad and killed the last Abbasid caliph. Hulagu was finally repulsed by the Mamluk forces of Egypt at a place in Palestine that would be called Ain Jalut (bloody spring) after the event. Hulagu returned to Iran where he spent the remainder of his life, mostly in Azarbaijan. Under the nominal suzerainty of Kublai Khan in China, Hulagu possessed the title Il Khan, or subordinate khan, a name passed on to his dynasty in Iran. Hulagu was buried on an island in Lake Rezaiyeh, the last known time that servants were buried with their Mongol lord.

Mongol power had peaked by this time, but they remained a superb military force because of tactics unique for the period: they used retreat and ambush and attacked only the flanks of an enemy's column. They also used agents for propaganda and had those refugees who survived their attacks carry supplies to the next city. Until the accession of Ghazan Khan in 1295—a Muslim and great-grandson of Hulagu—Mongol rulers had little success in

Tomb of Omar Khayyam, Neyshabur
Courtesy Embassy of Iran

restoring Iran to a measure of the prosperity it had known. In-
fighting among the Mongol elite lead to the bizarre murder of
several of them.

Ghazan, with the assistance of Iranian viziers (unfortunately no
vizier in a Mongol court died a natural death until 1324), began to
reconstruct the nation by lowering taxes on works by artisans,
encouraging agriculture by rebuilding and extending irrigation
works, and posting thousands of men along the caravan routes. By
protecting the trade routes, commerce increased dramatically.
Items from India, China, and Iran passed with ease across the
Asian steppes, and the contacts culturally enriched each of the
nations. Undoubtedly the most exciting legacy for Iran was the
development of a new style of painting based on a unique fusion of
solid, two-dimensional Mesopotamian painting with the feathery
and light brush strokes and other motifs characteristic of China.
Artists worked mostly in Tabriz, the Mongol capital, where they
joined potters using new techniques and architects who created
massive and highly experimental exteriors with elegant and under-
stated interiors.

Ghazan's nephew, Abu Said, also known as Bahador the Brave,
was the last great Mongol ruler. He mounted the throne at the age
of twelve, having been governor of Khorasan since the age of nine.
After his death in 1355, Mongol commanders, old Seljuq re-
tainers, and regional chiefs maintained petty dynasties—the
Salghurid, Muzaffarid, Inju, and Jalayirid.

The Mongols' land of Transoxiana had been divided into two
separate areas, Transoxiana proper and Turkestan, the leaders of
which were in constant rivalry with each other, frequently to the
point of war. Timur, also called Tamerlane (Timur, the Lame), son
of the governor of Samarkand, conquered Transoxiana proper and
by 1381 established himself as sovereign. He did not have the
huge forces of earlier Mongol leaders so his conquests were slower
and less savage than those of Genghis and Hulagu. Nevertheless
Shiraz and Isfahan were virtually leveled. Like the Mongols before
him Tamerlane had his cultivated moments. He ruled with the
administrative assistance of Iranians and was personally addicted
to architecture and poetry. The Timurid empire disintegrated
rapidly after his death in 1405. Mongol tribes, Uzbeks, and
Bayundur Turkomans ruled until the rise of a native Iranian dynasty, the first in almost 1,000 years.

Safavid Dynasty (1502–1736)

Iranians perceive the Safavids as the first native Iranian dynasty
since the Sassanian and thus the heirs of ancient Achaemenid
glory. The Safavids are Iranian to the extent that they had been
settled in Iran since the Arab conquests; there was naturally a
significant admixture of Iranian blood. They also intermarried
with Turks and Greeks. For example, the mother of the first
Safavid shah, Ismail, had a Turkish father and a Greek Christian
mother.

The Safavids did have a distinguished family line, however. They were direct descendants of Safi al Din, a famous Sufi mystic, who was descended from Ali, the Prophet's son-in-law. After Safi al Din's death, his descendants were shaykhs of the Safaviyya Sufi brotherhood. The Safavids had acquired considerable secular support when Safi al Din's son, on being offered a boon by Tamerlane, requested the release of a huge body of Turkish prisoners. The tribes of the released prisoners attached themselves to the Safavid family, embraced Shiism, and became *muwalis,* clients of the family.

The Safavids lived in Ardabil in eastern Azarbaijan, which was under the nominal suzerainty of a group of Bayundur Turkoman, the Aq-Qoyunlu (possessing white sheep). The Turkomans were powerful under their first leader, Qara Yuluk (Black Leech Uthman), but their power had declined by 1499 when the Safavid shah, Ismail, at the age of thirteen, began his attacks against them. By 1500 he had seized Tabriz from the Aq-Qoyunlu and was crowned shah, preferring this to the title Shaykh of the Sufis of Ardabil, his birthright title (see fig. 6). He proclaimed Shiism as the state religion and encouraged but did not force Sunni Iranians to become Shiites. Seven Turkish tribes of Azarbaijan, the Qizl Bash ("Red Heads," from their red turbans)—made famous in a modern Iranian novel of that name—joined him and together they took Iraq, Hamadan, Fars, Kerman, and Khorasan.

The Sunni Ottoman Turks, who then claimed the mantle of caliph, had become the major Islamic power in the west, and having secured Asia Minor they proceeded to advance east toward Iran. The memory of foreign invaders was fresh in the minds of Iranians, and they rallied around Shah Ismail and embraced Shiism. In 1514 the Safavids lost Tabriz, their first conqest and capital, to the Ottoman, Selim the Grim. The Safavids harassed the Turks and briefly recaptured Tabriz, but in 1523 Suleiman the Magnificent regained it for the Ottomans. Shah Tahmasp, Ismail's son, moved the capital to Qazvin, south of the Elburz Mountains, and maintained a court noted for its refinements. Like previous and subsequent shahs, Tahmasp received guidance, while dreaming, from Shia Imams, including Ali, who prompted him to renounce wine and prohibit the selling of it in his domains. He also, for reasons unknown, had his eldest son imprisoned from childhood. Fear of the potential power of sons appears frequently in the annals of Iranian history. Several shahs had their sons blinded and others had them killed; it had seemingly become an ingrained habit of the Mongols.

When Tahmasp's son, Ismail II, made the transition from prison to throne in 1576, his pathological mental state induced him to attempt the murder of his entire family, mostly with his own sword "to see whether it would cut." His fortunately brief reign ended with an overdose of opium and his ineffectual brother, Muhammad Khudabana, succeeded him. A nephew, Abbas Mirza, who had

41

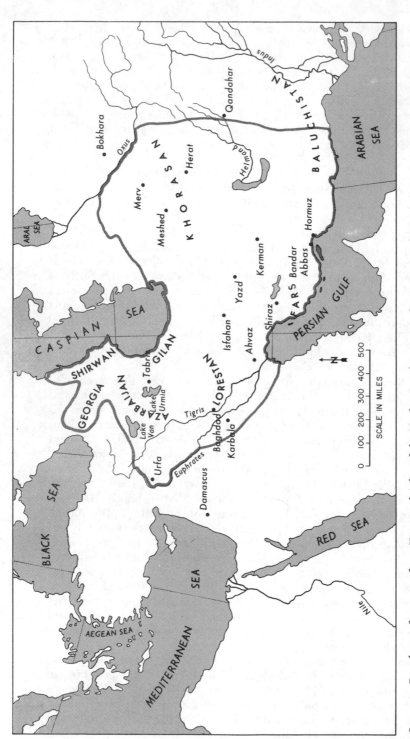

Source: Based on information from *Historical Atlas of the Muslim Peoples.* Amsterdam, 1957; and Marshall G. S. Hodgson, *The Venture of Islam,* Chicago, 1974.

Figure 6. *Safavid Empire, Ca. 1512*

escaped the family massacre, was Safavid governor of Khorasan and was encouraged by notables of the region to seize leadership. These local chiefs were concerned by the activities of the Turks, Georgians, and Uzbeks all along the Iranian frontier.

Abbas Mirza became shah in 1558 at the age of sixteen and ushered in a golden age of prosperity and development. One of his first acts was to sign a treaty of peace with the Ottomans, which enabled him to concentrate his security forces against the Uzbeks. Shah Abbas was noted for the magnanimity with which he treated ethnic and religious minority groups, a politically sound gesture that gave minority groups a sense of identification with the government and the larger body of the Iranian population. Kurdish tribes were moved to northern Khorasan to guard against the Uzbeks. With the eastern border secure, he moved against the Ottomans and rid Azarbaijan, Georgia, Kordestan, and Armenia of their presence.

Shah Abbas moved the capital from Qazvin to Isfahan in 1598 and rebuilt the city. Armenian artists were brought from Azarbaijan to beautify the city, along with scores of architects and builders from all over Iran. Isfahan became the most splendid city in the Middle East. Tabriz, Shiraz, Ardabil, and Meshed were also embellished. The holiest shrine in Iran, that of Imam Reza at Meshed, received extensive renovations, presumably to encourage Shia pilgrims to visit there instead of Iraq, where the major Shia shrines are located.

Shah Abbas opened Iran to European influences, originally in an effort to gain the support of the English against the Portuguese who had garrisons along both the Arab and Iranian coasts of the Persian Gulf. The Portuguese had never distinguished themselves by diplomatic niceties in the gulf and had steadfastly refused to pay the relatively small tribute that Iran had always demanded of those who ruled its gulf trading towns. In 1602 Shah Abbas evicted the Portuguese from Bahrain, and during the years between 1608 and 1615 tried ineffectually to drive them from Hormuz. During these years the English had slowly been acquiring prestige and making friends at the Iranian court. Sir Anthony Sherley and his brother, Robert, had entered the private service of the shah in 1600. When in 1617 Edward Connack carried a letter to the shah from King James I of England asking for support for the East India Company, he was extremely well received. The shah promised the English the port of Jashk from which to trade; granted them sole control of all silk leaving Iranian ports; and provided for the permanent presence of an English ambassador at court.

The Portuguese, who were experiencing increasing difficulties in maintaining their position due in part to their annexation by Spain in 1581, attempted unsuccessfully to block the ships of the East India Company from entering Jashk. In 1622 a combined English-Iranian attack on the Portuguese garrison at Hormuz and at a post on the island of Qeshm resulted in victory and in an agreement that customs collected in Qeshm and Hormuz would be shared by the Iranians and the East India Company. The English established their headquarters at Bandar Abbas, which became the center for political and commercial activities in the gulf for the next 150 years.

Shah Abbas made his military forays with a regular paid army, which had a special unit called the Friends of the Shah, composed of 20,000 infantry and 10,000 cavalry. Despite his improvements, open-mindedness,and appreciation of the arts, Shah Abbas has one hideous blot on an otherwise distinguished record: he blinded two of his sons and had the eldest put to death. Lacking sons capable of rule, therefore, he named as his successor his grandson, Safi. Shah Safi was passive but his son, Abbas II, who ascended the throne at the age of nine, managed to retrieve the city of Qandahar (in present-day Afghanistan) from Shah Jahan, the Mughal emperor of India, and to pacify the frontiers.

The next and the last two Safavid shahs were voluptuaries who ignored reality for the comforts of the seraglio. The Afghans had begun moving deep into the heart of the country and finally surrounded Isfahan. They cut off food supplies to the city and bided their time. Domestic animals were eaten, and the citizens of Isfahan were driven to cannabalism. Finally, in October 1722, Shah Husayn, dressed in mourning, went to the camp of Mir Mahmud, the Afghan leader, and passed the symbol of leadership to him.

Afghan power in Iran was short-lived. A son of the last Safavid shah leagued with an Afshari tribesman and together they ousted the Afghan forces. The Afshari tribesman, Tahmasp Quli Khan, then assumed power in his own right, and in 1736 was crowned under the name Nadir Shah. Nadir Shah was indefatigable in regaining occupied Iranian lands. He drove the Ottomans from Georgia and Armenia and harried the Russians until they evacuated their forces from the Iranian coast of the Caspian Sea. Hoping to expand his empire, Nadir Shah made several forays into India and defeated the Mughal army near Delhi in 1739. Fabulous treasures were brought back to Nadir Shah's capital at Meshed, including the Peacock Throne and other exquisite items, valued at the time at 87.5 million pounds sterling. Contemporary Iranians hold Nadir Shah in high favor for uniting Iran, but they fault him for permitting his army to live off the land and for his extortionate tax demands. When the army began to feel his tyranny, his bodyguard murdered him in 1747.

In the confusion and general rebellion that followed Nadir Shah's death, a great national hero, Muhammad Karim Khan Zand emerged and, except for areas of Khorasan, unified the nation. Karim Khan ruled from 1750 until 1779 but disdained the title of shah. He called himself *vakil al ruaiya* (attorney of the people). He encouraged the Europeans who had been frightened off by the Afghans to return, and under his peaceful and just rule, the Iranian nation began to heal.

The Rise of the Qajar Dynasty

Out of the chaos that in Iran always seemed to follow the death of a strong leader, a new dynasty arose. The Qajar dynasty originally had little to recommend it but brute strength and later held power by the cunning manipulations of one group against another. Considering the deficiencies of the Qajars, which were legion, their long reign until 1925 was in large part a function of the external tension created by the interests of Great Britain and Russia in Iran.

The Qajars, originally of Turkish stock, were settled in Gilan, south of the Caspian Sea. They had assisted the Safavids and Nadir Shah, but their fortunes fell as Nadir Shah's tyranny increased. One of the Qajars, Agha Muhammad Khan, had been a captive in Shiraz at the court of Karim Khan. He had been castrated as a boy by one of Nadir Shah's successors and understandably became embittered and obsessed with revenge. He escaped from Shiraz and united the Qajars and six other tribes that were related to them. He decided on Tehran as his center of operations and from there attacked the army of Luft Ali, the last of Karim Khan's successors. Luft Ali fled to Kerman where he was captured and eventually tortured to death. For sheltering the kindly Luft Ali 20,000 citizens of Kerman had their eyes put out. Agha was named shah in 1796. He controlled all of Iran before his assassination in 1797.

Fath Ali Shah (1797–1834), Agha's nephew and successor, was milder in disposition and chose to rely on a European power to shore up Iran's political decline. Fath signed a treaty with Napoleon in 1807. In exchange for arms to repell expanding Czarist Russia Fath granted Napoleon access to India through Iran. Iran fought sporadically against Russian incursions until finally ceding them Georgia by the Treaty of Gulistan in 1813. The Iranians lost again to Russia and in 1828, by the Treaty of Turkmanchai, the Russians gained Erivan and Nakhichevan and many important concessions.

The economic and naval benefits the Russians received from these treaties were unnerving to the British who were anxious to maintain their supremacy in the Persian Gulf and to feel secure about the foreign policy of nations adjacent to India, then under British rule. Fath Ali Shah died in 1834 and was succeeded by his grandson, Muhammad Mirza, who ascended the throne with both British and Russian support. The British began to regret their choice when Mirza, with assistance from the Russians, began his campaigns against the Afghans, focusing on the city of Herat. The Russians were intent on winning a warm water port for themselves and one possibility would have been a march along the Iranian-Afghanistan frontier. It was of little consequence that the Qajars, not the Russians, were taking the offensive against the Afghans. The Qajars would receive British censure, and later the Russians would exert pressure on the Qajars to achieve their objective. Iran was exceedingly vulnerable at this time, lacking both the technological expertise to make munitions and a large or effective army.

Mirza attempted to improve conditions in Iran by forbidding torture and the importation of slaves. He was able to devote more time to internal affairs when it became clear that he could not take Herat, where the resistance was organized by British officers.

In 1848 at the age of seventeen, Nasr al Din Shah succeeded his father, Mirza, and spent the first eight years of his reign suppressing revolts in various parts of the country. By 1856 he felt strong enough to invade Herat and occupied the city with the help of a pro-Iranian Afghani ruler. Meanwhile Great Britain had been engaged in hostilities against the ruler of Afghanistan and was supporting a pro-British Afghani ruler in Kabul. The British were enraged at the Iranian occupation of Herat and demanded the immediate evacuation of Iranian forces; the governor general of India declared war against Iran. The support Nasr al Din expected from Russia was not forthcoming, and he was forced to withdraw. In 1857 the Treaty of Paris was signed whereby Iran recognized the independence of Afghanistan and agreed to certain commercial privileges demanded by the British.

During the late 1800s most of Iran's boundaries were fixed. In 1847 the Turko-Iranian boundary was determined by a commission of Russians and British. In 1881, as a further outcome of the Treaty of Paris, Iran ceded half of Sistan Province to Afghanistan. As a result of Russian movements into the virtually independent territories of the Turkish Uzbeks—tribes around Khiva and Bokhara— the Russian-Iranian boundary in the northeast was fixed in 1884, and Iran thereby lost Merv. In 1893 the British set the boundaries between Iran and British India in the area then known as British Baluchistan, part of present-day Pakistan.

Russia and Great Britain were able to make significant territorial and commercial inroads into Iran because of the almost total lack of modernization within the country. An astonishing feature of Iranian history in this period was the ability of the Qajar shahs to retain internal power. To a certain extent, the fact that the then major powers were signing treaties with Qajar shahs and that British subjects were signing commercial contracts with them, legitimized their power and gave them the mantle of international protection. Nevertheless any benefits the Iranian people received as a result of Qajar rule were minute compared with their staggering needs, and unrest was growing. Further, local tribes, such as the Bakhtiari khans, were gathering strength and certainly would have been able to wrest power from the Qajars had it not been for the unique adaptation of oriental despotism by which the Qajars ruled.

By the end of the nineteenth century the Qajars ruled with an army of only 2,000 slaves. As Ervand Abrahamian notes, "The Qajars having no instruments for enforcing their will, were forced to retreat whenever confronted by dangerous opposition . . . And all the monarchs lived in terror of public violence whenever the weather and consequently the harvest was bad." The Qajar shahs used the titles King of Kings; the Asylum of the Universe; the Subduer of Climates; the Arbitrator of His People; the Guardian of the Flock; the Protector of the Unfortunate; the Conqueror of Lands; and the Shadow of God. In practice a shah was none of these, but he did have virtually absolute power over his subjects; the land, except that which he had already granted, was regarded as his personal property.

There was a small bureaucracy and therefore only the shah could grant privileges, monopolies, or trade concessions. There were only thirteen major categories of officials, and the shah either appointed or approved those in each category. The bureaucracy consisted chiefly of ministers (vizirs), accountants (*mustawfis*), and secretaries (*mirzas*), located both at the shah's court (*darbar*) and in provincial capitals. Major tribes were headed by *ilkhans*, each of whom had a representative (*vakil*) at court. At the religious level each major city had a *shaykh al Islam*, responsible for the Muslim community. In large towns this task was the duty of the *imam jumaah*, who organized the Friday prayers. The shah had complete control over the economic market as well and was able to fix both buying and selling prices and to appoint major mercantile figures: the guild leaders (*kadkhudas*—see Glossary), the heads of the merchant societies (*malik al tujjars*), the supervisors of guild products (*kalantars*—see Glossary), and the bazaar overseers (*mahtasibs*).

The Qajars neither possessed nor relied on a huge and localized army to enforce their will. Instead they relied on their authority alone and on the diverse nature of the population and all its attendant animosities. The population was widely scattered, and the isolation of many communities increased regionalist tendencies. In addition to geographical factors there were numerous linguistic components; even neighboring ethnic groups spoke different dialects and even languages. For example, in one relatively small area of the northeast lived Persians, Turkomans, Kurds, Shahsavans, Afshars, Tajuks, and Timurs. Religious differences within small areas were also significant: Sunni and Shia Muslims, Armenian Christians, Bahais, Assyrians, Jews, and Zoroastrians might live in close proximity. The Shia community was divided into two factions, Haydari and Nimati, and into three schools (see ch. 4).

When one group rebelled or even threatened rebellion, or committed a real or imagined injury against the shah, there were always potential enemies nearby for the shah to use as instruments of revenge. When the citizens of Nishapur revolted, the shah encouraged local tribes to devastate their lands. "Enemies" received booty, land, or satisfaction in return for their effort. Rebels carried the stigma for many years and "friends of the shah" were rewarded for extraordinary performances. "The city of Burujird was paying a special tax at the end of the century because a generation earlier the Shah had held the local population responsible for the death of his favorite horse . . . ." Sir John Malcolm, the first British emissary to Iran, attempted to explain British governmental machinery to the shah whereupon the shah replied, "Your king, then, appears to be no more than the first magistrate of the state. So limited an authority may be lasting but can have no enjoyment! I can elevate and degrade all the high nobles and officers you see around me."

While Iranian despots might enjoy local pleasures, their anachronistic system made them increasingly vulnerable to foreign economic pressures. Rapid industrialization in the West created demands for raw materials and for fresh markets for manufactured products; Iran was marked as a potential profitable area for such enterprises. The British and the Russians were the leading contenders. In 1889 Baron Paul Julius von Reuter, a British banker and news broker, received the concession for the creation of the Imperial Bank of Persia, and in 1901 William Knox D'Arcy, also British, obtained oil rights for all of Iran with the exception of the northern provinces (see ch. 10). Russia countered with brigades that came to be called the Persian Cossacks and were manned by Iranians under Russian officers. The Russians also secured a concession for the Discount Bank of Persia, which opened in 1891.

In 1896 Muzaffar al Din succeeded his father Nasr al Din and proceeded to neglect the nation and eventually to bankrupt it. Russia made two substantial loans, one early in 1900, by which time Russian officials controlled Iranian governmental finances, and another loan later that year. The total amount was for the equivalent of 32 million rubles, and although Russia was to receive 5 percent interest, it also received low tariff rates, road and railroad concessions, and related benefits.

Nationalism and Revolution

Exclusive of the humiliation of so many foreigners virtually administering the country and certainly exploiting it, popular unrest grew as taxes were increased on the peasants at the same time that *qanat* irrigation networks were falling into ruin. Nasr al Din had been assassinated by a religious nationalist, and after his execution a famous pan-Islamic intellectual, Jamal al Din al Afghani, discussed the antigovernment sentiment with Malkom Khan, a senior official in the Iranian foreign service. Two events appear to have catalyzed the growing movement against the government—Russia was defeated by Japan in the Russo-Japanese War of 1905, and later that year many disaffected Russians fled to Iran after an abortive uprising. These political refugees found many eager listeners for their revolutionary ideas.

Protest took the form of agitation for a constitution. Intellectuals, religious leaders, and merchants demanded that Ayn al

Dawla, the grand vizir, be dismissed from office, that the government refrain from incurring further debts, and that a "house of justice" for the safe expression of views contrary to the government be established. Initially religious and business leaders created a passive resistance movement by taking *bast* (mass refuge) in mosques in Tehran and Qom in December 1905. The shah agreed to all the demands and then reneged on the establishment of a house of justice. A widespread strike followed in July 1906. Ten thousand Tehran citizens fled to the British legation for *bast*. The city was paralyzed, and the shah was forced to capitulate. In August 1906 the shah dismissed Ayn al Dawla and appointed Mirza Nasr Khan as grand vizir.

More important, he granted a form of constitution that provided for a permanent representative Majlis (National Consultative Assembly). Elections were held, and the first Majlis convened in October 1906, with representatives from the nobility, landlords, businessmen, and the Islamic clergy (see Glossary). In January 1907 Muzaffar al Din died and was succeeded by his son, Muhammad Ali Shah, who has been aptly described by a close observer as "perhaps the most perverted, cowardly, and vice-ridden monster that had disgraced the throne of Persia in many generations." The unscrupulous shah took advantage of dissension within the Majlis caused by the failure of the merchants to supply agreed-upon funds and by the disaffection of many of the religious leaders toward secular aspects of the constitution. He reinstated as grand vizir Amin al Sultan, a brilliant but reactionary figure who had been exiled before Ayn al Dawla became grand vizir. Nevertheless the shah yielded to pressure and signed the Supplementary Law in 1907 which along with the 1906 document became an integral part of the Iranian Constitution (see ch. 6).

On August 31, 1907, Great Britain and Russia entered into an agreement by which Iran would be divided into three zones of commercial and protective influence. On the one hand, Russia was eager for an accord with Great Britain because the British had supported the constitutionalists' desire to rid Iran of Russian political influence. Moreover in the aftermath of its recent defeat by Japan, Russia was anxious not to lose any ground in central Asia. The British, on the other hand, were concerned because the Germans planned to build a railroad across the Middle East to the Persian Gulf where Great Britain had substantial investments. Russia's zone was across the northern part of Iran and included Tabriz, Rasht, Tehran, Meshed, and Isfahan. The British zone in the southeast was much smaller. The remainder was to be a neutral zone (see fig. 7). In May 1908 oil was discovered at Masjed Soleyman in southwestern Iran, located in the neutral zone.

Nationalistic opposition was growing because of the commercial partitioning, and the shah decided that the time was ripe to crush the nationalists. With support from the Persian Cossack brigade, commanded by a Russian colonel, the Majlis building was shelled,

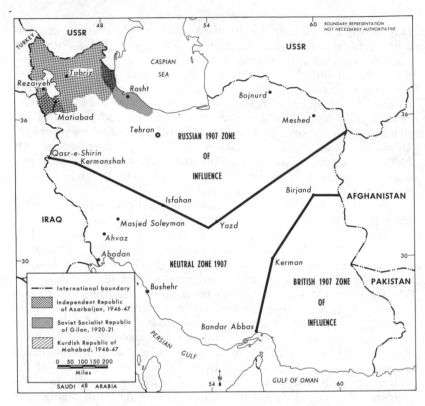

Figure 7. Foreign Zones of Influence, 1907–47

and there were several casualties among the nationalists. The response of the nationalists was swift. Forces were recruited from Tabriz, Rasht, and Isfahan, and civil war began. Czarist Russian contingents continued to support the shah and in July 1908 entered Tabriz on the pretext of safeguarding European lives and property. The occupation of Tabriz provided the incentive the constitutionalists (and others who merely hated the Russian presence) needed to consolidate their forces and influences. In July 1909 a tribal force of 5,000, led by a Bakhtiari chief, defeated the Persian Cossacks near Tehran and liberated the city. By this time the British were also siding with the shah and the Russians against the constitutionalists. Despite the odds the constitutionalists deposed Muhammad Ali who fled first to the Russian legation and then to Russia. In July his eleven year old son Ahmad Mirza was installed as shah by the nationalists, religious leaders, and the Majlis, which was also reestablished.

The task before the constitutionalists was enormous. They wished to unify the country, rid it of foreign political influences, and at the same time modernize it to the extent that it would be less economically dependent on and less vulnerable to foreign powers. Two parties with differing views on the nation's priorities emerged within the Majlis—the revolutionaries and the moderates. Progress was slow, and disagreements within the Majlis prompted the Russians in 1911 to encourage the exiled and deposed shah, Muhammad Ali, to attempt a comeback.

Meanwhile the consitutionalists asked the United States for advisers because the Americans had little vested interest in Iran and might serve to balance the inordinate dominance of Great Britain and Russia. The Americans dispatched William Morgan Shuster, who served as treasurer general in Iran and made immediate and substantial financial reforms. Although beloved by the Iranian people, Shuster's work was strongly opposed by Great Britain, Russia, and the shah's Council of Ministers. Russia showed its displeasure by advancing troops into Iran as far as Qazvin, killing many of the liberals at Tabriz and shelling the shrine of Imam Reza at Meshed, an act of sacrilege that has remained prominent in the minds of Iranians. Although the Majlis would not agree to discharge Shuster, the Council of Ministers finally acquiesced, and he left Iran less than a year after beginning his work.

The fourth nation to become involved in Iran was Germany, and German merchants and advisers began to achieve some prominence. The Iranian people were sympathetic to the Germans chiefly because they were neither British nor Russian and because they kept a low profile in Iran. Germany received support from many members of the Majlis at the beginning of World War I for these reasons and because an allied defeat might loosen the stranglehold Great Britain and Russia had on Iran.

Foreign Influence and the World War I Period

Although Iran had made a declaration of neutrality, British and Russian troops entered Iran shortly after war broke out. Because of Iran's geographical location and its neutrality, Tehran and other major Iranian cities became centers for espionage activites by Russian, German, and British agents. Their aim was to gain Iran's allegiance and to use Iran as a starting point for incursions into Afghanistan and other adjacent areas. Turkish forces were well inside the country before they were defeated by Russian troops. Major Percy Sykes arrived from India at Bandar Abbas and raised a force of 5,000 called the South Persia Rifles. Soon Sykes had the entire south under British control. In Shiraz a German agent, Wassmuss, was busy attempting to win the tribes over to the cause. Iran was torn by warfare, and peasants suffered from the exertions of extortionate landlords who, in the confusion, had no restrictive authority regulating their activities.

Because of the 1917 Russian revolution, most Russian forces had been withdrawn from Iran by the end of the war, and Great Britain became the dominant de facto power. The peace conference after the war rejected Iran's claims and instead, in 1919, Iran was presented with a British-drawn treaty that would have officially placed Iran under total British control. Ahmad Shah and his ministers vacillated about ratifying the treaty. Eventually popular pressure caused them to refuse. An anarchic situation prevailed in Iran. In 1920 Bolshevik troops had control of almost the entire Iranian Caspian Sea coast and with a separatist group proclaimed the short-lived Soviet Socialist Republic of Gilan. The following year Iran signed a treaty of friendship with the Soviet Union whereby, among other articles, the Soviets canceled all Iranian debts, denounced capitulations, ceded all Russian assets on Iranian soil, and agreed to withdraw all Russian forces. In return Iran's chief responsibility was to ensure that anti-Soviet groups would not be permitted to use Iran as a base of activities.

Reza Shah and the Establishment of the Pahlavi Dynasty

On February 21, 1921, while negotiations were taking place in Moscow on the Soviet treaty of friendship with Iran, a bloodless coup d'etat occurred in Tehran. It was led by a prominent Iranian journalist, Sayyid Zia al Din Tabatabai, and backed by the military forces of the Persian Cossack Brigade led by Colonel Reza Khan as minister of war and commander in chief of the army.

Tabatabai was stymied in his reform efforts; he resigned three months after taking office and fled the country. Reza Khan then assumed effective control of the government and remained its prime mover through several cabinet shufflings. In October 1923 Ahmad Shah, accurately assessing the situation, appointed Reza Khan prime minister and left the country for Europe and never returned. During 1924 royalties from the Anglo-Persian Oil Company (APOC) enabled a team of American economic consultants under Arthur C. Millspaugh to achieve a measure of financial stability. Spurred by the example of Turkey, supporters of Reza Khan and liberals began to agitate for the establishment of a republican regime. Reza Khan was enthusiastic at the idea of such a change, but conservative factions within the Majlis and prominent religious leaders were strongly opposed to the dissolution of the monarchy. In February 1925 the Majlis declared Reza Khan commander in chief of the armed forces for life, and he began to initiate changes that he hoped would spark national unity. Among other things he forbade the use of honorific military and social titles and set an example by choosing Pahlavi as his family name.

A new Majlis was called, and on October 31, 1925, the rule of the Qajar dynasty was declared ended. On December 12, 1925, the Majlis chose Reza Pahlavi as the first shah of a new dynasty, with rights of succession granted to his heirs. On April 25, 1926, the formal ceremony of coronation took place, and the next day Reza Shah's oldest son Shapur Mohammad (Mohammad Reza Pahlavi) was named crown prince. Despite the zenophobia that Reza Shah displayed in the interest of national unity and in the hopes of restoring Iran's lost pride, neither Great Britain nor the

Soviet Union opposed the 1921 coup nor the establishment of his dynasty.

Reza Shah Pahlavi, who ruled from 1925 to 1941, wished to Westernize and particularly to industrialize Iran while retaining or restoring those Iranian traditions not antithetical to modernization. Many of the devices used by Turkey's Kemal Ataturk were adapted to a monarchical setting. Arabic words were to be expurgated from the language wherever possible, veiling by women was forbidden, and eventually the Majlis passed a "uniform dress law" making the wearing of Western clothes compulsory. The adaptation of Western clothes was not a thoughtless gesture aimed at mimicking the habits of Western society. Tribal and regional costumes were too reminiscent of ethnic diversity and therefore of disunity. Further, he thought that the adoption of Western clothes would ease the transition of women from the home to the labor force. The use of Persia, the name Westerners and eventually Iranians came to call their country, was discouraged, and foreign mail that arrived addressed to Persia was returned to the sender.

Within Iran foreigners lost much of the prestigious stature they had by virtue of merely being foreign. Reza Shah enacted various restrictions for foreigners: they were prohibited from owning land; the activities of resident foreign businessmen and shopkeepers were circumscribed; and employees of the Ministry of Foreign Affairs were prohibited from marrying non-Iranians and from socializing with foreigners. Reza Shah's foreign policy also reflected his insistence on the necessity of becoming independent of foreign influence. The British-owned Imperial Bank of Persia lost the right to issue currency, and contracts with the APOC were renegotiated to include provisions more advantageous to Iran. Loans were not sought from abroad, and the system of capitulation was ended.

While he was still minister of war, Reza Khan had set out to meld the heterogeneous military bodies of Iran into one army. In 1926 the Majlis passed a universal conscription law that provided Iran with a standing army drawn from the peasantry throughout the country and released the government from its former dependency on tribal levies. The new army, eventually composed of approximately 40,000 men and equipped with modern weapons, had a highly centralized control, and Reza Shah's decrees were brought to and enforced in every part of the nation. There was great social upheaval because only words equivalent to miss, madam, and mister were tolerated, and the authority of nobles and tribal leaders was greatly diminished. The power and authority of the great merchant houses was also reduced because of governmental controls and monopolistic practices. The peasants experienced very real hardships because most of Reza Shah's revenue depended on taxes levied on essential items.

Religious leaders lost influence through a series of reforms and abolitions. They no longer had direct control over religious trust funds and of more importance, with the introduction of the French judicial system in 1927, they were no longer arbiters of civil law. Civil marriage and divorce codes were established, and special licenses were required for those who wished to wear so-called clerical garb. Religious teaching was placed under the aegis of state schools and various local religious phenomena, such as self-flagellation during the religious passion plays and public appearances by dervishes, were forbidden (see ch. 4).

After withdrawing in 1921 from the Gilan area around Rasht on the Caspian Sea coast, the Soviet Union refrained from further attempts at territorial expansion at Iran's expense during Reza Shah's rule; Soviet aggressive commercial policy, however, proved to be detrimental to Iran. By controlling the flow of Iranian exports and Soviet imports, the Soviet state trade monopoly established a balance of trade predominantly favorable to Soviet interests. In the late 1920s the Soviet Union used its control of Soviet-Iranian trade as economic pressure to obtain a favorable settlement of the Caspian Sea fisheries rights. Although the Soviet-Iranian relationship was not cordial, Reza Shah realized the necessity of maintaining commercial ties. In 1927 five pacts with the Soviets were signed chiefly relating to commercial, customs, and naval rights; several more followed in 1935.

As Reza Shah's reign progressed he became staunchly hostile to socialistic ideas and particularly to communism, which to him was a modern manifestation of the old Russian goal of controlling and subverting legitimate authority in Iran. Teachers, journalists, and community leaders who advocated any aspect of communism were jailed. In 1931, at the repeated urging of Reza Shah, the Majlis passed a law that outlawed communism and provided stiff penalties for those accused of spreading "foreign ideologies." Unfortunately there were no effective channels for explaining Reza Shah's goals to the people or for the people to express disagreement or dissent. In 1927 four political parties existed briefly, and Reza Shah said that a parliament without political parties was incomplete. Foreign observers, however, suggest that Reza Shah was too authoritarian to welcome or tolerate disagreement with his policies.

Like his predecessors, Reza Shah continued to look for another world power to counterbalance Soviet and British interest in Iran, which remained strong. As in the pre-World War I period, Germany assumed that role. In the 1930s Germany supplied Iran with heavy machinery, technicians, and advisers for some industrial ventures, and by 1939 Germany rivaled the Soviet Union for a dominant role in Iran's foreign trade. Germany, specifically Nazi Germany, also supplied the shah with the idea for "The Society to Guide Public Opinion." The society was described as a vehicle for acquainting citizens with the goals of the state through publications and lecture tours. Actually a propaganda effort, the society encouraged citizens to subordinate personal interests for the betterment of the state.

World War II and the Azarbaijan Crisis

On September 4, 1939, Iran declared its neutrality in World War II and expected to be able to continue normal commercial relations with powers from both sides. Relations between Great Britain and Iran deteriorated because Great Britain was preventing critically needed industrial equipment from reaching Iran from Germany and because Reza Shah refused Allied requests to expel all German residents from the country and—after Germany attacked the Soviet Union—to permit the shipment of Allied war supplies across Iran to the Soviet Union. Reza Shah perceived both requests as violations of Iran's neutrality.

On August 26, 1941, Great Britain and the Soviet Union simultaneously invaded Iran, the Soviets from the northwest and the British from across the Iraqi frontier and at the head of the Persian Gulf. The British destroyed the Iranian naval forces at Khorramshahr, causing many Iranian casualties. For three days Iran put up a token resistance and then acceded to Allied demands, which amounted to the occupation of Iran by British and Soviet forces. Reza Shah was aware that the Allies would never permit him to remain in power and on September 16 abdicated in favor of his son and legal successor, Shapur Mohammad, who on the same day ascended the throne as Mohammad Reza Pahlavi at the age of twenty-two. Reza Shah and several members of his family were then sent by the British first to Mauritius and then to Johannesburg, South Africa, where Reza Shah died in July 1944.

The new shah, who continued to rule in early 1978, was born on October 26, 1919. He had been carefully nurtured for the monarchy by his father. He was educated in Switzerland and then at the Military College in Tehran. The shah came to the throne facing both domination by the Allied powers and a chaotic internal situation. Reza Shah's tight political restraints over the country were no longer enforced, and many previously repressed groups began to reassert themselves. Tribal leaders secretly returned to their areas, regained lost authority, and resumed the old ways of tribal raiding and harassing sedentary villages. The Shia religious leaders who had been silenced regained importance. Many people went back to the traditional way of dressing, some women resumed wearing veils, and the religious leaders again became influential in education. Numerous political parties sprang up. Most lacked concrete programs, however, and restricted their discussions to complaints and newspaper invective supporting particular interests.

The occupation of Iran proved to be of critical importance for the Allied cause. Americans, British, and Soviets working together managed to move over 5 million tons of munitions and other war matérials across Iran to the Soviet Union. On September 9, 1943, Iran declared war on the Axis powers. In November 1943 at the Tehran Conference, President Franklin D. Roosevelt, Prime Minister Winston Churchill, and Prime Minister Josef Stalin agreed in the Tehran Declaration to give economic assistance to Iran after the war and to respect its independence, territorial integrity, and sovereignty.

The effects of the war and of Allied pressure were devastating for Iran, however. Food and other essential items were scarce and, as a result of severe inflation, very expensive. Cabinet officials changed with alarming frequency, and the Majlis elected in 1943 was unable to agree on priorities or to take any concerted action either to ameliorate Iran's condition or to ease the country's transition from an authoritarian to a more democratic regime.

New political parties had arisen during the war that were increasingly vociferous about the need for change. The most important was the Tudeh (Masses) Party, sometimes called the Democratic Party of Azarbaijan, which was their main area of activity (see ch. 12). The Tudeh Party was initially composed of a group of liberals and left-wing politicians many of whom had been imprisoned during Reza Shah's reign in the 1930s and had used their years in jail to organize a party in the Western sense of the word. Some of its members had studied for a time in the Soviet Union and belonged to the Communist International; others were men who felt that the Tudeh Party offered the best opportunity for seeing their political concepts brought to fruition. During the war the party came under the control of Communists, who were careful at first to minimize communist elements in the party platform in an effort to attract supporters from among the intelligentsia as well as the working class. They denied any revolutionary plans and did not demand nationalization of private property or collectivization of the land. The Tudeh Party's official platform seemed similar to that of many other parties. It advocated progressive labor legislation, improved standard of living for the peasants, reform of the judicial system, national industrialization, and elimination of foreign influences. For a time it succeeded in developing a joint front between its own and some liberal newspapers.

During the initial years of World War II the Allies agreed on most issues in Iran. Toward the end of the war, however, disagreements arose between the Soviet Union on the one hand and Anglo-American policies on the other. The Allies attempted to keep up a united front, but these disputes eventually resulted in repercussions in internal Iranian politics. During 1944 all three countries negotiated actively with the Iranian government for oil concessions. At that time the Majlis membership included many nationalist-minded Iranians. Under the leadership of Mohammad Mossadeq, they passed a resolution forbidding Iranian officials from entering into oil concession negotiations with foreigners while the war was in progress and foreign troops still on Iranian soil. During the debate in the Majlis, however, the Tudeh Party, which until 1944 had claimed to be disassociated with any foreign power, openly supported the Soviet claim for a concession while denouncing the British and Americans as colonial imperialists who wished to steal the natural resources of Iran. As a result the governing political orientation of the Tudeh Party became clear, and it began to lose some popularity among Iranian intellectuals.

Despite the loss of popularity among some groups, the Tudeh Party continued to increase its membership and to make sporadic attacks on Iranian police posts and army garrisons. Government reinforcements sent to Azarbaijan were countered by Soviet forces stationed west of the capital. In December 1945 the establishment of the autonomous state of Azarbaijan was announced and, a short time later in nearby Kordestan, the Republic of Mahabad was declared by the Kurds with a Russian-backed puppet government. Iran denounced the activities of the Soviet Union, which were clearly in violation of the Tehran Declaration, at the Security Council of the United Nations (UN). The Security Council suggested that Iran negotiate with the Soviet Union.

On March 2, 1946, the last British troops left, in accordance with the treaty signed when Great Britain and the Soviet Union entered the country in 1942. American forces had already been evacuated by the end of 1945. In March 1946 Ahmad Qavam al Saltaneh, an Iranian politician known for his friendly relations with the Tudeh Party and the Soviet Union, became prime minister of Iran and went to the Soviet Union to begin negotiations for the withdrawal of Soviet troops. He succeeded in obtaining a promise from the Soviet government to evacuate its army in exchange for Ahmad Qavam's agreement to sponsor in the Majlis an oil concession to the Soviets and to negotiate a peaceful settlement with the Azarbaijani rebels.

Partially because of remonstrations by the American and British governments directly and in the UN the Soviet Union eventually withdrew from Azarbaijan. The objective of obtaining oil concessions, however, was not abandoned by the Soviets. In March 1946 Tudeh Party demonstrations in front of the parliament building prevented the fourteenth Majlis from meeting in order to extend its expired term of office; this gave Ahmad Qavam effective control over the government. He then closed down anti-Russian newspapers and arrested certain conservative politicians, including Tabatabai, who had returned to Iran in 1943 to head the National Will Party. In August Ahmad Qavam reshuffled his cabinet and included three Tudeh Party ministers.

At the same time, five Iranian tribes in the south, including the Qashqai, revolted against the increased influence of the Tudeh Party and the Soviet Union in Tehran and against the conciliatory stance taken by the government toward the regime in Azarbaijan. Meanwhile pro-British Arabs in Iraq began agitating for the return of certain lands in the south of Iran to Arab rule. British troops from India were moved into Basra (in Iraq, about thirty miles northwest of Abadan). These steps were considered by observers to mean that the British government was unwilling to see the Iranian government fall under control of Moscow.

In October 1946 the shah ordered another cabinet reshuffle; Ahmad Qavam dismissed the Tudeh Party members and announced that he intended to occupy Azarbaijan with Iranian troops before holding elections for the fifteenth Majlis because the government of Azarbaijan had reneged on its promise to allow supervision of elections. In December Iranian troops moved into Azarbaijan forcing Jaafar Pishavari, the Azarbaijani leader, to flee to the Soviet Union, putting an end to the independent government there and also to the short-lived Kurdish Republic of Mahabad. The Soviet government did nothing to prevent the overthrow of their protégés in Azarbaijan and Mahabad, partly because of the American and British positions and partly because of its continuing major objective of obtaining a ratified oil concession in the northern provinces of Iran.

In July 1947 the fifteenth Majlis met with most of the members of the Democrats of Iran and took up the issue of ratification of the Soviet-Iranian oil concession. The Tudeh Party representation had been reduced to two members. A strong nationalist group of Majlis deputies called the National Front, led by Mossadeq, accused Prime Minister Admad Qavam of being willing to sell Iran's oil to foreign interests and urged the Majlis to reject the concession. The United States government, having taken a more active interest in the affairs of Middle Eastern states, indicated through its ambassador that the United States would support rejection of the concession by Iran. Early in October 1947 an agreement between the United States and Iran for American military aid went into effect. Encouraged by this new attitude, the Majlis refused to ratify the Soviet oil concession. Ahmad Qavam's political strength declined; he resigned as prime minister in December 1947 and a pro-Western cabinet came to office.

The Soviet Union, having withdrawn from the territory occupied in Azarbaijan, had also failed to attain its postwar objective of gaining oil control in northern Iran. The prewar British oil concession, however, remained in effect; shortly before he resigned, Ahmad Qavam had brought a bill before the fifteenth Majlis calling for renegotiation of this concession.

Mohammad Mossadeq and Oil Nationalization

The Azarbaijan crisis was resolved, and the Majlis was about to turn to more pressing internal problems when an assassination attempt was made on the shah in February 1949. Although two of the five shots fired at point-blank range hit the shah, he was only slightly injured and decided that this represented the second of a .series of miracles—the first being the recovery of Azarbaijan—and was a clear sign from God that the shah had a "mission for his country." The Tudeh Party was blamed for the incident and banned, and its adherents either fled into exile or were imprisoned. With a new feeling of internal security and calm, Iranian leaders announced their intention of intensifying the modernization and industrialization begun by Reza Shah.

In 1949 the Majlis approved the Seven Year Plan for industrial and agricultural development in Iran, which had been worked out by American financial advisers, and a plan organization was set up for its administration. This ambitious plan was to be financed in large part by revenues derived from the agreement with the AIOC, which was still operating under the terms of the 1923 agreement. Politically conscious Iranians were aware that the British government derived more revenue from taxing the profits of the AIOC than the Iranian government did through royalties. The nationalistic membership of the Majlis was determined to obtain a greater and as they saw it more equitable share of the revenue.

The shah's cabinets changed several times in 1948 and 1949, and each prime minister tried to reach a more favorable settlement with the AIOC. In 1949 new elections for the Majlis were held in an atmosphere in which the oil issue was of great importance. The government eventually worked out a compromise solution with the AIOC, but the Majlis rejected it. Mossadeq, a staunch nationalist, assumed the chairmanship of the Majlis committee on oil in 1950.

General Ali Razmara, named prime minister in June 1950, urged the oil company to listen to the demands of the nationalists in the Majlis, but he was at first unable to get any concessions beyond the ones made in the unsatisfactory 1949 compromise draft agreement. In February 1951, however, the company offered a fifty-fifty profit-sharing arrangement. This offer proved too late, since a campaign of intense nationalism had united the Majlis against "imperialism and foreign control" of all kinds. Late in February the oil committee of the Majlis asked Razmara to report on the practicability of nationalizing the oil industry. After consulting oil technicians and economists, Razmara reported that nationalization was not practicable or in the best interests of Iran. Four days later, on March 7, 1951, he was assassinated by Khalil Tahmeshi, a member of a militant religious group, the Fedayani Islam.

On March 15, 1951, the Majlis voted to nationalize the oil industry; and when the new prime minister, Hussein Ala, made no immediate move to take over the properties of the AIOC, the Majlis demanded that the shah appoint Mossadeq, then seventy-one years of age, as prime minister. Violent demonstrations supported the Majlis' demand.

Mossadeq was named prime minister on April 29, 1951, and his administration lasted until August 1953. At the outset Mossadeq displayed great skill as a leader of public opinion. He was supported, although not continuously, by the National Front, a heterogeneous group that included the Iran Party, the Toilers' Party, the neo-Nazi Sumka Party, the ultranationalist Pan-Iran Party, and the Fedayani, a group coalesced around Sayyid Abal Qasim Kashani, a fanatic religious leader. During Mossadeq's administration the nationalization law was put into effect, oil production in Iran almost came to a stop, and the Iranian government suffered greatly from the loss of oil revenues. The prime minister and his nationalist and anti-British religious followers were not trained as petroleum economists capable of working in the international oil market.

Moreover Iran had few trained technicians and engineers capable of continuing the production of oil once the British left. Great Britain, however, had many economic counteractions at its disposal. It was not dependent on Iranian oil for survival, and in fact there was a surplus of oil on the world market by 1953. In September 1951 Great Britain withdrew Iran's special sterling exchange facilities, banned export of commodities and matériel to Iran, and applied an embargo on Iranian oil that was observed by most European shippers—who were the primary distributors of Iran's petroleum products. By early 1952 the Iranian economy began to suffer from loss of foreign exchange and foreign goods.

The poorer people of Iran, however, were not at first directly affected by the loss of oil revenues and continued to hold Mossadeq in great esteem. Throughout his time in office he maintained a high pitch of excitement in the capital and to a lesser extent throughout the rest of the country. His major political weapons were the crowds that appeared in the streets to cheer his speeches against British colonial imperialists. The Tudeh Party resumed its activities. Mossadeq was not a Communist, but he did not suppress the Tudeh Party mobs because they supported him in his anti-British policies. Because of the emotional atmosphere throughout the country during this period, neither Mossadeq nor any other politician could have afforded to give the appearance of compromising Iran's position with regard to the oil issue, even had he so desired. Negotiations with the AIOC continued but, while protracted, were inconclusive.

In the summer of 1952 Mossadeq asked for absolute control over the government for a limited time. The shah refused and made his first attempt to challenge Mossadeq's authority by appointing a new prime minister. Four days of rioting by Mullah Kashani's Fedayani forced the shah to change his mind; Mossadeq was reinstated and for the remainder of 1952 possessed almost absolute control over the government. He consolidated his control by assuming the post of minister of war, a position traditionally appointed by the shah. He reorganized military units and weeded out those he considered potential dissidents. Contrary to what Mossadeq had led the people to expect, authoritarian and generally repressive measures were enacted as a result of special powers given him by the Majlis, which permitted him to make laws without the prior consent of the Majlis. Strict censorship laws came into force; strikes by government workers were prohibited;

martial law was extended; and elections for the Senate and for the Majlis were suspended. Diplomatic relations with Great Britain were broken off in October. By January 1953 the increasing economic difficulties and repressive government measures caused Mossadeq's popular support to erode. By the end of June 1953 some of Mossadeq's stuanchest and most important supporters not only had left the National Front but were strongly opposed to him.

By early August 1953 Mossadeq's authoritarianism had alienated so many of his supporters in the Majlis that he lost his majority. He therefore called for a public referendum on August 3 to abolish the Majlis, a referendum he claimed to have won. Taking advantage of the constitutional provision that on the abolition of the Majlis the shah could dismiss the prime minister, the shah replaced Mossadeq with General Fazouah Zahedi, a staunch supporter of the shah. Mossadeq refused to relinquish the government and arrested the shah's emissary. He then announced the deposition of the shah and the formation of a regency council to act for the shah. For four days, during which time the shah left Iran, anarchy reigned in Tehran. By August 19, however, General Zahedi had rallied the army behind the shah, arrested Mossadeq and his supporters, and assumed the premiership. On August 19 the shah returned to Tehran amidst great public enthusiasm. On December 2, 1953, Mossadeq was sentenced to three years of solitary confinement for high treason. After his release in 1956 he lived quietly and died in Tehran on March 5, 1967, at the age of eighty-seven.

After World War II Mossadeq and his followers described the United States as assuming Great Britain's former role of counterbalance to the Soviet Union in Iran, Turkey, Greece, and other parts of the Middle East and estimated that the United States would take major action to prevent Iran's turning to the Soviets for assistance. During the Mossadeq period, however, the United States declined to provide the massive financial aid that would have been required to make up for Iran's oil revenue losses. In 1950 the first United States economic aid agreement had been signed with Iran; and both technical assistance and military aid was continued and even showed an increase from its modest beginning during Mossadeq's rule. The amount of United States dollars that reached Iran in this way, however, was in no way sufficient to prevent the Iranian economy from suffering severely during the shutoff of oil revenues.

The royalist coup that displaced Mossadeq in 1953 was criticized in the Soviet Union but viewed favorably by Western powers. In fact most foreign and Iranian observers assert that British and American assistance—both official and private—ensured the success of the royalist coup. Diplomatic relations with Great Britain were restored by Iran on December 5, 1953. The United States had answered Prime Minister Zahedi's appeal for financial aid by a first installment of US$45 million in September. Zahedi's main support within Iran came from the army's high command and from most of the conservative political elements in the country.

Mohammad Reza Pahlavi and the White Revolution

It was only after the deposition of Mossadeq that the shah began to rule; previously he had only reigned. After 1953 he became the preeminent national leader and personality and introduced a program of national reforms and development known as the White Revolution (see Glossary). At the same time he took steps to diminish the substantial power of the Majlis and affirm his central authority over every aspect of government (see ch. 6). Elections in 1954 and 1956 for the eighteenth and nineteenth Majlis, respectively, were closely managed by the government, which played an important part in nominating the candidates and in supervising the balloting. The Tudeh Party continued to be outlawed, and Mossadeq's National Front, with its leader in jail, was prevented from obtaining substantial power in either of the assemblies.

Simultaneously the influence of the shah, his immediate family, and his close associates at court and in the national security forces increased. The prime ministers as well as other cabinet members were the personal choices of the shah, who also took an active part in determining the country's foreign policy. It was sometimes necessary, however, for the shah to accede to the advice or wishes of certain elite Iranian families of great wealth and power. Through their influence in the Majlis, they could affect the passage of legislation desired by the shah. These influential families tended to be conservative in action, rather than socially progressive (see ch. 5).

General Zahedi was prime minister until April 1955, and during this period governmental operations were unambitious but stable. Slow but definite progress was made in reestablishing Iran's relations with Western powers, dealing primarily with the oil question (see ch. 10). The resolution of the oil crisis in 1954 led to an increased policy of economic and political cooperation between Iran and states outside the Soviet sphere of influence.

Hussein Ala succeeded Zahedi as prime minister in April 1955 and began to initiate domestic reforms. Additionally on October 11, 1955, despite Soviet protests, Iran subscribed to the regional security arrangement initially known as the Baghdad Pact, which had been launched the previous February by Turkey, Iraq, Pakistan, and Great Britain. The United States was a supporting observer. After the disassociation of Iraq from the agreement in 1958, the structure was known by its formal name, the Central Treaty Organization (CENTO), to which Iran continued to adhere in 1977. On March 5, 1959, representatives of the United States and Iran, meeting at Ankara, Turkey, signed a bilateral defense agreement (see ch. 8).

Relations between Iran and the Soviet Union after the fall of Mossadeq were correct but not cordial. In December 1954 agreements with the Soviet Union were reached by which the latter undertook payment to Iran in settlement of World War II claims and further agreed to a joint frontier survey, commencing in August 1955. The shah visited the Soviet Union in 1956; the frontier demarcation commission completed its work in April 1957, when protocols were signed specifically defining the frontiers. Despite these accomplishments relations were less than cordial. Internal and external communist propaganda was frequently vituperative against the shah and his government until late 1962 and 1963, after which Iranian-Soviet relations improved.

With some countries of the Arab world, however, frictions developed and continued after 1960. Some causes of disagreement were of older origin, such as the boundary dispute with Iraq along the Shatt al Arab waterway (the Tigris River at the head of the Persian Gulf), which was not resolved until 1975 (see ch. 8). Another long-standing difference was the Iranian claim to the island of Bahrain and to other smaller islands in the Persian Gulf. Other differences of more recent origin lay in Iran's de facto recognition of Israel, which caused the severance of Iranian-Egyptian diplomatic relations in 1960, and in border incidents with Iraq connected with the Iraqi operations in the 1960s and early 1970s against dissident Kurds.

Relations with Jordan were consistently cordial, however, and in the late 1960s improved substantially with Saudi Arabia. The shah and King Faisal of Saudi Arabia were instrumental in organizing and supporting the Islamic Summit Conference held in Rabat, Morocco, in September 1969. Iran's relations with Afghanistan were generally good; riparian distribution rights to the Helmand River waters had been a source of some differences, but the boundary between the two countries had long been demarcated and accepted, and no critical international issues prevailed.

Internally much publicity was given during the middle and late 1950s to the need for firm action on chronic social problems, most of which had existed long before the Pahlavi dynasty came to power. These included overcentralization of government in the capital city and the resulting lack of control over their own affairs by provincial populations; concentration of land in the hands of a relatively few wealthy landlords; the enormous, often inefficient or venal bureaucracy; and the inequality of tax laws and the manner in which they were admininstered. As early as 1949 the shah had indicated a firm intention of instituting significant changes, beginning with agrarian land reform. Before these were initiated, however, a preparatory period of economic recovery and of political stabilization, both internal and external, was needed. The recovery and stabilization period continued through the 1950s and early 1960s.

Order was restored internally after 1953. The outlawed Tudeh Party attempted to organize conspiracies against the shah in January and August 1954 and at later times, but none succeeded.

During the recovery period in the late 1950s, however, internal political stresses developed, which were evident from the rapidity with which prime ministers changed. Zahedi's successors included Hussein Ala, who remained in office until April 1957; Manuchehr Eqbal, who resigned in August 1960; Jafar Sharif Imami, who resigned in May 1961; Ali Amini, who resigned in July 1962; Asadollah Alam, who resigned in March 1964; Hassan Ali Mansur, who was shot by a militant Muslim on January 21, 1965; and Amir Abbas Hoveyda, who was designated on Mansur's death. He in turn was replaced in August 1977 by Jamshid Amuzegar.

Martial law ended in 1957, and the foundation of a legal political party system was laid. The parties included the Maliyuun (National) Party, which was succeeded in the majority role by the Iran Novin (New Iran) Party and opposed by the Mardom (People's) Party. National elections were held in 1960 but were annulled by the shah because of supervisory irregularities. Elections were held again in January 1961. After this election the shah requested the Majlis to enact a new electoral law. Before the resignation of Prime Minister Imami in May 1961 his successor, Amini, sought to correct irregularities in the civil service, begin decentralization of administration, limit luxury imports, and initiate land redistribution reforms. Both houses of the Parliament—the sixty-member Senate and the 220-member Majlis—were dissolved pending development of a new electoral law. In July 1962, because of budget controversies and dissatisfaction over postponement of elections, Amini found it necessary to resign and was succeeded by Alam of the Mardom Party.

Prime Minister Alam, a firm advocate of close ties with the West and of land reform, was confronted almost at once by a disastrous earthquake that shook northwestern Iran in September 1962, causing an estimated 10,000 deaths. Surviving this crisis, his government assisted the shah in preparing a reform program, which the shah announced in January 1963 at the First All-Iran Farm Cooperatives Conference. This program became known as the White Revolution of the Shah and the People and, by the mid-1970s, as the Shah-People Revolution. The six principles embodied in the program were abolition of the feudal landlord-peasant system and redistribution of land; nationalization of public forest and pastures; compensation of former landlords by capital shares in government industry; profit sharing in all productive enterprises; ratification of a proposed new electoral law, including votes for women; and creation of a national literacy corps using educated youth in national service to raise the literacy rate (see ch. 3; ch. 11). The program was overwhelmingly endorsed in a national referendum in January 1963. By the end of 1963 the shah had distributed the crown estates to the land distribution scheme and the Pahlavi Foundation. Prime Minister Alam, who was a major landholder, also voluntarily distributed his land.

Early in June 1963 rioting occurred, inspired by the opposition of landlords and conservative Islamic clergy to land reform and the emancipation of women and by political pragmatists in the old National Front seeking to take advantage of political turmoil of any kind. At about the same time tribal disturbances created disorder in southern Iran. The shah and his government held fast, however; the armed forces and gendarmerie remained loyal, order was restored, and elections were conducted in September 1963. In these elections, in which women voted for the first time in the history of Iran, Alam and his National Union were overwhelmingly successful. The new Parliament, elected for four years by law, was formally opened in October 1963 by the shah, who was accompanied by Queen Farah Diba, whom he had married in late 1959. The shah called on Parliament to continue current efforts and to project a twenty-year program of reform and revitalization of the nation.

Alam resigned his office in March 1964 and was succeeded at once by Mansur, a former minister and progressive leader, who was shot on January 21, 1965, and died on January 26. This act did much to discredit conservative religious leaders. The shah called on Hoveyda, the minister of finance, to become the prime minister, and he did so with the unanimous support of the Majlis.

Serious internal opposition has steadily decreased since 1963, although in April 1965 another attempt was made to kill the shah. On September 15, 1965, Parliament conferred on the shah the personal title of Aryamehr, a word derived from the ancient pre-Islamic Achaemenian era meaning Light of the Aryans. In the elections of August 1967 Prime Minister Hoveyda and the Iran Novin Party received a large majority. That Parliament, the twenty-second session of the Majlis and the fifth session of the Senate, was declared open by the shah on October 6, 1967, in a speech from the throne called "The Revolution—New Dimensions." The next month, as a further evidence of progress, United States government economic aid was terminated as no longer required.

Formal coronation of the shah occurred at an impressive ceremony on his forty-eighth birthday—October 26, 1967—twenty-six years after his accession to the throne on September 17, 1941. In official proclamations the Iranian monarchy was held to be over 2,500 years old and therefore the oldest continuous monarchy on earth; in 1976 Parliament, at the request of the shah, approved a new calendar system that started with the coronation of Cyrus the Great. Under this system the Iranian year beginning March 21, 1977, was the year 2536 (see table A). Immediately after placing the crown on his own head, the shah crowned his wife as empress, the first woman in Iranian history to receive the honor.

The Majlis, meeting on September 7, 1967, had resolved that Farah should be recognized as regent in the event of the shah's death or incapacity before the twentieth birthday of the crown prince, Reza Cyrus. The oldest son of the shah and Farah, Reza

Cyrus, born on October 31, 1960, was formally designated crown prince at the coronation ceremony.

*   *   *

The most complete source for Iranian history is the peerless *Cambridge History of Islam* in eight volumes, which, in a series of essays by specialists, details religious, social, geographical, and economic as well as political history. Each essay also contains substantial bibliographic information. Noteworthy among single volume studies for the ancient period accessible to the layman are Jacques Duchesne-Guillemin's *Religion of Ancient Iran,* Jean-Louis Huot's *Persia I,* and Peter Moorey's *Ancient Iran.*

For the period of the Islamic conquest and its immediate aftermath in Iran, the most illuminating single volume is Richard Frye's *The Golden Age of Persia,* which benefits from Frye's thorough acquaintance with the whole of Iranian history. Roy Mottahedeh's scholarly and delightful article, "The Shuubiyah Controversy and the Social History of Early Islamic Iran," offers a wealth of insights on material frequently neglected by the political historians.

The late Safavid and the Qajar period have only recently received focused attention by scholars. Among the best of new works on the period are two of Algar Hamid's works, *Religion and State in Iran, 1978–1906* and *Mirza Malkum Khan.* Ervand Abrahamian's article, "Oriental Despotism: The Case of Qajar Iran," is a short but excellent treatment of the ruling patterns of the Qajars.

For the twentieth century, Nikki Keddie's "Iranian Politics 1900–05, Background to Revolution" is extremely helpful. Donald Wilber's works—*Riza Shah Pahlavi: The Resurrection and Reconstruction of Iran, 1878–1944* and *Iran: Past and Present,* which treats Iranian history from its beginnings through the establishment of the Pahlavis, with particular emphasis on the modern period—are excellent introductions to the modern period. Three works that mainly examine Iranian artistic developments are also valuable for social history: David Talbot-Rice's, *Islamic Art;* Reuben Levy's, *An Introduction to Persian Literature;* and Jan Rypka's weighty, *History of Iranian Literature.* (For further information see Bibliography.)

Chapter 3.   Demographic Setting and Education

DEMOGRAPHIC TRENDS DURING the years since World War II have profoundly effected the way in which the people live. According to preliminary results from the 1976 census—only the third in the country's history—the population totaled less than 34 million but may have been somewhat more. The annual population growth rate had increased from less than 2 percent in the early 1900s to about 3 percent in the 1960s and had subsequently leveled off or commenced a slight decline. It was not one of the world's highest growth rates, but it was a high one with important negative socioeconomic consequences, and by 1970 Shahanshah Mohammad Reza Pahlavi had formally committed the country to a family planning program. By the mid-1970s the program was reportedly showing encouraging results.

Population growth was also probably being slowed by urbanization; city families customarily have fewer children than rural ones. In the mid-1970s a little more than half the population was still rural, but country people were flocking to Tehran and other cities at a rate that was fast changing the pattern of population distribution.

There were numerous consequences of this shift. Standards of living in the cities were generally higher than in the countryside, but the migration worsened an already serious housing shortage and made necessary more schools and more health facilities.

The urban movement brought with it a corresponding change in the character of the labor force. In the mid-1970s agriculture was still the principal occupation, but agricultural employment was undergoing a progressive relative decline at the expense of higher urban employment in industry and in service activities.

Labor skills of all kinds were in such acutely short supply that trained personnel could command extremely high salaries, even by European standards. Unemployment was minimal, but there was considerable underemployment in agriculture and in the handicraft sector of industrial employment.

School enrollments were increasing, but the number of children flocking to the schools placed a severe strain on the capacity of a system that only a few years earlier had accommodated but a small proportion of the school-age population. The most effective thrust of the educational program during the 1960s and early 1970s had been directed at the reduction of illiteracy, but in the mid-1970s most of the rural population was still unable to read and write.

A large proportion of students at the university level studied abroad, and during the 1950s and early 1960s many of them failed to return to Iran on completion of their studies. In the 1970s it appeared that most of the professionally trained were returning because of the high salaries availabe. Physicians, however, were remaining abroad, and a shortage of doctors was among the most serious of the country's medical problems. Ample medical care was available in Tehran and the major urban centers, but in the countryside little was available. The population relied on occasional mobile medical teams and still engaged extensively in traditional medicine that involved herbal medicine and mystical practices.

In the mid-1970s a social security program reached less than 10 percent of the population, and there was considerable continued reliance on the family for the care of family members. The continued dependence on children by parents in their old age probably had an adverse effect on progress of the family planning program.

The shift of population from rural to urban brought with it a corresponding change in how much money families had to spend and how it was spent. The rise in petroleum prices in 1973 and 1974 meant enormous prosperity, and the per capita income in the mid-1970s was among the world's highest. For higher income families this meant purchasing automobiles and other luxuries at rates exceeded in few parts of the world.

In the changing demographic setting the role of women was becoming increasingly more significant and conspicuous, but in the Muslim tradition females continued to play a secondary role outside the family. Moreover males continued to outnumber females in the mid-1970s. The reason was not clear, but it appeared to stem from heavy childbirth mortality and from a continued tendency to give better care to male than to female babies. The data may also reflect a tendency in the censuses to undercount females.

Women represented a small minority of the labor force where they were engaged principally in factory work. A considerable number were domestic servants, but men made up nearly all the work force in stores and restaurants. Wearing veils had been banned since the 1930s, but veiled women could occasionally be seen, even in the streets of Tehran. Although the proportion of females in the schools was increasing substantially, they remained a minority. Significantly, perhaps, coeducation in the mid-1970s could be found only in institutions of higher education and in the literacy program (see ch. 5).

Population Structure and Dynamics

In December 1976 a government publication reported the preliminary count in the third national census, which had been conducted earlier in 1976, to have been about 33.5 million. Totals from the first (1956) and second (1966) census had been enumerated as 19 million and 25.3 million respectively. The counts appeared to have been substantially underenumerated, however, and were unofficially later corrected upward to 20.4 million and 27.1 million respectively (see table 2, Appendix A). For neither census year did the figures include counts for tribal and other unsettled populations, which in 1966 were calculated at 462,146 and 244,141 respectively. The preliminary findings from the 1976 population census did not indicate whether or not the unsettled populations were included in the total; and there may have been an underenumeration. In early 1977 it could be generalized only that there were at least 34 million people in Iran and that perhaps there were 1 to 2 million more.

During the first half of the twentieth century, estimates and scattered population surveys indicated that the population growth rate was irregularly increasing but that at the end of the period the average remained below 2 percent annually. During the 1956–66 period it had increased to 2.9 percent on the basis of enumerated census data.

The preliminary report on the 1976 census showed the current growth rate to have been 2.7 percent, presumably the average for the years since the second census. This is fairly consistent with the United Nations (UN) estimate of 2.8 percent annual average for the 1970–74 period. Other estimates and projections for the late 1960s and early 1970s indicated averages of 3 percent or more. The population growth rate in the mid-1970s had apparently stabilized at a little under 3 percent and perhaps had turned slightly downward. Neighboring Iraq and Jordan had rates well over 3 percent, but even the lowest rate indicated for Iran was above the world's average.

The leveling off or downward turn in population growth appeared to have been based directly on the increasing effectiveness of the family planning program to which the government was formally committed. Indirectly it was based on the improvement and expansion of the country's educational system and on the substantial and continuing movement of people from rural to urban areas, which had been in progress since World War II or earlier. Demographic studies throughout the world have made clear the inverse relationship between the amount of education of a mother and the number of her children. Similarly a shift in population to urban localities has invariably been accompanied by a drop in the population growth rate.

Data on vital statistics on which the growth rate was determined were incomplete. A United Nations Educational, Scientific and Cultural Organization (UNESCO) team during the mid-1960s estimated that only about 60 percent of the births and 35 percent of the deaths were recorded. On the basis of these limited data the UN estimated the birthrate for the 1965–70 period as slightly more than forty-five per 1,000 a little above the average of forty-two per 1,000 for southcentral Asia. For the same period the death rate was estimated at more than sixteen per 1,000; similar data from another source listed the death rate for the Muslim world as a whole at fourteen per 1,000. The UN estimated life expectancy at birth at an average of fifty years for both sexes during the 1965–70 period. Other UN data refined this figure to forty-eight years for men and fifty-two years for women. Yet another source covering approximately the same period showed life expectancy to have been fifty-one and one-half years and fifty-seven and one-half years for urban people and forty-seven and one-half years for rural dwellers.

Preliminary 1976 census data indicated 51.4 percent of the population as male, only slightly less than the 51.8 percent recorded for 1966. In a developed country the naturally greater longevity of women would have come into play, and females would have outnumbered males. In Iran the pattern seemed characteristic of a country in the early stages of development where a large number of women died in connection with childbirth, and one in which a male infant received a more adequate diet and thus enjoyed a better chance of survival. To some extent this has probably been true in Iran. In addition, however, the presence of young, unmarried women may not have been declared to the census enumerators by some heads of households.

It was a very young population. Age data for 1976 were not yet available in mid-1977, but according to a 1971 UN estimate the median age was between sixteen and seventeen, and only a little more than 3 percent was aged sixty-five or over. The extreme youth of the population had important socioeconomic implications in terms of the burden placed on workers by the number of children too young to be economically active, the increasing need for new jobs, and the enormous expansion that must be made in social security and other social services.

In the Central Plateau of Iran the population is remarkably homogeneous, having an Indo-European origin. In frontier regions there is greater ethnic admixture; Turkic-speaking people predominate in the northwest, Turkoman in the northeast, and Arabs in the southwest. Although in 1966 the nomadic tribal people were reported to constitute less than 2 percent of the total population, estimates ran to as much as 10 percent. Historically the tribes have played a significant role in placing monarchs on the throne and in supplying soldiers for the armies. Of particular importance were the Kurds, in the west, related to compatriots across the borders in Iraq and Turkey. Among other tribal people were the Bakhtiaris, Lurs, Baluchis, and Qashqais. In the northeast the once wild and feared Turkomans of Khorasan had for the most part been permanently settled (see Peoples, ch. 5). In general the degree to which the tribal population remained apart from the mainstream of national life was determined by the extent to which it resisted government efforts encouraging it to become sedentary. In the 1960s and early 1970s, however, the public education program was notably successful in providing mobile tent schools and vocational training programs to the still nomadic tribes (see Education, this ch.).

Immigration and emigration during the years since World War II were not of sufficient importance to have a statistically significant effect on population dynamics. On the basis of the scanty information available, emigrants are believed to have outnum-

Luri women weaving
U.S. Army photograph

bered immigrants and to have consisted largely of unemployed workers from the southern provinces who moved into the Arab states across the Persian Gulf in search of employment. In the early 1970s there were sizable Iranian settlements in the gulf area, particularly in Iraq, Kuwait, the United Arab Emirates (UAE), and Oman.

Of much more socioeconomic importance than the emigration into the Persian Gulf states was the qualitative population loss or brain drain resulting from the failure of a large proportion of the university students going abroad for higher education to return to Iran after completion of their studies. Conflicting estimates are given as to their number, but according to a 1976 foreign ministry report approximately 60,000 students were enrolled abroad.

Before 1965 it might have been concluded that a large proportion would never return to Iran. Several reports appearing in the mid-1970s, however, indicated that in most professional categories the brain drain might have been stopped or even reversed. In particular a 1976 study conducted by Tehran University's Center for International Studies reported the exodus as continuing in the case of physicians but that in other professions the number returning to Iran exceeded the number leaving. The study, covering the late 1960s and early 1970s, found that the country's industrial growth was proving effective in encouraging young people educated abroad to return and in attracting young professionals from other countries.

Family Planning

Despite possessing one of the world's higher population growth rates, Iran in the mid-1970s had a very low average population density, and although half the national territory consisted of desert, it did not as yet face the immediate problem of population crowding that was afflicting many other countries. Urban crowding was becoming apparent, however, and Iran had made an early start in recognizing the advantages in restraining and directing population growth.

Public instruction on family planning practices commenced in maternal and child health clinics as early as 1953, and official interest in the problem was aroused by demographic studies that appeared after the 1956 census, including a landmark study by the New York-based Population Council. Ministry of Health officials initiated visits to survey similar problems in Egypt and Pakistan, and these visits led to creation of the position of undersecretary for family planning in the Ministry of Health, charged with formulating a specific planning program.

The first Iranian project was initiated in 1967 with the establishment of a family planning center to promote the use of contraceptives and to make maximum use of Iranian physicians in the program. A more aggressive policy initiated in 1970 had a twenty-year goal of reducing the annual population growth rate to 1 percent (later, the target for the 1973–78 period was set at 2.6

percent). In 1974 it was reported that nearly 7,500 medical personnel and over 17,000 persons engaged in technical work in hospitals and clinics had taken courses and were participating in promoting the family planning program.

In the mid-1970s, however, some serious difficulties had not yet been overcome. Awareness of the program was severly limited by the fact that well over half the female population was illiterate and that in rural Iran where the program was most needed only a relative few could read and write. In the Zoroastrian system of beliefs, aspects of which became imbedded in Shia culture, there was a strong emphasis on the role and importance of children, and childbirth itself was regarded as a religious experience having profound implications (see ch. 4). Culturally, religiously, and politically children were enjoined to care for parents in their old age, a traditional attitude that stressed the importance of large families (see Welfare, this ch.).

During the late 1960s and early 1970s steady progress was made in overcoming ignorance and traditional attitudes toward birth control, and data available by 1972 showed that about 6.5 million contacts had been made with women who had come to the more than 2,000 clinical centers for advice or services. In 1974 the government estimated that the family planning techniques had reduced births by about six per 1,000. The shah prescribed that December 5 would be commemorated annually as Family Planning Day. By 1977 about 85 percent of the adult population was reported to have gained awareness of effective birth control methods, and 3,000 clinics had been established throughout the country.

Settlement Patterns

The urban sector of the population increased from about 33 percent of the total in 1956 to about 38 percent in 1966. Between 1966 and 1976 the urban sector grew at a rate three times that of the rural, and preliminary 1976 census data showed 16.3 million people, or 46.7 percent of the total, to be living in urban localities. An urban locality was defined either as one with a population in excess of 5,000 or as a *shahrestan* (district) irrespective of its size (see ch. 6).

The Iranian definition of urban is a highly restrictive one. In most countries a small base population is used—1,500 is probably the most common—but in Iran some population centers that are technically urban because they have more than 5,000 residents remain essentially rural in their characteristics. Most of rural Iran is made up of farm villages, localities with populations of fifty or more people. Still smaller populated areas are known as hamlets. The prevailing pattern of rural settlement is a nuclear one in which the houses of the farmers and perhaps an orchard are surrounded by fields. The line village is a rarity, and there are relatively few isolated farms in which the farm family lives on its own tract of land.

The area of greatest population concentration—urban as well as rural—lies in the western part of the country in an area west of a line drawn between the eastern flank of the Caspian Sea and the Persian Gulf (see fig. 1). In addition, a band of heavy population concentration extends farther to the east along the historic silk route to the ancient city of Meshed near the Soviet border.

Water availability is closely linked to population density— heaviest in and about the Elburz Mountains, which stretch laterally across the top of the country and the Zagros Mountains, which occupy most of its western flank (see fig. on topography and drainage, ch. 1). These mountain systems and their approaches incorporate agriculturally intermontane basins and piedmont valleys that include most of the best agricultural land, much of it farmed continuously or intermittently since antiquity.

The rest of the country consists principally of the Central Plateau, an almost unpopulated waste with hot summers and bitterly cold winters. It is one of the world's most barren regions in which closed basins have no outward drainage, and the only settlements occur in scattered oases and in the foothills of small interior mountain chains.

In the mid-1970s not much more than 14 percent of the national territory was under cultivation, but the amount was being increased by energetic government programs particularly in Khuzestan Province, where intensive agriculture had been practiced in antiquity, and in the Qazvin Plain farther to the north. The region of fastest rural population growth in Khuzestan was near the city of Ahvaz. The recently completed damming of the Rud-e Dez and dam construction and irrigation projects in progress on several other rivers in the area attracted people from other regions (see ch. 11). Other areas of particularly dense rural population concentration were found in Azarbaijan in the northwest, around Meshed in the northeast, and along the length of the Caspian littoral where about one-sixth of the country's farmers resided in an area of lush vegetation totally unlike that elsewhere in Iran.

The urban growth that has occurred since World War II has in part been a natural process in which rural villages have been converted into urban towns because of demographic increase. An equally important cause of urbanization was an internal migration made up almost entirely of a movement from rural to urban localities. According to one calculation about 90 percent of the migration that occurred between 1956 and 1966 consisted of an urban movement, and during the early 1970s the rural exodus was estimated at 500,000 annually.

Despite the population loss from urban migration, the rural population continued to increase. In 1900 there had been about 15,000 villages, but the total had increased to 48,500 in 1963 at the beginning of the national agricultural reform program (see ch. 11). By 1972 there were about 71,000 villages and about 22,000 hamlets. A substantial proportion of the villages created resulted from the progressive settlement of nomadic tribes that in 1900 made up more than 40 percent of the total population.

From 1900 to 1966 the number of urban localities increased from about 100 to well over 200. In 1966 there were twelve cities with populations of more than 100,000 compared with nine in 1956 and three in 1900.

During the years since World War II Tehran has made the only real gains through urban migration. Between 1956 and 1966 the population almost doubled. The rate of growth slackened thereafter, but in 1976 it had 3.4 million people. The metropolitan area exceeded 4 million, and urbanized Central Province contained about one-fifth of the country's population. In 1966 the only other centers with more than 400,000 residents were Isfahan, Meshed, and Tabriz.

Tehran, a relatively young city, is located at the foot of the Elburz Mountains at a site that in ancient times marked the intersection between the silk route to China and the north-south route between the Caspian Sea and the Persian Gulf. The city was founded as a walled bazaar early in the nineteenth century. It was later made the capital of Agha Muhammad Khan, founder of the Qajar Dynasty, and by 1900 it had a population of about 200,000 (see Rise of the Qajar Dynasty, ch. 2).

In the mid-1970s Tehran's population was not excessive when compared with the principal urban centers in many other countries, but Tehran was also an industrial center and there were specific limits on how much further the city could grow. It was estimated that by 1993 the city would have a population of 5.5 million, and the potential limit of available water supplies would have been reached.

For a variety of reasons during the mid-1970s the government was actively seeking a better spread of population and decentralization of economic activity. Large new industrial centers were being established in Isfahan and Khorasan provinces, and smaller ones near the cities of Kerman and Zahedan. Early in 1977 the prime minister reported the emphasis would continue during the sixth five-year plan commencing in March 1978 (see ch. 9).

Labor Force

In the mid-1970s there were about 10 million economically active persons in Iran, and a participation rate (number of workers as a proportion of the total population) of some 30 percent, about the same as that recorded for 1966. The figure was a consensus of estimates and did not include information on how many workers were employed in what occupations, or age and sex information. These data would be forthcoming from unrefined 1976 population census returns.

Agriculture remained the principal source of employment but had been declining progressively since World War II to the faster growing industrial and services sectors and their higher paying jobs. According to data compiled by the Statistical Service of Iran for the years 1956 through 1972, agriculture had employed 56.3

percent of the population in 1956, 47.5 percent in 1966, and 40.1 percent in 1972. During the same years industrial employment had risen from 20.1 percent to 26.5 percent and 29.4 percent; the services sector employment had been up from 23.6 percent to 26 percent, and 30 percent.

The relative decline in agricultural employment corresponded to the urban migration that was drawing workers away from the farms and into the factories. There were few amenities of life in the countryside, and worker income was low. The real gross domestic product (GDP) of agriculture fell from 26.1 percent of the total in 1963–64 period to 12 percent in the 1973–74 period (see ch. 11). The fifth plan (see Glossary) called for increased government expenditures on agriculture and related occupations.

The employment pattern in Iran was somewhat different from most countries in the sense that employment in rural areas by no means consisted entirely of work in agriculture and related activities. The larger villages were of sufficient size to support such traditional industries as bakeries, blacksmith and carpentry shops, and other service activities. Some of the large construction industry projects were located in the countryside and recruited labor from it; the government encouraged the growth of textile mills and artisan shops in rural environments.

Industrial employment rose by an estimated annual rate in the early 1970s of 14 percent as compared with 11 percent during the 1960s. Much new employment came from the few (3 percent of the total) large plants, which accounted for 65 percent of manufacturing production. A large proportion of the manufacturing labor force, however, was still employed in handicrafts in traditional shops of not more than three workers. New industrial employment opportunities programmed for the fifth plan consisted of 846,000 jobs in factories and mines; 528,000 in construction projects; and 36,000 in oil, gas, water, and power undertakings.

The proportion of the labor force in the construction industry was up from 6 percent of the total in 1966 to 8 percent in 1973, and fifth plan schedules indicated a continuing rise. The increase in construction employment was because of dam and road construction in the countryside, and it served as a kind of "transmission belt" in bringing surplus agricultural labor into the urban labor market.

Service employment rose to 30 percent of the total in the early 1970s as the largely capital intensive new industrial production was unable to absorb many of the job applicants who had left the farms or were entering the job market for the first time. In particular, employment was increasing rapidly in such peripheral services sector activities as custodial work, vending, and certain personal services.

The civil service makes up a substantial and growing portion of the labor force employed predominantly but not entirely in the services sector. It numbered about 200,000 in 1956, and the

Tehran press in 1974 estimated its strength at 400,000. Both professionalism and education have substantially increased since 1963 when some 23 percent of the civil service was illiterate. Wage scales in the 1970s were relatively low, but security and possibly other nonpecuniary benefits made the civil service career attractive.

With the urbanization of the labor force since World War II the working element became increasingly aware of its own identity. In particular, the mechanized sector of industry—up in number by 165 percent between 1956 and 1966—became a new social element, concentrated in the big cities. This largely skilled cadre made up an identifiable and socially aware group of potential value as a power base. The Tudeh (Masses) Party recognized this as early as the 1940s and sought energetically to recruit workers (see ch. 12). Later the government became concerned, and the economic and social betterment of this class became one of the six points of the White Revolution's (see Glossary) manifesto in 1963.

According to the 1966 census just under 1 million female workers made up 13.2 percent of the labor force; 12.5 percent of the girls and women over the age of ten as compared with 77 percent of the boys and men were in the economically active population. Over one-half of the female workers were wage and salary earners. They made up about one-fourth of the professionals and administrators and nearly one-fourth of the personal service workers but less than 8 percent of the office employees and 1 percent of the sales personnel.

The heaviest female concentration by sector or employment was in the manufacturing industry where some 60 percent of all working females were employed. Within the manufacturing sector women were employed most extensively in textile mills and in other labor-intensive operations requiring few skills and offering relatively low pay and in small, usually family-operated shops making up the traditional artisan-work sector of manufacturing. After manufacturing female workers were in domestic service and other personal services undertakings where they made up about 17 percent of all employment.

In mid-1976 it was announced that the Iran Woman's Organization in cooperation with the Ministry of Labor and Social Affairs was engaged in training female workers at vocational training centers to increase their skills, particularly in the electric industry and other light industries. The total number of female workers was calculated at 1.3 million. This, however, was relatively no greater than the 1.2 million estimated in a 1972 survey, or the 1 million counted in the 1966 census.

The shortage of skilled labor in 1975 was such that the minister of labor and social affairs pleaded with industrialists to refrain from "snatching" workers from their jobs by offering higher pay or fringe benefits. In 1976 observers projected a shortage of 721,000 skilled workers for 1978.

The most conspicuous bottleneck in the improvement of skills was a general lack of education. School enrollment was growing, but over half the labor force was illiterate and as such unable to absorb training effectively. A 1971 study of government employees, for example, determined that by becoming literate they could receive a salary increase.

At the level of popular folklore, it has become axiomatic to state that workers in the northern part of the country are "fast learners" and "better workers" than those in other regions. There may be some justice in this because historically the highly seasonal nature of agricultural work in the north meant that northerners developed a greater adaptability to new employment opportunities than workers in the south. Moreover there is some evidence that both rural and urban workers in the south are smaller in size, less adequately nourished, and less educated. There is, however, a much more clearly definable difference by region between skills and job opportunities in Tehran and the rest of the country. In the mid-1970s most of the best jobs and skilled workers were in the capital city where a large proportion of the labor force consisted of migrants from other parts of the country.

In the mid-1970s agricultural workers were among the least skilled. However, with the establishment of the Development Bank (Bank Omran), money received from the distribution of land under the White Revolution was being used in training schemes for the education and betterment of peasants (see ch. 11). Under this program experts were sent to each group of seventy-five families to teach techniques of land and water use, agricultural production methods, marketing, finance, and setting up rural cooperatives. Membership in cooperatives increased from 542,118 in 1964 to 2,598,328 in late 1975.

The incidence of skills was somewhat greater in the rapidly developing industry sector as well as in trades. A government labor authority suggested the possible necessity of shortening the university course for engineers to two years in order to produce the vocational teachers needed. Reliance was also placed on using foreign entrepreneurs to develop advanced skills.

At the professional level, skills were in the shortest supply of all, in large part because they were poorly adapted to needs. The universities were still turning out only a few of the badly needed business administrators and scientists and a great many liberal arts degree holders. In 1966 nearly 75 percent were employed in the tertiary or services employment sector.

The shortage of skills at all levels was worsened by a lack of mobility that caused one government manpower authority to describe it as "our biggest headache." Farm and industrial labor resisted movement from one locality to another even when the costs of transportation were paid, and the skilled urban worker, technician, and professional alike strenuously and often successfully resisted efforts to relocate in industrial complexes being developed in rural sites. The young engineer or business administrator willing to accept such assignment might expect a salary regarded as impressive in Western Europe or North America.

Overt unemployment in the mid-1970s was not regarded as a serious problem. It had been about 3.7 percent at the time of the 1966 census and was estimated at 3.5 percent in a 1975 International Labor Organization (ILO) study. In the mid-1970s Iran was a full-employment economy in which a substantial proportion of the unemployment counted was of a fractional nature (time elapsed in fitting the job applicant in the job) or was voluntary (resistance to relocating to a rural locality or to accepting a less desirable job).

There was, however, a great deal of underemployment. In the agricultural sector many landless farmers worked less than 100 days a year, and a 1972 study found 400,000 Iranians to be seasonally unemployed (principally in agriculture and in construction work). Overall an estimated 37 percent of the agricultural working force was underemployed. In the industrial sector numerous workers employed traditional skills, often a high order, which had been rendered obsolete by economic development. For example, Persian Gulf shipwrights still made superbly fashioned fishing craft, using age-old processes involving enormous amounts of time.

In the mid-1970s urban migration together with improving agricultural and industrial practices were reducing the rate of underemployment, and open unemployment had yet to become a serious problem. About 300,000 new workers were entering the labor force each year, however, and by the most optimistic assessment, the industrial sector was able to absorb no more than 60,000 to 70,000. The rapidly expanding services sector was expected to absorb most of the rest (see ch. 9). In fact the rapidly expanding economy of the mid-1970s developed a labor shortage, particularly of technical and skilled workers. Foreign labor was brought in to fill the gap and train Iranians, but the long-term problem was to increase employment opportunities.

Diet and Nutrition

For families able to afford the cost, almost any foodstuff available in the United States can be found in Tehran, although some imported items are very expensive. Avocados, pineapples, bananas, and other tropical fruits are not ordinarily available, but Persian melons (like cantaloupes) are plentiful and excellent, and citrus fruit, watermelons, pomegranates, and all of the most popular temperate zone fruits are regularly carried in the markets.

White potatoes and sweet potatoes are available at all times, and a full range of green vegetables is available seasonally. Mutton, lamb, beef, veal, and pork can usually be found, but there is a pronounced national preference for mutton and, as a consequence, beef is less regularly available and of uncertain quality. Seafood from the Caspian Sea or the Persian Gulf is marketed in limited quantities; Iranians consume little seafood, and the fishing industry is not well developed (see ch. 11). Pasteurized milk, cottage cheese, and other cheeses are regularly sold, but the purity of milk cannot be guaranteed.

Because of inefficient methods of preservation and distribution, the variety of foods available is seasonal throughout the country. In general late summer is a time of plenty, but at other times the diet of many tends to be restricted because of the unavailability of certain items. Most diets are good, but those of mothers and babies are often deficient for a variety of social and cultural reasons. Animal protein shortages could be rectified through increased production of fisheries and improved animal husbandry. Availability of vegetables and fruits could be improved by a reduction of losses in the field during the harvest and in storage and distribution practices.

Not all inhabitants of Tehran and other large cities can afford to buy the amounts and kinds of food available. In rural places limited availability of foods as well as limited purchasing power make for a generally inadequate diet, although the average farm family devotes well over half its consumption expenses to food. Diets in the dense rural population areas of the north and the east are relatively the best. In the provinces of the south and southeast, country people sometimes keep alive during shortages by consuming large quantities of grasses and locusts. The passage of a swarm of locusts is greeted with great excitement by small children who are not above catching the insects and consuming them alive.

Food consumption data for the country as a whole were not available in early 1977, but per capita consumption appears to have been rising substantially during the late 1960s and early 1970s. In Tehran the average diet in 1971 was reported to consist of 2,591 calories, 84.9 grams of protein (including 9.8 grams of animal origin). The total amount of fat consumption and the quantity of protein intake of animal origin were somewhat low, but the overall amounts were above the minimums generally considered safe. Data for the early 1970s reported by the ILO, however, showed a range countrywide in caloric intake of 2,073 to 3,121 calories, and village averages ranging from 1,550 to 2,500 in regions classified as low consumption to 2,550 to 4,170 in regions classified as high consumption. Within specific regions, there were sharp variations by household.

In the early 1970s the rising per capita income resulting from petroleum price increases was reflected in an apparently substantial increase in food consumption. In a 1976 report a government spokesman stated that per capita intake of poultry was up from 3.7 pounds in 1970 to 7.3 pounds in 1974 and that the red meat intake was up from 20.2 pounds in 1972 to 37.4 pounds in 1974. A government projection in 1976 anticipated that per capita red meat consumption would rise at a rate of a little more than 1 percent annually during the next ten years and that of rice and wheat by no more than 3 percent annually.

Most Iranians are not conscious of the need for a better diet if they can obtain adequate quantities of foods they are accustomed to eating. They feel the lack of customary items in the diet even if well-fed with unfamiliar dishes. Bread is the main staple, except in certain parts of the Caspian Sea areas, where no meal is complete without rice. In the bread area, rice may be a luxury; in the rice area, bread is relatively unimportant and is eaten mostly as a cake. Similarly apples and grapes are luxuries in the Caspian region where oranges grow abundantly. In Tabriz oranges are as highly desired as medicine, though apples and grapes are plentiful.

Among the foods most commonly eaten by lower income groups are a dish consisting of boiled wheat flour, onions and preserved meat, and a thick, spiced porridge of beans and barley served with flat bread and yogurt. Onions, tomatoes, cucumbers, and radishes are eaten, and a wide variety of fruits, including melons, grapes, dates, and figs, and pistachio nuts are popular. These contribute about 10 percent of the total daily caloric intake of low-income diets, but only 2 percent is derived from meats. Mutton is the most popular meat, followed by goat; the two account for about 80 percent of the total meat consumption. Beef, veal, and poultry are eaten when available. Fresh milk is rarely consumed, mainly because of the lack of refrigeration facilities, but yogurt made from sheep's milk is very popular.

The inadequate diet of young children is often rooted in social customs. Girls sometimes get less food than boys, and the oldest and youngest children in the family are given preferential treatment at meals, while those in the middle age ranges receive much smaller portions. Researchers at the Tehran Center for Food and Nutrition pointed out that fish from the Gulf of Oman and the Persian Gulf could provide the majority of the population with adequate proteins, but people living in the northern areas tend to reject fish caught in southern oceans, largely because of their unfamiliarity, while those living in the south refuse to eat certain kinds of fish for religious reasons.

Meals are taken three times a day. Breakfast is usually sweetened tea and bread. Lunch and dinner consist primarily of soup or stew accompanied by bread, cheese, and tea. Frequent glasses of tea, together with nuts, and sunflower or melon seeds are eaten as snacks. In wealthier homes pastries are served between meals. A dish of boiled rice and grilled meat, called *chelo kabob*, and a thick soup of yogurt, rice, and vegetables, are national dishes. Raw egg yolks and the spice, *sumac*, serve as a dressing for *chelo kabob* and other rice dishes.

The diet varies regionally. Along the Caspian Sea, for example, farmers breakfast on a bowl of rice and several glasses of sweetened tea. A farmer in the southern part of Fars Province may have a morning meal of tea, bread, and cheese. Lunch may consist of yogurt and leftovers from the previous evening. Dinner is almost always a hot meal of bread, vegetables, and kabob; a stew is served about once a week.

The diet of nomadic tribesmen consists almost exclusively of the products of their herds, supplemented with cereals. Honey and a sugary syrup made from grapes are commonly eaten. Clarified sheep's butter is the chief cooking fat. Wine is drunk extensively despite the Islamic proscription against excess in its consumption.

Housing

In early 1973 it was officially estimated that 1,625,000 housing units were available for 2,759,000 urban families and that for 3,489,000 rural families there were 2,908,000 units. There was, accordingly, a deficit of 1,715,000 units if the government's often stated objective of one unit per family were to be obtained. A side effect of this shortage was the extremely high occupation density, calculated at 8.1 persons per unit and 2.4 per room. The fifth plan sought to reduce these ratios to 7.7 and 2.1 respectively. Government planners, however, estimated that the country would need 200,000 new units per year if the goal of a separate unit for each family were to be realized.

The country's record of housing construction during the third and fourth plans had not been encouraging. Third plan funds allocated to housing represented about 2.4 percent of the gross national product (GNP) compared with 5 percent cited by the UN as the minimum necessary for a developing country. The proportion allocated under the fourth plan rose only to 4.6 percent, far from enough to make up for the low investment in the previous period. Under the fourth plan 256,000 housing units had been added by the private sector and 37,000 by the public; but during the period 120,000 new families were added annually to the population.

Under the fifth plan sectoral investment listing of principal items, housing investment rose sharply to rank first with 19.7 percent of the total (see ch. 9). Industry was second with 16.6 percent. In terms of units actually to be constructed, the target had originally been 740,000 units but had subsequently increased to 810,000. The private sector was counted on for 575,000 of this total, but observers commented that the goal would be an impossible one without substantial financial help from the government. Goals were placed higher than ever before, and more public funds earmarked for housing. At the beginning of 1976, however, housing construction in public and private sectors combined had never exceeded 100,000 units in any year.

The bulk of the new houses built in the 1960s were in urban centers where the populations were being swelled by migration from the countryside; during the early 1970s government housing efforts were focused on provincial towns rather than large urban centers, apparently as a phase of a general policy of encouraging population decentralization. The problem of providing enough housing in these smaller places was aggravated by the need to provide at the same time such support installations as schools, hospitals, and stores.

In at least one aspect the housing problem in Iran was less acute than in many or most other developing countries—there were relatively few shantytowns. Some did exist on the fringes of Tehran, Abadan, Ahvaz, and several other cities. In them people lived in makeshift huts using tin sheets, scrap wood, or whatever other materials might lie at hand. Their total populations, however, were estimated at no more than 30,000; in a great many countries the shantytown populations numbered in the millions.

The new houses in the mid-1970s were modern in terms of materials and design. In order to construct the units envisioned in the fifth plan some 3 billion bricks, 17 million tons of cement, 14 million tons of plaster and lime for finishing, 2 million tons of steel bars, and more than 200 million square feet of glass would be required. A public housing official in 1974 had commented that "mud huts can no longer serve our housing needs," but many of the more modest urban houses had been built of this convenient cost-free material. In the countryside mud-built villages gave the appearance of having risen spontaneously out of the earth from which the construction material had been derived.

In the mid-1970s only limited use had been made of prefabricated units, but readymade housing was attracting increasing interest. In 1976 a Ministry of Housing and Town Planning official noted that the oldest operating factories for producing prefabricated units had produced only enough material for 3,000 houses and that as yet no judgment could be made as to the use of these materials as a means of solving the housing shortage. The available information indicated otherwise. The Iran National Iron Smelting Company early in 1974 had announced its readiness to accept orders for a prefabricated sections plant by means of which it would be possible to erect a sixteen-story apartment building in two months. In 1975 a firm under joint American-Iranian management commenced erecting 2,000 units in Persian Gulf cities using an aluminum-form system and castable building material. In early 1976 the government announced plans for erecting two prefabricated sections plants in Tehran. The first was to be completed in 1977 and was to be used in the construction of 3,200 four-story units annually. At the end of 1976 a United States government publication announced that through an American-Iranian working group the Iranian government had indicated a desire to encourage suppliers of manufactured housing components to establish joint venture factories in Iran.

Multifamily dwellings, in many cases high-rise apartments, made up most urban construction in the mid-1970s. The new plants for building prefabricated units were designed for constructing apartments, and an entire new town built by private enterprise was to have a mixture of one- to four-story multifamily units plus high-rise buildings of twenty- to twenty-five stories. In 1975 the government announced that it would no longer make loans for single-family dwellings except for low-income groups. Multifamily dwellings were cheaper to build and, in Tehran in particular, the price of land for single-family units had become prohibitive.

Consumption Patterns

With a per capita annual income in 1976 estimated at the equivalent of US$1,600, Iranians had much more available to devote to consumption expenditure than people in most developing countries. The money, however, was very unevenly divided. According to a 1973 ILO survey, about 10 percent of the population lived at the apex of the income scale with 40 percent of consumption funds. The 30 percent at the bottom consumed only 8 percent.

Other factors also tend to distort the consumption pattern. In general urban people have considerably more money to spend than do rural, and the growing sophistication of urban markets make it possible for an urban family marketbasket to be far more varied than that of a rural family. In Tehran department stores and supermarket-type grocery stores sell an immense line of products. Patterns of consumption also vary by region, influenced by wide differentiations in wage scales. In the early 1970s a manufacturing worker in Kerman might earn only one-third of the amount received by a similar worker in the Central Province, and a male farm laborer in Gilan might receive 60 percent more wages than one in Kerman (see fig. on administrative divisions, ch. 6).

Accordingly in the mid-1970s there were a great many consumption patterns. The largest single consumption group, however, was still the average rural family. According to a 1975 ILO report, these families spent about 67 percent of their income on food and tobacco in 1965 and 1970. Among other principal expense items, housing and household expenses remained constant at a little over 13 percent, and clothing expenses declined from over 10 percent to about 9.5 percent of the total (see table 3, Appendix A). Corresponding data on urban expenditures were not available in early 1977, although it was probable that the average proportion expended on food and tobacco was much lower. The consumption patterns of tribal people were simple to an extreme and entirely different from that of other population elements. Their dependence on the market was minimal, and their purchases were confined to such basic needs as tea, sugar, salt, rice, flour, clothing, shoes, pots, dishes, rope, and tea glasses.

During the mid-1970s the government was following a policy of using funds from the petroleum price increases in 1973 and 1974 to influence the consumer market in certain basic foods. Subsidies were allocated to meat, wheat, barley, corn, rice, and vegetable oils. These basic foods and certain other articles were marketed at controlled prices. At the beginning of 1977 the Ministry of Commerce announced that the control of prices on goods and services deemed essential would continue until market forces became stabilized.

For the more prosperous urban dwellers the increased petroleum revenues had a substantial and immediate effect on expenditures. For example, 167,101 motor vehicles were sold at a cost equivalent to US$1.1 billion in fiscal year (FY) 1975 (see Glossary)—a rise of 46 percent from the previous year. The oil wealth, resulting in higher urban incomes, was not passed along to small farmers in terms of higher prices for their produce, however. Instead changes in the urban-rural terms of trade during the mid-1970s went against the farmers as food prices were held down, while the prices of other commodities were permitted to rise, in some cases behind substantial tariff protection.

Recreation

It is said that in Iran there are more holidays than working days. This is an exaggeration, but there are a great many days in which to some extent work is abridged. An Iranian almanac lists fifty-seven national and international holidays and twenty-nine commemorative dates and holidays. There are seventeen official holidays, and Friday is the Muslim sabbath. In addition work in many businesses ceases at noon on Thursday.

In general ample time is available to enjoy recreational outlets, although not all the numerous religious holidays are festive occasions. During Ashura, for example, the holiday commemorating the martyrdom of Imam Husayn, music on the radio is stilled and cafés, theaters, and nightclubs are closed (see ch. 4). Most other holidays, however, are greeted lightheartedly. Of these the most important is No Ruz, the Iranian new year. Although only two days are officially devoted to it, festivities often go on for two weeks and conclude only after the thirteenth day of the new year—an official holiday. According to tradition the festival dates back to legendary figures, and by the Achaemenian period the new year was a time for rejoicing. In the mid-1970s it had become the preeminent family day.

The favorite sport of many Iranians is a ritualized combination of wrestling and weightlifting that takes place in an athletic club or in a traditional *zurkhana* (house of strength). Wrestling bouts are preceded by weightlifting and other exercises, and the predominantly working-class athletic club members regularly stop on their way home from work for an hour or two of exercises. Organized on a close personal basis, these clubs are well-defined urban social units. The ritual of the itinerant champion has ceased, but wrestling remains in high esteem, and on his birthday the shah distributes prizes to outstanding wrestlers.

The responsibility for sporting events is shared by the Ministry of Education and the National Organization for Physical Education. There are federations for polo, sharpshooting, riding, fencing, cycling, swimming, ping-pong, weightlifting, boxing, rugby, hockey, skiing, mountaineering, volleyball, and basketball. Iranians assert that polo and backgammon originated in the region, although polo probably started elsewhere. Many sports contests take place in the great Aryamehr sports complex for which some facilities were still under construction in the mid-1970s. The central feature is a 100,000-seat stadium completed in 1971. Also completed were a sports hall seating 12,000 persons and four Olympic-sized swimming pools.

Rudaki Hall in Tehran offers a regular series of operas, concerts, and ballets, as well as performances of Iranian dances. A newly built amphitheater constructed in traditional design is used for folkloric plays and operas. Motion pictures are moderately popular; in 1972 there were 438 motion picture theaters and 282,000 seats throughout the country. Iran has its own film studios, and several hundred films have been produced since the first one in 1947.

In the mid-1970s television reached about 60 percent of the population, and 2 million receiving sets gave Iran the third highest Asian concentration after Japan and Hong Kong. By the end of the fifth development plan period television was expected to reach 70 percent of the population. Two powerful 2,000-kilowatt radio transmitters blanketed the country, and the estimated 10 million receivers, approximately one for every three people, provided extensive coverage.

For the urban upper and middle class an important activity occurs in the traditional *dowreh* (literally, cycle) system in which groups meet informally about every two weeks. The *dowreh* may be assembled for a single purpose, usually political or economic, or for various purposes. Meetings may take place at public places or in the houses of members, and the group may represent a single occupation or several related occupations. As a kind of men's club, some *dowrehs* have immense political influence. Coffeehouses and teahouses are also significant meetingplaces and act as a kind of continuous *dowreh*. In the mid-1970s there were more than 2,000 coffeehouses in Tehran alone, many patronized by customers following a particular occupation.

Welfare

Religious and social traditions profoundly influence attitudes toward welfare. There is a belief that fate determines living conditions, but an obligation is felt to help the needy in accordance with religious tenets. The giving of alms (zakat) is one of the pillars of the Islamic faith; according to the teachings of the Prophet Muhammad, a gift to the poor is a meritorious act in the eyes of God. As a consequence donors of real property and monetary bequests are anxious that their names be attached to their gifts. Charity donations may be distributed at any time, but Friday is regarded as a particularly appropriate day, and even those of modest means regularly distribute food to the poor.

Fundraising campaigns by charitable organizations are frequently subject to misuse, and people tend to doubt the honesty and efficiency of nonreligious private voluntary organizations. These organizations exist, and some play worthy and important charity roles; but the individual's basic responsibility is to himself, his family, and his friends. Family members care for each other in times of trouble and need. In general people are required by law to accept responsibility for their next of kin—in the vertical line whether ascending or descending—to the extent that they are able to do so without causing themselves undue hardship. Responsibility of parents for the care of their children is specifically required.

A traditional landlord-peasant relationship has prevailed for centuries. Although the peasant remained subservient to the landlord he could exert a checking power on him in various ways, and the landlord was expected to ensure the peasant's minimum welfare including food, clothing, and shelter during times of famine and pestilence.

In welfare matters the crown (the imperial family) expressed itself through several charitable organizations. The key entity in this category—the Pahlavi Foundation, funded by the personal fortune of the shah—was founded in 1961 to coordinate a group of social services in which the shah was interested. The foundation, which receives income from the shah's vast holdings in major industrial and commercial enterprises, supports a program for low-cost housing, operates moderately priced restaurants for workers, grants scholarships, and gives assistance to student hostels. It also supports cultural projects, such as low-cost book translations and a program for the preservation of national relics.

The Farah Pahlavi Charity Organization, under patronage of the empress, operates orphanages and day nurseries and furnishes direct aid to poor families. Other charitable undertakings are concerned primarily with improving health conditions. The Imperial Organization for Social Services is active in various social fields but is primarily concerned with extending medical care to low-income families. It has built and operates more than 100 clinics in rural areas and maintains hospitals in provincial urban centers to care for cases referred to them by the clinics. Free transportation to and between these institutions is provided for destitute people living in remote areas.

Princess Ashraf (the shah's sister) is active in welfare matters and serves as a kind of liaison between the throne and private charity. Among the private organizations the most important is the Red Lion and Sun Society. A member of the International Red Cross, it is organized under the honorary presidency of the shah and receives substantial government funds; in the FY 1976 budget it was allocated 1.2 billion rials (for value of the rial—see Glossary). The range of its activities approximates that of Red Cross or Red Crescent organizations elsewhere in the world.

The Institution for the Protection of Mothers and Infants maintains a network of maternity clinics, and the National Association for the Protection of Children operates foundling homes, places children for adoption, and maintains centers for the mentally retarded young. It also provides milk rations and a nutritionally balanced midday meal for needy children.

The National Association for the Protection of Lepers, founded by Empress Farah Diba in 1960, maintains special medical facilities and conducts an information program designed to further the care and rehabilitation of lepers. Associations for the care and support of defective persons and chronic invalids also function under imperial auspices. The Prisoners' Welfare Society furnishes aid to needy families of prisoners; it also maintains workshops, recreation halls, and tuberculosis and narcotic control centers for prison inmates. In addition chambers of commerce and the High Council of Women's Associations play important welfare roles.

The first workers in Iran to benefit from a public retirement program were government employees. At a time when no social security program was in force, the government program acted as a powerful incentive to employment in one of the public agencies. The first general disability and death legislation was enacted in 1954; additional legislation was enacted in 1960 and amended in 1968. It covered workers and their immediate families with respect to on-the-job accidents, pregnancies and childbirth, disability and old-age retirement, and survivors pensions. Old-age pensions were awarded to men at the age of sixty and to women at the age of fifty-five after thirty years of work; disability pensions were payable after a two-thirds loss of earning power. Pensions ranged from 25 to 100 percent of earnings, and a widow's pension was 50 percent of that of the insured worker.

According to a Ministry of Information and Tourism report, some 190,000 workers enjoyed social security coverage in 1957; the number had increased to about 500,000 by 1968, but only about 26 percent of all qualified workers were actually covered. According to the 1976 edition of an international yearbook, most of the 683,000 workers receiving protection were employed in large industrial and commercial firms.

Apparently much less than 10 percent of the working population during the mid-1970s received social security coverage, but a bill that in principle afforded social insurance to all Iranians became law in June 1975. The legislation was to be implemented gradually during a period of eight years, but the *Tehran Economist* observed skeptically that the earlier social insurance scheme had been headed by twenty-one different managing directors during its twenty-five years of existence and that it had never released an acceptable balance sheet. The prospects of the new program, it was implied, were not favorable.

Health

In 1970 it was estimated that in addition to the Ministry of Health (reorganized as the Ministry of Health and Social Welfare, but in 1977 again the Ministry of Health) no less than forty public and semipublic agencies and organizations participated in the administration of health matters. Most of the hospitals and out-patient facilities were in the public sector, but a large proportion of the doctors and most of the dentists devoted at least a part of their time to private practice.

Early in 1974 the shah was reported to have ordered health authorities to undertake a program leading to the provision of free medical care to the population. As initially reported the scheme appeared to be some kind of instant cradle-to-grave medical care for all. The program, however, proved to be initially applicable only to indigent and low-income people, and in mid-1974 it was reported in effect for 500,000 low-income people in three localities—where the government had signed contracts with specific hospitals for this purpose.

Free care or care under special arrangements was also available to government employees and participants in the social security programs through public facilities or contractual arrangements. Nevertheless a large part of the medical care program remained in the private sector or in the hands of charitable organizations.

Medical Personnel and Facilities

According to a March 1976 report there were 12,196 medical doctors and 1,728 dentists in practice in Iran. About 7 percent of the doctors and 16 percent of the dentists were women. The dentists included personnel in such specialities as orthodontics and periodontists, but the demand for dental specialties was limited. There was little understanding of oral hygiene, and one dentist commented that rotten teeth and gum diseases accounted for most of the dental ailments. Medical support personnel of all kinds were in short supply. During the 1970s according to one report, there were no more than 6,000 to 7,000 nurses and nursing auxiliaries, plus a few health workers.

The regional distribution of personnel was uneven to an extreme. In 1974 the patient-doctor ratio was reportedly 789 to one in Tehran and about 4,970 to one elsewhere. Of 3,538 medical specialists some 2,337 were said to be in practice in Tehran, where ninety-six of 119 psychiatrists and twenty-eight of thirty-one pulmonary specialists were to be found. The patient-dentist ratio was 6,642 to one in the capital city and 42,301 to one elsewhere.

In theory young Iranian physicians must devote years of practice to the rural villages where more than half the population resides. Young doctors are reluctant to accept the privations of rural life, however, and there has been considerable effort to evade this obligation, which has been described as one of the causes of the continued emigration of Iranian physicians. Many or most of the medical emigrants have gone to the United States, and in 1974 Iran ranked fifth among foreign countries supplying doctors to American hospitals. According to a government survey, in the early 1970s about 10,000 Iranian doctors were practicing abroad. The country was suffering from a severe doctor shortage, and during the early 1970s the Iranian Embassy in Washington was writing to the emigré physicians and arranging meetings with them in an effort to persuade them to return to their homeland.

In the early and mid-1970s Iran, according to a World Health Organization (WHO) study, needed at least 22,000 more doctors to supplement the services of the 12,000 in practice. An announcement in 1974 that the seven-year course of medical study would be shortened to four years to increase the production of doctors was greeted with some consternation by medical faculties; several commented that the production of a competent physician in four years was impossible. Under the fifth plan, however, provision was made for training "rural physicians" who would be prepared in four-year study programs for eight to twelve years of service in the countryside. They would be exempt from military service and on completion of their service, might return to medical school and complete the seven-year course of medical study.

Beginning in 1974 foreign doctors, midwives, and medical technicians were recruited to serve under contract. Unreported numbers of Pakistani and South Korean personnel arrived in 1974. More than 100 Indian doctors arrived in early 1975, and an additional 3,340 were said to be coming from India, the Republic of Korea (South Korea), and the Philippines. More than 1,300 foreign personnel were brought in by the Red Lion and Sun Society.

The most significant measure for alleviating the medical shortage, however, was the establishment of the Health Corps as one of the major undertakings of the White Revolution. Between 1964 and 1975 nearly 12,000 Health Corps personnel were assigned to duty in rural areas. They served eighteen months after an intensive six-month period of military-medical training. Likened to the "barefoot doctors" of the People's Republic of China, each Health Corps element was designed to provide medical services to 10,000 to 15,000 rural inhabitants, and under ideal circumstances worked with cadres of professional personnel. In 1976 it was reported that more than 7,000 corpsmen were being assisted by 2,147 doctors and 207 dentists.

According to a 1974 medical census there were 539 hospitals with 45,400 beds in Iran. A projection envisoned an increase in the number of beds to 60,000 by conclusion of the fifth plan in March 1978. In 1974 the principal administrator was the Red Lion and Sun Society with 172 hospitals and 8,647 beds. The Ministry of Health and the universities ranked second and third respectively. Private institutions maintained 119 hospitals with 6,370 beds, and welfare and charitable organizations had twenty-six hospitals with 2,500 beds.

About 7,500 beds were devoted to the care of tuberculosis, leprosy, and mental ailments. Like medical personnel, the facilities were heavily concentrated in Tehran where 40 percent of the beds were located. Rural hospitals were few, and the bulk of the care was provided by temporary and mobile units of the Health Corps, which provided curative services including ophthalmology and dental treatments, minor surgery, and maternal and child care as well as preventive services in the form of vaccinations and instructions in diet and nutrition.

In the mid-1970s the government proposed building several large 500-bed hospitals in provincial towns to replace the small hospitals that were unable to meet the needs of the regions. They were not, however, to be government operated but were to be offered for rent or sale to medical groups. In addition in 1974 the government announced plans to construct eighty-four health centers in towns of fewer than 40,000 inhabitants for provision of preventive and curative services. The plan called for the placement of one center for each 28,000 urban and 10,000 rural inhabitants; the scattered nature of the rural population made it necessary to plan rural facilities for fewer users.

In the mid-1970s medical facilities were in much better supply than medical personnel. One government health official remarked that facilities were available to meet the most urgent health needs if only enough personnel were available to staff them.

Health Hazards and Preventive Medicine

According to a sampling from urban hospital records, the chief causes of mortality in the early 1970s were infant diseases, gastrointestinal diseases, diseases of the respiratory system, and parasitic diseases. Of the contagious diseases reported in 1973, the most numerous were grippe and influenza, diarrhea, conjunctivitis, scarlet fever, whooping cough, pulmonary tuberculosis, and typhoid fever.

Although not figuring among the major causes of mortality, the incidence of heart disease was climbing and in 1974 was reported to have caused 28 percent of the registered deaths. The number of deaths from it supposedly tripled during seven years. Infarction was the most common cause of heart-related mortality.

Drug addiction is a serious health problem. With the increasing availability of opium during the nineteenth century, it was brought into use increasingly as a panacea for every ailment. Women used it for menstrual pain, men for fatigue or insomnia, and parents administered it to children as a tranquilizer during teething. As a consequence, during the first half of the twentieth century a large number of addicts developed among persons who used opium to relieve pain or stress. Heroin use increased but did not appear in substantial quantities until the 1960s when its use was reported primarily among young men between the ages of twenty and thirty (see ch. 12). There was also some use of marijuana. Despite Quranic prohibitions wine, beer, and vodka were produced locally, and alcoholism was a not uncommon problem.

In 1955 the shah banned poppy cultivation and imposed stringent penalties on opium use. In 1969, however, the government recognized that the total ban was not feasible, and limited opium production was permitted in conjunction with a government program for registration of addicts, rehabilitation of nonregistered addicts, and draconian penalties for traffickers. In 1975 there were 169,512 persons registered as addicted to opium and *shireh* (an opium derivative), and 180 tons of government opium were consumed. The number receiving supplies from illicit sources was estimated at 200,000 to 500,000.

An extensive vaccination campaign—to be carried out under the fifth plan—would consist of 135 million immunizations against measles; tuberculosis, diphtheria, tetanus, and whooping cough innoculations for infants and young children; poliomyelitis vaccine for the urban population up to the age of fourteen; and smallpox vaccinations and cholera innoculations for the entire population. By 1975 it was reported that 40 percent or more of the effective age-group had been reached in all categories. The plan projected that 70 percent of the targeted population would have been reached by 1978.

Water Supply and Sanitation

Polluted water supply was one of the main reasons for the high incidence of parasitic and gastrointestinal diseases. Tehran and other large cities had sanitary water systems, but the creation of a safe water supply was a major problem in the smaller towns and in rural communities. The disposal of waste was generally unsatisfactory in both cities and rural areas. There was a water-carried sewage system in Tehran, but it did not serve all sections of the city. Many other urban centers had only partial sewage systems, and most villages had none at all.

Traditional Beliefs and Practices

In villages life, death, health, and sickness are often attributed to God's will. Poor health is accepted in a spirit of fatalism, and medical aid is sought only when illness is so debilitating as to interfere with the daily work routine. There is a widespread belief in curative elements in nature, particularly in herbs, but incantations, magic formulas, and Quranic verses are also believed effective in warding off illness. The evil eye is thought to be a malicious spell cast through the eyes of a person or beast.

Ancient medical lore is found in the memory of people and in written works. The *Book of Healing* by the renowned Avicenna (Abu Ali al Husain ibn Abdullah ibn Husayn, 980–1037) is still read in Iran and widely known in Western countries. It contains descriptions of herbal medicines, dosages, and exercises, as well as general health rules. Because many medical problems are regarded as being within the area of the supernatural, they are sometimes handled by religious practitioners whose services are called on in efforts to assure potency, the birth of male issue, or the love of a certain person. There is a vigorous traffic in talismans, even in Tehran.

For serious illnesses the family may consult a village herbalist or a medical practitioner who may have had some Western medical training, and barbers are called on for circumcisions or dental extractions. Occult powers are attributed to midwives who are viewed as specialists in the diseases of women and children. In many areas midwives have been trained successfully in modern practices and provide a regular and important part of the official medical program.

Women are depended on to handle many health problems and to administer everyday remedies to members of the family. Mothers train daughters in traditional medical lore, using both magical formulas and herbs or foods according to particular rules for certain illnesses. The Islamic faith prescribes certain measures of hygiene, including periodic baths, and ritual washing before prayers. Most villages of any size have at least one public bath, which is regarded as a symbol of cleanliness and well-being. Traditional and religious medical practices are not exclusive and, in the countryside in particular, are used as supplements for modern pharmaceutical products and the occasional visits of a mobile health team.

Education

Engraved over the doorway to the headquarters of the Ministry of Education in Tehran is the quotation: "He Who Has Knowledge Has Power." Until well into the twentieth century, however, education remained largely irrelevant to the Iranian way of life. As recently as 1972 only 62 percent of the primary-school age population was actually in primary schools, and most of these were in urban localities. The small secondary-school system existed almost solely as a means for preparing students for a university level education that only a relative few would obtain; and technical and vocational skills were learned on-the-job rather than in the classroom.

Education and textbooks were nominally free at both primary and secondary levels, but small fees continued to be charged. A fee of 5 rials was assessed against the use of every book used in the state schools in order to subsidize the activities of the Literacy Corps, and secondary schools assessed a general fee of 1,500 rials plus a sports fee. University education was free to students who had served in the military, the number of years equal to the time in the armed forces. In 1976 more than 90 percent reported studying under these terms.

With the growth of public education during the early 1970s expenditures increased correspondingly. Expenditures for the school year ending in 1973 had been 37.9 billion rials, and the budget estimates for 1976 totaled 126.3 billion. It was a period of soaring expenditures, however, and as a proportion of the total budget the amount allotted to education dropped slightly from a little more than 10 percent to 8 percent.

Iran has been in a socioeconomic takeoff stage, and school facilities and enrollments have increased precipitously since World War II. Observers have been wont to attribute the growth to a release of pent-up popular demand for schooling. It is difficult, however, to see the increase as it occurred in Iran in exactly those terms for, in rural localities at least, education had little to do with the village style of life. Attainment of an education did not mean higher income for the farmer; there were few books or magazines to read; and the schoolmaster in villages where schools existed did not occupy a particularly honored place in the village society. In the mid-1970s about 3 million primary-school age children were still not in school, and the most frequently given explanation for their nonenrollment was parental objection.

The educational system during the 1970s was at midstream in a period of massive change as well as of enrollment growth. Previously the school system had consisted of a six-year primary cycle followed by lower and upper secondary cycles of three years each. Changes set forth in 1969 and implemented on a progressive basis beginning in the 1972 school year (the year ending in 1972) reduced the primary cycle to five years and introduced a guidance cycle of three-years' duration during which the student's capabilities were to be explored and his future course of study, if any, was to be determined. Students remaining in school after completing the cycle were to follow a four-year course of study in general or academic schools, leading to further study at the university level or technical schools. Curricula of two or four years' duration at technical schools would prepare students for direct employment as skilled workmen or middle-grade technicians. Limited access to institutions of higher education was also provided. The changeover from the old system was not completed until 1976 and, with the beginning of the 1977 school year, the new system was revised by reducing the general or academic cycle to three years and introducing a one-year program devoted exclusively to university preparation.

Administratively the country in the mid-1970s was divided into four school regions and 180 school districts. The new system was decentralized to the extent that reforms and innovations were implemented gradually by district, and day-to-day administration was conducted at the district level. The principal administrator was the minister of education who was assisted by eight deputies, four of them in charge of the four regions. Pursuant to a 1969 decree, however, higher education was detached from the Ministry of Education and placed under the newly created Ministry of Science and Higher Education, which was also charged with administration of the country's extensive overseas scholarship program and with overall educational planning.

In large part creation of the new ministry was aimed at remedying a seriously deficient program of academic research. University enrollments were rising so rapidly during the early 1970s that the university system was hard put to make places for the flood of applicants, and the professors—most of them part-time—were unable to devote many hours to research, or to anything beyond delivering lectures and presiding over classes. There was a lack of determination to formulate a long-term and coherent science pol-

Urban primary school in session
Courtesy Embassy of Iran

icy or prospective, and no organization had been created to rationalize the resource allocation process and to integrate research efforts with national needs. A UNESCO consultant studying scientific research in the mid-1970s concluded regretfully that it did not yet exist in Iran. One notable exception was the highly respected Faculty of Education at Tehran University, which concerned itself with the educational research and training of high-level education rather than training classroom teachers.

Although primary-school enrollments during the 1960s and early 1970s increased at lower rates than those at other schools, enrollments doubled between 1963 and 1973 when almost three-fourths of all students in the regular school system were enrolled at the primary level (see table 4, Appendix A). The relative superiority of the urban schools over those in the countryside was evidenced by the three kinds of primary institutions in existence. There were predominantly large urban schools, 4,453 in 1972, offering complete primary programs; regular rural schools, numbering 10,749, smaller in size but for the most part (80 percent) offering a complete primary program; and 10,556 incomplete Army of Knowlege schools, existing at the fringe of the regular school system as part of the program administered by the Literacy Corps. These offered only incomplete primary programs of four years' duration, and the one or two teachers in each unit were young people meeting their national service requirements by serving in these schools.

There was an acute need for additional school buildings. Scarcity of land in major cities and a lack of building materials and technical know-how in the villages were the most pressing but not the only aspects of this problem. In the mid-1970s some authorities felt that the lack of suitable buildings was already slowing down the normal expansion of primary education, and in a 1976 speech the prime minister urged that every available room and every mosque or similar public facility be pressed into classroom service.

The importance of primary education and its relevance, at least in the urban environment in the early 1970s, was underlined by a study that found the return to education to be much higher from urban primary schooling than from schooling at any of the higher levels. Essentially this meant that a worker's productivity and his earning power were increased more from having gone to primary school than from having gone to school at any other level. Worded differently it meant that the acquisition of literacy coupled with a few simple mathematical skills enabled a tradition-directed people to free themselves from traditional modes of living and enter the mainstream of national life.

In this sense the most important education available in the mid-1970s was not in the regular school system at all but in the literacy program schools. As recently as 1977 only about 37 percent of the adult population was literate, and illiteracy was extremely high among the older rural people. The literacy program was established by the shah in 1963 as a key element of his White Revolution, aimed primarily at socioeconomic development in the countryside. It had a 1973 enrollment of 8.2 million as compared with 3.4 million in the entire regular school system. In addition to bringing up the literacy level, the Literacy Corps had a socially unifying effect of enormous significance. The corpsmen were high school graduates and, as such, almost necessarily urban dwellers. By fanning out into the countryside they did much to create mutual understanding between the urban and rural sectors, thereby contributing considerably to the process of nationbuilding.

The lower returns to education above the primary level resulted principally from a circumstance common to education in most developing countries. A large majority of the students entering secondary school wanted academic schooling, preparing them for universities rather than technical education preparing them for jobs. Although the technical institutions registered a 450-percent enrollment increase between 1963 and 1973, the highest attained by any category of school, in 1973 they represented only a little more than 6 percent of the total secondary-level enrollment, and industry continued to rely on on-the-job training rather than on the school system for skilled personnel (see Labor Force, this ch.).

It was in large part to correct this lopsided enrollment pattern that guidance-cycle schools were introduced beginning in 1972. In addition, beginning in 1977 the four-year general or academic cycle was to be reduced to three years and a one-year program of preparatory studies designed exclusively for university-bound students added. At the same time comprehensive schools offering both practical and technical studies facilitating lateral transfer to other kinds of schools were to be established for students who had not determined the specialization most suitable for them.

The experience in many other developing countries, however, has been that the preference of students for academic schooling is much more than a superficial one. Given the choice they will enroll in academic schools even though their chance of university matriculation is minimal. It appeared therefore that a better balance between academic technical enrollments in Iran could be achieved only by reforms much more draconian than those that had been made or were in progress in 1977.

In 1973 the enrollment in institutions of higher education was only about 8 percent of that in the academic secondary schools, and the secondary school graduate's chances of gaining admission to a higher level were correspondingly limited. Although universities and medical schools had flourished during the Middle Ages, the first modern institution, Tehran University, was not founded until 1934. In the early 1970s its enrollment made up about one-third of the university total throughout the country, and its infrastructure consisted of seventeen faculties and fourteen affiliated colleges and institutes (see table 5, Appendix A). There were eight other universities, and seven more were either projected or in various stages of planning. Three of the nine were partially autonomous; the others were fully state controlled. The language of instruction was Farsi in all universities other than Pahlavi University where English was used.

The universities made up about one-half of the enrollment in institutions of higher education. There were also approximately 100 higher level institutes including twenty-five private entities. Although some were permitted to award degrees, they enjoyed considerably less prestige than the universities and were much more specialized. Some, sponsored by various government agencies, led to public employment in fields such as public administration, telecommunication, and railroads. Others were higher technical institutes and institutions offering schooling in fields such as commerce, management, business, computer science, and the performing arts.

Undergraduate university degrees were formerly conferred after three years of study, but law (an undergraduate program) was extended to four years, and the extension of other programs followed. Medical schools already had seven-year programs, and later the faculties of enginering and architecture extended their curricula to five years. Graduate studies were available in medical schools and in two-year arts and law programs at Tehran University.

Universities were organized into faculties, components resembling but more self-contained than academic departments in American universities. They offered complete courses of study, and as a consequence there was a considerable duplication in course offerings. In universities as well as in secondary schools there has been a pronounced preference for academic studies. As recently as 1970 over half the collective enrollment was in liberal arts or humanities as compared with 15 percent in engineering and technological disciplines, although the popularity of technical studies and of engineering in particular was increasing during the early 1970s. The overwhelming majority of those completing technical studies, however, gravitated to government service and office employment concentrated in Tehran, and even those engaging directly in productive occupations were reported to show little aptitude for fitting their knowledge into industry and modern management programs.

A 1968 study revealed that only 7 percent of the students in one of the larger universities used its library, and the director of one of its major academic components deplored the fact that students did not listen carefully to lectures and were not in the habit of taking lecture notes. At a later date the university's chancellor prohibited the distribution of lecture notes, which the students who had failed to attend classes memorized for examinations.

Dedication to the idea of social progress and change on the part of university students could be more readily found among the

Aerial view of Tehran University
Courtesy Embassy of Iran

substantial number studying abroad than among those in Iran. As recently as 1950 the number in the country's institutions of higher education (24,000) had probably been exceeded by the number abroad. In the mid-1970s the exact enrollment in foreign universities was not known, but 60,000 was the figure most frequently used. The majority was in the United States, and most of the remainder were in the Federal Republic of Germany, (West Germany) and the United Kingdom.

Students going abroad for university-level education frequently voiced concern over what they viewed as an absence of civil liberties in Iran (see ch. 12). This discontent coupled with attractive job opportunities abroad caused a disturbing number of students during the 1960s to remain abroad after completion of their studies, but during the early 1970s this trend seemed to have abated, and a large majority of the students were returning. The major exception was the medical student who continued to remain abroad in the face of a serious doctor shortage at home, probably because of superior working conditions in the country were he had obtained his schooling (see Labor Force, this ch.).

Students who returned to Iran before 1960 constituted a significant element in Iranian society of the 1970s and enjoyed particular prestige. Having attended a prestigious foreign institution was of such importance that graduates sometimes included this fact on a business letterhead. University graduates formed into informal but discernible groups in which those who had engaged in studies in the United States were socially differentiated from those who had studied in Western Europe, and both were differentiated from the products of the domestic university system. A returned engineering graduate could often identify more readily with a returned humanities graduate than with a fellow engineer educated in Iran.

Private secular education was almost nonexistent before World War II, but by 1966 it was officially reported that 8.4 percent of the primary students and 26.4 percent of the general secondary students were in private schools. The proportions were not great, but the schools were supported by substantial tuition fees and were able to offer the best facilities. Well-to-do parents customarily enrolled their children in them. The private school system had developed ostensibly to meet the country's need for more schools and to raise educational standards, but in the late 1960s and early 1970s it had become increasingly clear that a dual system of education had emerged and that it was strengthening rather than eliminating social stratification. The government became increasingly concerned over the socially divisive influence of private education. As a consequence the abolition of all private schools and their absorption into the public system was decreed, though by early 1977 the decree had yet to be fully implemented. Its implementation would bring about a generally stricter control over the school system and a general raising of standards. It would also mean heavier pressure on the public system, particularly in schools above the primary level.

Although the Iranian population is made up of linguistically as well as ethnically diverse elements, the Farsi language is used as the language of instruction throughout the school system, except in a few private schools. This is in part a practical matter resulting from the diversity of languages represented, but it is also deliberately used as a means of unifying the various population elements. The education of the nomadic tribal people has represented a particular challenge in this respect, and in the mid-1970s it appeared to have been a challenge effectively met.

The history of tribal education dates from the late 1950s when a directorate general for tribal education was established; a one-year teacher-training school in Shiraz was expanded, and other tribal school facilities were added in that city. In addition tent schools were established in Fars Province to accompany tribal people in their wanderings, and an observer reported that although Farsi was not the mother tongue of the young students and their illiterate parents were not able to help them with their lessons, most of them were able to read and write after a few months. Parents could be seen gathered a short distance from the school tent following the lessons and attempting to repeat the teachers' words.

By 1971 some 38,000 students, including nearly 7,000 girls, were attending the tent schools, and between 1963 and 1973 over 3,000 teachers had been trained for service in them. Only a few were female, but not many years earlier it would have been impossible to imagine tribal women working as schoolteachers. In the mid-1970s the success of the tribal schools had not yet been fully evaluated in Fars Province to which it was still confined. If deemed successful the schools would be extended beyond Fars Province to include such other nomadic groups as Kurds, Baluchis, and Turkomans.

A statement prepared in 1971 by the Ministry of Education for presentation in an international publication stated that there was no distinction made by sex in Iranian education and that the ministry gave priority to raising the national education standard for women. The same statement, however, included statistics showing that in 1966 females made up only 34 percent of the enrollment in primary schools, 30 percent of the enrollment in general secondary schools, and 24 percent in institutions of higher education. The 17-percent female enrollment in vocational schools at the secondary level was for the most part segregated in schools giving instruction in such traditionally female undertakings as home economics.

Moreover coeducation, even in the mid-1970s, was the exception rather than the rule. Women had first been admitted to Tehran University in 1954, but in the mid-1970s coeducation for the most part was to be found only in institutions of higher education, in rural schools where isolation and small student bodies made segregated education impracticable, and in the literacy program schools. In 1972 about 95 percent of the urban primary schools were single-sex institutions, but 68 percent of the rural units were coeducational. Girls made up only a small minority in rural schools enrollments, however, and illiteracy among village women was almost total.

Female enrollments in schools of all kinds edged upward during the early 1970s, and by 1976 some 42,789 women were enrolled in institutions of higher education, constituting more than 28 percent of the student body. By 1972 some 47 percent of the teachers in public primary schools and 24 percent of those in the public general secondary schools were women. It seemed that education was proving itself a powerful force in bringing about the socioeconomic emancipation of women. It could as well be argued, however, that the progressively improving status of women was making educations for them increasingly possible.

With the increase in school enrollments at all levels, a serious teacher shortage developed, and although it was officially determined in 1972 that 62 percent of all primary teaching personnel were academically qualified, the calculation was probably a generous one, and the level of qualification was probably much lower than in the rural schools. Finding teachers, qualified or otherwise, to serve in rural classrooms has been a particular problem. Energetic and ambitious young people have been enrolling in teacher-preparation programs as a means of escaping the rural environment rather than of returning to it. A large proportion of the rural teaching staff has been made up of young people performing their national service and by former Literacy Corps teachers who have returned to teach in rural areas after undergoing a short period of regular teacher training.

Training for primary teachers is furnished in teachers colleges or normal schools at the secondary level, which offer a regular general school curriculum plus courses in psychology and pedagogy. Agricultural and vocational subjects are also taught, and in colleges for women home economics is substituted for physics and chemistry. In order to encourage young people to become primary teachers, free room and board are provided as well as free tuition.

Secondary teachers are trained at the Teachers Training University and in other institutions of higher education. They must in theory earn bachelors' degrees in order to qualify for secondary teaching, but in 1970 an acute shortage of qualified personnel caused the Ministry of Education to establish centers where candidates could qualify for the lower secondary academic positions after completing a two-year course. In the mid-1970s only a little over half the teachers at the secondary level were graduates of any kind of higher level program, but the Teachers Training University was the prototype for higher teachers colleges, which were developed at five provincial universities in the mid-1970s.

Neither primary nor secondary teaching has proved particularly attractive to young people, and the quality as well as the quantity of teachers produced have suffered accordingly. In 1969 primary technical salaries were raised substantially, and private school-teachers and teachers holding temporary appointments were made eligible for social security benefits. This was significant because only a small minority of the labor force at the time was eligible for participation in the social security program (see Welfare, this ch.). Both the economic and the social status of secondary teachers were somewhat higher than for primary level personnel. The modest social prestige derived by secondary teachers, however, probably came more from having attended an institution of higher education than from being a teacher.

Institutions of higher education in the early 1970s suffered acutely from a lack of full-time professors. The average teaching load at the undergraduate level was only five or six hours a week. An instructor was usually required to serve eighteen years, irrespective of merit, before becoming a full professor. Salaries were low, and independent wealth or the holding of one or more outside jobs was a virtual necessity for the university teaching aspirant.

Chapter 4. Religious Life

IN 1977 MUSLIMS composed approximately 98 percent of the population of Iran, a figure that has remained relatively constant for three centuries. Ninety percent of the Muslims adhere to a form of Islam known as Ithna Ashari or Twelver Shiism. Iran is the only country in the world where there is or has ever been a Shiite majority. Most of the remainder of the Muslims are members of the Sunni branch of Islam and are most numerous among the Kurds, Baluchi, Turkomans, and Arabs (see ch. 5). Officially recognized—as opposed to proscribed minorities, such as the Bahais—are the Jews, Zoroastrians, and Christians who number somewhere between 420,000 and 500,000.

By the time Islam was introduced into Iran by conquest in the seventh century, the country had already experienced a long and continuous religious development based on Zoroastrianism (known originally as Mazdeanism), which included an ethical system, a highly developed ritual, and a dogma, the basics of which would be familiar to most monotheists. Although conversion to Islam was rapid among certain classes, it was not until the tenth century that Islam became thoroughly entrenched. Much of the opposition had been fervently nationalistic rather than religious in tone. But by the tenth century Muslim Iranians of both the Sunni and Shia branches had melded Islam with the native cultural milieu: philosophy, literature, and the plastic arts treated Islamic themes in traditional Iranian ways. The Iranians, for instance, blithely ignored the Islamic ban on representations of the human figure and included not only respected religious leaders but also the Prophet in their exquisite miniature paintings.

Gradually Shiism acquired more adherents. It was easier to identify with this deeply emotional, mystical, and esoteric form of Islam that focused on a series of martyrs and tragic disasters wrought mostly by Arab hands than with Sunnism, the more exoteric branch of Islam. Popular sentiment was confirmed when Shiism was adopted as the state religion by the Safavids, the first native dynasty to rule the whole of Iran since the advent of the Arab Islamic conquerors (see Safavid Empire, ch. 2). Thereafter Shiism could also be used as a tool of state to arouse popular opposition to the growing power of the Ottoman Turks who were Sunni.

The result has been that Shiism, because of its tenets and because of the direction and shaping given the religion through its development in Iran, has emerged as the national expression par excellence of the Iranian people. Because Shiism has been the state religion since the sixteenth century, religious leaders acquired tremendous prestige and influence as the interpreters of the comprehensive legal system, which was largely derived from shariah, Islamic religious law, and as social arbiters. Historically the shahs of Iran have given considerable leeway to the religious leaders because Shiism, more than any other interpretation of Islam, supports a monarchical system. In 1977, under the terms of the Constitution, the shah of Iran is symbolically identified as a caretaker until the last Shiite Imam, who went into occultation (hiding) in A.D. 939, reappears to rule the state (see Shia Dogma, this ch.). Traditional religious values and modernization, however, came into conflict even before the extensive reforms of Reza Shah, the founder of the ruling Pahlavi dynasty, and his son, Mohammad Reza Pahlavi.

The *mujtahids* (religious authorities—see Glossary) had never fully supported the Constitution, although some religious leaders were among its foremost proponents during the campaign for its adoption in 1906. Contending that the Constitution, as adopted, contravened higher religious law, many did not feel themselves bound by its provisions or by the acts derived from it. Some actively led opposition to it; others learned to live with it. The same disparate views were recognized in subsequent national issues. The government, for its part, confirmed the constitutional guarantees for Shiism, continued to encourage the spread and strengthening of Muslim beliefs—while banning some of the more extravagant Shiite practices—and limited the spheres of influence of the *mujtahids* to a much smaller area than before.

The political leaders of 1977 retained traditional religious precepts but promoted national symbolism, some of it non-Islamic. The words of law and the actions of leaders scrupulously followed the spirit of high moral purpose and the dependence on divine guidance, but functions in religious and political fields were being increasingly delineated.

The shah has attempted to maintain a balance between secular and religious authority in promoting modern social and economic programs. At the same time he has sought the support of the religious leaders in furthering national consciousness. Many observers feel, however, that although the religious leaders lack a political power base, they offer the only solid opposition to certain governmental policies. On the popular level Shiite Islam, and particularly the culture and world view emanating from it, influences much of Iranian behavior regardless of whether the individual is an illiterate peasant or a member of the middle or upper classes. And as the distinguished scholar Sayyid Nasr notes, "even among the modernized, who outwardly seem completely secularized, there exist many traditional tendencies which in a people of less elastic mentality would not be conceivable."

According to the noted Iranian analyst James A. Bill, in 1977 there was a large religious revivalist movement in Iran among young people. In defiance of secondary school and university regulations, "a significant percentage" of young women had been attending classes wearing the black veil, or the chador. One woman from the University of Isfahan said, "I am making a statement," when asked why she had reveiled. Religious study circles where political and social topics are discussed in the light of Shia doctrine, also have become quite popular. These movements apparently were expressive of dissatisfaction with the direction of Iran's social and political developments and as such were forms of political opposition.

Pre-Islamic Religions

Because of the early development of high cultures in Iran, formalized religions existed well before the arrival of the Indo-European tribes at the end of the second millennium B.C. These early religions were polytheistic and appear to have included the deification of natural elements, particularly, earth, fire, and water. The followers of these ancient religions conceived of good and evil as opposing forces within nature, a common conception among ancient peoples. They also perceived of existence as a struggle between good and evil in an ethical sense, however, which was not a common idea in the ancient world.

Zoroastrianism (Mazdeanism) had, in its earliest period—the Mazdayasna—six major and equal deities, the Amesha Spantas. That the Amesha Spantas included female deities suggests a mingling of the religious ideas of the matriarchal local people with those of the patriarchal Indo-European invaders. Early Mazdeanism had much in common with that of the Hindu Vedas because of the ethnic and linguistic origins of the invaders of both Iran and India. It was highly developed with a dogma, eschatology, and priesthood by the time its chief prophet, Zoroaster (also known as Zarathustra), a priest from Media (modern Azarbaijan), reformed the religion most probably in the seventh century B.C. Zoroaster introduced certain refinements and additional rituals as well as a strict behavioral code. He stressed individual responsibility for the welfare of the community and proclaimed Ahura Mazda as the paramount deity and the creator of man. He attributed to Ahura Mazda qualities of wisdom, purity, goodness, and light.

Other gods were subordinated to helper status with the exception of Ahriman, a satan prototype, who, as the embodiment of evil, was in constant conflict with Ahura Mazda. Ahriman was responsible for such natural calamities as the floods, droughts, and earthquakes that plagued Iran and for disease and death. Zoroastrianism is considered monotheistic because of the belief in the superiority of Ahura Mazda, but functionally Ahriman was considered to be as powerful, and many Zoroastrian rituals are designed to repel his tremendous influence. An individual has the choice of yielding to Ahriman's temptations and forfeiting heaven, but because Ahriman can also cause disasters to be visited upon the entire community, the priesthood, called the magi, was empowered to impose severe penances for infractions of the religious code.

The corpus of Zoroastrian beliefs were contained in the Avesta, a holy book of seventy-two chapters believed to have been revealed to Zoroaster by Ahura Mazda through divine inspiration. Only a small part of the Avesta has survived: the Gathas, hymns to Ahura Mazda, and seventeen chapters of the Yasna, which contain the core of Zoroastrian dogma as well as ritualistic directives for daily life. The Yasna is an important source for the ancient history of Iran and one of the most cherished cultural documents of the Iranian people.

Zoroastrians believe that man has free will to shape his eternal destiny. At death the soul passes over an "Accountant's Bridge," a safe and easy passage to heaven for those who have adhered to the Zoroastrian dictum of "good thoughts, good words, and good deeds." For those who have not followed the precepts or who have omitted the enormous number of prescribed daily rituals, purgatory or hell is the punishment. Good and bad angels exist respectively to aid or to plague man in his daily spiritual struggle. The heart of sacred ritual is the fire temple, maintained by the magi. In the austere temples fires burn constantly, as a symbol both of Ahura Mazda's light and of the divine spark in every human soul. Typical sacrificial offerings are milk, butter, meat, and consecrated water. Earth, air, fire, and water are considered sacred by Zoroastrians, and to avoid sacrilege the dead are arranged in concentric circles in dakhmas, or towers of silence, where vultures quickly consume the flesh. During the Achaemenid period, the kings were the only ones entombed, but their corpses were first dipped in wax so they would not pollute the earth.

There are over 1,000 common substances and circumstances that can pollute the individual; very early, therefore, a caste system developed that relegated certain pollutive activities, such as herding, tilling the soil, and keeping the towers of silence to certain social groups (see Ancient Iran, ch. 2). As Jacques Duchesne-Guillemin notes, Zoroastrianism is not so ethical a system as it appears at first sight: "In real life, the Mazdean is so constantly engaged in so intricate a battle against contagion of death, a thousand causes of impurity and the menace of demons present everywhere, even in his sleep, it cannot be often that he has the sense of leading his life freely or ethically."

Zoroastrianism was probably not the dominant religion of Iran until the middle of the Achaemenid period when the months of the civil calendar were named for Zoroastrian deities. Its influence was strongest under the Sassanians when it was made the state religion, and the caste system was used as a tool by the shahs to keep the society static and apolitical. Regardless of the change of fortunes that Zoroastrianism has experienced in Iran, Zoroastrian elements formed the matrix for Iran's subsequent religious development, and every Iranian religion displays certain motifs or characteristics associated with it.

During the period between the Achaemenids and the next native dynasty, the Sassanians, Iran was opened to Hellenistic religious influences from the west. Alexander the Great, and after him the Seleucids, were extremely tolerant of religious differences, and Greek gods, particularly Heracles, existed side by side with Zoroastrian deities. Additionally hybrid religions appeared, the most important of which would cause worldwide repercussions.

The Cult of Mithra

An example of one of these hybrid religions was Mithraism. Mithra was worshiped as a god in Iran before Zoroastrianism became firmly established. Ultimately he was incorporated into the Zoroastrian pantheon as a helper god or intermediary between Ahura Mazda and man. The cult of Mithra as a mystery religion acquired many believers during the Greek occupation and soon spread throughout the civilized world. Mithra was a righteous god and the preeminent god of battle, capable of striking terror in the hearts of his enemies and ensuring victory to his worshipers. Mithraism had a moral code, or *entolai*, based on commandments Mithra had handed down to his followers. There was a strict discipline, with a long initiation process and a hierarchical series of grades through which the devotees passed. A chief element of the Mithraic cult was the supernatural bull that Mithra, somewhat against his own inclinations, was forced to slay for the good of mankind. From the sacrificed bull then sprang animals and beneficial plant life. Part of the initiation into the Mithraic cult was the baptism of the initiates who stood in a pit under a grate over which a bull was sacrificed. The blood had redemptive qualities, and after this sacrament the novice possessed the grace to be saved. There was also a communal holy meal where wafers of bread were blessed and distributed to the communicants. Ahriman remained the great foe, but the position occupied by Ahura Mazda in Mazdeanism was replaced by the Unconquerable Sun, Sol Invictus. Because of the association with the sun Mithra's birthday was celebrated just after the winter solstice on December 25, long predating the Christian use of the date for Christ's birthday.

Mithraism had naturally a strong appeal to armies, and the cult spread quickly from Iran to Mesopotamia and Asia Minor where it absorbed astrological concepts. At its floruit Mithraism was the religion of the Roman army, and Mithraic temples have been found as far west as Roman Britain, built by the soldiers encamped there. Mithraism was a strong rival to Christianity but, because its adherents were mostly soldiers and since only men could join the cult, it never developed a significant following among settled communities. With the decline of the Roman Empire in the west, Mithraism gradually disappeared but not before it had influenced Zoroastrianism and several other major mystery religions, most notably Christianity.

Manichaeism and Mazdakism

Despite the Sassanian state's adoption and protection of Zoroastrianism, two heretical movements developed during the Sassanian period that attracted large followings. Both constituted rebellion against religious authority and against the social constraints inherent in Zoroastrianism. As the power of the Zoroastrian priesthood grew it began to alienate many members of the middle and lower classes for whom the Zoroastrian social system had little to offer.

In the third century A.D. Mani, a religious reformer from the Iranian satrapy of Iraq, preached a revised form of Zoroastrianism. His religion was sharply dualistic in the Zoroastrian tradition, but he depicted man as the creation of the power of darkness who therefore needed to atone by means of extreme asceticism, prayer, and rejection of the material world. Because these heretics perceived man as intrinsically evil and benighted, an intercessor was necessary to act as guide (a continuing theme of Iranian religion), and Mani introduced himself as a divinely appointed guide and intercessor. Shah Shapur I (A.D. 241–272) protected and encouraged Mani. The magi gathered their forces, however, and under Shah Bahram, Mani was executed in 274. Manichaeistic cults eventually ranged from China to France. In the twelfth century in France a large group of Manichees, called Albigensians, were executed to a man by the central authority.

In about A.D. 500 Mazdak, another religious reformer, appeared and advocated a kind of religious communism. Working from the basic Zoroastrian dualistic system as had Mani, and holding to Mani's view that salvation lay in abstinence from worldly pleasure, Mazdak insisted that strife, greed, and unhappiness came from the unequal distribution of goods, services, and lands. Animal food was shunned as having too excitable an effect on the senses, and women were regarded as communal property. Mazdak found a patron in Shah Kobod, who saw in the movement a chance to check the exordinate power possessed by the Zoroastrian magi. Kobod embraced Mazdakism and proclaimed it to be the national religion without, as far as can be determined, following through on the practical elements of the religion. The aristocracy and the magi rose against Kobod, and his throne remained unoccupied for three years until he recanted and ordered the massacre of some 10,000 Mazdakeans, including Mazdak.

The lack of religious tolerance evidenced by the extermination of Mazdakeans was unusual for Iran. There were several Jewish communities since Achaemenid times and a much larger body of Christian sects. The Sassanians particularly welcomed and encouraged dissident Christian sects, such as the Nestorians, because of their rivalry with the only obvious threat to Iranian power, the Byzantine Roman Empire at Constantinople.

A significant development within "orthodox" Zoroastrianism during the late Sassanian period was Zurvanism, a philosophical religious school that attempted to apply Greek philosophy to basic Zoroastrian precepts. On the popular level, it was widely believed that Shah Khasrow I (A.D. 531–579) would return at the end of the world to save Iran.

Islamic Conquest

True religious reform or social change could not come from within the Iranian system because of the entrenched power of the magi and because the monarchy benefited from the tight control the magi gave them over the populace. The power that eventually toppled the Sassanian Empire and radically changed its social structure and religious orientation was the army of Muslim warriors from Arabia, which, as a result of two decisive battles— Qadisiyya in 637 and Nihavand in 641—established itself as the new power in Iran.

The religion the Arab warriors brought to Iran had been articulated by Muhammad, a member of the powerful Quraysh tribe of Mecca in western Arabia. There was tremendous social disruption and disintegration in Mecca when Muhammad was born there in A.D. 570. The Quraysh were a northern beduin tribe but had failed to maintain the more humane of bedu values in their sedentary commercial setting. Tribal solidarity was weakened, and strong tribal members gave little protection to weak and poor ones. As an impoverished orphan and a member of a weak clan Muhammad was sensitive to the moral malaise of Mecca. He was raised by his grandfather and then by an uncle, Abu Talib. At twenty-five he married a wealthy widow of his tribe, the forty-year-old Khadijah. He began to work in her caravan business and came into contact with the Jews, Christians, and Zoroastrians in southern Arabia who were active in the trade.

In 610, while meditating in one of the caves around Mecca, Muhammad began to receive a series of divine revelations through the medium of the Angel Gabriel. After a period of self-doubt he began preaching the message he had received to his extended family and then to his tribe. These divinely revealed messages were eventually collected in the Quran, the holy book of the Muslims. The religion Muhammad preached came to be called Islam, a derivation from the Arabic word for submission and obedience. Teaching a stern monotheism at a time when the Arab tribes worshiped many nature gods, Muhammad and his small band of followers were ridiculed and persecuted for more than a decade by members of their own tribe because of the danger to Meccan economic life that Muhammad's gospel posed. Income from the pilgrimage to the many gods of the shrine of the Kaaba, which was under the jurisdiction of the Quraysh, was secondary only to the profits of trade. Other business and social arrangements would also be affected if Muhammad's message of monotheism and status determined by piety proved popular.

In A.D. 622 tribal leaders forced the small band of converts to seek refuge elsewhere. They were invited to Yathrib, the present-day city of Medina, about 250 miles to the north of Mecca, where Muhammad had already made converts. It is this movement, the hijra, known in the West as the Hegira, that marks the beginning of the Islamic calendar. Eight years later the Muslims were able to retake Mecca, which became the center of the Islamic religion. The principal shrine, the Kaaba, was cleansed of its idols and rededicated as the temple of Abraham and Ishmael, who are believed to be the builders of the modern temple. (Traditional belief accounts for three earlier temples at the same site.)

After the Hegira Muhammad rapidly gained converts among the Arab tribes. By the time of his death in 632 he had united most of the Arabian Peninsula, both religiously and politically, and had created a zealous and virtually unbeatable military force. The first several caliphs (literally, successor, the supreme political leaders of the Islamic community after the death of Muhammad) continued the campaign to expand the area under Islamic law. Within a century holy war, or jihad, brought a vast area from China to North Africa and Spain under Islamic rule.

Iran fell under the sway of Islam during the first twenty years of Islam's aggressive drive. By 650, after about fifteen years of resistance, the armies of the Sassanid Empire gave way before the onslaught of the small but inspired Arab forces. Iran fell under Arab domination, and Arab influence became strong. While Islam had much in common with Zoroastrianism, it was also very attractive to potential converts because its social system seemed to clear away caste distinctions. The Muslim theology and ritual and the egalitarian character of its social message was simple and attractive to the common people of Iran who had long been subjected to the exacting rule of the Zoroastrian magi, but the new religion spread slowly outside the major cities. For 150 years Iranians resisted the Arab conquest and the forced introduction of a foreign religion, and it was not until the end of the eighth century that Islam was accepted by a sizable majority of Iranians.

The Arab victory was decisive; it permitted little organized, effective military resistance. Opposition was manifested in a series of politicoreligious movements within the framework of Islam; some gave vent to anti-Arab and anti-Islamic sentiments, but most movements sought to modify the political and religious order to allow more scope to Iranian culture and interests (see Islamic Conquest, ch. 2).

Between the seventh and fifteenth centuries Iran was dominated first by the Arabs and then by the Islamized Seljuq Turks and the Islamized Mongols. Most of these foreign rulers were adherents of the Sunni branch of Islam. When a native Iranian dynasty, the Safavid, was able at last to assert its control over all Iran at the beginning of the sixteenth century, it declared the Shiite form of Islam to be the official religion of the country, and it has since remained the official religion.

Iran has made considerable contributions to Islam under both Sunni and Shia rule. Once having accepted Islam, the Iranians championed it, expanding the realms of the Islamic empire deep into Asia. Before Shiites became the majority in Iran it was a major center for Sunni Islamic studies producing some of their greatest theologians and scholars—al Bukari, Abu Hamid al Ghazali, and Fakhr al Din al Razi—and no other area in the Middle East has produced mystics of the genius of Sanaai, Nizami, Jalal al Din Rumi, and Hafiz.

Basic Islamic Beliefs

The fundamental article of faith of Islam is the *shahada* (to give testimony), a monotheistic testimonial declaration: "There is no God (Allah) but God and Muhammad is his Prophet." To become a Muslim, one is required to recite the *shahada* in full as an expression of unquestioning belief and in the presence of two Muslim witnesses. Muslims believe that Islam is the fulfillment of the Judaeo-Christian tradition. That is, just as Christians believe that Judaism has been fulfilled since the arrival of Jesus Christ, the Messiah, so do Muslims believe that with the revelation of the Quran, God's final message to man has been received. They do not, however, believe that either Christ or Muhammad is the Messiah. And in the Sunni orthodox branch of Islam there is no messiah at all; rather it is the duty of each Muslim to seek to bring about the correct ordering of society by positive personal example, by conducting business in prescribed Muslim ways, and by regulating his social interactions to those consonant with Muslim directions.

There is a concept of sin in that certain things are *haram* (forbidden) while others are *hallal* (permitted) and a whole range of activities that have a moral value between the two. Forbidden acts include *shirk* (the attribution of divine qualities to anyone but God), fornication, adultery, and the consumption of pork, carrion, blood, or any intoxicating substance. There is a much stronger emphasis, however, on sins of omission, that is, on the failure to perform good acts.

Because of the social milieu into which Islam was introduced, there are many references in the Quran to right dealings with people, particularly with those of inferior status, e.g., "Neglect not the orphan and turn not the beggar away" (Sura 93). A Muslim is judged at death and is sent to heaven or hell, depending on the sum total of his life's acts. Because of the Islamic connection with Judaism and Christianity, Muslims believe in the divine origin of several of the Old and New Testament scriptures: the Pentateuch, the Psalms, and the Gospels. They are recommended reading for Muslims although it is believed that God's message had been tampered with either out of deliberate self-interest or lack of skill in transmission or translations. The prophets of the Judeo-Christian tradition and of Zoroastrianism are also regarded as prophets by Muslims. The foremost of these are Adam, Noah, Abraham, Moses, Jesus, and Muhammad, the greatest and "the seal of the prophets," meaning the final prophet to be sent by God. Muslims believe in a satan, who tempts men, and in angels who are messengers of God and guardians of men.

Shia Branch of Islam

Despite the minuteness of Quranic directives and despite the thousands of nondivinely inspired sayings of the Prophet Muhammad and his companions collected in eleven volumes called hadith, there was great confusion at his death as to who the next temporal ruler or caliph should be. The election of Abu Bakr and Umar, the first two of the four "rightly-guided caliphs," was unanimous. But Uthman, the third orthodox caliph, had encountered opposition during and after his election to the caliphate. Ali, the Prophet Muhammad's cousin and husband of the Prophet's only living issue, Fatima, had been the other main contender for the caliphate, but his pietism seemed certain to dislodge vested-interest groups who preferred the more conservative Uthman as more likely to continue the policies of Umar. Discontent increased, as did the formal opposition to Uthman led by Ali. Ali's personal opposition to Uthman was based on religious grounds. He claimed that innovations had been introduced that were not consonant with Quranic directives. For most of the other members of the opposition, economics was the key factor, but this too acquired religious overtones.

As a result of a too rapid military expansion of the Islamic movement financial troubles beset Uthman. Many beduin had offered themselves for military service in Iraq and Egypt. Their abstemious and hard life contrasted with the leisured life of many in Mecca and Medina who were enjoying the benefits of conquest. The volunteer soldiers questioned the allocation of lands and distribution of revenues and pensions. In Ali they found a ready spokesman.

Groups of malcontents eventually left Iraq and Egypt to seek redress at Medina. Reforms were promised to them, but on their return journey to their posts they intercepted a messenger to the governor of Egypt commanding that the rebels be punished. The rebels turned mutinous and beseiged Uthman in his home, one of them finally slaying him. Uthman's slayer was a Muslim, and among the rebels was a son of Abu Bakr, the first caliph. The Muslim world was very shaken. Ali had not taken part in the siege and was chosen caliph.

Two opponents of Ali then enlisted Aisha, a widow of the Prophet Muhammad but not Ali's mother, and together they demanded the lex talionis for Uthman's death, pointing the finger at Ali. The three went to Iraq to seek support for their cause. Ali's forces engaged theirs near Basra; Aisha's two cohorts were killed, and Ali was clearly victorious. Muawiya, a kinsman of Uthman and the governor of Syria, then refused to recognize Ali and demanded the right to avenge his relative's death. Ali's forces met his at Siffin near the great bend of the Euphrates River. This was, perhaps, the most important battle fought between Muslims.

Muawiya's forces, seeing that they were losing, proposed arbitration. Accordingly two arbitrators had to decide whether or not Uthman's death had been deserved, which would give his slayer executioner status rather than murderer status and would remove the claims of Uthman's relatives. Their decision was against Ali, who protested that the verdict was not in accordance with shariah and declared his intention to resume the battle.

Ali's decision came too late for the more extremist of his followers. Citing the Quranic injunction to fight rebels until they obey, they insisted that Ali was morally wrong to submit to arbitration, which would be the judgment of men as opposed to the judgment of God, which would have been revealed by the outcome of the battle. Those who felt this strongly withdrew to Nahrawan. Known as Kharajites from the verb *kharaja* (to go out), their secession had far-reaching political effects for the Islamic community in the centuries that followed. Before resuming his dispute with Muawiya, Ali appealed to the Kharajites and when that failed, massacred many of them. Many of Ali's forces deserted him, furious at his treatment of pious Muslims, and Ali was forced to return to Kufa (present-day Karbala in Iraq) and await developments within the Islamic community.

A number of leaders of the Islamic community met at Adruh in Jordan, and the same two arbitrators for Siffin worked on a solution to the succession problem. At last it was announced that neither Ali nor Muawiya would be caliph. Abd Allah, son of Umar, was proposed. The meeting terminated in confusion, and no final decision was reached. Both Ali and Muawiya bided their time in their separate governorships: Muawiya (who had been declared caliph by some of his supporters) in newly conquered Egypt and Ali in Iraq. Muawiya contented himself with fomenting discontent among those only half-committed to Ali. While praying in the mosque of Kufa, Ali was murdered by a Kharajite; Muawiya induced Ali's son Hassan to decline any claim, and Muawiya was declared caliph by the majority of the Islamic community. He became the first caliph of the Umayyad dynasty.

The importance of these events for the history of Islam cannot be overemphasized. They created the greatest of the Islamic schisms—between the followers of Ali, the Shiat Ali, known as Shiites, and the upholders of Muawiya, the Ahl al Sunna, the Sunnis, who hold that they are the followers of orthodoxy.

The death of Ali, henceforth a martyr, ensured the future of the Shiite movement and quickened its momentum. With the single exception of the Prophet Muhammad no man has had a greater impact on Islamic history. The Shiite declaration of faith is: "There is no God but God; Muhammad is the Prophet of God and Ali is the Saint of God." Ali's elder son, Hassan, received the title Lord of all Martyrs because it was popularly held that Muawiya had him poisoned. Yazid I, Muawiya's son and successor in 680, was unable to contain the opposition that his strong father had vigorously quelled. Several groups rose against him, partially out of hatred at a strong government and partially because they thought a more rigorously theocratic government would satisfy their needs. Ali's younger son, Husayn, refused to pay the commanded homage and fled to Mecca where he was asked to lead the Shiites, who were mostly Iraqis, in a revolt against Yazid I. Ubayd Allah, governor of Kufa, discovered the plot and sent detachments to dissuade him. At Kufa, Husayn's band of 200 men and women followers, unwilling to surrender, were finally cut down by about 4,000 Umayyad troops. Yazid II received Husayn's head, and Husayn's death on the tenth of Muharram A.D. 680 continues to be observed as the most important day of mourning for all Shiites.

Shia Dogma

Shiism is often viewed as a deviant or heretical form of orthodox Islam. However, Shiism is the result of schism and, as scholars of Shiism correctly observe, the elements for a Shiite interpretation of Islam are present in the Quran as well as in hadith. Certainly the catalyst for the development of a Shiite entity and movement was the political turmoil created over the question of the temporal successor to the Prophet Muhammad and the ensuing murders of Ali and his sons. Shiites maintain, however, that Sunni-Shia polemics are not as much a matter of who should have succeeded the Prophet as they are about the function of the office of the successor and the qualifications of the man to hold it.

 The distinctive institution of Shiism is the Imamate, which includes the idea that the successor of the Prophet be more than merely a political leader. He must have *walayat*, the ability to interpret the inner mysteries of the Quran and of shariah; only those who have *walayat* are free from error and sin (*masum*) and have been chosen by God (*nass*) through the Prophet.

The Imamate began with Ali, who was also the fourth of the orthodox or "rightly guided caliphs." Ali is the key figure of the Imamate because it is his descendants who are the Imams. Shiites point to the close lifetime association of the Prophet and Ali. When Ali was six years old, he was invited by the Prophet to live with him and is considered by Shiites to be the first person to make the declaration of faith to Islam. He also slept in the Prophet's bed on the night of the hijra when it was assumed that the house would be attacked by unbelievers and the Prophet stabbed to death. He fought in all the battles the Prophet did except one, and the Prophet's choice of Ali as the husband of his only child was especially significant. Also significant is a hadith that records the Prophet as saying, "God placed the children of all the prophets in their backbone but placed my children in the backbone of Ali."

In Sunni Islam an imam, meaning *he who sets an example* is the leader of congregational prayer. When Ithna Ashari (Twelver Shiism) Shiites use the term, they are referring to the twelve divinely designated descendants of Ali's sons, Hassan and Husayn, who were wrongly denied their right to rule the Islamic community. Shiites reject the legitimacy of rule of all but the first four caliphs (Ali was the fourth). Shiites use the term *imam* instead of *caliph* because *caliph* has a strictly temporal connotation, and for them the ruler of the Islamic community has spiritual as well as temporal duties. None of the Twelve Imams, with the exception of Ali, ever ruled the Islamic empire. Each Imam chose a successor "by divine guidance" before his death, usually from among his sons.

For Shiites the Twelve Imams were like a combination of king and pontiff in exile. There always remained the hope that Shias would assume the rule of the Islamic community, and the existent Imam would be installed in his rightful place. Because Sunni rulers were cognizant of this hope, the Imams were the object of constant surveillance and therefore endeavored to be as unobtrusive as possible and to live as far as was reasonable from the capitals of the Islamic empire. The Eighth Imam, Reza (Ali ibn Musa), was designated crown prince for a time by the Sunni Caliph, Mamun, and was the only Imam to reside in or to die in Iran. His death at Caliph Mamun's orders encouraged Shiites to redouble the security and secrecy with which they surrounded the Imams. The later Imams were usually in hiding, which the Shiites called occultation *(ghybate)*.

Because of the persecution generally experienced by the Imams while Iran was ruled by the Umayyad and even the Abbassid caliphs, Imam Reza resided in Medina in Arabia. Caliph Mamun, the incompetent successor and son of Harun al Rashid, decided to designate Reza as his successor to avoid the usual conflict between groups that supported the Iman and those that supported the caliphate during transitions of rule. He invited Reza to join him. Reza's popularity grew too quickly, partially as the unexpected result of Mamun's intellectual soirees where Reza's learning brought him a tremendous following of scholars, including many who were not Shia. Poison, the chief cause of mortality among Imams, was administered to Reza, and his relatives attempted to flee to escape further disaster. The treachery of Mamun toward the Imam's family confirmed an already prevalent feeling among Shias that the Arab Sunni rulers were an untrustworthy lot.

The Twelfth Imam, Muhammad al Muntazar, was five years old when the Imamate descended upon him "through Divine Command and by the decree of his forefathers;" in the tenth century. Muntazar is usually known by his titles of Imami Asr (the Imam of the Period) and Sahib al Zaman (the Lord of the Age.) Because of the danger of assassination, he was hidden from public view and appeared only to a few of his trustworthy deputies *(naib)*. Sunnis claim he died at the age of five or six. From the Shiite point of view he went into minor occultation *(ghybati sughra)* by divine command as soon as he assumed the office, and in 939, some seventy years later, he began the major occultation *(ghybati kubra)* which will last until the divine command is given for him to manifest himself as the Mahdi or Messiah. Because Shias believe he is

121

spiritually present—some also claim him to be materially present as well—he is beseeched to reappear in various invocations and prayers. His name is mentioned in wedding invitations, and his birthday is one of the most jubilant of all Shiite religious holidays.

The five Shiite principles of religion *(usal al din)* are belief in divine unity *(tawhid)*; prophecy *(nubuwwah)*; resurrection *(maad)*; divine justice *(adl)*; and the belief in the Imams as successors of the Prophet *(imamah)*. The last two principles are not accepted by Sunnis.

Implied in the Shiite principle of the *imamah* is that the Imams, because of the special qualities they alone possess, are imbued with a redemptive quality as a result of their sufferings and martyrdoms. And, although they are not divine, they are sinless and infallible in matters of faith and morals. The latter principle is very similar to the notion of papal infallibility in the Roman Catholic Church. Roger Savory observes that these formulations were designed to establish the superiority of the Shiite Imams over the Sunni caliphs, but at the same time they supplied Islam with an infallible authority in an incarnate form. The idea that man needs an intermediary between himself and God is an Iranian idea that long predates Islam and can be found in' several Iranian religions, as is the idea of the savior or messiah (mahdi) who will come in the future to redeem man and cleanse the world of corruption. To expect that the mahdi, who is the last (Twelfth) Imam, really will reappear is a religious virtue *(intizar)*.

Two distinct and frequently misunderstood Shia practices are *mutah* (temporary marriage) and *taqiyah* (religious dissimulation). *Mutah*, that is, marriage with a fixed termination contract subject to renewal, was practiced by Muslims as early as the formation of the first Muslim community at Medina. It was banned by the second caliph and has since been unacceptable to Sunnis, but Shias insist that if it were against Islamic law it would not have been practiced among the Imams. *Mutah* differs from permanent marriage in that it does not require divorce to terminate it because the contractual parties agree on its time span. It can be for a period as short as an evening or as long as a lifetime. By making the *mutah*, the sexual act is placed within the context of shariah and is not considered adulterous; offspring are considered legitimate heirs of the man.

Mutah was most commonly practiced while traveling and during such periods of great unrest within the community as war. Shia scholars observe that because it is not unknown for men to seek sexual pleasure outside of permanent marriage, it is necessary to place such unions under the framework of shariah for the protection of the woman and any potential offspring. The word *mutah* derives from the same Arabic root as that for contentment, *istamtatum*, and its sanction is from the Quranic Sura 4, Verse 24: "And those of whom you seek contentment *(istamtatum)* give unto them as a duty." While *mutah* is no longer acceptable as legal from the point of view of the Iranian government, it nevertheless continues to be widely practiced in Iran. A couple can make the *mutah* contract discretely and without witnesses and thus avoid committing an act believed to be sinful if undertaken without religious sanction.

Taqiyah is another practice condemned by the Sunni schools as cowardly and irreligious but encouraged by Shiism. A person resorts to *taqiyah* when he hides either his religion or disavows certain religious practices to escape probable or definite danger of death from those who are opposed to his beliefs. Shias cite both Quranic injunctions (Sura 3, Verse 28) and the behavior of the Prophet in the case of Amar ibn Yazir who pretended to turn away from Islam and to reaccept idol worship rather than face torture and death. The Prophet condoned Amar's actions and said that Amar had accomplished his duty. *Taqiyah* can also be practiced when not to do so would bring definite danger to the honor of the female members of the household or when a man could be made destitute as a result of avowing his beliefs. Because of the persecution experienced frequently by Shia Imams, particularly during the period of the Umayyad and Abbasid caliphates, the need for *taqiyah* has been continually reinforced by historical realities.

Religious Obligations of Shia Islam

In addition to belief in the five principles of faith, Shias have seven major pillars of faith as opposed to the five of the Sunnis. The pillars detail the performances necessary to implement the principles of the faith.

The first pillar, the *shahada* (recitation of faith) "There is no God but God; Muhammad is the Prophet of God and Ali is the Saint of God," is said on many occasions. In addition to its use in prayers, the *shahada* is recited into the ears of a newborn child and is chanted at the bedside of the dying.

The second pillar is *namaz* (ritualized prayer), which Shiites perform three times a day, as opposed to the five observed by Sunnis. Ritual ablution is required before the prayer to orient the individual to the act of prayer and to symbolically cleanse him from the activities and distractions of the world. The believer faces the direction of Mecca and prays in Arabic, because the elements of ritual prayer are from Quranic passages and are therefore perceived as of divine origin and unchangeable. Dual editions of the Quran in Farsi and Arabic are in great use, and most Iranians read the Quran in Farsi translation. The *namaz* are committed to memory.

They must be made in a clean place, and for this purpose special rugs are often used although some Shias prefer to pray on clean earth, in memory of Husayn's death in the dust of battle. Many Shiites use a small tablet (*mohr*) made of clay from the environs of the tombs of Ali or Husayn to which they touch their foreheads during prostration. Daily prayers may be said at home or in a mosque. Congregational prayer is an occasion when the one who delivers the sermon, in the course of the prayers, may comment on political matters of importance to the religious community. Because of the absence of their political leaders (the Imams), Shiites do not place much importance on congregational prayer.

Zakat, or almsgiving—the institutionalization of generosity—is the third pillar. Zakat is based on a percentage of a person's income and is paid during the fasting month of Ramazan. It is used for the poor and for the upkeep of charitable and religious institutions. In addition to zakat, many Iranians also pay *khums*, one-fifth of one's income, which is given to sayyids (or seyyids), descendants of the Prophet Muhammad.

The fourth pillar fasting *(sawm)* during Ramazan—the ninth month of the Islamic year commemorates the revelation of the Quran to Muhammad. Shiites fast daily during the month from first light to the time the sun sets. During the daylight hours Muslims abstain from food, beverages, smoking, and sexual contact. This fasting does not have a penitential quality as do Christian fasts; rather it is a way of encouraging sympathy for those in need by directly experiencing hunger, thirst, and other privations. Zakat is paid during Ramazan because it is presumed that empathy with the poor will be greatest during this period. Those forbidden to fast are pregnant or lactating women, the sick, children, and travelers on arduous journeys. Iranians usually begin fasting after puberty, and while they are encouraged by adult family members to fast, they are never forced to, since it must be a voluntary act. Fasting appears to be widespread in Iran, although it is not as universally practiced as in most Muslim countries. Some restaurants are open during the day, particularly in Tehran.

Evenings during Ramazan are times of great festivity once the fast is broken. Parties, street entertainment, and, in more religious homes, the reading of the Quran continue until daylight. Shiites have a three-day period of mourning during Ramazan, commemorating the stabbing and eventual death of Ali. During this time Quranic verses and hadith are recited as well as special prayers and sayings of the Imams. Some of the prayers take four or five hours to recite.

On the first three days of the following Islamic month, Shawwal, the end of the fast is celebrated by the Id al Fitr, or little feast. Most Iranians, who would not otherwise do so, join in congregational prayers on the feast day.

The fifth pillar is the hajj, the pilgrimage to Mecca and Medina, during the last month of the Islamic year, Zul Hijjah. Every Muslim should attempt once in a lifetime to make this pilgrimage, which commemorates Abraham's willingness to sacrifice his son Ishmael by his servant woman Hagar (or, as presented in the Pentateuch, his son Isaac by his wife Sara). The performance of the hajj is highly ritualized, and specific religious activities are performed between the eighth and thirteenth days of the month, culminating in the Feast of the Sacrifice, the Id al Adha or Qurban. On the Feast of the Sacrifice, sheep are sacrificed by Muslims everywhere and by the pilgrims at the hajj rites. Half of the meat must be given to the poor, while the remainder is con-

Meidane Shah, Isfahan
Courtesy Iran Information and Tourism Center

sumed by the family. The sacrifice is widely practiced in Iran by those who can afford it. But for all classes it is a day of special rejoicing. Many Shias feel that the pilgrimage to Imam Husayn's tomb in Karbala is of equal merit as the hajj to Mecca, and thousands of Iranians visit Karbala annually.

Shias add two additional pillars to the five of the Sunnis. The sixth is jihad, or holy war, in which a Muslim must engage if Islamic lands or institutions are under attack. The seventh pillar is the old Zoroastrian dictum, "good thoughts, good words, and good deeds."

Religious Institutions and Organizations

As in all Muslim countries the single most important religious center is the mosque. Activities within a mosque vary greatly in Iran depending on whether it is in a rural or urban setting and particularly whether or not it is connected to a holy shrine.

Maktabs, village mosque schools for primary education chiefly of a religious nature, continue to exist, though in small numbers, since the educational reforms of Reza Shah. In urban centers a mosque may be connected to a religious school, the madrasah, where advanced religious training is available. Students live on the premises and are given full financial support from money garnered through endowments, zakat, or from the offerings of pious Muslims. Unlike madrasah systems in Sunni countries, there is no fixed curriculum or period of study, although students may specialize in transmitted sciences (*naqli*), in Islamic law, which in the Shia system includes Quranic exegesis, or in the intellectual sciences (*aqli*), which include Islamic philosophy, theology, and logic. Some students remain with the madrasah system their entire lifetimes, progressing from students to teachers. The madrasah at Qom is the largest (more than 6,000 students as of 1974), but sizable madrasahs exist in Tehran, Isfahan, and Meshed. Smaller madrasahs are located throughout Iran because wherever there is a teacher, there can be a madrasah, on however modest a scale.

There appears to be considerable frustration among *mujtahids*, or madrasah scholars, because of the few opportunities available to them outside of the madrasah system. The teachers of religion in the state school system are not, as a rule, madrasah graduates but instead are university graduates who have become *mujtahids* as a result of theological studies within a university curriculum. The religious leaders regard this as an infringement on one of their chief areas of influence and income. Some observers note that as a result of the segregation of the power of the religious leaders and scholars, they represent the most consolidated opposition to many of the government's programs (see ch. 7).

There are approximately 1,154 holy places in Iran, which vary from crumbling sites associated with local saints to the spectacular and often visited shrines at Qom and Meshed. The more famous shrines are usually huge complexes that include the mausoleum of the holy person, a mosque, a madrasah, and a library. The shrine of the Eighth Imam, Imam Reza, at Meshed is the country's largest and holiest. In addition to the usual shrine accoutrements Imam Reza's shrine contains hospitals, dispensaries, a museum, and several mosques located on a series of courtyards surrounding his tomb. The shrine's endowments and gifts are so large that at every meal 1,000 people are fed free. There are no special times for visiting the shrines, although naturally the Shiite holy days and special months receive more pilgrim traffic. The Iranian government estimates that approximately 3 million people visited Meshed in 1976.

Visitors to the shrine represent all socioeconomic levels. Whereas piety is a motivation for many, others come to seek the baraka (grace or general good fortune) that a visit to the shrine ensures. Most commonly a pilgrim is there as a petitioner, to ask the spirit of the holy person to act as an intermediary between the pilgrim and God for some specific boon. It is not uncommon for students who are going abroad for further education to make a pilgrimage to Meshed before the journey.

The shrine of next importance is the tomb at Qom of Imam Reza's sister, Hadrati Masuma. Sufis are particularly attracted to Masuma's tomb because she died a virgin and virginity, or that psychic state when one's spirit is attracted and opened to God alone, is an important Sufi mystical stage before one can bring forth or express the spirit of God within (see Deviant Religious Movements, this ch.).

Of the four shrines next in importance three are also those of Imam Reza's relatives, whose histories are indicative of the relationship between religious feeling and nationalism in Iran. Hadrati Abd al Azim, a relative of Reza's, is entombed at Rey near Tehran and Shah Chiragh, Reza's brother, at Shiraz.

Another important shrine is that of the great Sufi leader Sayyid Nematollah Wali at Kerman. Lesser shrines either of the relatives of Imams or sufis may be differentiated by the speciality of the holy person. For example, the shrine of Khizr, Elijah, the Green Man, is chiefly visited by women who are unable to bear children. Iranians of all socioeconomic levels will travel to shrines that are located in remote and geographically difficult locations; there is usually a little shrine in most towns of any size for people to repair to in times of difficulty.

Because these holy intermediaries are able to intercede for the dead as well as for the living, cemeteries are located in the shrines that have the greatest baraka. In 1932 the Iranian government prohibited the international practice of shipping corpses (approximately 200,000 a year) by air to Isfahan and then to Karbala where Imam Husayan is buried. This practice of shipping corpses to holy sites remained a common practice in 1977; Qom and Meshed were the principal recipients of the bodies.

The constant movement of pilgrims from one part of Iran to

another has had important effects in mitigating the parochialism of regions. Pilgrims continue to act as major sources of information about conditions in different parts of Iran.

The chief but not exclusive means of financial support for all religious institutions is the waqf, an Islamic religious foundation by which lands, pastures, wells, and even fruit-bearing trees are given in perpetuity as an act of piety. A person is chosen to administer the waqf in accordance with the wishes of the donor and, although the Iranian government has established a waqf department in an attempt to organize bequests, in many cases the administrator of the waqf or his descendants retain the power over the endowed property. The department of waqf was one of the by-products of the 1963 referendum, which empowered the government to lease waqf lands for a period of ninety-nine years to the peasants who traditionally worked the waqf lands with an assurance to the religious institutions that the sources of revenue would continue to flow. Many leaders of the religious establishments thus affected perceived this as a deliberate governmental attempt to lessen one of their traditional areas of authority and to win the allegiance of the peasants at the expense of a revered custom (see ch. 11).

Organization of the Shiite Religion

Islam provides no body of priests to intervene between man and God. In theory and for all practical purposes, a Muslim is free to minister to his own religious needs and duties. The explanation of the Quran and the hadith to common people and largely non-Arab Muslims, however, required men versed in religion. As Islam became organized into a system, it provided a clerical class, which acquired considerable authority and prestige. It was to this class that the authority to decide points of law and religious conduct came to be relegated.

Among Shiites the religious authority lies with the *mujtahids*, men who, by virtue of their proficiency in the science of religion and their attested ability to decide points of religious conduct, act as leaders in their community on matters concerning the particulars of religious duties. Laymen are free to follow any *mujtahid* in such particulars. Usually several *mujtahids* concurrently attain prominence and attract a large following. Occasionally a *mujtahid* achieves almost universal authority. Such authority was held by the late Hussein Tabatabai Borujerdi (d. 1961), who resided in Qom and bore the title of *ayatollah*, the highest honor a Shiite leader can be given. After his death in 1961, wide recognition as spiritual leader of Shiite Islam developed for Ayatollah Moshen Tabatabai Hakim. Hakim died at Baghdad on June 1, 1970, at the age of eighty-four and Ayatollah Azem Shariamadari succeeded him.

To become a *mujtahid*, one must complete a course of religious studies and receive authorization from a qualified *mujtahid*. Of equal importance is either the explicit or the tacit recognition of a man as a *mujtahid* from laymen and scholars in the religious community. The mullah, who works at the community level as a leader knowledgeable in religious precepts, is not as extensively schooled.

Religious schools are often associated with mosques and follow a traditional curriculum. The chief centers of study are at An Najaf in Iraq and at Qom. Other important centers are Meshed, Tehran, Tabriz, Zanjan, Isfahan, and Shiraz. The Theology College of Tehran University helps train teachers to give the religious instruction that forms part of the curricula of elementary and secondary schools. Anyone who studies theology, earning a doctorate in Islamic theology and jurisprudence, and who is found morally and spiritually pious and qualified, is given a letter of authorization either from an official Shiite center—at Qom, An Najaf, or Meshed—or from the Theology College of Tehran University and thus becomes a *mujtahid*.

Iranian clergymen wear a white turban and an aba, a loose, sleeveless brown cloak, open in front. If the clergyman is a descendant of the Prophet, he wears a black turban and a black aba.

A combination of dogma, ritualism, devotional practices, and mystical beliefs form the main body of popular Shiite religion. Great merit is attributed to the ritual mourning for the martyrs of Karbala, and the highly stylized shedding of tears for Husayn and for the House of the Prophet gains spiritual credit for the participant. Ali is the most important hero of religious legend, and his name continues to be the most popular name for males. The so-called usurper caliphs are execrated, and their names are never given to children. Execration of Yazid and Shemr, who murdered Husayn, is considered a meritorious deed. It is believed that God ordains the circumstances and the people one encounters throughout life—and from this is derived the notion of fate, or *taqdir*—but man can use those circumstances and achieve salvation or misuse them and merit hell.

Two angels record one's deeds and present their records on the Day of Judgment. The first night after a person dies he is visited by the two messengers of God, who hold threatening maces made of pillars of fire in their hands. He is questioned regarding his faith. If he cannot assert his belief in the unity of God, the prophethood of Muhammad, and the leadership of Ali, and if he does not remember the names of the Twelve Imams, his chances for salvation are lessened. If he passes the test, however, he has a good chance of finding a mediator from the House of the Prophet to remit his sins.

Ritual purification is a great concern. Under no circumstances is human flesh to be eaten. Fire, water, and earth, under certain conditions, are purifying elements. Running water, or a body of stagnant water of a certain size, must not be defiled by unclean elements. It is most important to perform correctly the ritual ceremonies involved in acts of worship; otherwise the act of worship is invalidated and must be repeated. Some persons make a living by publicly explaining points of ritual. Funeral rites are elaborate. Vows of charity and piety are frequently made for the fulfillment of a wish. A person who has asked for the granting of a wish often symbolizes this request by slaughtering a sheep or by attaching a padlock or a shred of cloth to the door or some other part of a shrine, even to holy trees.

There is virtually a cult of Ali in Iran. Many homes have a painting of him set in an enshrined niche, and gold medals with his portrait are worn by many in all classes. In times of trouble Ali, not Allah (God), is exclaimed; and whenever an example is called for, whether in social discourse or business dealings, anecdotes about Ali occur much more often than those of the Prophet. The hadith of Ali are collected in a volume that is regarded with almost the same reverence as the Quran and is probably read more often.

Two religious practices, unique to Shia Iran, combine those elements of cathartic religious tragedy and beauty so beloved by Iranians. The *rawda* (literally, garden) is a series of religious sessions during which the *rawda khwan*, a person gifted in the techniques of sermons and laments who is not necessarily a *mujtahid*, delivers powerfully emotional sermons and recites and sings laments on the subject of the deaths of the Prophet or the Imams. The government sponsors *rawdas* in mosques during Muharram and Safar. In addition they are given in private homes, throughout the year, usually as *nadhr*, the fulfillment of a vow for some special favor asked of God. Anyone may go to a *rawda*. Black flags on the door indicate that a *rawda* will be held. Weather permitting they are held in a garden. Some of the particularly pious attach loudspeakers outside of their houses so that those who cannot fit inside the house may still benefit from the *rawda*.

The holding of a *sufra* is similar but is usually strictly confined to women. *Sufras* are held to fulfill *nadhr*, and a woman will invite her friends to a lavish feast prepared with meticulous and highly ritualistic care. A female *rawda khwan* will recite and chant during the meal. After the performance, the remainder of food is distributed among the poor and the participants and is believed to possess baraka. The success of both the *sufra* and the *rawda* is judged by the number of people who are moved to weeping.

Despite the Islamic prohibition against magic, it is widely practiced in Iran where it is combined with Islamic motifs. The magical use of Quranic phrases is a traditional science, and certain phrases or formulas are well-known for their specific application. *Dua*, short prayers that include the names of Sufi saints or imams, may be carried on the person or inscribed on rings and amulets. The *dua niwis*, the writer of the correct *dua* for a specific situation, and the *rammal*, the practioner of geomancy, enjoy a brisk trade in urban and rural areas.

Iran has major religious holidays throughout the year. New Year, No Ruz, is the continuation of the Zoroastrian New Year and, although the celebration naturally contains many pre-Islamic elements, it has become strongly Islamicized. The Quran is placed on a table along with young plants and the *haft sin* (seven things that begin with the letter *s*). Blessings are recited for the Prophet and his family, and prayers are offered. Joyous religious festivals are the feasts at the end of Ramazan; the feast of the sacrifice during the hajj month; the birthdays of Muhammad, Ali, and the Imams; and the Idi Ghadir, which commemorates the day when Ali was chosen as successor to the Prophet.

Tragic religious events are more numerous than the joyful: the most important is Ashura, the death of Husyan on the tenth of Muharram. Mourning begins on the eve of his martyrdom, and the procession of self-flagellation occurs on the day itself. There is open weeping and exclamations of sorrow on the streets as the procession passes. *Taaziehs*, highly emotive passion plays, are performed depicting the events of his martyrdom.

The deaths of the Prophet, Ali's other son, Imam Hassan, and of Imam Reza, all occur in Safar. The attack and eventual death of Ali on the twenty-first of Ramazan is understandably a major event. Other mourning holidays are for the deaths of Ali's wife, Fatima, and of the other Imams.

Deviant Religious Movements

After the acceptance of Shiite doctrine as the official religion in the sixteenth century, there were many schismatic movements, partly encouraged by the Shiite principle of *ijtihad* (personal reasoning, derived from the Arabic word meaning *to struggle*). The follower of *ijtihad* is permitted to study rules and regulations and their sources, draw his own conclusions, and follow his conscience on procedural matters without reference to the authorities. This code of personal responsibility is open to anyone who can make an intelligent judgment. The two most important deviant movements that exist in modern times are Sufi mysticism and Bahaism.

In the ninth century, as the conquering Arabs adopted a way of life at variance with the puritanism of the early period of Islam, the Sufi movement was formed by Muslims who felt that worldly pleasures distracted from the true concern of the believer with the salvation of his soul. They also believed that materialism was supporting and perpetuating political tyranny. They prescribed meditation that over the years became formalized. The Sufis believe love of God is the only real condition; all else is illusion, and sense and reason are inadequate to explain these facts. Their name is generally believed to come from the rough white wool (*suf*) that they wore as a symbol of their asceticism; some scholars, however, claim the name came from the Greek word *sophos* (knowledge).

By the tenth or eleventh century the Sufis had developed a semiliturgical poetic service with a significant musical content. Influenced by Christianity and pre-Islamic mystery religions, their mystic love of God sought outlet in religious fervor. Some became so preoccupied with the contemplation of divine perfection that they sought ecstatic trances, eventually by prescribed phases, as a means of identifying with God. Mystic poetry and music were developed to a high degree as aids in achieving their selfless state. As a result, Sufi poets were among the greatest contributors to Iranian art.

A number of Sufi brotherhoods were established during the early centuries of Islam, many of which continue to exist. In the late 1960s one Kurdish sect had members in nine Middle Eastern countries. One of the brotherhoods, which came into being in the thirteenth century, was that of the whirling dervishes (from the Iranian word meaning *poor*), mendicant ecstatics known for their gyrating dances performed while in a trance, a condition heightened by the gyrations. Dervishes and other Sufi orders maintain loose organizations and hold private meetings at which the traditional ritual chanting of Sufi poetry and invocations are carried on.

A *khaniqah*, the tomb of a dead Sufi master or the teaching center of a living one, continues to be a vital religious institution in contemporary Iran and is actually a complex of centers. It houses rooms for spiritual training as well as accommodations for *fuqara* (disciples) and for visiting Sufis. The ceremonies of the *khaniqah* are opened to the public on such special occasions as birthdays of the Prophet Muhammed and the Imams and on the mourning holidays. In addition to the *fuqara* who reside there and the public who occasionally visit, there are others from all socioeconomic classes who may go once a week to the *khaniqah* for instructions in Sufi spiritual techniques. The meeting of these people on a frequent basis is socially significant because it is one of the few Iranian institutions that cuts across all classes and where there are exchanges among the members of all groups.

The major Sufi orders, most of which have branches in other countries, wield considerable influence in shaping contemporary cultural life, particularly in the fields of philosophy, music, literature, and painting. Because of the Sufi orientation to the esoteric or mystical truths of Islam, Sufism is attractive to those Iranians who, while living in the real world, nevertheless seek spiritual realization. Because the emphasis is on the development of the inner self and because Sufism may be approached and appreciated on any intellectual level, it draws, though not necessarily or exclusively, from groups that are not otherwise religious in the traditional sense of outward practice. In order of their size and influence, the following Sufi orders are most prominent in Iran today; the Nematollahi, which has centers throughout the country; the Gunabadi, chiefly in Khorasan; the Dhahabi in Shiraz; the Qadiri in the Persian Gulf area and in Kordestan; and the Naqshbandi, also in Kordestan.

The Bahai movement had its origin in the eighteenth-century heretical beliefs of the followers of Shaykh Ahmed Ahsai, who taught that the hidden Imam was a creative force with which contact could be made through a human intermediary, the Bab (door). In 1840 Mirza Ali Muhammad of Shiraz proclaimed himself

Dervish carrying flag ornamented with symbol of Shiite resistance
U.S. Army photograph

to be the Bab and gained the following of many tribal leaders. The Babi movement grew rapidly and assumed the character of a militant new faith at considerable variance with Shiism. The Babis interpreted the Quran as largely allegorical and represented the resurrection as a manifestation of divine spirit. Claiming to be Muslim nevertheless, they taught that all religions have elements of truth, peace, brotherhood, and tolerance. The heretics were severely persecuted by the Shiite leaders, and many were put to death, including Ali Muhammad.

A number of the Babis escaped, however, and followed Hussein Ali Baha Ollah, a disciple of Ali Muhammad, who declared himself the expected manifestation of the divine spirit, the messiah of all religions, and the promulgator of a new era. The followers of Baha Ollah, known as the Bahais, were pacifists (unlike the Babis) and preached respect for the law. They advocated universal brotherhood of man and legal equality between men and women. The Bahai movement was spread throughout the world; it has small groups active in Western Europe and the United States and claims a world membership of 500,000. The Bahais have been severely condemned by the Shiite clergy; the Bahai religion, while not under active suppression, is not legally recognized in Iran.

In addition to the Sufis, who may be appreciated as representing the mystical aspect of Islam, and the Bahais, who are now totally outside the theology of Islam, there are several sects active in Iran today that fall somewhere in the middle of these two interpretations. Of these dissident sects, the Ismailis are the oldest and were very numerous in Iran during the medieval period. They were originally part of the larger Shiite movement but split from the main body of Shiites during the ninth century over the question of the rightful successor to the Imamate. They claim only seven imams but have a religious leader, Aga (or Agha) Khan, forty-ninth descendant of their last imam. The largest number of Ismailis are in other countries, but in 1977 several thousand resided in Iran, chiefly in the Elburz Mountains.

Two smaller groups—the Ali Allahi and Ahl i Haqq—are concentrated in Lorestan but have also spread to Mazandaran, Kordestan, and some of the southern provinces. Although still a part of the Islamic tradition, these two sects emerged from politicized Sufi orders, and members of these two religious groups ignore the shariah and many Muslim devotional practices.

Minority Religions

The official recognized minority religions are Judaism, Christianity, and Zoroastrianism. Each of these groups is permitted to sustain an organization, to elect a representative to the Majlis (the lower house of Parliament), to maintain religious schools, and to publish periodicals. They are, however, restricted in their political activities since non-Muslims cannot occupy command positions in the armed forces and cannot achieve policymaking positions in the government.

In mid-1977 there were an estimated 80,000 Jews in Iran, living mainly in Tehran, Isfahan, Kashan, Hamadan, and Shiraz. Since 1948 some 45,000 Jews have migrated to Israel. Iranian Jews form one of the oldest Jewish communities in the world, and through more than 1,000 years of living among the Iranians, have become physically and spiritually very close to the majority population. They have preserved, however, a rather conservative, closed religious life. They are fully protected by the Constitution.

In the twentieth century the Jewish community achieved importance in the commercial life of the major cities, particularly Tehran, and Jews have entered the professions, most notably pharmacy, medicine, and dentistry. They have their own hospitals and academic and technical schools and are the only ethnic group that is considered 100 percent literate. The Jewish shrine to Esther and Mordecai is at Hamadan; the tomb of Daniel is supposed to be located near Ahvaz.

Native Christians are limited almost entirely to the Semitic Assyrians, numbering about 30,000, who live around Lake Rezaiyeh and in Tehran, and to the Armenians, totaling approximately 250,000, living mainly in Tehran and Isfahan. Most Assyrians belong to the Assyrian Church of the East, formerly and mistakenly called the Nestorian Church. As a result of Western missionary work in the twentieth century, four distinct denominations also exist, including Roman Catholic and Protestant groups. Adherents to these four Christian groups were estimated at approximately 30,000 in the mid-1970s. Most Armenians belong to the Gregorian Church under the Catholicos of Cicile at Beirut. This has led to a political split in the Armenian community as many Armenians continue to recognize the leadership of the Catholicos of Echmiadzim at Yerevan in Soviet Armenia, who claims to represent the entire community.

Armenians have long been free to enter the economic and social life of Iran. They have achieved a relatively high standard of living, have maintained a large number of religious schools, and are entitled to two seats in the Majlis. An annual feature of their worship is a pilgrimage to the ruins of the Church of Saint Thaddeus, founded over 1,500 years ago, in the area that became West Azarbaijan. The strong National Armenian Committee represents the interests of the religious community.

The foreign community of business and diplomatic people make up the bulk of the remainder of the Christians. They have churches in major cities, where services are conducted in European languages.

*   *   *

One of the best treatments of Shiism in Iran is Sayyid Hossein Nasr's article, "Ithna Ashari Shiism and Iranian Islam." Roger Savory's article, "Land of the Lion and the Sun," is useful as an overview of Shiism within the historical context of Iran. Allamah Tabatabai's work, *Shiite Islam*, is the most complete and authoritative treatment of the subject from the point of view of a religious leader and a devout practitioner of Shiism. Fritz Meier's article, "The Mystic Path, the Sufi Tradition," is an excellent overview of Sufism, but a more complete discussion of Sufism and its spiritual methodology can be found in Leleh Baktiar's beautiful book, *Sufi, Expressions of the Mystic Quest*. For a general study of esoteric Islam, Frithjof Schuon's *Understanding Islam* remains unsurpassed. It does presume, however, some acquaintance with the basic features of Islam. (For further information see Bibliography.)

Chapter 5. Social Systems

IN THE LATE 1970s Iran's social system was seeking to accommodate new forces of social change. The principal social division was between urban and rural society, the former having three levels, or classes, that were crosscut by a division between traditional and modernizing sectors. The upper class was defined by political and familial connections and by access to wealth. A minute elite at the top of the upper class was singled out by its members' access to the shah, who determined and not infrequently altered the membership of the elite (see Shah and Political Power, ch. 7). The middle class included a burgeoning, Western-oriented group pressing for changes in basic behavioral patterns and for rights and privileges heretofore reserved to the upper class. The main divisions in rural society included distinctions not only between villagers who owned property and those who were propertyless but also between villagers and the seminomadic or nomadic tribesmen. Rural inhabitants in general and the nomadic tribesmen in particular were less conscious than urban dwellers of national institutions and less imbued with a sense of Iranian identity. Forces of change were at work there, too, though less obvious than in urban centers.

Successive invasions of peoples speaking Indo-Iranian, Semitic, and Turkic languages produced a heterogeneous population displaying a wide range of physical, linguistic, and cultural variation. Physical differences were lessened by millennia of intermarriage; each of the languages absorbed accretions from the others; and cultural differences became less distinct in the course of long contact. Nevertheless the present-day population is aware of the divisive factors that stem from different ethnic origins, and this attitude, although lessening, remains an important barrier to the development of a sense of national identity.

The most important element in the population are the speakers of Indo-Iranian languages who, in 1977, comprised about two-thirds of the population. They represent one of the branches of the nomadic peoples who moved southward out of Central Asia about 4,000 years ago. The speakers of Indo-Iranian languages are not a homogeneous group. In present-day Iran they are represented not only by the speakers of Farsi (or Persian as it is commonly known outside Iran), which has been established by the government as the official language, but also by sedentary Kurds, seminomadic and settled Lurs and Bakhtiari in the Zagros Mountains in western Iran, and by seminomadic and nomadic Baluchi along the southeastern rim of the country.

The extended family traditionally has been the basic social unit. It gained early acceptance in a predominantly agrarian society and was later reinforced by Islamic beliefs and practices. The family continues to be the most important unit of society, providing its members with identity, security, and social orientation.

Languages

Indo-Iranian

Linguistic specialists generally divide Indo-Iranian dialects and languages (branches of the Indo-European language family) spoken in Iran into two groups: Western and Eastern. The Western group consists of Farsi and its two distinct dialects, Gilaki and Mazandari; Tajik, Tati, Talishi, Kirmanji (Kurdish), Baluchi, Parachi, Ormuri, and the languages and dialects of central and southwestern Iran; and Luri, Sivandi, and Gabri, and the dialect of Qumzari. The Eastern group is composed of Afghi (Pashtu and Pakhtu), Ossetic, Yaghnobi, Munjani, and Pamiri.

Educational instruction and government business are conducted in Farsi. It is the mother tongue of over half the population and is spoken as a second language by a large portion of the rest. Many different dialects of Farsi are spoken in various parts of the Central Plateau, and people from each city can usually be identified by their speech. Shirazis are considered to speak the purest Farsi. Some dialects, such as Gilaki and Mazandari, are distinct enough to be virtually unintelligible to a person from Tehran.

In its historical development Farsi is the result of three successive stages. Old Persian was used from at least 514 B.C. to A.D. 250. It was written in cuneiform and used exclusively for royal proclamations and announcements; it was not the language of common speech or commerce (which was Aramaic, a Semitic language). Middle Persian or Pahlavi dates from A.D. 250–900. It was the official language of the Sassanid Empire and the language of the priesthood (see table A). It was written in an ideographic script called Huzvaresh, which was mastered almost exclusively by the scribes. An example of Huzvaresh is given by Ibn al Muqaffa (d. A.D. 757), a well-known translator of Middle Persian into Arabic: when a scribe wished to convey the idea of *meat*, he wrote the Aramaic word *bisra* but read it as *gusht*, which is the Persian word. Dari, a variant of Middle Persian, was the court language.

Farsi, or Modern Persian, a continually evolving language, began to develop about A.D. 900. With the advent of the Islamic conquest in the seventh century and the eventual conversion of the population to Islam, Arabic became the official, literary, and written language, although not the language of court records (see Islamic Conquest, ch. 2). Farsi borrowed extensively from Arabic, not only the Arabic script but also certain elements of construction and vocabulary. In the course of centuries many Turkic words entered Farsi as well.

As part of the Indo-European language family, Farsi is distantly related to Latin, Greek, the Slavic and Teutonic languages, and English. This relationship can be seen in such cognates as *beradar* (brother), *pedar* (father), *mader* (mother), and *medal* (medal). It is a relatively easy language for English-speaking people to learn compared with any other major language of the Middle East. Verbs tend to be regular; nouns lack gender and case distinction; prepositions are much used; noun plural formation is regular; and word order is important. The difficulty of the language lies in the subtlety and variety of word meanings according to context. The language is written right to left in the Arabic script with several modifications. It has four additional consonants, *pe, che, zhe,* and *gaf,* making a total of thirty-two letters. Most of the letters have four forms in writing, depending on whether they occur at the beginning, in the middle, or at the end of a word, or stand separately. The letters stand for the consonants and the three long vowels; special signs written above or below the line are used to denote short vowels. These signs are used only in dictionaries and textbooks, which means that a reader must have a substantial vocabulary to understand a newspaper, an average book, or handwriting.

Farsi speakers regard their language as extremely beautiful, and they take great pleasure in listening to the verses of medieval poets. The language is a living link with the past and is important in binding the nation together. When Reza Khan became shah he assumed the dynastic name Pahlavi in order to use the lure of this Middle Persian language.

The Kurds speak a variety of closely related dialects collectively called Kirmanji. Kirmanji is part of the northwestern division of Iranian languages. Arabic and Farsi words and phrases have entered Kirmanji over the centuries. The dialects are divided into northern and southern groups, and it is not uncommon for the Kurds living in adjoining mountain valleys to speak different dialects. The small body of Kurdish literature is written in a modified Arabic script. Luri and the related Bakhtiari languages are closer to Old Persian than is Kirmanji, but they remain distinct languages. Baluchi belongs to a different subbranch of Indo-Iranian languages and is more closely related to Pashtu than to Farsi. Few Iranians learn these languages, which they regard as distinctly inferior.

There is no accepted standard transliteration of Farsi into Latin letters, and Iranians write their names for Western use in a variety of ways, often following French spelling habits (see Preface). The most profound dispute, however, exists between those who think Farsi should be transliterated in conformity with the rules for Arabic and those who insist that, since Farsi is not a Semitic language, it should have its own rules. Within Iran nationalist sentiment, recalling the widespread Iranian empires before the Islamic conquest, makes sporadic efforts to diminish the Arabic element in Farsi usage. These efforts, associated with deliberate secularization of society and restrictions on the influence of Muslim theologians, are opposed by those who point to the Quran and the language in which it is written as the ultimate source of truth. An attempt was made under Reza Shah to romanize written Farsi, but this was opposed by religious leaders and abandoned.

Turkic and Arabic Languages

The Turkic languages belong to the Ural-Altaic family, which includes many languages of Soviet Asia and western China as well as Turkish, Hungarian, and Finnish. The Turkic languages spoken in Iran tend to be mutually intelligible. Of these only Azarbaijani is written to any extent. In Iran it is written in the Arabic script, in contrast to the Azarbaijani in Turkey, which is written in the Roman script, and that in the Soviet Union, which is written in the Cyrillic script. Unlike Indo-European languages, Turkic languages are characterized by short base words to which are added numerous prefixes and suffixes, each addition changing the meaning of the base. They are also distinguished by their vowel harmony, which means that the kind of vowel used in the base word and the additives must agree. Thus lengthy words might be filled with *o's* and *u's* or with *a's* and *e's* but not with mixtures of the two.

The Arabic dialects spoken in Khuzestan Province and along the Persian Gulf coast are modern variants of the same older Arabic that formed the base of the classical literary language and all the colloquial languages of the Arabic-speaking world (see fig. on administrative divisions, ch. 6). Arabic is a Semitic language related to Hebrew, Syriac, and Ethiopic. There is therefore no linguistic family relationship between Arabic and Farsi. Arabic continues to be the language of prayer. Many children, especially in the villages, learn to read the Quran, though without understanding it. Arabic words actually incorporated into Farsi have been modified to fit the Persian sound pattern. Persians of the southern coast often learn Arabic for commercial reasons.

Like other Semitic languages Arabic is based on three-consonant roots, whose meanings vary according to the combinations of vowels that are used to separate the consonants. The written language is rendered difficult by the tendency to ignore the vowels or to indicate them by minimal diacritical marks.

The Assyrians around Lake Rezaiyeh speak Aramaic dialects related to the older Syriac. In addition to their religion, this is a significant binding force that attracts them to the Assyrians of other Middle Eastern countries. Armenian is an Indo-European language, but it is entirely incomprehensible to a native Farsi speaker. Almost all Armenians in Iran speak Farsi in addition to their native tongue, and many also know at least one Western language.

Western Languages

Educated Iranians are often literate in one or more European language as well as Farsi. For many decades French was widely learned by the educated groups. It was the language of diplomacy, and it appeared on postage stamps and paper currency. English has been rapidly replacing French in diplomacy and commerce; it has attained wide use in the military because of American and British military influence (see Foreign Influence, ch. 13). The majority of educated Iranians speak English rather than French as their first foreign language. German had been of importance to the military, and many Iranians have studied in the Federal Republic of Germany (West Germany). Some also have learned Russian. Westernized Iranians in the cities have found it necessary to learn English and French terms to describe the many Western concepts and material objects that have been introduced.

Peoples

Indo-Iranian Speakers

Approximately two-thirds of the inhabitants of Iran are speakers of one of several Indo-Iranian languages. Farsi is the official language of the country and the language native to the majority of the population. Aside from the Persians who speak Farsi, other major ethnic groups who speak Indo-Iranian languages are the Kurds, Lurs, Bakhtiari, and Baluchis.

Persians

The terms *Persian* and *Farsi* are sources of confusion. In a political context, particularly in an international one, the term *Persian* is often used to include all who live in Iran. As a rule the Iranian government uses the term to designate those speakers of Indo-Iranian languages who are settled rural or urban dwellers. As a result groups of settled Kurds, Lurs, or Bakhtiari, which most ethnographers treat separately, are officially included as Persians. Most scholars limit the term to those nonnomadic and nontribal people who form the majority population of central Iran and the inner slopes of the surrounding mountains and who speak one of several mutually intelligible dialects of Farsi.

Thus restricted the Persians constitute the largest ethnic component in the country. They predominate in the major urban areas of central Iran—in the cities of Tehran, Qom, Isfahan, Shiraz, Yazd, and Kerman—and in those areas of the plateau where there is enough water to permit settled farming.

In music, poetry, and art the Persians consider themselves—and are generally considered by other groups—as the leaders of the country. This feeling is strengthened by a consciousness of a heroic past and a rich literary heritage with which most upper- and middle-class Persians are intimately familiar. The more highly educated Persians form a large segment of the upper class, fill the majority of government positions, and are most subject to Western influence. Most Iranians abroad belong to this group.

The vast majority of Persians belong to the Shia branch of Islam, the official religion of Iran; but their way of life is still conditioned to some extent by their pre-Islamic Zoroastrian faith. A few thousand Persians, many of them in the area of Yazd in the center of the country, still practice Zoroastrianism (see ch. 4).

Gilani and Mazandarani

Along the southern Caspian coast live two major groups—the Gilani and Mazandarani—closely related to the Persians but speaking dialects that cannot be understood by Persians in Tehran. They are also distinguishable by their colorful dress and their mode of living. They are a rustic people, settled farmers and fishermen, considered rough and unsophisticated by the Persians of Tehran and the other plateau cities.

The Gilani, particularly, have long harbored separatist sentiments, and revolutionary leaders succeeded in establishing a short-lived socialist republic in the confused period after World War I. Reza Shah was from Mazandaran, and the crown accumulated considerable property in the rich coastal provinces. Economic development has linked them more closely to the central government, and the distinctions between the Gilani and Mazandarani and the Persians are in the nature of regional differences. Most Gilani and Mazandarani speak standard Farsi as well as their own dialects. Because Russian influence long existed in this area, it is understood as a second language by many, particularly the older generations.

Kurds

Approximately 3.5 million Kurds, one-third of the entire Kurdish population of the Middle East, live in Iran. They are one of the largest ethnic groups in the country, numbering about one-tenth of the population. Approximately 130,000 Kurds are refugees from the 1958 and subsequent Kurdish rebellions in Iraq. The Kurds are concentrated in the Zagros mountain area along the western frontier from the north of Khuzestan Province to the Soviet border. This region includes most of West Azarbaijan and Kordestan provinces and part of Kermanshahan and Lorestan provinces. They form the basis for the rural population and predominate in Kermanshah, Sanandaj, Mahabad, and other cities of the area.

There are also scatterings of Kurds in Fars, Kerman, and Baluchestan va Sistan provinces. Approximately 300,000 Kurds live in a small area of northern Khorasan because of a government decision in the seventeenth century to move Kurdish tribes there to break the power of their concentrations in western Iran and to defend the area from Turkish raiders. Approximately 80 percent of the Kurds are settled; the others practice seasonal migrations.

The Kurds are related to Persians by their language and ethnic origins. Ethnographers believe the Kurds to be descendants of the Medes who migrated from the Eurasian steppes in the second millennium B.C. and mingled with the indigenous population. The Kurds differ from the Persians in their social organization, their form of Islam, and to some extent in their physical appearance.

Whether settled in rural or urban areas, or seminomadic, most Kurds retain a tribal form of social organization, although the position of the chief is less significant among the settled Kurds. More than forty Kurdish tribes and confederations of tribes are recognized. Many of the tribes are feudally organized under a chief clan (*ashiret*) and depend on serf clans (*rayet*) that pay taxes and owe allegiance to the chief clan. They follow the Sunni branch of Islam, an important difference that sets them off from most of the population. There are, however, a number of Kurds in the Kermanshah region who adhere to Shia beliefs. Additionally many Kurdish tribal leaders profess Shia Islam, which is more useful to them politically.

Manifesting an independence of spirit throughout Iranian history, the Kurds at times have been a restive element in the society, fighting among themselves as well as against outsiders. Attempts at Kurdish autonomy occurred twice in the 1900s. In 1919 a Kurdish chief, Ismail Aga, led an unsuccessful rebellion. During World War II the short-lived Komeleh Kurdish Republic (known by Western historians as the Republic of Mahabad), supplied with arms from the Soviet Union, came into existence (see World War II and the Azarbaijan Crisis, ch. 2). In 1947 the movement was quelled by the Iranian army, and twenty of the leaders were hanged in Mahabad.

In mid-1962 Shahanshah Mohammad Reza Pahlavi, in an apparent attempt to placate the Kurds, asserted that the government would make special efforts to improve educational and economic opportunities in Kurdish areas. He began a program of fostering Kurdish-language broadcasts and publications and of forcing absentee landlords with large holdings to sell their property to the government for distribution among the landless peasants. Many Kurds have migrated to towns and cities to increase their opportunities for employment and education: quite a few have gained positions in the government. Much of the tension that had impaired earlier relations between Tehran and the Kurdish population has been largely eliminated by such factors as extension of government control to the provinces, construction of new roads, hospitals, and schools, adoption of the land reform program, and establishment of closer contacts between the government and the people.

Lurs and Bakhtiari

South of the Kurds in the Zagros chain live the Lurs and Bakhtiari, two ethnic groups related to the Kurds but staunchly maintaining their distinctness. Tradition among both the Lurs and Bakhtiari indicates that they were once a united group that divided about 1,500 years ago because of a quarrel among the leaders. Knowledge of any tribal unity between these two groups and the Kurds is lost in prehistory, but some Iranian scholars believe the Kurds were at one time a part of the Lur peoples. Both the Lurs and the Bakhtiari are Shia Muslims, and both groups speak languages related to Farsi.

The Bakhtiari are concentrated in an area extending southward from Lorestan to Khuzestan and westward from Isfahan to within fifty miles of the Iraqi border. Approximately 40 percent of the Bakhtiari are settled. They are divided into two main tribal groups: the Chahar Lang (Four Legs) are located in the northwest and until the middle of the nineteenth century retained the leadership of all the Bakhtiari tribes; the Haft Lang (Seven Legs), the southwestern group, have been more closely associated with modern Iran than the Chahar Lang and in some instances have proved quite influential.

Typically each group considers itself descendants in the male line of a single progenitor. Each is controlled by a single ruling family whose political power is buttressed by substantial wealth in herds and arable lands. It is the practice for the position of khan (ruler) to be held for a period of two years by the leader of one tribal group and the junior position of beg by the leader of the other group, after which the posts are reversed for the next two years. Members of the ruling family spend much of their time in Tehran, returning to the tribal areas only to handle major tribal matters, such as leading the tribes on their semiannual trek across the mountains between summer and winter pasture.

Historically the Bakhtiari provided the military forces for many Iranian rulers but remained aloof from the functioning of the central government in Tehran. In 1908, however, Sardar Assad, then a chief of the Haft Lang, returned from Europe an outspoken nationalist and democrat. At the time the constitutionalists were locked in a power struggle with the Qajar monarch, Muhammed Ali Shah. In 1909 Assad and his brother led a force of Haft Lang to Tehran and won a nationalist victory there that resulted in the reestablishment of the Constitution of 1906 (see Rise of the Qajar Dynasty, ch. 2). Since that time the Bakhtiari have remained the most powerful of the southern tribes. Assad's family has supplied many of the governors of Kerman, Yazd, and Isfahan. Assad's brother was prime minister for a short time in 1918, and Assad was minister of war during the early part of Reza Shah's reign. He is credited with settling the tribal problem with a minimum of bloodshed. Until his exile in 1962, General Teimur Bakhtiar was one of the most powerful men in Iran, serving first as military governor of Iran and then as chief of the National Intelligence and Security Organization (Sazeman Ettelaat va Amniyat Kashvar—SAVAK).

Despite the governmental activities of certain of the Bakhtiari, most of the tribesmen continued to follow their traditional lifestyle and became the objects of three campaigns by Reza Shah to break British influence and the power of the Bakhtiari in the oil field region, located in Bakhtiari territory. In late 1977 most of the Bakhtiari appeared to retain many of their traditional ways, including seasonal transhumance, despite continued governmental efforts to settle them. The Bakhtiari khans have national importance and are considered part of the traditional elite. The sons of wealthy Bakhtiari are educated in Tehran and sent abroad for higher education. Although the Bakhtiari tribespeople have expressed dissatisfaction at the often ostentatious life-style enjoyed by the khans residing in Tehran—and feel that the khans have little interest in their welfare—there appeared to be no concerted movement against the khans, and it seemed unlikely that the old leaders would soon be replaced.

The Lurs live south of Kordestan in the Zagros mountain chain northwest of Bakhtiari territory. They are centered in Khorramabad, the only urban area in Lorestan that existed before 1950; several of the more than sixty Luri tribes reside in Fars, Khuzestan, and Ilam va Poshtkuh provinces. The Lurs, like the Bakhtiari, are divided into two major groups: the Posht-e-Kuhi, meaning "from behind the mountains," and the Pish-Kuh, "this side of the mountain." The Posht-e-Kuhi are more numerous, and most continue to follow a nomadic existence in Ilam va Poshtkuh Province. Approximately half the Lurs are settled farmers, and most of these are Pish-Kuh.

The Lurs, totally nomadic until 1900, traditionally have been considered among the fiercest of Iranian tribes, frequently preying on the villages of Lorestan. Reza Shah ordered several campaigns against the Lurs, but the campaigns had little permanent effect. In 1927 the Lurs revolted, and by 1928 two military garrisons were established in the heart of their territory. Since then the Lurs have revolted periodically but with no lasting success. The nomadic Lurs of Ilam va Poshtkuh augment their income by smuggling guns, opium, and other illegal traffic from Iraq. The sedentary eastern Lurs have been beset by numerous problems since their settling: extreme poverty, land erosion, and denudation of forest areas. For the most part they farm on the sharecropping system, and although the landlords are themselves Lurs, they have come to identify with the landowning elite and appear to have little sympathy for their fellow settled tribesmen.

The Baluchi

The Baluchi—who comprise the majority of the population of Baluchestan va Sistan—number about 600,000 in Iran and are part of a larger group that forms the majority of the population of Baluchistan in Pakistan and of some areas in southern Afghanistan. As members of the Sunni branch of Islam they are separated in religion from the majority of Persians. The Baluchi occupy the Makran highlands in the southeast corner of Iran. This area stretches north along the Pakistani border and comprises some of the least inviting country in the world.

About half of the Baluchi are seminomadic or nomadic; the others have become settled farmers. Tribal organization remains intact among nomadic and seminomadic Baluchi; tribal patterns of authority and obligation have also been retained by settled Baluchi. They are among the most difficult tribal group for the Iranian government to control, in large part because of the great difficulty of communications between Tehran and Baluchestan va

Sistan. As a result they remain one of the poorest and least advanced peoples in Iran.

Most of the principal Baluchi tribes in Iran border Pakistan or Afghanistan. They are the Yarahmadzai, the Nauri, the Gomshadzai, the Saravan, the Lashari, and the Barazani. Two other important tribes, the Sadozai and Taherza, live on the coast of the Gulf of Oman.

Others

The groups here described by no means exhaust the different Indo-Iranian-speaking ethnic groups in Iran. Small groups of nomadic and seminomadic tribes are mingled with Turkic- and Arabic-speaking groups in the southern part of the Iranian plateau. Others, related to groups in neighboring Afghanistan and the Soviet Union, are found in Khorasan. Also in Khorasan are an estimated 25,000 Tajiks, a settled farming people that some ethnographers believe to be among the original Indo-European invaders of Iran. Distinguishable—but comparatively smaller Indo-Iranian-speaking ethnic minorities—are the following settled tribes: the Hazareh, Barbari, Teimuri, Jamshidi, and Afghani in Khorasan; the Qadikolahi and Palavi in Mazandaran; and the Sasani and Agajani in the Talesh region of Gilan.

Turkic-Speaking Ethnic Groups

The second major element of the population is composed of various Turkic-speaking ethnic groups. Beginning in Achaemenid times, nomadic Turkish peoples migrated steadily out of central Asia into the area that became known as Iran. In the eleventh century they were united under the Seljuqs and established their dominion over much of the Middle East, from the Oxus River north of Afghanistan to Mecca in the Arabian Peninsula. The animosity between Turks and Iranians, engendered by this conquest and intensified by the incursions of the Mongols in the thirteenth and fourteenth centuries, continues to affect relations between Turkic and Farsi speakers.

The Turkic speakers are concentrated in northwestern Iran, where they form a majority of the population in East and West Azarbaijan provinces; in northeastern Iran, where many small Turkish groups are mixed with Persians, Kurds, and Arabs; and in Khorasan Province and southwestern Iran, where nomadic Qashqai and Afshari tribes form enclaves in primarily Persian areas. Except for the Azarbaijani, most Turkic groups are tribally organized, and many continue to follow a nomadic or seminomadic life. Most of them have learned to speak and understand Farsi, but they have not been assimilated with the Persians to the point of giving up their language and customs.

The Azarbaijani

By far the largest Turkic-speaking ethnic group are the Azarbaijani—most of whom are concentrated in the northwest corner of Iran where they form the majority population between the

Qashqai children attending tent school
Courtesy U.S. Agency for International Development

Caspian Sea and Lake Rezaiyeh and from the Soviet border south to the latitude of Tehran. Their language, Azarbaijani (also called Azari), is structurally similar to Turkish but with a strikingly different accent. They are mainly settled farmers and herders; their village life does not appear to differ markedly from that of the Persians. They also share the Persians' adherence to the Shia branch of Islam.

The Azarbaijani of Iran are identical in language and way of life to their relatives across the border in the Azarbaijani Soviet Socialist Republic. The Russians have long had an interest in acquiring the Iranian area and uniting the Azarbaijani under their protection. During and immediately after the two world wars they controlled the area and in December 1945 established a short-lived communist-led independent state. As among the Kurds, the Iranian government is trying to strengthen the allegiance of the Azarbaijani to Iran.

Qashqai

The second largest Turkic group in Iran are the seminomadic Qashqai, numbering about 500,000. They are one of the best organized tribal confederations in the country. Composed of fifteen major tribes and many minor ones, they move between summer pastures in the highlands south of Shiraz and winter pastures north of Shiraz. Their migration is among the longest and most difficult of any of the nomadic tribes. In 1977 few Qashqai were permanently settled. The majority of the Qashqai are Shia Muslims.

The Qashqai were extremely powerful in the nineteenth century, virtually dominating Fars Province and including as their clients the entire Khamseh confederation, a group of five Arabic-and Turkic-speaking tribes. Under their most notable leader, Khan Solat ud Doleh, their strength was great enough to defeat the British-led South Persia Rifles in 1918. Reza Shah's campaigns in the 1930s against them were successful because the narrow pass on the route from their summer to winter quarters was blocked, and the tribe was starved into submission. Solat and his son were imprisoned in Tehran where Solat was subsequently murdered. Many Qashqai were then settled on land in their high country which is 6,000 to 8,000 feet above sea level. A specialist on Iranian tribal affairs, Oliver Garrod, noted that in the first ten years after enforced settlement many of the Qashqai died from disease, famine, and exposure; the health of others—particularly the younger generation—appeared to have been permanently impaired.

The Qashqai and other tribes returned to nomadic life after Reza Shah's exile in 1941. By 1946 all the southern provinces were in rebellion, and the Qashqai had reverted to pillaging villages and robbing on the highways. Army and government officials were driven out of the area. The Qashqai, however, reduced in numbers and disorganized after the settlement, were never able to garner their previous strength and independence. They revolted again in the 1962–63 period over the question of land reform, which the Qashqai viewed as another governmental attempt to wrest away their land. A full-fledged army campaign was brought against them, and by 1964 the area was somewhat pacified, although few of the Qashqai actually settled. Barbara Wilson, a researcher on tribal affairs, cites the Qashqai as an extreme example of the difficulty of integrating a subgroup into the political and social community on the national level.

Others

Many other Turkic-speaking groups are scattered throughout Iran, but mainly along the northern tier of provinces. The fifty or more nomadic Shahsavan groups abut the Azarbaijani on the east. They may number as many as 180,000, but most sources treat them with either the Azarbaijanis or Turkomans. They have a long history of staunch support for the ruling dynasties since Safavid times (see table A, Preface). The Qajars, from whom came the royal family that Reza Shah dethroned, form an enclave among the Mazandarani. Some are settled farmers; others retain their nomadic way of life. The Turkomans and Qarepakhs are small nomadic tribal groups in Khorasan. Qarepakhs also live along the south shore of Lake Rezaiyeh in Azarbaijan.

One of the largest and most scattered of the Turkic groups is the Afshars; estimates of their number run as high as 400,000, but there are probably fewer than 100,000 in Iran. A seminomadic people who speak a language akin to Azarbaijani, they are found along the shore of Lake Rezaiyeh, around Zanjan, on the edges of Kordestan, south of Kerman, and in Khorasan. These scattered groups share no consciousness of their identity, nor any political unity, but they nevertheless differentiate themselves from the groups that surround them. Several other Turkic groups, more accurately described as confederations of tribes than as ethnic groups, are found near the Qashqai and Lurs. Among them, Turkic-speaking tribes are allied with Persians and Arabic tribes mainly to defend their interests in pastureland against more powerful neighbors.

Arabs

Estimates of the number of Arabs in Iran vary greatly, but there are probably fewer than 500,000. They predominate in Khuzestan Province and along the coastal plains bordering the Persian Gulf; scattered groups are located in central and eastern Iran. In general they are tribally organized. Most are nomadic herders, but in Khuzestan Province and along the Persian Gulf many carry on a seminomadic or sedentary existence. They raise cattle, sheep, and camels; they also grow cereals, rice, and dates. Many are fishermen, and several thousand are employed as unskilled workers in the oil industry.

The Arabs mingle with their surrounding Persian and Turkish neighbors, and there is no sense of ethnic unity among the scattered Arabic settlements. Their sense of loyalty toward the government in Tehran is subject to question, for historically these Arab groups have regarded themselves as separate and have usually been so regarded by their countrymen. Their ties and interests lie more with the Arabs in Iraq and across the Persian Gulf than with Iran, but there is no apparent sense of irredentism among them. Their adherence to Sunni Islam strengthens their differentiation from the Shia Iranians. The government has made no special effort to improve their cultural or economic level or to draw them into national life.

Other Minority Groups

An important criterion for identifying a minority group in the country is religion. The nonsettled populations have had fewer advantages in education and economic development because the government has concentrated on Tehran and other urban centers. Theoretically all Muslims (Turkic speakers and Arabs, as well as Persians) have the same political rights. Non-Muslims, however, have not been allowed to vote for delegates to the Majlis (the lower house of Parliament) on the same basis as Muslims, but have been allotted a fixed number of representatives (see ch. 6). The economic lot of Armenian and Jewish minorities is gradually improving, however, because younger generations have gained education through privately sponsored school systems and have moved into the middle class.

Armenians

About 270,000 Armenians were living in Iran in mid-1977. Some were settled by Shah Abbas in the sixteenth century just north of Isfahan, where they pursued their crafts as weavers, goldsmiths, and tailors, and others have become located in East and West Azarbaijan provinces, near Turkey, and in their traditional homeland, which is now part of the Soviet Union. About half the Armenians live in Tehran, and several thousand work in the oil fields of Khuzestan Province. They are largely an urban people—craftsmen and traders. In the cities they tend to live apart from the Muslim population and maintain their own schools, Armenian-language newspapers, and social life. Most are literate in both Armenian and Farsi and are relatively well-educated. They have not recently been permitted to occupy important positions in the Iranian diplomatic corps and army, but they have never been actively persecuted by the government. They have maintained a sense of group solidarity and have developed a solid middle class.

The Armenians for the most part are Christians of the Gregorian persuasion, whose patriarch is either the Catholicos of Echmiadzin near Yerevan (150 miles north of Tabriz in the Armenian Soviet Socialist Republic) or his rival the Catholicos of Cicile at Antelias (about five miles north of Beirut). Clergy from Soviet Armenia were at one time active among the Iranian Armenians and had some success in exploiting their sense of community with their coreligionists in the Soviet Union. Several thousand emigrated to the Soviet Union during the World War II period and, except for occasional interruptions by one government or another, emigration has continued. Since 1949 most Armenians have adhered to the Catholicos of Cicile. Another sizable group of Armenians is made up of Catholics of the Eastern rite (see ch. 4).

Jews

The Jews have been in Iran since ancient times. It was the Achaemenid kings Cyrus II and Darius I who permitted them to return to Jerusalem from their Babylonian captivity. Through centuries of close association they have become physically and culturally almost indistinguishable from the Persians.

Most Jews retain a strong adherence to Judaism, tend to be orthodox, and conserve the ancient Jewish values. Family life is generally very close-knit. In mid-1977 there were an estimated 85,000 Jews in Iran, living mainly in Tehran, Isfahan, Hamadan, and Shiraz.

The Jews, unlike the Armenians, were long confined to ghettos, from which they were emancipated only at the beginning of the twentieth century. Many, however, continue to live in their own quarters of the cities. Iranian Jews had less opportunity than Jews in other Middle Eastern countries to become skilled artisans or businessmen. Their activities were limited largely to small-scale trading and moneylending. Since the 1920s they have gained increased importance in the bazaars of Tehran and other cities, and some of the younger generation have acquired enough education to enter into the professions, particularly pharmacy and medicine.

In 1977 the Jews were the only group in the country that was 100 percent literate. There has been little anti-Jewish feeling in Iran, probably because the Jews have remained a small and impoverished people there. They have fewer schools than the Armenians, no press, and no means to preserve their own language. The Jews speak Farsi or, in western areas, Kurdish or Syriac. They have been helped by a number of international Jewish organizations, including the American Joint Distribution Committee, which introduced electricity, water, and sanitation into the Jewish community.

Assyrians

In mid-1977 there were approximately 32,000 Assyrians. The traditional home of the Assyrians in Iran is along the western shore of Lake Rezaiyeh, but immigration has taken many to Tehran and other urban areas of western Iran. Most of those who remain in East and West Azarbaijan provinces are farmers, but many are employed as mechanics in the cities, and many others are in the oil industry in southern Iran. A mountain people, they have a reputation as fierce fighters.

Language and religion provide a strong cohesive force and give the Assyrians a sense of identity with their coreligionists in Iraq and elsewhere in the Middle East and also with the Assyrian Federation of the United States. Linguistically they are distantly related to the Arab-speaking groups. Most of them adhere to the Christian faith, mainly to the Assyrian Church of the East (sometimes mistakenly called the Nestorian Church). The Assyrian Church of the East is regarded by many theologians as the oldest church in Christendom. Beginning in the late nineteenth century the Anglican Church of Great Britain and the Presbyterian Church of the United States sent missions to help renew the Assyrian Church of the East, with the result that many Assyrians belong to denominations of Protestant Christianity; one group is Roman Catholic (see ch. 4).

Zoroastrians

Zoroastrians form a small religious minority, numbering probably not more than 36,000 who, through centuries of intermarriage and isolation from their Muslim Persian relatives, have become distinguishable in language and way of life. They are concentrated in Tehran, Yazd, and Kerman, where they have accumulated considerable wealth as merchants and land speculators (see ch. 4).

Structure of Society

The Iranians have a very strong sense of class structure. They refer to the groups, commonly called the upper, middle, and lower classes in the West, as first, second, and third levels of society. The class consciousness of Iranians is highly developed. Iranians are always aware of their social position vis-à-vis other members of society. This is expressed in *taarof*, the elaborate ceremonies of ritual politeness, which are used in virtually every social interaction. The kind of *taarof* used differs according to the relative status of the individuals involved. William Beeman, a linguistic anthropologist, maintains that "*taarof* is the active, ritualized realization of differential status in interaction. It underscores and preserves the integrity of culturally defined status roles as it is carried out in the life of every Iranian every day in thousands of different ways. Iranian youth cry in despair at its pervasiveness, but they are powerless against it, and practice it themselves even while complaining about it." Honor (*gheyrat*) and face-saving (*aberu*) are components of the *taarof* system; thus while an underling must recognize authority, he can retain his dignity. Reza Arasteh notes that the use of *taarof* lessens the possibility of insult to one's self-respect; "Persians strive to avoid humiliating or criticizing others; they may agree with another's statement merely to avoid publicly embarrassing him."

Urban Society

It is only in the urban sector that Iran's basic three-class social system can be discerned. The tribal chiefs and the formerly great landlords who might be expected to form the upper class of rural society in fact reside in the provincial capitals, such as Isfahan and

Shiraz or, as is increasingly the case, in Tehran. Iran's modern middle class of government bureaucrats, professionals, technicians, and industrial managers is totally confined to urban areas as is the traditional middle class of affluent bazaar merchants, Islamic clergy (see Glossary), and independent artisans.

Historically the stimulus for urbanizaton came from a political impetus and not primarily from economic factors, as in the West. Politics is the main occupation of the city, and other occupations revolve around it. Regardless of wealth one does not have a secure position in the upper or upper middle classes without access to the political apparatus. For this reason wealth and politics seek each other out, the former to obtain security, the latter to offer service in return for economic benefit. This alliance is the basis for the Iranian upper class.

Formerly members of the upper class with strong provincial ties, that is, those who had their power or wealth bases in the provinces, could afford to live away from Tehran. In many cases, because Iran has been traditionally a highly regional society, it was necessary to do so to safeguard one's interest. Because of the increased centralization of Iran—a deliberate governmental policy—and because the government's military machine can penetrate everywhere and overcome any nongovernmental force, those who would safeguard their provincial interests move as closely as possible to the heart of the system—the shah's court of Tehran.

The domination of Tehran over the workings of the country is evidenced by the preponderance of Iran's elite who reside there and especially by the large number of the younger generation of the upper class who were born in Tehran. In his study of the political elite, Marvin Zonis noted that only five members of the political elite—and they were religious leaders—did not reside in Tehran. The opportunities for social mobility in Tehran are disproportionately greater than in other cities. It is where the elite lives, forms contacts, and spends its money and favors. It also provides the educational services that spawn the growing modern middle class as well as the infrastructure to support the occupations of such a class.

Zonis cited the following statistics based on data available in the late 1960s: 73 percent of all university students in Iran were studying in Tehran; 69 percent of those who had any college education lived there; 33 percent of all secondary students studied there; and 34 percent of all literate Iranians lived there. Although the rural peasants were slowly acquiring a voice, the relative insignificance of them and of other groups in the rural sector make the urban-hinterland designation for the demarcation of Iranian society more appropriate than urban-rural.

The upper class, or elite, historically comprised the shah and his family and court, the great landlords, the highest religious dignitaries (*ayatollahs* and *mujtahids*), and the leaders of the larger tribal federations. As a result of innovations and developments in

155

the economic, military, and political sectors, the elite has been expanded to include high-level government administrators from families with a tradition of service to the throne, general officers of the military and security forces, highly respected professional men, and the wealthiest industrialists and representatives of commercial interests. Although no longer the ruling dynasty and precluded by the Constitution from holding the highest political positions, members of the Qajar family retain important political, economic, and social status. In 1977 the upper class was estimated to comprise less than 1 percent of the total population.

Members of the elite tend to be involved in numerous complex interrelationships. Some members of the Senate, which included many members of the elite, were also on the boards of several industrial and commercial enterprises and were owners of a large number of villages. Since an important prerequisite for entry into the elite has usually been belonging to a "good family," blood and marital relationships tend to bring together important segments of the elite. Until the land reform measures most political leaders were also large landowners, and many of the Islamic leaders held a number of lucrative trusteeships over property endowed for religious purposes, waqf land.

In spite of all the prestige and power the ruling elite did not enjoy real security even before the reform movement. There is no strong group or class cohesion even at the top. The members react individually or by family to the favor or displeasure of the single individual at the apex of the entire social hierarchy, the shah. One of the conclusions of Zonis' study was that because of such factors, the behavior of the political elite emerged from and was based on four attitudinal characteristics: political cynicism, personal mistrust, manifest insecurity, and interpersonal exploitation. Studies by other observers identified the same or similar characteristics in the society as a whole.

The middle class underwent considerable changes during the 1960s and 1970s, the most important of which was its rapid expansion. The class may be divided vertically into upper and lower middle-class strata and horizontally into modern and traditional groups.

The members of the upper middle stratum are drawn from the same occupational sources as the upper class. They are found in lesser positions in the civil service in Tehran or in top positions in provincial cities, in positions just below command level in the military, in important but not outstanding positions in commerce and industry, among professionals who have not achieved recognition as being at the top of their profession, in positions of religious respect, and finally as landowners of local influence but not important enough to be consulted when new policies are being considered for the rural areas. They include latecomers to the cause of the Pahlavi dynasty, younger offshoots of old upper-class families, members of families too actively associated with the

Qajar dynasty but powerful enough to hold on to some of their former glory, those who through choice or fate have not acquired a foreign education or some other essential of upper-class status, and men of unusual ability who could never hope to attain upper-class status for reasons having to do with their ethnic origins or religious adherence. The Bahais are the most conspicuous example in this category.

Because political connections are the key to social status, the upper middle stratum continually hopes that some political change will bring them as individuals into the upper class. The lower middle class is made up of small retailers, craftsmen, low-level government employees, mullahs, and related occupations. Generally they are less well educated and less well paid than members of the upper middle class. Like the upper middle class they have a strong dislike for manual work, preferring desk jobs, especially with the government. The members of this stratum do not, however, have the hope of the upper middle stratum that fate will propel them into the upper class. They are too far away from the dividing line, and they do not have the economic resources, family background, or political connections to take advantage of a shift in the political scene. Their main concern appears to be that they do not lose their social niche and fall into the lower class.

The middle class is also divided into modern and traditional groups. The modern middle class consists of those persons with Western education employed in government services, the professions, and the universities, whereas the traditional middle class includes bazaar merchants, mullahs, and wealthy guild members.

The two groups differ greatly in their origins and outlook. The modern middle class stems from the development of a modern bureaucracy originating in the late nineteenth century. This group was significantly expanded in the 1960s and 1970s, largely as a function of the greater access to education and wealth. James A. Bill notes that, "One of the most profound unintended consequences of the White Revolution is the accelerating growth of the professional middle class." Bill pays special attention to the modern middle class that he calls "The Professional-Bureaucratic Intelligentsia." He views them as an alienated class for the most part and the class that is most vociferous about the need for system transformation. This group, whose power position comes primarily from talents or skills acquired from a modern formal education, increasingly refuses to participate in or is at least intensely frustrated by the personal maneuvering and manipulation that are necessary for advancement in society.

The civil service reforms of 1966 strengthened the position of this group. The reforms introduced competitive examinations and provided that advancement would be based on education and skill rather than on traditional criteria. Once in a position in the civil service, however, individuals have found that traditional methods for retaining a position or securing another position have continued to obtain. Additionally in the six-point reform program in 1963—the White Revolution—nobles and landlords were struck from the list of those who supervise national electoral procedures and replaced by the workers and peasants, but no reference was made to any professional middle class, a snub that further alienated this class. It is precisely this class that is most needed to implement industrialization and other modernization of society. The government is aware of this and is recruiting members into government service and rewarding them for special achievement, apparently with the expectation that this will lessen their efforts to emphasize merit rather than personal connection as the basis for advancement. By 1977 some members had been successfully integrated into the system but many others had not, and intraclass struggles were rife.

Members of the urban lower class can be distinguished by their traditional dress, linguistic use, extremely high rate of illiteracy, and performance of manual labor. They are generally uneducated and have little understanding of the political process. Urban influences and separation from customary social and economic structures, however, make inoperable the traditional rural behavioral patterns and relationships. Members of the lower class have not defined their role in urban society nor have they adopted a new set of values to cope with the problems of the urban environment.

The gap between the lower middle class and the lower class is greater than that between the upper middle class and the upper class. In terms of values, attitudes, and expectations, a member of the lower middle stratum may identify more closely with the upper class than with the lower class.

In the past members of the urban lower class did not take political initiative, but many willingly responded to the call for mob action when it came from a patron who was evidently politically secure. Their cooperation has been disdained by the modern middle class, and even the Tudeh (Masses) Party failed to organize them effectively. At various times they were used as hired mobs in the petty struggles of rival members of the elite but also notably in the overthrow of Mohammad Mossadeq (see Mohammad Mossadeq, ch. 2).

Among the leaders of the lower class groups are employers, influential bazaar merchants, wholesalers, concessionaires, police officers, and mullahs. The occupational hierarchy within the lower class runs from the migrants and casual laborers at the bottom to the regularly employed factory workers and those in government service, such as office boys, postal employees, and low-ranking members of the police force, at the top. In between there are bazaar porters, streetcleaners, car washers, mechanics, journeymen and apprentices in the bazaars, domestic servants, gardeners, newspaperboys, peddlers, distributors, and unskilled factory and service workers.

Servants form an important segment of the urban lower class. They work in the houses of upper- and middle-class families and come from all age-groups. Traditionally they were employed on a permanent basis, remaining with the same family and providing recruits over generations. A deep personal loyalty based on mutual rights and obligations existed between employer and servant. The employer supposedly had the responsibility of caring for his servants' welfare even when they became too old to work or when they left their employer for family reasons. Female servants were often widows or deserted wives who depended on such employment for the support of dependent children. During the 1970s this traditional relationship was breaking down, especially in Tehran and the larger cities,as servants moved from master to master in hope of improving their security.

Beggars make up a distinct group within the urban lower class. They depend on the Islamic obligation of charity, and as a consequence many claim some religious association. There have been some serious attempts to remove beggars from city streets and resettle them in rehabilitation centers where they can learn a trade. No noticeable success has been achieved in this regard, and many beggars prefer to continue their endeavors.

Industrial developments have tended to improve the economic and social situation of the urban lower class. Experts anticipate that the growth of the industrial sector will provide employment for those rural workers displaced by mechanization in agriculture. Industry is also expected to absorb the growing number of women who enter the labor market each year (see. ch. 9).

Political Influence and Social Status

Officials and those associated with the government in any capacity occupy the first stratum in urban social structure. They are expected to be men of advanced education, gentlemen, and experts on Iranian culture. Recognition of individual rank and prestige is given great importance, and professional titles are widely used as a means of gaining such recognition. As men of importance, officials enjoy many privileges and prerogatives that they are assumed to merit and need not justify in terms of any standards of morality or performance.

Officialdom is organized along strictly hierarchical lines. In general governmental positions in small towns in the provinces are at the bottom of the ladder. The closer one gets to the shah as the center of political power, the higher one's status. In such a situation rivalry for promotion is acute; there is little cooperation among members of the government. Protocol in relations with superiors is strictly observed. In their dealings with the public officials are conscious that they represent the powerful political apparatus of the state. They are also aware that their careers depend on their satisfying their superiors. They are reputed to prefer to take no acton at all rather than risk any criticism from their superiors.

Among officials, politicians and civil servants are not clearly differentiated. Politicians resemble civil servants in that both are appointed for an indefinite tenure and act primarily to please superiors. Lateral shifts between the civil service and political positions are frequent. Consequently the two roles are intimately related, and it is not unusual for the same individual to engage in both activities at the same time, regardless of formal title. Socially the two roles also are equated, for one carries the high status achieved in one role into the other role. As expected many civil servants and politicians on this level come from "good families." For them public service is primarily a source of social status and political protection.

A military unit is stationed in or near most cities. The command level of the military and the chiefs of SAVAK constitute another segment of the upper class. The military is the special favorite of the shah because it provides security both for the present regime and the present social structure. The military quite often do better than persons of comparable status in the civil service. Certainly they have better facilities and privileges, which are resented to some extent by the officials. Socially they mix with civilians but are prohibited from fraternizing with foreigners. Upon retirement some military leaders of unquestioned loyalty to the regime may enter the upper levels of the civil service. Such individuals had acquired a reputation for greater honesty and strength than regular officials, at least in government circles, but this reputation was shattered in 1960 when some of the top generals holding important civilian posts were taken into custody and charged with corruption. In the mid-1970s senior navy officers were charged and convicted of corruption, and rumors of other corrupt military officials were widespread (see ch. 13).

The military do not have any special esprit de corps in spite of special treatment. On the command level in particular they are jealous of each other, as are other Iranians in similar positions. They hope to make a personal contact as high as possible in the power structure, especially with the shah, to ensure a secure future. The shah plays on this opportunism, and thus political authority completely dominates the military who understand that they owe their social position and economic benefits directly to the regime's confidence in them. The military are a potential source of subversive activity, but since the early 1950s the shah has been taking no chances that the military will strike out on its own. Loyalty is enforced in the ranks, and on the command level the shah plays divide and rule, forbidding generals, for instance, from fraternizing with each other.

The highest ranking officers still tend to come from prominent, upper-class families, many having a long history of military service. Junior officer positions are increasingly being filled by educated young men of middle and, less frequently, lower class backgrounds. The nomadic and seminomadic tribal groups furnish very few officers. There is, however, more opportunity to gain prestige and to achieve upward social mobility in the military than in society at large. There are competitive examinations for admission into officer candidate programs, partially to dilute the strong relationship between certain families and military service. But personal recommendations are still necessary for entrance into the officers corps, and the shah's personal approval is needed for promotion beyond the rank of major (see ch. 13).

Professionals and high-level technicians, including doctors, lawyers, engineers, and some educators form another element in the upper class. The professional group make up about 3.5 percent of the labor force.

Traditionally the professions have been associated with government service or the leisure group of landlords. At one time all education was the monopoly of the upper class. Individuals studied under Islamic scholars or, in the twentieth century, went abroad in limited numbers. Reza Shah shattered this monopoly, partly in order to build up his own following against the Qajar forces. He increased and secularized the internal educational capacity of the country and sent abroad many young men who did not come from the old landed families, whose position he was attacking. These early recruits, especially those who had gone abroad, have grown to maturity and are the nucleus of the top professional group in the universities and in private practice. Many are in government service as heads of the technical departments established by Reza Shah. The group has expanded as new opportunities for professional services have risen as, for example, in the Plan and Budget Organization.

Professionals do not constitute a unified group. The older generation, especially those who went to France, are humanistically inclined and are scholars of Iranian culture, defending the purity of the Farsi language, dominating university circles, and looking down on the technically trained and more practically oriented younger generation. Although European in most of their habits, they are wary of being associated too closely with the outside world, especially with new ideas that could undermine their privileged position.

Many of the newer professionals, even physicians, have adopted this outlook, but others have attempted to introduce modern technical standards into their work and indirectly into society. They are often frustrated by resistance from colleagues and from government civil servants who depend on the older tradition for survival. If the newer professionals are not willing to accept administrative positions either in public or private life, they stand to lose potentially superior status, because technicians traditionally are underlings to gentlemen-generalists. The professionals then are fighting not for their status alone but for a change in Iranian social structure. Most succumb, a few protest but go along, and a small number leave Iran in disgust. The newer professions conceivably could afford the opportunity to practice skills without interference; for example, engineering does not have the heritage of law and medicine. But engineers rarely are ready to work with their hands and dominate their aides in such a way that technology has been subordinated to the Iranian way of doing things instead of acting as an agent of change.

The use of titles is the norm for all members of the professional class. Such constantly used status designators alert others as to their relative position and are naturally a source of social satisfaction for the achievers.

The number of modern industrialists and merchants has been expanding along with the industrial and commercial sectors of the economy. A few of these persons were born into the middle or lower classes, and others are former landlords who realized that protecting the self meant extending beyond agriculture.

In the course of the White Revolution (see Glossary) the shah encouraged the large landholders to invest the bonds they received from the sale of their land in industry. Although the majority of the great landholders who were forced to sell appear to be merely holding their bonds, those who invested in industry have fared extremely well, having as they did the cooperation and to a certain extent the patronage of the shah. In this particular instance the land reform program therefore served the added interest of the shah in providing capital for industrial development. These men are among the private sector industrialists who own or operate factories; others are among the private merchants who work in partnership with foreign concerns or act as their agents in Iran. Because many factories have been built and are operated by the government, the upper-class industrialist may be a government official; it is both economically and socially beneficial for an official to become the administrator of a government enterprise.

The wealthy upper-class modern merchants, especially those in partnership with foreigners in Iran or acting as Iranian agents, prefer doing business on the main streets of the city to the bazaar. They are educated and knowledgeable in modern technology and commerce. Many have been trained abroad, especially in West Germany and the United States, and consequently are learned in European languages and ways unlike their bazaar counterparts. They also may have foreign wives whom they have married while abroad, like other members of the upper class.

The upper-class modern merchants are committed to the Pahlavi regime. Many of their fortunes came out of the economic changes introduced by Reza Shah from which they directly benefited as early backers of the dynasty. But economic and political security is as elusive to this group as it is to the bazaar merchants, since the modern merchants depend just as heavily on official favor to ensure their status and even their economic life. For example, especially upper-class merchants in Tehran have speculated heavily in real estate, hoping for spectacular profits from population increase and inflation. Access to government sources determining which property will be favored with new construction ensuring high rentals is vital if fortunes are to be made and financial disaster averted.

Private sector industrialists are also dependent on government favor to secure building materials—which may come from abroad—for assistance in obtaining raw materials, for marketing the finished product through government purchases or export aid, and for a benevolent labor relations policy to ensure operation of the enterprise at minimum cost and with a minimum of strife. One of the keys to dependence is based on the fact that most enterprises are established and operated on the basis of loans and not on acquired capital from operations, and it is the government that controls or supplies loan capital.

In return for such benevolence the government forces the enterprises to hire unneeded workers to keep down unrest, levies unpredictable national and local taxes, and permits civil servants, unless properly mollified, to apply nuisance regulations. The result is that industrialists view enterprise as the merchants view commerce—as a means to make as much as possible as soon as possible in any way possible. The proceeds are hidden away or used for conspicuous consumption—just about anything except reinvested for plant improvement. One scholar has suggested that the smallness of most industrial operations is the direct result of such inhibitions.

Land ownership was both the traditional mark of security and social superiority and the principal source of economic support for that social position. Most of the former great landlords of present-day Iran received their holdings—which in many cases ran into hundreds of villages—as payments for their services to the shah. Reza Shah appropriated over 2,000 villages in the richest areas of Iran, most of which had belonged to members of the Qajar ruling family. Rich merchants also bought land with their surplus capital as a means of gaining recognition as members of the elite. These landlords resided almost without exception in the cities. In most cases they never visited their property; this situation often extended to more than one generation. These absentee landowners were more likely to own a whole village and even many villages, rather than a fragment of a village. In contrast resident landowners usually owned only a part of the village or held a share interest in it, and their families had long been residents of the area; the extent and value of the property was almost always less than that of the absentee landowners.

The land reform program stipulated that large landowners could retain a small portion of their property, the exact size being determined by local land distribution committees; the remainder was purchased by the government for distribution among the landless peasants. Having lost their principal means of support, the former owners were forced to seek alternative sources of income.

Their influence over rural affairs was being assumed by local government officials, by elected village representatives, and by small landowners. Nevertheless those who actually lost their properties still constitute an important part of the urban class, either through traditional prestige or through their diversification into more profitable areas.

The landlords as an influential and prestigious group have by no means been eliminated by the Shah-People Revolution, however. Rather the group membership has undergone some change. Mechanized or large-scale agricultural enterprises were exempt from the reforms and these owners, as well as those close to the royal court, have not been negatively affected. In other instances new investors in the agricultural sector are rapidly rising in social prestige.

The upper class includes the leaders of Shiite Islam (*ayatollahs*) and prestigious religious scholars (*mujtahids*—see Glossary). The religious leaders are immediately identifiable by a particular kind of black or white turban that only they may wear (see ch. 4). Increasingly they are well educated and have experienced life beyond their local and national boundaries. They usually come from important families and add further to family prestige by becoming religious scholars. They maintain strong family bonds, and since most marry, religious social prestige can be handed down from generation to generation. In many periods of history the clergy have been immensely powerful politically, but since the time of Reza Shah and the ensuing increased secularization of the state they have been forced to restrict their activities to the spiritual realm. Given the all-embracing character of Islamic law, however, the religious leaders and the government entertain very different notions as to the dividing line between the secular and the religious, and this has led to considerable conflict. Increasingly the religious leaders feel disenfranchised of their rightful role in society.

In one area, however, the role of the religious clergy has been encouraged rather than diminished by the government. The upper-class religious clergy have traditionally given sanction to the monarchy. In the Shiite conception, the shah is but the caretaker for the last, hidden Imam until that Imam reappears to unite church and state under his personal rule (see Shia Branch of Islam, ch. 4). That this is passive approval is shown by the fact that Reza Shah had no particular difficulty in winning the support of the upper-class clergy once he was in power. The support is important, however, since to many Iranians, especially to the peasants, the religious sanction to the authoritarian state makes rebellion a religious sin, *fitna*.

Many important religious leaders wield power through positions in bazaars, especially if they are spiritual heads of guilds. They use such positions and their pulpits to bargain with the government for privileges for their followers and themselves. The religious leaders of the bazaar have a reputation for troublesome behavior. They have closed bazaars and led followers out on strike or riot to support their demands. It was this kind of religious activity that Reza Shah tried to suppress, but he was only partially successful. Such religious activity surfaced in the 1951-53 period when Mossadeq was prime minister and was even more pronounced in the summer of 1963 when religious leaders led uprisings and incited riots over the issue of land reform, which affected waqf properties, and over the issue of women's suffrage. By late 1977 there had been no repetition of such events; but the dissatisfaction of religious leaders to the increased secularization of society appeared to have percolated downward, and the government may have underestimated both the power of religious leaders over some of the populace or the popular reaction to such secularization. In 1977 there appeared to be a burgeoning religious movement, notable particularly among the student body who may have been protesting a variety of things but who chose to protest in a highly traditional manner. Some university women were—in violation of the law and for the first time in their lives—wearing veils, and male students rioted on one campus, demanding separate facilities for women. This is tied into the larger pattern of social dissent in Iran. Since there is no available vehicle whereby the system may be challenged from within (active political malcontents risk ostracism, exile, or imprisonment) the traditional or religious route of dissent is the only in-society alternative.

Market Town Society

A market town is commonly a large village settlement of a few thousand people situated on a main thoroughfare, such as a provincial highway. It acts as a geographic, economic, and social link between rural and urban areas. Villagers from outlying districts may come to the market town to find supplemental employment, to obtain certain items not available in their own villages, to market crops, to see friends, to report births and deaths, and to have a marriage performed and registered. Those villagers living where there are no schools or teachers may send their children to school at the nearest market town.

The social structure of the market town is essentially urban. The dominant positions in the community are held by the mayor, heads of gendarmerie units and of government bureaus, and perhaps the leading mullah. The next level is represented by the leaders of the bazaar, small landowners, and lower level mullahs.

The next group or middle stratum includes petty civil servants, small shopkeepers, and the bulk of the gendarmerie. At the bottom of the social scale are the illiterate workmen, messengers, servants, beggars, and other drifters who continually move from community to community.

Social mobility in the market town tends to be horizontal rather than vertical. Except for a few persons at the bottom of the society, most persons in the market town are oriented toward urban life and expect to improve their social position by moving there when the opportunity arises. This movement from the rural to the urban areas is reflected in the changing demographic patterns and economic trends of the country.

Village Society

Significant changes have occurred in the structuring of social relationships in the village as a result of land reform and other programs begun by the shah in the early 1960s. Most government programs were still being implemented in 1977, but initial efforts have been substantial and indicate the essential nature and direction of social change for the future.

By 1977 much of the property owned by the traditional powerful absentee landlords had been purchased by the government and resold to the peasants farming the land. Other factors contributing to the reshaping of village society were the expansion of the school system, the new rights of peasants to elect their own representatives to local and national offices, the establishment of village cooperatives, and the creation of the government's revolutionary corps organizations to aid in rural development (see ch. 6).

Traditional Social Structure

Social organization in the village was traditionally less stratified than that in the urban areas, but basic social relationships and patterns of interaction could be identified. At the top of the village social structure was the landlord; his *kadkhuda* (agent; literally, little god—see Glossary), and sometimes the head of the local gendarmerie unit. Below them in the middle stratum were small peasant landowners, craftsmen, mullahs, and small merchants. The lowest level contained the vast majority of landless peasants and workers. Except for those in the highest stratum most persons had little knowledge of life beyond the village. The landlord or the *kadkhuda* acted as the intermediary between the villages and the city.

Before land reform implementation the dominant social relationship at the village level was that between landlord and peasant. This relationship was not conducive to social or economic development, and social mobility was almost impossible. Those at the top justified their position by pointing to customary practice and Islamic beliefs. The peasant never had permanent title to his land and was always afraid of being displaced. The system discouraged any initiative on the part of the peasantry and failed to provide a forward-looking leadership concerned with promoting social, economic, and political advancement.

Before land reform leadership in the village commonly came from the *kadkhuda*. Villages owned by more than one person might have several *kadkhudas*, whereas others had none at all. The landlord, particularly an absentee landlord, rarely met the peasants who farmed his land; his orders were conveyed to the villagers by the *kadkhuda*.

The landlord customarily selected the *kadkhuda* with the approval of the government's officials in the local areas. The *kadkhuda* often came from the village he served. In some villages the position was hereditary. He might be a village headman, a notable or a notable's relative, or a villager in whom the landlord had confidence. After 1930, in addition to representing the land-lord's interest, the *kadkhuda* was recognized by the government as an official for channeling government information and instruc-tions to the villagers. He assisted the gendarmerie in seeking military conscripts and in collecting taxes. In some cases where villagers owned their own land, the villagers selected a headman whose responsibility it was to represent their interests.

Individual peasants had little opportunity to improve their economic or social position while in the village, and they had no political rights. The landlord had the means to enforce his decisions, even against the peasants' will, and he could always call on the local police or judiciary for assistance. He was usually not interested in upgrading the peasants' life, especially if it meant risking his own social position. Government services, such as loans, tended to go to the landlord rather than to the peasant and were often used for purposes other than those for which they were intended. Government agents appeared infrequently in the villages and did little to ensure that their advice was followed. Many improvements were actively opposed by the landlords on social grounds, regardless of mutual economic benefit.

Modernizing Forces in Rural Society

One of the stated objectives of the White Revolution and particularly land reform, was to reshape the traditional economic and social relationship between landlord and peasant and to raise the standing of the peasant. The shah felt that the country could not modernize without the participation of the peasants, and since the peasants of Iran have never been revolutionary in any way, there was no danger in ameliorating their condition.

The redistribution of land was viewed by the shah as a necessary step in this process. From the start it was recognized that land redistribution would not achieve the desired results unless it was accompanied by a program of financial and technical assistance. It was in this framework that the rural cooperatives, the Agricultural Development Bank, and other projects were created. The rural cooperatives, for example, were organized to assist the small independent farmer by providing services that were previously the landlord's responsibility. The effectiveness of the rural co-operatives and of other parts of the land reform program have been somewhat reduced because of the serious shortage of trained personnel to implement changes or to assist villagers to do so (see Land Reform, ch. 11).

By a slight margin the majority of the total population continued in the late 1970s to live in villages that ranged in size from a few to several thousand people. Settlements with 5,000 or more inhabitants may be rural in composition, but for demographic reasons they are classified as urban centers. Some villages are situated near highways and have modern facilities, whereas others are less accessible and less developed. Villagers in remote areas may have to travel a considerable distance to the nearest town having a teacher, doctor, newspaper, or motion picture theater.

The larger landowners who constitute the highest stratum of the village social scale are not totally unlike the former absentee landlords; the two groups actually were closely associated in the years before land reform. The next level of society consists of small, independent landowners who farm their own plots. They may have an outside source of income, but they count on farming as their main economic resource. Lower in the social hierarchy is a group of small landowners who do their own farming and do not participate in any nonagricultural work. They cannot afford to employ hired laborers on their farms, as do many of the larger landowners, and they are more dependent on the operation of rural cooperatives and other government assistance. The number of small, independent landowners and persons engaged in some form of nonagricultural activities has increased considerably since the land reform measures were applied in the early 1960s.

The lowest stratum of village society includes a large group of landless peasants. They are engaged as agricultural workers during the farming season, and many migrate to nearby towns and cities to seek work during the slack periods.

Between the larger landowners on the one hand and the small landowners and agricultural workers on the other is a group of landless persons who occupy themselves exclusively with nonagricultural endeavors. This group includes shopkeepers, moneylenders, vendors, and others.

When the absentee landlords were dispossessed of their property, their need for *kadkhudas* disappeared. During the first stages of land reform in the early 1960s, a *kadkhuda* achieved leadership in a village because he was already the village headman and held a dominant position in the society or because he was elected by the villagers. Otherwise the government took it upon itself to appoint a headman at that time; however, the duties of the *kadkhuda* had not been redefined, and his role in society was uncertain.

The *kadkhuda* is no longer appointed by the government; usually the position is elective. He does not represent a single, large landlord, and therefore he can be more responsive to the needs and demands of the local people. He acts as a liaison between the villagers and the government and attempts to settle disputes between individuals and families before it becomes necessary to call in the police or gendarmerie. In some villages he competes for prestige and influence with government officials,

Scene along an irrigation canal in Khuzestan Province
WORLD BANK PHOTO (Ray Witlin)

members of the clergy, gendarmerie officers, and other prominent individuals.

In the late 1960s the government announced that elected village councils would be established throughout the country, and the first councils were in fact elected in 1973 (see Local Government, ch. 6). The councils usually consist of five members and a headman elected by the villagers. In every village informal leaders meet the important daily needs of the inhabitants.

Intravillage unrest is commonly caused by disputes over water or by ethnic-religious differences. Conflict over water is widespread and often results from the storage of supply as well as the vagueness of customary rights regarding use.

Many villages have mixed ethnic or religious composition, whereas others are extremely homogeneous. There is no fixed pattern of intravillage relations; a village composed of several different ethnic or religious groups may be peaceful, whereas another village with a homogeneous population may have continued friction. There is, however, usually no residential segregation on an ethnic or religious basis.

There is less cooperation between villages than within a single village. Attempts to form marketing and credit cooperatives, which depend on joint action, have had only limited success (see Organization of Agriculture, ch. 11). The growing demand for education, along with other social, economic, and political developments, has given the villagers more incentive to cooperate. The schools in particular encourage cooperation among young people because they offer regular opportunities for mixing in such programs as crafts and sports. Children from neighboring villages may share a school, and leaders of different villages may join to discuss mutual problems and find ways to solve them. Villagers are also learning that limited government facilities can be made available only if sufficient numbers of villagers are organized to use them.

Tribal Society

Because of the difficulties of data collection among the tribal groups due to the reticence of tribal members and the remoteness of much of their territory, only rough approximations of their numbers are available. Professor Afshar Naderi, an Iranian tribal specialist, estimated that in 1975 there were 4.5 million people who identified themselves with a tribal group. Most tribespeople—nomadic, seminomadic, or sedentarized—inhabit the mountainous rim surrounding the Central Plateau. Within that area the greatest concentration of the tribal population is in the south of Iran where the climate is mild but where the land is considerably less fertile.

Most of the tribes are remnants of three major invasions: the Arabs, the Seljuq Turks, and the Mongols. In the period before the Pahlavi dynasty the tribes possessed a great deal of power and influence. In many cases they were virtually autonomous nations and would negotiate for extensive land rights particularly when the government needed troops. After Reza Khan suppressed separatist movements in Gilan, Khuzestan, Kordestan, and Khorasan in the early 1920s, he then moved against the tribes with his small but effective Western-trained armed forces. His object was twofold: to break the authority and power of the great tribal leaders, who posed a threat to his centralization of power, and to gain the allegiance of power holders in urban centers, who resented the sporadic incursions of tribespeople into their areas.

In addition to military maneuvers against the tribes, Reza Khan used such economic and administrative techniques as confiscation of tribal properties and holding chiefs' sons as hostages. Eventually many tribespeople were subdued and placed under the administration of the army. Some were given government-built houses and forced to follow a sedentary life. When Reza Shah abdicated in 1941, many tribal groups returned to their nomadic or seminomadic life-styles.

In the 1960s the government began to develop educational, health, and vocational training services to ameliorate conditions among the tribes. In view of the almost universal illiteracy, particularly among nonsedentarized tribes, the educational services, almost totally directed to children, are expected to have the result of giving these children a greater attachment to the state and mitigating tribal separateness. Training is always given in Farsi, which is in virtually all cases not the native language of the tribespeople (see Peoples, this ch.). Many tribal confederations have a paramount leader *(ilkhan)*. Individual tribes are headed by a khan or beg. *Kalantars* (see Glossary) head the subtribes and *kadkhudas*, the clans.

Each tribe holds or claims the use of a fixed territory. If nomadic it claims both winter and summer territories and the right during specified seasons to use the connecting migration routes. The tribes are composed of clans *(tayefeh)*, each with its own recognized area of farmland and pasture and its own hereditary leadership. The smallest unit is the tent. The norm is that a tent contains a nuclear family and a few dependents.

With the exception of the Kurds and Arabs, who are chiefly sedentary, most migratory tribes are seminomadic, practicing seasonal transhumance in the spring and fall. Frequently summer and winter camps are as far as 200 miles from each other so each migration, with families, flocks, and household equipment, may take two months. In some tribes a few people, usually women, will remain in the *qishlag*, the winter quarters, to harvest grain. Similarly some tribesmen may remain permanently quartered in the *yaylaq*, the summer camp, to protect the grazing area from encroachers.

The Family

For almost all Iranians the reciprocal obligations and privileges that define relations between kinsmen, from the parent-child bond to more distant ones, are more important than those associated with any other kind of social alignment. Economic, political, and other forms of institutional activity are significantly colored by family ties, even if the nature of these activities is not necessarily determined by such ties. Such statements hold not only for the biological family of parents and offsprings but also for the aggregate of kinsmen, near and distant, who, taken together, represent "the family" at its outermost boundary.

An influential family is one that has its members strategically distributed throughout the most vital sectors of society, each prepared to support the other in order to ensure family prestige and family status. Each of the more dominant families of Tehran has its cadre of professional men, businessmen, and statesmen. Business ventures are likely to be family affairs; often large business loans can be obtained simply because the owners are recognized as members of "good" families. Political activities also follow family lines. Traditionally the members of one family may join the foreign service, another, the Ministry of Interior or the army. Kinsmen are expected to support one another; the successful members are obligated to assist the less successful ones. The nepotism involved in this system has been a positive value to Iranians and has not been considered by them to be a corrupting factor. A man without family ties has little status, if any, in the society at large. If the tie is severed, the consequence for the individual and his immediate dependents has some of the force of exile, reducing his security in a hostile world.

The reputation of a family is of concern to its members and to others as well. Its honor must be jealously protected. Individuals can be judged by the status of their families. One is from a good family; another is from a less reputable one. At the same time it is the achievements of individual members and heads of households that gain the family what reputation it has. Acknowledged near and distant kinsmen contribute, therefore, to one another's status in the general society by their individual acts insofar as they are observed as belonging to the same family. Thus the rise or fall of a family may be marked as the fortunes of its members are made or founder. Of course there are probably no more than a few households in any large family that carry the burden of determining its reputation among outsiders. Quarrels and dissension can put severe strain on the group, but the primary obligations must still be met.

Religious law and civil law support the sanctity of the family in diverse ways, defining the conditions for marriage, divorce, inheritance, and guardianship. In the past the civil code has tended to reinforce the religious one, but more recently some disparity between them has developed. Nevertheless both are constrained to protect the integrity of the family.

The head of the household—father and husband—exacts obedience and respect from others in the family. In principle they are expected to submit to his will. In return he is expected to support them, to satisfy social as well as material needs. He is more than a strict disciplinarian; he also may be a focal point of love and affection, and family members feel a strong sense of duty toward him. It is not uncommon for considerable inner conflict and irresolution to result when traditional norms and values are questioned by young Iranians who try to reconcile their values with their father's values.

There are innumerable ways in which a husband's or father's authority may manifest itself in his interaction with other members of his family. The religious law, without contradiction from civil law, defines a wife's relation to her husband as one of submission. This injunction does not necessarily countermand the postulate of "harmonious coexistence." Submission refers to the husband's right to expect his spouse to perform wifely duties. In general such duties involve responsibility for the care of home and children; in particular they include her willingness to provide sexual gratification at his bidding. A woman must help her husband maintain his status and in effect the family status. For example, the civil code specifies that the "husband may forbid his wife to accept a job that is degrading to him or her." This statement has been interpreted to suggest that if a position is not degrading a wife may take it without her husband's permission. This is a questionable interpretation, since the decision as to what is or is not degrading must necessarily be left to the husband. Otherwise he would not be in a position to forbid but only to transmit a decision made for him.

The father is usually the legal custodian of his children, whether or not he remains husband to the mother. As such his authority over them is undisputed. As for a daughter the force of his statement can be no better illustrated than with the observation that by law she must receive her father's express permission to marry. The law does not prescribe similarly for the son. However, the authority of his position as head of the household throughout the years of a son's rearing continues to give the father considerable power and influence over him, even when it might be possible legitimately to circumvent decisions made for him. For example, a son may be given more freedom of choice in the decision as to whom he should marry; however, parental prerogative will prevail. It remained so even in early 1978 as profound changes were being wrought throughout the society. Economic dependence, if no other, often determines a son's subordination to his father's wishes.

In general it may be said that dominance in the Iranian family is determined both by age and sex—older dominates younger, male dominates female. Where these two factors cancel each other, as in the position of a mother in relation to a son, a special mode of behavior can be expected. She is a source of solace; she is more likely to cajole than to dictate; and she is a form of affection made overtly evident. This contrast to the father's behavior is particularly apparent with children in early childhood stages. She is an intermediary, striving to reconcile father and son at times of strain.

Where the sex factor is canceled out, as between a mother and daughter, the former dominates in the relationship, somewhat similar to the manner in which a husband dominates a household in general. A daughter, by all accounts, is formally at the bottom of the heap, having neither age nor sex working on her behalf.

In relations with a brother, a daughter's age is insignificant as far as the structure of the household in general is concerned; she is separated from him in interests and activities early in their rearing, reflecting the different aspirations the family has for sons and daughters. Daughters will become primarily wives and mothers. Religious law—conformed to by civil law—prescribes the mode of inheritance for daughters. A brother also remains a potential male protector should his sister be cast out by her husband. Moreover even before this contingency arises, when a girl has reached the age at which she may move more freely beyond the scrutiny of her parents but has not yet acquired a husband as protector, the brother assumes the responsibility of assuring her virtue and her dignity. Should she divest herself of one or be divested of the other, a brother usually takes action to redress the wrong he perceives. After marriage as well, should her behavior stain the family honor, a brother may reprove her as surely as a husband. The law recognizes merely a token difference: a man is absolved of legal guilt if he kills his wife after catching her in an adulterous act and is subject to imprisonment for a period of from one to six months if he kills his daughter or sister under the same circumstances.

Marriage regulations as defined by the civil code represent modifications of the religious law. There is no basic disagreement between the two, but the code emphasizes the civil character of marriage. According to official statistics over 150,000 marriages occur annually, or about 6 per 1,000 inhabitants. The marriage rate is higher for skilled and unskilled workers than for the upper and professional middle class because of the increasing tendency of these groups to delay marriage until the completion of the male's education. In 1977 the average age for marriage was almost nineteen years. The average age for marriages for women was nineteen in urban areas and seventeen in rural areas; the figures for men were approximately twenty-seven years and twenty-five years respectively.

The civil code forbids marriages for females under the age of eighteen and for males under twenty unless a court injunction is obtained. An injunction may allow a female to marry as young as thirteen and a male, fifteen. In practice, however, an enormous number of marriages, which simply are not recorded in the Public Register, occur below these ages. Nine years of age or the onset of the first menses—whichever occurs earlier—is the minimum age under Islamic law. In villages and tribes this religious law is often used to rationalize the marriage of young girls. In a 1971 study of twenty-five villages near Tehran and Isfahan, 37 percent of the females had married before the age of thirteen; 57 percent between fourteen and eighteen; and only 6 percent between the ages of nineteen and thirty.

The selection of a marriage partner is determined by customary preference, economic circumstances, and geographic considerations. Among the Zoroastrians and other minority groups, the choice may be restricted by religious practices. The socially defined line within which one is not permitted to marry is drawn around primary and secondary kin. The prohibited group includes grandparents, parents, brothers and sisters, sons and daughters, uncles and aunts, nieces and nephews, and grandchildren. The children of paternal and maternal siblings as well as more distant cousins are beyond this exogamous barrier and traditionally represented frequent marriage partners. Paternal parallel cousins, the children of their fathers's brothers, have been a somewhat preferred marital choice. This kind of consanguineous marriage has been declining, and it is much less frequent in urban than in rural areas.

The selection of a marriage partner may generate a conflict between the male and female members of a kin-group. In the search for a sutiable partner, the patriarch and male kinsmen customarily hope to form an alliance with a family of wealth and power. The women often share this hope but are also concerned with selecting an individual who will fit into the kin-group. Cousin marriages are sometimes advantageous in resolving these conflicting interests.

Marriage arrangements in villages tend to follow traditional lines. When a young man is judged ready for marriage, his parents will visit the parents of a girl they believe to be a likely candidate. If the girl's parents show similar interest in the union, the conversation generally turns to money. There must be an agreement as to how much *shirbaha* (a form of bridewealth or marriage payment) will be given to the girl's family at the time of marriage. The *shirbaha* compensates the girl's family for her loss. The sum varies according to the wealth, social position, and relationship of the families.

A time period usually elapses between the betrothal and the signing of the marriage contract. During this interval the young man is expected to perform small duties for his future father-in-law, such as serving tea or running errands. Bride service occurs among some nomadic tribal groups. The young man spends time at the home of the bride, where he is permitted to talk to her and is frequently served lunch by his future mother-in-law; in this manner he comes to know his future wife and her family.

The courtship period ends on the signing of the marriage contract. This step may be completed at a notary's office in the city or before a mullah, who acts as a government representative for this purpose. One significant feature of the marriage contract is the *mahr,* a stipulated amount of wealth that is guaranteed the wife. It may be given to the woman at her husband's death or paid to her in the event of divorce. It provides security for the wife when her husband is no longer prepared to maintain her. Sometimes the marriage contract also states whether or not the future wife is a virgin.

After signing the contract there are festivities and preparations for the actual union; relatives and friends give small money contributions to the bride and groom. During most of the festivities the prospective bride and groom are separated, each at his or her own house. The women of the village visit the bride inside her house; the men usually gather outside the house of the bridegroom. The public celebrations of the men are intended to show the wealth of the young man's father and to gain prestige for the family. In the evening the boy's relatives come for the girl, and the *shirbaha* is presented to her father. The girl is taken to her husband's house, which is customarily located in his father's compound.

Marriage customs in urban areas tend to follow those practices in Europe and the United States, at least among the middle and upper classes. The *shirbaha* may sometimes be paid in installments and is even eliminated if a substantial *mahr* is guaranteed. A study of urban workers in Tehran in 1963, however, indicated that their marriage practices and methods of choosing a partner differed little from those of the villagers. About one-fourth of the working men and boys had independently decided to marry and had chosen their own brides without parental interference; a significant portion of the choices involved girls from within the larger kin-group. More than 80 percent of the workers' wives came from their kin or residential unit or from the local area. Few meetings between boys and girls took place outside these boundaries, and the parents interviewed stressed their disapproval of boys and girls meeting without parental consent.

Polygyny in Islam is regulated by tradition and by the Quranic prescription that permits a man to have up to four permanent wives at one time provided he can treat them equally. The civil code conforms to religious law in this respect with certain caveats enacted in 1967 and with further restrictions in the Family Protection Law that was passed in June 1975. A man cannot take a second wife except in nine cases: consent of the first wife; inability of the wife to have coitus; the wife's disobedience to her husband; the wife's suffering from insanity or refractory diseases; convictions of the wife; narcotic addiction; abandonment of family life; barrenness; or the wife's absence without a trace. Figures were not available in 1977, but the number of polygynous marriages appeared to be declining, and most such marriages were among the older generation.

Mutah, a special form of marriage known as temporary marriage, had traditionally been practiced by Shia Muslims (see Shia Dogma, ch. 4). Although a number of *mutah* marriages exist, this practice, too, is on the decline and is banned by the Family Protection Law.

Before promulgation of this law divorce was authorized in conformity with Muslin law at the will of the husband and was usually effected through repudiation of the wife by the husband. The wife could not divorce her husband but could have her marriage annulled if her husband were insane, impotent either at the time of the marriage or afterwards, or castrated. The new law provides a wife increased protection and allows her to initiate divorce proceedings if the husband deserts or mistreats her. A husband must obtain a certificate of incompatability and must have the permission of a court of law.

On the average one marriage in six ends in divorce; in Tehran, however, the average is one in four. Ten percent are divorces by mutual consent, 15 percent are initiated by women, and the rest by men. The divorce rate is highest in cases where there is a great discrepancy in age. In a study of several villages one out of three girls who had been married between the ages of ten and fifteen to men at least forty years old—a not infrequent arrangement— ended in divorce.

The Status of Women

Considerable progress was made in the struggle for women's rights during the 1960s and 1970s. Indications were that this trend would continue. The women's movement in Iran began in the late nineteenth and early twentieth centuries in response to Western liberal thought, which found acceptance among some influential social groups. At that time only a few upper-class women actively participated in community activities. In 1977 the movement continued to be mainly an urban phenomenon, led and supported by women from upper-class families, including Empress Farah Diba, who is one of their chief spokeswomen. Nevertheless the idea of giving greater freedom and responsibility to women has received much criticism and opposition from all sectors of society, particularly the religious leaders.

A meeting of the Oriental Feminine Congress held in Tehran in 1932 called for the right of women to vote, compulsory education for boys and girls, equal salaries for men and women, and an end to polygyny. From the time of its establishment in the mid-1930s Tehran University has admitted women; in 1936 Reza Shah banned the veil. As part of the White Revolution the shah has done much to improve the status of women. Women were enfranchised in 1963 and are allowed to hold public office. The Family Protection Law and various changes in the country's economic policies have helped women make gains toward equality with men.

About 13 percent of the female labor force was employed in 1977, compared with 68 percent for men. In actual numbers about 1.4 million women were employed in 1972: 64 percent in industry;

11 percent in agriculture; and 22 percent in all phases of the service industry. As of June 1976 women representatives held twenty-one of the 268 seats in the Majlis, and there were two female senators. In early 1978 women had been or were occupying such posts as: minister of education; the head of the State Factories Department; the head of the Tribal Affairs Department; and ambassador to Denmark. In 1975 two of the 383 district chiefs were women; eighteen of the 105 undersecretaries were women, and two mayors were women. The numbers of professional women in 1976 by occupation were: 86,399 women in the civil service; 248 dentists; 316 lawyers; 350 engineers; 20,101 nurses and midwives; and 793 physicians (of a total of about 10,000).

* * *

The Arasteh book, *Man and Society in Iran*, is a relatively brief but useful survey of traditional and modern Iranian society. Important class studies of Iranian society include Marvin Zonis' *The Political Elite of Iran* and James A. Bill's *The Politics of Iran: Groups, Classes and Modernization*. Bill's article, "Modernization and Reform from Above: The Case of Iran," is also instructive. Nikkie Keddie's article, "Stratification, Social Control and Capitalism in Iranian Villages Before and After Land Reform" and Ann Lambton's study of land reform and rural cooperatives in *Iran Races the Seventies*, are thoughtful and thorough treatments of the subject. Jan Rypka's *History of Iranian Literature* remains unsurpassed as a work of general reference. (For further information see Bibliography.)

Chapter 6. Governmental System

IRAN IS A constitutional monarchy in which Shahanshah Mohammad Reza Pahlavi—the shah for short—has played a very active role in decisionmaking and in the execution of government policies. Both in theory and in fact the shah is the most important national symbol and the most powerful political force. He is not only the royal head of state but the head of the executive government and the real source of legislative power.

The governmental system is based on the constitutional framework laid down in 1906 and 1907 and modified in later years. The operation of the government is to conform to the principle of checks and balances among the legislative, executive, and judicial branches. The separation of powers has little or no substance, however, in light of the all-pervasive preeminence of the shah in all manifestations of the govenment. The shah personifies the authority, power, and legitimacy of the state and the government. The monolithic unity between the monarchy, on the one hand, and the state and the government, on the other, has been further reinforced by the conversion of Iran to a single-party political state in March 1975. In announcing the formation of the Iran National Resurgence Party (Rastakhiz-e-Mellat-e-Iran) or, more popularly, the Rastakhiz Party, the shah declared that Iran would henceforth be guided by "a single philosophy and goal aimed at protecting the country's interests in the present as well as in the future."

In 1977 the shah's government was continuing the multifaceted program of modernization that was inaugurated in 1963 under the label White Revolution (see Glossary) but later was redesignated the Shah-People Revolution (see ch. 7). This ambitious undertaking is aimed at, among other things, the socioeconomic betterment of the people, industrial development, modernization of the armed forces, and a wide range of reform in the government.

Despite the inertia of tradition, the shah's programs appeared to be gaining ground, depending on the intensity of his personal interest in a target area. In the governmental domain high on the list of intended changes were streamlining bureaucratic agencies and functions, eliminating judicial red tape, stamping out corruption, and decentralizing official functions to local government units. It was through this vaguely defined scheme of devolution of power that the shah sought to bridge the gap between the government and the people. The age-old pattern of deference to the central government remained deeply embedded, however; to most Iranians the government still meant the shah and his deputies and agents in Tehran.

Constitutional Framework

In 1977 the imperial state of Iran was based on the constitutional framework set forth in 1906 and 1907 and as later amended in 1925, 1949, 1957, and 1967. The two fundamental documents—

the original constitution of 1906 and the supplementary constitution of 1907—known officially as the Constitution of Iran, were among the world's constitutions longest in effect.

The Constitution of 1906 was drafted shortly before Iran's first Majlis (National Consultative Assembly) was opened in October 1906 to mark the country's rudimentary beginning in constitutional practice and representative government. It was an outgrowth of increasing protests against corruption in government and of pressures for checks on absolute monarchy. The 1906 document contained fifty-one articles dealing mainly with the organization, authority, duties, rights, and procedures of the Majlis, the lower house; its provision for an upper house or senate was framed in language indicating that it would be formed at an unspecified future date.

During 1907 interest in constitutionalism remained high, and a supplementary constitution was drafted and promulgated in October. The supplement consists of over 100 articles divided into sections dealing with general principles, a bill of rights, the doctrine of separation of powers, the rights of the lawmakers, the rights of the throne, executive ministries, courts, local councils, finance, and the military establishment.

Among the general principles is the declaration that the state religion shall be the Jafari interpretation of Shiite Islam. Procedures are carefully laid down to ensure that the legislation conforms to the "sacred precepts of Islam;" in practice, however, the procedures have not been rigorously implemented (see ch. 4). Another provision states that the principles of the Constitution may not be suspended wholly or in part. The safety and property of foreign nationals residing in Iran are protected except as subject to the laws of the country.

The supplementary constitution guarantees the rights and liberties of the people, including equal protection under the law and the rights of personal security and of personal honor. Generally the bill of rights is conditioned by the proviso "except in conformity with the law." The supplement states that the right of the people to be secure in their persons, houses, private correspondence, and effects shall not be violated without due process of law. No one may be deprived of property "except in cases authorized by religious law" and without just compensation. The people are also guaranteed safety from summary arrest or summary exile. Additionally the people are assured freedom of the press and of publication and the right to assemble peaceably and form societies not prejudicial to religion and public order. Censorship is forbidden except for violation of the press law or for heretical reasons. The supplementary constitution also contains provisions for compulsory education and free public schools. All higher and primary schools are to be placed under the direction and supervision of the government.

In the mid-1970s it was quite clear that Iran's achievements in education and in lowering illiteracy were impressive. Human rights as guaranteed in the Constitution were, however, a subject of dispute. In their reports issued in 1976, the Geneva-based International Commission of Jurists and the London-based Amnesty International, which describes itself as "a worldwide human rights movement which is independent of any government, political faction, ideology, economic interest or religious creed," deplored violations of civil and political rights in Iran. In denying the validity of these reports, the Iranian government consistently portrayed itself as being in the forefront of the struggle for human rights; it hastened to add that Iran would in no way allow any detractors of either internal or foreign origin to undermine its "forward march toward greatness," nor would it permit Iranian territory to become a haven for terrorists (see ch. 7; ch. 12).

The powers of the state are in theory divided into legislative, executive, and judicial. These powers, as stipulated in the supplement, "shall always remain separate and distinct from one another." The legislative power is derived from and shared by the monarch, the Majlis, and the Senate; any of the three may introduce legislation, but all three must approve it. The enactment of financial and budgetary bills is reserved, however, to the Majlis. In addition the Majlis is to be solely responsible for "the explanation and interpretation of the laws." The executive power is reserved for the monarch and is to be exercised in his name by his ministers. The judicial power is to reside in two kinds of courts: the temporal courts in secular matters and the religious courts in matters relating to shariah (Islamic law).

In actuality the separation of powers was more apparent than real because the governmental system bore the stamp of the personality of one man, the shah. In the mid-1970s the monarch remained all-pervasive in the government and in the political arena, and any attempt to understand the Iranian governmental system without reference to the preeminence of the shah would be at best inadequate (see ch. 7).

The Constitution can be amended through a two-stage process. First the Majlis and the Senate (each by a two-thirds vote), on their own initiative or on a proposal by the cabinet, must make a decision, subject to the concurrence of the monarch as to whether one or more articles of the Constitution require revision. Then a constituent assembly must be elected and convened by royal order, its members being equal to the combined total of the two chambers of Parliament. The decision of this assembly requires a two-thirds vote of its membership as well as the assent of the monarch for promulgation.

Expressly forbidden from any constitutional amendment are provisions relating to "the Holy Religion of Islam and the official creed of the country which is the Jafari doctrine of the Shiite Sect with twelve Imams and its tenets, or to the Constitutional Monarchy of Iran." These matters are proclaimed to be "unchangeable for eternity."

The Monarchy

The constitutional monarchy, under the law, is defined as "the person of His Imperial Majesty Reza Shah Pahlavi and his male descendants in succession." The shah holds extensive powers and prerogatives expressly set forth in the Constitution, and his authority is futher enhanced by the mystique that is traditionally attached to his office and his person (see ch. 7). He represents the sovereignty, mentioned as "a trust confided, by the Grace of God" to him by the nation.

In his oath of office the shah is to swear before the Majlis to exert every effort to preserve the independence of Iran, to defend the nation's rights and territorial integrity, protect the Constitution, reign according to law, and promote the state religion. In carrying out his constitutional duties since his ascension to the throne in 1941, the shah has performed symbolic as well as substantive roles more powerful, in both relative and absolute terms, than any previous Iranian ruler. Unlike the constitutional monarchs of other countries, he has taken a personal interest in the affairs of state and played a direct and decisive role in the decisionmaking process. For example, according to political scientist Marvin Zonis, the shah: "personally without the aid of advisory councils, alter ego, or close confidants, makes the thousands of decisions that allow the government to function. From the appointment or promotion of officers in the army to the decisions as to whether or not to pave the main street of Tabas, His Imperial Majesty is the arbiter."

The shah is not only the head of state and chief executive but also commander in chief of the armed forces (see fig. 8). His executive powers are absolute; he is personally "free of responsibility," but all ministers, who act in his name, are accountable to both chambers of the legislature. The declaration of war is made by the shah. His signature is required on all bills before they become law. The shah may also call special sessions of Parliament and dissolve either or both houses, but new elections must be held within thirty days.

The mode of succession is spelled out in the Constitution as amended in 1967. By right a son born to the wife of the monarch becomes heir to the throne, provided his mother is Iranian. If there is no male child the monarch may nominate a crown prince, a regent, or both, subject to assent by the Majlis; however, neither a crown prince nor a regent may ever be a member of the Qajar family (see Rise of the Qajar Dynasty, ch. 2). In the event of transfer of the throne, the crown prince is to perform the functions of a monarch on reaching the age of twenty.

The Constitution as amended in September 1967 enables the wife of the shah—the *shahbanou* (empress)—and mother of the crown prince to rule as a regent if the shah were to die or were

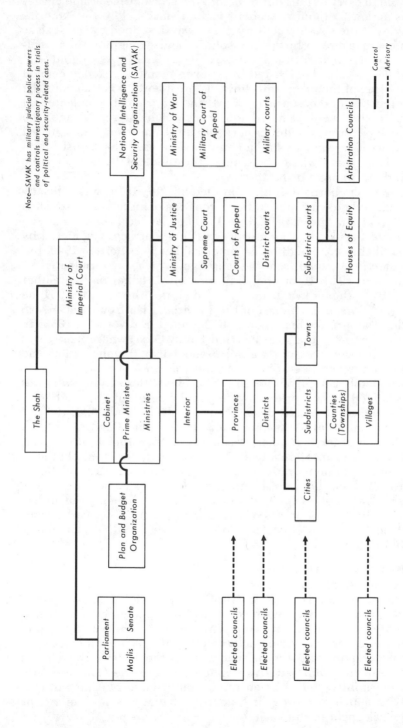

Figure 8. Organization of the Iranian Government

Note—SAVAK has military judicial police powers and controls investigatory process in trials of political and security-related cases.

Control ———
Advisory - - - -

The Shah

Ministry of Imperial Court

Parliament
Majlis | Senate

Cabinet
Prime Minister
Ministries

Plan and Budget Organization

National Intelligence and Security Organization (SAVAK)

Ministry of War
Military Court of Appeal
Military courts

Ministry of Justice
Supreme Court
Courts of Appeal
District courts
Subdistrict courts
Houses of Equity

Arbitration Councils

Interior
Provinces
Districts
Subdistricts
Counties (Townships)
Villages
Cities
Towns

Elected councils
Elected councils
Elected councils
Elected councils

unable to carry out his duties before the crown prince came of age. This action, without precedent in Iran since before the Arab invasions of the seventh century A.D., was described by the shah as "a new measure to further consolidate and strengthen the principles of a constitutional monarchy in Iran." As regent the *shahbanou* is to be assisted by a seven-member regency council consisting of the prime minister, the presidents of Parliament, the chief justice of the Supreme Court, and other notables selected by her. In the event of her death, resignation, or remarriage, the council performs the duties of regent until a new one is designated by a joint session of Parliament. In any case the Constitution stipulates that "whoever assumes the office of Regent shall be forbidden to ascend the throne."

The shah, born in Tehran on October 26, 1919, was officially proclaimed crown prince at the coronation of his father, Reza Shah the Great, on April 25, 1926. In 1939 he married Princess Fawzia, sister of Faruk, then king of Egypt, in a marriage negotiated by Reza Shah. One daughter, Shahnaz Pahlavi, was born in 1940, but no male heir issued from the marriage, which was terminated by divorce in 1948. Upon the abdication of his father on September 16, 1941, the crown prince ascended the throne. In 1951 he married Soraya Esfandiari of the Bakhtiari clan from Isfahan. No child was born of this union, which ended in divorce in 1958. In December 1959 the shah married Farah Diba, whose family was from the provinces of Azarbaijan and Gilan. Farah's father and grandfather had been officers in the Iranian army.

On October 31, 1960, Farah bore an heir, Reza Cyrus, who was proclaimed crown prince by imperial decree on November 1, 1960, and ceremonially designated as such on October 26, 1967, at the coronation of Mohammad Reza Pahlavi and Farah. In March 1963 a daughter, Farahnaz, was born; in April 1966 a second son, Ali Reza; and in March 1970, a second daughter, Leila Fatima.

Protocol, administrative, financial, and estate matters related to the royal household are handled by the minister of the imperial court. He receives his budget from the government, but unlike other cabinet members is responsible to the shah, not Parliament, and does not participate in cabinet sessions dealing with policy deliberations.

Central Government
Executive Agencies

The shah exercises his constitutionally vested executive power through the cabinet, which consists of his appointees—the prime minister and other ministers. Although in theory the prime minister is chosen by the Majlis and the other cabinet members by the prime minister, it is the shah who has the decisive voice in the choice of his administrative deputies. Under the Constitution a cabinet minister must be an Iranian citizen and Muslim and may not be a prince of the first degree, that is a son, brother, or paternal uncle of the shah.

The ministers are constitutionally answerable to the two chambers of the legislature, may be questioned by them, and may be dismissed, individually or collectively, by a no-confidence vote of a majority of either chamber. They may also be impeached by either chamber but may be tried only by the Supreme Court sitting as a court of first instance. Under the law ministers are prohibited from assuming any other salaried office and from evading responsibility by invoking royal privileges.

In August 1977 Jamshid Amuzegar was appointed prime minister, replacing Amir Abbas Hoveyda who had been in office since 1965. Under the immediate supervision of the prime minister were several cabinet-rank ministers of state, several executive assistants to the prime minister (sometimes called deputy prime ministers), deputy ministers of state, and several directors general. Among the more important agencies under his direction were the Plan and Budget Organization, which handles planning and budgetary matters; and the National Intelligence and Security Organization (Sazeman Ettelaat va Amniyat Kashvar—SAVAK), which is in charge of internal security and political crimes (see ch.9; ch.12).

As of late 1977 the cabinet consisted of the prime minister and twenty-one ministers in charge of agriculture and natural resources; commerce; cooperatives and rural affairs; culture and arts; economics and finance; education; energy; foreign affairs; health; housing and town planning; imperial court; industry and mines; information and tourism; interior; justice; labor and social affairs; post, telegraph, and telephone; roads and communications; science and higher education; social welfare; and war. In addition there were five ministers of state, the first of whom served as deputy to the prime minister for development and economic affairs; the others were, respectively, in charge of Iran National Resurgence Party (Rastakhiz-e-Mellat-Iran or, more popularly, the Rastakhiz Party) affairs, parliamentary affairs, Plan and Budget Organization, and women's affairs. Four additional ministers of state served without specific portfolios. Each ministry was manned by a civil service staff under a permanent undersecretary (also called deputy minister) who, together with career officials serving as directors general and division heads, provided departmental continuity.

In the mid-1970s the conditions of service affecting government employees were basically governed under the Civil Service Code of 1966, which was a major revision of Iran's first civil service law adopted in 1922. The 1966 law sought to bring about uniformity in conditions of employment, strengthen internal discipline, reduce overstaffing, and eliminate the chronic problems of red tape and irregularities. In 1966 it was officially anticipated that at least several years would be needed to bring about desired changes. In the mid-1970s changes were still under way.

The Civil Service Code provides for two categories of government employees: established career and contracted. The code also introduced a single system of grades for public servants on the basis of seven grades, each having fifteen steps. The same salary scale was to apply to all according to grade and step level. (This provision was amended in 1975 so that teachers, doctors, engineers, and other professional personnel would be paid according to different salary scales.) Base salaries were to be subject to change according to a cost-of-living index. Recruitment was to be based on competitive examinations.

Political appointees, members of the armed forces, police, and gendarmerie were exempt, with some exceptions, from the Civil Service Code. Also excluded were SAVAK, the Ministry of the Imperial Court, all agencies and public corporations operating on a commercial basis, and self-governing municipal authorities under locally elected councils. In addition, under an amendment announced in 1975, judicial personnel, members of scientific committees affiliated with universities, members of the state-owned higher scientific institutions, and members of the Ministry of Foreign Affairs were declared exempt from the civil service law; separate laws were to govern these special categories. The change was apparently designed to give higher salaries to and boost the morale of these highly specialized professionals.

The civil service was under the jurisdiction of the State Organization for Administrative and Employment Affairs attached to the prime minister's office. As of May 1976 there were 350,000 career civil servants, not counting those exempt from the civil service law. The exempt officials, including the members of the defense, police, and security agencies, would probably add an estimated 500,000 to the total on government payroll.

For years the need for so-called administrative revolution was widely discussed and even officially emphasized. As a result, in October 1967 the shah announced—as the twelfth point in the White Revolution (see Glossary)—a program designed to revitalize government institutions, improve administrative performance, and strengthen local government bodies through decentralization (see ch. 7). The program called for, among other things, better training of civil servants, increased efficiency in government operation through the application of latest principles and techniques of organizational management, rigorous supervision and inspection, and introduction of a merit system. These reforms were designed to make the government more responsive to grass-roots needs by eliminating administrative delays and most of all by stamping out corruption in the government.

In the mid-1970s irregularities and corruption were apparently widespread, as reflected in the government's renewed campaign against offenders. This drive was intensified, especially after January 1976, when the shah publicly deplored the persistence of "corruption of every kind" in Iran and singled out "administrative corruption," which he said would not be tolerated. The monarch also stated that every Iranian had "the duty of standing up to corruption" and of waging "a merciless struggle" against it until it was eradicated.

The Legislature

The legislative branch is bicameral. In 1977 the Majlis, or lower house, had 268 deputies popularly elected (in June 1975) for a four-year term from single-member districts. By special provision five seats were reserved for religious minorities: two for the Armenian community and one each for the Zoroastrian, Jewish, and Assyrian-Chaldean communities (see ch. 4). Although provided for in the Constitution of 1906, the Senate was not formed until 1950. It has sixty members, half of whom are elected and half of whom are royally appointed—all for a four-year term. Of those elected, fifteen must be from Tehran and fifteen from the provinces; those appointed must be divided in the same way. For election and appointment as well, all provinces are entitled to at least one seat; two seats each are assigned, however, to the more populated provinces with capitals in Tabriz, Meshed, and Shiraz.

Legislative sessions are generally open to the public and the press, subject to the maintenance of order and decorum as prescribed by the rules of Parliament. The speaker of the Majlis, who is elected by its members, may call a closed session at the request of ten deputies or one cabinet minister. The term of both chambers is concurrent, elections being held on the same day for both. Parliament opens its annual sessions in October, the anniversary of the inauguration of the first Majlis in 1906. The power to call special sessions of Parliament or to dissolve either house, separately or at the same time, is vested in the shah. He is also empowered to adjudicate cases of disagreement twice occurring on any bill before the two houses.

Bills may be introduced by the shah, prime minister, cabinet members, or by any deputy or senator. Legislative work is done in committee; after deliberation by the appropriate committee a bill may be brought to a vote of the Majlis. More than half of the members must be present for a vote to be taken; a bill is approved when it secures a majority of more than half the members present in the house at the time the vote is taken. The bill is then passed on to the Senate and, if approved, becomes law upon receiving the shah's assent. Budget and financial bills are voted on only by the Majlis, but the Senate has an advisory role in their enactment. Money bills may be enacted despite royal veto by a three-fourths majority of the Majlis. The members of Parliament are granted immunity from judicial action.

The way in which Parliament was constituted and operated in 1977 differed from the pre-1975 period. This was occasioned by the shah's decision in March 1975 to dispense with Iran's multiparty system and establish instead a one-party system under the Rastakhiz Party (see ch. 7). Before this action parliamentary elections had been a contest between two or more parties, and the legislature had opposition as well as progovernment deputies. After 1975, however, membership in Parliament was open only to those who supported the government, that is, those who were "loyal to the Constitution, Monarchy, and Revolution." Thus the candidates in the parliamentary election in June 1975 were all members of the government-sponsored party and once elected could not register any parliamentary objections to government bills or policies. As one Iranian source put it, all bills were approved "almost unanimously" inasmuch as the list of debaters was no longer drawn on the basis of pros and cons.

Nevertheless, in an obvious move to encourage the flow of internal communication within Parliament, almost immediately after the election of June 1975 the government formed what it called two wings in the legislature. Members of Parliament were free to join either of the two wings according to their preference. The wings were not to be regarded as parliamentary blocs in terms of majority and minority but as an entirely new, nonpartisan arrangement aimed at promoting government activities.They were likened, according to former Prime Minister Hoveyda's statement in July 1975, to "the bed of two rivers in which torrents of various ideas flow, causing the two rivers to roar but uniting and harmonizing them."

The Legal and Judicial Systems

At the close of the nineteenth century Iran had two bodies of law: the shariah and urf, or secular law. (Technically the Arabic term *urf* means tribal or customary law.) These were administered separately by the Muslim clergy through the religious courts and by the civil government through the secular courts. Neither system was standardized or codified in the modern sense, and jurisdiction was vague. This judicial dualism and attendant confusion received critical scrutiny from Reza Shah, especially during the 1926–28 period.

The judicial reform of the late 1920s was based mainly on the French model and the Judicial Organization Law of 1909 as amended in 1927 and 1928. The minister of justice was installed as head of the judiciary; special powers voted to him by Parliament in 1927 were used to bring about a sweeping reorganization and secularization, and by the mid-1930s all courts had been effectively brought under his authority. The judicial authority of the Islamic clergy (the qadis and ulama) was substantially curbed, and the religious courts were in effect relegated to a secondary place in the administration of justice (see ch. 4). Nonetheless, in light of the strong Islamic bent of the Iranians, especially in rural areas, religious branches were retained in some civil courts to deal with cases of marriage, divorce, inheritance, and related matters. Laws governing marriage and related family matters were in secular form, but care was taken to ensure that the Islamic traditions sanctioned by the shariah were taken into account as far as circumstances warranted.

Iran's legal codes were inspired mainly by the Napoleonic codes. These included the codes of civil and criminal procedure issued in the 1909–12 period and amended later; the penal code enacted in 1925, amended in 1940; the commercial code that evolved during the 1924–33 period; and the three-volume civil code adopted in the 1928–33 period. In the mid-1970s efforts to modernize the various codes were continuing under the State Law Codification Organization. The purpose of this body was to review all laws and regulations issued since 1907 and evaluate their consistency and relevance. Also under way was an attempt to determine whether Anglo-Saxon judicial procedures could be adapted to the French-inspired Iranian judicial system. In December 1974 the minister of justice formed a commission, the findings of which might eventually become a basis for change in investigative and trial procedures (see ch. 12).

The independence of the judiciary is constitutionally stipulated, but the judicial system, except for the military courts, is actually controlled by the executive branch—specifically by the minister of justice and the prime minister acting as chief executive surrogate of the shah. Judges of all ranks are appointed by the shah through the prime minister and the minister of justice; in most cases their promotion and transfer are also subject to executive determination, but they may be removed from the bench only through due process of law or if they resign.

The extent to which the judiciary is independent of executive interference could not be readily ascertained in 1977. The question of judicial autonomy was apparently a long-standing one as evidenced in a commentary that appeared in the May 7, 1974, issue of the weekly *Khandaniha* in Tehran. This commentary, attributed to the newspaper's publisher, A. Amirani, deplored the continued absence of judicial independence "almost half a century" after the same problem had been publicly decried by a government minister in 1926. As a remedial step the commentary suggested that the judiciary be placed under a chief justice elected by the people or by the judges from among elderly dignitaries who supposedly had no material interests—such as prominent religious leaders who would not be tempted by "money, women, threat and intimidation" and whose only aim would be to dispense justice. Such a step, according to the commentary, would forestall the practice of the judiciary surrendering "parts of its functions" to an unspecified "administrative office of the executive."

The highest tribunal of the land is the Supreme Court, sometimes referred to as the Court of Cassation. The court of highest appellate authority, it is divided into eleven branches. The Supreme Court is also the court of first instance, among other competences, in the trial of cabinet-level offficials and adjudicates jurisdictional disputes between civil and military courts as well as disputes between judicial and other government agencies. The chief justice of the court is appointed by the shah on the nomination of the minister of justice, as is the attorney general, who is a member of the Supreme Court.

Below the Supreme Court are courts of appeal or high courts, which are located in the provincial capitals; these courts consist of civil and criminal chambers that hear appeals from lower primary courts. A criminal chamber also has authority in the first instance over serious crimes. Lesser civil and criminal cases are tried before the district *(shahrestan)* courts. Below them are the subdistrict *(bakhsh)* courts, which, in addition to civil and criminal responsibilities, hear appeals from decisions of the lowest courts in Iran—the houses of equity in the villages and the councils of arbitration in the cities (see ch. 12).

The work of the county and district courts, long noted for delays stemming from the complexity of legal procedures and the heavy work load, has been considerably eased since the mid-1960s when the houses of equity and arbitration councils were created as part of the shah's multifaceted reforms designed to provide equitable, inexpensive, and speedy justice for the masses. They are operated by locally elected lay justices of the peace chosen from among reputable local citizens, and cases are adjudicated as far as possible on the basis of common law (see ch. 12). Evidently the houses of equity and the arbitration councils have been well-received by the people; this is probably because the adjudicatory functions traditionally performed, and often abused, by the landlords, clergy, and police were gradually being replaced by the civil courts.

The judiciary also has a number of special courts. These include the Criminal Court for Government Employees; a religious court in Tehran with branches in some provinces; a judges disciplinary tribunal; juvenile courts; a fiscal court (for fiscal fraud); and the regular military courts, which under the control of the Ministry of War play a major role in the trial of those charged with political offenses (see ch. 12).

Local Government

As of December 1977 there were twenty-three provinces *(ostan)* (see fig. 9). A province is headed by a governor general *(ostandar)*, who is appointed by the shah on the advice of the minister of interior and serves as principal executive agent of the central government, reporting directly to the minister of interior. All provincial and local administrative matters are under the supervision and control of the Ministry of Interior. Changes in administrative boundaries are made from time to time by the ministry in response to regional development needs. Formerly there were a number of subprovincial units called governorates *(farmandari)*, but by the end of 1976 the last one had been elevated to provincial status.

Each province is divided into districts *(shahrestans)*, headed by governors *(farmandars)*; each district, into subdistricts *(bakhsh)*, each administered by a lieutenant governor *(bakhshdar)*, and cities and towns; each subdistrict, into counties or townships *(dehistans)*, under a sheriff *(dehdar)*; and each township into villages *(deh)*, under a village headman *(kadkhuda*—see Glossary). With the exception of village headmen, who are locally elected, local administrative heads are appointed by the minister of interior. In 1977, however, the pattern of central appointment was being modified somewhat, albeit under government supervision, to encourage local selection as part of growing official emphasis on administrative decentralization.

Large urban municipalities may have district status. Cities and towns have municipal government with a mayor and council locally elected or designated by a division of municipal affairs in the Ministry of Interior on recommendation from the provincial governor general or governor. The mayor of Tehran, a special case, is appointed by the shah on recommendation of the minister of interior and with approval of the cabinet.

The Constitution of 1907 provides a basis for local government by stipulating that provincial and district councils be formed through elections. The first tangible effort in that direction occurred in 1962 when a bill was enacted for the establishment of these and other local councils in the municipalities and villages.

The evolution of local government, however, proved more complex than the proponents of constitutionalism had envisioned. Tradition continued to weigh against official efforts to modify by decree the age-old pattern of centralized, authoritarian rule based in Tehran. Invariably all decisions, major and minor, were made in Tehran, and those affecting regions outside the seat of the central government were implemented through local officials appointed by the central government. For generations the primary duties of these officials were to collect taxes and enforce law and order. There was no uniform set of procedures or code of conduct applicable to all local authorities, and the quality and effectiveness of local administration varied widely from region to region. The dispensation of justice depended heavily on the personality or disposition of local officials, who were more often than not susceptible to the influence of landlords and Islamic clergy. Public accountability was unheard of, and few actions, if any, were initiated locally.

Inevitably the country's political power, best talents, wealth, and means of production were concentrated in Tehran and to a lesser degree in a few other metropolitan centers. Gradually but steadily Iran came to grips with the two major problems of urban-rural inequity and regional underdevelopment. The Shah-People Revolution was designed in part to cope with these problems (see ch. 7). The government's increased attention to the need for decentralization and the strengthening of local government, especially since late 1967, was based on the shah's comprehensive administrative reform program. Simply stated it sought to bring

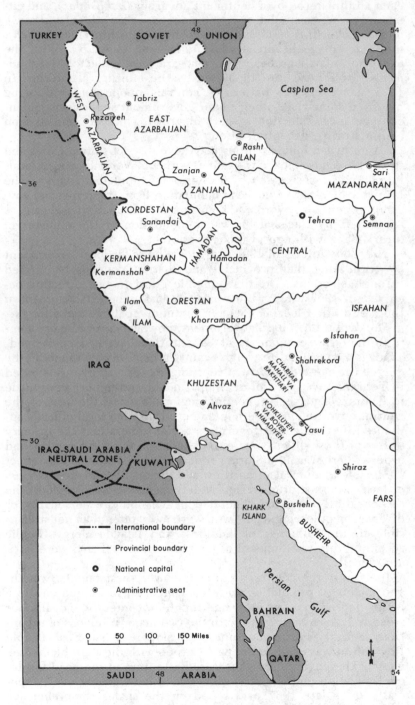

Figure 9. Administrative Divisions, December 1977

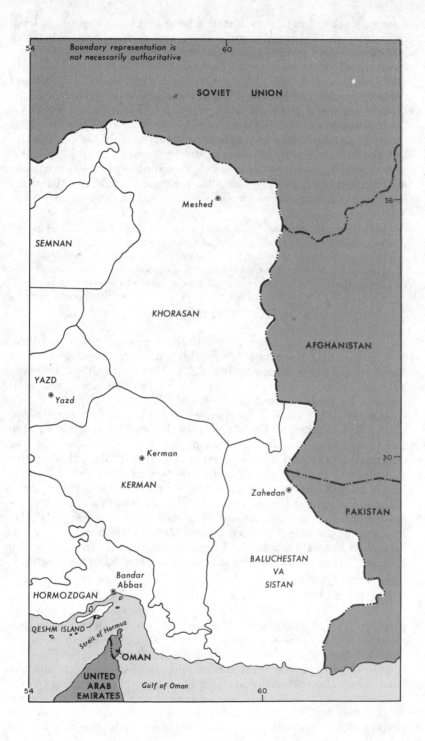

Boundary representation is
not necessarily authoritative

SOVIET   UNION

Meshed ⊙

SEMNAN

KHORASAN

AFGHANISTAN

YAZD

⊙ Yazd

⊙ Kerman

KERMAN

Zahedan ⊙

PAKISTAN

BALUCHESTAN
VA
SISTAN

Bandar
Abbas

HORMOZDGAN

QESHM ISLAND

Strait of Hormuz

OMAN

UNITED
ARAB
EMIRATES

Gulf of Oman

about a devolution of power to the local levels, to encourage local initiatives and innovation, and to enlist grass-roots participation in a wide range of government-sponsored programs.

The first local elections for city and town councils took place in 1968 and were followed by elections for provincial and district councils in 1970. The first village councils were formed in 1973. Under law these councils, except at the village level, are given limited authority to initiate local projects and supervise their implementation; they are specifically responsible for community development, health, education, finance, and other local matters.

In actuality, however, the development of local government was more apparent in form than in substance. Tehran's English-language *Kayhan International* commented on August 31, 1974:

> At the moment provincial administration is not particularly efficient or well-staffed. Despite talk of local autonomy, control still tends to be firmly in the hands of authorities in Tehran. Elected councils exist at the provincial, district, town, and even village level. But, town councils aside, these elected bodies do not play a very effective role in local affairs. Even the town councils have been able to plan only a limited role as vehicles for public participation in local decisionmaking.

Among the reasons cited were: limited powers given the local councils; lack of necessary funds; the tendency of central government officials to control provincial activities; unhealthy influences brought to bear on local bodies by "local notables;" and self-seeking by some elected members of these councils.

As a result the issue of local government was closely scrutinized by the Commission on Local Councils that had been established in 1973 under the Ministry of Interior. By 1976 evidently little had changed. In the May 10, 1976, issue of *Ettelaat,* Manuchehr Ganji commented that various decisions were still made "at the upper levels of administrative apparatuses" in Tehran and thus: "Centralization beyond the bounds of activities within Tehran has resulted not only in work being performed more sluggishly but also in drawing the most creative and educated elements in the provinces and *sharestans* more and more to the capital each day, due to the fact that political power has been concentrated in the capital."

Electoral System

Elections to the Majlis, the Senate, and the local councils in the provinces, districts, cities, towns, and villages are held under the provisions of an amended law passed in January 1963. These provisions, which were designed to bring about sweeping electoral reforms, gave women the right to vote and hold elective office and required prior voter registration and possession of an identity card. They also ended the practice of electoral involvement by two or more government agencies by naming the Ministry of Interior as the sole supervisory body; the ministry was to carry out its responsibility through local supervisory councils, the members of which were to be appointed by provincial governors general, or indirectly elected. In an attempt to curb the self-serving influences of landlords and aristocrats often brought to bear on the rural and economically weaker voters, the 1963 reform excluded landlords and aristocrats from membership in local supervisory bodies. The social groups allowed to be represented on the supervisory councils after 1963 were the Islamic clergy, businessmen, tradesmen, workers, and farmers. During 1976 an additional change was being considered for the representation of women, members of local councils, self-employed people, retired people, and university personnel.

Voters must be Iranian citizens in good standing at least twenty years of age for the Majlis election and at least twenty-five for the Senate election and have resided in their respective electoral districts for at least six months. All active-duty members of the armed forces, gendarmerie, and police are barred from voting in the jurisdictions in which they are stationed or exercise authority. Also barred from electoral participation are princes of the first degree, cabinet ministers, and senior civil service officials. Government officials of lower grade may be eligible for candidacy but are expected to resign their posts if elected.

Candidates for the Majlis must be from thirty to seventy years of age, Iranian citizens in good standing, literate, and except in the case of those running for religious minority seats, Muslims. Senatorial candidates must be Muslims of at least forty years of age and must be drawn from among reputable leaders of government in retirement and from the business and academic community and the clergy. Candidates for provincial and other local councils must be at least twenty-five years of age, able to read and write Farsi (or Persian as it is commonly known outside Iran), and have resided in their respective localities for at least two years.

Iran is divided into 268 electoral districts for the Majlis, and one or more provinces serve as a single senatorial constituency for a total of fifteen elective seats. Electoral boundaries are to be redrawn from time to time to account for increased population at the ratio of one Majlis deputy for every 100,000 people. Parliamentary election is conducted by direct secret ballot. For the parliamentary election of June 1975 there were about 800 polling stations. The eligible voters totaled about 25 million—14 million for the election to the Majlis and 11 million for the Senate. The voter turnout was about 47 percent, up from 30 percent in 1971.

City, town, and district councils are directly chosen, but the provincial councils are not. Candidates to the district council must be endorsed by thirty to 150 lawful voters; their competency must be reviewed by a committee composed of the provincial governor general or governor, provincial departmental heads in charge of justice, health, education, and finance; and two "local dignitaries." Voters are allowed to cast ballots for only those candidates on the approved list issued by the screening committee. Each district council is entitled to elect two members to the provincial or governorate council. Apparently the indirect procedure is designed to weed out candidates considered objectionable by government authorities.

* * *

The Iranian governmental system remains a relatively unexplored subject; few comprehensive studies are available. Among the monographs considered useful to the understanding of the subject is the 1957 edition of *Iran,* edited by Herbert H. Vreeland for the Human Relations Area Files. Also helpful is *Iran Past and Present* by Donald N. Wilber. The annual editions of *Iran Almanac and Book of Facts* offer current information on a wide range of categories, but the information is sometimes inconsistent and inaccurate. The monthly *Profile on Iran* issued by the Embassy of Iran in Washington occasionally provides insight into the structure and working of the governmental system. (For further information see Bibliography.)

Chapter 7. Political Dynamics

IN MARCH 1975 Mohammad Reza Pahlavi, the Shahanshah of Iran, decreed that "a new political structure" would be established to replace the old two-party system. The new structure was named the Iran National Resurgence Party (Rastakhiz-e-Mellat-e-Iran) or, more popularly, the Rastakhiz Party. Thus without any forewarning, Iran was placed under a one-party system. As ensuing events were to bear witness, however, the innovation did not affect the reality of the Iranian political process, which in early 1978 continued to center on the shah. The shah remained the heart and sinew of political power and decisionmaking. In fact, if the one-party experiment proved successful, the shah-centered authoritarian rule might well become even more unassailable.

The Rastakhiz Party is not a political party in a conventional sense. It does not engage in partisan struggle for power, which in the eyes of nearly all Iranians remains the exclusive preserve of the shah. Rather, the one-party system is envisaged as a political instrument designed to animate the proverbially apathetic citizenry and to mobilize them into the government-controlled mainstream of political life.

The shah's decision to create the Rastakhiz Party evolved from his desire to stimulate empathy with and participation in the political process by the citizenry. In his judgment, the active involvement of all Iranians was essential to the immediate challenge of a rapidly industrializing society and, more important, to the task of making Iran one of the world's foremost powers by the year 2000—the task set by the shah in March 1975. What the shah saw at that time was the critical need for nothing less than total commitment to the three supreme and governing principles; the monarchy, the Constitution, and the White Revolution (see Glossary)—the "revolution" that the shah set in motion in 1963 as a comprehensive national program of socioeconomic and political modernization. These principles would be translated into reality, the shah concluded, only when the masses were willing and prepared to become actively involved in the process of nation-building. There was little doubt that the previous pattern of tutelage would continue under the one-party experiment; what was new was the shah's belief that Iran's leap to grandeur would be materially hastened if the people were better motivated, more productive, and prepared to accept greater discipline.

In 1977 it was at yet unclear whether the Rastakhiz Party had achieved any of the results desired by the shah. The organization certainly had a far-flung network throughout the country and a claimed membership in the millions. But noticeably absent from the political scene was the effervescence of mass spontaneity; the tradition of cynical indifference was far more ingrained than had been suspected. Political opposition existed among ultraconservative religious elements, intellectuals, university students, and radical groups of both leftist and rightist persuasion. It appeared unlikely, though, that the shah would be troubled by political destabilization of any major proportions. Opposition was scattered, ephemeral and ineffective; and organizational outlets were virtually nonexistent. As a result the most likely issue appeared to be the future of systemic integrity on the eventual passing of the shah from the political scene. It is axiomatic that a political system that is identified in popular view with a single national leader—however stable it may be—contains seeds of instability. Once the leader departs a new consensus is required to sustain the effectiveness of the system, and the search for a consensus, whether through constitutional means or otherwise, frequently proves to be painfully divisive.

The symbolism of continuity associated with the monarchy is an undeniably important historic source of strength for the shah. Equally potent are the military, the ultimate guarantors of his power. The loyalty of the army has been an important stabilizing factor, as has been the effective if sometimes harsh manner of political control exercised by an array of secret police and security organizations at the personal disposal of the shah (see ch. 12).

Shah and Political Power

The monarchy, with its many dynasties and varying fortunes, has for centuries been the principal single source and center of political power, and so it continued in 1977 (see table A). The shah wields extraordinary power as head of state, chief executive, and commander in chief of the armed forces (see ch. 6; ch. 13). Unlike constitutional monarchs in most other countries, the shah is actively involved in decisionmaking, playing a pivotal role as the most important formulator of national goals, priorities, and key policies.

The manner in which the shah exercised his power in the 1970s was significantly different from the way power had been wielded several decades earlier. Before the advent of the Pahlavi dynasty in 1925, the power hierarchy was relatively diffuse. Although the monarchy was the most influential of all power groups, its special position was often checked by the balancing forces of such traditional elements as wealthy landlords, tribal leaders, wealthy urban merchants, army officers, and the Muslim clergy (see Glossary), particularly those *mujtahids* (religious authorities) known as *ayatollah* (see ch. 4). No single group could preempt wealth and power to the exclusion of others. Balance between these elements was considered natural in maintaining order and stability.

Aside from the monarchy, none of the traditional power groups was necessarily exclusive. Membership could and often did overlap on the basis of landownership. A senior army officer or a provincial governor could and probably would be a member of one of the wealthy families with extensive landholdings, long accepted as a principal requisite for access to power elite. Tribal leaders, whether residing in Tehran or encamped in distant and inaccessible regions, were also among the largest landowners, as were Islamic religious interests. An urban merchant might also be a landlord.

The traditional power structure had not been nearly as centralized as it was in the 1970s. Royalist rule inside the capital region of Tehran was seldom questioned, but outside the region it was a different story. What little influence the monarchy could exert over distant provinces waxed and waned depending on the loyalty and strength of local governors and tribal leaders. Many of these tribes had their own customs, traditions, and languages and were tenaciously loyal to their own regions; in effect they were virtually independent of rule by Tehran. The existence of scattered pockets of power did not necessarily pose a threat to central authority, however. Local powers usually failed to coalesce into alliances against royal authority partly because of their own mutual rivalries and partly because of the generally successful tactic of divide and rule used by various dynasties.

Informality and personal connections were the time-honored rules whereby political power, whether exercised by the shah or some lesser figure, was stabilized and distributed. These rules underlay the traditional network of multipurpose friendship circles known as *dowrehs* existing at all social levels. Most Iranian men belonged to two or more *dowrehs*, some of which were exclusive. Established informally for social, cultural, recreational, intellectual, or political purposes, a typical *dowreh* had an average of fifteen members of similar educational experiences, sharing common interests or social backgrounds. The members would meet periodically, on a rotating basis, in individual houses to discuss issues or ways to advance mutual welfare.

For influential members of society, the *dowreh* was especially important because it offered personal connections through which to gain access to important positions of power. The informal forum enabled members not only to discuss mutual reciprocity but also to reinforce their sense of partnership against a rival *dowreh*. In addition the *dowreh* acted as a communication channel through which information could be transmitted. A bazaar rumor, originating or inserted into the *dowreh* and often untrue or half-true, was nevertheless rapidly communicated within and across social classes. Rumor could also originate from within the inner circles of power as a means of partisan competition.

In the 1970s the *dowreh* system remained essentially unchanged and was ubiquitous as an important nexus of social life second only to family (see ch 5). Equally true was the continuing relevance of the *dowreh* in contemporary politics, which were being fashioned to a remarkable degree by the traditional methods of harmonizing conflicts and of promoting interests through informal, behind-the-scenes maneuvers. There were formal institutions, such as political parties, the legislature, voluntary associations, and bureaucracies through which the individuals could articulate their interests, but on the whole these were viewed with suspicion and as impersonal and inaccessible. There were some indications that, given the difficulty of overt political dissent, a growing number of students and intellectuals withdrew into these *dowrehs*, a symptom of political cynicism and alienation long prevalent among the politically aroused segments of the population.

Despite the timeless nature of the *dowreh* system, relationships between various components of the power structure have undergone significant changes in recent decades. The single most salient feature of these changes has been the steady centralization of power in the hands of the shah—not only in spatial terms but also in functional terms—all at the expense of the traditional land-based wealthy families.

The realignment of power relationships was perhaps inevitable. Socioeconomic changes, coupled with the relentless strengthening of the government under modernized, and modernizing, army and bureaucratic agencies, have had far-reaching implications for the political life of the country in general and for the socioeconomic bases of power in particular. The growth of modern economic sectors created new sources of wealth and power. A strong, mobile, and centrally directed army meant a sharp decline in tribal autonomy. The government sponsorship of a rival secular educational system, as distinguished from the religious education controlled by the *mujtahids,* also had major consequences, not the least of which was the steady erosion of clerical power, once considered virtually impregnable.

The transformation of the power hierarchy has been especially noticeable since the shah's sweeping land reform and other measures initiated in January 1963 (see Shah-People Revolution, this ch.). Of these measures, land reform proved particularly unpopular with wealthy landowners, religious leaders, and some tribal leaders. For years the dominant force in the Majlis, the lower house of Parliament, these traditionalists had managed to circumvent the shah's earlier though similar but milder land reform proposals. Thus in announcing his scheme for the abolition of the peasant-landlord tenure and sharecropping systems and for the redistribution of landed estates, the shah expressed concern that "forces of black reaction and red destruction" might attempt to sabotage the land reform program.

His statement proved prophetic. Faced with the certainty of a further reduction of their status and power, the conservatives criticized the agrarian reform as unconstitutional. They were joined in their opposition, for different reasons, by loosely organized former party politicians and by remnants of the outlawed communist Tudeh (Masses) Party (see ch. 12). These groups sought revenge for past political defeats suffered at the hands of the shah. Rioting broke out in Tehran in June 1963, as oppositionists stirred mob action that resulted in extensive destruction in the bazaar area and adjoining sections and disruption of usual activities. During this time the long-simmering dissidence among some smaller tribes in southern Iran flared into open rebellion. These disturbances were directed against government controls of tribal movement and armament and, to a lesser degree, against the reforms initiated by the shah.

In Tehran security forces contained the violence within a week of the attempted mass uprising. Similarly within weeks the tribal unrest in the southern region subsided, and public order was restored throughout the country. During this unrest, the national police and the gendarmerie rather than regular army troops were used in both Tehran and tribal areas. Critically important throughout the year was the fact that no defection of regular forces occurred; this demonstration of loyalty was widely regarded as evidence of the shah's firm control of the army and security forces.

Equally significant was the fact that the ill-fated challenge of the traditionalists meant the emergence of the shah as the absolute ruler. He no longer had to confront the obstructionist parliamentary tactics of traditional power groups. For the first time he was able to initiate a dialogue directly with the broadest possible segments of the population, i.e., the peasants and workers. The shah found his position additionally strengthened by the fact that he could now effectively preempt the often ambiguous rhetoric and programs of nationalist and radical opposition with his own land reform program.

In 1977 the military and security establishments continued to be the keystone of the shah's ruling structure. These organizations appeared unlikely to emerge as a disloyal, independent political force. The officer corps generally enjoyed special status in society, owing in part to the shah's personal interest in improving its morale through higher salaries and fringe benefits; moreover all officers above the rank of major owed their status to the shah who personally approved their promotions and assignments. The possibility of a military coup was also minimized by the effective operation of the National Intelligence and Security Organization (Sazeman Ettelaat va Amniyat Kashvar—SAVAK). SAVAK is not alone, however, in secret police functions; it is joined by other military intelligence arms with overlapping responsibilities that are designed to ensure mutual surveillance (see ch. 12).

Thus according to responsible observers, the security and intelligence agencies are infiltrated by agents working for and reporting to separate bodies unknown to one another. The heads of the agencies in return report periodically or as often as deemed necessary directly to the shah. The possibility of collusion between these bodies is foreclosed by a procedure that does not permit interagency coordination or cooperation. The same rule also applies to the shah's generals, who are forbidden to visit Tehran or to meet with any officers of the same rank or responsibility without, according to political scientist Marvin Zonis, the shah's "personal, case by case, permission." These vertical procedures not only encourage competition for the shah's recognition and approval but also place at the disposal of the shah the exclusive advantage of cross-checking the integrity and performance of generals as well as intelligence and security agencies. In addition the shah maintains close rapport with his generals and key bureaucrats through frequent face-to-face discussions, underscoring the importance of personalism as a central feature of political life.

Iran is no exception to the political axiom that a society cannot thrive on law and order alone without demonstrating some measure of responsiveness. Stability depends in the final analysis on the credibility of a regime with respect to its intentions and the effectiveness of its actions in coping with the varied needs of society. Numerous efforts were under way in the 1970s to narrow the distance between the shah's government and the people. Development projects in socioeconomic fields were being implemented on a massive scale because of the abundant oil revenues.

Results were mixed, however, as a result of the lack of indigenous skills, labor shortage, inefficiency, waste, general lagging in building socioeconomic infrastructures and, according to the shah, corruption in the bureaucracy (see ch. 9). The gap between rich and poor appeared to be steadily widening, at a time when the aspirations of a growing middle class and urban industrial work force to a better way of life were being aroused. All these were concomitants of a rapidly modernizing society, a society that was seeking to leap from its recent feudal past into one of the world's leading industrial powers in as short a time as possible. The stability of the shah-centered power structure was not an immediate issue in 1977, nor was it likely to be strained for some time to come. The capacity of the regime to cope with pressures from the grass roots for more rapid satisfaction of unfulfilled needs may be severely tested, however.

Generally the shah sought to remedy the situation with firmness, coupling it with frequent spurts of anticorruption drives. On a more positive level, he has rewarded qualified people with government positions by way of recruitment or promotion; this policy of co-optation has helped to boost morale and efficiency at the top echelons of the government, especially in those highly professional and technocratic units responsible for economic planning and management and for external and defense matters.

As a group these talented individuals usually possessed university educations, many earned at home but a very large number abroad. They constituted the nucleus of a rapidly expanding new class of administrative-economic-technical-managerial elites, some holding high-status positions in the cabinet, Parliament, key ministries, diplomatic service, and major public corporations; the most prized of these corporations was the National Iranian Oil Company (NIOC) (see ch. 10). Except for a few highly placed individuals personally trusted by the shah, however, most members of the new class belonged on the periphery of the power structure.

The shah's method of co-optation was applied also to a small number of former career politicians and intellectuals who had been in opposition to the regime and who had once wielded influence disproportionate to their number. Many of these individuals were induced into government service of one kind or another, depending on their qualifications and talent, by impressive salaries and other emoluments. This tactic sometimes proved effective in diffusing political tensions, actual and potential, and hence forestalled the possibility of dissidence getting out of control. Economic inducements were undoubtedly an important factor in some cases for collaboration with the regime; evidently demoralization played no small part. Some Iranians were made to realize the futility of disagreeing with the shah inasmuch as the price of dissent proved very costly. What is more, virtually no channels existed through which political interest could be aggregated except through a framework approved by the shah.

The shah may be the practitioner of what he once called "the most strict authoritarianism," but he is by no means dogmatic or insensitive to the ebb and flow of events at home and abroad. An astute tactician, he caused a change in the leadership of the cabinet in August 1977 when he replaced Amir Abbas Hoveyda as prime minister—a post he had held since 1965—with Jamshid Amuzegar, the fifty-four-year old minister of interior. The change was made amid mounting symptoms of infrastructural constraints on industry and other undesirable consequences of imbalanced economic growth, agricultural stagnation, and an inflation rate close to 25 percent a year. The seriousness of the situation was underlined by the shah's decision to appoint technically experienced new men to the ministries of energy, industry and mines, housing and town planning, and agriculture and rural development and to the Plan and Budget Organization. Later in August the shah ordered all ministers and other senior officials to declare their private income and assets in yet another effort to stamp out corruption and to restore popular confidence in government officials.

The cabinet reshuffle came at a time when the shah appeared to be taking steps, if somewhat haltingly, toward lessened restrictions on political debate. Signs of relaxation in his tough stance against political dissenters were discernible in early 1977, coinciding with President Jimmy Carter's strong emphasis on human rights as a major theme in United States foreign policy. Specifically political relaxation was evident in the release of some political prisoners and the modification of legal procedures designed to protect the rights of those accused of political crimes. It was also reported that the use of what some observers called "torture" was suspended. At the end of 1977 it was unclear whether these developments would lead to a somewhat freer political climate or amount to no more than what some critics called "cosmetic" maneuvers.

Framework for Political Activities

In 1977 the trial and error of organized political activity was still in effect, a process under way intermittently since its embryonic beginnings at the start of the twentieth century (see Nationalism and Revolution, ch. 2). At the center of this process was the Rastakhiz Party whose real purpose was to act as the political arm of the shah and his regime in an effort to educate the public and to inculcate in them the importance of discipline and participation.

Background

Political parties abounded in Iran in the years after the end of World War II, but their impact on the national scene was minimal. With the exception of the communist Tudeh Party—formed in 1941 but outlawed in 1949—no party had any notable continuity, any national or even regional following, or any organizational structures outside Tehran. In most cases the parties were little more than a collection of loosely organized cliques centering on one or two charismatic personalities. The parties or cliques existed more often than not at the sufferance of the shah and attracted little popular following. Essentially political activities continued to be a function of personalism, and the notion of channeling popular aspirations through formal, Western-style organizations has not taken roots in the country.

Various parties that mushroomed in the 1940s appealed to a bewildering variety of conflicting and frequently vague popular sentiments, loosely identified with conservative traditionalists, religious fanatics, students and intellectuals, bazaar merchants, socialists, nationalists, communists, anticommunists, and so forth. In 1949 Mohammad Mossadeq set out to unify these disparate elements into a single political force and establish himself as its leader; he succeeded partly as evidenced by the establishment of the National Front, which he headed without associating himself with any of the groups affiliated with it. During his prime ministership from 1951 to 1953, however, Mossadeq caused alienation within the National Front and outside it as well with his increasingly erratic and arbitrary use of power. In consequence effective support for him did not coalesce in his fateful confrontation with the shah and army royalists in August 1953 (see Mohammad Mossadeq and Oil Nationalization, ch. 2). After the Mossadeq crisis, nearly all political party activity ceased. Subversive groups were broken up and hunted out, and others became inactive or quiescent as the central authority of the shah and his army-backed government was restored and the period of recovery begun.

In 1957, his power more firmly established than previously, the shah moved to create a two-party system that was designed to provide an orderly means of resolving political conflicts and legitimizing the shah's cautious reform and development policies. Stability and control were important considerations in this move in the light of the Mossadeq crisis that had nearly toppled the monarchy in 1953. (Reportedly the system was set up mainly as a tactic to help obtain United States aid.) If party politics were to be resumed, it would be under a condition whereby the government could firmly control the political scene. As to the significance of the two-party system, the shah stated that effective loyal opposition would not only keep the majority party alert and honest but also energize responsible public discussions of issues "free from the strait-jacket of one-party rule or the one-party state."

The "opposition" Mardom (People's) Party was set up first in 1957 under Asadollah Alam, a confidant of the shah's. The government party, the Maliyuun (National) Party was formed in 1958 under the leadership of Prime Minister Manuchehr Eqbal. The platforms of the government-sponsored parties were barely distinguishable from one another, both calling for social reform, economic development, constitutionalism, nationalism, and loyalty to the shah. There was some difference in membership; the Mardom Party, in addition to Alam's own political circle or *dowreh*, represented the generally dissatisfied elements seeking greater shares in the existing pattern of power or value distribution; the Maliyuun Party membership included a large bloc of civil servants and others already associated with the government or receiving substantial benefits therefrom.

Both parties proved erratic as much because of unremitting personality conflicts as because of the lack of popular interest. In December 1963 the function of the majority, or government, party was assumed by the newly organized Iran Novin (New Iran) Party. When its leader, Prime Minister Hassan Ali Mansur, was assassinated by a religious fanatic, Mansur's brother-in-law, Hoveyda, then minister of finance, was called on by the shah to be prime minister and at the same time secretary general of the party. This meant that the Maliyuun Party, which retained some strength in Parliament, continued the role of a minority party through early 1963.

Until the early 1970s the Iran Novin Party continued to act as the shah's political agent. It enjoyed an overwhelming majority in the Majlis. The Mardom Party remained a distant second in terms of representation in the Majlis. A third opposition group was the small but vocal Pan-Iran Party, which was strongly nationalist; active after 1965, the party demanded among other things the annexation of the Bahrain Islands and support for the Kurds in Iraq (see ch. 8). In 1970 a splinter group from the Pan-Iran Party formed the Iranian Party as still another opposition force.

The Rastakhiz Party

What was purported to be an approximation of a Western-style bipartisan system came to an abrupt end on March 2, 1975, when the shah ordered a new political structure established under a single government-sponsored political party. In so doing he stated that all Iranians who were loyal to the monarchy, had faith in the Constitution, and supported the Shah-People Revolution "must enter the new political structure." Not surprisingly all existing parties announced their dissolution on the same day and joined the Rastakhiz Party.

Under the charge of Prime Minister Hoveyda, who was to double as party secretary general "for at least a two-year term," the Rastakhiz Party was intended as a permanent institution that, according to the shah, would endure well beyond his own lifetime. But more significant, it was charged with the responsibility of invigorating the people, whom the shah, perhaps correctly, assessed as lethargic and unresponsive. The Rastakhiz Party was supposed to bring an end to the decades-old problem of alienation.

Participation was seen as evidence of loyalty to the monarchy and of commitment to the regime. Thus the shah could not have been more emphatic when he said in March 1975: "Everyone must be man enough to clarify his position in the country. He either approves of the conditions [the three principles concerning the monarchy, the Constitution, and the Shah-People Revolution] or he does not." An Iranian not joining the Rastakhiz Party nor accepting the three principles would be regarded, as the shah put it, "a traitor" who should be "in an Iranian prison" or who should leave the country forthwith or who should not in any event have "any expectations" or benefits from the regime. As for an individual who was not a traitor and yet who did not believe in the three principles, that person would be "free" in the country, provided that he was not antinationalist.

The shah was confident that all qualified Iranians would either "enter this new political structure or clarify his position as of tomorrow or as soon as possible." Among the first groups that he believed would join the Rastakhiz Party were workers, farmers, professors, and educators. Teachers as a whole were expected to shoulder "a great responsibility" for the training of the people in view of "the goals we have set out to achieve in order to develop our country to such a stage in three years, and an even higher level in eight years, and an even greater one in 13 years, and in the next 25 years to reach such a standard, which I think, will make Iran one of the five top nations in the world. Achieving such objectives is impossible with a handful of uneducated and illiterate individuals. . . ."

In inaugurating the new political setup, the shah clearly anticipated the potential problem of complacency that often accompanies a one-party political system. It was decreed, therefore, that the Rastakhiz Party should have "political wings" as an internal safeguard against self-indulgence and ossification and to ensure that various points of view were brought to bear on the political process. The shah left little doubt, however, that the "spirit of constructive criticism" he spoke of would be tolerated only as long as the fundamental and primary position of the three principles was not brought into question.

The new party came into being officially on May 1, 1975, when 5,000 delegates approved a party constitution in a hastily assembled convention. The party charter provides for a congress that convenes once every four years; a central council chosen by the congress whose delegates are elected by party branches at the ratio of one delegate for every 1,000 party members; an executive board whose fifty-five members are elected by the central council; and a thirty-one-member political bureau that is headed ex officio by the prime minister. The Political Bureau, in the nature of membership, is the most prestigious of all party organs; in addition to the prime minister, it has as its members a varying number of cabinet ministers; two deputies, each representing the lower and upper chambers of Parliament; a secretary general and deputy secretary general; and other influential figures chosen by the Executive Board from among its own members.

The party operations, which are financed by the government, are under the direction of a secretary general who is elected by the congress for a four-year term, renewable for a second and last term; the election is only a formality since the secretary general is picked personally by the shah. Party branches are located in Tehran and at the provincial, township, district, town, and village levels (see Local Government, ch. 6). Membership is open to all Iranians over the age of eighteen; excluded are members of the armed forces, Iranians domiciled abroad, nomadic tribesmen, seasonal migrant workers, prisoners, and the mentally incompetent.

Within ten days of its inception, the Rastakhiz Party began to focus on elections for the twenty-fourth Majlis whose term was to start in September 1975. The first under the one-party system, the election was scheduled for June 20. At the end of May the party announced a list of some 900 nominees out of about 7,000 applicants. In selecting the candidates, the party emphasized the importance of efficiency and talent, of representation for all socioeconomic groups including workers, farmers, university professors, schoolteachers, and officeworkers, and of "new faces," including women, who had no previous political experience. Loyalty and trustworthiness were doubtless overriding considerations.

Nearly all incumbent members of Parliament (268 deputies for the lower house elected every four years and thirty for the Senate—the balance of thirty senators are appointive) wanted to contest the election, but less than one-half were approved by the party (see ch. 6). All in all candidates with previous political or government experience accounted for about one-half of the total nominees.

Each seat was contested by two to four candidates (more in some districts) who ran as members of the Rastakhiz Party, but the party itself was not involved in electioneering for or against any individual candidate. Campaigning was notable more for the intensity of individuals advertising their personal qualifications or achievements or both than for their eagerness to dwell on issues of the day. Debates, when they occurred at all, were distinctively discreet, not surprisingly because the one-party platform of the Rastakhiz Party, reflecting the will and wisdom of the shah, obviated the necessity for further improvement or the need for disagreement. In those areas where candidates were relatively unknown to the voters, wealth and money were decisive factors because of the high costs of campaign advertising.

Acting in concert with the government, the party did undertake a massive media campaign to ensure the highest possible voter turnout. Voting was stressed as a civic duty not to be taken lightly. In fact the party's daily newspaper, *Rastakhiz*, once warned in an editorial that nonvoting would amount to "treason against experimentation with democracy." Rumors of possible actions against the nonvoters circulated in Tehran and elsewhere—without any official attempt to deny or discredit—until two days before election day. In the end slightly more than 40 percent of the eligible adults registered and cast ballots.

According to Iranian sources, the larger turnout in 1975 (as compared with 30 percent in 1971) was attributable to the fact that voters had a large number of candidates to choose from in each constituency (in 1971, only one or two candidates). Also cited was the absence of any conflicting and confusing campaign rhetoric or promises. It was asserted that an even higher turnout would have been possible if the Rastakhiz Party had had more time to educate the public and prepare itself organizationally, especially in the rural areas. Nearly 80 percent of the deputies and almost 50 percent of the senators elected were new faces; generally they were younger and better educated than their predecessors. (Occupational breakdowns were not available in late 1977.) The 1975 election was officially pronounced as free—the freest ever—and successful.

In July the party organized two separate wings: the "progressive liberals" wing under Amuzegar and the "constructive liberals" wing under Hushang Ansary. The *Financial Times* (July 28, 1975) observed that these "confusingly similar" wings or blocs reflected "a fairly genuine division of opinion within the establishment." Whereas the progressive bloc argued that economic growth was important as an end in itself "but too high a price should not be paid," the constructive bloc is said to have chosen the path of "maximum growth despite the consequences." Viewed in this light of differing emphasis, the election of Amuzegar in October 1976 as the first full-time secretary general of the party appeared to signify the pragmatic if somber awareness on the part of the shah and his advisers that the regime should address a lengthening list of infrastructure issues. The shah's appointment of Amuzegar as prime minister in August 1977 further underscored the sense of urgency facing the regime. Mohammad Baheri was chosen to succeed Amuzegar as secretary general.

As of July 1977 the Rastakhiz Party claimed 6 million party members or about 46 percent of those eligible to join the party's 50,000 chapters. About 50,000 members were considered to be "advanced" cadres. From all indications the party's all-out efforts to embrace a cross-section of the population were less than successful, despite the claim of "the public's enthusiasm and demand actively to participate in party affairs."

The Shah-People Revolution

The year 1963 was a turning point in the shah's relentless effort to stabilize the political scene, to accelerate nationbuilding, and to enhance the image of the regime as the promoter and guardian of popular welfare. Concretely this effort took the form of what was at first called the White Revolution of the Shah and the People but has since come to be called the Shah-People Revolution, an ambitious program of modernization through multifaceted reforms. The revolution, though sometimes dubbed by detractors as the "forgotten revolution," was still under way in 1977 albeit with uneven results. The shah and his regime, not the people, remained the principal moving force of this revolution from above.

From the political standpoint, perhaps the most significant result of the Shah-People Revolution is the consequence it has had on the diminishing importance of the landowning class as the traditionally important base of support for royal power (see ch. 5). The failure of landlords and their conservative allies to neutralize the shah's land reform measure in 1963 meant the removal of the last vestiges of obstructionism from the political scene (see ch. 11). The shah's preemption of power has since that time been effortless.

As first announced on January 9, 1963, the shah's reform program consisted of six points. The first point, always foremost in the evolution and implementation of reform goals, was abolition of the peasant-landlord tenure system and the redistribution and sale by the government of all landed estates—in excess of one village—on easy terms to the peasantry. Later, individual holdings of even one village and its associated lands were precluded (see ch. 11). The second point was public ownership, or nationalization, of forests throughout the country in the interest of conservation and better utilization.

The third point called for public sale of state-owned industrial enterprises to private corporations and individuals in order to finance agrarian development and create investment opportunities for the public in general and, in particular, for former landlords who were to be compensated by the government on a scale proportional to the landlords' own prior declarations and payment of taxes. The fourth point provided incentives for increased labor productivity by profit-sharing arrangements between industrial workers and owners to the extent of 20 percent of net corporate earnings.

The fifth point involved granting voting and political rights to women, thus extending equal and universal suffrage to all Iranian citizens regardless of sex. The sixth point, striking like the others at a chronic social ill, called for the formation of an education corps, called the Literacy Corps, from high school graduates who, during their military conscription period, would act as primary-school teachers and multipurpose village-level workers in rural areas to eliminate illiteracy, superstition, and ignorance (see ch. 3).

Between 1963 and 1965 three more points were added to the shah's program. The first of these, constituting the seventh point, was set forth in 1964 and directed toward improvement of health services. The Health Corps, paralleling the earlier Literacy Corps, was formed to bring free medical attention to rural areas and to provide training in sanitation and health standards.

The eighth point called for modernization of farm life and agricultural methods and the increase of farm productivity. To this end, the Development and Agricultural Extension Corps was formed. The ninth point, announced in 1965, dealt with the problems of justice and law at the village or small municipality level where long delays and distances had traditionally hampered or prevented prompt administration of justice. Local courts, called adjudication councils in towns and houses of justice or houses of equity in villages, were formed at these levels to hear local cases of a minor nature and settle them pragmatically, rapidly, and equitably. In 1968 the Equity Corps was established, parallel to the existing three corps, to assist in the operation of these local courts (see ch. 6).

In 1967 the shah's revolution was broadened to cover three additional areas. Thus the tenth point directed nationalization of water resources for better conservation, research, and judicious use. The eleventh point called for an extensive program for urban and rural reconstruction. The twelfth point, also of long-standing interest to the shah, prescribed an administrative reorganization and revitalization of government agencies. Under this final point came the overhaul of the Civil Service Code and the emphasis on decentralization and the development of local institutions, increasingly urged by the shah in 1969 and 1970 (see ch. 6).

The twelve-point program became more inclusive in 1975 with the addition of such subjects as the expansion of the industrial ownership base (thirteenth point); price fixing, improvement of the distribution system, and antiprofiteering measures (fourteenth point); additional measures for free education (fifteenth point); provision of free baby food up to the age of two (sixteenth point); and social security for all Iranian citizens, especially for rural inhabitants (seventeenth point). The first two of these additions were announced in August 1975 and the remainder in December 1975.

The Royal Family
Courtesy Embassy of Iran

In October 1976 the shah declared that a new or second phase in his revolution had begun; this pronouncement was coupled with his emphatic exhortation to the people to rise to the challenge of achieving a great civilization through more hard work and more sacrifice. Coinciding with this development, the shah had a lengthy interview with the editor of the leading Iranian daily newspaper, *Kayhan*, during which he revealed his concern about the general state of affairs in the country. Robert Graham, Middle East correspondent for the *Financial Times* (July 25, 1977), quoted the shah as saying: "We have not demanded self-sacrifice from people. Rather we have covered them in soft cotton wool. Things will now change. Everyone shall work harder and shall be prepared for sacrifices in the service of the nation's progress." The usually insightful correspondent also reported:

> This was the first real indication that the carefree party atmosphere of the past three boom years, when oil revenues seemed to have the necessary alchemy to solve all Iran's problems, was now past history.

> The shah hammered home the point that oil alone enabled the Government to subsidise food prices, provide free education, the trappings of a welfare state—and one day in the not too distant future this oil would run out. Unless people were prepared to work harder, produce more, and pay higher taxes, there would be nothing to replace oil.

The second phase was envisaged as a period of austerity. It would hopefully bear witness to a more effective campaign against corruption, waste, and inefficiency; the Iranian scene was described by Graham as follows:

> Everyone has been taking as much as they could get out of the system—bribes, commissions, cheating the Government on taxes, minor fiddles and big swindles—and giving very little in return. No one really cared, except the few harassed officials and individual businessmen concerned that there was a labour shortage, that money had been wasted on frivolous projects, that important plants were a year behind schedule. Some businessmen themselves preferred not to look to the future but transfer profits to bank accounts in Switzerland, houses in London, flats in the South of France, or farms in California.

In early November 1976 the shah issued a decree establishing a special imperial commission to monitor performance in all sectors of the economy and to expose glaring instances of waste and inefficiency. Among the problems that the high-powered commission was told to investigate were: waste in the agricultural and industrial subsectors; eliminating congestion in ports; more rapid educational development; identifying causes or shortcomings relating to some unfinished development projects; remedial steps to cope with deficiencies in cooperatives and rural affairs; improving social insurance and health insurance measures; and the need for a comprehensive and more effective program to deal with the shortage of electricity.

The seriousness of the shah's resolve to alter the endemic mood of distrust toward officialdom and to cope with the pressing problem of urban population was underscored on August 17, 1977, when two more points were added to the program of the Shah-People Revolution. The eighteenth point directed that the government should take steps to ensure within three years that the rise in urban land prices not exceed the annual rate of inflation. Some countermeasure was considered urgent in view of rising urban housing costs amounting to as much as 60 percent of wages. The nineteenth point directed "all senior Iranian civil servants" to declare on specified dates "all assets belonging to them, their wives, and their dependent children." It stated that the use of official positions for personal gains had no place in Iranian society.

Political Orientation

The political orientation of the Iranian people—from the shah at the top down to the grass roots—continued in the late 1970s to display the aspects of both old and new Iran. These two aspects were complementary in some ways and incongruent in others. For years the shah has sought to minimize the area of incongruity that he believed was obstructing Iran's march toward modernity. As he has expressed it, modernization is not only imperative as an end in itself but as a means of elevating Iran to a state of grandeur "as great as that of any of the most advanced nations of today." He is determined, in his words, "to put an end to all the social inequalities and all the factors which caused injustice, tyranny and exploitation, and all aspects of reaction which impeded progress and kept our society backward." What the shah seeks to accomplish is the construction of "a new society" that is uniquely Iranian in form and in substance. The shah-people revolutionary program continues to reflect his resolve to accelerate the transition from old to new. From all indications this transitional process will continue under the shah's absolute direction. Paradoxically tradition will militate against this process as much as it will help the shah compress it.

The old norms and attitudes concerning public affairs had featured the simple expectation that the monarch and the government would provide the services of public protection and order in a feudal society. In exchange, royal absolution had been accepted, passively, by the people throughout the centuries, as long as these benefits were maintained. The government and its officials, however, were usually associated with taxes, arbitrary impositions, exploitation, and foreign influence and consequently were to be avoided as much as possible. The government was at best mistrusted as a vehicle through which the powerful wealthy families furthered their personal aggrandizement in consort with their highly placed relatives and friends in Tehran. The distance between officialdom and the masses was formidable, and as a result the people had little or no expectation that the ruling class would initiate any change or reform for the benefit of other than the members of the power elite. Indifference and acquiescence became deeply rooted.

The monarchy was the principal focus of identification for most Iranians in traditional times. The shah was popularly viewed, regardless of parochial attachment to ethnic and regional separatism, as the ultimate embodiment of authority and power. He was a father symbol known to most remote villagers and tribesmen. Thus familiarity with the traditional role of the monarchy was the strongest political common denominator when Reza Shah came to the throne in 1925 and continued to be so in the 1970s. The shah serves as a bridge or link between traditional and modernizing Iran.

In the 1970s this link was especially pronounced in the traditional political norms or values accentuating the absoluteness of authority. The shah inherited a political legacy whereby his effectiveness depended on unqualified obedience to and compliance with his authority. The severity of authoritarianism was tempered somewhat by the shah's effort to cast himself in the role of a benevolent father and teacher and by his effort to reach out to the people. The shah was religious in his conviction that with the judicious application of his 'moral power' he could lead the nation to greatness "without having to rely on totalitarian measures or to wait for slow evolutionary processes to achieve his aims" of modernization.

The shah held the view that, with an enlightened leadership, the weight of tradition would not necessarily be an obstacle to progress. The wisdom of this thinking was confirmed partly in the continued stability Iran enjoyed under his highly personalized and activist leadership. This stability, however, had weaknesses spawned by the innocence of tradition. The preponderance of the monarch as the focus of power and decisionmaking and the ritualized adoration that surrounded the personality of the shah were so overwhelming that, for most Iranians, nothing else seemed to matter insofar as the object of political identification was concerned. Not surprisingly, intermediary institutions between the government and the people remained relatively underdeveloped. Efforts were under way after 1975 to interest the citizenry, in affairs of state through active involvement; the absence of spontaneity, however, underscored the staying power of traditional indifference. The widely shared mood of mistrust toward bureaucrats as a whole remained unabated.

In the 1970s loyalty, law and order, discipline, hard work, and participation were among the most frequently and most strongly emphasized tenets of political education conducted in the shah's Iran. These values were to be realized according to the needs, temperament, and tradition of the Iranian people. The term *westernization* was not in general use, nor was the concept of democracy accepted without qualification. The Iranian leadership would rather substitute the term *industrialization* for *westernization* and continued to insist that Iran had its own democracy, one that they claimed was superior to that found in advanced Western nations. During an interview with an Italian journalist in October 1973, the shah was emphatic in his statement that he would not want any part of democracy if that democracy meant freedom of expression and representation as they were found among Western nations. This point was made in order to underline the importance of discipline, control, and commitment as critical ingredients not only in leadership but also in the political orientation of the citizenry.

* * *

Given the fact that the single most dominant political phenomenon of Iran is identified with Mohammad Reza Pahlavi, *Mission for My Country* (1960) and *The White Revolution of Iran* (1967), both authored by the shah, should engage the attention of all students of Iranian affairs. The shah-centered Iranian political elites and political processes are the subjects of analyses by political scientists James Alban Bill and Marvin Zonis in their seminal studies, *The Politics of Iran: Groups, Classes and Modernization* and *The Political Elite of Iran,* respectively. Among other useful readings are: Rouhollah K. Ramazani's "Iran's 'White Revolution': A Study in Political Development" in *International Journal of Middle East Studies* and Nikki R. Keddie's "The Iranian Power Structure and Social Change 1800–1969: An Overview" in *International Journal of Middle East Studies.* Robert Graham's contributions to *The Financial Times* on the Iranian political scene in the 1970s provide a synoptic yet insightful view of the society, as does Richard T. Sale's "Shah's Vision of Progress Clashes with Iran Reality" in the *Washington Post.* Hassan Mohammadi-Nejad's "The Iranian Parliamentary Elections of 1975" in *International Journal of Middle East Studies* provides a glimpse of the Rastakhiz Party in action. For a chronology of political events in Iran, the *Iran Almanac* published annually in Tehran may be consulted. (For further information see Bibliography.)

Chapter 8. Foreign Relations

AS THE DECADE of the 1970s drew to a close, Iran had attained a position of international respect and a stable pattern of foreign relations. Factors contributing to the country's favorable foreign policy milieu included sustained internal political stability under the shah, rapid economic development, changing relationships among the major powers, and most of all Iran's status as a major producer and exporter of oil. Domestic stability made for continuity in the direction and structure of foreign relations; tangible gains in efforts to compress the process of transition from backwardness to modernity tended to generate confidence in Iran's capacity to shape its own future in an uncertain world; the importance of peaceful coexistence as a basis for relationships between superpowers also had its ripple effect on Iran's increasingly pragmatic bent in external affairs; and the country's oil resources gave the shah a powerful instrument with which to influence the course of foreign interactions to Iran's advantage.

During the 1970s Iran's principal concern in foreign relations was focused, as it had been in the two preceding decades, on its ties with the Soviet Union, its neighbor to the north and an historic overland threat to Iran's territorial integrity, and the United States, with which the country had a mutual security agreement. With these superpowers Iran had cordial and cooperative relations especially in the economic and technological fields. Equally important, however, Iran's major external concern was centered on its relationships with its immediate neighbors in the Persian Gulf area. The security and stability of the area was considered in Tehran a matter of overriding national interest that should be safeguarded through the collective action of littoral states. Iran's concern about the security of the gulf area has been especially evident since Great Britain, the traditional stabilizing influence in the region, withdrew its military forces from the Persian Gulf by the end of 1971. In practical terms this concern has been translated into the shah's determination to build up and strengthen Iran's own defense posture and into his readiness to respond to any destabilizing situation in the gulf region. As a corollary, in 1972 the shah's "security perimeter" was extended to the Indian Ocean with the acquisition of port facilities for the Iranian navy in Mauritius. This development lent substance to the shah's resolve to play a leading role as a regional power in the Middle East and as a littoral state of the Indian Ocean.

By the mid-1970s it had become clear that the shah attached growing importance to the need for the development of nuclear technology. This was born of the realization that the country's conventional energy resource, oil, would be seriously depleted by the end of the century; hence the need for an alternate source of energy. Emphasis was on the peaceful use of nuclear technologies.

Cooperation was under way with the United States, France, and the Federal Republic of Germany (West Germany), among other countries, to find a new and comprehensive approach to nuclear energy compatible with the needs of nonnuclear nations.

Framework For Foreign Relations

Principles

Government statements of principles and policies, especially since 1963, have stressed that Iran has entered a new era of independent national policy in international relations. The enunciated principles on which foreign policy is to be based are: support of the United Nations (UN) and its role in peaceful settlement of international disputes; peaceful coexistence and cooperation with all nations regardless of sociopolitical differences; rejection of war as an instrument of statecraft; preservation of peace, including efforts to ban nuclear tests, to establish zones free from nuclear weapons, to use nuclear energy for peaceful ends, and to effect universal disarmament; regional cooperation; removal of gaps between rich and poor nations; the eradication of illiteracy, disease, and hunger; and strengthening defense forces for protection of Iran's territorial integrity, pending effective universal disarmament.

Evolution

Since 1900 foreign relations have evolved through successive phases in which policy objectives had to be geared to internal capabilities and the realities of regional and international situations. From the start an underlying, twofold goal has persisted: to maintain national identity and to attain independent national action.

From 1900 to the immediate years after World War II the conduct of foreign relations principally involved accommodation between the intrusive great power influence of Great Britain and the Soviet Union (Czarist Russia before 1917). This accommodation included an effort to find a third force to help maintain the balance and prevent the further loss of power or territory or even the possible loss of national identity. The principal third powers to which Iran turned were Germany, before both world wars, and the United States, as exemplified in the economic administration missions before and after World War I (see Rise of the Qajar Dynasty, ch. 2). The minimum goal was attained; the country was never subjected to a colonial status. But when Iran emerged from World War II and from the Soviet intrusion in Azarbaijan in 1946, it was so weakened as to make independence of action unrealistic. The postwar years were characterized by a defensive foreign policy that nevertheless benefited from a complex combination of diplomacy and of external as well as internal events to forestall postwar Soviet objectives.

After World War II there emerged three distinct schools of thought concerning the country's foreign policy direction. The

Ceremony at the tomb of Reza Shah the Great
Courtesy Embassy of Iran

first of these, identified with the shah and his advisers, endorsed alignment with the United States and the West; the second, represented by the Tudeh (Masses) Party, favored alliance with the Soviet Union; and the third was associated with the political elements collectively known as the National Front, which, under the leadership of Mohammad Mossadeq, called for nonalignment.

The nonalignment view of Mossadeq was strongly influenced by the country's experience in the preceding 150 years of being caught between Russian imperial expansion in the north and Great Britain in the south. Proponents of nonalignment maintained that a close association with the West would simply result in the United States replacing Great Britain in Iran, as British imperial power declined after the independence of India in 1947. When Mossadeq became prime minister in 1951 he continued to speak of nonalignment, but foreign policy attitudes were increasingly phrased in terms of xenophobic nationalism, directed in particular against Great Britain. The objective of the National Front and of Mossadeq was nationalization of the oil industry and of the Anglo-Iranian Oil Company. Nationalization legislation was passed by the Majlis (the lower house of Parliament) on March 15, 1951, and subsequently carried out by Mossadeq with results that, by 1953, were economically disastrous (see Oil Industry, ch. 10).

The decade after the political victory of the shah and his royalist military supporters over Mossadeq in 1953 reflected the shah's full control of power over both internal and external matters (see ch. 6). Since 1953 all lines of policy and major features of its implementation have centered on the monarch. During the 1953-63 period foreign policy was essentially defensive, the overriding objective being to ensure the internal processes of political consolidation and economic recovery.

These processes were aided substantially by alliances with the West, together with extensive United States economic and military aid that had not been received in like measure in Mossadeq's time. The shah's policy, however, did not place exclusive reliance on the West in general or on the United States in particular. Simultaneously he undertook the delicate task of maintaining correct relations with the Soviet Union, eventually improving them. Iran's pragmatism was grounded historically in its experience of interactions with foreign powers; it took into account the prevailing international situation at any given time and considered the realities of the country's capabilities and resources.

By the early 1970s Iran's international position had been transformed from its early dependency and defensiveness to one of self-confidence and independence. Its improved national position resulting from domestic economic growth and political stability enabled Iran to support a more assertive policy, especially in the Persian Gulf and in regional Middle Eastern affairs.

Administration of Foreign Affairs

In the government's conduct of foreign relations perhaps the greatest asset has been the country's extensive natural resources, notably petroleum and natural gas. Enormous oil revenues have enabled it to develop considerable capabilities; by the late 1970s a relationship of interdependence had been established with all industrialized nations in economic fields as well as in weapons procurement. Moreover the Iranian government has used financial aid as an instrument of external policy in dealing with both developing and industrialized nations and international organizations.

Another major factor in Iran's perception of its foreign policy environment and of its role in it has been the shah's intensified efforts to build up a strong military force. A powerful defense posture is seen as essential not only for Iran's immediate self-preservation from external threat but also for the security of the Persian Gulf and other areas including the Indian Ocean. The shah has stated that Iran's security is directly linked to the security of the Persian Gulf and that his government would therefore be prepared to give military assistance to any regional country requesting it.

The decisionmaking process in foreign policy, like other government policies in the country, is centered on the shah. Any change in Iran's orientation in international affairs must be decided by the shah, as must any major foreign policy decision. The shah frequently takes direct part in international negotiations by going on state visits to various countries and receiving important persons on their visits to Tehran. He also is known to offer his good offices for arbitration in some cases. Because of the role that the shah plays in foreign affairs, the position of foreign minister is of less importance than some other portfolios in the cabinet. Apart from the shah, Empress Farah Diba and Princess Ashraf Pahlavi, twin sister of the shah, are also active in foreign affairs as emissaries of goodwill and friendship.

The several hundred career officers of the Ministry of Foreign Affairs hold positions of prestige in society and are drawn from the higher levels of the well-educated political and social elite. They serve under the foreign minister, who is assisted by one deputy minister and several undersecretaries each with specific areas of responsibility including political affairs, planning, administration, cultural and social affairs, information, parliamentary affairs, and international and economic affairs. The next level of staff organization includes directorates for area-oriented political affairs involving Europe-America and Asia-Africa, and several functional directorates for administration, economic affairs, consular affairs, coordination, information, and press. These directorates were further divided into geographical subareas and other functional units.

In late 1977 diplomatic relations were maintained with more than 120 nations, of which about one-half were served by resident missions. Representation was less in Southeast Asia, Latin

America, and Africa than in the Middle East and Europe. The importance that the Iranian government attaches to foreign relations was evidenced in part in the sharply increased expenditures for the Ministry of Foreign Affairs. The budget for fiscal year (FY—see Glossary) 1976 was four times the amount appropriated for FY 1968.

Iran and International Organizations

Iran was a member of the League of Nations and is a charter member of the UN. It belongs to all its specialized agencies and has been active in the deliberations of the political, economic, social, and humanitarian committees and agencies of the world organization.

Iran has demonstrated a keen interest in furthering the political, economic, and social objectives set forth in the Charter of the United Nations. It has consistently supported measures to deal effectively with such issues as nuclear nonproliferation, disarmament, decolonization, illiteracy, human rights, the status of women, peaceful settlement of disputes between nations, and international terrorism.

The Iranian government takes great pride in its active interest in seeking to eradicate illiteracy and to end all forms of discrimination against women. In 1965 it contributed US$700,000—the equivalent at the time of one day's military spending—to the United Nations Educational, Scientific and Cultural Organization (UNESCO) to combat illiteracy. Most closely associated with Iran's efforts to improve the status of women throughout the world has been Princess Ashraf, who headed the Iranian delegation to the annual session of the UN General Assembly in the 1970s. She was Iran's chief delegate to the International Women's Year Conference in Mexico City in 1975.

Another source of pride, evident in frequent official pronouncements, has been Princes Ashraf's—and Iran's—interest in the field of human rights. In 1968 the First International Conference on Human Rights, commemorating the twentieth anniversary of the Universal Declaration of Human Rights of the United Nations, was held in Tehran. In December of that year Senator Mehrangez Mancherian, the president of the Women Lawyers International Association, received an award from the Human Right Commission of the United Nations; in 1970 Princess Ashraf was elected chairman of this thirty-member body, succeeding the French Nobel Prize winner, René Cassin. The princess also has been her country's official representative to the Human Rights Commission in the 1970s. She reflects the view of the shah that the human rights charter, noble as it is, may vary from country to country in practical application.

For years Iran wanted to see the UN play a constructive role in the establishment of what it called "a new international economic order," that is, an order envisaged as one in which the countries producing raw materials receive better prices for their products and achieve a more favorable position in the economic balance in the world. Its interest in the world body has been heightened especially since December 1976, when representatives of both industrialized and developing nations meeting in Paris to reach an equitable and reciprocal basis for economic and trade relations failed to produce any satisfactory results. The Iranian government apparently holds the view that, given the failure of the so-called north-south dialogue, efforts to bridge the gap between developed and developing countries should be pursued more actively through the United Nations Conference on Trade and Development (UNCTAD). Essentially the aspirations of the developing nations, with which Iran identifies itself for the moment, to a fair international economic order can be fulfilled only when there is a more productive north-south dialogue. According to the Iranian government the dialogue should focus on four major areas: the establishment of new principles and rules for rational, efficient use and conservation of the world's natural resources; the need to restructure the world trade system to ensure market stability and to improve the terms of trade for the developing nations; reform in the international monetary system; and greater assistance by advanced, industrialized nations for the developing, poorer nations.

As a major oil producer and exporter, Iran is a founding member of the Organization of Petroleum Exporting Countries (OPEC), made up of Algeria, Ecuador, Indonesia, Iraq, Kuwait, Libya, Nigeria, Qatar, Saudi Arabia, United Arab Emirates (UAE) and Venezuela; Gabon is an associate member (see Appendix B). This organization has a board of governors, a secretariat, and an economic commission. Its mission is to coordinate petroleum policies among the member countries and to generally safeguard their oil interests. OPEC conferences are held at least twice yearly. Iran has maintained the position in the 1970s that oil should not be used as a political or economic weapon against consuming nations and that the pricing of oil should be linked to the fluctuations of industrial and manufactured commodities from advanced nations. In view of the lingering effects of recession caused by the 1973–74 oil crisis on industrialized nations, which in turn depressed oil demand in 1976 and 1977, the Iranian government expressed the view in 1977 that a temporary freeze on oil prices might be necessary. The shah himself underscored the need for a temporary freeze in 1978 after his talks with President Jimmy Carter in Washington in mid-November 1977.

Relations with the United States

The arrival of two missionaries from the United States in 1829 marked the first reported contact with Americans. But it was not until 1851 that official efforts were undertaken to formalize relations between Iran and the United States, and then more than thirty years passed before the first American diplomatic mission was established in Tehran in 1883. The principal motive of the United States before 1900 was to protect the interests and lives of the increasing number of American citizens living in Iran, mainly as missionaries, who were instrumental in the early development of missionary schools and hospitals.

During World War II the United States, for the first time, became actively involved in Iranian affairs. In the immediate postwar years it supported Iranian resistance to continued Soviet troop presence in the north of the country and Soviet sponsorship of the separatist movements—in Mahabad and in neighboring Azarbaijan—centered in Tabriz (see World War II and the Azarbaijan Crisis, ch. 2). This support reflected the international tensions of what came to be known as the cold war. After the political crisis of 1953 that culminated in the overthrow of Mossadeq, emergency financial aid was made available by the United States and was followed by extensive programs of economic and military assistance. By 1953 it was evident that the United States had replaced Great Britain as the nation of primary importance in Iranian foreign policy.

Iran became linked with the West militarily in 1955 through what was formally known as the Pact of Mutual Cooperation (sometimes called the Baghdad Pact) but was renamed the Central Treaty Organization (CENTO) in 1958 after Iraq withdrew from the pact (see ch. 2). The United States did not officially join CENTO but is represented by an "observer" delegation at all ministerial meetings and participates in the work of various standing committees; in fact its military representative serves as the head of the combined military planning staff of the organization (see Defense Mission and Operations, ch. 13).

The legal basis for the United States-Iran defense link is the bilateral defense agreement that the two countries signed in March 1959. This pact commits the United States to take "such appropriate action, including the use of armed forces, as may be agreed upon" in the event of attack against Iran—subject to the Constitution of the United States. For its part Iran is obligated to use military and economic assistance for the purposes intended in preserving its independence and integrity. This agreement may be terminated by either party through written notice one year in advance.

The United States also extended such assistance as sales of surplus agricultural commodities and technical assistance for economic development. Because of the substantial progress achieved by Iran in the 1960s United States economic aid was terminated in November 1967, as was United States military grant assistance. In 1977 the United States remained, however, the principal supplier of Iran's military imports and continued to maintain a large advisory group (see Foreign Influence, ch. 13).

Relations between Iran and the United States deepened also in the economic and trade areas. Mutual interests were promoted through a Joint Commission on Economic Cooperation set up in November 1974. Also actively involved in the expansion of trade and cooperation between the private sectors of the two countries were the United States-Iranian Chamber of Commerce seated in Tehran and the United States-Iranian Business Council. The result has been a sharp increase in the level of participation by private American firms in the development of Iran's economic and social infrastructure. Cooperation was also evident in the mid-1970s in educational and cultural areas. Roughly fifty American universities were assisting in one form or another Iranian educational and public institutions. As of mid-1977 there were approximately 60,000 Iranian students enrolled in various colleges and universities in the United States. In 1977 the number of American citizens working in Iran in various areas totaled about 31,000.

Relations with the Soviet Union

Relations with the Soviet Union have been of particular interest since medieval times and have been increasingly so since the modern era. Throughout the nineteenth century Czarist Russia extended its political authority over various territories north of the present-day boundaries of Iran. Russia invaded Iran twice in the twentieth century and twice allied itself with separatist movements in the northern parts of the country. Since 1946, however, the Soviet Union has not attempted an overt campaign to establish its authority over any part of Iran. It did try to use the Tudeh Party to gain influence in the central government, but its success in this endeavor has been extremely limited because of the severity of the government crackdown on party members (see ch. 12). Soviet efforts to influence the direction of internal and external policies of Iran has included clandestine radiobroadcasts directed to Iran.

In the years after the failure of the Soviet effort to annex Iranian Azarbaijan in 1946, relations with the Soviets fluctuated widely. Moscow did not welcome the overthrow of Mossadeq in 1953 but was apparently ready in 1954 to improve ties with Iran by agreeing to delimit the boundaries between the two countries. In 1955, however, Soviet tactics changed after Iran's decision to commit itself to the Western bloc by joining the Baghdad Pact. Hostile propaganda broadcasts against the shah's government were stepped up, and the Soviets asserted the right to invade Iran if they felt threatened by a Western military alliance based in Iran.

The shah made a state visit to the Soviet Union in 1956, during which he assured the Soviets that Iran would not accommodate hostile bases. During 1957 and 1958 three agreements were negotiated between the two countries: the boundary commission set up in 1954 completed its work, and a protocol defining the frontier from Turkey to Afghanistan was signed; an agreement for joint use of the waters of the Aras and Atrak rivers for irrigation and electric power was negotiated; and an agreement was reached on the question of transit between Iran and the Soviet Union.

After the military coup of 1958 that caused Iraq's departure from the Baghdad Pact, the Soviet government saw an opportunity for decreasing Western influence in the Middle East. It offered a new nonaggression pact in exchange for Iran's rejection of the CENTO alliance. Ensuing negotiations were unsuccessful and were broken off in February 1959. Iran responded to Soviet pressure by concluding a bilateral defense agreement with the United States in March 1959. During the next several years relations with the Soviet Union were cool.

Iranian-Soviet relations began to improve in September 1962 when Iran declared that it would not allow offensive anti-Soviet missiles to be based on Iranian soil, one objective of the Soviet negotiators during the abortive talks in early 1959. In October 1962 an Iranian cultural mission went to the Soviet Union, and in November the transit accord that had been negotiated in 1958 was finally signed in Moscow. In the following month the instrument of the border agreement reached in 1957 was exchanged. The Soviet government also sent economic and technical experts to Iran to discuss the issues of frontier water resources, fishing, and trade.

In January 1966 Iran concluded an agreement with the Soviet Union for supply of natural gas beginning in 1970; in return the Soviets offered to advance economic credits, build Iran's first steel mill complex at Isfahan, and provide other development facilities, as well as construction equipment for a pipeline from the northern part of Iran to the Caucasus. This agreement set the tone of growing economic and technical cooperation between the two countries in later years. Cooperation was also evident in another area: in August 1973 the two countries signed an anti-hijacking agreement. Under this accord hijackers of civilian airplanes were to be extradited on request regardless of their motive. In late October 1976 Iran returned a Soviet pilot who had flown a light plane across the border in the previous month and had requested political asylum in the United States. Shortly after that two of the Soviet-financed clandestine radio stations broadcasting in Farsi (or Persian as it is commonly known outside Iran) were reported closed down.

Further evidence of economic cooperation was a US$3 billion five-year barter agreement reached between the two nations in mid-October 1976. Additionally a protocol was signed in December for economic and technical cooperation whereby the Soviet Union would provide assistance for construction in Khorasan Province of an industrial park said to be one of the world's largest. The Soviet Union also promised at that time to assist in the expansion of the Aryamehr steel mills in Isfahan.

In 1977 the degree of satisfaction expressed by the shah over Iran's economic and technical ties with the Soviet Union was not readily apparent in noneconomic affairs. There were nagging suspicions in Tehran that the Soviet Union continued to support, albeit indirectly, the anti-shah and anti-Iranian aspirations of the outlawed Tudeh Party. Soviet support of Marxist rebels in the Dhofar Province of neighboring Oman and the Soviet naval buildup in the Indian Ocean were among other sources of Iranian apprehensions over Soviet intentions toward the Persian Gulf in general and Iran in particular. The shah was also believed to be concerned about the possibility that the Soviet Union might be using Cuba as an instrument of its interventionist policy in Africa and elsewhere.

Regional Relationships

Turkey, Pakistan, Afghanistan, and India

Relations with Turkey, Pakistan, Afghanistan, and India in 1977 were amicable and without dispute over any major issues. Interchange with Turkey and Pakistan took place not only bilaterally but also within the framework of CENTO and the Regional Cooperation for Development (RCD). Afghanistan and India were not members of these regional arrangements, and relations with them continued on a bilateral basis.

CENTO is based on the Baghdad Pact between Turkey and Iraq signed in Baghdad on February 24, 1955. The treaty consisted of eight articles whereby the contracting parties agreed to cooperate for mutual security and defense, to refrain from interference in each other's internal affairs, to receive applications from other states desiring membership, to form special agreements among themselves that might be useful for implementation, and to set up a government council at ministerial level. Great Britain acceded to the pact on April 5, 1955; Pakistan, on September 23; and Iran, on October 12. The United States did not become a full member but joined the military, economic, and countersubversion committees as an active participant; the pact also established separate bilateral mutual defense relations with Iran, Turkey, and Pakistan in 1959. Iraq, after the coup of July 1958, renounced the pact. Headquarters were then shifted from Baghdad to Ankara.

CENTO was an important support to Iran's security during the years after its formation when cold war tensions were high. Military planning and joint exercises were carried out, and developments in the transportation and communications infrastructure were undertaken. As major cold war tensions eased after 1962, however, the original rationale for the alignment was seen by government spokesmen to diminish. The failure of CENTO powers to intervene on behalf of Pakistan during the Indo-Pakistani war of 1965 also contributed somewhat to Iran's disenchantment. Nevertheless in 1977 Iran remained a member, and the organization itself remained prepared to take an active role should the international situation so warrant. In May 1977 the Iranian government hosted the twenty-fourth session of the ministerial council of CENTO, at which time the treaty members and the United States reaffirmed their resolve to contribute to the peace, security, and stability of the CENTO region. The ministers accepted the invitation of the United States to hold the next session of the council in Washington in early 1978.

As the military and political needs underlying CENTO appeared to diminish, Iran, Turkey, and Pakistan established the RCD in July 1964 in order to promote economic, trade, and cultural relations. The RCD was charged with responsibility for the promotion of free movement of goods through trade agreements; the eventual establishment of a joint chamber of commerce; the initiation of joint development and construction projects; the improvement of rail and road links; the promotion of tourism; and the exchange of students and cultural missions and related projects.

Among the recent steps taken to promote cooperation among RCD members was a declaration of intention, issued in the Turkish city of Izmir in April 1976, to set up a free trade zone and to increase cooperation in tourism and financial and economic areas. In March 1977 the foreign ministers of the three nations formally signed an agreement, known as the Izmir Pact, providing for the creation of a free trade zone and the establishment of a regional development bank and a technology college in Tehran. The RCD administrative secretariat is located in Tehran.

Iran's relations with Afghanistan were friendly as evidenced in increasing economic and technical cooperation between the two countries. In March 1973 the two nations reached an agreement on sharing the water in the Helmand River basin area: when the agreement came into effect in 1977 it put an end to this ancient dispute. The river lies mostly in Afghanistan but flows into a basin area in Iran, and the Iranian government long contended that upstream dams to be constructed by Afghanistan would reduce the water available to Baluchestan va Sistan Province (see fig. on administrative divisions, ch. 6). The 1973 accord would ensure the flow of a fixed quantity of water to Iran throughout the year. In May 1975 when Afghanistan's President Mohammad Daud Khan visited Tehran, the shah offered, as he had done in 1962, to mediate a dispute between Afghanistan and Pakistan over the long-standing problem of Pakhtunistan. At that time the two heads of state discussed the possibility of a Meshed-Kabul railroad link. The two countries are connected by a highway through which Afghanistan has access to the Persian Gulf at the port of Bandar Abbas.

With India there is no common boundary, but both have a strong if potentially competitive interest in political and economic regional affairs. During much of the 1960s relations with India were strained. Iran, linked with Muslim Pakistan in both CENTO and the RCD, tended to sympathize with Pakistan in its dispute with India over Kashmir as was the case during the Indo-Pakistani hostilities of 1965. Differences also were evident with regard to Middle Eastern policies in which India, having neither de jure nor de facto relations with Israel, supported the Arab cause more definitely.

Relations began to improve after the shah's visit to India in January 1969. In a joint communiqué the two countries expressed support for UN Security Council Resolution 242 of November 22, 1967, calling on Israel to withdraw from territories occupied in June 1967. More important, however, the communiquè contained former Prime Minister Indira Gandhi's endorsement of the shah's position that peace and security of the Persian Gulf was the responsibility of the littoral states and that outside powers should keep out of the gulf region. Iranian-Indian ties have become perceptibly cordial since Gandhi's return visit to Tehran in April 1974, at which time the two nations reaffirmed their view that major powers should keep out of the Indian Ocean and that the ocean be declared a zone of peace. The visit also marked the beginning of close economic cooperation between the two countries.

Iraq

The pattern of power rivalry in the Persian Gulf remains unchanged between Iran and Iraq, but the two countries have maintained cordial ties since they normalized their relations in 1975. Cordiality was made possible as a result of settling the dispute over the boundary at the Shatt al Arab waterway (see fig. 1).

The border with Iraq, extending southward from the junction with Turkey, was demarcated in 1914. The southern terminal area was described in the frontier treaty negotiated between Iraq and Iran under British auspices in 1937. This treaty specified that at the head of the Persian Gulf in the waterway known as the Shatt al Arab or, in Farsi, the Arvand Rud, the international boundary should lie in part at the low water mark on the Iranian side, thus leaving the Iranian petroleum shipping site at Abadan with less sea-lane than the channel median line would have provided.

These provisions had long been a source of contention between the two countries, Iran insisting that the 1937 treaty had been imposed on it by "British imperialist pressures" and that it was in violation of common international practice. The shah's government claimed as the proper boundary the thalweg line. The issue came to a head in 1969 when Iraq in effect told the Iranian government that the Shatt al Arab was an integral part of Iraqi territory and that the waterway might be closed to Iranian shipping. Almost immediately two Iranian vessels supported by naval elements traversed the waterway; they met no Iraqi interference. Neither, however, did Iraq indicate a willingness to abandon the 1937 treaty and negotiate a new one.

Diplomatic relations were severed by Iraq in December 1971, the Iraqi government charging clandestine Iranian complicity in a plot to overthrow the Iraqi government. Iran denied the accusations. In the wake of some forty executions in Iraq, the Iranian press denounced the neighboring government as attempting to divert attention outward in order to conceal its own weakness. Nonetheless the two countries reestablished formal relations in October 1973 in order to present a united front against Israel during the Arab-Israeli war. The facade of unity was shattered, however, in early 1974 when the two countries clashed in a border dispute.

Through Algerian mediation Iran and Iraq agreed to normalize their relations in March 1975 and signed a border treaty three months later in Baghdad. The treaty defines the common border along the Shatt al Arab estuary on the basis of the thalweg line based on depth. It also specifies land frontier lines to run according to maps worked out for the 1914 border agreement. The normalization pact also includes mutual commitment to the prevention of sabotage from either side of the border. Almost immediately the Iranian government withdrew its support from the Kurdish separatist movement inside Iraqi territory, and many of the Kurdish leaders were reported to have fled to Iran.

Under the 1975 agreement Iran and Iraq also pledged to address the problem of displaced Iranians and Kurds. The Iranian government would help resettle about 97,000 Kurdish refugees in Iran if they refused to return to Iraq. For its part Iraq agreed to consider compensation for the property of some 65,000 Iranians who had been expelled through the mid-1970s.

The Persian Gulf States

On December 18, 1968, Great Britain declared that it did not "intend to maintain commitments in this part of the world [the Persian Gulf area] after [its] withdrawal is concluded by the end of 1971." This statement had been preceded by a similar announcement on January 16, 1968, when British Prime Minister Harold Wilson disclosed plans to cut defense expenditures sharply and to withdraw forces from east of Suez including the Persian Gulf. The British commitments included matters of foreign policy and military presence or controls varying in degree and, as of January 1968, involved Kuwait, Bahrain, Qatar, the seven princely Trucial Coast States, and the Sultanate of Muscat and Oman.

The announcement was received with alarm in many countries and dependencies where for decades the British had been the key stabilizing factor. For his part the shah grew apprehensive about the possibility of a politicomilitary vacuum in the Persian Gulf region once the British forces withdrew. On January 27, 1968, the shah expressed Iran's readiness to cooperate with any littoral state to ensure the security and stability of the region. This readiness was born of the realization that the vital sea-lanes passing through the Strait of Hormuz and the security of the approaches to the Persian Gulf should be safeguarded if only because Iran's trade and oil export depended on uninterrupted use of these sea-lanes.

In a significant effort to clear the way for a favorable regional environment, Iran in 1970 relinquished its historical claim to Bahrain; the issue was settled peacefully through the framework of the UN. Equally significant, relations with Saudi Arabia, Iran's biggest neighbor and rival on the gulf littoral, improved steadily; this was especially true after October 1968 when the two countries concluded a continental shelf agreement regarding the seabed rights in the Persian Gulf. In this accord Iran's claim to the island of Farsi and Saudi Arabia's sovereignty over the island of Al Arabiya, both in the middle of the Persian Gulf, were recognized.

The 1968 agreement set the stage for continued improvement of relations. In January 1972 the two countries signed their first agreement to undertake joint economic and industrial ventures. In April 1975 the shah visited Saudi Arabia to cement mutual relations; this visit was returned by King Khalid in May 1976. Among the topics discussed was the issue of joint security in the Persian Gulf. Evidently there was no agreement on the issue; the shah at that time expressed the view that if the littoral states of the gulf failed to agree on common security, Iran would defend the gulf area alone. Observers suggested at the time that rivalries among Iran, Saudi Arabia, and Iraq for dominance in the area might be at the root of the continued disagreement on gulf security.

Relations with other littoral states were cordial. Warmth was lacking, however, in relations with the UAE, known until 1971 as the Trucial Coast States or the Trucial Shaykhdoms. The source of lingering strain was the Iranian occupation in November 1971 of the islands of Abu Musa and the two Tunbs islands, all of which are strategically located astride the narrow entrance of the Strait of Hormuz and hence regarded as vital to the protection of Iran's lifeline. Iran and the UAE reportedly reached an unspecified working arrangement over the disputed islands to which the shaykhdoms of Sharjah and Ras al Khaymah, two of the seven areas of the UAE, and Iran had historical claim.

The seriousness with which the shah views the security of the Persian Gulf and of the approaches to it was unmistakably clear as early as 1972. At that time, at the request of the Sultan of Oman, the shah sent military assistance including helicopters and pilots to Dhofar Province to help pacify guerrilla rebellion festering there since the mid-1960s. More military help was sent there in 1973 and 1974, the shah declaring that his country could not survive the presence of any hostile forces close to the entrance to the Persian Gulf. The task force of Iranian troops had grown to about 3,000 by the end of 1976; but in January 1977 it was announced in Tehran that many but not all of the Iranian troops were being withdrawn from Oman because "calm" had been restored. In May 1976 the shah stated that if Iranian troops had not intervened in Oman, Dhofar Province "might have become another Angola."

Other Arab States and Israel

Relations with Arab states outside the Persian Gulf area were generally cordial. The main bonds are geographical association in the Middle East and the cultural and religious ties of Islam. The principal area of difference in 1977 continued to lie in Iran's attitude toward Israel, with which de facto political and commercial relations have existed since 1960. At that time Egypt's President Gamal Abdul Nasser unilaterally broke diplomatic relations with Iran without notice. In the years after 1960 the shah consistently maintained that relations with Egypt could be restored at any time in the same manner they were broken—that is, through action initiated by Egypt. Relations began to improve gradually after the Arab-Israeli conflict of 1967. By early 1970 negotiations were under way, mediated by Libya, for resumption of ties between the two nations, and in January 1971, after Nasser's death, Egypt and Iran formally normalized diplomatic relations.

Iran is a Muslim country but not an Arab country or a member of the League of Arab States (Arab League) and therefore is not bound by the determinations of the league. An Israeli aid-and-trade technical mission is located in Tehran, and about 50 percent of Israel's oil imports come from Iran. Iran buys some manufactured goods from Israel and has air transport connections. Israel has expressed a desire for formal diplomatic relations, which Iran has declined, along with any other form of formal political or military commitment.

Iran has consistently backed the UN Security Council Resolution 242 of November 22, 1967, calling for Israeli evacuation of occupied territories and has voted for unimplemented UN resolutions calling for the return or compensation of the Palestinian refugees. However, it has resisted Arab requests that it cut off oil shipments to Israel and sever all other connections. Iran supports a peaceful solution but without total victory for either side. In June 1967 the shah stated, "Although we have never concealed our sympathy toward the Arabs, we could not elude our firm belief that no country has a right to threaten another with extinction." And in May 1976 when King Khalid paid a visit to Tehran, the shah said that the existence of Israel was a "reality" and that the Arab countries should recognize the Jewish state in return for Israeli withdrawal from occupied territories.

In October 1973 Iran backed the UN Security Council Resolution 338 of October 22, 1973, adopted in the wake of the Arab-Israeli war, which called on all parties involved to terminate military activity and to seek a basis for enduring, permanent peace. In September 1975 the Iranian delegation to the UN reaffirmed its position that Israeli forces should be withdrawn from territories occupied in the June 1967 war, including Jerusalem, that the legitimate rights of the Palestinian people should be reinstated, and that all parties in the Arab-Israeli confrontation should be guaranteed the right to survival.

In March 1977 Iran and Egypt, in addition to reaffirming their familiar positions on the Arab-Israeli situation, agreed that a Geneva peace conference should be reconvened with the participation of all parties concerned including the Palestinian Liberation Organization. They also condemned Israel's policy of settling Jews in the occupied territories. Among other agreed points were that the Middle East should be declared a nuclear-free zone; that the peace and security of the Indian Ocean should be the principal responsibility of the littoral states; and that outside powers should keep out of the region. In November 1977, after Egyptian President Mohammad Anwar as Sadat made a dramatic visit to Israel, the Iranian government lauded the president and extended full support to his courageous peace initiative.

* * *

This chapter is based on information and analysis found in the numerous sources listed in the bibliographical section. The following works were particularly useful: Peter Avery's "The Many Faces of Iran's Foreign Policy" in *New Middle East* (1972); *The Foreign Relations of Iran: A Developing State in a Zone of Great-Power Conflict* (1974) by Shahram Chubin and Sepehr Zabih; Alvin J. Cottrell's *Iran: Diplomacy in a Regional and Global Context* (1975); and Rouhollah K. Ramazani's *Foreign Policy of Iran, 1943-1974* (1975). (For further information see Bibliography.)

Chapter 9. Character and Structure of the Economy

A KEY TO understanding the economy as well as aspects of social and political life in Iran in the late 1970s is the determination of its leaders to modernize. Some observers attribute the motivation to develop to the desire of Shahanshah Mohammad Reza Pahlavi to elevate Iran to a position in the world similar to its past periods of greatness. Others see the motivation as the shah's effort to aggrandize his current position and ensure his place in Iranian history. Still others see the intense effort to develop as a natural response to the poverty and difficult life so long the condition of the vast bulk of the population. To these observers the probability that oil revenues will begin to diminish in a few years adds urgency to the efforts to modernize. Perhaps all of these reasons contributed to the leaders' determination to raise Iran's economy to the current level of Western Europe by the 1980s.

Modernizing the economy is not a new goal. The first efforts began in the early 1800s when attempts to introduce more modern production techniques resulted in the import of skilled workers and equipment from Europe (see ch. 10). These and subsequent efforts had barely discernible effects even after 100 years. By the 1920s there were only a handful of relatively large and modern plants, producing such simple commodities as textiles, bricks, and flour. The bulk of the population was still engaged in subsistence agriculture, cultivating in the same manner and probably on the same land as their great-great-grandfathers (see Traditional Land Tenure and Farming System, ch. 11). Urban areas were few; the population was dispersed and transportation primitive. Production of nearly everything was geared to small, local markets. Production of crude oil was the exception. Modern techniques, modern management, and modern transport moved ever-increasing quantities of oil to international markets, but the oil industry remained largely a foreign enclave with little initial impact on the domestic economy. During the first century of effort social, political, and economic conditions were not favorable to economic development.

A more systematic and comprehensive development effort began in the 1920s after the founding of the Pahlavi dynasty. The handicaps to modernization centered on the aridity of the land. Only a small part could be cultivated—where rainfall was adequate or irrigation water could reach. Great distances of difficult terrain separated areas under cultivation, making commercial farming or distribution of other products difficult and costly. People existed in isolated pockets of relatively small groups. Perhaps a quarter of the population were nomadic tribesmen who were largely a law unto themselves. Unifying and modernizing a population under such circumstances—changing their economic, political, and social customs and mores—is expensive, difficult, and time-consuming at best. At worst, there are prolonged periods of revolution and anarchy as groups contend for power. Economic development requires political stability for a number of reasons. The two Pahlavi shahs have sought to maintain peace and stability while instituting far-reaching economic, political, and social changes.

The country has as assets in its effort to alter the economic structure a sizable population (over 3.4 million in 1977) and an assortment of natural resources as a base for modern industry. Many of the resources were newly discovered and barely exploited. There are commercial deposits of iron ore, coal, nonmetallic minerals, and nonferrous minerals, particularly copper, the reserves of which appear large and rich. Most important the country has large deposits of natural gas, some claim potentially the world's largest, and crude oil. The oil deposits were large, but they have been exploited since 1908. Unless important new fields are discovered, oil production should soon stabilize and begin to decline about the mid-1980s. By the early 1990s domestic consumption will about match production, leaving little or no oil for export (see ch. 10). By 1978 the production and export of oil had provided a significant and increasing source of revenue in foreign currencies to help finance modernization of the economy. Oil exports should continue to be an important source of revenues through the 1980s. Oil revenues, unlike the returns from most export industries in developing countries, accrue to the government, providing the leader a key instrument for influencing the pace and direction the economy takes.

By 1978 more than half a century of economic development had wrought tremendous changes. Change, as is often the case, had been uneven geographically and in terms of groups of people, however. The accomplishments so far and the problems remaining to achieve a level of living comparable with present-day Western Europe comprise the remarkable and challenging story of Iran's economic development.

Growth of the Economy

Many observers have noted the considerable growth and change in Iran's economy since the 1920s. Then the population was largely illiterate and impoverished, ekeing out an existence from a semifeudal agricultural system and handicrafts. By late 1977 Iran ranked fifteenth among noncommunist countries in terms of gross national product (GNP), and per capita GNP amounted to about US$2,200. Assessing the growth with any precision over the last half a century is impossible, however, because of the lack of statistical data in the early years.

An Iranian economist calculated that GNP was about 5 billion rials (for value of the rial—see Glossary) and that per capita GNP was approximately 500 rials (equivalent to about US$50) in 1926. If this latter figure is compared with the official (preliminary) estimate of per capita GNP of 140,000 rials (approximately US$2,000)

Copper bazaar, Isfahan

in fiscal year (FY—see Glossary) 1976, the average increase was about 17 percent a year (in current prices) above population growth. This is an exceptionally high rate of growth and casts some doubt on the accuracy of the early calculation, but it suggests that the rate of growth was substantial.

The first official estimate of GNP was made in the early 1960s for FY 1959. The estimate of GNP amounted to 284 billion rials compared with 4,040 billion rials in FY 1976 (in current prices), an average rate of growth of nearly 17 percent per year. Measuring economic growth in terms of current prices includes price inflation also. The rate of growth of GNP in terms of constant prices was 9.4 percent a year over the same period. Measurement in terms of constant prices in this instance is unsatisfactory, however, because it eliminates the tremendous increase of revenues the country received for oil exports in the 1970s. The jump of oil prices provided an increased command over resources; it was a very favorable swing in the terms of trade and should be incorporated in evaluating real economic growth. A completely satisfactory statistical solution for measuring growth for the ecomony in real terms (eliminating normal price inflation) for Iran or other Organization of Petroleum Exporting Countries (OPEC) does not exist for the 1972–75 period when the price of energy rose dramatically (see Appendix B). The general conclusion about the period between FY 1959 and FY 1976 is that real growth of the economy was appreciably higher than 9.4 percent a year and considerably less than 17 percent a year but still substantial over a sustained period.

Economic growth tended to accelerate as new investment added to the output of goods and services, but there were fluctuations around the trend. The period in the early 1950s after nationalization of the oil industry temporarily halted oil production was particularly depressed. Although World War II was disruptive, the local purchases and promotion of various services by Allied forces stimulated economic growth. Since 1959 gross domestic product (GDP) increased consistently although slowly in the early 1960s in the aftermath of a boom period in the late 1950s. GDP increased an average of 10.1 percent a year between FY 1962 and FY 1967 in current prices (9.8 percent in constant prices) compared with 17.1 percent a year between FY 1967 and FY 1972 in current prices (11.4 percent in constant prices). The increase of GDP between FY 1973 and FY 1975 averaged a phenomenal 41 percent a year in current prices because of the tremendous increase in the price of oil.

Not all groups or regions have shared equally from economic growth. Rural inhabitants (amounting to 47 percent of the population in the 1976 census) had per capita incomes in the early 1970s in the neighborhood of two-fifths of the national average and one-fifth of those of urbanites. The rural population had far less access to schools, health care, electricity, piped water, and other facilities. In part this was a regional disparity. Many farmers in areas favored by heavier rainfall, basically the northwest and north central parts of the country, had incomes above the national average from such crops as rice, oranges, tea, and tobacco. Population density was usually greater in the wetter areas, facilitating the provision of such services as roads, schools, and health clinics. The population in more arid regions was dispersed, frequently isolated by lack of roads, and without much change in their way of life or standard of living from that of their forefathers. Per capita incomes in some of the regions and among some nomads ranked with the very poor in other developing countries.

In 1977 urban dwellers as a whole had higher incomes, a better variety of goods including food, urban amenities, educational opportunities, and more social mobility. Nearly two-thirds of the urban population was ranked as middle class in 1971, a very large increase from the period before World War II. Cities provided a powerful attraction to the poorer segments of the rual population, and migration continued in 1977. The responses to a survey on the causes of rural migration to urban centers by an Iranian agency were interesting, however. More than two-thirds of the responses in 1964 concerned jobs; but in 1972 only about one-fourth concerned jobs and about two-thirds indicated a move to urban centers to join family members. Nonetheless there was a substantial number of quite poor urban dwellers, about one-third of the urban population in the early 1970s. Some had no jobs and were supported by relatives. Construction work and employment in small manufacturing shops, with relatively low pay and long hours, were where new arrivals, the illiterate, and the chronically poor were employed.

Urban areas had not shared equally in the growth. Tehran and nearby towns had benefited the most from development of industry, transportation, and other services. Incomes were higher, and living was generally better in Tehran. Some urban areas, mostly oil centers and cities in East Azarbaijan and Gilan, were closer to conditions in Tehran and better off than the other cities and towns in benefiting from economic development.

The aim of the Pahlavi dynasty had been to achieve equity in the benefits of development. Numerous measures have been instituted, many entailing far-reaching social changes, but equal development had not been achieved by 1978, in part because of the magnitude of the task. Building roads linking all villages of a dispersed population and placing schools, clinics, electricity, and other facilities in them, for example, could not be accomplished unless other important projects were sacrificed. The government has aroused expectations, however. Some observers have noted during the 1970s that Iranians appeared more concerned with what they think they should have and less in comparing their conditions with what others have. At some point in the future the government may have difficulty meeting the rising expectations of the population (see ch. 7).

Structural Change

Growth of the economy wrought major shifts in its structure. The pace of structural change was slow at first. The increasing flow of oil revenues first stimulated the expansion of government and the import and distribution of foreign consumption goods. Reza Shah, after unifying the country, involved the government in building roads, railroads, and industrial plants and extended such services as health and education. The fast growing sectors with higher paying jobs attracted workers to government employment and to construction, trade, transport, and the oil industries. Because many farmers came to urban centers to increase their incomes, the migration created demand for housing, services, and consumer goods. New growth sectors emerged, such as manufacturing and utilities. Changes in the structure accelerated along with growth.

By FY 1959 the economy was much more diverse. Instead of contributing the bulk of the economy's output as in the 1920s, agriculture's share of GDP was only 30 percent. The oil industry contributed 16 percent of GDP; manufacturing (including mining, water, and power), 11 percent; transportation and communications, 10 percent; government services, 8 percent; domestic trade, 8 percent; and construction, 5 percent. A number of sectors contributed the remaining 12 percent of GDP (see table 6, Appendix A).

By FY 1975 the oil industry, manufacturing, and government services each contributed more to GDP than agriculture. The value added by the oil industry surpassed that of agriculture in FY 1969, that of manufacturing (including mining, water, and power) in FY 1973, and that of government services in FY 1975. The rapid increase of oil prices in the 1970s quickly made the oil industry's share of GDP very large. Other sectors may also become more important than agriculture in the future.

The slow growth of the agricultural sector became measurable in FY 1959. Between FY 1960 and FY 1970 the value added by agriculture (including livestock, forestry, and fishing) increased at an average rate of 4 percent a year in constant prices (5.9 percent a year in current prices), just above population growth. Between FY 1970 and FY 1975 the agricultural sector grew at an average rate of only 2.1 percent a year in constant prices (15.8 percent a year in current prices), less than population growth. As a result, when urban incomes rose rapidly in the 1970s and more food and a wider variety were needed, imports had to increase rapidly. The country switched from one largely self-sufficient in foods to one heavily dependent on imports.

Many factors contributed to the slow growth of agricultural output. In the 1970s inadequate moisture and primitive cultivation techniques were still important restraints on increased farm output (see ch. 11). The lack of roads and adequate transportation kept production in some farming areas from progressing beyond

Pahlavi Dam across the Dez River in the southwest
WORLD BANK PHOTO *(Ray Witlin)*

the subsistence level. Land reform, when it broke up the source of wealth and political power of large landowners, disrupted the economic organization in the countryside, which had not been adequately replaced by cooperative organizations by 1978.

The government had undertaken many measures to help agriculture. In particular large dams and irrigation projects had been initiated, and large-scale farming (agribusiness) had been promoted. The agribusinesses, many with foreign investors and management, may become successful in the future. The combination of agribusinesses and the larger, more productive farms could begin to accelerate the growth of the agricultural sector in the late 1970s. Whether farm production accelerates will depend in part on government price policy. Before 1978 the government had been more concerned with the cost of food for urbanites, keeping the price low for equity and perhaps political reasons. Desirable as this may have been for a large part of the population, it undercut efforts to stimulate agriculture, the source of income for about half the population.

By FY 1975 the oil and manufacturing industries together accounted for just slightly less than half of GDP. The oil industry was no longer a foreign enclave but largely a government-controlled operation, and manufacturing was a rapidly expanding sector, promoted by government investments and policies (see ch. 10). Growth in manufacturing (including mining, water, and power) averaged 12.7 percent a year in constant prices (13.4 percent a year in current prices) between FY 1960 and FY 1970. Between FY 1970 and FY 1975 manufacturing value added increased by an average of 17 percent a year in constant prices (26 percent a year in current prices). In FY 1975 employment in manufacturing for the first time exceeded that in agriculture. About 40 percent of manufacturing employment was in the textile industry; food and furniture production were large employers also. The oil industry increased at an average rate of 6.8 percent in constant prices between FY 1960 and FY 1975, but the growth in terms of current prices, about 24 percent a year, was closer to the real growth because it took into account the real increase in command over resources provided by the rise in the price of oil.

Emphasis on development of the petroleum and manufacturing industries might create problems in the future because neither employed many workers where modern, capital-intensive technology was used. In 1975 total employment in the petroleum industry amounted to about 90,000 workers and in manufacturing about 3.5 million people. In 1977 the economy suffered a labor shortage, requiring thousands of expatriate technicians and many imported workers. If the population continued its high rate of increase, there could be a time when creation of jobs became important although the shortage of skilled workers and technicians was expected to persist for several years. Much would depend on developments in other sectors, particularly agriculture, and how fast skills improved in the domestic work force.

Construction activity has been a small but important portion of the economy, accounting for about 8 percent of GDP in FY 1975. The rate of growth averaged 11.2 percent a year in constant prices (22 percent a year in current prices) between FY 1960 and FY 1975. Residential construction, however, lagged considerably behind demand.

Until the 1970s housing construction was largely left to the private sector, which concentrated on medium- and high-cost dwellings. The concentration on expensive housing partly resulted from high land and construction costs and insufficient credit. Purchasers of dwellings often had to put down 40 to 50 percent of the total price and pay off the balance usually in ten years. This situation limited the number and kind of residences built. The housing shortage of the 1960s became acute in the early 1970s. In FY 1972 there were about 1.9 million urban dwellings for approximately 2.6 million households, with lower income groups suffering the most.

In the early 1970s, in the face of the increasingly serious shortage, the government began public housing projects and various measures to promote private building. Contracts were let to foreign firms to supply materials and labor and to build 500,000 housing units. Plants to build prefabricated houses and to produce building materials were ordered from abroad. Public land was made available for housing projects; speculative real estate transactions were curbed; and financial resources were increased for credit institutions that made loans for residential construction. Budget allocations for housing increased, reaching the equivalent of US$1.3 billion in FY 1976.

Between 1973 and March 1978 a total of over 1 million housing units were to be constructed. By late 1977 it was unclear whether the housing goals had been met, but most observers reported an acute housing shortage even for high-cost dwellings. Various factors, including shortages of building materials in the oil boom years and a greater than expected influx to urban centers of rural and foreign workers, may have contributed to the housing shortage, but a continuing deficiency between the housing needs and the residential units available appeared a likely prospect for the future.

The service sector was quite large, accounting for 34 percent of GDP and employing about 30 percent of the labor force in FY 1975. Government was the most important service, contributing 10 percent of GDP in FY 1975. In that year there were about 313,000 government civil servants, the bulk of whom were teachers employed in education. The civil service increased by an average of 28,000 employees between FY 1968 and FY 1972. In late 1976, as a result of the shah's edict to reduce waste of human and material resources, government departments began cutting back staffs as much as 25 percent. Some experts claimed there were about 20,000 unnecessary jobs in the government. Figures were not available to indicate how seriously government employment might be cut, but if the Iranian bureaucracy was like its counterparts in other governments, the number of civil servants would not diminish much.

Transportation and communications, a service subsector contributing 4 percent to GDP in FY 1975, had a long history. Twenty-five centuries ago Cyrus II developed a highway and a form of pony express extending from the Iranian capital to the Aegean Sea to expedite communications in the empire. Unfortunately little improvement took place after that. By the twentieth century, transportation and communications lagged seriously behind development in other countries. Concessions to foreigners in the late 1800s and early 1900s gave some impetus to modernizing transportation and communications, but extensive development essentially started in the 1930s. An expensive catch-up effort began. Funding for transportation and communications increased from the equivalent of US$677 million in FY 1974 to US$1.2 billion in FY 1976, yet there were deficiencies in 1977.

The catch-up effort in transportation was difficult and costly because of the size of the country and the rugged terrain. Most emphasis was given to linking the major population centers and economic areas by rail and road, the main arteries of which formed a squiggly T pattern with the crossbar extending from the northwest corner to the northeast along the lower edge of the Caspian Sea (see fig. 1). The vertical ran through Tehran down to the Persian Gulf. By 1977 the railroad extended southeast to Kerman, and roads and air travel linked much of the country.

The southern link of the T between Tehran and the gulf was the most intensively used transportation corridor, accounting for half of all road and two-thirds of all rail traffic. This leg handled considerable domestic traffic to and from the southern industrial and population centers as well as much of the foreign trade. About three-fourths of the country's international commerce passed through the Persian Gulf ports of Khorramshahr, Bandar Shahpur, Bushehr, and Bandar Abbas. Khorramshahr, the best equipped and most important port, primarily handled private sector trade. Bandar Shahpur was largely the port of entry for government imports. These ports were linked to Tehran and the rest of the T by rail and road. The remainder of the foreign trade largely passed through road and rail links with Turkey and the Soviet Union in the northwest corner and via two minor ports on the Caspian Sea.

During the oil boom years of the mid-1970s imports increased greatly and exceeded the capacity of the transport system. Neither the ports nor the transportation system leading away from the ports could handle the volume of goods. As a consequence long lines of ships stacked up, some waiting months to unload and adding more than US$1 billion a year to freight costs. Considerable waste resulted in terms of goods that spoiled, extra charges that were required for freight to Iran, and disruptions to production and construction schedules. Priority was given to expansion of port and transportation facilities. By 1976 the six major ports had a capacity of 12 million tons with expansion projects under way that would increase capacity to 29 million tons by 1980. By late 1977 unloading delays at the ports were essentially cleared up although it was not certain whether the piled up goods around the ports had been delivered to the purchasers.

By late 1977 the transportation system had advanced considerably from the 1920s when pack animals carried imports from the gulf to the capital, but much remained to be done. The capacity of the most heavily used portions of the main road network was to be expanded and feeder roads extended to open up the many isolated agricultural areas to commercial farming. Plans were drawn to double-track and electrify part of the railroad system and to extend the system, including additional connections with neighboring countries; the system would have its first links with Afghanistan and Pakistan.

The government-owned and -operated telecommunications facilities expanded rapidly after the early 1960s as a result of accelerating investments. By 1978 a substantial part of an integrated national telecommunications system had been constructed by a consortium of international firms. There were more than 550 microwave stations in an 11,000-mile network covering a large part of the country. Transmission capability included telegraph, television, and data communications. The system had international links to many parts of the world via satellite and other connections. In addition the National Iranian Radio and Television Organization had some television transmission and relay stations that reached about 60 percent of the population in 1977 although far fewer received television broadcasts (there were an estimated 1 million sets in March 1976) probably because the sets were costly. Eleven towns had computerized telex facilities and telex links to major countries.

The major criticism of the telecommunications system came from the public who could not get telephones. In early 1977 there were about 800,000 telephone lines, nearly double the number five years earlier when there were about 150,000 customers waiting as long as two years for a telephone. The increase of incomes and business activity increased the demand for telephones, making it doubtful that the number wanting a telephone had diminished by 1977. The government was steadily expanding facilities and planned to increase the number of lines to 2.2 million by early 1982. Most exchanges were direct dial, and local manufacturers produced a considerable amount of the telecommunications equipment.

Banking System and Monetary Policy

Modern banking and insurance came late to Iran but, protected and stimulated by the government and expanding economic activity, they became one of the fastest growing parts of the economy. The value added by banking and insurance increased at an average rate of nearly 19 percent in constant prices between FY 1960 and FY 1975 and accounted for 6 percent of GDP in FY 1975. Banking was the primary activity; the insurance industry was barely started and played a negligible role in accumulating funds to finance development, largely because life insurance and other forms of insurance were little used by the bulk of the population.

Before the modern era credit was available only from non-institutional lenders such as relatives, friends, wealthy land-owners, and the moneylenders of the bazaar. Interest rates were usually high to exorbitant. In 1977 these noninstitutional sources of credit were still active, particularly in the more isolated rural communities where they might still be the only source of credit. Institutional banking had spread rapidly since the late 1960s, however, and by 1978 almost all small towns were served by at least one bank.

Modern banking arrived in 1888 with the opening of a branch of a British bank. This bank was taken over by a second British bank, the Imperial Bank of Persia, founded in 1889 by Baron Paul Julius von Reuter, who had obtained the first oil concession in Iran. The Imperial Bank concession permitted it to issue paper currency as well as conduct commercial business. Because of British-Russian competition a Russian bank was established in 1891. After the 1917 revolution the Soviet government took over ownership, and in 1977 it was the only bank with more than 50 percent foreign ownership—actually 100 percent Soviet owned. A few additional foreign banks were established. Before the 1920s the governments borrowed from foreign banks, and a substantial public debt accumulated.

In 1925 the government established the first Iranian bank, subsequently named Bank Sepah, using accumulated retirement funds for military personnel. In 1928 Bank Melli Iran (National Bank of Iran, also fully government owned) was established. It became the government's bank and undertook central bank functions, including note issue and regulatory tasks. Gradually Iranians replaced the expatriate staff. At various times departments have been split off from Bank Melli to form new banks.

Entry of foreign banks was effectively curtailed between 1926 and the 1950s and local banks encouraged. Some socioeconomic characteristics of Iranian society held investors back before World War II, however, and only government banks were established. The first private Iranian bank, Bank Bazargani Iran, was founded in 1949 and grew into one of the five largest banks. Subsequently several more Iranian banks were established, some with minority foreign participation.

By the late 1950s the need for a central bank was apparent. Bank Melli was overburdened with commercial banking, government bookkeeping, enforcing foreign exchange laws, and regulating banking and credit. Moreover commercial banking and central banking functions conflicted. Therefore legislation was enacted creating a separate central bank.

In 1960 Bank Markazi Iran was established as the central bank. Later legislation further defined its powers and responsibilities. The bank had responsibility for note issue and authority to control variables affecting the value of the currency; it acted as banker for the government—keeping accounts, marketing government securities, maintaining foreign exchange reserves, and overseeing international transactions; it set standards for and supervised financial institutions; it established credit and monetary policies; and it had authority to take a variety of measures to enforce credit and monetary policies. The laws also limited foreign participation to 40 percent in any Iranian bank (except the Soviet bank formed much earlier); subsequently the central bank limited foreign ownership in a new bank to 35 percent.

By 1977 the banking system consisted of the central bank, twenty-four commercial banks, twelve specialized banks, and three savings and loan associations. The commercial banks had more than 7,400 branches including a few in other countries. All towns had at least one banking office, permitting the banks to mobilize savings throughout the country. The specialized banks mostly focused on a particular kind of lending—e.g., industrial or agricultural loans, although three regional banks specialized in financing local development projects. In addition some seventy foreign banks (primarily from the major industrial nations) had representative offices in Iran, but they could conduct no local banking business; their purpose was to smooth trade relations.

At times the idea had been broached that Iran should become an international financial center because of the country's stability and facilities. Urgency was added by the civil war in Lebanon in the mid-1970s and the virtual demise of that center. Substantial legal changes would be required, however, which would reduce the government's extensive influence on the country's financial affairs. In 1976 the head of the central bank said changes to convert Iran into an international center in the foreseeable future were unlikely. Instead the authorities would concentrate on developing domestic banking and local financial markets to meet the needs of the expanding internal economy.

Commercial Banks

The banking system was highly concentrated, controlling about four-fifths of the financial assets in the country. The commercial banks accounted for more than one-half of the total assets in the banking system, the specialized banks for about one-tenth, and the central bank for the remainder. Deposits with commercial banks increased considerably, from the equivalent of about

US$750 million in 1963 to about US$18 billion in January 1977. The increase was particularly rapid after the oil boom and was concentrated in time and savings deposits. The commercial banks lent primarily to the private sector for generally less than a year. A substantial part of commercial bank lending financed domestic and foreign trade. Commercial banks played an important role in short-term financing for agriculture but extended little consumer or housing credit.

The country had a comparatively large number of commercial banks, but five dominated the rest, accounting for 75 percent of total deposits and 70 percent of commercial loans in FY 1976. In terms of assets Bank Melli was by far the largest with 546 billion rials of total assets, nearly 29 percent of the assets of the commercial banking system. It had about 1,600 branches in Iran and in foreign countries and acted as the central bank's agent outside of Tehran. Bank Saderat, a privately owned bank, had assets of 348 billion rials and 2,900 branches. The three other large banks were Bank Sepah, Bank of Tehran, and Bank Bazargani Iran. Bank Melli and Bank Sepah were government owned. Only the Bank of Tehran had foreign participation.

Specialized Banks

Specialized banks were formed to channel credit to particular areas in the private sector in which the commercial banks were reluctant to become involved. In 1977 there were three banks specializing in long-term development financing for industry, two for agriculture, two for construction, two for housing, and three for regions. The government owned some of the banks and actively encouraged the others. Their source of funds was largely from the government, from share capital, and from borrowing, almost exclusively from abroad. A few accepted deposits or had other contributory sources from which to lend.

The specialized banks usually made loans for several years and in some cases became part owners in projects. The government set the interest rates and kept them at concessionary levels to encourage private sector activity. Lending by the specialized banks was highly concentrated in FY 1975, 56 percent going to industry and 29 percent to agriculture, leaving only 15 percent for all other activities.

The largest and most active of the specialized banks was the Industrial and Mining Bank of Iran (IMDBI), which was owned by domestic shareholders and twenty-two foreign institutions. It primarily financed large private industrial projects, and 95 percent of its financing had been for over five years. IMDBI financing in FY 1975 amounted to 88 billion rials compared with 270 billion rials of credit by all the specialized banks.

Overview

The Iranian banking system was relatively well developed. Through branch offices it was able to tap funds scattered in various parts of the country and channel them into investments. The government had extensive influence through formal regulations, government ownership, and treasury funds to control the amount of credit and direct it in desired directions. There were problem areas, however, which the authorities were attempting to remedy.

Development of banking had been rapid, and the individual parts had yet to meld. Some groups, basically small industry and agricultural investors, lacked access to credit facilities because they fell in between the gaps in the fractured structure. Banks themselves, again mostly smaller ones, suffered because of a lack of an active interbank money market where those in need could obtain funds from those that had excess liquidity. The range of credit instruments was small, making it difficult for banks and others to achieve balanced investment portfolios. Banking services had yet to attain the range and sophistication that were available in other countries, partly because bank staffs were not as thoroughly trained.

Monetary Policy and Inflation

Monetary policy aimed at price stability while mobilizing and channeling financial resources into economic development. During the 1960s after establishment of the central bank, substantial economic growth was achieved with remarkable price stability. The official wholesale price index increased only about 17 percent between FY 1960 and FY 1970, an average annual rise of about 1.6 percent. In the 1970s, however, prices accelerated upward. The wholesale price index increased about 9.5 percent a year between 1970 and 1976. The increase was sharpest in 1973 and 1974 when the index increased 11 and 17 percent respectively. Consumer price indexes behaved much like the wholesale price index.

Although Iranian statistics were not as complete or reliable as in more developed countries, they certainly indicated much less price stability in the 1970s than in the 1960s. Critics argued that the rate of price increases was higher than the official index, exceeding 25 percent a year in the 1974–76 period, because the index used official prices whereas many commodities were available only at prices substantially above official prices. The situation was serious enough for an official campaign to halt price gouging by merchants. Officials and critics agreed that prices had risen alarmingly and that inflation imposed severe burdens on the population.

The cause of the increase in prices was beyond the control of the monetary authorities and the central bank. In an economy such as Iran's (other oil exporters and some industrial nations experienced the same phenomenon) where oil revenues accrued to the government, spending those revenues internally had a multiplier effect on the money supply and added to the demand for the existing supply of goods and services. Rapid increases of government expenditures became the primary determinant of the money supply and a major factor in the behavior of prices. When oil revenues rose rapidly in the early 1970s and government expenditures followed, the money supply expanded, increasing by 61 percent in FY 1974, for example. The expansion of government domestic expenditures was the basic cause for the inflation although worldwide inflation and rapidly rising prices for imported goods between 1972 and 1974 added to domestic sources.

A number of measures were invoked to combat inflation. The monetary authorities attempted to minimize the multiplier effect on the money supply by increasing the cost of borrowing and reducing the amount of credit available. Imports were increased by lowered duties, by reduced quantitative restrictions, and by much larger government purchases of foreign goods. Physical constraints at the ports and in other parts of the transportation system limited the ability of imports to satisfy demand, however. Subsidies were increased on basic goods to keep their prices down, and in 1973 a serious price control program was mounted. In 1975 fiscal authorities decided to lower the rate of increase of government expenditures, partly because of inflation and strains in the economy and partly because demand for Iranian oil slackened.

The fight against inflation continued in 1977. Imports remained at a high rate, and physical constraints had eased. The monetary authorities maintained controls on the supply of credit. Most important continued restraint in the growth of government expenditures limited the increase of liquidity and the money supply; in FY 1975 growth of the money supply was 36 percent, and it was expected to have increased slightly less by March 1977. Other monetary indicators also improved. The effect on prices was not discernible, however. The official wholesale price index increased 10 percent between January and June 1977, suggesting that the earlier large increases in liquidity were sustaining a high demand for goods and services. By early 1978 it was not clear how soon inflationary pressures would abate.

International Trade and Finance

Imports afforded the only way to improve conditions for the population. Hence the authorities annually used a large share of the foreign exhange received from exports to purchase goods abroad, such as foods, medicines, and machinery. Imports (excluding military) increased from US$688 million in 1960 to US$12.8 billion in FY 1976, an average increase of about 20 percent a year. Imports accelerated sharply after 1973 (increasing by 77 percent in FY 1974 and 77 percent in FY 1975 because of the large investment program and government imports to fight inflation. Imports increased by about 10 percent in FY 1976.

Imports of intermediate goods primarily for industrial processing and to a lesser extend for construction have been the most important category since FY 1960 (see table 7, Appendix A). Their share of total imports fluctuated because of various factors (accounting for 52 percent in FY 1976), but the trend in absolute amounts has been upward. Intermediate goods will remain a large share of imports into the 1980s because they are required for continued growth in manufacturing and construction. Imports of consumer goods varied over the years, reflecting such factors as the size of harvests, growth of domestic manufacturing, and the amount of foreign exchange available. Consumer goods were 18 percent of total imports in FY 1976. Imports of machinery and equipment gained in importance mostly at the expense of consumer imports, reflecting the government's policy of industrialization.

Imports came primarily from noncommunist industrialized countries, accounting for 75 percent of nonmilitary imports in FY 1976. The Federal Republic of Germany (West Germany) was the largest supplier in FY 1976, accounting for 18 percent of imports, Japan 17 percent, and the United States 15 percent. India and the Republic of Korea (South Korea) were the most important suppliers among the developing countries, accounting for 2 and 1 percent respectively of total imports. Communist countries were minor suppliers, accounting for only 4 percent of Iran's imports in FY 1976.

A primary goal of Iranian planners is to lessen the country's dependence on oil exports, which amounted to about 96 percent of total exports in FY 1976. The magnitude of the task is readily apparent, and urgency exists because oil production will soon stabilize and then begin to decline (see Oil Industry, ch. 10). The rapid growth of machinery imports since the oil boom was partly to develop export industries and partly to produce domestic goods that could replace imports before foreign exchange earnings from oil began to fall. Progress had been achieved in both import substitution and developing export oriented manufacturing, but reaching the goal of non-oil exports on the order of US$40 billion a year in fifteen to twenty years would require tremendous growth. In fact non-oil exports have declined steadily since FY 1973 and amounted to about US$543 million in FY 1976.

The bulk of non-oil exports has been traditional commodities (see table 8, Appendix A). Carpets and cotton accounted for a large portion of non-oil exports and particularly of traditional goods. Cotton has been the most important non-oil export in years of a good crop. In years of a poor cotton crop carpets became more important. Carpetweaving is an important industry, employing nearly 800,000 workers and substantially contributing to incomes in rural areas. About 80 percent of carpet production was exported in the mid-1970s. The traditional carpet industry or its exports were not likely to expand appreciably because of the demand for labor and higher wages in other activities. Most other traditional exports came from the agricultural sector, which experienced slow growth.

Planners counted on the growth of exports of new industrial products to lessen the dependence on oil; they wanted to accelerate the trend that emerged after the early 1960s. Exports of new industrial products grew at a faster rate than traditional exports although they still were of much less importance. Substantially increased exports of industrial products will face two very important hurdles in the future, however. Industrial production will have to be more efficient and competitive in price than it was before 1978. Inflation, and particularly the rapid increase and high level of wage costs since the oil boom, further complicated growth of industrial exports. The second hurdle to be surmounted for exports of industrial products to grow is the willingness of the industrialized countries to purchase more of these products. This has been a constraint on economic development for some developing countries.

The bulk of non-oil exports went to industrialized countries. In FY 1976 West European countries purchased about 37 percent of non-oil exports, communist countries (predominately the Soviet Union and Eastern Europe), 27 percent, the United States, 7 percent, and Japan, 3 percent. Most of the remainder of non-oil exports went to nearby areas, particularly Arab countries on the gulf. Major trade partners in FY 1976 were West Germany, 16 percent; Soviet Union, 15 percent (excluding natural gas); United States, 7 percent; Italy, 6 percent; and Saudi Arabia, 5 percent.

Trade and Exchange Controls

The basis for control of trade and foreign exchange dates from the 1930s when the country was struggling to gain control of its destiny and to find funds for development. Legislation gave the government a monopoly of foreign trade and legal control of foreign exchange balances. Subsequent laws made alterations, but the government retained strong powers.

Although the government exerted considerable influence over trade, it left actual trade operations primarily to private traders. The regulatory system for imports largely consisted of the tariff schedule, a commercial benefit tax, a list of authorized and unauthorized imports, and an annual regulations for trade. The tariff schedule was passed by the Majlis (the lower house of Parliament) and remained in effect over a period of years. The commercial benefit tax was applied to the value of an import and was, in effect, the same as a customs duty. The government set the tax rate for each commodity and thus, by changing rates, altered the effective tariff schedule without waiting for changes in the tariff laws. The list of authorized and unauthorized imports also contained a list of goods that could be imported under specified conditions. The regulatory system for imports gave the government considerable flexibility in adjusting total imports and the composition of imports to the economy's needs and the anticipated foreign exchange earning each year.

Control of imports became less stringent with the passage of time. The initial aim of import controls was to produce revenue. As industrialization progressed, protection of infant industries became an additional objective. During the inflationary period of the mid-1970s, controls were considerably relaxed to encourage more imports. Tariffs and commercial benefit taxes were reduced and sometimes eliminated for needed commodities, and import procedures were made easier. At the same time there was an official awareness of the need to reduce protection of industries relatively well established, but by 1977 it was not clear the extent to which maturing industries had become exposed to foreign competition.

Except for a few products such as petroleum and gas, which were government monopolies, exports were freely permitted. In fact expansion of exports was increasingly encouraged. Incentives included exemption of income taxes on profits from exports, concessionary credit for export industries, refund of all custom duties paid on raw materials used in producing exports, and the provision of services and facilities to help develop foreign markets. By 1977 exports had not responded to policy stimulation to the degree desired by officials nor that needed by the economy.

The central bank exercised control over foreign exchange. Legally it regulated all exchange transactions, but in fact it established rules under which commercial banks handled operations. The rules became progressively more liberal. In January 1974 most of the few remaining restrictions were removed and exchange procedures simplified. Subsequently the rial and major foreign currencies were essentially freely convertible by citizens and foreigners, although the central bank maintained a supervisory role. Unauthorized moneychangers on the streets were illegal but tolerated by the authorities.

Balance of Payments

The jump in oil revenues dramatically altered the balance of payments. Before FY 1973 a consistently favorable trade balance was usually more than offset by the large net service payments (primarily the earnings of the foreign oil companies), leaving a net negative balance on current account (see table 9, Appendix A). Receipts and payments were balanced largely by government borrowing abroad. Borrowing had to increase to stay ahead of debt repayments causing the external public debt to rise during the 1960s and early 1970s. In FY 1973 the increase of oil revenues was sufficient to create the first favorable current account balance in many years, which, with a substantial rise in public and private borrowing, produced a favorable balance of payments and an increase of the country's international reserves.

In FY 1974 and FY 1975 the much higher level of oil revenues permitted Iran for the first time to become a major exporter of capital. Public borrowing was drastically reduced and debt repayment accelerated. Foreign loans with the more onerous terms were repaid ahead of schedule in FY 1974. A foreign aid program was started, and the government began large-scale investments abroad, aid and investments totaling US$2.4 billion in FY 1974 and US$2.9 billion in FY 1975. Even with the outflow of capital, the balance of payments showed a favorable balance of US$5 billion in 1975. The country's international currency reserves increased from US$1.2 billion in 1973 to US$8.4 billion in 1974. By FY 1975 a small decrease in oil revenues, combined with increased imports and larger capital exports, produced a negative balance of nearly US$1 billion. International reserves were US$8 billion at the end of March 1976. By August 1977 reserves had reached US$11.6 billion, a 41-percent increase since the end of FY 1975 because of increased earnings and a sharp reduction of government foreign aid and investments.

Foreign Aid and Investments

Except for a small irrigation project in Morocco in 1967, Iran's aid program essentially started in FY 1974. Large-scale foreign investments started at the same time. By the end of 1976 total aid and investment commitments exceeded US$13.5 billion, of which about US$6.7 billion had already been paid out. Data were not published on the different programs nor on the recipients. Moreover without data on terms it was impossible to distinguish between concessionary loans that qualified as aid, from credits provided as good risk commercial investments, even if the recipient was a developing country. The fragmentary information allowed only partial description of foreign aid and investment.

The major outlines of the aid program were available by late 1974, by which time commitments had reached about US$3.8 billion. Bilateral commitments were made with: Egypt for US$1 billion of which US$250 million was for reconstruction of the Suez Canal Zone, US$400 million was for industrial development, US$200 million was to finance imports, and the rest was for several other projects; India for US$900 million of which US$500 million would cover oil shipments over five years and US$400 million for industrial and mining development in India; and Pakistan for US$643 million of balance-of-payments support and development projects. Bilateral commitments were also made with a number of other developing countries but for much smaller amounts. In addition Iran agreed to provide a US$1.2 billion loan to Great Britain as well as funds to some other developed countries.

Multilateral aid commitments were above US$2 billion to United Nations agencies including the International Monetary Fund (IMF) and the International Bank for Reconstruction and Development (IBRD, also known as the World Bank) by March 1976. The bulk of this aid (US$1.5 billion) was for an IMF oil facility. Iran's commitment to the OPEC Fund was US$210 million in FY 1975.

Relatively little was known about the government's foreign investments or the proportion they constituted of the aid and investment program. Fragmentary information was published occasionally, such as the investments in a West German firm. In 1974 Iran bought 25 percent interest in the Krupp steel works in West Germany, and in October 1976 Iran bought 25 percent of the shares in the overall Krupp holding company, which had 125 subsidiaries and affiliated companies in twenty-five countries. The value of the purchases was not announced. Subsequently agreement reportedly was reached for Iran to purchase part ownership of a Krupp subsidiary in Latin America.

Share purchases in some other large firms, mostly West European, have been reported. In 1975 Iran purchased part of France's interest in a gaseous diffusions plant owned by several West European countries. Negotiations for Iran to purchase part interest in an American airline, Pan American, and an independent oil company, Occidental, reportedly fell through. The purpose of foreign investments varied: in some cases it was strictly commercial, for the rate of return, but in others it was to help meet the country's need for materials, to help in marketing Iranian products abroad, and to help transfer modern technology and management to Iranian industries. Krupp firms, for example, had some projects in Iran, and observers expected that benefits would flow to Iran's budding steel industry and other industries from the Krupp relationship.

Disbursements under the aid and investment program were available only from the budget in lump sums. Expenditures on the program amounted to US$2.4 billion by FY 1974, US$2.5 billion in FY 1975, US$1.5 billion in FY 1976, and US$1.1 billion in FY 1977. The declining amounts reflected the government's increasing financial pinch. The prime minister stated in his budget presentation to the Majlis for FY 1977, for example, that no new foreign aid commitments would be made in FY 1977 but that funds were included to cover payments to Egypt, India, Pakistan, France, and Great Britain based on earlier negotiations.

External Public Debt

Iran's external public debt (obligations over one year) more than doubled between FY 1969 and FY 1975. In March 1976 it amounted to US$7.1 billion of commitments and US$4.6 billion of disbursed credits. Nearly half of the debt committed was owed other governments. Supplier credits amounted to US$1.6 billion, private lenders (largely banks) US$1.1 billion, and international organizations, such as the World Bank, US$909 million. Of the disbursed aid, other governments provided US$2.7 billion, international organizations US$600 million, suppliers US$700 million, and banks US$600 million. The public debt included loans to government companies and agencies, but it was not clear whether credits for defense-related equipment were included.

An estimated repayment schedule of the above debt by World Bank experts projected principal and interest payments of US$1.3 billion in 1976. Debt servicing would slowly decline to about US$880 million in 1980. Even in the year of heaviest repayment, 1976, debt servicing would amount to only 5 percent or less of foreign exchange earnings. Iran appeared a good risk to foreign lenders, and observers anticipated increased borrowing as the country went ahead with some large and costly development projects.

The government, including its subsidiary institutions, borrowed substantial sums after 1975. The two budgets anticipated total foreign credits to amount to about US$2.6 billion in 1976 and US$2.9 billion in FY 1977. There were reports of various loans negotiated including a US$500 million credit to the government that was discussed for nearly a year before it was signed in January 1977. Bank credits alone probably exceeded US$1.4 billion in 1976 and may have amounted to about US$1.5 billion in 1977. Increased use of supplier credits was also reported after 1975. The country's external debt had increased by early 1978 and probably would continue to rise as long as large investments were made in infrastructure, natural gas and petrochemicals, and basic metals. A banker's view of Iran was perhaps reflected in a study by a large international bank that estimated the country's net foreign assets amounted to US$22 billion after the external debt was deducted.

Foreign Investment in Iran

Direct investment by foreign countries in Iran's non-oil sectors has been officially encouraged since the 1950s. Organizations were established to foster direct investments, official guarantees were given against uncompensated expropriation, financial incentives were provided, and legislation was passed to permit transfer of profit and capital abroad. Direct investments totaled 22.5 billion rials (more than US$300 million) between FY 1968 and FY 1975. Japan had provided the most foreign private capital (40 percent), largely because of substantial investments made since FY 1972. Other major investors in order of importance were the United States, West Germany, Great Britain, and France. The major sector of investment was chemicals, including pharmaceuticals and petrochemicals; foreign capital participated in many sectors, however, such as large-scale agriculture, banking, automobile industry, and hotels.

The response of foreign investors was small in terms of the economy's needs, the amount of domestic investment, and the prospects for profitable investments. The size of the market, the improving economy and rising personal incomes, and the official inducements should have appealed to foreign investors. It is not clear why greater amounts of foreign capital did not enter, but some observers suggested it was partly because of conflicts in the government's attitude. While the official attitude encouraged private foreign investors in general, there was considerable nationalistic sensitivity about specifics. In banking, foreign interests were limited to 35 percent, for example, and foreign capital was excluded from some industries. The program, which started in 1975 and required private Iranian companies to sell 49 percent of their shares to the public, further confused foreign investors. The potential existed for greater direct investments, but a more consistent series of signals was needed for the potential to be realized.

Role of Government

In the late 1970s the public sector was large and still growing; the government was a strong force throughout the economy. This happened more by accident than by design and not because of a socialist philosophy and a policy of nationalization. It was an accident that by tradition the government owned those things not owned by individuals. The government assumed ownership of natural resources because nobody else owned them. When oil was discovered the government received payments. It was a fortuitous circumstance that the oil deposits were large, putting ever-larger sums in the government's hands to distribute. It was also accidental that a series of weak rulers, whose courts were corrupt and who overspent and accumulated debts for the country, preceded the age of the automobile and the growing importance of oil (see Rise of the Qajar dynasty, ch. 2).

When Reza Shah became ruler, his aim was to correct the abuses and neglect of the past. He reformed the government, brought the budget into balance, and repaid the country's debts. He also set out to improve conditions for the bulk of the population by building schools, constructing roads, and increasing health facilities. He built up the government in the process because the private sector was unable or reluctant to undertake many of the fundamental tasks. The economic philosophy of Reza Shah and his son who succeeded him (the present shah) has been for the government to do what the private sector could not or would not do and for the government to act as referee to see that benefits were spread among the population. The idea of sharing benefits was a major cause of much of the government's influence in the economy even if a wide disparity remained in the distribution of income and wealth.

In 1978 a government monopoly existed over such natural resources as oil, mineral deposits, water, fishing rights, forests, and grazing lands, and over many industries, such as railroads, airlines, communications, and basic steel, petrochemicals, and copper. The government also had a monopoly on production and/or sale of opium, tobacco products, sugar, and a few other commodities. Some of the government monopolies, such as communications and railroads, were formed in the 1930s in order to establish a national system that the small companies then existing could not undertake. Monopolies in basic steel, petrochemicals, and copper were decreed relatively recently after the private sector failed to develop the industries because of the huge investments (including infrastructure) required. The private sector can and does participate in subsequent levels in these industries, such as producing steel and copper products. The private sector dominates in most of the economy although government firms operate alongside privately owned ones in some of the more modern parts of the economy, such as banking.

The government's economic influence extended far beyond the

impact of the government-owned companies. The government set prices where it had monopolies, such as fuel's and electricity, and also for such other items as credit, rents, basic foods, farm produce, and some farm inputs. The government also regulated various aspects of economic life and provided prohibitions and incentives to encourage changes by the private sector. Much of the government's economic intervention was aimed at achieving the shah's stated socioeconomic goals (see Shah-People Revolution, ch. 7).

The announced objective of the White Revolution (see Glossary) was social justice. Its concern was not so much economic growth itself as a more equal distribution of the benefits of growth. In effect it said every person was entitled to a decent minimum of the essentials of life including education and medical care. Some of the points, such as establishing a social security system, were more easily implemented than others, but nearly all of the points required time to make an impact, particularly such problem areas as raising the levels of literacy and education.

A fundamental part of the revolution dealt with broadening the ownership of the means of production. The land reform program was successful in redistributing estates, depriving a conservative group of their source of wealth and power to frustrate other social and economic changes (see Land Reform, ch. 11). Although increased farm production was not an objective in land reform, greater output probably was hoped for. Land reform favorably altered some of the relationships affecting crop cultivation, but others were adversely affected and combined with the sector's systematic problems to retard growth of agricultural production.

Sale of public businesses and profit sharing for workers were the two original points that pertained to industry. The proposal for sale of state enterprises aimed at broadening the base of industrial ownership, mobilizing part of the funds to finance land reform, and providing investment opportunities to landowners who had sold their estates to the government under the land reform. Of about 200 government businesses (mostly power plants but including the railroad, oil company, and others), fifty-six factories (largely food and textiles) were designated for sale. Ten were purchased outright, and majority ownership shares of three more were sold. It was not clear how many of the remainder were sold, but critics contended that only the profitable ones were sold, and the taxpayers were stuck with the unprofitable plants.

An outgrowth of the program was formation of the Industrial Development and Renovation Organization (IDRO) in 1967 as a government holding company to improve the factories the government could not sell. IDRO went on to become quite active in fostering industrial development. In 1977 two of its projects, requiring investments totaling more than US$4 billion, were industrial parks in which the Soviet Union and the Krupp firm were separately contributing technical assistance.

The industrial profit-sharing plan, as it finally evolved, required firms to set aside a portion of profits not exceeding 20 percent for distribution to its workers. By 1976 about 200,000 workers in 2,000 private firms and 110,000 employees of government-owned enterprises participated. The yearly bonuses varied, and in exceptional cases might amount to three or more months' pay, but most bonuses were much less. It was questionable how much the bonus system contributed to increased productivity and feelings of participation once the novelty was gone.

In April 1975 a thirteenth point was added to the Shah-People Revolution, and was followed by a law in June calling for the expansion of the ownership base. It required sale of 49 percent of the shares of private industrial firms and 99 percent of the shares in public plants (except oil, gas, steel, and copper). Workers in the plants had priority in purchasing shares, followed by other workers and farmers and finally by the general public. A group was formed to designate the large private firms whose shares must be sold, to set the price for the shares, and to supervise the sale. A list of 320 private factories was issued of which 106 firms had to sell 20 percent of their shares by March 1976. Additional sales were scheduled, but the program was to be completed by October 1978. Foreign interests were allowed to retain 15 percent ownership in light industry, 25 percent in a number of other industries, and 35 percent where advanced technology or export markets were concerned.

Financial institutions were established to provide concessionary credit to workers and farmers and to facilitate sales to others. The objectives were to mobilize funds for additional investment, to improve distribution of income and wealth, to increase workers' feelings of participation, and to blur the distinction between workers and management in an attempt to lessen chances of labor problems. By mid-1977 some 220,000 persons had purchased shares in 159 major industrial firms, but the real impact of the program was unknown. The forced selling entailed risks. It might discourage some foreign and domestic private investors. Conversely it might lessen the power and wealth of some family empires that posed a potential challenge to the shah's power, and it might stimulate purchases of shares by a broad section of the population. The program was initiated at a time when real estate speculation was extremely high, and excess liquidity was in the hands of many.

Budget

The central government's budget is the primary tool for influencing the economy. It does not contain all of local government (e.g., provinces, districts, municipalities, and villages) financing, but a large portion of local funding is included because it comes from central government expenditures. Municipalities are the main subordinate jurisdictions with significant although limited taxing powers; they raise some of their own revenues from such sources as property taxes, vehicle fees, and business licenses. The emphasis on administrative decentralization in the mid-1970s indicated that local government fiscal activity might become larger in subsequent years. Even though some local revenues and expenditures were excluded from the central government budget, the exclusion was a minor part of the public sector.

Aside from financial transfers to subordinate jurisdictions, the budget contains revenues and expenditures for a growing number of public commercial and industrial enterprises (at least 50 percent government owned). There were 144 registered state companies in 1976. In addition the budget contained funds for over fifty welfare, cultural, and charitable nonprofit organizations such as universities. The government-owned companies and the nonprofit organizations have their own budgets, only a consolidated summary of which is in the government budget.

Articles and discussions on Iran's budget sometimes include and sometimes exclude revenues and expenditures of public profit and nonprofit organizations, frequently without explicit notation of what has been included. Moreover the central government and many subsidiary agencies borrow funds at home and abroad that are included in total revenues in some information about the budget. In this chapter the focus is on the central government's operations; revenue and expenditures of profit and nonprofit organizations have been excluded, and domestic and foreign borrowing have been treated separately from revenues in order to show means of financing deficits (see table 10, Appendix A). These differences are significant. In FY 1976, for example, total government revenues from all sources including deficit financing amounted to 2,960 billion rials and expenditures to 3,105 billion rials, compared with revenues of 1,744 billion rials and expenditures of 1,791 billion rials when government businesses and public borrowing were excluded.

Budgeting procedures have changed frequently. This improved the value of the central government budget as a fiscal tool and as a planning document but at the expense of a consistent series of statistics that were comparable over several years. Beginning with the establishment of the Plan Organization in 1947 and preparation of development plans, there were two separate budgets. The development budget received a portion of oil revenues (80 percent for many years) to finance development expenditures. The Plan Organization also had authority to borrow at home and abroad to finance development costs. Current expenditures were in the "ordinary budget," which was largely financed by the government's non-oil revenues.

The development and ordinary budgets were consolidated into a single document in 1966, but in effect they remained separate entities until 1973. In 1973 revamped procedures abolished the separate sources of funds for ordinary and development expenses and made a more accurate distinction between current and development expenditures. In addition a significant portion of defense spending was handled differently in 1973 and subsequent years. As a result budget data since 1973 are not strictly comparable to earlier years. Fiscal experts consider the new budgeting system a significant improvement over the previous system.

In 1977 the Plan and Budget Organization retained responsibility for preparation of the budget, relying heavily on the Ministry of Economy and Finance for data concerning current expenditures. It also made many of the decisions about financing, relying on advice from the Ministry of Economy and Finance and the central bank when appropriate. Financial controls over budget transactions were exercised by the Ministry of Economy and Finance. Implementation of budgetary actions was lodged with appropriate operating ministries.

Revenues

Government revenues increased sharply from 53 billion rials in FY 1962 to 302 billion rials in FY 1972, an average increase of 19 percent a year. A still more dramatic increase, to an anticipated 2,145 billion rials, occurred between FY 1972 and FY 1977, an average increase of about 48 percent a year. The tremendous growth of revenues prompted a corresponding jump in expenditures.

During the 1960s oil revenues and non-oil revenues increased more or less evenly, and the share of each hovered around one-half of total revenues each year. In the mid-1970s, however, oil revenues rose extremely fast as a result of actions by OPEC (see Oil Industry, ch. 10; Appendix B). In FY 1970 oil revenues were just marginally less than non-oil revenues, but in FY 1974 oil revenues amounted to 87 percent of total revenues. By FY 1977 anticipated oil revenues had dropped to 65 percent of total revenues in the proposed budget as oil revenues leveled off and tax collections increased. The worldwide economic recession and reduced purchases of Iranian oil by oil-importing countries in the 1975–77 period caused oil revenues to fall below what they would usually have been, however, exaggerating the trend.

During the 1960s Iranian officials focused on increasing non-oil tax revenues, particularly direct taxes on personal and business income. A major reform in the tax laws occurred in 1967 that nearly doubled the yield of direct taxes in two years. The 1967 legislation was complex, containing many definitions, establishing schedules for various kinds of income, and providing a number of exemptions and allowances. The taxes applied to foreign and domestic businesses and individuals. Further legislation in the 1970s increased direct taxes even more sharply and for the first time made direct taxes more important (FY 1975 and FY 1976) than indirect taxes. Direct taxes amounted to about 11 billion rials in FY 1967 compared with 177 billion rials in FY 1976. Direct taxes on businesses (129 billion rials in FY 1976) were far more important than individual income taxes (48 billion rials), and government corporations paid substantially more taxes than private sector businesses.

Like most developing countries Iran traditionally relied on indirect taxes (customs duties and excise taxes) for most of its revenue not associated with oil. Indirect taxes accounted for 72 percent of non-oil tax revenues in FY 1962, 60 percent in FY 1972, and 45 percent in FY 1976. Customs duties and related fees on imports were by far the most important indirect taxes and were the most important single source of non-oil revenues until corporation income taxes increased sharply in FY 1975 and FY 1976. The declining importance of indirect taxes in the mid-1970s was partly the effort to rely on direct taxes and partly reduction of indirect taxes, particularly those affecting imports. Imports were encouraged to fight inflation and reduce protection of domestic industries. Excise taxes were levied on vehicles, petroleum products, alcoholic beverages and soft drinks, telephones, and phonograph records, for example. Imported luxury cars were heavily taxed in the mid-1970s.

Non-oil, nontax revenues increased considerably in recent years, reflecting receipts from government monopolies and businesses and the income from foreign investments. The government tobacco monopoly regularly produced revenue for the government, for example. Income from government companies amounted to 23 billion rials in FY 1976. The return on foreign investments was 18 billion rials. Government sales of goods and services amounted to 17 billion rials in FY 1976, and miscellaneous items accounted for the remainder of nontax revenues.

The flow of oil revenues and particularly the rapid increase in the 1970s freed Iranian officials from the necessity to develop the tax system. As a consequence the tax base was narrow, focused on consumers generally and the urban, salaried middle class specifically. Import duties and excise taxes were easily collected and were traditionally the basic source of non-oil revenues. Development of income taxes, largely since 1967, again concentrated on those easily collected—taxes on government corporations, and the withholding of personal income taxes by large corporate employers. Informed observers believed the tax burden was light, even for the personal incomes most heavily taxed, because of the numerous exemptions.

In 1977 fiscal authorities were aware of the deficiencies and were attempting to improve the tax system. Considerable success had been achieved in restructuring major revenue sources, especially toward direct taxes. The share of tax revenues went from 14 percent in FY 1974 to 30 percent in FY 1977 with a corresponding decline in the share of oil revenues. An obstacle to continued expansion of direct taxes was the numerous exemptions provided in the tax laws. Personal income from certain sources was exempted or only partially taxed. Lavish exemptions had been provided businesses, particularly industry, to encourage private investment. For example, plants locating at a distance from Tehran, firms listed on the stock exchange, agricultural activity, export industries, approved housing projects, and many other businesses received partial or full exemptions for several years. Some experts suggested that many of the exemptions were excessive and no longer appropriate for the future when oil revenues would be declining.

The tax concessions stimulated discussion about the objectives of fiscal policy. Some experts suggested that taxation be refined to achieve social goals. Although land was taxed in various ways, real estate, for example, was still favored as a haven for funds because capital gains were lightly taxed; real estate received other tax benefits. Wealth was taxed at inheritance, the burden depending partly on the number of heirs, but it was not clear that the tax system prevented the passing on of large estates through various evasive tactics. Most observers, however, expected the authorities to use taxation primarily for revenue purposes, relying on other measures to effect equitable distribution of income and wealth. The consensus was that tax revenues could be substantially increased wihout undue burden if a political decision was taken to proceed with an unpopular measure.

Expenditures

The shah's broad goals of military power, economic development, and social advancement required huge investments. Each year the available funds were spent toward achieving these goals. Since the early 1960s the priorities in allocation of funds have been defense, economic development, and social and welfare measures. Factors affecting revenues, particularly those from oil exports, also affected expenditures. Less than anticipated oil revenues caused periods of financial stringency; the most recent, in FY 1976 and FY 1977, required slowdowns of expenditures.

Defense has been the most important current expenditure, amounting to 19 percent of the central government total in FY 1963, 24 percent in FY 1972, and 30 percent in FY 1976. Some expenditures associated with defense, such as housing and other construction, may be included in the budget under other headings. Purchase of military equipment, primarily from other countries, has been treated in the budget as a current expense and not as a capital item. Before 1973 equipment purchases from abroad were partly financed by foreign loans. Military equipment imported under loans was included in the budget only to the extent of annual repayment of principal and interest on the loans. In FY 1973 and subsequent years, a large part of military equipment imports was paid for in cash, which caused a somewhat artificial increase in defense costs.

Nonetheless defense expenditures climbed rapidly alone with the jump in oil revenues. At United States Congressional Hearings it was reported that Iranian purchases of American military equipment alone amounted to about US$10 billion between 1972 and 1976, the peak occurring in 1974 when purchases amounted to nearly US$4 billion. Although the United States was Iran's major source of military equipment, there were additional purchases from other countries (see Budget, ch. 13).

Most current expenditures cover the recurring expenses of government operations. Personnel costs are a substantial portion of current expenditures. Pay raises for government employees have added to the growth of administrative expenses. Part of the increased oil revenues were channeled into greater government services—free elementary education beginning in FY 1975, for example. Interest on the public debt increased significantly in recent years. In addition the government subsidized prices of a number of basic commodities, such as foods (sugar, meat, eggs, and cereals) and materials (cement and fertilizer), during the inflationary period in the mid-1970s. Subsidy costs had increased to more than US$1 billion in the FY 1976 budget. Current expenditures were rising rapidly in the mid-1970s; they had always been substantially higher than development expenditures.

Development expenditures primarily cover the investments in plant and equipment for future economic and social growth. Development expenditures were 28 percent of total expenditures in FY 1963 and 35 percent in the FY 1976 budget, reflecting an accelerating development effort. The jump in oil revenues permitted the inclusion in the budget of payments advanced for imports to be delivered later of 176 billion rials (approximately US$2.5 billion) in FY 1974 and 112 billion rials (approximately US$1.7 billion) in 1975. Prepayments were 102 billion rials in the FY 1976 budget. Priorities and allocations of capital expenditures are discussed under Development Planning in this chapter.

The jump in oil revenues produced adverse side effects on expenditures. The lack of financial constraints no longer required close scrutiny of all spending. Financial management relaxed. The rapid expansion of government spending in the mid-1970s resulted in considerable waste of resources and serious inflation. By FY 1977 fiscal authorities were attempting to exert greater control over government spending.

Deficit Financing

Since the early 1960s the government has had to borrow to balance the budget. Only in the oil boom years of FY 1974 and FY 1975 did the central government budget show a surplus. Domestic borrowing was primarily from the banking system, particularly the central bank, although the monetary authorities promoted development of the domestic market for treasury bonds in the mid-1970s. An unofficial estimate of the internal debt (probably including borrowing by public corporations and agencies) amounted to about 370 billion rials in March 1976, of which about 280 billion rials was in government bonds.

The government also borrowed in foreign countries to finance part of the budget deficits. The external public debt continuously increased during the 1960s, and debt servicing became a growing but not a major burden. In FY 1974 the authorities began to use part of the increased oil revenues to repay ahead of schedule the country's foreign debt, particularly the loans with the more onerous terms. Since then there has been a net outflow of capital caused by the accelerated repayments, prepayments on equipment to be imported at a later date, and the initiation of an aid and investment program in foreign countries (see Balance of Payments, this ch.).

The jump in oil revenues in FY 1974 provided Iranian planners only temporary respite from fiscal pressures. In FY 1975 the authorities anticipated a growth of oil exports and revenues greater than materialized because of a reduced demand in oil importing countries. Sharply rising expenditures produced signs of a cash flow problem and the beginning of moderation in government spending. Preliminary results for the year showed a budget surplus of only 2 billion rials compared with 142 billion rials in FY 1974.

Efforts to control expenditures increased in FY 1976. Some projects were postponed or canceled while completion dates for others were extended. Foreign aid was cut sharply, and foreign borrowing hit a record high of more than US$1 billion. The proposed budget anticipated a deficit exceeding US$1 billion, but initial accounting indicated that the combination of moderation in spending and greater than anticipated revenues brought the budget toward a balance.

The fiscal authorities were more than a month late preparing the FY 1977 budget because of the uncertainty about prospective oil revenues under OPECs two-tiered pricing system. In the proposed budget oil revenues were expected to be US$19.3 billion compared with US$20.3 billion in FY 1976. Non-oil tax revenues were expected to increase to 421 billion rials. Non-oil, nontax receipts were also expected to increase to produce 1,939 billion rials of total central government revenues.

Expenditures in FY 1977 were budgeted at 2,275 billion rials compared with 1,910 billion rials in FY 1976. Current expenditures were to be cut back—primarily administrative expenses although a small reduction of defense expenditures was anticipated. Development expenditures by social and economic ministries were to be substantially increased, however, accounting for the rise in total expenditures. The proposed deficit of 336 billion rials, far exceeding any previous deficit, was to be financed by domestic and foreign borrowing. Data for part of the year suggested that oil revenues were higher than anticipated and the deficit smaller than expected.

Iranian leaders recognized that government spending after the jump in oil revenues was excessive and not sustainable. The shah called for moderate spending and growth. In 1977 a new government was installed partly to correct imbalances in the economy and to draw up plans for the next planning period with investments the economy could absorb (see ch. 6). During the late 1970s and early 1980s government expenditures will rise less rapidly and in closer relationship to the increase in revenues than occurred in the mid-1970s if the current policy prescriptions are followed. Many observers anticipated a continuing rise in expenditures—only a moderation in the rate of increase—because oil revenues probably will continue to rise in the 1980s, and the leadership has the option to increase taxes to finance expenditures they judge sufficiently important.

Development Planning

Formal development planning began with formation of the Plan Organization in 1947; it was renamed the Plan and Budget Organization in 1973. High economic officials of the government provided guidelines from which the plan was formulated. Planning had a direct impact on the public sector through allocations of capital expenditures. In Iran's mixed economy, however, the planners had no direct power over private sector investments and development; instead they had to rely on indirect measures such as fiscal and financial incentives.

The Planning and Budget Organization's power and responsibilities have varied. It was originally responsible for planning and executing all development activities. By the mid-1970s it was responsible for preparing the current and development budgets, evaluating the performance of ministerial development activities, and coordinating planning and budgeting activities nationwide, as well as preparing annual and five-year plans. Except for broad, multiministry projects that the organization planned and implemented, the ministries proposed and executed approved development projects in their sector, freeing the organization from the large executive burden it had carried in the early years. It no longer disbursed actual funds or managed foreign loans, both functions having been regained by the Ministry of Economy and Finance. The trend was toward freeing the organization from executive functions so it could focus more on planning. Many experts rated the personnel as very capable and the organization's performance as very good and far superior to most parts of the government. In fact some feared that having ministries execute development projects instead of the organization would slow project completions although the administrative change was desirable in the long run.

The basic development strategy was to speed growth by concentrating on the latest technology in large-scale, capital-intensive industry. Expansion of the infrastructure, of course, preceded development of industry. The planners often built ahead of demand, creating physical and economic incentives for the private sector. Creating employment opportunities had not been a primary concern because the population was not that large. Diversification in industry was a goal, partly to free the economy from its dependence on oil, although the planners recognized that at first there would be excessive dependence on oil revenues for the capital to diversify. Diversification would work toward import substitution, and large-scale industry would mean that many plants produced for export to achieve the economies of scale. The Planning and Budget Organization was pragmatic in its approach to development planning and also used a variety of supplementary measures to adjust to particular problems or peculiarities of society.

The role of agriculture reflected the pragmatic approach. At first agriculture was expected to grow with the economy, furnishing food for the population and materials for industry. Accordingly agriculture received large allocations of development funds. When farm output lagged, its role was reduced. The country clearly lacked a comparative advantage for farm produce to become significant export, and food could be imported cheaply and paid for with industrial products. The worldwide food shortages and high international prices of the early 1970s caused another reassessment. Iranian planners anticipated the possibility of a more severe international food shortage in a generation as population pressures make themselves felt. Prudence, therefore, dictated an effort to attain self-sufficiency in grains, still leaving the country an importer of other foods. The planners also realized that industrialization required continued growth of the agricultural sector. By 1978 attention was again directed toward increasing farm output.

The First Development Plan, 1949–55

The first plan anticipated development expenditures by the government of 21 billion rials (approximately US$650 million). Plan allocations included 25 percent of total expenditures to agriculture, 14 percent to industry and mining, and the rest to infrastructure and social development. Financing was to come from oil revenues and foreign and domestic loans. Foreign credits failed to materialize, domestic loans were considerably less than anticipated, and when the oil industry was nationalized in 1951, oil revenues ceased. The effect on the plan was disastrous. Major goals were not reached, and unpaid obligations remained at the end of the plan.

The Second Development Plan, 1955–62

Under the Consortium Agreement in 1954 oil exports resumed, and the second plan was drafted (see Oil Industry, ch. 10). Planned government development expenditures amounted to 70 billion rials (approximately US$930 million) of which transportation and communication received 33 percent, agriculture and irrigation received 26 percent, public utilities and social services received 26 percent, and industry and mining received 15 percent. A proportion of oil revenues (initially 60 percent and climbing to 80 percent) was allocated as the primary means of financing the plan. Oil revenues increased faster than expected, and government expenditures exceeded the plan in some sectors. In 1958 the plan was revised, and expenditures increased 20 percent, to 84 billion rials. The sectoral allocations were largely unchanged.

The rapid increase of oil revenues and government spending created boom conditions. Part of the plan called for two multipurpose dams and extensive transportation construction, elements needed for future growth; but because of their huge costs and long gestation time, they contributed to inflationary pressures. Consumer goods production increased rapidly, encouraging a high rate of private sector investment, partly financed by short- and medium-term foreign loans. By 1960 a period of consolidation was needed, however. The IMF prepared a stabilization program that the government carried out. In spite of the adverse effects the boom laid the foundations for future growth. The economy, including per capita income, grew rapidly, and new attitudes toward industrial investment were generated in the private sector.

The Third Development Plan, 1962–68

The third plan (five and one-half years) attained greater sophistication. Broad macroeconomic goals were combined with investment targets. The primary objective was to raise real GNP (in constant prices) by an average of at least 6 percent a year. An average rate of 8.8 percent was achieved, and real per capita GNP increased at an average rate of 6.5 percent a year. Higher than anticipated oil revenues caused the growth rates to exceed the plan by a wide margin, but rapid growth was not confined to the oil sector. Non-oil GDP rose by an annual average of 8.7 percent (in constant prices). Gross domestic fixed capital formation increased an average of 18 percent (in real terms) a year.

Investments were originally planned to be 140 billion rials by the government and 160 billion rials by the private sector. Actual investment reached 451 billion rials. Planned government development expenditures were revised upward to 230 billion rials. Actual government expenditures totaled 205 billion rials and private investments, 246 billion rials. Major sector allocations under the revised plan were transportation and communications, 25 percent; agriculture, including irrigation, 21 percent; industry, 12 percent; and health and education, 15 percent. Only public sector industrial investments fell seriously behind the plan.

The Fourth Development Plan, 1968–72

The fourth plan stepped up the pace of economic growth. The target rate of growth of GNP in constant prices was set at an average of 9 percent a year, and per capita GNP was to reach 26,900 rials (approximately US$359). Fixed investments needed to reach the growth targets amounted to about 810 billion rials. Private sector investments were to total 366 billion rials and government development expenditures, 443 billion rials. Financing was primarily from oil revenues (about 80 percent was assigned to development), plus about 150 billion rials of foreign loans.

276

The growth target was exceeded. GNP in constant prices increased by a remarkable average of 11.9 percent a year. Total investment was 918 billion rials, of which government development expenditures were 507 billion rials. In 1968 public sector development expenditures for the first time exceeded private investment. Again, increasing oil revenues enabled revision of planned government development expenditures upward to 524 billion rials. Actual expenditures reached 97 percent of the revised target, and spending in all sectors was close to revised goals. Actual expenditures on industry and mining (113 billion rials) were followed by transportation and communications (110 billion rials) and oil and gas (57 billion rials). Other important sectors were electricity, water, housing, education, health, and agriculture. Agriculture investments were originally set at 65 billion rials but cut to 42 billion rials in the revision; actual investments were 41 billion rials.

A number of very large projects were under construction during the fourth plan. Examples were a steel mill, an aluminum smelter, a petrochemical complex, a tractor plant, and a gas pipeline leading to the Soviet border. Substantial cost overruns on many of the large projects accounted for the higher spending goals. After investigating the causes of the cost overruns, the Planning and Budget Organization took a number of steps to prevent their recurrence. It was not clear how successful the measures would be because the fundamental cause was lack of experience and competence by a great many individuals, foreign and Iranian, government and private.

The Fifth Develpment Plan, FY 1973-77

The fifth plan, approved in early 1973, was outrun by circumstances almost from the beginning. Tremendous increases in oil revenues removed financial constraints on investment. The leaders decided to use the additional funds to maximize growth. A radically revised fifth plan was prepared by 1974. Total fixed capital investments were raised from 2,460 billion rials to 4,699 billion rials (nearly US$70 billion), almost doubling. Public sector development expenditures were increased from 1,550 billion rials to 3,119 billion rials (about US$46 billion).

Spectacular quantitative goals were set in the revised plan. GNP in constant 1972 prices was to triple, from 1,165 billion rials in FY 1972 to 3,686 billion rials (about US$55 billion), an average rate of growth of 25.9 percent a year in real terms. Per capita GNP (in 1972 prices) was to increase at 22.3 percent a year, reaching 102,665 rials (about US$1,520) by FY 1977. Gross domestic fixed capital formation was to increase (in 1972 prices) by 29.7 percent a year and 38 percent a year in the public sector.

The bulk of investments were to be made in the economy (see table 11, Appendix A). About two-thirds of public and private fixed capital formation was concentrated in housing (925 billion rials), manufacturing and mining (846 billion rials), oil and gas (792 billion rials), and transportation and communications (583 billion rials). Most private sector investment was expected in housing and manufacturing.

Economic expansion on such a scale was certain to create problems, and they surfaced soon. Ports became clogged and the transportation system overburdened in spite of considerable expansion of capacity. Labor became scarce, and wages soared. Shortages of commodities pushed up prices. By 1975 the leaders recognized that expansion had to be restrained—that the revised goals could not be met.

Failure to meet goals was not economic stagnation. Substantial growth was achieved by the end of the third year (March 1976). GNP in constant prices increased at an annual average rate of 21.7 percent over the three years. Fixed capital formation in the public sector amounted to 1,037 billion rials (33 percent of planned investments), and private sector investments had exceeded 700 billion rials. Capacity in most sectors was considerably expanded providing the base for future growth.

Present-Day Problems

In a little more than fifty years Iran had made remarkable economic progress, much of it concentrated in the 1960–77 period. By September 1977 per capita GNP had reached US$2,200. The economy had climbed to fifteenth among the nations of the world. Yet much remained to be done. In particular the economy was still dependent on oil revenues for growth. A basis for self-sustaining growth was still ahead.

The time frame for action appeared set. Oil revenues would be declining by the mid-1980s unless major new fields were discovered. Modernization had created an expanding appetite for imports. Exports had to be found to earn foreign exchange by the time oil revenues began to decline, or the modern economy would slowly starve to death. There were good export prospects in numerous industries, such as copper, aluminum, and petrochemicals, but a combination of low efficiency, partly fostered by trade barriers in the domestic market, and a continuation of the voracious internal demand for goods could seriously hamper development of exports.

Declining oil revenues will require more discipline and efficiency in the economy than existed in early 1978. The private sector will become increasingly dependent on domestic savings and profits for growth momentum. Government consumption and investment will require a higher level of taxation. Altering fiscal and monetary policies will require delicate handling if the desired goals are to be achieved while improving initiative and efficiency without seriously disrupting market forces.

A constraint on growth lay in the government itself and affected nearly all other obstacles because of the sheer size and structure of government. The shah, using a few able men, had considerably improved administration and planning since the 1950s, but much more efficiency was needed to improve the government's own performance and to avoid dampening the private sector's dynamism. A start had been made to decentralize the highly centralized governmental apparatus. Delegation of authority speeded up reaction time and, to the extent that it spread away from Tehran, tapped the energies and expertise of local people dealing with local development problems.

Rapid economic growth had created disparities among groups. Vast differences in incomes and amenities separated the growing middle class and the poor, urban and rural inhabitants, and various regions in the country. Closing the gaps was necessary to enlarge the domestic market, for the poor could afford to buy only bare necessities. The government had made a determined effort since the early 1960s to locate industry away from Tehran and toward regional centers. A very large part of public sector industrial investment in the fourth and fifth plans was in regional centers—largely those already partially developed. The renewed interest in agriculture would help close gaps if the policy decisions and implementation were good. Some observers suggested that the time was near to tip the balance away from economic efficiency and more toward social justice to prevent tearing the social fabric. This required innovative ideas and very tough decisions to meet perhaps the country's most difficult challenge.

Government leaders and planners were keenly aware of the many problems and were seeking solutions. Various ideas had already been tried. Some helped, and some did not. If the right combination of ideas and actions could be achieved, Iran's future would be bright. The country would rank high among the nations of the world before long, based on its strong economy. If the right combination could not be found, an experiment, costly in money and human terms, to achieve rapid growth would have failed.

*   *   *

Iran: An Economic Profile by Jahangir Amuzegar, an up-to-date, comprehensive, authoritative, and detailed study of the economy and economic policies, should be the first source for those seeking more information. "Oil Income and Financial Policies in Iran and Saudi Arabia" by Henry E. Jakubiak and M. Taher Dajani published in *Finance and Development*, an IMF publication, provided an incisive survey of financial developments between 1973 and 1976. The *Iran Almanac and Book of Facts*, published by Echo of Iran, carries considerable statistical and textual material pertaining to the economy. The Embassy of Iran in Washington publishes two periodicals, *Iran Economic News* and *Profile on Iran*, which report current developments. *Profile of Iran*, April 1977, surveyed the banking system. "Iran: A Special Report", February 1977, published by the *Middle East Economic Digest*, surveyed the economy. The IMF *International Financial Statistics* (monthly) contains recent statistics about important aspects of the economy. Abdol-Majid Majidi, Minister in Charge of the Plan and Budget Organization, in an article, "Iran 1980–85: Problems and Challenges of Development," published in *The World Today*, set forth a broad review of economic achievements and future problems. (For further information see Bibliography.)

Chapter 10. Industry

IRAN'S LONG HISTORY and periods of greatness have inter-mittently induced nationalistic feeling in rulers and subjects (see ch. 2). In relatively recent times the feeling was manifested in efforts to modernize the economy and abolish widespread poverty. In the early 1800s Iran's ambassador in London saw techniques and skills that he introduced into Iran to improve the quality and quantity of manufactures by artisans and craftsmen. Additional efforts were made to modernize industry, but very little success had been achieved by the early 1900s. The discovery of oil in 1908 brought Western technology and production methods to the economy, but they long remained almost exclusively confined to production and refining of oil and had little direct impact on the rest of the economy.

In 1925 Reza Shah established the Pahlavi dynasty and com-mitted himself to restoring national pride and establishing control over the country's destiny. His government actively intervened to change economic conditions and establish a base for modern industry. Rising oil production and revenues helped finance pro-jects, but there were periodic tensions between the government and the oil company because the government lacked control of the oil industry and of the flow of funds to finance industrial develop-ment.

When Reza Shah's son, Mohammad Reza Pahlavi, took control of the government in 1941, he was even more firmly committed to industrialization. In the 1940s he instituted national plans to establish priorities and allocate scarce resources in order to speed up modernization of the economy. Nationalistic feelings led to nationalization of the oil industry in 1951, creating political and financial chaos until oil production resumed in late 1954. As a result of the Consortium Agreement reached in that year between the government and a consortium of foreign oil companies, the terms of settlement that permitted oil production resumed, albeit slightly, but left the oil companies' control virtually intact; the agreement did, however, dramatically increase the government's share from each barrel of oil produced. The combination of the larger share and rising oil production provided the government with increased revenues to finance industrial development, but there never was enough money for all that needed to be done. In 1961 the government joined with other major oil exporting countries to form an organization, the Organization of Petroleum Exporting Countries (OPEC), whose members acted in concert to increase each country's control over its own production and to maximize its revenues (see app B).

By the early 1960s the country remained predominantly agri-cultural. Manufacturing was primarily in small shops and cottage industry. Handweaving of rugs was still a major activity, and rugs were an important export product. Large-scale, modern factories were few and were confined largely to consumer products, primarily food processing and textiles. But the economy was changing. Transportation had improved, able managers and some skilled workers had appeared, and urbanization and incomes had increased. The shah believed it was time for a greater effort toward industrialization. He instituted a program—called at first the White Revolution (see Glossary) and by the mid-1970s the Shah-People Revolution—and government planners gave priority in allocating investment funds to manufacturing. As a result manufacturing output grew rapidly, and many new industries were established between 1962 and 1972. There was an impressive range of new products from domestic manufacturing, including iron and steel products, machine tools, agricultural implements, and tractors, communications equipment, television sets, refrigerators, assembled cars and buses, and petrochemical products.

In 1973 the government concluded an agreement with the consortium members, thus achieving full control over the oil industry, including pricing, that had eluded it in the 1954 Consortium Agreement. Plans were made for the long-term development of oil and the integration of the oil sector into the rest of the economy and economic planning. Use of the gases produced as by-products of crude oil was given particular attention so that this natural resource would no longer be wasted. Between 1973 and 1974 OPEC members sharply increased the price of oil and the share the government received. As a result the government's oil revenues jumped from about US$4 billion in 1973 to more than US$21 billion in 1974.

The much higher oil revenues freed the planners from financial constraint in economic development. A large number of industrial projects, many of considerable size, were undertaken during the fifth plan (1973–77) (see Glossary) period. Government investments were concentrated in petrochemicals and basic metal industries as well as the oil industry. Private investors, domestic and foreign, were to furnish 64 percent of the US$11 billion of planned investments in manufacturing between the 1973–74 period—fiscal year (FY—see Glossary) 1973 and FY 1977. The economy proved incapable of absorbing such feverish growth, and some projects were postponed and completion dates extended for others. Nevertheless industrial production was growing at close to 20 percent a year, and a diversified industrial base was erected. The economy might not reach the goal of being equivalent in the mid-1980s to some West European economies of the mid-1970s, but it was expected to come close. By FY 1975 manufacturing and mining (excluding electric power and construction) had become more important in value of output than agriculture and contributed about 10 percent of gross domestic product (GDP). The oil sector of course dominated the economy, accounting for 38 percent of GDP.

Oil Industry

From the beginning the oil sector has been important to the economy but never as dominant as in the Arab oil-exporting states across the Persian Gulf. Iran's large population and somewhat diversified economy counterbalanced the importance of oil. In 1960 the oil sector's contribution to GDP was 16 percent and in 1970, 22 percent. It was not until 1969 that the oil sector's contribution to GDP exceeded that of agriculture even though agriculture had low productivity and a very slow growth rate. The dramatic increase of oil revenues between 1973 and 1974 also affected GDP and the oil sector's share of it. In FY 1976 the oil sector's contribution amounted to 40 percent of GDP. The impact was similar for government finances; oil revenues accounted for 46 percent of total budget revenues in FY 1970 and 85 percent in FY 1974.

The capital-intensive nature of the oil industry meant that it provided relatively little employment. In FY 1975 the oil sector employed about 90,000 people—about 0.5 percent of the total work force and about 2 percent of the workers employed in industry. Expatriates employed in the oil industry numbered about 1,400 in FY 1973. In the 1930s and 1940s, however, oil field employment had been quite large because of government pressure on an oil company to hire persons sent to it. After 1954 foreign oil companies began sharply reducing the excess staff, contributing to opposite trends. Oil field employment declined rapidly while production rose. Oil industry employees often carried modern skills and techniques into the rest of the economy when they quit working for the oil companies.

Official government estimates of the country's oil reserves were unavailable, but statements by officials indicated there were about 60 to 70 billion barrels in 1976. Extensive and expensive secondary and tertiary recovery techniques were planned to extend the life and increase the amount of oil that could be drawn from the fields. Data published by the government-owned National Iranian Oil Company (NIOC) indicated that planners expected oil production to peak in about 1977 or 1978 and stabilize for about seven years; by the mid-1980s oil production would begin to decline unless significant new reserves had been discovered by then. In the mid-1970s Iran was the world's fourth largest producer of crude oil and the second largest exporter of petroleum, but the country's importance as a source of oil will probably diminish by the mid-1980s.

Early Development of the Oil Industry

Oil, bitumen, and natural gas were known to Persians in antiquity. Oil was used in lamps, in asphalt, and in waterproofing boats and water conduits; natural gas was used in fires at temples of the fire-venerating Zoroastrians. These petroleum products were collected from natural seepages until modern times.

When the commercial significance of oil became apparent in the 1860s, a worldwide scramble for oil began. Survey parties investigated the natural seepages in Iran and just across the border in Czarist Russia. By 1874 drillers had discovered oil at very shallow depths (little more than 100 feet in some cases) near Baku on the western side of the Caspian Sea in the present-day Soviet Union (though just north of the Iranian border and in territory formerly belonging to Iran). The fields proved large and continued to produce in the 1970s. The Baku discoveries stimulated Russian interest in the northern area of Iran.

Oil in Iran proved more elusive. The first concession was let in 1872 to a naturalized British citizen, Baron Paul Julius von Reuter (who later founded the news agency of that name), but Czarist Russia's hostility caused the Iranians to cancel the concession. In 1884 a concession was let to a foreign firm to drill near seepages in Fars Province. Their efforts failed. Reuter obtained another concession in the late 1880s but did not find oil. Interest in Iranian oil lapsed until near the end of the century when two French explorers returned to report abundant evidence of oil. A British banker, William Knox D'Arcy, who had made a fortune by financing the Australian gold strike, became interested. His negotiator won a concession in May 1901 from the shah (who was in need of funds), after skillfully evading any objections from the Russians.

D'Arcy received a sixty-year exclusive concession "to search for, obtain, exploit, develop, render suitable for trade, carry away, and sell natural gas, petroleum, asphalt, and oxocerite throughout the whole extent of the Persian Empire," with the exception of five northern provinces bordering Russia. The concession area was originally about 480,000 square miles (larger than the United States east of the Mississippi River). The Iranians received about 20,000 pounds sterling in cash, 20,000 pounds sterling worth of stock in the company to be set up, 16 percent of the company's annual net profits, and a fixed sum of about 1,800 pounds sterling a year.

Drilling started considerably to the west of where oil was eventually discovered. Heat, disease, and hostile tribes hindered exploration. The last problem was easiest to solve; large payments to the tribes made them bodyguards instead of marauders. D'Arcy spent millions of pounds in financing the exploration and was close to bankruptcy several times. He dickered with French bankers for financing until the British government heard of it. The British government appealed to his patriotic interests and committed a British oil company, in which the government had an interest, to provide some funds. The British government also used diplomacy and some British troops to continue the exploration effort. Finally on May 26, 1908, oil was found at Masjed Soleyman (Mosque of Solomon) in Khuzestan Province.

In 1909 the Anglo-Persian Oil Company was formed to exploit the oil field and explore the rest of the concession. About this time the British navy was preparing to convert its ships from coal to oil, but the British Empire had little oil. The prospects in Iran appealed to several British officials. By 1914 the change to oil for the navy was under way; just before World War I broke out, Winston Churchill's oratory contributed to passage of a bill in the British Parliament, empowering the British government to purchase a 51-percent interest in the Anglo-Persian Oil Company. The company received a forty-year contract to supply fuel to the British navy but at a secret price substantially below market prices. The company name was changed in 1935 to Anglo-Iranian Oil Company to conform with Reza Shah's policy (see ch. 2). The name became British Petroleum (BP) after the consortium was formed in 1954. BP will be used hereafter to refer to the company in its various manifestations.

Additional wells were drilled, and pipelines, a sea terminal, and a refinery at Abadan were constructed. Production amounted to 43,000 tons (see Glossary under *barrels* for conversion factor) in 1912. Production increased rapidly, amounting to 1.4 million tons in 1920 and 5.4 million tons in 1927. The worldwide depression of the early 1930s contracted foreign markets, but production reached 10.3 million tons in 1937. During the early years of World War II production dropped, amounting to 6.6 million tons in 1941, after which it began to rise again. Production reached 19.2 million tons in 1946 and 31.8 million tons in 1950.

Oil revenues began to mount along with production. The government had received a cumulative total of 1.3 million pounds sterling between FY 1912 and FY 1918. Annual oil revenues amounted to 585,000 pounds sterling in FY 1920 and 1.3 million pounds sterling in FY 1930. The worldwide depression of the early 1930s caused BP's profits to drop, and Iran's oil revenues fell to only 307,000 pounds sterling in FY 1931 in spite of higher crude production. Oil revenues amounted to 4 million pounds sterling in FY 1940 and 16 million pounds sterling in FY 1950. Until 1925 oil revenues went primarily into the private purses of the rulers. During the Reza Shah regime oil revenues were incorporated into a budget to finance government expenditures, including development projects.

By 1950 Iran was the world's fourth largest producer of crude oil, accounting for about 6 percent of world production. Proven reserves amounted to about 13 percent of the world total. BP had drilled 453 wells, laid more than 2,100 miles of pipelines, installed refining capacity amounting to nearly 5 percent of the world's total, and constructed three major ports, 1,500 miles of roads, and schools, hospitals, and housing. The cumulative total of oil payments to the government was approximately 120 million pounds sterling. Nonetheless oil revenues had been a small part (perhaps 10 percent) of the value of oil exports and amounted to less than 15 percent of the government's annual total budget revenues. The oil industry had had only a small impact on the economy; it remained essentially a foreign-owned and -operated enclave apart from the rest of the economy.

Almost from the beginning of the concession there were disagreements between the government and the oil company over revenues. The Interpretive Agreement, reached in 1920, temporarily quieted matters. When revenues fell sharply at the beginning of the depression, Iran cancelled the concession. Great Britain took the case to the League of Nations in 1932. Before the league reached a decision, a compromise was worked out that significantly modified the original concession. Royalty payments were changed from a share of company profits to a fixed amount per ton of oil produced. Minimum payments to the government were established, and the life of the concession was extended by thirty-two years (until 1993), although the concession area was reduced about 80 percent.

Nationalization of the Oil Industry

The visibility and eminence of the oil company and the disagreements between the government and company officials on various issues contributed to antagonism toward BP's presence in the country. Popular opinion was easily inflamed, for example, by reference to the secret discount price of fuel for the British and to the fact that BP paid more taxes to Great Britain than to Iran. But some observers believed that a change in popular attitudes—a pride in country that began with the Reza Shah regime—brought about the nationalization of the oil industry.

Occupation of Iran by Soviet, British, and American forces during World War II and abdication by Reza Shah in 1941 intensified nationalistic feelings (see ch. 2). These feelings were further aroused when Soviet occupation of the northern provinces continued after the end of the war. A promise of a fifty-year oil concession extracted by the Soviets from the Iranian government in exchange for withdrawal of troops was never honored. After the withdrawals of foreign troops, BP became the focus of nationalistic sentiments. The Majlis (the lower house of Parliament) instructed the government to investigate and renegotiate the BP concession because Iran was being deprived of its full share of oil revenues.

While the government conducted its investigation, BP submitted the Supplemental Agreement to the Iranians in 1948. In 1947 Venezuela had obtained a fifty-fifty profit-sharing arrangement with oil companies (in effect an income tax of 50 percent on net profits of in-country oil production—see Appendix B) that raised Venezuela's oil revenues substantially. Iran's Supplementary Agreement would have raised its receipts per barrel of oil produced by roughly 100 percent and reportedly would have yielded about the same amount of income as a fifty-fifty profit-sharing agreement. The prime minister was satisfied with the agreement, but it was rejected by the Majlis as not enough. In

Roadbuilding outside of Malayer
WORLD BANK PHOTO *(Pierre Streit)*

February 1951 a draft proposal to nationalize Iran's oil industry and all of BP's properties was submitted to the Majlis, and it was adopted on April 30, 1951.

In 1951 Iran's oil industry virtually ceased to operate. The pool of trained Iranian personnel was sufficient to operate only a small fraction of the facilities. More important the oil companies provided no help and refused to purchase or transport Iranian oil. The boycott remained until the Consortium Agreement was reached in late 1954. The virtual halt of crude production in the largest Middle East oil producer at that time did not materially affect the oil companies; production was increased elsewhere, particularly in Kuwait. The halt caused serious political and economic consequences for Iran, however (see ch. 2).

National Iranian Oil Company

The National Iranian Oil Company (NIOC) was formed after nationalization to continue oil operations; its charter was not approved until 1955, however. It is a commercial company wholly owned by the government, which determines major policies. NIOC pays taxes on its net profits.

The charter assigned the government's ownership of the country's oil and natural gas resources to the administration of NIOC and gave it the unrestricted right to search for oil and to produce, refine, and distribute petroleum products, including a complete monopoly of domestic sales. The 1957 Petroleum Act accorded NIOC the legal power to grant permission to Iranian or foreign companies to search for and produce crude oil outside the consortium's area and to form wholly owned subsidiaries. The important subsidiaries formed were the National Petrochemical Company (NPC), established in 1966, the National Iranian Gas Company (NIGC), established in 1966, and the National Iranian Tanker Company. In addition NIOC operated a pipe-rolling mill in Ahvaz and participated in several foreign ventures, such as a refinery in India and exploration and development in the North Sea with BP. NIOC was conceived as, and by 1977 had become, a large oil company with wide-ranging interests.

NIOC has been one of Iran's more efficient and effective organizations. The technical ability required in the oil business meant that talent and competence—rather than family connections alone—counted in appointment and promotion, and as a result NIOC developed some of the country's most able managers and administrators. NIOC activities have steadily expanded into all phases of the oil business. The most apparent deficiency has been foreign marketing of Iranian petroleum. The international oil industry in general and the consortium members in particular hampered NIOC's penetration of international markets, and its direct sales abroad increased slowly. The 1973 Sales and Purchase Agreement provided NIOC with more crude for export, and direct sales subsequently increased. In 1976 NIOC's direct sales abroad amounted to more than 1 million barrels per day (20 percent of total oil exports), a considerable increase over earlier years.

In the 1960s NIOC resorted to barter arrangements with some communist countries, exchanging oil for factories and equipment, in order to increase its direct sales as well as the country's overall exports. Government control of production and trading companies in communist countries facilitated the arrangements. In 1976 and 1977 NIOC attempted to negotiate barter terms with other countries, such as Great Britain, Italy, France, and the United States, primarily for military equipment and large plants. The terms became quite complex. An aircraft manufacturer, for example, had to arrange with an oil company for the refining, transport, and sale of oil products before receiving payment for aircraft exports. Many oil companies and some governments disapproved of barter transactions. By late 1977 a few minor barter transactions had reportedly been arranged, but observers doubted that barter deals would attain much significance because of the complicated arrangements and additional risks encountered by foreign exporters.

Consortium Agreement

On October 29, 1954, the nationalization issue was settled by the Consortium Agreement signed by NIOC (representing the Iranian government) and a consortium of the major international oil companies. The consortium was expanded in 1955 to include a number of smaller American independent oil companies. BP accepted the principle of nationalization and of NIOC ownership of oil reserves and facilities. NIOC authorized the consortium, of which BP was the most important member (40 percent), to carry out operations on its behalf. BP received compensation for the assets it gave up. The other consortium members paid, primarily in installments of US$0.10 per barrel of oil exported, a sum equivalent to 510 million pounds sterling. The Iranian government paid 25 million pounds sterling over ten years as settlement of claims and counterclaims. By the 1970s BP had received compensation and suffered little loss from nationalization.

NIOC and the government referred to the Consortium Agreement as an agency contract, implying that the consortium merely handled the technical operation under the supervision of NIOC. Many observers, however, viewed the Consortium Agreement as only a slight modification of the usual concession agreement because NIOC lacked a complete voice in petroleum operations. The consortium established production levels and prices and made the decisions on exploration and expansion.

The consortium members formed two companies under British laws, the Iranian Oil Participants (to hold the shares of the operating companies in Iran) and the Iranian Oil Services (to provide personnel and supplies for the operating companies). Iranian Oil Participants formed two subsidiaries under the laws of the Netherlands to conduct operations in Iran: the Iranian Oil Exploration and Producing Company and the Iranian Oil Refining

Company, together commonly called the Iranian Oil Operating Companies (IOOC). The IOOC received the right to explore for and produce crude oil and natural gas in a defined area known as the Agreement Area and to refine petroleum products for export at the Abadan refinery. NIOC was to handle some support functions, such as housing and medical services.

The Agreement Area covered about 100,000 square miles in southwest Iran, basically the former BP concession area. All of BP's former fields except the Kermanshah oil field, which with the Kermanshah refinery was taken over by NIOC, were included in the Agreement Area. In 1977 the Agreement Area accounted for nearly all of Iran's important fields and for over 90 percent of crude production. The consortium concession was for a period of twenty-five years and renewable for another fifteen years. Only minor modifications occurred before 1971; the Consortium Agreement was essentially voided by the 1973 Sales and Purchase Agreement.

The operating companies did not market or export oil. Individual consortium members established their own trading companies, which bought the oil for export before or after refining. The IOOC charged the full cost of production plus a fee for the oil sold to the trading companies. The trading companies were taxed by the government on their profits. NIOC had the right to buy as much oil as it needed for domestic consumption from the operating companies. In addition NIOC was entitled to 12.5 percent of crude production (royalty payment), which it could resell to the trading companies or market abroad. In the 1960s the consortium agreed that NIOC could export larger amounts to markets not supplied by major oil companies, essentially Eastern Europe.

The agreement incorporated the fifty-fifty profit-sharing arrangement standard among Persian Gulf oil exporters. The higher tax made Iran's revenues four times as high as in the prenationalization period. In 1964 the royalty payment became an operating expense instead of part of the tax payment, raising the government's effective share of consortium operations to more than 56 percent. Other OPEC members made the same change. OPEC members, including Iran, raised tax rates rapidly in the 1970s (see Appendix B).

Opinions differ about the effects of nationalization. Some experts believed that Iran accepted essentially the same terms in 1954 as those offered by BP in 1949—that the same results could have been achieved without the sacrifice of oil revenues and the ensuing economic chaos. Other experts, taking the longer view, point to the formation of the NIOC and the training of Iranians in petroleum affairs; still others believed that political and social conditions were such that nationalization was inevitable.

Other Concessions

Iran's Petroleum Act of 1957 was one of the first comprehensive and well-prepared petroleum laws of a major oil-exporting country. It recognized NIOC as the owner of all the country's oil resources and broadened NIOC's powers and functions. To diversify petroleum development NIOC was authorized to divide the country, including offshore areas, into numerous districts and open them to exploration through bidding by foreign oil companies. NIOC was empowered to enter into joint ventures or any other legal arrangement with foreign companies. NIOC was to hold not less than 30 percent ownership in a joint venture, but in fact it never had less than 50 percent. The act prohibited any foreign oil company from holding too large an area, and it contained broad guidelines concerning payments and taxes. Agreements were to last only twenty-five years (with three renewals of five years each), and relinquishment was scheduled. NIOC was to set aside at least one-third of the exploitable area as national reserves.

Almost as soon as the act was passed, a joint venture agreement was signed with an Italian firm, and in 1958 one was signed with an American firm. NIOC entered into six more joint ventures in 1965 and three more in 1971. NIOC's partners were primarily state oil companies or small international companies, although a few of the major international companies participated after first denouncing the joint venture arrangements.

The joint venture agreements were referred to as seventy-five-twenty-five agreements because 50 percent of the net profit of the foreign oil company was paid to the Iranian government and one-half of the remainder went to NIOC as an equal partner. The joint ventures before 1971 did not require a royalty payment. Iranians made up half of the board of directors of the operating company, although the foreign oil company named the managing director until the 1971 joint venture agreements. The foreign oil company put up the money for development costs; if oil was found, NIOC usually paid its share of exploration and development costs out of proceeds from production. There were many additional provisions. In general the 1971 joint ventures were even more favorable to Iran than the ones signed earlier.

In 1966 Iran initiated a new form of agreement with foreign oil companies called service contracts. The foreign company had no ownership rights in Iran but was simply a contractor of NIOC paid with crude oil. The foreign oil company undertook exploration with its own funds and would loan NIOC funds for development if oil was found. NIOC would set aside 50 percent of any oil discovered for the national reserves and would sell a specified proportion of the remainder to the foreign oil company contractor at cost plus 2 percent. The contract would last twenty-five years from the beginning of commercial production of oil. In addition NIOC would pay the foreign company for its exploration costs and development loans (including interest) from production. There were a number of additional provisions. The service contracts greatly increased NIOC's control over all operations, and some Iranian officials claimed they would increase the government's take to about 90 percent. The companies holding the three service contracts let by 1977 had not discovered oil.

The joint ventures had discovered some fields, most of them offshore, but their combined production never exceeded 10 percent of the output from the consortium area. Production from joint ventures amounted to about 453,000 barrels per day in 1976. Moreover joint ventures did not provide the seventy-five-twenty-five profit split they were supposed to. Some economists calculated that, at least before 1973 and for a number of reasons, Iran's revenues per barrel of oil were substantially higher from the consortium than from any of the joint ventures. In addition economists argued that the service contracts were not as favorable as they appeared. Nonetheless concessions let since formation of the consortium provided the government with considerably greater control of petroleum operations and provided training for Iranians not possible in the consortium.

Sales and Purchase Agreement, 1973

In 1973 the Sales and Purchase Agreement replaced the Consortium Agreement even though the latter had originally been drawn to extend to 1979. The participation agreements signed by several Arab oil-exporting states of the Persian Gulf area by which they obtained 25-percent ownership in major oil operations in their countries were a major cause (see app B). Iran had opposed the participation agreements because they appeared unworkable. When they were successful, and particularly when the buy-back provisions increased revenues from each barrel of oil produced, Iranian officials moved to obtain at least equal benefits. Negotiations with the consortium were started in July 1972, and the Sales and Purchase Agreement was signed in July 1973 although the effective date was March 21, 1973.

The most important feature of the agreement, which was to last for twenty years, was that NIOC became sole owner-operator in the consortium area and thus became responsible for exploration, development investment, production, and pricing—the complete control that had been lacking in the Consortium Agreement. The IOCC was replaced by a new nonprofit service company, Iranian Oil Service Company (IOSCO), incorporated in Iran and subject to its laws. The IOSCO carried on exploration and production of crude oil—but not refining—in a revised area assigned by NIOC. The service contract was for five years and was to continue unless terminated by NIOC or the former consortium members.

Under the new agreement NIOC obtained crude oil needed to meet domestic requirements and a stated quantity for export, which was 5 percent of total output in 1974 and would increase to about 18 percent by 1981. The trading companies of the former consortium members could take the remaining production from the Agreement Area, but NIOC could export the surplus that the trading companies did not buy. NIOC took over management of the Abadan refinery and preemptive right to take about 100,000 barrels per day of products for the domestic market. NIOC would process up to 300,000 barrels per day for the trading companies.

The price to the trading companies for crude oil delivered by NIOC to tanker terminals or the Abadan refinery included four elements. The most important to Iran was the balancing margin clause, designed to give Iran financial benefits at least equal to those obtained in the future by other oil states in the Persian Gulf. The other elements of price included operating costs (originally set at about US$0.10 per barrel) and payments for development expenditures. Because NIOC was responsible for capital funds (which were expected to be quite large during the first five years as recovery techniques were improved in the older fields), the agreement provided that NIOC would furnish 60 percent of the funds and receive interest in the selling price of crude. The trading companies were annually to advance NIOC the other 40 percent of investment funds as prepayment of crude oil purchases. In 1976 and 1977 difficulties arose over the payments of these contributions by the oil companies to NIOC's capital investment budget. A royalty (initially 12.5 percent of posted price) was also included. The agreement furthermore stipulated that all payments to Iran and NIOC were to be in United States dollars.

NIOC's production policy also was broadly outlined. Installed capacity and production were to rise between 7 and 8 million barrels per day by about 1977. Production would remain stable until around 1984 and decline thereafter. Domestic consumption was expected to increase as output declined and by 1993 would about equal total production, leaving little oil for export.

Production and Revenues

Production rose quickly as soon as the Consortium Agreement was reached in 1954, and it increased steadily through 1974 (see table 12, Appendix A). Production amounted to 329,000 barrels per day in 1955 and to 6.0 million barrels per day in 1974, an average annual growth rate of 16.5 percent. The growth rate averaged 13.5 percent in the 1964–74 decade. In 1975 production declined to 5.3 million barrels per day primarily as a result of a worldwide recession and reduced consumption in industrialized countries. In early 1976 the price of Iranian heavy crude was reduced by 9.5 percent to bring it into line with heavy crude from other gulf states. The reduced price combined with some economic recovery in oil-importing states pushed production upward to about 5.9 million barrels per day in 1976 according to preliminary estimates. Production dropped sharply in January 1977 because of a build up of stocks by importers in late 1976 and the two-tiered pricing adopted by OPEC in December 1976 (see Appendix B).

Iran's proven crude oil reserves were estimated at about 60

billion barrels in 1974, enough to last about thirty years at current rates of production. By 1976 price increases and enhanced recovery programs raised the estimates of recoverable reserves to between 60 and 70 billion barrels. NIOC had planned expensive investments, primarily to pump gas back into the fields to increase recovery of crude oil, but it was uncertain by 1977 how much of the program would be implemented. Additional fields would probably be found, but not many observers anticipated discovery of large fields. The fields discovered since 1964 had been small. Iran's crude oil for export was blended into two grades—light [34-degree on the American Petroleum Institute (API) gravity scale] and heavy (31-degree API)—and usually exported in the ratio of about 55 percent light and 45 percent heavy.

The bulk of oil production was exported, primarily as crude oil. Growing domestic consumption reduced the export proportion, but domestic consumption was minor. In 1976 exports of crude and products amounted to 272 million tons, internal consumption to 23 million tons. Exports of refined products have been small, generally less than 10 percent of the total tonnage of petroleum exports and closer to 5 percent in the 1970s. The bulk of petroleum exports went to Western Europe and Japan. American imports of Iranian oil increased after the 1973 Arab oil embargo, and by the mid-1970s Iran supplied about 7 percent of American crude oil imports.

Oil revenues increased more rapidly than production, primarily because of the actions of OPEC. The posted price of Iranian light crude was US$2.17 per barrel in 1948 and US$1.79 per barrel between 1960 and 1970 (although the actual market price had fallen to about US$1.30 to US$1.40 per barrel by early 1970). At the Tehran meeting in 1971 OPEC members began unilaterally to increase posted prices. By September 1973 Iran's posted price for light crude was US$2.99 per barrel, and the government take was US$1.75 per barrel. Iran's posted price was increased to US$5.09 per barrel and the government take to US$3.18 in October 1973. Posted prices were increased by 130 percent effective January 1, 1974; Iran's light crude became US$11.87 per barrel and the government take more than US$7.00. As OPEC countries increased tax rates and royalty fees, Iran benefited through the balancing margin clause of the Sales and Purchase Agreement. Iran's take rose to about US$9.74 per barrel in late 1974.

Iranian officals strongly advocated that OPEC members adopt a uniform pricing system. In Decemer 1974 OPEC adopted such a system, establishing a single posted price of US$11.25 and a selling price of US$10.46 per barrel for Arabian light crude (34 degree API) and a government take of US$10.12 per barrel, Iranian light was increased to US$11.62 per barrel in September 1975 in line with OPEC's price increase. Iran's posted price was increased by 10 percent to US$12.81 per barrel on January 1, 1977, in accordance with the decision of eleven OPEC members.

Saudi Arabia and the United Arab Emirates (UAE) increased the posted price of their light crude by 5 percent to US$12.09, contributing to the fall in Iran's exports and revenues in early 1977.

The 50-percent tax on oil company operations in Iran that became effective with the Consortium Agreement in 1954 considerably boosted the country's oil revenues and stimulated efforts to develop the economy. Minor adjustments to the methods of calculating taxes and royalties, along with increasing production, caused oil revenues to increase from US$90 million in 1955 to US$1.1 billion in 1970, an annual average increase of 18.2 percent, which was slightly higher than the growth rate of production. Revenues were not increasing rapidly enough to generate funds for the country's development projects and military build up, however (see ch. 9; ch. 13). In the 1960s NIOC sought in various ways to increase production and sales of petroleum to consortium members in order to obtain additional funds. Iran's activities in OPEC increased toward the same end and brought dramatic results in the 1970s. By 1973 oil revenues had increased to US$4.4 billion, an annual increase of about 60 percent since 1970. In 1974 oil revenues increased to US$21.4 billion, nearly a fivefold increase from the previous year. Iranian officals increased economic and military expenditures accordingly.

The unexpected worldwide decline in oil consumption in 1975 caused Iran's production and oil revenues to fall after expenditure commitments had already been made, causing a budget deficit of about US$2 billion in FY 1976 (see ch. 9). Iranian officials charged the consortium members with failure to fulfill their 1973 contract commitments to purchase oil and failure to make the required loans to NIOC for investment expenditures. Iran also pushed strongly for large increases in OPEC's posted prices in order to obtain sufficient revenues to meet expenditures. Iran's advocacy of a 15-percent price increase at the December 1976 OPEC meeting was welcomed by other members in need of funds, but when Saudi Arabia increased prices only 5 percent for 1977, that move threatened to intensify Iran's budget problems. OPEC's two-tiered pricing system created sufficient uncertainty about future revenues that Iranian officials delayed for several weeks the presentation of the FY 1977 budget to the Majlis (see ch. 9).

Refineries and Terminals

Iran had six refineries in operation at the beginning of 1977 with a combined capacity of more than 800,000 barrels per day. All contributed to the domestic supply of petroleum products, although the Abadan refinery produced primarily for export. The high cost of transportation in Iran led to regional location of refineries. Pipelines brought the crude oil from the fields to the refineries for processing and essentially regional distribution of products.

The Abadan refinery was completed in 1912 and enlarged many times. It has been the world's largest refinery at various times, and

Tankers and supertankers taking on oil for export

an expansion (to 600,000 barrels per day) scheduled to be completed in 1978 will again make it the world's largest refinery. Its capacity in 1977 was 470,000 barrels per day. Until NIOC took it over in 1973, the refinery had always been operated by foreign oil companies. It produced a wide range of products and had considerable flexibility in its product mix. It was one of the world's main "balancing refineries"—i.e., product mix was easily adjusted toward products in short supply in particular markets. About 20 percent of production had gone to the domestic market in the early 1970s, but in 1973 NIOC obtained the preemptive right to about 25 percent of production for local consumption. It was linked by pipeline to several fields in the former Agreement Area and to a sea terminal. A pipeline for products ran to Tehran and had branches extending north and west to Tabriz and east to Meshed (see fig. 10).

The Abadan refinery produced more than just petroleum products. One purpose in its original construction was to provide income and employment in Khuzestan Province. This it did well, reportedly employing some 46,000 people by 1964, most of whom were Iranians. Oil men claimed that a comparable refinery elsewhere would need only 4,000 to 5,000 men. After the Consortium Agreement, efforts were made to reduce inefficiency. By 1964 Abadan employed only 18,000 Iranians, but production costs were still high. In 1960 it reportedly cost US$0.66 to refine a barrel of oil there—and about US$0.4 in a comparable refinery elsewhere. By 1972 employment of Iranians at Abadan had dropped below 10,000 in spite of larger facilities and greater production. Refining costs were about US$0.58 per barrel in 1973.

Employment at Abadan diminished for foreigners as well as for Iranians. About 260 expatriates were employed in 1958 compared with forty-five in 1970. After nationalization, Iranians were increasingly placed in positions of responsibility. By the early 1970s, for the first time, the refinery's general manager was an Iranian, and Iranians filled most technical and administrative positions at all levels. Their talent and competence were acknowledged by their counterparts in private oil companies. The refinery had become the main training center for topflight executives. By the mid-1970s recruitment of key technical and managerial personnel for many of Iran's big new projects started at the Abadan refinery.

The other refineries were much smaller than Abadan. Two were located near Tehran to supply that main consumption area. Both were built and operated by NIOC. The first was completed in 1968 with a capacity of 85,000 barrels per day, increased to 110,000 barrels per day in 1972. It produced a full range of products including lubricants, special products, and sulfur. Tehran's second refinery was completed in March 1975 with a capacity of 100,000 barrels per day. It included a unit to produce 95,000 tons a year of multigrade motor oils and a unit to produce 256 tons daily of bitumen. Both refineries were supplied by pipelines from the southwest oil fields. A pipeline also carried petroleum products from the Abadan refinery for distribution in the capital area.

The Kermanshah refinery came onstream in 1935 with a capacity of 2,000 barrels per day. Its crude came from a field close to the Iraq border. NIOC took over operation of the field and refinery in 1954. The refinery was rehabilitated in 1972, and capacity increased to 20,000 barrels per day. NIOC planned to increase capacity again (to about 80,000 barrels per day) in the late 1970s. The Shiraz refinery was completed in 1973 with a capacity of 40,000 barrels per day. It produced a full range of products for distribution in southern and eastern parts of the country. A topping plant, constructed in the 1930s, operated at Masjed Soleyman. It supplied oil for the domestic market and sent distillates by pipeline to the Abadan refinery.

In 1975 construction was started on an 80,000-barrel-per-day refinery in Tabriz to supply the northwest area of the country. It was scheduled to begin operation in early 1978. Petroleum consumption had increased rapidly in the northwest, and a pipeline had been completed by 1976 from Tehran to Tabriz to supply products for the area. The pipeline would be used to supply crude to the refinery when it was completed. A 200,000-barrel-per-day refinery was planned for Isfahan, the second largest city, but construction had not started by 1977. A 130,000-barrel-per-day refinery was also planned near Meshed to supply the northeast region; in 1977 this area received its petroleum products by pipeline from Tehran.

Since 1973 NIOC had negotiated with several foreign oil companies concerning construction of large export refineries in Iran. Iranian officials wanted to move in this direction to gain the value added and employment for their economy, but the negotiations faltered in 1975. Firm commitments still appeared to be lacking in 1977. Part of the problem was excess refining capacity in the world since 1974, as well as refinery construction in several oil-exporting countries. According to some experts a more fundamental consideration lay behind the stalled negotiations. They believed that the industrialized countries were fearful of a shift of refineries to producing areas because it made their economies more dependent on a single source of supply. When refineries were located in industrialized countries, it was easier to buy crude from several sources according to availability, price, strategic interest, or other reasons. Nonetheless observers expected that Iran would build one or more additional export refineries in the future.

Khark Island was the principal sea terminal, handling much of the export of crude from the consortium area. It was the world's largest offshore crude terminal. It could berth ten tankers of up to 500,000 deadweight tons. Refined products were exported from Bandar Mah Shahr, which had been the crude oil terminal before construction of the Khark Island installation. There were additional small sea terminals for individual areas.

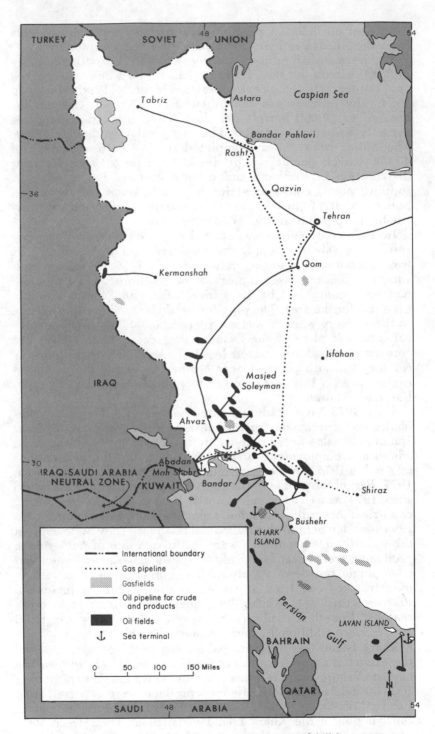

Figure 10. Oil and Gasfields plus Major Pipelines

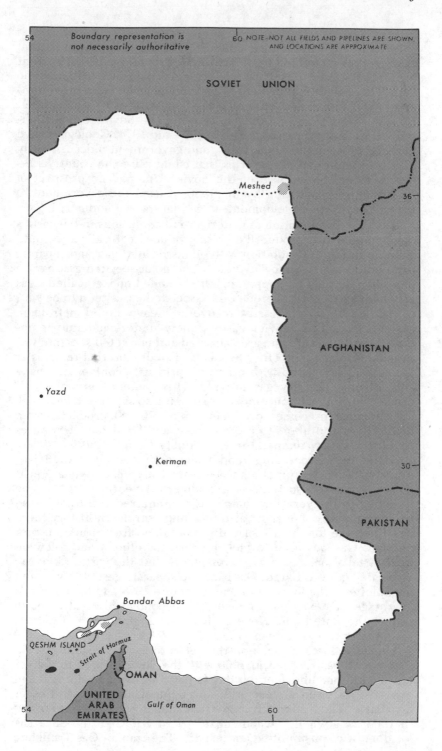

Natural Gas

In early 1977 Iranian gas officials reported that proven natural gas reserves amounted to 377 trillion cubic feet and that current exploration could raise reserves to more than 593 trillion cubic feet. These figures represented a sharp increase from proven reserves of 270 trillion cubic feet at the beginning of 1974 and placed Iranian reserves second only to those of the Soviet Union. Substantial gas discoveries occurred in 1973 and 1974. Geologists have noted numerous gas-prone areas, and government officials clearly expected additional discoveries that could raise the country's reserves even above those of the Soviet Union. The prospect of declining oil production by the 1980s caused the government to invest heavily in development of the natural gas industry.

The same combination of materials and conditions in the earth's development that produced oil also produced natural gas. Natural gas is found both in solution with oil (associated gas) and separate from crude oil (nonassociated gas). The nonassociated gas may be in a separate field or trapped in a high-domed pocket (called a gas cap) above a deposit of crude oil. Associated gases tend to be wet, containing relatively easily recovered heavy liquid petroleum gases (LPG). The heavier gases liquefy under moderate temperature and pressure and are extracted and marketed separately as propane, butane, and other products. The dry gas that remains or is found unassociated with crude oil primarily contains methane and ethane. The dry gas provides an excellent burnable fuel, usually burning without smoke or soot; it also supplies a feedstock for chemical processes producing some 70,000 products, from textile dyes and fibers to protein foods and fertilizers. Dry gases require very low temperatures to liquefy (about $-260°F$).

Collecting, processing, and transporting gas is expensive. Transportation by pipeline is easiest. Only recently has technology improved so that, as a commerical venture, gas can be liquefied to the very low temperatures required and transported by special ships. For most of Iran's long petroleum history there was little use for the associated gas obtained from crude oil production. Gas was used to fuel the Abadan refinery and a few oil field installations, such as power plants, but the vast bulk of the associated gas was flared. Gas caps and separate gasfields were left unexploited. The low cost of energy before 1974 and the country's low stage of development made it uneconomical to attempt to collect the flared gas. Nevertheless the dissipation of a natural resource troubled Iranian officials.

A major effort was made in the 1960s to use associated gas. An agreement was reached in 1966 with the Soviet Union to deliver up to 1 billion cubic feet per day to pay for Soviet equipment and expertise to build a steel mill, an engineering plant, and other assistance. The National Iranian Gas Company (NIGC) was formed in 1966, as a wholly owned subsidiary of NIOC, to produce gas for domestic consumption and export. The Iranian Gas Trunkline

(IGAT) was built to bring gas from the southwest oil fields to the Soviet border at Astara on the Caspian Sea and commissioned in October 1970. Spur lines branched off to major Iranian cities to supply gas primarily for industrial use. The pipeline had a capacity of 1.6 billion cubic feet per day at the beginning of 1975. In 1976 exports to the Soviet Union were about 328 billion cubic feet, and revenues were nearly US$150 million for the year.

The early estimates of the cost of the IGAT system were the equivalent of US$470 million, which some pipeline experts considered at least 25 percent above what a similar system would cost elsewhere. Actual costs reportedly were about US$700 million, an example of the serious cost overruns on many Iranian projects. The original sale price of gas at the Soviet border was the equivalent of US$0.187 per 1,000 cubic feet. Economists familiar with the project concluded that the IGAT system would have difficulty paying for itself from export proceeds, let alone for the steel mill and other equipment. Several price increases negotiated with the Soviet Union had increased the foreign exchange earnings of the system. In 1975 the price of gas at the Soviet border was increased to the equivalent of US$0.57 per 1,000 cubic feet. Cumulative export earnings through June 1976 were about US$600 million, suggesting that many more years of gas exports would be required to cover the costs of the pipeline and industrial plants.

As a result of the IGAT system, other local gas pipelines, and a government policy to encourage use of gas in industry wherever possible, domestic gas consumption had been expanding at about 20 to 25 percent a year in the 1970s. One of the world's largest natural gas liquids (NGL) refineries was completed at Bandar Mah Shahr in 1970 to process dry gas for the Abadan refinery and the IGAT system and to produce propane, butane, and natural gas for the domestic market and export. Bottled gas was widely used in houses because dry gas distribution to residential areas was limited. Several petrochemical plants were built using gas as feedstock. Power plants and other large industrial users converted to gas as it became available. Yet only about 40 to 45 percent of associated gas was used in the mid-1970s (see Appendix A for production and consumption statistics). More than half the gas produced was still flared.

When the era of cheap energy in the industrialized world ended in 1974, economic justification and funds became available for development of gas resources. Four major goals emerged: to increase gas exports, to increase domestic industrial use of gas, to build petrochemical plants using gas, and to reinject huge quantities of gas into the oil fields to increase the amount of recoverable crude oil. The fifth plan (1973–77) guidelines for the gas industry anticipated investments of US$2.5 billion: US$1 billion from the NIGC, US$0.77 billion from the government, and the remainder from foreign companies. The plan stated that the gas industry would not be subject to financial limitations, however, indicating that the planners had assigned considerable priority to the expansion of the gas industry.

A major twenty-year export agreement was signed in November 1975 for Iran to deliver about 1.3 billion cubic feet per day of gas to the Soviet Union, which in turn would deliver gas to the Czechoslovakian-West German border. The Soviet Union would consume Iranian gas in the south and deliver gas to the Federal Republic of Germany (West Germany) from the Soviet gasfields. The difference between the amount of gas delivered to the Soviet Union and to West Germany was the Soviet transit fee although it could also be paid in agreed-upon currencies. West Germany would keep 40 percent of the gas, and 26 percent would be delivered to France and 13 percent to Austria. Czechoslovakia subsequently arranged to take 21 percent of the gas. A second pipeline, probably parallel to the IGAT pipeline, would be financed and built by Iran, requiring an investment likely to exceed US$1 billion. The pipeline was to be completed and deliveries to start by 1981, but full capacity would not be reached until 1984. Original estimates indicated that Iran would earn about US$2 billion from gas export over twenty years, but Iranian officials reported in early 1977 that gas export would earn US$12 billion. Construction had not started as of early 1977.

In the 1970s Iranian officals had discussed exports of liquefied natural gas (LNG) with several international companies. The project proposal closest to conclusion appeared to be with a consortium of American and Belgian companies. Letters of intent were signed in December 1974. The agreement called for Iranian exports of LNG equivalent of 2 billion cubic feet of gas per day and rising to 3 billion cubic feet of gas per day in the mid-1980s. Required investments would amount to about US$6 billion. The liquefied gas would be marketed in the United States, Western Europe, and Japan. Iranian revenues would amount to about US$300 to US$500 million a year, totaling close to US$10billion over the twenty-year contract.

Domestic projects to use gas were numerous. One long-term development project concerned fields on Qeshm Island near Bandar Abbas (see fig. 1). Producing, gathering, and processing facilities were to be developed during the 1970s and 1980s to bring gas to Bandar Abbas and eventually to the interior town of Kerman. Among the projects to be built to use the gas were a direct-reduction steel mill with an initial annual capacity of 2 million tons, a large power plant at Bandar Abbas, and the important copper mine and smelter in Kerman Province (see fig. on Administrative Divisions, ch. 6). The pipeline, supplying the town of Meshed from a large gasfield near the Soviet border in Khorasan Province, would be extended westward about 500 miles to towns near the southeast corner of the Caspian Sea. The pipeline would eventually supply a very large (1,400 megawatt) power plant and a direct-reduction steel mill to be constructed. In the area around

Ahvaz, a number of plants were to be built by the early 1980s, including a direct-reduction steel mill and a power plant, requiring expansion of the gas supply existing in the mid-1970s. Existing petrochemical plants were to be expanded and additional ones built. Gas, as a proportion of total energy consumption, was expected to increase from one-tenth in 1974 to over one-third by the mid-1980s, exclusive of that used in secondary recovery techniques in the oil fields.

The most ambitious gas-using project was the recovery technique, i.e., the injection of gas into older oil fields to increase crude oil recovery. The procedure had high priority because Iranian officials expected it would substantially increase amounts of recoverable crude oil. Moreover perhaps 85 percent of the gas would itself be recoverable after the oil field was no longer productive. Reinjection had already started in some fields by 1975 and would increase through the 1970s and early 1980s. When fully implemented, reinjection could require about 13 billion cubic feet per day, a very large program requiring an amount of gas equivalent to about one-fourth of total United States gas production. Reinjection would absorb all associated gas production (4.5 billion cubic feet per day in 1975), eliminate flared gas (over 2 billion cubic feet per day in 1975), and require large quantities of additional gas from gas caps and gasfields.

It was natural that Iranian officials would attempt to exploit the country's large gas reserves when funds became available from the rapid increase of oil revenues in the 1970s. Exploitation became even more attractive as a means to partially offset the prospect of declining oil exports by continuing crude production through secondary recovery techniques and also by freeing more oil for export by switching domestic energy consumption to gas. But the program proposed was extremely ambitious.

By 1977 there were indications that gas exploitation projects might be slowed and some perhaps cancelled. Journalists reported that officials were disappointed with the results of secondary recovery techniques so far achieved, and the gas injection program was the most important determination of the rate of gas exploitation. Ardor for LNG projects had reportedly cooled because of the huge investments required. Moreover the delays at ports, difficulties with construction schedules, and shortages of men, materials, and funds might delay completion of projects (see ch. 9). Nevertheless some observers expected many of the gas exploitation plans to be implemented but at later dates than originally proposed.

Domestic Consumption of Petroleum

Wood and dung provided most of the country's energy until oil was discovered, and its products became available. Low incomes and lack of transportation provided little incentive to BP to increase sales of petroleum products in Iran. Through the 1920s petroleum consumption was largely confined to the northern part of the country, particularly Tehran, and most oil products were imported from the Soviet Union. The rest of the country continued to use traditional fuels. After 1932 BP received a monopoly of internal distribution of petroleum products that lasted until nationalization in 1951. Construction of the Iranian railroad before World War II and construction of road networks during the war by Allied forces contributed to greater distribution and consumption of petroleum products.

NIOC was given a monopoly of domestic petroleum distribution at nationalization, and it became the largest and most important activity of NIOC. Prices were set by the Cabinet, however, and uniform prices were established throughout the country for various petroleum products. NIOC had to absorb the subsidy costs created by high transportation rates as distances from the refineries increased. Moreover NIOC investment priorities did not always conform to schedules of the government's planning organization, at times creating a lag in petroleum facilities needed for economic development. Although NIOC's distribution department appeared to have avoided acute shortages, there was some discussion in 1976 of establishing domestic distribution as a separate entity in an effort to mesh petroleum supplies to development plans.

A study of energy demand in 1969 determined that 74 percent of total energy used was petroleum products and 14 percent was natural gas; coal, wood, dung, and hydroelectricity together made up the remainder. Projections indicated that by 1982 petroleum would account for 60 percent of the total energy consumed and natural gas 34 percent. In 1973 diesel fuel and industrial fuel oil each made up about roughly one-fourth of the petroleum products consumed and kerosine about one-fifth. In 1974 residential and commercial users accounted for 31 percent of domestic petroleum consumption, industry 27 percent, and road transport 20 percent. In the mid-1970s kerosine was the primary household fuel and occupied a significant part of most household budgets, particularly among low-income groups. The price of kerosine was a sensitive issue.

Between 1967 and 1972 domestic consumption of petroleum products increased at a rate of more than 11 percent a year and amounted to about 220,000 barrels per day in 1972. NIOC projected consumption to increase at just under 9 percent a year between 1973 and 1993; consumption would therefore amount to 851,000 barrels per day in 1985 and 1.5 million barrels per day in 1993. By 1993 consumption would match production, and exports would cease. Thus Iran was facing an increasingly stringent energy balance. Lags in constructing gas facilities or electric power plants would increase petroleum consumption and halt oil exports sooner. More rapid industrialization than anticipated would probably have the same effect. The problem facing the planners was readily apparent. Export industries had to be developed to furnish the foreign exchange the country needed before oil exports ceased in fifteen or twenty years.

Other Industry

The oil sector long remained a foreign-operated, export-oriented enclave in the economy. The exploitation of the country's oil reserves initially had only a limited impact on the rest of the economy, but there was an effect. The increase in incomes, urbanization, growth of various institutions, and development of roads and other forms of transportation gradually increased the possibilities for industrial development. By the 1960s investment in and production by manufacturing establishments began to accelerate. Iranian officials decided to use the huge increase of oil revenues of the mid-1970s to hurry up the industrialization process. By 1977 large investments were being made in manufacturing as well as mining and electric power to expand the country's industrial base.

Early Industrialization

Several major factors kept the economy from modernizing over the centuries. Aridity limited productivity and incomes in agriculture (see ch. 11). Distances were great and transport difficult between the small concentrations of people, limiting most production to local markets. Power and prestige were attached to owning land, thus restricting investments in more risky undertakings such as manufacturing. These and other constraints had to be overcome before new economic patterns could emerge.

A discernible effort to break the economic stagnation started in 1820. The Iranian ambassador to London brought a steam engine and several British workers skilled in various industries to Iran. The object was to establish factories that would produce industrial goods that were readily available in Europe. In the 1850s skilled Iranian artisans and craftsmen were sent to European cities to learn modern methods of production. These measures resulted in the establishment of several factories between the 1820s and 1920s. Most failed because of the lack of a skilled work force, the inability of Europeans to adapt to life in Iran, the lack of efficient management, transportation, and communications, and the lack of a social and political environment conducive to industrialization. As a result only a few plants survived the competition of cheap imports from Europe. By 1920 there were three successful cotton textile plants, a saw mill, two match factories, a knitting factory, a soap factory, some urban workshops, and small plants producing brick and tile. Most manufacturing was cottage industry and produced Iran's famed rugs and other textile and leather products, which were important foreign exchange earners.

Reza Shah accelerated the movement toward modernization. His initial and very important contribution was to unify the country and establish internal security, which had been lacking for many years (see ch. 2). He also used the government to stimulate industrialization. He favored more factories than less, state factories to privately owned, and big plants to small ones. He believed in capital-intensive production, and World War II prevented installation of one of his favored projects, a steel mill ordered from Germany. By 1940 sixty-four state factories had been established. They had been financed by internal sources—the National Bank of Iran and the government budget—without recourse to foreign funds. Twenty percent of the budget was allocated to economic development by the 1940s. During Reza Shah's regime transportation and other ancillaries to economic development were improved, the most significant of which was completion in 1938 of the trans-Iranian railroad (850 miles).

The petroleum industry had a limited direct effect on the economy, but the cumulative indirect effects began to mount. Skills employees learned in the oil industry diffused into the rest of the economy when they left, raising, albeit slowly, the level of the work force. The rise in incomes and greater urbanization expanded markets for local manufactures. The oil company itself became an important buyer for local products and services. The increased availability of motor fuels at low prices accelerated the growth of modern transport. Most important, however, was the growth of oil revenues that enabled the government to participate directly in industrialization.

One hundred thirty-six new factories (employing ten or more workers and providing employment for more than 40,000 workers) were built between 1926 and 1947. There was a particularly rapid growth between 1934 and World War II. By 1947 total industrial employment amounted to about 100,000, approximately 39 percent in large-scale (for Iran) plants. Manufacturing's contribution to GNP had increased from near zero in the 1920s, to about 5 percent in 1947. Industry did not rank very high, but the structure of the economy was changing. Most manufacturing attempted to substitute local products for imports and was concentrated in food processing, textiles, and other consumer goods; some plants produced chemicals, soap, paint, cement, and glass. Nearly all industry in this period depended on local materials for processing. The scale of production was small by international standards and geared almost exclusively to the local market where domestic products enjoyed an advantage over imports because of higher transportation costs.

Natural Resources

A large variety of mineral resources were long known to exist, but only in recent years has a start been made to conduct surveys and establish commercial potentials of known deposits. By 1977 about one-half the country had been surveyed, but less than one-fifth had been explored on the ground. Exploration permits covered about 5 percent of the country and were issued only to government organizations. Iranian officials expected substantial additional discoveries from continuing exploration.

Minerals have been discovered in many parts of the country. In

1975 estimated reserves of some of the more important mineral deposits were 114 million tons of iron ore with a metal content of 35 to 62 percent; 1 billion tons of copper ore, much of it high grade; 10 million tons of lead and zinc ore; 12,000 tons of antimony ore; 720,000 tons of manganese ore; 7 million tons of chromite; 300 million tons of coal; and 12 million tons of sulfur (apart from oil). In addition there were extensive deposits of limestone, glass sand, clay, construction rock, and marble.

Mining statistics were fragmentary and outdated. In 1973 there were 555 mines and quarries in operation, employing about 21,300 workers. Nearly 14,200 of the workers were employed in coal mines and in the production of nonmetallic minerals for the construction industry; nonmetallic minerals were the largest mining activity in terms of employment and value added, followed by coal and iron ore. Some ores—chromite, zinc, and lead—and rock sulfur were exported. Some minerals produced in 1972 were 1 million tons of coal; 980,000 tons of iron ore; 220,000 tons of lead and zinc ore; 1,000 tons of copper ore; 180,000 tons of chromite; and 5.2 million tons of limestone.

Planned government investment in mining and quarrying between FY 1973 and FY 1978 amounted to about US$1 billion; additional sums were expected from domestic and foreign private investors. A major focus was a twenty-year project—costing initially about US$450 million—to exploit the copper ores near Kerman, estimated at about 400 million tons and possibly over 800 million tons. Officials expected copper products to become a major foreign exchange earner as oil revenues declined. About US$170 million was to be invested in developing large, high-grade iron ore deposits north of Bandar Abbas to supply growing domestic requirements. Plans called for production of 4 to 5 million tons of concentrated ore by the early 1980s. The government was also developing coal mines in Kerman Province to supply the iron and steel industry. A private consortium was being established to build a colliery and to mine rich seams of top-quality coal in the northeast.

Electric Power Base

The lack of adequate electric power was an important constraint on industrial development until the late 1960s. Power generating facilities through the 1950s were primarily small diesel units owned by local private and municipal companies or attached to industrial installations. Tehran had the largest facilities. In the late 1950s the government initiated a power development program based on three dams that would generate electricity. A power authority was created in 1963, and its functions were incorporated into a ministry responsible for water and power in 1964. In 1965 the electric power industry was nationalized in order to build a large, integrated system. In 1967 all generating facilities were government controlled except generators attached to industrial plants. In 1977 the Iran Power Generation and Transmission

Company (TAVANIR), a government-owned company formed in 1969, owned and operated most generating and transmitting facilities, but regional entities distributed electricity to final consumers and had some generating capacity. Some plants still had generators.

During the 1960s the government made a major effort to expand the electricity supply and build a national system. Generating capacity increased from about 440 megawatts in 1963 to 2,800 megawatts in 1973, including about 300 megawatts in isolated units throughout the country. About 30 percent of capacity was in hydroelectric installations. Gross generation of electricity increased from 1.9 billion kilowatt-hours in 1963 to 10.4 billion kilowatt-hours in 1972, an average increase of about 21 percent a year. Government generators supplied 72 percent of electricity generated in 1972; the rest was supplied by private industry. In 1972 public sector sales of electricity were 46 percent to industry, 19 percent to commercial enterprises, 19 percent to residential users, 8 percent to rural users, and the rest to miscellaneous consumers.

Only about one-fourth of the population had electricity available. About 2,000 miles of transmission and distribution lines had been constructed by 1972, which was the start of a national system. Two smaller, separate networks centered on Kerman in the southwest and Meshed in the northeast.

The fifth plan anticipated a growth in demand for electricity of about 21 percent a year, requiring generation of about 24 billion kilowatt-hours by 1978. The original plan allocation of investment funds was about US$1 billion to increase installed capacity to 6,200 megawatts by 1978 and to increase transmission lines to nearly 6,000 miles. In 1974 the fifth plan goals were sharply raised as oil revenues jumped. Investment funds for electricity were increased to US$4.6 billion (6.6 percent of total fixed investment). Up-to-date figures were unavailable in early 1977, but the presumption was that the original schedule was being met or surpassed. Major projects that were to be completed by 1978 included 1,000 megawatts of capacity at Reza Shah Kabir Dam, northeast of Masjed Soleyman on the Rud-e Karun, with transmission lines to Arak, Ahvaz, and Isfahan; increased generating capacity at Shiraz, Isfahan, and Arak, and linking of these industrial areas to the main grid; and substantially increased generating facilities at Bandar Abbas and the copper mines near Kerman and transmission lines to link these areas to the southeast transmission network.

During the 1960s and early 1970s the rapid increase of manufacturing, the greater urbanization, and the extension of electric lines to more of the population placed a considerable burden on planners to build ahead of demand. They did not always succeed even with extensive foreign advice. For example, industrial development was temporarily held up in the vicinity of Bandar

Abbas because of insufficient power, and by mid-1977 brownouts and blackouts occurred frequently, disrupting industrial production. Nevertheless many experts approved the approach of building a network with large, interconnected power stations rather than the more costly and inefficient construction of separate facilities for each impending local shortage. The near doubling of investment goals for the fifth plan compounded the problem of keeping the power supply ahead of demand, however, for it meant a substantial increase in industrial consumers.

To meet the challenge, Iranian officals opted for nuclear power plants to meet part of the demand for electricity. Discussions were held with several countries, and press reports discussed several possible transactions. Two contracts were reportedly signed for four plants, but it was not certain by early 1977 that all obstacles had been cleared. West Germany was to supply two of the nuclear power plants (with a capacity of 1,200 megawatts each), and France was to supply two (with a capacity of 900 megawatts each). The plants were pressurized water reactors using enriched uranium and would be sited near the Persian Gulf because of the need for large quantities of water for cooling. Each was a turn-key project; i.e., the manufacturer was to supply everything needed for the plant to become operational, including training. The German plants were to be completed in 1981 and 1982, the French plants in 1983 and 1984. More nuclear plants were to be added later. The decision to go to nuclear power, though perhaps questionable on economic and technical grounds, stemmed from policy decisions to develop non-oil energy sources in the coming decades.

Industrialization Since World War II

After World War II industrial growth accelerated, becoming the most dynamic sector of the economy by the mid-1970s. Simple statistical measurements for the period were lacking to show the growth because a consistent and relatively accurate set of national accounts was not established until the end of the 1950s. Several factors contributed to accelerating industrialization. An important one was the shah's decision to have national plans drafted to guide the allocations of resources for systematic economic development. The plans provided a means of noting the development of industry before national accounts became available.

In 1946 an American firm was hired to study the economy and formulate a development program. The results were reviewed and modified by the government and adopted for the period of the first plan (see Glossary), FY 1949 through FY 1955. Primary emphasis was given to agriculture and the infrastructure, but industry and mining received 14 percent of the plan funds (see ch. 9). The primary goal for industry in the first plan was to renovate the established industries that had received little maintenance or replacement of equipment during the war. The first plan relied heavily on oil revenues for financing. The sharp decline of oil revenues during the nationalization crisis kept development expenditures to about 20 percent of those planned, crippling the program. Nonetheless two cement mills and four sugar refineries were built or expanded, raising cement production from 56,000 tons in 1949 to 132,000 tons in 1955 and production of refined sugar from 27,000 tons to 76,000 tons over the same period. Construction or expansion of several chemical plants, a dried-fruit processing factory, and a dairy processing facility also started.

During the first plan large plants were usually established by the government. They were generally unprofitable because of overstaffing and inexperienced management. The private sector established several thousand small, consumer-oriented industries despite the difficulties created by the nationalization crisis. Discriminatory exchange rates and tariff concessions provided a favorable environment for the private sector.

The second plan, covering September 1955 to September 1962, was a more sophisticated document than the first; however, administrative problems continued. Various difficulties caused delays and large cost overruns, particularly on big projects. A number of the projects were included in agriculture and infrastructure, which together received 56 percent of planned expenditures. Three large dams and considerable expansion of railroads, highways, ports, and airports were completed during the plan. Manufacturing and mining received only 7 percent of government development expenditures. An integrated textile mill, two cement plants (to provide cement for dam construction), and a sugar mill were the major additions in the public sector.

The private sector provided most of the growth in manufacturing. The number of industrial enterprises increased from 45,000 in 1957 to nearly 70,000 in 1960; the industrial work force increased by 20 percent in the same period. Legislation in 1956 provided protection to foreign investors, and a significant inflow of foreign investment began, amounting to nearly 400 million rials (for value of the rial—see Glossary). Most foreign investment went into chemical, pharmaceuticals, rubber tires, and batteries. Three major industries were notable; between 1955 and 1962 expansion of total capacity (private and public) in textiles increased from 60 million meters (one meter is equal to 39.37 inches) to 418 million meters; in cement, from 132,000 tons to 1.2 million tons; and in sugar refining, from 85,000 tons to 217,000 tons.

The next economic plan covered five and one-half years, and subsequent plans covered five years each. The third and fourth plans, FY 1963 to FY 1972, provided a convenient period to mark the growth of industry and the impact of the shah's efforts to modernize the economy. In addition national account data became available for the period providing statistical measurements.

Between FY 1962 and FY 1972 manufacturing made remarkable progress. Output of the industrial sector increased at an average rate of 12.9 percent a year, and gross value added, in constant prices, averaged 12.3 percent a year. During the decade the direct contribution of manufacturing to total economic growth was over 15 percent in real terms, and its share of GDP increased from 12 percent in 1962 to 14 percent in 1972. Employment in manufacturing increased from approximately 1.2 to nearly 2 million, accounting for about 38 percent additional employment opportunities.

Domestic investments in industry increased from 5 billion rials in 1962 to 65 billion rials in 1972, which was about a ninefold increase even after adjustment to constant prices. Net fixed investment in manufacturing amounted to 63 billion rials in the third plan and 250 billion rials in the fourth plan. The gross flow of foreign private capital (excluding the oil industry) amounted to nearly 13 billion rials, about one-half of which came from the United States. About one-half of foreign private investment was in petrochemicals, chemicals, pharmaceuticals, and rubber products.

During the same period investment shifted noticeably away from nondurable consumer goods toward basic metals (steel and aluminum), capital goods, chemicals and petrochemicals, construction materials, and motor vehicles and other consumer durables. Nondurable consumer goods received 63 percent of net fixed investment in manufacturing in the third-year plan but only 25 percent in the fourth plan, though increasing in absolute amounts from 39 billion rials in the third plan to 63 billion rials in the fourth plan. Investment in basic metals increased from 1.4 billion rials in the third plan to 60 billion rials in the fourth plan as a result of government construction of a large steel plant. Investment in chemicals also increased sharply. The investments affected output. Several new products appeared for the first time (e.g., paper, fertilizers, steel pipes, aluminum, diesel engines, electric fans, and insulated cables). Output of detergents, sheet glass, iron profiles, gas stoves, television sets, refrigerators, and passenger cars also increased sharply.

The shift in investments caused a rapid increase of the value added by durable and capital goods (an annual average of 21 percent) and intermediate goods (an annual average of 19 percent). The value added of nondurable consumer goods increased at an annual rate of about 11 percent. The value added of intermediate, durable, and capital goods accounted for a substantial part of the value added by manufacturing during the decade.

The changing structure of industry toward vertical integration of production laid a solid base for future growth. A few large-scale plants accounted for nearly two-thirds of the value added by manufacturing, however, which created difficulties for the planners' goal of improving income distribution. A survey in 1969 showed only 239,000 paid employees in 5,100 urban manufacturing establishments employing ten or more people. The bulk of the work force engaged in manufacturing, more than half of whom were unpaid, worked in small urban shops of ten or fewer workers, or in such cottage industries as rug weaving. The data suggest that most small-scale enterprises benefited little from the rapid economic growth. The government was aware of the problems and attempted to take remedial steps because of the potential contribution small-scale business could make toward employment, income distribution, and regional diversification goals. Although before 1972 government assistance was limited, more help was planned in the fifth plan, particularly for small shops that had a potential to become modern.

Many factors contributed to the rapid industrial diversification of the economy in the 1960s. The years of investing in the infrastructure, the rising incomes and urbanization of part of the population, the increasing skills of the work force, the changing social conditions, and the growth of attitudes and institutions conducive to industrial investment were examples of a process described as maturation of the economy. Moreover the growth of oil revenues and their payment in foreign exchange supplied funds for development, including a large volume of imports that provided a flexibility often lacking in other developing countries.

The objective of the Pahlavi dynasty has been, from its beginning in 1926, industrialization of the country. The government intervened in many ways to achieve its objective. Some efforts were indirect, such as land reform. Many were direct, such as government investment in large-scale projects and fiscal incentives to private investors. In general government policies have been flexible, adjusting to changing conditions.

Import substitution was the basic strategy. Initially domestic production concentrated on such basic consumer goods as textiles and food processing. By the 1960s import substitution moved into more complex products, such as production and processing of basic metals, and more sophisticated final products, such as consumer durables. Government policy encouraged import substitution through high tariff protection, import quota systems, generous fiscal incentives, direct government investment, credit facilities, and legislation protecting foreign investors.

The government's main objective was to create an industrial base incorporating modern technology. Often large projects had large cost overruns above initial cost estimates, reducing the competitiveness of the project's products under normal conditions. The government also enforced a policy of dispersing industry into various parts of the country to reduce the excessive concentration that had developed near Tehran. The government was willing to accept extra costs to achieve a somewhat balanced growth in various regions. Cost conditions or competitiveness was not the prime concern in laying the industrial base, however. Nonetheless investigations by economists in the early 1970s did not find all Iranian industry inefficient. Government policy has been sufficiently flexible so that production costs for some products were competitive with those in other countries, although some remained considerable higher.

By the fifth plan remarkable progress had been made in industry. Industry, including mining, power, and construction, contributed 22 percent to GDP in FY 1972. There were incipient problems, but the foundation for additional development was in place.

Industry in the Fifth Plan (FY 1973–77)

The original fifth plan was drafted in 1972 and adopted in early 1973. The prospect of tremendous increases in oil revenues that immediately followed posed a choice for officials. Essentially the choice was to follow the fifth plan as drafted and invest excess funds abroad for future use or put the additional funds into the economy for maximum growth in the shortest time. An in-between policy was adopted that attempted to limit the amount of investment in the domestic economy to the amount it could absorb without inflation and resource waste (see ch. 9).

The revised fifth plan raised planned fixed investments in manufacturing by 50 percent over the original plan to US$11.6 billion (US$4.1 billion in the public sector and US$7.5 billion in the private sector), the largest investment other than housing. Substantial investments were also allocated to electricity, development of gas resources, and mining as ancillaries to industrial development. Over half the revised investment goals for manufacturing were in basic metals (30 percent) and chemicals and petrochemicals (21 percent). The remainder of planned fixed investments were spread among all other industries. Clearly basic metals and petrochemicals had been assigned priority in development expenditures.

Up-to-date data were unavailable in early 1977 to access accurately the performance in the fifth plan. Actual government investments in public sector manufacturing in the first two years and budget allocations for FY 1975 amounted to nearly 70 percent of the total for the entire five years. The high level of business activity and shortages of various commodities reportedly caused a high level of private sector investment in industry. The growth of value added (in constant prices) in industry and mining in each of the first three years reportedly exceeded the average 18-percent growth rate of the plan.

There was considerable doubt about the industrial sector's ability to meet some of the more spectacular quantitative fifth plan goals by the end of the plan period, March 1978. Cement production, for example, was 5.4 million tons in FY 1975 compared with planned production in FY 1977 of 20 million tons; fertilizer production was 440,000 tons in FY 1975 compared with planned production in FY 1977 of 1.7 million tons; and steel production was perhaps 1 million tons in FY 1975 compared with planned production in FY 1977 of 10 million tons. Observers anticipated slippage in completion schedules for many of the larger projects. Even if sufficient additional capacity was installed in time, some economists expected that start-up problems would keep production in many industries below quantitative goals by the target date.

Although some goals might not be met within the plan period, there was evidence of a surge in the industrial sector. More investment was being made in plant and equipment during the fifth plan than had been accomplished in the four previous plans combined. The range of products the economy produced was rapidly expanding. For example, the automotive industry no longer just assembled foreign components; domestic manufacturing supplied an increasing proportion of the parts. The volume of production was also rising rapidly. Most observers agreed that the fifth plan would considerably increase the importance of industry in the economy and remake the country's image from that of primarily a producer of oil and handwoven rugs.

Steel

The steel industry was scheduled for rapid expansion even though it was relatively new in the Iranian economy. Reza Shah had ordered a steel mill in the 1930s, but World War II kept it from being erected. A steel mill became an Iranian symbol of economic progress, but discussions produced no results until an arrangement was reached with the Soviet Union in 1966 for the Soviets to construct an integrated iron and steel complex and a heavy engineering works in return for Iranian exports of natural gas (see Oil Industry, this ch.).

The Soviet-supplied steel mill was situated at Isfahan, primarily because of the availability of water. In addition Isfahan was centrally located, being relatively close to iron and coal deposits, natural gas from the oil fields, and the major steel consuming center of Tehran. The National Iranian Steel Corporation, a government-owned company, was formed to build and operate the plant. The basic equipment included conventional blast furnaces fueled by natural gas, coke ovens, steel converters, continuous casting equipment, and rolling mills. The Soviets also helped build training facilities, a residential town, and mines for coal and iron ore as part of the steel mill project.

The steel mill was designed for three stages. The initial stage was to produce 750,000 tons of ingot steel; a second stage would increase capability to about 2 million tons. A third stage could be added to raise production to 5 to 7 million tons. Part of the infrastructure was constructed for eventual maximum output, creating problems of evaluating the cost and efficiency of the plant. The plant cost considerably more than originally planned.

The first stage of the steel complex was formally commissioned in early 1973 but had some start-up difficulties. The most serious was shortage of high quality coking coal. The problem was reportedly solved by mixing various Iranian grades with about 7 to

10 percent of imported coal. Some trouble was also reported with the rolling mills. Production reached about 600,000 tons in 1975 and was scheduled to reach 1.9 to 2 million tons by 1977. Expansions under way would raise capacity to 6 million tons. There has been discussion of expanding capacity to about 15 million tons by the mid-1980s.

Privately owned plants and a subsidiary of NIOC produced steel products. The first steel operations began in 1966 at the Shahryar group's mills, using scrap and imported billets to produce reinforcing rods and light structural shapes. By 1975 this private company had facilities for 400,000 tons of steel products. The Ahvaz Rolling and Pipe Mills Company's plant became operational in 1971 with a capacity of 150,000 tons of hot coil strip and 40,000 tons of black and galvanized pipe. Completion of an expansion that would more than double capacity was scheduled for early 1977. A 1-million-ton slab and plate mill was also under construction, and completion was scheduled for 1979, when it would receive steel from a new government steel mill scheduled for completion at the same time. NIOC operated two mills (annual capacity totaling 200,000 tons) to produce pipe for the oil and gas industry.

From these modest beginnings the steel industry has greatly expanded. In 1973 the government decided not only to enlarge the steel complex at Isfahan but also to build five new ones as part of the government monopoly over basic iron and steel. The five new plants all incorporated the relatively new and advanced technology of direct reduction of iron ore by natural gas. A separate government organization, the National Iranian Steel Industries Company (NISIC), will own and operate the plants.

By mid-1977 the plant at Ahvaz was furthest along. It had a capacity of 2.5 million tons of sponge iron and 1.5 tons of steel. Its reported cost was US$650 million. It incorporated three different direct reduction processes and served as a testing ground to find the one most suitable for future use. The first two units were completed in 1977 with an initial capacity of 1.5 million tons of sponge iron. The third unit was scheduled for completion in 1978. The plant would use imported ore—initially from Sweden and eventually from India—under a twenty-year agreement arranged earlier.

A US$1-billion project was signed with a British company to build a gas reduction plant at Isfahan. It was scheduled to be completed in 1980; capacity reportedly would be about 1.2 million tons of liquid steel.

Another agreement was signed with an Italian company in late 1975 for a plant to be constructed near Bandar Abbas. Capacity would be 2.8 million tons of liquid steel, partly for Iran's automotive industry and partly for export. The project had an estimated cost of US$3 billion, which included a town, port facilities, and a desalination plant to produce the necessary fresh water.

Progress was reportedly slow, partly because the original site was on a geological fault and partly because of infrastructure problems caused by the lack of development in southern Iran. A severe earthquake in the area in March 1977 may have further delayed construction. Iron ore was to come from near Kerman, requiring mine development and construction of a railroad to bring the ore to the plant.

Two additional steel mills have been discussed for sites in Khorasan Province in the northeast and on the Persian Gulf near the large gasfields. By 1977 it was not clear whether studies had been completed and contracts let for these projects. The NISIC entered a joint venture with a French company for a US$200 million plant to produce 220,000 tons a year of special alloy steels, largely for Iran's motor industry.

Government officials indicated that in 1973 Iran's steel consumption was 2 million tons, 4.5 million in 1975, and probably 5.5 million in 1976. Consumption was expected to increase about 20 to 25 percent a year into the 1980s, requiring production of about 15 million tons annually by 1985 if substantial imports were to be avoided. The goal posed very formidable problems in coordinating such related investments as transportation, power, water, housing, and mining, plus plant construction, which involved technology new to Iran. Most observers anticipated lags and delays that would cause extension of schedules, but a rapid increase of iron and steel production was expected nonetheless. Experts doubted, however, that the steel industry had much potential for export within the next ten years.

Copper

Copper products appeared to offer a potential for export earnings. In 1977 the rich Sar Cheshmeh copper deposits southwest of Kerman were being exploited. Proven deposits were 430 million tons of high-grade ore, and the deposits might hold as much as 850 million tons of ore. It was one of the richest mines in the world. A government-owned company was developing the mine, smelter, and refinery with foreign help. Production from the mine was expected to begin in late 1977 or 1978. When mining and smelting reached full capacity, annual production would reach about 200,000 tons of blister copper. An electrolytic refinery was scheduled for completion in 1978 that would finish the ore processing to nearly pure copper. Copper deposits near Yazd appeared promising and might be processed at the Sar Cheshmeh facilities later.

Domestic consumption of copper was about 30,000 to 35,000 tons in 1976 and projected to reach about 85,000 tons per year by the early 1980s. The projections led officials to anticipate exports of pure copper above 100,000 tons a year, worth US$200 to US$300 million for a few years at least. The amount of copper or copper products for export will depend on the amount of time required to reach full production and how rapidly domestic consumption increases. Some observers expected that domestic

Refinery operation, part of budding complex industry

consumption would grow faster than anticipated, reducing the amount of copper available for export.

Aluminum

In the early 1970s an aluminum smelter with an annual capacity of 45,000 tons was built at Arak in cooperation with an American firm. The smelter turned out about 40,000 tons of aluminum ingots in FY 1975 from imported materials. About 18,000 tons were consumed domestically and the rest exported. The smelter was being expanded to have an annual capacity of 120,000 tons by early 1978 with planned production of 110,000 tons of ingots. By 1977 studies were completed and financing arranged for construction of a plant to produce aluminum sheet from the smelter's ingots. The government was also considering construction of a second smelter with a capacity of 150,000 tons a year, but it would not be completed during the fifth plan (by March 1978).

Petrochemicals

The shah long advocated development of petrochemical industries, and Iran was the first major oil exporter in the Middle East to build sizable plants. He wanted Iran to gain the large value added from processing hydrocarbons into chemical products. The fact that associated gases otherwise being flared could be used as feedstock made petrochemicals even more attractive.

The first plant to produce fertilizers was constructed near Shiraz in 1961. Additional plants followed. In 1966 a government company—National Petrochemical Company (NPC), a subsidiary of NIOC—was formed to develop the industry. The government required that the NPC participate at least 50 percent in basic petrochemicals; private industry, including foreign companies, could develop industries further along in the processing chain or participate with the NPC in basic petrochemical development. By 1976 the NPC had directly invested US$450 million in five complexes—at Shiraz, Abadan, Khark Island, Ahvaz, and Bandar Shahpur. The public sector dominated petrochemicals, but the private sector had built some plants, most of which were on a modest scale.

In 1975 production from the NPC plants was over 300,000 tons of ammonia products, phosphate and compound fertilizers, soda ash, and nitric and sulfuric acid. Fertilizer production was about half of the estimated annual domestic consumption of 750,000 to 800,000 tons. About 40,000 tons of polyvinylchloride, 12,000 tons of detergents, 16,000 tons of carbon black, and 30,000 tons of sodium tripolyphosphate were produced in 1975. Exports of petrochemical products reportedly amounted to about US$300 million in the mid-1970s.

Revisions in the fifth plan in 1974 called for investment of nearly US$2.5 billion in chemical and petrochemical plants (primarily the latter), and an annual growth of 27 percent in the value added. Production goals for FY 1977 included 1.7 million tons of fertilizer, 2 million tons of petrochemicals, 1.9 million tons of aromatics, 591,000 tons of plastics for the tire industry, 100,000 tons of monocellular proteins for animal feed, and 250,000 tons of raw materials for the synthetic fibers industry. By 1976 the NPC had committed US$640 million to expanding existing plants.

The largest addition to the petrochemical industry was a US$1.9 billion complex under construction at Bandar Shahpur in 1977. It was a fifty-fifty joint venture between the NPC and a consortium of Japanese firms to produce the basic products, olefins and aromatics, of the petrochemical industry. The complex consisted of three units: a salt electrolysis plant to convert 400,000 tons of salt into 250,000 tons of caustic soda and 200,000 tons of chlorine gas; a cracking unit to process 120,000 barrels a day of natural gas liquids into ethylene, propylene, and butadiene; and a reforming unit to process 24,000 barrels a day of naphtha to produce benzene and xylenes. Production was scheduled to begin in 1979 or 1980, although slippage on a project of this size would not be surprising.

At the start of the fifth plan officials viewed expansion of petrochemicals as export oriented. Even in 1977 some officials anticipated that about one-third of increased production would be sold abroad. Other officials were less optimistic because of very large increases in domestic consumption between 1974 and 1976. By 1977 the increase of fertilizer production, for example, was expected to be completely consumed domestically, leaving none for export by the end of the fifth plan. Negotiations for the Iranian-Japanese complex stalled for a while because officials decided Iran needed more of the production for domestic use, diminishing the amount Japanese industries could obtain. It remained to be seen how much the growth of petrochemicals would contribute to future export earnings, but it was clear that Iran intended to continue a high rate of investment in petrochemicals through the mid-1980s.

The Legacy of Rapid Growth

The rapid industrialization of the fifth plan was not without problems. The planners overestimated the amount of investment the economy could absorb. The volume of investment overtaxed the human and physical capacities of the economy. Shortages of materials and labor appeared, increasing the costs of each. Additional imports were ordered to ease the shortage of materials, but the ports and the transportation system could not handle the volume. By early 1977, however, the long line of ships waiting to unload was largely gone, and delays amounted to only fifteen days. Shortages were easing; cement and bricks, for example, were reportedly available without black-market prices. The worst of the inflationary pressures may have passed, but their legacies were left.

The rapid infusion of money accelerated the demand for goods far beyond that foreseen. The increased demand was for all kinds of products, not just consumer goods and construction materials. As a result many projects that originally were intended to produce partly for export probably would find their production consumed domestically. Many observers expect that the country will not be much better off by the 1980s in finding export products to replace oil as petroleum production begins to decline.

The high rate of demand and rapidly increasing prices created favorable circumstances for private sector investment in manufacturing. It was unclear, however, how enterprises established between 1972 and 1976 would fare when the economy cooled down and efficiency and low production costs gained importance. A large number would nonetheless be spared competition from imports by protective tariffs and quotas.

The question of efficiency applied to both the private and public sectors. Official policy had long focused on constructing industrial capacity, leaving low costs and efficiency to be solved later. It was recognized that many public sector plants were overstaffed. The rapid increase of wages—30 to 40 percent in 1975 and 1976, when labor was short and could demand wage hikes—compounded the problem of reducing production costs. The government pledged in the fifth plan to study closely and to adjust protective barriers so as not to create large distortions in prices and resource allocation, but this was not the same as making efficiency paramount. Until the emphasis shifted to low production costs and protective barriers were lowered, industry would continue to avoid production for export where competition was keen, preferring instead the less demanding conditions of the domestic market. Some economists expected industrial products to remain a small source of foreign exchange and a poor substitute for oil revenues until efficiency replaced installed capacity as an official objective.

* * *

A wealth of material exists on the international oil industry. Morris H. Adelman's *The World Petroleum Market* is a basic study of the industry although somewhat overtaken by events since 1973. *Power Play* by Leonard Mosley, *The Seven Sisters: The Great Oil Companies and The World They Made* by Anthony Sampson, *Making Democracy Safe for Oil* by Christopher T. Rand, the U. S. Congress Ninety-Third Congress (Second Session) Senate Subcommittee hearings on *Multinational Corporations and United States Foreign Policy Part 7*, August 7, 1974, and OPEC's *Annual Statistical Bulletin* contain considerable information pertaining to the international oil industry and to Iran. *Development of the Iranian Oil Industry International and Domestic Aspects* by Fereidun Fesharaki and *Iran: Economic Development under Dualistic Conditions* by Jahangir Amuzegar and M. Ali Fekrat cover aspects of Iranian industry including the oil sector. *Profile on Iran* (issues June 1975, July 1975, August 1975, and May 1976 compiled and published by the Iranian Embassy, Washington) provides broad surveys on oil, gas, and petrochemicals; the issue of April 1976 contains a survey of non-oil industry. The *Iran Almanac and Book of Facts,* published approximately yearly by Echo of Iran in Tehran, contains a variety of statistics and information on Iran's economy including oil and manufacturing. (For further information see Bibliography.)

Chapter 11. Agriculture

AGRICULTURE'S SIGNIFICANCE IN the economy began to decline with the first moves toward modernization. From overwhelming dominance in the early 1900s, in the mid-1970s agriculture employed only about 40 percent of the labor force, and the sector's output (including fishing and forestry) contributed less than 10 percent of gross domestic product (GDP).

During the 1960s and the early and mid-1970s the government took numerous steps to boost agricultural production. Nevertheless the rate of agriculture output advanced only haltingly, most farmers continued to engage in subsistence production, and the volume of imported foodstuffs soared in response to progressively increasing demand (see ch. 9). Between the mid-1950s and the mid-1970s the population increased by more than 50 percent. During the early 1970s sharp increases in world petroleum prices caused a spurt in the amount of money available for spending, and the volume of imported agricultural produce expanded correspondingly.

Among the government projects designed to increase agricultural production, the most ambitious was an extensive dam and irrigation network construction program that was still under way in the late 1970s. The data on land use in late 1977 were frequently contradictory, but in approximate figures the data indicated that of the country's 407.5 million acres, about 123.5 million were arable, i.e., if water were available the soil could be cultivated. Of this arable land only about 50 million acres had ever been cultivated, and in any given year less than 23 million acres were tilled, the remainder lying fallow, a common practice in the dryland farming of marginal land. In 1974 about 9.4 million acres were under irrigation, and an estimated 11.8 million acres were under dry farming. Iran's hopes for increasing agricultural production were based mainly on a significant expansion of the amount of land under irrigation.

Of the measures taken by the government to alter the agricultural sector of the economy, the most significant in social and political terms was the land reform program set in motion by the White Revolution (see Glossary). According to Ann K. S. Lambton, a prominent scholar on the subject, the goals of the program were "political and social," and the program "was intended first to break the political and social influence of the landowning class and secondly...to bring about the emergence of an independent peasantry." By the late 1970s most observers agreed that the power of the large landowners as a class had been greatly diminished, but there was sharp disagreement as to whether an independent peasantry had emerged.

Before 1962 over half of the land that was farmed either regularly or occasionally was owned by large, frequently absentee landlords. Another 10 to 20 percent was owned by religious trusts or endowment organizations known as waqf (pl., *awqaf*). Most of the land was farmed by sharecroppers or tenant farmers occupying small plots of land. The three-stage land reform program forced many but not all landlords to sell all or part of their holdings to, for the most part, the sharecroppers or tenants already farming the land. The managers of the public waqf properties, the proceeds of which were used for public purposes, were eventually forced to enter into ninety-nine year leases with their sharecroppers and tenants. The government purchased the land owned by the private waqf—the proceeds of which were used for private purposes—and resold it to those who had been farming the land. Only a few of the landless farm laborers received land, and in the late 1970s members of this group continued the vast migration to the industrial centers, especially Tehran (see ch. 3).

By the early 1970s the land reform program was defined as completed. The government stated that about 2.3 million former sharecroppers and tenants had become owners of small and usually scattered parcels of land. Several thousand others had signed long-term leases.

The land reform program had not required the landlords to divest themselves of such various categories of land as orchards and land that they were personally farming with mechanical equipment and paid labor. There were several thousand generally prosperous farms in this so-called commercial sector. In addition the government was actively encouraging the establishment of large agribusiness operations in which foreign capital was urged to participate. The minimum size of such undertakings was 1,000 hectares (one hectare is equal to 2.47 acres), and in some instances former sharecroppers who had just received title to and begun payment on land were forced to sell their land and move.

The agribusiness holdings included some land already under irrigation, but most of the holdings were in areas scheduled to come under irrigation in the late 1970s. The cost of preparing the land to receive and use the water from the irrigation canals greatly exceeded the preliminary estimates, and some foreign entrepreneurs who had invested capital in the early 1970s pulled out. A few firms have remained, however, and in the mid-1970s the government invested more of its increased oil wealth in this aspect of farming as part of its continuing effort to decrease its food imports, which in 1977 reached an all-time high.

Land and Water

The amount of fertile soil in the country is limited. Although the data were inconclusive and the definitions used sometimes vague, observers generally agreed that 50 percent or more of the nation's total land area was desert, wasteland, or barren mountain range of no agricultural value. About 11 percent was forested, about 8 percent grazing or pastureland, and about 1.5 percent was made up of cities, villages, industrial centers, and related areas. The remainder included land that was cultivated either permanently or on a rotation, dryland farming basis (about 14 percent) and land that could be farmed with adequate irrigation (about 15 to 16 percent). Some observers treated the latter category as pastureland.

In most regions the natural cover has been insufficient to build up much organic soil content, and on the steeper mountain slopes much of the original earth cover has been washed away. Although roughly half of Iran is made up of the arid Central Plateau, some of the gentler slopes and the Persian Gulf lowlands have relatively good soils but poor drainage (see fig. on topography and drainage, ch. 1). In the southeast a high wind that blows incessantly from May to September is strong enough to carry sand particles with it. Vegetation can be denuded, and the lighter soils of the region have been stripped away.

In mountain valleys and in areas where rivers descending from the mountains have formed extensive alluvial plains, much of the soil is of medium to heavy texture and suited to a variety of agricultural uses when brought under irrigation. Northern soils are the richest and the best watered. The regions adjacent to Lake Rezaiyeh and the Caspian Sea make up only about 25 percent of the country's area but produce 60 percent or more of its major crops (see fig. 11).

In places where the water table is high and capillary action has lifted moisture to the surface, evaporation salts have accumulated. Thousands of square miles of territory, particularly in the Central Plateau and in the south, have acquired these salt-encrusted surfaces. For the most part, dryland soils have high unleached mineral content and are deficient in hydrogen and humus, thus poor for farming. Poorly designed and structured irrigation without proper drainage has ruined some good soils, but elsewhere small areas of desert soils have been made productive by flushing out excess soluble salts and building up organic content.

Water is so scarce and valuable a commodity that in the 1970s it was still sometimes possible to see a farmer watering his crop by carefully pouring a few drops of water from an old tin can on each individual spike of wheat. All water resources were nationalized by 1967 legislation, and the Ministry of Water and Power was established.

The amount of rainfall is sufficient to adequately water only about 10 percent of the country. In addition to being scanty, rainfall is seasonal; most falls during the rainy months between October and March, and much of the seasonally watered land becomes parched during the dry season. It is also unevenly distributed by area. Near the Caspian Sea rainfall averages about fifty inches a year, but in the Central Plateau and in lowlands to the south it seldom exceeds four to five inches, far below the ten to twelve inches usually required for dry farming.

In the north the Elburz Mountains act as a brake to rain clouds

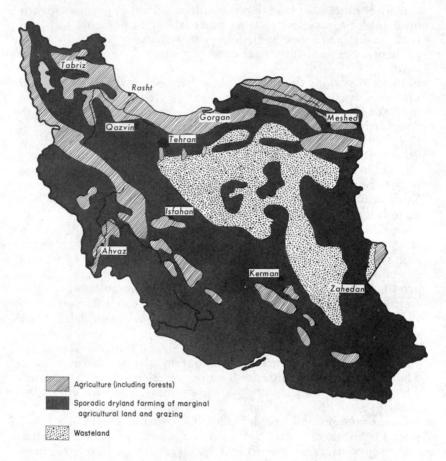

Agriculture (including forests)

Sporadic dryland farming of marginal agricultural land and grazing

Wasteland

Figure 11. Land Use, Mid-1970s

moving southward from the Caspian Sea. Rain falls plentifully; the northern slopes of the mountains remain covered by a heavy rain forest, and at lower levels the hillsides are covered with lush vegetation. South of the mountains this is not the case, and Tehran is surrounded by barren moors on which the only greenery to be seen results from carefully tended plantings. Parts of Khuzestan Province are watered by rivers descending from the Zagros Mountains, but toward the east aridity increases progressively in an area bordered by the Persian Gulf and the Pakistan frontier (see fig. on administrative divisions, ch. 6). It was in this region in 35 B.C. that the lack of water and blazing heat combined to destroy a large part of the army of Alexander the Great, returning from India.

Immense seasonal variation in flow is characteristic of Iran's rivers. The Rud-e Karun and other rivers passing through Khuzestan carry water during periods of maximum flow that are ten times the amounts borne in dry periods. Several of the government's dam projects are on these rivers. In numerous localities there may be no precipitation until a series of sudden storms accompanied by heavy rains dump almost the entire year's rainfall in a few days. In addition to causing floods and local damage, the runoffs are so rapid that they are useless for agricultural purposes.

Scarcity of water and the means for making use of it have proved a formidable constraint to agricultural development since ancient times. To make use of the limited amounts of water the Persians developed man-made underground water channels called *qanats* (also *ghanats*), in use in present-day Iran. A *qanat* is a gently sloping tunnel conducting water from a well or spring usually located at the base of a mountain system to a village or villages located on an alluvial fan. It is built by sinking a series of vertical shafts every several yards along the course of the tunnel to provide ventilation for the workmen below and to allow extraction of the dirt. The chief advantage of the *qanat* is that it avoids the heavy rate of evaporation to which surface channels are subject. The chief disadvantage is a lack of flexibility; the flow cannot be controlled, and water is lost when it is not being used to irrigate crops.

In the mid-1970s an estimated 60,000 *qanats* were in use, and new units were still being dug. Some of the working *qanats* were centuries old; there was evidence to suggest that the system dated back 3,000 years. On the moors adjacent to Tehran, an observer standing on high ground could still see indentations in the earth formed by collapsed ventilation shafts that mark the course of ancient subterranean watercourses.

The tunnels vary greatly in length but average about three miles. Typically three or more supply water for a village of 1,000 to 2,000 inhabitants. After it reaches the village, the tunnel continues by force of gravity into the areas under cultivation through surface irrigation channels known as *jubes*. Maintenance of *qanats* and *jubes* is an important and costly operation that was traditionally conducted by the estate owner. Making new provisions for *qanat* and *jube* maintenance has been one of the many problems faced by the administrators of the land reform program.

Legislation enacted in 1930 prescribes that a person who constructs or reclaims a *qanat* acquires ownership of the vacant land irrigated by it except where there are other *qanats* in the locality or where the land has been enclosed. *Qanat* water may be distributed in various ways: by use for a specified period of time; by division into a number of shares; by a dam or sluice; or by opening outlets through which the water flows to each plot of land. Where land is operated on a crop-sharing basis, the various plots have prescriptive rights to a certain share of the water supply. Anyone bringing new land into cultivation must buy water from someone with water available for sale. When a *qanat* serves more than one village, each village has a customary right to the water for a certain period of time. So important is the system to the agricultural economy and so complex is the procedure for allocating water rights that a large number of court cases regularly deal with adjudication of conflicting claims.

A second traditional irrigation method common in hillside farming involves digging channels from rivers and streams in order to carry water directly into the cultivated fields. The water is usually diverted into these channels by temporary wooden or gravel structures. The resulting networks are often complex and require careful control.

A third method involves the use of water drawn from wells. At the end of World War II only a small number of wells were in existence, and very limited use had been made of well water except in the date palm groves of the southern lowlands. The tempo of well drilling increased substantially during the 1960s, however, and by 1970 some 7,400 deep wells were producing groundwater for irrigation in various parts of the country.

On the basis of hydrological surveys indicating the existence of large subterranean water resources, the government has sought to assist farmers with credit and equipment to drill new wells. A goal of 1,000 new wells drilled annually was being attempted during the mid-1970s, although in some areas pumping was seriously depleting groundwater supplies. In some localities, however, the stoniness of the ground frustrates modern well drillers, and a drilling rig can be seen standing idle while workers endeavor to sink a shaft manually.

The most spectacular as well as the most extensive development in the field of water management during the years since World War II has been the construction of large reservoir dams for irrigation and industrial purposes. Between 1957 and 1975 twelve of these dams were completed, and another four were under construction.

Dam construction has centered in the southwestern province of Khuzestan. In 1955 the government commissioned a New York consulting firm to prepare a comprehensive study of what was designated the Unified Development of the Natural Resources of Khuzestan. A final report was submitted in 1959, and the government set up the Khuzestan Water and Power Authority (KWPA) to organize its implementation.

The rivers of Khuzestan rise high in the Zagros Mountains. The upper courses flow in parallel stretches before cutting through the surrounding mountains in extremely narrow gorges called *tangs* in regions often too precipitous for roads or even tracks. The configuration, however, provides good dam sites. The Khuzestan plain lying below the mountains had been virtually neglected for centuries, but as the site of the ancient kingdom of Elam it was a cradle of civilization (see Ancient Iran, ch. 2).

The first of the major dams to be built, the Mohammad Reza Shah Dam on the Rud-e Dez, was completed in 1962. The project, modeled after the Tennessee Valley Authority, was the first modern irrigation undertaking to have a significant impact on the Iranian economy. It was designed to transform the arid land of the Khuzestan plain and to satisfy a large part of the country's electricity requirements (see Electric Power Base, ch. 10). After the first years of operation the dam had achieved only a small proportion of its original goals, and the government determined that the lands below the dam and other dams nearing completion required special administration. As a consequence in 1969 a law was passed nationalizing irrigable lands downstream from dams. The lands below the Mohammad Reza Shah Dam were later leased to newly established domestic and foreign companies that became known as agribusinesses (see Organization of Agriculture, this ch.).

Traditional Land Tenure and Farming System

Traditionally rural landownership fell into one of five major categories. Most of the land was divided into large estates (*omdh malaki* or *arabi*) owned by proprietors who leased or rented plots of land or, more frequently, parceled them out to sharecroppers; more often than not, these were absentee landlords who delegated responsibility to a resident manager. Peasant-owned properties (*kordah malaki*) were for the most part small plots owned and operated by farmers who sometimes employed workers during periods of peak activity. Most of these owner-operated holdings were on isolated patches of land in mountain valleys. Other lands were waqf properties, in which profits or rents were assigned for charitable uses of a public or private character. Except that waqf properties were usually leased rather than sharecropped under waqf managers, the administration of the lands differed little from those of the individual landlords. Public domain lands (*khalisati dulati*) were those retained by the government, and crown lands (*amlaki saltanati*) were the personal estate of the shah.

It was officially estimated in 1951 that less than 0.5 percent of the total population owned 56 percent of the land under annual or occasional cultivation; between 14 and 20 percent was owned by peasant proprietors; some 15 to 25 percent consisted of waqf properties; and public domain and crown lands each made up about 5 percent of the total. Because no cadastral surveys had been made, the exact proportions of lands owned by category could not readily be determined.

Although as much as 75 percent of the population depended on the land, Iran had proved unable to achieve self-sufficiency in food production. The land tenure system had produced a prevailing stagnation in agricultural production because neither landowner nor tenant farmer had much incentive to increase production by using new farming techniques.

The concentration of land in the hands of a few large holders dated from the beginning of the nineteenth century, or earlier, but had been furthered in the late 1920s and 1930s by Reza Shah's practice of rewarding loyal service by granting large estates. It was further advanced by the purchase of land as an investment by Iranians who had become wealthy in trade or in some other endeavor, particularly after World War II. In addition in numerous villages that required a common supply of water from the *qanat* systems, which were too expensive for the farmers to construct and maintain, holding irrigated land tended to grow progressively more concentrated.

In 1962 it was officially estimated that 10,000 of the country's 49,000 villages—farming areas made up customarily of about 50 to 500 inhabitants—belonged to landlords who owned seven or more villages each; another 5,000 villages belonged to those owning five or six villages each. These divisions included tribal villages owned as private holdings by tribal leaders. One landlord in Khorasan Province was reported to own 136 villages; and four landlords owned most of the villages in Kordestan Province.

There were three common methods of operating the farmlands. The most common was sharecropping under the supervision of the landlord or the *kadkhuda* (village headman—see Glossary). A 1930 law made the *kadkhuda* an agent of the government on behalf of the people in the village or group of villages in which he served as well as the representative of the landlord. Alternatively the landlord might lease or rent to another individual who assumed the role of landlord in dealing with sharecropping peasants who actually worked the land. Finally peasant owners and tenants farmed their small plots directly with the help of families and hired labor. On tribal lands, however, a system of communal distribution was applied.

In practice ancient customs that regulated landlord-peasant relations differed substantially from the prescribed legal regulations. Sharecroppers seldom had a written contract or any security of tenure, the landlord or lessee could discharge a peasant at will (though custom militated against such action), and a male heir usually continued to work the land after the death of the head of the family.

The landlord often left to his *kadkhuda* the administration of his land, including assigning plots to sharecroppers, determining the crops to be grown, planting instructions, and the cultivation, harvesting, and distribution of the harvest. The *kadkhuda* was chosen and paid by the landlord, subject to the approval of the provincial governor. The system tended to minimize peasant initiative and sense of identification with the land.

In most but not all parts of the country, the crop was divided at harvesttime between the peasant and the landlord according to the five factors of production (land, labor, water, animals, and seed), the supplier of each receiving 20 percent of the crop. The formula varied in application. For example, where land could be dry-farmed because of adequacy of rainfall the water unit was eliminated; the extent to which the peasant sharecropper supplied seed, animals, and labor varied in different localities, but peasants seldom had capital, storage space, or managerial ability to buy and store seeds. Some sharecroppers owned oxen, but oxen were more frequently owned by independent operators who rented teams in exchange for up to 20 percent of the harvest.

Thus a peasant's share could range from about 20 percent to as high as 60 to 75 percent of the harvest. Occasionally the government attempted to increase a peasant's share by legislative action but with limited success. Peasants, however, traditionally had certain rights and privileges that tended to maximize their meager incomes. They were authorized to use the village communal pasture for grazing their animals and to collect shrubs from the pastures for use as fuel. Peasants were allowed to plant fruit and nut trees from which they retained the produce (although landowners usually discouraged this practice), and women had the right to glean any grain left in fields after harvesting.

Conversely the landlords traditionally required certain services of peasants beyond the regular cultivation of the crops. This took the form of *bigari* (unpaid labor) and consisted of a certain number of days of work performed by a male of the family and by one of his animals. *Bigari* was levied according to the amount of land farmed, the amount of water used, or by the number of sharecroppers engaged. It was used in the construction of buildings, irrigation work, roadbuilding, or in the cultivation of the landlord's private garden. The service was practiced on public domain and crown lands as well as on private estates.

Contributing to the prevailingly low income level was the customary decline of prices for grain at harvesttime when peasants were in poor bargaining positions. Some landlords were even able to force peasants to sell their shares at arbitrarily fixed prices on threat of withholding water or other necessities during the ensuing season. The sharecropping peasant was constantly plagued by debt. Loans, if available at all, were given by the landlord against the security of the next crop. Before 1961 the government's Agricultural Cooperative Bank shunned peasants and lent only to landowners who often used the money to speculate on land or, in turn, lent to peasants at high rates. Interest rates charged by moneylenders were very high, usually from 20 to 40 percent and sometimes as high as 60 percent.

Although sharecroppers and tenant farmers—who made up the majority of the peasantry—fared badly, the economic situation of the small landholder was not far superior. The land farmed, particularly in poorer areas of the country, was often submarginal in size, and the small landholder was forced to supplement his income by offering his services part-time as a farm laborer or by engaging in nonfarm activities in the off season. His harvesttime problems were generally similar to those of the sharecropper. He was ignorant of market conditions outside his village, lacked a cooperative marketing association to help him in fixing a price for produce, possessed no savings, and had no transportation to carry produce to a better marketing area.

The plight of a farm laborer was even worse than that of a small landowner or a sharecropper because he lacked the security, however scanty, of a sharecropping arrangement or of permanent rights to the land. Because of a lack of demand elsewhere for his unskilled services, he was tied to his village of origin where he worked by the day for a miniscule cash wage or a portion of the harvest.

Traditionally peasants remained in their villages of origin, and the typical peasant worked for the landlord family that had employed his forebears during previous generations. This pattern began to change soon after World War II as peasants—in particular the farm laborers—began to flock to urban centers in search of work and a better way of life. The process caused increasingly serious disruption of agricultural production and at the same time gave rise to such new urban problems as crowding, unemployment, and increased demand on limited availability of public utilities (see ch. 3).

Land Reform

Shortly after 1900 a series of land reform measures were enacted, directed at modifying the proprietary relationship between landlord and peasant. For the most part, however, they were limited to particular areas or forms of ownership and either were never implemented or were made ineffective by poor planning and administration.

Most of the land transfers of the early years of the twentieth century involved infertile and poorly cultivated properties in the public domain. Initially the property was sold to the private sector because of its marginal value and the government's chronic need for funds. In 1921 the government announced that public domain lands would be distributed to peasants in order to free them from landlord domination, but the project was abandoned after a few months. In the late 1920s some public land was sold to individual peasant farmers, and several laws and decrees during the 1930s resulted in the distribution of certain public domain lands.

The collective effect of the several land distribution schemes during the first half of the century was minor, and land reform in its real sense is generally agreed to have commenced in 1950 with the issuance by the shah of a program for the distribution and sale of the crown lands. Distribution of these lands was suspended during the prime ministership of Mohammad Mossadeq (1951–53) but was later resumed, and by 1962 some 42,403 smallholders in 517 villages had received plots of land averaging almost twelve acres per plot but varying greatly in size. In 1955 a law was passed prescribing distribution of the public domain lands, and the distribution of these properties actually commenced in 1958.

Advocates of sweeping land reform had hoped that the large landlords would follow the example of the crown lands and public domain distribution programs by voluntarily giving up at least a portion of their holdings. These hopes were not realized, and in 1960 general land reform legislation was enacted by Parliament. Landlords, however, were able to attach so many amendments to this legislation that its intent was largely frustrated. It was in this atmosphere that the shah, in a January 1963 meeting of the Farmers' Congress, declared the first six principles of the White Revolution on which subsequent social and economic development would be based (see ch. 7). The number of principles was soon expanded to twelve and by 1977 had reached nineteen.

The first principle called for rural land reform and led directly to enactment of the 1962 Land Reform Law, a key piece of legislation that was implemented during the 1960s in three different phases. The program set forth as its goal the massive transfer of lands to peasants in all parts of the country. The obstacles were numerous. The continued opposition of the landlords and Islamic clergy (see Glossary), who controlled vast amounts of waqf lands, was accompanied by a general feeling of incredulity on the part of nearly everyone. A cadastral survey had never been made, and in fact there was no land survey department. In addition financing of the program's cost was inadequate, and administrative officials had no experience in land redistribution and quite literally made up specific rules as they gained experience.

The first phase of the three-phase land reform program was aimed at distribution of the large estates throughout the country. It permitted the landlord to retain only one complete village, or equivalent portions of villages, and called for the sale of all other holdings to the farmers already tilling the soil. The government took over the remainder of the estate by paying the landlord one-tenth of its cost and guaranteeing payment by the farmer over a fifteen-year period.

The second phase, introduced in 1965, dealt with the remaining villages that were still retained by landlords. Depending on the region, ex-landlords were permitted to retain up to 2,470 acres of land, provided that it was in orchards or under mechanical cultivation. Other land was to be divided by sale or lease to the occupying tenants and sharecroppers. The second phase provided also for the formation of agricultural cooperatives by stipulating that, as a precondition to taking title to the land, the new landowners had to join the village or regional cooperative.

The third phase of the reform program was aimed at improving living conditions of farmers through the introduction of modern economic and technological methods. Initiated in 1968, the third phase called for the establishment of agricultural corporations and encouraged the development of rural cooperatives. In addition a 1969 amendment to the Land Reform Law provided for the abolition of all tenancies and the sale of the land to the occupying tenants.

At the end of 1966 the government announced that land reform, insofar as it concerned the distribution of land, was completed. The statement apparently was made to remove feelings of insecurity on the part of freeholders and the remaining landlords, because the actual process of distribution continued into the 1970s. In March 1974 the government announced that nearly 20 million acres of farmland had been acquired by the government and distributed to 2.3 million families, one-third of whom had been landless. Most foreign observers doubt that one-third had been landless, and most earlier reports had emphasized that almost all the land was being distributed to the occupying sharecropper or tenant.

Although some data were available on the average size of the holdings of the new landowners, the averages tended to be meaningless. For example, two or three acres of irrigated, rice-growing land near the Caspian Sea were vastly more valuable than twenty or more acres of marginal nonirrigated land near Shiraz or Kerman where only a few acres could be farmed in any given year and where droughts were frequent.

The land reform legislation stipulates that the Islamic law of inheritance, which provides a precise formula for the division of all property at the death of the property holder, will not be observed. In an effort to prevent a further fragmentation of already small and usually noncontiguous plots of land, the legislation states that each heir is to receive a certificate showing his or her share of ownership. In late 1977 information on the implementation of this part of the program was not available. It was known, however, that many religious leaders continued to be opposed to what they viewed as a contravention of divine law.

The program was not without other severe critics. Provision had not been made for many or most of the landless farmworkers. Other related socioeconomic problems, such as availability of credit and of water resources, had been neglected.

A more general criticism of land reform held that instead of creating a productive and independent peasantry it led only to the further consolidation of the powers of the state over the rural scene. Although the peasant became proprietor of a small plot of ground, in most instances he continued the marginal existence of a subsistence farmer. It was the central government rather than the peasant farmer that had gained at the expense of the unseated landlords.

Moreover land reform meant the destruction of *boneh*, a system of cooperation between landlord and sharecropper or tenant that had evolved through the centuries and, however imperfect, had served as a means of socioeconomic interaction. Its destruction without adequate replacement was seen by some critics as a disastrous by-product of land reform. The new agricultural cooperatives were devised as replacements for *boneh*, and farmers were virtually compelled to join the cooperatives (see Organization of Agriculture, this ch.). Critics, however, asserted that relatively few farmers were active cooperative members and that the cooperatives themselves were not much more than credit organizations.

Supporters of land reform regarded it as a landmark achievement. Even those observers who concluded that land reform had not substantially improved the status of most peasants, acknowledged that the process had extended their awareness of social and economic matters. They had yet to enter the mainstream of national life, but they could no longer be considered *roaya*, the Farsi word for the traditional peasant farmer. The word in English most closely approximating this term is *serf*.

No exact count has ever been made of the number of landlords displaced by land reform. The holdings of those with more than seven villages were distributed first, and gradually the holdings of those with five or six and finally those with one or parts of one or more villages were effected. Leases that had been made pursuant to earlier phases of the program were converted into sales. Many landlords attempted to circumvent the program by transferring their properties to relatives, but the government retaliated by seizing these properties, paying only the nominal prices at which they had been transferred. Landlord opposition was overcome with the assistance of the police and local governors who were required by law to cooperate with the land reform officials. The relative ease with which the landlords were displaced reflected the growing and overwhelming power of the shah (see ch. 7).

Organization of Agriculture

During the mid-1970s a large majority of the more than 2 million farm families (or about 11 million people) that had received properties during the land reform program continued to live at or near the subsistence level. Although these families made up the bulk of the farm population, their farms were relatively small, and they occupied only about one-third of the agricultural land.

In terms of number of families involved, next in size was the so-called commercial sector, consisting in large part of former landlords who had been able to retain all or a part of their holdings. Depending on the definition, this sector included as many as 650,000 families farming plots ranging in size from twenty-five to 12,350 acres. According to a narrower and probably more realistic definition, however, the commercial sector was made up of farms of such productivity as to make them responsive to usual market forces and to provide their owners with reasonable levels of income. Particularly productive in this sector were the mechanized farms of up to 2,470 acres that had been exempted from land-reform distribution. The farms making up the commercial sector produced nearly 50 percent of the value added in agriculture and in so doing enjoyed relatively extensive capital assets, borrowing power, and managerial and technical competence.

Between 1969 and 1972 five large private agribusinesses were established in Khuzestan Province on the newly irrigated lands below the dam on the Rud-e Dez. The agribusinesses were developed to take advantage of the economies of large-scale production while conserving state development funds and bringing foreign technical know-how into the country. All but one of the first five enterprises was established with foreign business partners.

The new agribusinesses were granted leases of not more than thirty years for areas of at least 2,470 acres. The cost of constructing roads and irrigation and drainage canals for the leased properties was divided between the government and the lessee; the latter was responsible for land leveling, building structures, maintenance, and related costs. Sugarcane, alfalfa, corn, wheat, cotton, and other crops were to be produced on a large-scale.

Some 150,000 acres had been allocated to the four businesses set up by Iranians with foreign partners, but by 1973 only 20,150 acres, or 13.4 percent, had been brought into production. The undertakings had met with mixed results, ranging from considerable success in the introduction of sugarcane to what appeared to have been a disastrous failure in a cotton-growing venture. At the end of 1975 total investment in agribusiness was reported to have reached 20 billion rials (for value of the rial—see Glossary), 45 percent of which was provided by the Agricultural Development Bank in the form of loans and equity participation and the balance provided by private domestic and foreign investors.

A feature article appearing in an October 1976 edition of the *Financial Times* of London concerning the agribusinesses was headlined "A Most Troublesome Experiment" and described the venture as generally a failure. Defenders of agribusiness, however, pointed out that their initially poor performance had resulted from heavy infrastructure costs and bottlenecks in the economy. The projects were expected to justify their planning and make a sizable contribution to the country's agricultural output. Early in 1977 their defenders seemed to have won the day in the sense that the minister of agriculture and natural resources was reported as having approved fifteen new large agribusiness projects to be implemented by the private sector in the northern provinces of Gilan and Mazandaran.

Somewhat less ambitious in concept than agribusinesses have been the farm corporations or joint stock companies. Designed in particular for land reform beneficiaries residing in depressed areas, the first came into being in 1968. By the end of 1975 some eighty-nine farm corporations were in operation, consolidating the lands of 816 villages; plans called for increasing the number to 143 by conclusion of the fifth plan (see Glossary) in 1978. The average farm corporation included 300 families and had a land area of up to 2,470 acres. The goal of the corporation system was to provide a means of raising members' incomes by mechanizing production, a maximum use of manpower, and the acquisition and use of modern farming techniques.

A corporation is formed in any village or group of villages where at least 51 percent of the land-owning farmers vote for it affirmatively. Once the corporation is formed, the farmer-members transfer their land-use rights to it and receive shares in proportion to the amount of land surrendered. Farmers receive wages and dividends from their shares as employees of the corporation. Government experts who designed the farm corporation program state that the participants will derive a much higher income from their wages and dividends than would have been possible had they tilled their own small plots individually. The government provides grants-in-aid to the corporations; furnishes machinery, farm equipment, fertilizer, and seeds at low prices; and makes available credit facilities and technical assistance. The farm corporations have suffered from inability to attract experienced managers, however, and peasant farmers have been reluctant to accept the loss of independence entailed in joining a corporation. Information was incomplete in late 1977, but the corporations seemed neither to have been well received nor as successful as hoped.

A variation of the farm corporation is the agricultural production cooperative, established in 1971. Like the farm corporation it is designed to raise agricultural productivity in depressed areas, but it is more flexible and has less central control. Members retain their individual land rights but engage in joint production, establishment of irrigation facilities, road construction, and other undertakings of mutual interest. Economies are also brought about by pooling equipment and marketing. Some twenty-four production cooperatives were in existence by 1976, and sixty were to be established before conclusion of the fifth plan.

Distinct from the production cooperatives were the rural cooperative societies that were assisted and promoted by the Central Organization of Rural Cooperatives, a public agency established in 1963 to give assistance to the subsistence farming sector. Each of these units covered several villages and had an average of about 200 members. In mid-1977 more than 2 million families (almost the total number benefiting from land reform) were reported participating in 2,800 cooperatives. The government asserted that the cooperative program was a great success, with most of the farm population participating. It would appear, however, that much of the apparent success could be attributed to rules of the land reform program that made membership in a rural cooperative a requisite for receiving land. The cooperatives provided a variety of services including credit, marketing, distributing consumer goods, and developing nonfarm activities. However, they were active primarily in channeling credit from the Agricultural Cooperative Bank, which is represented by some 200 rural branches as well as by agencies and mobile units; in other activities their achievements have been limited. In 1975 the cooperatives were reportedly marketing less than 1 percent of the value of agricultural output.

Government Investments in Agriculture

The vertiginous increase in world petroleum prices occurred during the course of the fifth plan, and as a consequence the amounts originally allocated in the plan were subsequently more than doubled. The amount allocated to the agricultural sector was raised by 95 percent, a little less than the average. This revision of the plan called for an annual growth in the country's gross national product (GNP) of 25.9 percent. The annual growth target was a modest 7 percent for agriculture and 8.3 percent for livestock raising as compared with 18 percent for industry, 16.4 percent for services, and 51.5 percent for petroleum and natural gas.

The revised fifth plan allocated 296.7 million rials to agricultural development, a figure nearly six times the investment under the fourth plan. It amounted to about 6.6 percent of the total fifth plan development allocations. As reported at the beginning of 1976, however, disbursements were running well behind schedule, with only 18 percent used by the end of the second year and probably less than 40 percent allocated by March 1976.

Agricultural development policies pursued during the fifth plan continued under the premise that bigger is better. Priority was to be given to large farm units capable of using technically advanced capital-intensive processes leading to high yields in relatively short time periods, and the agribusinesses and the farm corporations most nearly met these requirements. For subsistence farmers, emphasis was placed on joining the new rural cooperatives. Toward the end of the fifth plan, however, there were some indications that the government might be giving increased attention to the previously neglected medium-sized commercial farms.

Looking forward to agricultural development under the sixth plan, in late 1976 the minister of agriculture and rural development announced that a preliminary report by the Agricultural Planning Committee foresaw self-sufficiency in the production of wheat, pulses, sugar, poultry, and eggs by the end of the sixth plan period in March 1983.

The statement by the minister occurred on the fifteenth anniversary of land reform, and he emphasized that agricultural production had doubled during that period. During the same period, however, industrial production had much more than doubled, agricultural imports had risen monumentally, and the country's population had increased by nearly 50 percent. Foreign observers could not foresee a period when Iran would be self-sufficient in grain production.

Farming Practices

Farming methods used in the 1970s by most farmers were for the most part not much different from those used for millennia. Credit facilities had been improved, and there was some use of fertilizers and mechanized equipment in the newly established agribusinesses and farm corporations, but subsistence farming continued to be prevalent (see Organization of Agriculture, this ch.).

Traditionally the lands occupied by the sharecroppers were divided into plots based on a share of the village water or, more commonly, on the amount of land that could be cultivated by a yoke of oxen. A farmer, assisted by his wife and children, tended one to three of these plots, which varied in size from one to nine acres and frequently were not contiguous. Plowing was still done with an ironshod plowshare similar to those that had been used two millennia earlier. With it, a farmer and a yoke of oxen could plow between one-fourth and one-half of an acre in a ten-hour day. Sowing was done by hand, and the plow and a piece of lumber were dragged over the furrows to cover the seeds and press them into the ground. Hoes were generally unknown. A limited amount of weeding was accomplished by hand, and threshing and winnowing grain were done by hand or with the help of animals.

Before the land reform program of the 1960s, the peasant family or a group of peasants drew lots to determine which fields, from those made available for village use by the landlord or by his resident agent, would be cultivated. Under this system there was little incentive for the peasant to improve the plot through proper cultivation, crop rotation, and the use of fertilizer. There was no opportunity for attachment to a particular plot of land to develop, although there was considerable resistance to moving from one rural locality to another. When farm people moved it was to abandon the rural environment altogether. Government planners had hoped that as a consequence of land reform the rate of urban migration would slow. In the mid-1970s, however, there was no evidence that such a trend was developing.

Seasonal and year-to-year variations in precipitation and river flows, archaic water distribution systems, unleveled land, and poor seed beds have combined to make uniform water distribution impossible. Yields of wheat and other crops under irrigation have not been much greater than the yields from dry lands during years of adequate rainfall. Irrigation, therefore, has been regarded as much as an insurance against crop failure as a means of obtaining high yields.

The older irrigated lands have been tilled to a depth of five or six inches for so many centuries that a compact hard pan has built up retarding water penetration and root development. Crop residues that might enrich the soil are usually consumed by sheep and goats or removed for fuel or construction of buildings. Each summer season, lands that have been left fallow almost dry out completely.

The third plan (1963–68) had as one of its objectives the mechanization and improvement of farming—by using tractors, modern tools and equipment, fertilizers, and improved seeds. The effort failed in part because of poor timing. The large estate owners were reluctant to invest in the development of their lands in the face of the looming threat of land reform. Under the third plan period, however, the Agricultural Machinery Sales Agency was established and has promoted the use of mechanical equipment by extending easy credit terms to farmers.

Mechanization of agriculture progressed slowly during the late 1960s and early 1970s; the accomplishments in this sector were summarized by the minister of agriculture and rural development in a 1977 address celebrating gains achieved during the fifteen years since enactment of land reform legislation. The number of farm tractors in use had increased from 3,000 to 50,000, and the amount of chemical fertilizer used had soared from 50,000 tons to between 700,000 and 800,000 tons a year.

Crops

Over 75 percent of the land cultivated in any year was devoted to growing wheat, barley, and other grains. Cotton, sugar beets, fruits, and nuts took up most of the remaining cultivated area (see fig. 12). In order to encourage and stabilize crop production, the government in 1974 issued a decree providing price supports for wheat, barley, corn, sugar beets, rice, beans, peas, and oilseeds.

Grains

Wheat is an essential staple for most of the population. Bread is the most important single item in the diet everywhere except in certain parts of the Caspian lowlands where a meal is not considered complete without rice. The small farmer endeavors to produce enough grain to make his own bread, and wheat and barley are planted on dry-farmed and irrigated lands and on mountain slopes and plains. Wheat is used almost exclusively for human consumption, but barley is used mainly as animal feed (see table 17, Appendix A).

The combined 1975 output of corn and sorghum was estimated at 77,000 tons, up about 44 percent over the previous year. These crops, used primarily for animal feed, were still of minor importance, but plantings were increasing rapidly in response to a growing feed demand. Most of the production came from the Caspian littoral, the remainder from the Zagros highlands. The two crops are fairly new to Iran where the concept of a crop grown specifically for animal feed is itself novel. Sorghum, in both grain and forage varieties, appears better adapted than corn to Iranian growing conditions, but imports of 300,000 tons of corn in 1976 and 508,000 tons in 1977 as compared with 150,000 tons of sorghum in 1976 indicated a strong preference for corn. To encourage corn production, improved seeds were made available by the government at low prices during the mid-1970s. Corn prices were guaranteed, and low-cost loans to encourage production over a five-year period were offered.

Rice is the only crop grown exclusively under irrigation. The long-grain rice of Iran grows primarily on the wet Caspian lowlands in Gilan and Mazandaran provinces where heavy rainfall

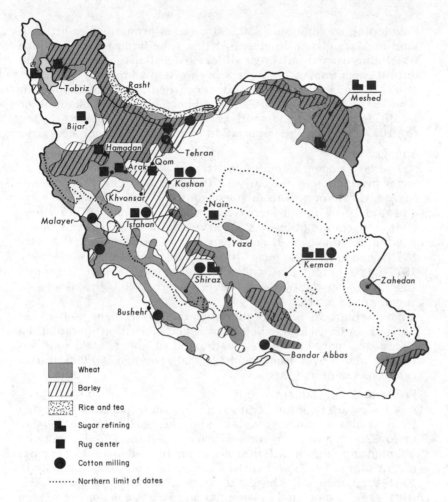

Figure 12. *Agricultural Regions and Locations of Processing Centers for Agricultural Products, Mid-1970s*

facilitates paddy cultivation. Population growth and the rising standard of living have stimulated production of the fine quality rice that could find a steady export market should volume of output permit. During the late 1960s the government sought to improve productivity by bringing in Taiwanese and Japanese experts to set up a rice-improvement project. At about the same time the completion of malaria eradication in the marshy Caspian region led to a large-scale movement of people into that area, making additional workers available for rice cultivation. By the mid-1970s much of the previously marshy littoral had been reclaimed for paddies, and completion of the Safid Rud Dam made ample irrigation water available.

In early 1977 the Ministry of Agriculture and Rural Development contracted with a British firm to produce a master plan for developing an additional 230,000 acres of primarily rice-growing land in Mazandaran Province. At that time intensive rice culture was being carried out in six different locations. The bulk of the output came from 690,000 acres in the Caspian provinces of Gilan and Mazandaran, but 13,350 acres had been developed in Khuzestan, and limited acreages had been developed in four other localities in central and southwestern Iran. Nevertheless during the 1977 crop year the importation of 326,000 tons was necessary.

Sugar

The government's ambitious attempt to gain self-sufficiency in sugar production by the early 1970s was frustrated by the exceedingly fast rate of growth in sugar consumption. During the early and mid-1970s output increased annually at a rate of 5 to 6 percent, but consumption was up at a rate of 10 percent or more. Production of beet and cane sugar was increased during the early 1970s, and in 1974 the Agricultural Development Bank projected a 1977 sugar output that would permit a small export of refined sugar. During that year, however, nearly 300,000 tons of raw sugar were imported.

To supplement sugar production, the government in 1976 reportedly initiated a large beekeeping and processing operation at a site near Qom. Production, estimated at about 2,000 tons annually, was derived from some 120,000 hives and 360,000 swarms in baskets and mud jars.

Fruits and Vegetables

A wide variety of temperate zone and subtropical fruits ranging from apples to pomegranates, and the world-famous Persian melons, are grown in Iran. Citrus fruits are found along the Caspian and Persian Gulf littorals and in limited quantities in parts of the south. Peach and apricot production occurs principally in East Azarbaijan and Khorasan. Grapes, produced in many localities, are dried or used in winemaking. Iran is a major exporter of dried apricots and raisins.

It is also one of the world's leading producers of dates, which are grown on inland oases and along the length of the Persian Gulf coast, where in the poorer villages they often are eaten as a substitute for bread. During the nineteenth century huge date estates were established along rivers; salt was leached from the adjacent lands and networks of irrigation canals dug. Date culture led to the establishment of the city of Khorramshahr. Export sales for the 1976 crop year included 35,000 tons of dates.

Vegetable Oils

The demand for vegetable oils as a substitute for animal fat has risen sharply. In the late 1960s the government embarked on a campaign to stimulate the oilseed industry by providing loans, distributing seeds, purchasing the produce, and constructing storage facilities. The program was slow in gaining momentum, however, and success was limited. Because the crop yield per acre tended to be low and production costs high, farmers soon lost interest and production flagged. In 1972 about 60 percent of the vegetable oil consumed was imported.

Cottonseed is the most heavily produced, but it is a by-product of cotton boll production, and as such its output is not responsive to the needs of oilseed processing facilities. During the early 1970s, however, soybean production was growing rapidly under the influence of guaranteed prices and mechanized cultivation. The beans were cultivated on medium-sized commercial farms and had a yield averaging 1 to 1.3 tons per acre.

In the mid-1970s farmers sold their oilseed harvests to five large companies operating eighteen crushing plants and eleven refineries for the production of hydrogenated vegetable fats. In 1976 some 250,000 tons of vegetable oils were imported—all but a few thousand tons consisting of soybean oil—and imports were expected to rise to 300,000 tons for 1977.

Cotton

Cotton culture has been practiced since antiquity, but commercial-scale production in modern times did not commence until the early 1930s when American varieties were first imported to supplement native strains. Cotton is consistently the country's most valuable cash crop—as well as a major export item—but variations in weather, pest infestations, and swings in world prices have made its profitability irregular. In addition, in the 1970s such primitive cultivation practices as broadcasting seeds and harvesting by hand continued to be practiced.

Tobacco

Tobacco—a moderately important cash crop and a state monopoly—has been produced for about 300 years, principally in the northern provinces of Gilan and Mazandaran and on the Gorgan plain. Acreage allotments for tobacco culture are controlled by the Tobacco Monopoly Organization. The leaf tobacco is sold to four government factories producing cigarettes, and a significant proportion is *tanbacco* (a form of coarse tobacco) for smokers of hookah pipes. In 1977 the monopoly continued to import about one-third of the tobacco used.

Tea

Tea is the national drink, although the custom of drinking tea—known locally as *chai*—was originally imported from Russia. Tea is so much a part of the national life that those who can afford the luxury of servants are awakened to a glass of tea, and the ritual serving of tea regularly precedes business meetings. Production and distribution of the crop are strictly controlled by the National Grain, Sugar, and Tea Organization.

Introduced in 1907 when the first Indian seeds were planted, tea is produced in the lowland areas near the Caspian Sea in Gilan and Mazandaran provinces in small plots averaging about thirty-five acres. Producers have chronically suffered from earnings too low to encourage improving either the quality or the quantity of their crops, and Iranians have developed a preference for imported Indian tea. Moreover smuggling is extensive and has had an adverse effect on the domestic market. Beginning in the late 1960s, however, there was some improvement in the quality of native tea owing to the better use of fertilizers, introduction of better bushes, and technical guidance obtained from experts brought in from the Republic of China (Nationalist China).

Other Crops

Pulse production of beans, chick-peas, lentils, and peas was estimated at 160,000 tons for 1976, an increase of 17 percent over the preceding year. Imports were negligible, but consumption was rising sharply and increased imports in the future appeared probable. Exports are restricted by government policy.

Estimates concerning annual potato production during the mid-1970s varied from 300,000 to more than 500,000 tons. Production is customarily sufficient to meet demand, but during late 1975 potatoes became scarce throughout the country and 50,000 tons or more were imported from India. Consumption was increasing, and there was a growing demand for frozen and dried potato products.

In 1976 the output of pistachio nuts, almonds, and walnuts totaled about 30,000 tons, a gain of 35 percent over the previous year. Exports were about 12,000 tons, a decrease of some 3,000 tons from 1975. The falloff resulted from lower production rather than from increased domestic consumption. In the mid-1970s a negligible amount of walnuts and about 2,000 tons of peanuts were imported annually. Nuts were grown in many parts of the country, but production was most bountiful in the south. Pistachios, the leading nut crop, grow wild in many places but were cultivated with particular success in Kerman.

Cultivation of poppies, the basic raw material for opium, was banned during the early 1960s but resumed in 1969 on a limited scale and under strict government control. Harvests supposedly were rigorously policed, and the planted area was regulated according to the requirements of the population addicted to opium (see ch. 12). No production figures were available in late 1977, but about 600 tons of opium were produced annually from about 50,000 acres planted to poppies.

In the mid-1970s a small natural silk industry was being expanded with the aid of Japanese technical assistance. Production of 8.2 million pounds annually by the end of the fifth plan period was expected.

Certain commercially valuable wild plants and shrubs and their saps and resins are regularly collected, usually for export. Gum tragacanth, one of the most important, is gathered mainly in the provinces of Fars, Kerman, Isfahan, and Lorestan. Annual production amounts to between 2,500 and 3,000 tons, a sizeable proportion of the world's supply. Gum arabic, gum asafetida, galbanum, colocynth, and licorice are also gathered. Indigo,

Tea cultivation in the north
Courtesy Embassy of Iran

saffron, and gallnuts supply dyes for the carpet industry, and henna trees are found in the south near the cities of Abadan and Ahvaz and in Kerman Province.

Livestock

Including dairying and poultry breeding, livestock breeding accounted for approximately 40 percent of the value of agricultural production in the mid-1970s. Sheep breeding predominated. The bulk of the red meat consumed was mutton; wool for the textile and carpet industries and the skins of Persian lambs were important commodities. Goats were raised primarily for their wool and milk but also for meat. Little beef was eaten; cattle were used principally for milk—converted into yogurt, cheese, and other dairy products that provided a substantial amount of the food and income of rural people—and as draft animals. Poultry raising was gaining in importance, particularly in the vicinity of Tehran.

Because nomadic tribesmen and villagers remained generally averse to outside enumeration of their livestock, only rough estimates were available concerning the size of the animal population. According to government estimates of livestock and poultry in rural areas during 1974, sheep were most numerous at 30 million head. Goats were next, 14 million, followed by cattle, 5.5 million, and pigs, 150,000. There were also 60 million poultry, 2.1 million asses, 500,000 horses and mules, and 150,000 camels. The numbers were similar to or somewhat lower than those reported during the late 1960s, except that the supply of poultry increased sharply and in the late 1970s was continuing to grow.

Because of the methods used to raise livestock there was not much increase in their numbers and consequently in the meat supply. Both sheep and goats were kept by nomadic tribesmen—about fifty head per tribal family—and by sedentary villagers who supported a few animals as a sideline to crop cultivation. The tribesmen relied so heavily on livestock that they constituted the central theme in tribal life, as the search for pasturage prompted their seasonal migrations. With diets consisting of grass and shrubs, both village and tribal animals were often diseased and malnourished, and the return from these animals in meat, milk, hair, and hides was low.

The economic status of the nomads tended to be somewhat better than that of the small subsistence farmers and markedly better than the landless farm laborers. The nomadic economy was based mainly on livestock raising. Nomadic tribesmen were not required to divide the returns from their flocks, but head taxes and other special levies were exacted by the tribal chief. In addition to the returns from their livestock—which provided their principal support—they earned small cash incomes from fruits and nuts harvested from the orchards and date groves on their tribal lands and from the sale of charcoal made by burning scrub oaks. Largely self-sufficient, they needed money only for a few items, such as

Pastoral scene in the southeast
Courtesy U.S. Agency for International Development

sugar, tea, clothing, matches, arms, and ammunition.

Sheep and goats are raised together although the ratio of sheep to goats varies—for example, there were more sheep in Khorasan and more goats in Yazd. Up to 40 percent of the goats yield mohair for textile production and are used for milk. In recent years mechanization of dryland farming has progressively reduced the amount of wasteland available for grazing, and overgrazing has been severe on the natural range. Lambs are born in spring, and stock is sold in the fall for fattening; the number sold depends largely on the prospects for winter feed supplies and immediate cash needs. The availability of stock for fattening is accordingly irregular from year to year and will become increasingly so as cropping of cultivable areas increases and as areas available for wintering become more restricted.

The government has begun construction of state meat complexes with fattening, slaughtering, and meat-packing facilities such as the one at Marv Dasht in Fars Province. These complexes were being complemented by several livestock collection centers located on the migratory routes of the herdsmen. The Marv Dasht complex annually supplied slaughterhouses in Shiraz, Isfahan, and Tehran with about 365,000 head of fattened sheep during the mid-1970s and had established an annual target production of 1.5 million head. There were about 400 municipal slaughterhouses located nationwide, but about one-half of the slaughter was carried out on farms or in backyards. The State Meat Organization controlled the large Tehran slaughterhouse, which handled an estimated 15 percent of all commercial slaughtering.

Several large, modern poultry operations have been installed, and more were planned, particularly around Tehran, with British, West German, and Dutch participation. American firms had not participated in these ventures, but in early 1977 a joint Iranian-American group applied for credit from the Agricultural Development Bank to establish a major poultry complex at Qazvin, west of Tehran. The complex would ultimately have an annual production capacity of 5,600 tons of poultry in packed form as well as 7 million chicks. In 1977 poultry meat production was estimated at 215,000 tons, consumption at 245,000 tons.

According to a mid-1970s study some 51 percent of the animal protein in the Iranian diet was derived from milk. Sheep and goat meat accounted for 18 percent, and 13 percent came from beef and other animal meat. Eggs accounted for 9 percent, poultry meat for 6 percent, and a scanty 1 percent came from fish.

Much of Iran's milk is produced by small farmers for the local village (farms often consisting of from one to four cows or other milk-producing animals). The total volume of milk from sheep and goats slightly exceeds that from cows. With relatively low per capita milk consumption and extremely high income elasticity in the mid-1970s, the demand for milk and milk products increased rapidly, particularly in urban localities. To meet the growing demand, the government has successfully encouraged the setting up of large dairy units with 100 to 500 milk cows. Many, imported as calves from the United States and Israel, were high-quality Holsteins.

Work began in late 1976 on the country's largest milk production center a few miles from Shiraz. On completion in 1981 it will house 10,000 purebred cows. The complex will cover nearly 10,000 acres, of which half will be used for pasture and the production of fodder. A total of 5,000 Holstein cattle will be imported, and their number will eventually double through artificial insemination.

As reported in 1976 there were ten pasteurization plants in operation, the two largest having capacities of 300 tons of milk per day. Eleven new plants—each with a capacity of 150 tons per day—were under construction with assistance from Sweden and Denmark. Much had been written concerning the prospects of dairying on improved pastures in the fertile Caspian area. Because of the Caspian weather, however, it seemed doubtful that output from these pastures could be substantially raised. Given Iran's climate and lack of technical experience, further development of large intensive operations based on purchased fodder appeared to be a better solution to the problem of satisfying the rising demand for high-quality dairy products.

Domestic wool production of almost 20,000 tons in the mid-1970s was not enough to accommodate the needs of the country's famous carpet industry. During 1975 some 18,000 tons of raw wool and over 3,000 tons of wool yarn were imported, principally from New Zealand, Australia, Argentina, and South Africa.

Fishing

Fishing provides employment for about 12,000 persons, many of whom are small independent operators using primitive equipment and techniques. They work the fishing grounds of the Caspian Sea and the Persian Gulf, the country's two important fishing areas, where a variety of species can be found. During the late 1960s and early 1970s the catch averaged about 5,000 tons and 20,000 tons respectively. Although frozen fish from the Caspian and the Persian Gulf are available in Tehran markets, long distances separate most of the population from the fishing grounds, and in most parts of the country distribution and storage facilities are inadequate. Iranians are not fish eaters by tradition, and a mid-1970s analysis of animal protein in the Iranian diet determined that only about 1 percent was derived from fish.

Commercial fishing is controlled by two state-owned enterprises, the Northern Fishing Company operating in the Caspian Sea and the Southern Fisheries Company in the Persian Gulf and the Gulf of Oman. Sturgeon, white salmon, whitefish, carp, bream, pike, and catfish predominate in the Caspian and sardines, sole, tuna, bream, snapper, mackerel, swordfish, and shrimp in the Persian Gulf.

The Caspian sturgeon is of particular importance because it produces roe or caviar. Known as gray pearls, the Iranian caviar is said to be the finest in the world and commands a startlingly high price. In early 1977 fresh beluga malassol caviar was available in the United States at US$100 for fourteen ounces. The Soviet Union and West European countries, however, were the principal importers.

During the 1960s and early 1970s caviar production fluctuated between 150 and 200 tons a year from a sturgeon catch averaging 1,500 tons. The caviar output during 1977 amounted to 200 tons, but increasing pollution in the Caspian Sea posed a serious threat to future production. In addition evaporation coupled with a diminished flow of water from the Volga and other rivers lowered the level of the Caspian, the world's largest landlocked sea, at a rate that had caused a ten-foot drop in its waters since 1945. In general the Caspian fishing industry faced a dubious future.

Persian Gulf fishing prospects appear considerably brighter. About 200 species of fish, of which 150 are edible and the remainder are suitable for industrial use, are found in the Persian and Oman gulfs, and Persian fishing craft in the mid-1970s were beginning to venture into adjacent portions of the Indian Ocean. Under the terms of a 1976 protocol, assistance was being received from the Republic of Korea (South Korea), and plans had been made to double the southern zone catch. The fishing fleet was to include twenty large South Korean trawlers in addition to thirty-three trawlers operated by the Southern Fisheries Company and affiliated fishermen's cooperatives.

Forestry

Of an estimated 44.8 million acres of forest lands and coppices, only about 8 million acres near the Caspian Sea can be regarded as commercially productive. Forests once abounded elsewhere, but centuries of grazing by sheep and goats (which eat the young tree shoots) and exploitation by charcoal burners have had ruinous effects. The remaining 36.8 million acres consist principally of brushlands from which little timber can be produced.

A plentiful rainfall, mild climate, and long growing season have combined to create dense rain forest of high quality timber in the Caspian region. There is an extensive growth of temperate-zone hardwoods including oak, beech, maple, Siberian elm, ash, walnut, ironwood, alder, basswood, and fig. About half of the Caspian forests consist of these trees; the remainder are a low-grade scrub.

The Zagros Mountains in the west and areas in Khorasan and Fars provinces abound in pistachio, oak, walnut, and maple trees. Shiraz, the capital of Fars, is renowned for its cypresses.

During the 1940s indiscriminate overcutting of the Caspian forests reduced once lushly forested areas into barren mountainsides. Moreover, a large part of the timber felled was wasted because high transportation costs dictated that all but the most valuable parts of the trees be abandoned.

In order to curtail the indiscriminate forest destruction the government in 1967 moved to nationalize all forests and pastures. A forest service was established, and by 1970 more than 3,000 forest rangers and guards were employed, and 1.3 million saplings had been planted on 1.3 million acres of land. Reforestation activities have continued, and in 1976 the program had matured to the point that Iranian forestry experts were loaned to the United Arab Emirates (UAE) to participate in projects designed to stabilize shifting sand dunes by tree plantings.

*   *   *

In the absence of a first-rate present-day overview of the Iranian agricultural scene as a whole, the periodic agricultural report, *Iran: Agricultural Situation*, by the American Embassy, Tehran, provides useful data. *Water Resource Development in Iran* by Peter Beaumont provides a good summary of a critically important aspect of Iranian agriculture. *The King's Vista: A Land Reform Which has Changed the Face of Persia* by D.R. Denman provides a laudatory version that can be set off against Robert Graham's "A Most Troublesome Experiment: The Failure of Large Commercial Farming in Iran," a short and highly critical look at one phase of land reform. At the time of publication in 1969, Ann K.S. Lambton's *The Persian Land Reform 1926–66* was by far the most comprehensive study of land reform and in late 1977 remained an important benchmark for further studies. (For further information see Bibliography.)

Chapter 12. Public Order and Internal Security

THE MAINTENANCE OF internal security continued to be a primary concern of the government of Iran in the late 1970s, despite the fact that it appeared to be the most durable and stable regime in the Middle East. Since the late 1950s Shahanshah Mohammad Reza Pahlavi has personally guided the development of an efficient, by Middle East standards, system of security-related law enforcement. During the mid-1970s foreign news, television reports, and human rights groups charged that Iran's law enforcement agencies sometimes engaged in repressive measures against nonviolent dissidents. The shah responded to these charges in a number of ways, one being the promulgation in December 1977 of a series of reforms designed to protect the civil rights of those accused of subversion or related activities. In early 1978 the implementation of the reforms had just begun, and it was not possible to determine their extent and efficacy.

The administration of justice in the cases of more common legal offenders had improved considerably in previous decades, yet those improvements rarely received the attention of foreign observers. The institution and expression of a system of people's, or lay, courts during the 1960s and 1970s were giant steps toward reducing the backlog of minor cases and raised markedly the public's regard for the legal system and its ability to adjudicate common legal matters in an efficient and just manner.

Internal Security

Internal turbulence and instability in Iran date from the beginning of its recorded history (see ch. 2). Tribal rivalries have been a continual feature since the invasion of Indo-European peoples during the second millennium B.C. Terrorism has deep historical roots as well; the term *assassin* is of eleventh-century Iranian origin. Religious-inspired violence by individuals and groups demanding a purer interpretation of Islam dates back to the seventh century A.D. Each of these internal security problems has persisted to some degree into the twentieth century, but the problems facing the shah in early 1978 were minor compared with those confronted by his predecessors on the Peacock Throne.

In modern times the primary vehicle of religious fanaticism was Fedayani Islam, founded by Nabab Safavi in the early 1940s with the express purpose of overthrowing the shah to establish a more purely Islamic state. Many assassinations and attempted assassinations during the late 1940s and early 1950s were attributed to the Fedayani, but in the mid-1950s most of its leaders were arrested, and many were "shot while trying to escape." Remnants of the Fedayani joined terrorist groups active in the 1970s, and other conservative Muslim elements continued to oppose the secularization of Iran under the shah.

361

Communist-inspired threats to security originated in 1920, the date of the first congress of the Adalat (Justice) Party, which had been formed among Iranian oil workers. The government was initially tolerant of communist unionization and other activities, but in 1929 several communist leaders were arrested for their revolutionary declarations, and in 1931 the Adalat Party was declared illegal. The party remained active nevertheless until 1937, when most of its leaders were jailed. In 1941 British and Soviet occupation forces set free all political prisoners. In the following year the freed communist leaders organized the Tudeh (Masses) Party.

Because communism remained illegal under the 1931 law, the Tudeh Party posed as nationalist-inspired, advocating progressive labor legislation, social insurance, improved living conditions for peasants, price controls, equality for minority groups, and the elimination of foreign interference. During the mid-1940s the Tudeh Party gained control of about half the Iranian press, controlled most of the country's unions, held legislative and cabinet positions in government, and claimed a membership of 750,000. In 1945 the Tudeh Party, under the protection of Soviet occupation forces, was instrumental in establishing autonomous republics in Azarbaijan and Kordestan. A year later, after Soviet troops left the area, the republics collapsed. The party was promptly outlawed in 1949, however, when a member attempted to assassinate the shah.

The party survived a period of repression, and when in 1952 a court ruled that party members could not be prosecuted for upholding communist doctrines, Tudeh Party members once again came into the open. The Tudeh Party thrived under Prime Minister Mossadeq, but in 1954, after he was ousted by the shah, a large Tudeh organization of military officers with loyalty to Mossadeq was discovered and vigorously suppressed. Some of the party's top leaders were killed, some jailed; a few managed to escape into exile, but the party never recovered from this blow.

The Tudeh Party suffered from factionalism in the 1960s; by 1977, operating in exile in Leipzig, Democratic Republic of Germany (East Germany), it had lost its membership and importance. In 1973 the Bureau of Intelligence and Research of the United States Department of State estimated the membership of the Tudeh Party at 500, but it is likely that the number was smaller by 1977. Perhaps its most significant activity, the operation in Bulgaria of a clandestine radio station, Peky-e-Iran (Radio Iran Courier), mysteriously ceased in 1976.

The emergence during the mid-1960s of a pro-Peking faction within the Tudeh Party, which historically had been strictly pro-Moscow, cut deeply into the party's effectiveness. Possibly even more important, the infiltration of government security agents into several Tudeh-sponsored groups in the late 1960s led to personal recriminations among party leaders; one result was that

Reza Radmanesh, the party's longtime secretary general, was ousted in 1970 and replaced by Iraj Eskandari, who remained in that position in early 1977.

A further constraint on the Tudeh Party was the gradual improvement of Iran's diplomatic relations with two of its neighbors, the Soviet Union and Iraq, which historically have provided the bulk of the party's moral and material support (see ch. 8). As official relations have improved, these two governments have withdrawn their support for the illegal communist party. The thaw in relations with Iraq, however, dates only from March 1975, and occasional allegations of Iraqi support for supporters of the Tudeh Party continued to strain Iran's relations with Iraq in 1977.

It was difficult to ascertain the nature of party activities. From its East German headquarters the party published a monthly newspaper, *Mardom*, and a quarterly journal, *Donya*, each with small circulations. It was alleged that the Tudeh Party offered guidance and support to terrorists inside Iran and to various dissident groups in exile and Iranian student groups abroad, but this connection could not be verified.

Other opposition parties in exile have surfaced from time to time in the 1970s, but by 1977 they appeared all but defunct. These included the Free Iran Movement headquartered in Paris and the National Front organization (backers of former prime minister Mossadeq), which operated primarily from Iraq.

Another internal security problem that had all but disappeared by 1977 was that of tribal dissent by various groups demanding autonomy from central government control. Historically, and as recently as the 1960s, this had been evident among the Qashqai, the Bakhtiari, the Kurds, the Arabs, and the Baluchi tribes in various parts of the country. By the mid-1970s these presented no actual threat, although during the mid-1970s Iranian military personnel provided support for the government of Pakistan in its efforts to eradicate the active Baluchi rebellion in that country. This covert support clearly reflected the Iranian government's fear that the Pakistani rebellion might spill over into the Iranian province of Baluchistan, which is populated with tribal kin of the Pakistani rebels and has a rugged terrain suited to guerrilla insurgency.

In the mid-twentieth century terrorism appeared and disappeared in a somewhat cyclical manner. Between 1970 and 1976 there was a steady increase in the use of terrorist violence by groups that presented no threat to the shah's hold on the reins of power but were a persistent nuisance and embarrassment to the monarchy. These groups have survived despite internal strife owing to ideological and personal differences, a continual loss of membership before government firing squads and in gun battles with security police, and infiltration by security police. A series of gun battles with Tehran police made terrorists extremely visible during mid-1976, but terrorist activity subsequently declined markedly. In 1977 terrorists were estimated to number fewer than 1,000.

Iranian terrorists are extremely clandestine and have virtually no contact with the press. Identifying specific terrorist groups and their ideologies is both difficult and misleading. To quote a research project conducted by career military officers studying at the United States Air University, "Terrorist groups in Iran have repeatedly changed their names, and it is virtually impossible to pinpoint the responsible group. Organizations are constantly changing, new alliances are formed and new factions break off from parent groups."

The official press has further confused the situation by consistently referring to terrorists operating in 1976 and 1977 as the "Islamic Marxist group." This term correctly identified the ideology of a large part of the terrorist opposition, but it suggested that terrorists were unified, which they were not, and in fact there probably was no organization with such a name.

Informed foreign sources name two major terrorist groups operating in Iran in early 1977: the People's Strugglers (Mujahidin-e Khalq) and the People's Sacrifice Guerrillas (Charikha-ye-Fedaye Khalq). The most important group, the People's Strugglers, has changed its name at least three times since its formation in 1960 under the name of the Iranian Freedom Movement Association. The People's Strugglers' rank-and-file membership was primarily religiously oriented (that is, struggling for a more purely Islamic state than exists under the present-day government), but its leadership cadre seemed to be oriented more toward a Marxist ideology. The People's Sacrifice Guerrillas seemed to be a more purely Marxist-oriented group. These two groups operated largely independently of one another, but they did apparently collude from time to time.

In 1977 the primary activity of terrorist groups was mere survival in the face of the considerable effort put forth by security officials to exterminate them. Their primary offensive activity was the assassination of Iranian security officials and United States military and defense-related personnel stationed in Tehran, using guns and homemade bombs. Their victims in the early 1970s included Iranian General Ziaddin, chief of military courts in Tehran (April 1971); Iranian Major General Said Taheri, National Police official with a key role in combating insurgency (August 1972); Brigadier General Reza Sandipour, another important security oficial (March 1975); United States Air Force Brigadier General Harold Price, chief of the Air Force section of the United States Military Advisory Group in Iran (May 1972); United States Army Lieutenant Colonel Lewis Hawkins, also of the United States military mission (June 1973); Colonel Paul Shaeffer and Lieutenant Colonel Jack Turner, United States Air Force officers in the mission (May 1975); and three civilian employees of

Rockwell International Corporation advising the Iranian military (August 1976).

President Richard M. Nixon's 1972 trip to Iran was marred by a series of bombings, including one explosion at the tomb of the shah's father shortly before Nixon and his host were scheduled to arrive. On numerous other occasions United States facilities and property have been victimized by less significant terrorist activities, and in December 1970 there was an unsuccessful attempt to kidnap United States Ambassador Douglas MacArthur. The life of the shah, of course, is constantly in danger, and kidnap and assassination plots against him and the royal family are uncovered on occasion. The nature of the victims and the professional manner in which assassinations have been carried out indicate that the terrorists are highly discriminating in choosing their victims, have a rather sophisticated surveillance system, and are well trained in assassination methods.

By the mid-1970s terrorist activity rarely deviated from this pattern of assassinations. This had not been the case only a few years previously. In February 1971 a large guerrilla band attacked a post at Siahkal in Gilan Province and battled with security forces there for a week before succumbing. Although it apparently was an isolated incident, the Siahkal affair has become an important symbol to Iranian revolutionaries. More common in the early 1970s were bank robberies and armed holdups to support the terrorists financially. The lack of armed robberies by terrorists during the mid-1970s has been attributed to their having gained considerable financial support (as much as the equivalent of US$400,000 yearly) from Libyan President Colonel Muammar Qaddafi and the Popular Front for the Liberation of Palestine. In addition to external financial support, Iranian terrorists have allegedly received training from the Palestine Liberation Organization, the People's Republic of China, Iraq, and Cuba.

Another restive element opposed to the government in the mid-1970s was to be found among the some 60,000 Iranian students studying abroad. Active dissidents among them comprised a small, but highly vocal minority. Of over 50,000 Iranian students estimated to be in the United States, for example, fewer than 3,000 were believed to be members of the Iranian Students' Association (ISA), the most important of the various organizations of university students abroad. The ISA operated worldwide, though its strongest bases were in Western Europe and the United States, from which it carried on an active propaganda campaign in support of "the Iranian armed struggle" and against the shah, the National Intelligence and Security Organization (Sazeman Ettelaat va Amniyat Kashvar—SAVAK), and what it termed "institutionalized repression in Iran." Other dissident student groups, such as the pro-Peking Toufan group in Italy, were less active. Several analysts have noted that student leaders, once their education is completed, often accept government employment in Iran, thus effectively diffusing their opposition to the regime.

The ISA also organized occasional demonstrations; in 1976 one in Paris and another in Houston erupted in violence and mass arrests. Another demonstration took place during the shah's November 1977 state visit to the United States, when violence erupted near the White House as several thousand Iranian students demonstrated their opposition to the shah while a nearly equal number of demonstrators were expressing their support for the visiting monarch. Nearly 100 people were injured in the confrontation between hooded (to avoid identification) anti-shah demonstrators, the police, and the shah's supporters, many of whom were allegedly paid to go to Washington from as far away as San Francisco to counter the expected student demonstrations. The incident represented the largest demonstration to date by dissident Iranian students studying abroad and the first time counterdemonstrations were staged.

Within Iran's borders, government security measures had, by 1976, largely eliminated organized, open expressions of dissent. Opposition political parties, labor unions, peasant organizations, and university student groups either had been made illegal or remained under the close scrutiny of security officials. As a result these usual vehicles of nonviolent protest were largely quiescent, although antigovernment demonstrations did occasionally occur. In 1963 and in 1970 major riots, precipitated in universities but subsequently becoming more widespread, brought vigorous responses by security officials. Two days of rioting in Qom, eighty miles south of Tehran, in June 1975—accounts differ as to whether they were precipitated by militant Muslims, followers of Mossadeq, or Marxist-oriented students—left ten dead, 100 wounded, and hundreds more under arrest. During late 1977 and early 1978, after several months of relaxation of past stringent security measures, a series of large demonstrations erupted into riots and were attributed to a variety of dissident elements.

At the time of the shah's November 1977 trip abroad, Tehran witnessed political disturbances in the form of student strikes, street demonstrations by over 10,000 persons, and the wide circulation of a letter, signed by fifty-six prominent Iranians, calling on fellow citizens "to raise their voices against absolute rule." Those protests, clearly timed to call President Jimmy Carter's attention to the human rights situation in Iran, lasted almost two weeks and ended, according to a correspondent for the *Financial Times*, with the arrest of between 250 and 600 demonstrators.

On January 9, 1978, a demonstration by conservative Muslims was held in the holy city of Qom to express their long-standing opposition to the shah's reforms in such areas as land reform, which has resulted in the expropriation of mosque lands, and the emancipation of women, which many religious leaders feel to be in violation of sacred Islamic laws. Attempts by the police to disperse the demonstrators resulted in several deaths. On February 18, after a call for a general strike by Iran's most powerful *mujtahid* (see Glossary) to highlight the period of mourning for those killed in Qom, a far more serious disturbance erupted in Tabriz, precipitating the worst riots since those of 1963. After two days of widespread arson directed at the city's banks, movie theaters, and hotels, the army moved in to patrol the city. The government reported that twelve persons were killed and some 250 arrested before order was restored.

Observers of these events pointed out that the reemergence of massive protest demonstrations was possible because of the recent liberalization in the shah's stance toward the nonviolent expression of dissent. In an interview shortly after the riots, the shah confirmed his commitment to continue his liberalization, but at the same time warned that the dissident movement was "completely illegal," and that he "will not let it get out of hand."

Law Enforcement Agencies

Since 1953, when the shah consolidated his personal control of the government, Iranian law enforcement agencies have undergone a major transformation. The Imperial Iranian Gendarmerie—the rural police—and the National Police have more than doubled in size and, with generous increases in their budgets, have attained a high degree of professional effectiveness. More important the secret police organization, SAVAK, was established in 1957 and given ultimate responsibility for the maintenance of internal security. Twenty years later SAVAK was one of the most powerful and pervasive institutions of government.

The principal motivation behind this impressive upgrading of the nation's law enforcement agencies has been the shah's intense concern with matters of internal security since the turbulent decade after World War II. Another concern has been reducing the nation's historically high crime rate, an effort that apparently has met considerable success (see Incidence of Crime, this ch.).

This is not to say that Iranian law enforcement agencies were without problems, some of which were the product of the Iranian political process, in which the shah was virtually omnipresent in governmental decisionmaking (see ch. 7). As was the case in most areas of government activity, law enforcement officials tended to defer to the shah or his confidants for guidance and direction even in matters of relatively minor importance. Predictably this often led to inefficiency and inertia in cases that called for immediate decisions.

The second problem, lack of interagency coordination and cooperation, stemmed from the horizontal manifestation of the same principle of Iranian politics. This was emphasized by Gerald T. McLaughlin in his 1976 study of Iranian drug policies: "Coordination and cooperation—between the National Police and the Gendarmerie—[are] not fostered because the existence of such cooperation could lead to the development of close personal relationships between officers of both branches, which ultimately could become a threat tó the Shah's power." Although McLaughlin is concerned specifically with the promotion of a more effective drug policy, his conclusion undoubtedly holds true in other areas of overlapping jurisdictions, such as internal security. In 1978 it was reported that considerable efforts were being put forth to improve cooperation among law enforcement agencies.

Third, despite considerable improvement (particularly within the National Police), the upper ranks of police officers continued in 1977 to be permeated with armed forces personnel. This situation was destructive to morale among the lower ranking officers, who saw little hope of advancing into positions apparently set aside for military personnel.

Finally, and also despite considerable improvement, law enforcement agencies—SAVAK in particular—continued to suffer from a poor public image both at home and abroad, as repressive and sometimes arbitrary in their enforcement of the law. Although it was difficult to assess the Iranian population's image of the police, during the early 1970s those Iranians who held views contrary to the monarch feared, to some extent, the "long arm" of Iranian law enforcement officials. In 1978, however, a Department of State spokesman said that recent liberalizations had removed much of the fear of arrest for the nonviolent expression of dissent.

Imperial Iranian Gendarmerie

In 1977 the Imperial Iranian Gendarmerie numbered approximately 75,000 men and operated under a 1976–77 budget the equivalent of approximately US$417 million. The gendarmerie is under the direction of the Ministry of Interior in peacetime but in the case of war or national emergency would be transferred to the jurisdiction of the Ministry of War. Its law enforcement responsibilities extend to all rural areas and to small towns and villages of fewer than 5,000, encompassing some 80 percent of Iran's territory and about 60 percent of its population.

The gendarmerie has had an uneven record of progress since its founding in 1911, but since World War II it has undergone complete reorganization and constant reevaluation and reform, and by the 1970s it had developed into a vast, professional rural police force. Originally set up under the Ministry of Finance to control rural banditry so that taxes could be collected in the lawless countryside, the gendarmerie was organized and commanded by Swedish officers in its formative years. When Reza Pahlavi was crowned as Reza Shah in 1926, he absorbed the gendarmerie into the army in an effort to consolidate central government authority. This organization remained unchanged until 1943, after the abdication of Reza Shah in favor of his son, when the gendarmerie was given organizational autonomy under the Ministry of Interior. It retained this autonomy in 1977.

Of considerable assistance in the reform efforts has been the

United States Military Mission to the Imperial Iranian Gendarmerie (known as GENMISH), which originated in 1953 and was terminated in 1976. Consisting of approximately twenty United States military officers and ten civilians, GENMISH assisted in the gendarmerie's reorganization and gave advice on organizational and training matters.

The duties of the gendarmerie have expanded considerably since its early assignmet to suppress rural banditry. By the 1970s the missions included, in addition to routine rural police functions, the apprehension of smugglers of narcotics and other contraband, the maintenance of internal security and border security, traffic control on highways, and acting as an adjunct to the army in time of war or national emergency. Since 1972 the gendarmerie has also been placed in charge of the National Resistance Force, a widespread though largely inactive, militia organization charged with training citizens in the defense of their homes and villages.

In a more abstract sense perhaps the most important function of the gendarmerie was its role as the manifestation of central government authority to much of the Iranian population. In a country with such a disparate population whose allegiances have historically been directed toward local authorities, the importance of this function can scarcely be overemphasized. Personnel of gendarmerie posts (of which there were over 2,000 in the 1970s) routinely patrol their assigned areas, serve government notices, settle disputes, and exchange news in addition to providing police protection. In this way, and in their capacity as highway patrolmen, the gendarmes can keep aware of any unusual incidents and the passage of strangers. In short a key gendarmerie function is to gather intelligence in the vast, sparsely populated regions of the country.

In the mid-1970s gendarmes had a fairly wide range of modern equipment, including light aircraft, large Huey and small helicopters, some forty patrol boats, armored patrol cars and jeeps, trucks, and motorcycles. Most of this equipment had been recently acquired, and the improvement in the mobility of the gendarmerie has been accompanied by the installation of a nationwide radio network linking all posts.

The gendarmerie uses the same basic uniform as the army, has the same rank structure, and patterns its organizational structure after that of the armed forces (see ch. 13). The largest gendarmerie unit is the district, of which there were fourteen in 1975. Districts, in turn, are divided into two or more regiments, each headquartered in a provincial town. About a third of the districts operate at brigade strength. Each regiment controls about six companies, whose command posts are located in smaller municipalities. Finally company areas are apportioned among posts— located in villages, at road junctions, and in strategic rural areas— which are the basic gendarmerie unit. Gendarmerie posts are of squad size and are usually under the command of an officer and two or more noncommissioned officers. Central headquarters is located in Tehran. In addition to its stationary units, the gendarmerie contains numerous mobile units that are able to carry out sustained pursuit of hostile persons or groups.

Some gendarmes are conscripts who have completed their military service or inductees selected for this duty rather than for the army (see ch. 13). Many are volunteers. Most officers come from the military. In special cases the army lends officers to the gendarmerie, but they retain their army rank and eventually return to their own units. Except for inducted enlisted personnel who serve for two years, the usual enlistment period is five years and the reenlistment period three years. Most gendarmes make the service a career; many stay in for twenty years, the minimum period required to obtain retirement benefits.

Promotion for enlisted men is based on length of service, ability, and the recommendations of their immediate commanders. The same system of promotions is used by the army and the National Police. A panel of examiners, appointed by the commanding general, must pass on all promotions. The appointment of all senior officers must be approved by the shah, and the seniormost appointments are made by the shah.

Historically morale among gendarmes has been low; low pay and poor living conditions in isolated posts led some officers to supplement their meager existences through illegal activities. Corruption was widespread, and the gendarme was generally hated and feared as a repressive agent who often sought extortion payments from those he was expected to serve. Since the 1940s reforms in the pay and living conditions of gendarmes combined with a crackdown on corrupt officers have greatly improved the morale of the gendarme and his image among rural Iranians. Reforms have been designed to improve the caliber of personnel and provide them with greater incentives to be conscientious; included are higher pay, recognition of personal achievement, improved retirement benefits, medical benefits, new educational programs, and a higher standard of recruitment. The pace of the reforms accelerated markedly during the 1960s, and the improvement in the quality of gendarmerie personnel has been accompanied by significant increases in its budget allocations. To improve the public image of the gendarmes, they have been used to aid villagers with such humanitarian projects as health programs and relief in time of earthquakes or other natural disasters.

National Police

In 1977 the Iranian National Police operated with approximately 40,000 men, under a fiscal year (FY) 1976 (see Glossary) budget equivalent of about US$300 million. Like the gendarmerie, the National Police come under the direction of the Ministry of Interior. Their responsibility for law enforcement includes all cities over 5,000 in population, which numbered over 150 in the late 1960s and undoubtedly considerably more by 1977. In addition to the usual urban police activities, the National Police are responsible for passport and immigration procedures, issuance and control of citizens' identification cards, driver and vehicle licensing and registration, railroad and airport policing, and prison management.

The origins of the National Police go back to the beginning of the twentieth century when first Italian, then Swedish, advisers offered police training to Iranians and founded the first school for the training of police officers. It was not until 1921, however, that Reza Khan, shortly after his assumption of power, brought the various departments under the central control of the Ministry of Interior. In its formative years the National Police was essentially a paramilitary force, and as late as the 1960s its military heritage was reported to be reflected in the complexion of the force. By the mid-1970s, however, most of the military officers in the upper ranks, whose presence had been a cause of dissension among officers below them, had been reassigned to the armed forces; in almost all respects, the National Police was a civil police force modeled after those in Western societies.

The demilitarization of the National Police has been accompanied by the upgrading of the quality of personnel, the modernization of virtually all aspects of their operations, and the doubling of the size of the force between the mid-1950s and the mid-1970s. During much of this period these efforts were aided by the Public Safety Division under the United States Agency for International Development (AID), which worked principally in the areas of training, communications, narcotics control, and traffic control. This AID training mission was terminated during the 1960s.

Perhaps the greatest advance has taken place in the area of recruitment and training of personnel. Whereas in the past a large number of recruits were illiterate, were unsuited for police work, and received little in the way of training, by the mid-1970s recruiting had become highly selective, and training was required throughout the policeman's career.

The pride of the force was the National Police University in Tehran, which housed training facilities for officers and patrolmen. To be accepted for officers' school, the applicant must have a high school diploma and meet exacting physical and mental standards. Only about 10 percent of candidates for officers' training meet the requirements. Those who do spend three years studying police sciences and university-level subjects; the successful cadet graduates as a second lieutenant with a university-level (licentiate) degree. Successive promotion depends on length of service, quality of performance, and further training at higher grade levels.

Upon reaching the rank of lieutenant colonel the officer again enters the university for the nine-month Senior Officer's Course, which consists of training in such fields as modern police tactics, administration, and planning. This course, designed to offer expertise in management, is mandatory for further promotion.

Recruit patrolmen also train for three months at the National Police University before becoming law enforcement officers. In addition to passing this course, enlisted men must pass a literacy test, show proof of grade school education, and pass a physical and mental examination. In-service training for both officers and enlisted men consists of a series of twelve-week courses in a variety of subjects, including criminal investigation, traffic regulation and control, civil disturbance control, narcotics law enforcement, prison management, and radio communications.

The National Police are organized along hierarchical lines; routine activities are carried out by city headquarters, certain functions that exceed city jurisdiction are conducted by provincial headquarters, and those exceeding provincial jurisdiction are the responsibility of national headquarters in Tehran. Organization is also horizontal; there are scores of different bureaus responsible for various police activities—including selection and recruitment, prisons, traffic, communications, narcotics, passports and immigration, identification, intelligence—and several that are responsible for the welfare of police personnel. The number of bureaus in the National Police has multiplied since the early 1960s as have the responsibilities and efficiency of the force.

The Iranian government is extremely proud of the modernization of its National Police. The government claims that urban dwellers no longer fear walking streets alone, as was the case as recently as the early 1960s. This assertion may slightly overstate reality; however, it is certainly true that through demilitarization, which has allowed the career police officer to attain the highest ranks within the National Police, and through substantial budget increases (fourfold between FY 1970 and FY 1976), which have allowed salaries, benefits, and allowances to be standardized at an attractive level and enabled the expansion of the force and improvement of the equipment, the National Police have attained a degree of professionalism and morale far above their pre-1960s public image as inefficient and corrupt officials to be feared rather than respected.

SAVAK

After its formation, under the guidance of United States and Israeli intelligence officers, SAVAK quickly developed into a strong arm of government control. Its first director, General Teimur Bakhtiar, was widely reputed for his brutality. In 1961 Bakhtiar was suspected of intent to seize power from the shah and was dismissed; nine years later he was assassinated. His successor, General Pakravan, was also dismissed by the shah in 1966 on charges of ineffectiveness in handling opposition elements. The shah then gave the assignment to General Nematollah Nassiri, a trusted childhood friend and classmate who continued as director in early 1978.

Basic data concerning SAVAK is not publicly available, but information from a variety of sources serves as an indicator of its importance within Iranian society. The exact strength of SAVAK is unknown, although informed United States government sources estimate the number of full-time personnel at 10,000. The agency is also widely believed to employ a large number of part-time informants: William J. Butler, of the International Commission of Jurists, has estimated this number to be as high as 200,000. SAVAK is reported to have a generous amount of funds available to it, although its budget allocation is hidden within the Iranian national budget. Full-time SAVAK agents are said to receive salaries above those of regular civil servants.

SAVAK is attached to the Office of the Prime Minister, and its director, who is appointed by the shah, assumes the title of Deputy to the Prime Minister for National Security Affairs (sometimes referred to as Deputy Prime Minister). Though officially a civilian agency, SAVAK has close ties to the military; many of its senior personnel, in addition to the director, are officers of the armed forces. Another childhood friend and close confidant of the shah, General Hossein Fardust, was deputy director of SAVAK until the early 1970s, at which time he assumed the directorship of the Special Intelligence Bureau, which operates inside the monarch's palace independently of SAVAK.

SAVAK was founded with the purpose of rounding up members of the outlawed Tudeh Party; but in the twenty years of its existence it has expanded its activities tremendously to fullfill the mission of gathering intelligence and neutralizing opposition to the shah. One such activity in which SAVAK plays a primary role is press censorship and control of intellectual expression. By 1977 the government controlled distribution of all the nation's newsprint; and, although books were not censored before publication, private citizens with literature considered subversive were liable to arrest and imprisonment, and Iranians who authored such materials were subject to police harassment and possible imprisonment or exile. Ahmad Faroughy, one of the growing number of dissident Iranian intellectuals living abroad, described the mechanisms of press censorship in 1974 as "a special SAVAK press section [that] recruits political journalists who are imposed upon the press. Not only are these journalists mandated as censors, but all major articles dealing with important political events inside or outside Iran are written by them, SAVAK decisions concerning the orientation of a given subject being final and without appeal." During 1977 there was evidence of liberalization in the mechanisms of censorship, and freedom of intellectual expression was reported to have expanded significantly.

Another method reportedly used by SAVAK in the control of the nation's internal security was the widespread and continual surveillance of actual and potential trouble spots. Universities, labor unions, and peasant organizations were especially subject to overt and covert infiltration by SAVAK agents and paid informants; SAVAK is also active in foreign countries where there is a perceived threat against the Iranian government, although this mission is secondary to the domestic functions. Foreign missions include gathering intelligence related to external threats to Iran's national security, especially from neighboring countries, and infiltrating student and other groups potentially hostile to the shah.

The latter activity proved to be an embarrassment to Iran when in September 1976 Malek Mahdavi, a first secretary of Iran's diplomatic mission to the United Nations office in Geneva, was expelled by Swiss officials on the charge that he had engaged in "prohibited intelligence activity" as an agent of SAVAK. United States Secretary of State Henry Kissinger subsequently declared that there undoubtedly were SAVAK agents attached to the Iranian Embassy in Washington.

The domestic functions of SAVAK officials, as spelled out in the 1957 legislation establishing the agency, include the responsibility of acting as examining magistrates under the jurisdiction of military courts. This power has in effect made SAVAK a law unto itself, having legal authority to arrest and detain suspected persons virtually indefinitely. SAVAK operated its own prisons in Tehran (at least two, the Committee Prison and Evin Prison) and, according to some, throughout Iran where prisoners were detained while awaiting trial. There was no institutional check, with the exception of the shah, on these activities. In the words of one prominent Iranian as quoted in a document of the International Commission of Jurists "the trouble is that once you are arrested by SAVAK there is no place to go." The widespread fear of SAVAK alleged by Iranian exiles and student groups is largely attributed to its dual role as both police and judicial authority (see Administration of Justice, this ch.).

Incidence of Crime

Though extremely sensitive to criminal activity, the Iranian government has only recently begun to keep statistics on the incidence of crime. Although these statistics, which are compiled by the General Department of Police, are questionable—the total reported number of crimes is only a small fraction of the number of cases brought to court yearly—they do offer a general idea of the relative importance of certain crimes (see Administration of Justice, this ch.) (see table 22, Appendix A). Many forms of crime have been stabilizing or even falling for several years. Police proudly assert that Tehran's streets are safe, even for women and children at night. Less traditional forms of crime are on the increase, however. Traffic accidents and violations have skyrocketed as the number of automobiles in Iran's large cities, particularly Tehran, has grown rapidly. Corruption in government continues to be a persistent problem and ever since new laws passed in the mid-1970s brought nationwide attention to the problem of hoarding and profiteering by retail merchants, its incidence has been widely reported in the press.

One major source of criminal activity—the smuggling and use of illegal narcotics—has been scrutinized by foreign observers and considerable information has been made available. McLaughlin, in his survey of drug problems and policies in Iran, emphasizes that drug abuse has traditionally been a social as well as a law enforcement problem in Iran, dating back to Arab military campaigns in the seventh century A.D. Little the government has done in modern times, including the ban on poppy cultivation in 1955 and the 1969 reversal of this policy and adoption of legal poppy cultivation and opiate distribution under government auspices, has brought any significant reduction in the problem.

In the mid-1970s the government distributed some 180 tons of opium a year to 170,000 legally registered addicts. Nevertheless it was estimated that some 400,000 Iranians were illegal users, making a total of nearly 2 percent of the population either legal or illegal opium users. Other illegal drugs were also in evidence, but their use was far less widespread. The abuse of heroin, a relatively new problem in Iran, was said to involve about 40,000 users. Use of *shireh* (the residue from smoking opium) and hashish also was fairly widespread. Drugs of Western origin, including LSD, cocaine, and barbiturates, have recently been introduced into Iran. Abuse of these drugs occurred primarily among the young middle class, especially students returning from the United States or Western Europe.

Opium was the only illegal drug of domestic origin. Much of the illegally consumed opium was said to be sold illicitly from crops grown by the government, although it was smuggled from Turkey and Afghanistan as well. The Afghan border was an especially active locus of smuggling operations, said to be conducted at least in part by large Mafia-style organizations. Gendarmerie and customs police were instructed to maintain a constant vigil for smugglers, and large-scale gun battles with well-armed bands of smugglers near the Afghan border were a common occurrence. For a wide variety of reasons, which include the willingness of many border officials to take bribes, McLaughlin concluded that Iran's drug enforcement policies were inadequate and that the problem of abuse of illegal drugs in Iran was likely to worsen in the future.

Administration of Justice

The modern Iranian system of the administration of justice stems from reforms undertaken early in the twentieth century. From the proclamation of the Constitution of 1906 as amended in 1907, when a systematic approach to the establishment of courts first came into being, until the laws of 1932 and 1936—which respectively brought all legal matters into secular courts and made it mandatory for all judges to hold degrees in secular law—clerical authority, stemming from the traditional Islamic shariah law, gradually gave way to a system of secular law courts and procedures adapted largely from French law. Although the administration of justice was thus placed exclusively in the hands of secular authority, the influence of Islamic law on the Iranian legal system remained, even if generally subordinated to that of the more modern French system.

Another flurry of reforms took place in the mid-1960s when people's courts, called Houses of Equity in rural areas and Councils of Arbitration (sometimes called adjudication courts) in urban areas, were introduced to relieve the backlog of cases in the traditional court system. A decade later these courts had expanded greatly in number and were widely proclaimed to be successful.

Although the people's courts had made great strides in alleviating the case backlog, in 1977 the administration of justice continued to operate with several apparent difficulties. First of all was the chronic shortage of personnel with legal training. In spite of the fact that formal legal training is not required of judges or attorneys practicing in the people's courts Iran was not able to train a sufficient number of persons in the legal profession to fill its need. During the mid-1970s about 1,500 people were admitted to the practice of law each year from the country's two law schools, one at Tehran University (public) and the other at National University (private), both located in Tehran. A third law facility was planned for the city of Qom. A shortage of professionally trained judges was equally evident; the approximately 2,000 serving throughout Iran worked long hours to keep pace with the mounting caseload. It has been reported that the Ministry of Justice had difficulty in recruiting young lawyers for the judiciary because university graduates did not want to live in remote provinces and that it was not uncommon for judges to return to private practice because of low salaries.

In the mid-1970s judicial functions were exercised by the ordinary courts under the supervision of the Ministry of Justice, which included a hierarchy of courts for criminal and civil proceedings and several special courts for juvenile offenders, government officials, and members of the judiciary; locally elected people's courts; and military courts functioning under the Ministry of War.

These military courts handled, by law, a number of cases that in Western countries would be considered civilian, criminal matters. Their expanding jurisdiction in this regard was raising strenuous opposition from some quarters. Supporters of the increasing jurisdiction of military tribunals argued that military authority was an essential means of expanding the power of the central government over areas of the country with traditionally strong regional allegiances, that military judges were more efficient, honest, and loyal than their civilian counterpart, and that swift, harsh judgments were necessary in cases involving certain crimes. Opponents argued that military justice denies the accused of due process and that fundamental civil rights are consistently violated within a system that is essentially closed to the view of outsiders.

Civilian Criminal Courts, Procedures, and Penal Code

The Supreme Court, or Court of Cassation (Divan Kehvar), is the highest court in the land, seated in Tehran and having jurisdiction over the entire country (see ch. 6). It consists of the attorney general, a public prosecutor, and eleven branches, each of which consists of four justices. It has the power to hear cases involving the prime minister, ministers, and acting ministers; acts as the highest court of appeal in criminal cases involving punishments from two months' imprisonment to execution (in appeals from military tribunals this power must be authorized by the shah) and in civil cases involving amounts greater than 3,000 rials (for value of the rial—see Glossary); and settles jurisdictional disputes between lower courts.

The provincial courts, variously known as courts of appeal, courts of assize, and criminal high courts, operate in provincial capitals as courts of appeal in civil and criminal cases and as courts of first instance in criminal cases involving punishment of over two years' imprisonment. In hearing criminal cases, three judges sit unless the offense involves a maximum sentence of life imprisonment or death, in which situation five judges hear the case. There are no juries. In 1973 there were seventy-six provincial courts, and there were plans to expand the number to eighty-four during 1978.

The primary courts of the first instance are county (also township) courts, which have civil jurisdiction in controversies involving more than 50,000 rials and criminal jurisdiction over offenses punishable by more than one month's and less than three years' imprisonment. In general these courts hear misdemeanors, whereas the provincial courts hear felony cases. The county courts also act as courts of appeal from lower courts in both criminal and civil matters. Each county court consists of several judges, an investigating officer, and a prosecuting attorney. In 1973 there were 340 county courts throughout the country, and it was planned to expand the number to 398 during 1978.

The next lowest ordinary tribunals are called district courts. Each district court consists of one judge, who tries civil cases involving less than 50,000 rials and criminal cases with maximum sentences up to one month's imprisonment, generally referred to as minor offenses, or contraventions. District courts also review cases tried by the Houses of Equity and Councils of Arbitration, but seldom are judgments reversed. In 1973 there were 286 district courts, and there were plans to expand the number to 390 during 1978.

As a part of the shah's White Revolution (see Glossary), people's courts were inaugurated during the mid-1960s to relieve the burden of minor cases in the ordinary courts and to render swift judgments in such matters by a group of the defendant's local resident peers. By 1973 the number of Houses of Equity had grown to over 8,000, expected to be nearly 12,000 by 1978. Since their beginning in 1966 the number of Councils of Arbitration had grown to over 200 by 1975 and was expected to be 300 by 1978. The importance of these courts can be measured by the fact that in the 1973–74 period people's courts settled more than 600,000 of a total of about 1.6 million cases settled in all courts. This fact has greatly alleviated the case burden and, according to an official of the Ministry of Justice, has allowed the average time between arrest and trial to shrink from three or four years—before the time of the people's courts—to five or six months. The composition and jurisdictions of the two kinds of people's courts vary only slightly.

Houses of Equity consist of three regular members, or justices, and two alternates, all of whom are elected every three years by the local community from among the village elders. There is no remuneration, although it is considered an honor to serve, and justices are not required to be versed in legal matters or even to be literate. Young people from the Literacy Corps and from the Judicial Corps (law graduates in alternative service to military conscription) are available to render necessary assistance (see ch. 3). Their civil jurisdiction is extensive, involving claims up to 10,000 rials or, in the case of movable property, up to 50,000 rials with the consent of both parties. They also hear cases of family disputes. Criminal jurisdiction is more limited; they hear cases of trespass, unlawful occupation, and disturbance of the peace and may impose fines only up to 200 rials. More serious offenders may be detained by order of the village courts, which may also gather evidence to be used by higher courts.

Parties to litigation in the Houses of Equity pay no fee, and procedure is informal, based on common law. Trials were generally thought to be fair, and the village courts had inspired considerable confidence among rural dwellers in the ability of the judicial system to solve minor disputes and offenses in a swift and equitable manner.

Councils of Arbitration are found in cities of more than 5,000 people and function similarly to the Houses of Equity. The composition of these courts is identical, although justices in the Councils of Arbitration often are literate and receive a nominal compensation for their services. Criminal jurisdiction is wider; these courts may try cases in which the maximum penalty is up to two months' imprisonment and/or a fine of 20,000 rials. They may also impose fines for traffic violations.

The judicial system also contains several kinds of special courts that try special offenders or special categories of offenses. Juvenile courts, which try persons from ages six to eighteen, have existed since 1959 and contain a judge and five counselors. Offenders under the age of twelve are tried separately from older juveniles. Only those over twelve can be detained in penal institutions. Most cases are dealt with by way of warnings or by measures for re-education either within or outside the family.

The Criminal Court for Government Employees tries government workers and others who carry out official government duties, particularly for cases of extortion, corruption, embezzlement of funds, and abuse of authority. Because of the large caseload, minor offenses of this nature are dealt with in ordinary courts. The Criminal Court for Government Employees has the power to impose any punishment short of the death penalty; appeals go directly to the Supreme Court. Several other special courts, such as the Judges' Disciplinary Tribunal for dealing with offenses committed by judges, are of relatively minor importance.

The code of criminal procedure in force in 1977 was adopted in 1912 but has undergone considerable revision through the years. Investigation into alleged offenses is entrusted to the Imperial Iranian Gendarmerie in rural areas and the National Police in urban areas. They are allowed to hold suspects for up to twenty-four hours. If sufficient evidence is found, a warrant is issued by a magistrate or the public prosecutor. Under certain conditions the public prosecutor may grant a stay of prosecution, though not in the case of felonies. Provisional detention, which before 1974 was allowed for an unlimited period, has since been limited to two months for alleged misdemeanors and four months for felonies; though common under military jurisdiction for serious crimes, provisional detention is rarely used under ordinary criminal procedure. The vast majority of the accused are released on bail, or bail with surety provided by a third party, or on their own recognizance with a promise not to leave the jurisdiction of the court.

Trials are often delayed for considerable periods, but this situation has been greatly relieved by the expansion of the people's courts. If the defendant cannot afford a lawyer, the court may appoint defense counsel; in the case of felonies, the accused must be provided with counsel according to law. There is nothing comparable to a writ of habeas corpus, and a person may be tried in absentia, whether in or out of the country. Despite a constitutional provision for the presence of juries during political trials and those involving the press, in fact all trials are held without juries, although they are open to the public unless ordered in camera. Oral pleas are put by both the prosecutor and the defense, and witnesses are questioned by both parties. Although the law specifically states that the burden of proof lies with the prosecutor, great weight is placed on the police report, and the defendant has a heavy burden to overcome its contents.

There is only one stage of appeal, which may lie equally on questions of law and of fact. The appeals court may reverse the decision of the lower court or may make the sentence either more or less severe.

The penal code of 1925, as amended over the years, governs the operation of the penal system. The classification of offenses follows the French model: contraventions, or minor offenses, carry fines of from 200 to 5,000 rials; misdemeanors are punishable by prison terms of from six days to three years and fines greater than 5,000 rials (however, every sentence of imprisonment for up to thirty days must be changed by the judge to a fine of between 5,000 and 30,000 rials); and felonies, which carry sentences of more than two years' imprisonment. There are three degrees of imprisonment for felonies: the first degree carries two to ten years of imprisonment; the second degree, three to fifteen years; and the third degree, life imprisonment or execution.

An important amendment to the penal code in 1960 enumerates additional penalties when there is a serious probability of a future offense against the security of the nation. These include professional restrictions, restrictions on domicile (for a period of one month to three years) and, for a foreigner, expulsion. This law also authorizes the detention of the insane in asylums, of repeated recidivists in deportation camps, of vagabonds in work camps or in agricultural colonies, of alcoholics or drug addicts in medical treatment centers, and of juvenile delinquents in reeducation centers. In addition several supplementary or complementary penalties that restrict certain individual rights may be imposed under specified conditions.

Penalties generally are greater for recidivists. The law also provides for the suspension of sentences, though not at the time of pronouncement. There is no probation system; those released early receive no supervision. Provisions are made for the granting of amnesty to prisoners, but much more common is clemency, which is granted by the shah on a regular basis to prisoners tried by military tribunals.

Military Courts, Procedures, and Penal Code

Since the overthrow of Prime Minister Mohammad Mossadeq in 1953, the military has assumed a progressively greater role in the judicial system of the nation (see ch. 2). This fact stems from the expansion of the jurisdiction of military tribunals in the prosecution of civilians. In addition to trying offenses by military personnel, these courts, which are under the direction of the Procurator General of the Armed Forces, hear cases involving civilians accused of crimes against the state or against the shah, armed robbery on highways, smuggling and production of narcotics and, since 1974, sabotage and hoarding or profiteering by merchants, which are considered threats to the security of the state (see ch. 13).

Military tribunals consist of primary courts and courts of appeal. In 1968 there were reported to be twenty-nine primary courts and ten courts of appeal in the country. These were permanent courts and were attended, depending on the severity of the offense, by either three or five active-duty officers of senior rank.

Procedures of criminal prosecution and penal matters are enumerated in the Military Justice and Penal Law of 1938, as since amended. The investigation of offenses by civilians subject to military jurisdiction is entrusted to SAVAK. SAVAK officials are given considerable powers in their investigations, including that of acting as military magistrates, which gives them the power to arraign and detain suspects. The Constitution requires that a prisoner be arraigned within twenty-four hours of arrest but, because SAVAK officials act as magistrates, a prisoner may be held indefinitely by SAVAK without seeing a judge. In 1976 independent observers reported that more than three-quarters of those held in detention under military jurisdiction had not been convicted of a crime (see Law Enforcement Agencies, this ch.).

During the early and mid-1970s there were frequent allegations that SAVAK agents tortured prisoners during interrogations. These charges were extremely difficult to substantiate or refute, however, as the military judicial system under which SAVAK operated was essentially closed to the view of outsiders. Several investigatory agencies, including the International Commission of Jurists, Amnesty International, and the Subcommittee on International Organizations of the Committee on International Relations of the United States House of Representatives, conducted investigations into these allegations during 1976. Among those testifying, Reza Baraheni, an Iranian poet living in the United States, was the most insistent in his allegations that he had been tortured by SAVAK agents.

The widespread publication of these charges and the sudden worldwide interest in issues of human rights contributed to the subsequent decline in reported allegations of torture. When asked in an October 1977 interview on the Columbia Broadcasting System program "60 Minutes" whether torture was still used in Iran, the shah replied in his usual candid style, "not the torture in the old sense of torturing people, twisting their arms and doing this and that. But there are intelligent ways of questioning now." In its February 1978 human rights report the United States Department of State reported that in recent months it had received "significantly fewer allegations of torture in Iran than was the case in previous years and [it] does not believe torture has been used recently."

A dispassionate review of the Iranian legal system conducted in 1976 under the auspices of the International Commission of Jurists concludes that "it seems beyond dispute that offenders arrested, interrogated and imprisoned by the SAVAK do not enjoy the same rights as the offenders triable before the ordinary courts." The detained prisoner remains incommunicado and without counsel during the official examination by the military examining magistrate. Pursuant to legislation enacted in December 1977, the defendent may make his "choice from among civilian defense attorneys" after the completion of the investigation.

Military tribunals are usually held in camera; between March 1972 and April 1977 no foreign lawyers or journalists had been admitted into hearings before military courts. Most of what is known about the conduct of military trials comes from witnesses before March 1972. An Amnesty International report dated November 1976 states:

> The accused has no right to demand that witnesses against him or her be called and has no right to cross-examination. The only witnesses heard by the tribunal are the defendants themselves. The prosecutor proceeds by reading into evidence the findings of the SAVAK investigation, including confessions, if any. . . . The prosecution is not required to produce in court evidence referred to in the SAVAK files and the defense is not allowed to introduce evidence to support the defense case other than the testimony of the defendant. In practice the defendant is assumed guilty.

There is one stage of appeal. In theory one may appeal the verdict of the Military Court of Appeal to the Supreme Court; but doing so requires the consent of the shah and in fact has been extremely rare. After such an appeal the only legal recourse of the convicted lies in asking the clemency of the shah. Clemency in individual cases is exceptional, but the shah does grant broad clemencies, often of hundreds of prisoners, on certain occasions, such as his birthday and the anniversary of the ascent of the Pahlavi dynasty. Although accounts vary as to the numbers released on such occasions Pars, the official Iranian news agency, announced that nearly 5,000 prisoners were freed between March 1976 and January 1977 as a part of the celebration of the fiftieth anniversary of the Pahlavi dynasty. In March 1978 the shah indicated that continuing clemencies had reduced the number of political prisoners (that is, those tried in military courts on security-related charges) to 2,000. Opposition groups, however, maintained that the true figure was significantly higher.

The military penal code, in general, provides for stiffer penalties than the penal code used in ordinary proceedings. Executions are not uncommon and are highly publicized in the official Iranian press. On July 14, 1974, the government announced that 239 drug smugglers and peddlers had been executed in the preceding two and one-half years. A conservative estimate would put official executions ordered by military courts for all kinds of crimes at over 100 a year. Most executions involve those who were armed at the time of their arrest. A 1975 reform of the military code also provided for life imprisonment for a wide range of security-related crimes and stipulated five years as the minimum sentence for crimes involving state security. It also stated that a person would be exempted from prosecution and punishment if he gave information to authorities before the matter was discovered. In addition offering information that facilitated the investigation of a matter after it was discovered by authorities reduced the penalty considerably.

In December 1977 several amendments were made to the law governing criminal procedure in military courts, which promised a liberalization in the conduct of trials of civilians. In camera trials were forbidden except "in exceptional cases where a public session may be deemed to be against the public order, national interest or against accepted moral standards." In addition the accused was allowed, for the first time, to choose counsel of his choice, and defense counsel was given additional time to study the case before trial. The February 1978 annual human rights report conducted by the Department of State expressed guarded optimism concerning the reform: "Although procedures in this [military] court have not adequately protected due process, some potentially significant improvements in this system were instituted during the past year."

Prison System

The prison system is officially under the jurisdiction of the Ministry of Justice, but the Ministry of Interior and the armed forces also play a considerable role in its operation and management. There are three classifications of prisons in Iran: police jails, under gendarmerie supervision in rural areas and under the supervision of SAVAK and the National Police in urban areas, used for preventive detention and short-term prisoners; court prisons, under the criminal courts, used primarily for sentences of intermediate duration; and penitentiaries, under direct military supervision, for long-term sentences. Every city and town has a prison. Tehran has two large prisons, including Qsar, the largest in the country, which had approximately 6,000 inmates in 1970.

In the past Iranian prisons were reportedly poorly administered and were criticized as lacking facilities for the provision of basic amenities. Since the 1960s, however, there has been a fairly successful effort to upgrade prison conditions. The emphasis of this reform effort has been on providing jobs to inmates. In the mid-1970s thousands of prisoners were working within prisons in the manufacture of such items as rugs, appliances, and shoes. Others worked plots of land both inside and outside prison walls. Prisoners are paid for their work, although emphasis is on the vocational rehabilitation aspects of the work rather than on its monetary remuneration. Prison reform also emphasized literacy training, from which thousands are reported to have benefited.

The prison reform has also produced a large number of so-called open prisons, where prisoners are allowed to work outside the prison without being subject to systematic supervision, although they remain under lock and key most of the time. The work involved is usually road work, construction, or forestry and agricultural work, which may be for the benefit of the state or on contract with private enterprises.

In 1969 the Qezelhesar Detention Center, a prison with some 1,200 inmates southwest of Tehran, became a model prison for the reform program. In addition to the above amenities, inmates are provided with sports facilities and small huts available for conjugal visits.

Despite continuing efforts to expand reforms, such as those at Qezelhesar Detention Center, allegations of poor prison conditions continued to be voiced in the 1970s. Conditions apparently

varied considerably from one institution to another and depended
heavily on who the inmate was. According to William J. Butler of
the International Commission of Jurists, "If the arrestee is an
elite, or an author, or a writer, he goes to the best jails. . . . Some
jails are like country clubs. One of the jails in Tehran is very
famous because it has gardens and all kinds of things."

In contrast Amnesty International says the following about
prison conditions facing the less fortunate inmate: "Food is usually
inadequate and of poor quality and this often leads to mal-
nutrition, food poisoning or chronic illness. Medical treatment is
practically non-existent and prisoners are hardly ever seen by a
doctor, sent to hospital or allowed to receive medicines. Discipline is severe and in cases of indiscipline prisoners may be put
into solitary confinement for anything up to three or four months."

Iranian officials denied that poor treatment of prisoners continued to exist in 1978. In that year the Department of State noted
that foreign journalists and the International Committee of the
Red Cross were allowed to visit Iranian prisons in 1977 and concluded that "We believe the Iranian Government is committed to
prison reform and that prison conditions have indeed improved."

Conditional liberty may be granted a prisoner who has served
half his sentence in the case of a misdemeanor or two-thirds in the
case of a felony, or after twelve years' imprisonment if the sentence is life imprisonment. Conditional liberty is not available to
recidivists. Specific conditions for conditional liberty are fixed by
the court that grants it. The prisoner is set free, but his actions are
watched carefully by prison officials with the help of the National
Police and gendarmerie. Prisoners convicted by military tribunals
are said to suffer the loss of all civil rights for a period of ten years,
regardless of the length of their sentence.

* * *

The subjects of this chapter are discussed in a multitude of
works of widely differing value and points of view. A good introduction to human rights questions and the legal system in Iran,
presenting a variety of points of view, is the report on the hearings
before the Subcommittee on International Organizations of the
House Committee on International Relations entitled *Human
Rights in Iran*. The most articulate and outspoken criticism of the
system of internal security is found in the writings of Reza
Baraheni. The official views on the subject are best represented in
Kayhan International, an English-language daily from Tehran.
Probably the most complete and balanced discussion of Iran's legal
system and security apparatus is *Human Rights and the Legal
System in Iran*, written by William Butler and Georges Levasseur
under the auspices of the International Commission of Jurists.
Gordon B. Baldwin's "The Legal System of Iran" is another valu-
able discussion. For a discussion of problems in law enforcement,
Gerald T. McLaughlin's study of Iranian drug policies is an excellent and in-depth study. Those interested in present-day

problems of internal security (as of February 1977) will find little published that presents the situation accurately. One accurate, though brief, discussion of terrorists is found in the chapter devoted to Iran in *A Compendium of European Theater Terrorist Groups* by Raymond W. Goodman, Jr., et al. (For further information see Bibliography.)

Chapter 13. Armed Forces

DURING THE 1970s the Imperial Iranian Armed Forces were rapidly becoming one of the outstanding military forces of the developing world. Because of burgeoning oil revenues, Iran did not have to make the choice between guns and butter, being able to pay cash for the most sophisticated weapons available while also supporting an ambitious development program. Well aware of Iran's history of foreign military occupation and perceiving potential military threats from every border, Mohammad Reza Pahlavi, the Shahanshah of Iran, argued that Iran's growing military strength was necessary to protect its growing economic strength. Already clearly the strongest military power in the Persian Gulf region in 1977, the shah sought a place for Iran among the world's strongest powers by the end of the century. Iran was a signatory of the nuclear nonproliferation treaty. However, John C. Campbell, Director of Studies and Senior Research Fellow at the Council on Foreign Relations, questioned the long-run effectiveness of this commitment: "The Shah disclaimed any ambition to make Iran a nuclear power; but he left little doubt that if other middle powers took that path, Iran would also."

After the 1971 withdrawal of British troops from the Persian Gulf region, Iran assumed the vital mission of defending the gulf and the Strait of Hormuz, the sea-lane through which passed some 60 percent of the world's oil. Nevertheless many outside observers argued that Iran's arms build up exceeded anything necessary for its defense needs. Its growing arsenal did serve, to some extent, as a deterrent to political instability in the Persian Gulf region and also carried considerable prestige value for the nation in world affairs and for senior military officers within Iranian social and political life. The armed forces were clearly subordinate to their commander in chief, the shah, and they constituted a strong and vital political power base for the monarch.

The United States, under the so-called Nixon doctrine whereby aiding local armed forces is a preferred policy to direct United States military presence or intervention, has played an essential role in upgrading the Iranian armed forces. By 1976 more United States security advisers were in Iran than anywhere in the world. More important the United States was Iran's major arms supplier; after a 1972 agreement between President Richard M. Nixon and the shah, the United States sold the armed forces some of the most sophisticated of its nonnuclear technology. Aircraft dominated American military sales to Iran, though a wide variety of other equipment—including tanks, artillery and missiles, destroyers and submarines, and radar and intelligence gathering systems—was involved as well. The absorption of these vast quantities of technologically advanced matériel would present the Iranian armed forces with its major challenge of the late 1970s and early 1980s.

Historical Background

The importance attributed to the armed forces in Iran is difficult to understand without a knowledge of the nation's 2,500-year-old military tradition. The proudest moments of Iran's history stem from the military conquests of the Achaemenid rulers of the seventh and sixth centuries B.C. (see Ancient Iran, ch. 2). The Persian troops that carved an empire in western Asia and launched expeditions into Europe and Africa were said to number up to 360,000 and comprised a highly efficient fighting machine. To this day, the "10,000 Immortals," which were the Achaemenid kings' own troops, remain symbols of military prowess and valor.

The conquests by such great Achaemenid leaders as Cyrus the Great and Darius I mark the zenith of Iranian military history. In more modern times only the army of Nadir Shah, which defeated the Mughals of India in 1739, experienced a degree of military success and its accompanying prestige. Since then nearly all efforts to expand or defend existing territory have failed. During much of the nineteenth and early twentieth centuries, Iran found itself subject to occupation by military forces from Russia and Great Britain; in 1907 it was divided into spheres of influence under an Anglo-Russian convention. During World War I, Iran's weak Qajar Dynasty was powerless to prevent the dramatic increase of British and Russian intervention that came about despite Iran's declaration of neutrality (see Rise of the Qajar Dynasty, Ch. 2).

At the conclusion of World War I, the armed forces consisted of four separate military units as well as several provincial and tribal forces that the government could call on in times of emergency; but more often than not the provincial and tribal forces fought government troops enforcing centralization. By far the most effective government unit was the 8,000-man Persian Cossacks, a brigade created in 1879 and commanded by Russian officers until the 1917 revolution when its command passed into Iranian hands. The gendarmerie was a force of some 8,400 commanded by Swedish officers. Organized in 1911, its primary mission was to safeguard internal security. The 6,000-man South Persia Rifles, financed by Great Britain and commanded by British officers, was organized in 1916 to combat tribal forces stirred up by German agents during the war. The Nizam, or palace guards, once the core of the Qajar forces, had deteriorated to an ineffective unit of some 2,000 men.

Reza Khan (later Reza Shah, founder of the Pahlavi dynasty) assumed leadership of the Persian Cossacks after the expulsion of its Russian commanders. In 1921 he led several thousand troops who joined with civilian conspirators to overthrow the Qajar regime; he subsequently became minister of war in the new government (see Reza Shah and the Establishment of the Pahlavi Dynasty, ch. 2). Reza Khan recognized the importance of a unified army to the modern nation and immediately dissolved all independent military units and created a single national army—the first in Iranian history.

Reza Khan was determined to minimize the use of foreign officers in the new army. Only a few Swedish officers were allowed to remain; the majority of officers were Iranians drawn from the Persian Cossacks. Understanding the need for Western military know-how, Reza Khan continued to send officers to European military academies, particularly to St. Cyr Academy in France.

As the army grew in strength (40,000 in 1925), Reza Khan gradually assumed control of the central government under the provisions of martial law. In 1925 he persuaded the Majlis (the lower house of Parliament) to pass universal military conscription into law. Soon afterward Reza Khan assumed the throne.

If the strength of the newly unified army elevated Reza Khan to the throne, it was also his primary source of power during his reign as Reza Shah Pahlavi. The army was used to put down tribal rebellions, break strikes, and uphold the authority of the central government under the shah. Although the mission of the army was officially presented as defense against external aggression, it in fact acted to defend the shah's regime against any and all opposition.

The army always received an extraordinarily large portion—between 30 and 50 percent—of total yearly government expenditures. Modern armaments were purchased, and in 1924 and 1927, respectively, an air force and navy were created, though they remained as branches of the army until 1955. Two military schools were established during the 1930s, but the majority of officers continued to be trained in Europe. Officers assumed key government posts and became a privileged sector of society, being well paid and receiving considerable amenities, including large tracts of land, for their loyalty. Disloyalty, which surfaced in a series of attempted military coups, was dealt with harshly.

By 1941 the shah's army of some 125,000 troops appeared to be a remarkable advancement from the motley units of twenty years earlier. Nevertheless an invasion in August 1941 by British and Soviet Union forces proved the ineffectiveness of the Iranian military in full-scale modern warfare. Although Iran was again officially neutral at the outset of World War II, the shah's sympathies lay with Germany, and the Allied troops invaded Iran after the shah refused to eject Iran's considerable German population and to allow shipments of war supplies to transit Iran en route to the Soviet Union. Within three days the Iranian army was decimated: virtually the entire air force and navy were destroyed, and conscripts deserted by the thousands. Having lost his power base, Reza Shah abdicated in favor of his son.

The young shah immediately faced the enormous task of rebuilding an army that was not only defeated and demoralized, but was also feared by the vast majority of Iranians for its brutal role in upholding the regime of his father. In 1942 a United States military mission was invited to advise in the reorganization effort, and considerable progress was made by emphasizing strength through quality rather than large numbers of troops. In 1946 the newly reorganized army participated successfully in putting down a separatist rebellion in the province of Azarbaijan. The Majlis nevertheless remained suspicious that a strong military might again become a political instrument of the shah and used its power over the military budget to limit the army's growth.

The Majlis gradually gained more control over the management of the armed forces, and in 1952 Prime Minister Mohammad Mossadeq demanded and received the portfolio of minister of war. During the year in which he held the position, Mossadeq made changes in the high command, dismissed many officers loyal to the shah, and introduced other measures designed to make the armed forces loyal to him rather than to the commander in chief, the shah. Officers who were dismissed by Mossadeq played a key role in the coup d'etat of August 1953 that removed the prime minister and returned the shah to power (see Mohammad Mossadeq and Oil Nationalization, ch. 2).

After the overthrow of Mossadeq, several hundred officers and noncommissioned officers who belonged to military cells of the communist-leaning Tudeh (Masses) Party were arrested and about twenty-four executed. By 1955 the shah had consolidated his command over the armed forces, and he began a program of upgrading the military by creating separate air force and navy branches. The upgrading and modernization proceeded at an accelerating rate into the late 1970s.

Place in National Life

From the mid-1950s through 1977 the Imperial Iranian Armed Forces assumed an ever-expanding role in society. During this period the shah made a conscious effort to create a good public image of the country's military establishment. While they were available as a means to combat internal opposition to the shah, the armed forces in the 1970s were rarely visible as a source of repression. In fact the armed forces were engaged in numerous nationbuilding activities (especially in the area of education) that directly benefited the civilian population. Although occasional evidence suggested that some civilians resented the privileged place of the armed forces in Iranian society, the unreserved hostility expressed after the fall of Reza Shah was gone and much of the population, particularly the nation's elite, was proud of the armed forces as a source of prestige and a symbol of Iran's new and expanding power.

Budget

The budget of the armed forces is prepared by the Ministry of War in consultation with the shah and his closest military advisers and is presented by the prime minister to the Majlis for approval. The military budget consistently takes the highest priority in the allocation of government expenditures; from 1946 to 1976 the

Imperial Iranian paratroopers on parade
Courtesy Embassy of Iran

budget for defense rose continually, both in absolute terms and as a percent of the nation's gross domestic product (GDP).

Precise levels of military expenditures are difficult to determine. For example, various important defense-related activities, such as the Military Industries Organization and all facility construction, are not budgeted to the Ministry of War. Furthermore amounts spent often differ significantly from those budgeted, as revenues—larger or smaller than those anticipated—become available during the fiscal year. The Stockholm International Peace Research Institute indicated a nearly eightfold increase, in terms of constant 1973 dollars, in defense expenditures in the 1967–76 decade—from the equivalent of US$752 million to US$5.7 billion. Using current price figures, the International Institute for Strategic Studies indicated a nearly twenty-five-fold increase during that decade—from US$389 million to US$9.5 billion. Although actual defense expenditures probably differed slightly from these figures, they do clearly indicate a process of rapid growth. The most spectacular increases came during the period of rising oil prices: from 1972 to 1975 Iranian defense expenditures increased almost tenfold in money terms. By 1976 defense expenditures were estimated at the equivalent of nearly US$300 per capita, some 17.4 percent of GDP, and approximately 30 percent of all government expenditures.

The leveling off of budgeted defense expenditures for fiscal year (FY—see Glossary) 1977–78 reflected the shortfall in oil revenues during the previous year. Plans for the continued rapid growth of defense spending were scaled down; and ambitious projects, such as the naval facility at Chah Bahar and the Military Industrial Complex at Isfahan, were postponed. In observing Iran's 1976 revenue problems, United States Senate staff personnel concluded that "the defense budget [was] unlikely to increase significantly in future years and may have peaked in 1976–77." Oil revenues, which permitted the rapid increase of defense expenditures during the early 1970s, will continue to be the key variable in determining defense spending in the immediate future (see ch. 9).

Iranian defense planners were attempting to cope with the problem of oil revenue shortfall by making barter arrangements—exchanging oil for arms—with foreign suppliers. Major barter agreements were made with British and French firms, and discussions were under way in late 1977 for similar agreements with American firms.

The importance given to modernizing the military arsenal was apparent in the defense budget. During the mid-1970s some 60 percent of the budget was consistently used for the purchase, production, and renovation of armaments, while expenses for personnel consumed between 20 and 25 percent. The remaining 15 to 20 percent was allocated to maintenance and operations.

Noncombat Functions

Since the 1963 inauguration of the White Revolution (see Glossary) the armed forces have participated in a variety of civil action programs designed to benefit the civilian population and improve the public image of the armed forces. Through these programs, the armed forces have engaged in the construction of roads, housing, schools, and public baths, and have provided pivotal aid during epidemics and frequent earthquake disasters.

The White Revolution also spawned three noncombat military corps—the Literacy Corps, Health Corps, and Development and Agricultural Extension Corps—that have had favorable effects on civil-military relations. The army conscripts men above its military requirement to staff the corps, which are funded by civilian ministries. Corpsmen consist of high school and university graduates who receive basic military training and training relevant to their future assignments for about six months and spend the remainder of their two-year·conscription period in the field.

Between 1963 and 1977 some 150,000 conscripts served in the Literacy Corps, which was by far the most successful ongoing civic action project. Although its primary function was to provide the equivalent of a fourth grade education in rural areas where illiteracy is extremely high, the corps has also promoted national unification through teaching Farsi (or Persian as it is commonly known outside Iran) to thousands of hitherto non-Farsi speakers in addition to raising the esteem of the armed forces among both the educated corpsmen and the rural population they served. Some corpsmen reportedly remain in their assigned villages after being discharged as civilian teachers.

The Health Corps consisted of graduates of medical, dental, pharmacy, and nursing schools and high school graduates trained as paramedics fulfilling their conscription obligation. Several members formed a team that operated from a central clinic and traveled extensively to serve a widely scattered rural population. From its beginning in 1964 until 1977, a total of some 14,000 conscripts served in the Health Corps.

The Development and Agricultural Extension Corps was assigned a wide variety of duties in rural development, including introducing modern agricultural methods, setting up model farms, administering inoculations, combating pests, and constructing farm buildings and feeder roads to aid in marketing. Between 1965 and 1977 over 32,000 conscripts served in the corps.

The increasing involvement of the armed forces in such traditionally civilian occupations has contributed to the growing efficiency of the military bureaucracy relative to the civil service. Skilled armed forces personnel were often called on when civilians failed, i.e., in June 1977 when the air force was put in charge of construction of Tehran's new international airport after the project's civilian director was found guilty of embezzlement.

In addition to civic action programs, the armed forces were increasingly involved in the administration of justice. Traditionally the military courts have been used to try civilians in cases involving treason or breach of internal security. During the 1970s the definition of these offenses was considerably expanded, and military courts additionally were given jurisdiction over counterfeiting, narcotics violations, armed robbery, and hoarding or profiteering by merchants. The armed forces worked closely with the National Intelligence and Security Organization (Sazeman Ettelaat va Amniyat Kashvar--SAVAK) in cases involving civilians, and the penalties were likely to be more severe than those emerging from the regular courts (see ch. 12).

Political Role

Although the character of the political role of the armed forces had changed dramatically since the regime of Reza Shah, in the 1970s the military continued to play an essential though more subtle political role. Official pronouncements denied such a role, citing prohibitions against voting or political party affiliation by active military personnel; but few analysts would deny that the armed forces play an essential role in upholding the political authority of the shah (see ch. 7).

During the reign of Reza Shah, military personnel dominated ministerial posts and a wide variety of other sensitive political positions. Under his son this practice gradually declined, and by 1977 General Reza Azimi, the minister of war, was the only uniformed cabinet member. Military officers continued, nevertheless, to assume a variety of less visible positions within ministries and other government institutions. Important positions in the internal security apparatus, including the director of SAVAK and key posts within the National Police, were held by military officers. However, this practice declined as these agencies became able to provide their own leaders.

Another way in which the armed forces were visibly active under Reza Shah was their pervasive use as a source of political repression. Since the end of his reign, however, the internal security role under the shah has continually diminished as Iran's police agencies have gained increasing proficiency. Some army units remained trained for such functions, nevertheless, and aided the gendarmerie and National Police during large-scale disturbances in 1953, 1963, 1970, and 1975 (see ch. 12).

The riots that followed the overthrow of Prime Minister Mossadeq in 1953 taught the shah the importance of retaining the loyalty of the armed forces. On the one hand, the shah closely scrutinized officer personnel, reviewing personally all promotions above the rank of major and watching the public and private activities of individual officers using military intelligence and SAVAK agents. The efforts to ensure loyalty also extended to the troops, whose first order of duty each morning is to pray for, among other things, the welfare and longevity of the shah. On the other hand, senior officers continued to be well rewarded for their loyalty by receiving salaries and amenities that clearly placed them among the nation's elite.

Foreign observers have asserted that one motivation for Iran's massive arms purchases has been to build loyalty within the military. There is little doubt that the new arms are a source of prestige to the officer corps and gives them a considerable stake in the present political system. In addition the task of assimilating new weapons has left senior officers little time for political activity.

Thus there seemed little prospect in 1977 that the armed forces would pursue any political activity independent of the shah or contrary to his expressed goals and wishes. Indeed, their favored position within the government budget, their increasing bureaucratic efficiency, and the elite status of senior officers within society gave the members of the officer corps a tremendous stake in preserving the status quo; hence, they provided a key base to the political power of the shah.

Although all major defense related decisions are made by the shah, a few senior officers play an important advisory role, using their influence to ensure the continued privileged position in society and in the government's budget. For example, Air Force General Hassan Toufanian, the vice minister of war in charge of weapons procurement, was a proponent of higher oil prices so that the armed forces could continue their high level of arms acquisition.

Defense Missions and Operations

Missions

Since the founding of the Pahlavi dynasty and the subsequent creation of the unified Imperial Iranian Armed Forces, their officially stated mission has been the defense of the nation against foreign aggression. The domestic mission of subduing opposition to the regime was, in fact, the primary function of the armed forces well into the 1960s. Although this mission was retained in the 1970s, its importance receded as law enforcement agencies assumed an increasing burden of the internal security mission and as Iran's expanding role in regional and world affairs necessitated renewed emphasis on defense functions.

Iran's defense mission has traditionally been oriented toward the protection of its 1,250-mile border with the Soviet Union. Fears that the Soviets would try to gain access to warm water port facilities through Iran were reinforced by the Soviet occupation of parts of northern Iran after World War II. Until the mid-1960s the majority of Iranian troops were stationed in the north, reflecting the primacy of this mission. As relations with the Soviet Union improved—and as perceived threats shifted to the Persian Gulf and the border with Iraq—the protection of the northern border has become a secondary but by no means insignificant mission (see ch. 8). Realizing the impossibility of surviving a Soviet invasion, the armed forces strive to be capable of delaying a Soviet advance long enough to allow the intervention of Iran's Western allies.

In the 1970s the principal mission of the armed forces was to protect Iran's oil-based economy from a variety of perceived threats. The scope of this mission expanded during the decade from the defense of Iran's oil fields, refineries, and the sea-lane out of the Persian Gulf through the Strait of Hormuz, to the maintenance of stability within the potentially volatile Persian Gulf region. In the late 1970s plans were under way to include the defense of the sea-lanes of the Indian Ocean.

Until the Algiers Agreement with Iraq in March 1975, Iran perceived an imminent military threat to its oil installations located near the Iraqi border. A 1972 Soviet-Iraq treaty increased the flow of sophisticated Soviet military weapons to Iraq. Iran's continued support of the Kurdish rebellion in northern Iraq increased tensions between the neighbors, who had long disputed the Shatt al Arab demarcating borders near the Persian Gulf (see fig. 1). Under the terms of the Algiers Agreement, Iran terminated its aid to the Kurdish rebels in Iraq, and Iraq accepted Iran's claim to a thalweg (the middle of the main navigable channel of a waterway that forms a boundary between states) division of the Shatt al Arab and to other boundary adjustments (see ch. 8). Relations improved considerably. Nevertheless in 1977 the protection of the oil fields and facilities against any future threat remained a vital mission of the armed forces.

Iran's assumption of a major role in the defense of the Persian Gulf was conceived in the early 1960s, but it was not until the 1968 British announcement of the withdrawal of its troops from the region that this mission was implemented. Attempts to form a multilateral gulf security pact failed, and since 1971, when the last British forces withdrew from the Arab shaykhdoms, Iran has been, in effect, the self-proclaimed sole defender of this vital area.

The twenty-six-mile-wide Strait of Hormuz is a particularly vulnerable point in Iran's oil-lanes. The impressive upgrading of the navy and the shifting of its major facilities from Khorramshahr on the Iraqi border to Bandar Abbas on the strait reflected the importance of protecting this choke point, which the shah has often referred to as Iran's "jugular vein."

As Iran's military capabilities increased, its mission to protect the oil-lanes of the Persian Gulf expanded to include the maintenance of the generally pro-Western status quo in the region surrounding the gulf. The shah has stated that the success of an Arab socialist movement in any of the oil-producing states of the Arabian Peninsula would pose a threat not only to the West's major source of imported oil but also to Iran. In addition Iran has pledged to uphold the integrity of Pakistan in the face of its separatist movements.

Military planning in the late 1970s was geared toward building the capability of defending sea-lanes outside the Persian Gulf. Commonly referred to as Iran's "eastward-looking defense policy," this projected mission would expand Iran's defense of its commercial shipping interests into the Indian Ocean. Major steps toward making this mission operable had been undertaken by 1977, including obtaining naval port facilities on the island of Mauritius, beginning construction of a massive triservice base at Chah Bahar on the Gulf of Oman near the Pakistani border, and acquiring long-range weapons. Because of the immense investments still to be made, however, outside observers believed it would be well into the future before Iran would have the operational capacity to police this vast area.

Foreign critics of Iranian military policy in the mid-1970s argued that Iran's ever-growing military arsenal was already larger than necessary to fulfill its legitimate defense missions. The shah scoffed at suggestions that the armed forces may be used for purposes of territorial aggrandizement, responding in 1974 "What do I need more territory for? All I am concerned about is the security of my country, and Iran's security is intimately related to security and stability of the Persian Gulf region." Iran's growing military arsenal, it was argued, is necessary as a deterrent to possible forces of destabilization within the region of its economic interests.

Operations

For two decades after their defeat during World War II, the Iranian armed forces did not engage in regular combat. On several occasions between 1971 and 1977, however, Iran's military forces fought in small-scale operations. Limited as they were, these engagements enabled the largely untested forces to gain important combat experience.

In the early 1970s border skirmishes between Iranian and Iraqi ground forces occurred regularly. The most intense period of fighting was between October 1972 and May 1974, when there were at least ten major exchanges of fire, several of which cost the lives of fifty to 100 soldiers. Though hostilities ceased after the 1975 Algiers Agreement, the majority of Iran's ground forces continued to be deployed near the Iraqi border.

On November 30, 1971, one day before the expiration of the treaties that made Great Britain responsible for the protection of the tiny Persian Gulf shaykhdoms, Iranian military forces occupied three islands near the Strait of Hormuz—Abu Musa and the two Tunbs islands, belonging to Sharjah and Ras al Khaymah respectively. There was no resistance to this swift operation, which used the navy's hovercraft to transport the occupying troops. Iran had long laid claim to these islands, but the immediate justification for the occupations was the islands' strategic importance to the defense of the Strait of Hormuz and the "power vacuum" created by the British withdrawal. Some Iranian military facilities were subsequently installed on two of the islands.

Twice during the mid-1970s Iran has provided military assistance to neighboring governments enabling them to overcome internal rebellions. In 1976 a variety of informed sources reported that a small number of Iranian counterinsurgency forces, along with helicopter support, were deployed in Baluchistan Province (in Pakistan) to combat the separatist rebellion there. This covert support, even though on a very small scale, reflected fears that the rebellion might cross into Iran, which also contains a considerable Baluchi tribal population.

A more significant combat operation involved Iranian (along with British and Jordanian) support for Sultan Qaboos of Oman against insurgents of the Popular Front for the Liberation of Oman in the western province of Dhofar. From late 1972, when Qaboos requested Iranian military aid, to January 1977, when the shah began withdrawing troops after the revolt had been crushed, the Iranian military presence grew from some 300 to about 3,000. The bulk of these troops consisted of ground forces with limited training in counterinsurgency, but logistics support and reconnaissance were provided by air force and navy personnel.

Accounts of the performance of Iranian troops in Oman were mixed; the most favorable reports were with respect to aircraft and helicopter operations. Casualties were significant (210 Iranian soldiers were reported killed in 1976 alone), a fact attributed to the lack of combat experience. The rapid rotation of troops enabled some 10,000 to 15,000 soldiers to gain some combat experience during the four years but undoubtedly contributed to Iranian casualties. One Iranian reconnaissance plane was shot down when it strayed into the air space of the People's Democratic Republic of Yemen [Yemen (Aden)].

After the 1977 withdrawal, Iranian aircraft continued to patrol Omani air space. Iran was proud of the results of its operation in Oman: the rebellion had been crushed, Iranian troops had gained combat experience, and notice had been served that Iran would back up its military mission to preserve the status quo in the Persian Gulf region. The shah stated that he would continue to fulfill his mission in the future, whether or not his troops were invited to intervene.

Iran also participates in regularly scheduled war games conducted under the auspices of the Central Treaty Organization (CENTO). CENTO, whose members include Turkey, Pakistan, Iran, and Great Britain (the United States participates as an observer), was founded as the Baghdad Pact in 1955 during the height of the cold war. As political and military conditions have changed over the years, CENTO has declined in significance, but its joint maneuvers remained important training exercises for the Iranian armed forces. The most significant—the yearly maritime maneuvers known as Midlink—have usually been staged from Iranian waters. These mock combat operations have been important testing grounds for the rapidly expanding air and naval military forces.

Finally Iran participates in United Nations peace-keeping missions. In 1977 nearly 400 Iranian soldiers were deployed in the

United Nations buffer zone in the Golan Heights as part of the United Nations Disengagement Observer Force (UNDOF).

Organization, Size, and Equipment

The shah is constitutionally designated supreme commander of the armed forces, and important decisions regarding Iran's defense needs are made by him. He exercises operational control through the supreme commander's staff, a joint organization that loosely coordinates the activities of the three services. The chief of the supreme commander's staff—in 1977 General Gholam Reza Ashari—was second in command; the staff included a vice chief of staff and directors of personnel, intelligence, operations, logistics, plans, communications, and fiscal matters. Though within the chain of command, the supreme commander's staff served more as a coordinating than a command body, and the three service chiefs were encouraged to consult directly with the shah.

The minister of war—in 1977 General Reza Azimi—was not, as a cabinet minister, in the military chain of command. His primary concerns were legislative and budgetary matters. The vice minister of war, General Toufanian, was in charge of implementing the shah's decisions regarding arms procurement and thus was a highly visible and important figure during the 1970s.

Army

During the late 1970s the army, formally known as the Imperial Iranian Ground Forces, was undergoing a rapid increase in strength; that year it was a largely mechanized and armored force of about 220,000. In late 1977 its former organization into three army corps, with headquarters in Kermanshah, Tehran, and Shiraz, was dropped; divisional commanders subsequently reported directly to the army commander. The army contained three armored divisions, each with six tank battalions and five mechanized infantry battalions; four infantry divisions; four independent brigades (two infantry, one airborne, and one special force); and the Army Aviation Command (one infantry division and one independent infantry brigade formed the Imperial Guard). These combat units, backed up by the usual complement of support units, were said to be 85 percent operational, though some outside observers doubted this claim.

During the mid-1970s, fully 80 percent of Iran's ground forces were deployed along the Iraqi border, though official sources maintained that a large portion of these could be sent anywhere in the country within twenty-four hours by means of air force transports (see fig. 13). Troop deployment was expected to shift south during the late 1970s with the opening of the Chah Bahar facility.

Army equipment has been purchased from many countries, including the United States, Great Britain, France, the Federal Republic of Germany (West Germany), Italy, and the Soviet Union. This mix of weapons greatly complicated maintenance and supply procedures, and during the 1970s considerable effort was put into standardization by developing local production of basic

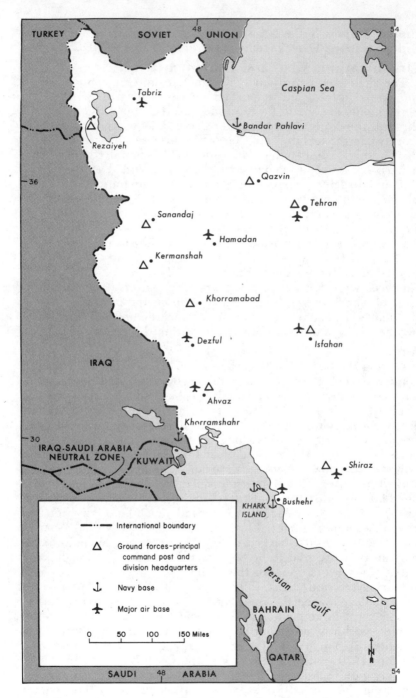

Figure 13. Disposition of Major Units of the Armed Forces, 1977

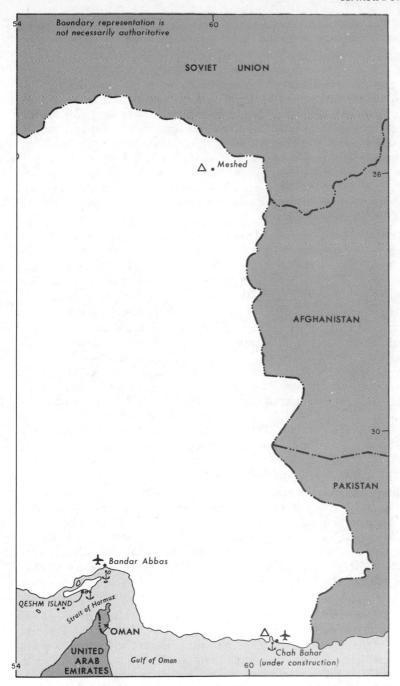

Source: Based on information from U. S. Congress, 94th, 2nd Session, Committee on Foreign Relations, Subcommittee on Foreign Assistance, *U.S. Military Sales to Iran,* Washington, 1976; Karl L. Santone, "Iran: Power in the Persian Gulf?", Maxwell Air Force Base, 1974; and *Defense and Foreign Affairs Handbook 1976–77,* Washington, 1976.

infantry weapons and local maintenance facilities for equipment of foreign manufacture.

In 1977 basic infantry rifles, machine guns, selected calibre mortars, and small-arms ammunition were produced locally, but virtually all heavier equipment was of foreign origin. Armored personnel carriers were from the United States and the Soviet Union and antitank missiles from the United States and France. Armored units were supplied with medium and light tanks of American and British origin, and about 1,200 British-made Chieftain tanks were being delivered to augment the 760 in the inventory. They were equipped primarily with Soviet antiaircraft guns and American surface-to-surface gun systems (see table 19, Appendix A).

The rapidly growing Army Aviation Command, whose main operational facilities were located at Isfahan, was largely equipped with American aircraft, although some helicopters were of Italian manufacture. In 1977 army aviation operated some sixty light fixed-wing aircraft, but its strength lay in its fleet of some 700 combat helicopters.

The Royal Armaments Factories in Tehran were the major local source of ordnance, producing small arms, a wide variety of ammunition, and such explosives as mines and grenades. Other local small-arms production took place in French-, Swedish-, and German-licensed factories. A planned major increase in Iran's armaments maintenance and production capacity was centered on a huge military industrial complex located near Isfahan, scheduled to be completed by 1980. Initially this facility will maintain and produce spare parts for Chieftain tanks and eventually will service all the army's armored vehicles as well as contribute to the manufacture of ordnance material. In addition a military electronic complex was being developed in Shiraz.

Negotiations took place with several foreign companies during the mid-1970s to manufacture major weapons in Iran. As of early 1978 one such contract had been signed with Bell Helicopter for coproduction of a utility helicopter. It was clear, nevertheless, that the Iranian army would continue to improve its local arms industry in order to relieve its long-standing dependence on foreign manufacturers.

Navy

The Imperial Iranian Navy was by far the smallest of the three services, with about 30,000 personnel in 1977. Long neglected in favor of the army and air force, the navy was in the midst of a rapid increase in personnel to some 40,000 by the late 1970s in order to expand its ability to defend the region's sea-lanes. These ambitious plans received several setbacks in the mid-1970s, including a major scandal in which the commander of the navy, Admiral Ramzi Attai, was relieved of duty after his conviction of corruption. In addition government revenue shortfalls forced major construction projects and equipment purchases to be postponed. Nevertheless considerable advances in organization and equipment were evident by 1977 under the command of Vice Admiral Kamal Habibollabi.

After many years of being based at Khorramshahr, by 1977 the bulk of the navy's fleet had been shifted south to the newly completed base at Bandar Abbas. The navy's third major base was at Bushehr, and smaller bases were on Khark Island, Hengam Island, and at Bandar Pahlavi. Bandar Pahlavi was the major training facility and home of the small Caspian Sea fleet, which consisted of a few small patrol boats and a minesweeper. The projected naval base at Chah Bahar is not likely to be completed until well into the 1980s.

The navy contained an air element, composed of an anti-submarine and minesweeping helicopter squadron, and a sizable transport battalion. In 1977 the navy also supported two marine battalions and planned to increase its marine strength considerably.

The navy's fleet was entirely of foreign origin. Great Britain had traditionally been their main supplier, but during the 1970s American vessels became more evident. In 1977 the Iranian fleet included one British-made and two American-made destroyers, four British-made frigates, and some sixty smaller vessels, including fourteen British-made hovercraft (see table 20, Appendix A). Iran's hovercraft, which function primarily for amphibious assault and logistics support, represent the largest fleet of such vessels in the world. They give the navy unique maneuverability around the shallow shores of the Persian Gulf and were used successfully in the 1971 occupation of Abu Musa and the Tunbs islands.

Major purchases from the United States were due to arrive during the late 1970s and early 1980s. These included four Spruance-class destroyers equipped for antiaircraft operations, among the most sophisticated destroyers in the world, and three diesel powered Tang-class submarines. There were also reports in 1977 of negotiations with Great Britain for the purchase of four cruisers capable of launching aircraft. These new vessels, to be based at the Chah Bahar facility, would give Iran escort and patrol capabilities in the Indian Ocean.

Before the mid-1970s, all Iranian ships had to go to foreign ports for major repairs. Since that time, Iranian shipyards have begun to assume much of the responsibility for maintenance. The most important such facility was the newly completed Fleet Maintenance Unit at Bandar Abbas.

Air Force

The Imperial Iranian Air Force has spearheaded the modernization of the armed forces. In 1977 it was by far the most advanced of the three services and among the most impressive air forces in the developing world. It was said to be the pride and joy of the shah, who is a qualified pilot and extremely well informed on modern air weapons systems. Numbering some 40,000 officers and men in 1973, the air force had grown to 100,000 in 1977 and was expected to grow further by 1980. In 1975 General Mohammad Khatami, the long-time air force commander, was killed in an accident; in late 1977 the command of the air force was in the hands of Lieutenant General Amir Hossein Rabii.

Air force headquarters are located at Doshan-Tappeh, near Tehran, and major bases are spread throughout the western half of the country. The principal base, Mehrabad, just outside Tehran, is the largest air base in the Middle East as well as Iran's major civil airport. Other major operational bases in the mid-1970s were at Tabriz, Bandar Abbas, Hamadan (Shahroki Air Base), Dezful (Vahdati Air Base), Shiraz, and Bushehr. Three new operational bases were under construction near Ahwaz, and at Isfahan (Khatami Air Base) and Chah Bahar, the latter two being near completion in 1977.

In 1977 the combat portion of the air force was organized into fifteen squadrons with fighter and fighter-bomber capabilities and one reconnaissance squadron. Support was provided by one tanker squadron, four medium and one light transport squadron, some sixty helicopters, and three SAM battalions. Aircraft on order, though not received as of late 1977, will double the number of fighter squadrons. The total of more than 400 combat aircraft in 1977 will, based on confirmed orders as of late 1977, increase to over 650 by 1980 (see table 21, Appendix A).

The air force is even more impressive for the quality of its nearly exclusively American procured equipment than for its size. Iran's aircraft has steadily improved over time. Whereas Iran once purchased aircraft that had become outmoded in the United States arsenal, in the 1970s its purchases were of progressively more sophisticated planes, culminating in the F-14A fighter, which was among the most advanced weapon of the United States Navy. In 1977 Iran wanted to carry this process one step further by contributing to the research and development of the new F-18 fighter, a plane not yet part of the United States military arsenal.

The sophistication of its equipment, particularly its fighters, gives the air force an impressive defensive and potentially offensive capability. The F-14A swing-wing Tomcat fighters were equipped with Phoenix missiles, capable of locating and destroying six targets simultaneously from a range of fifty miles or more. The capability of the F-4 (the backbone of the Iranian air force) and F-14A fighters has furthermore been enhanced by the acquisition of a squadron of Boeing 707 tankers, which extends their combat radius to 1,400 miles with inflight refueling.

The air force also assumed the burden of the air defense mission. There, too, modernization was apparent. Iran's early warning radar system, built in the 1950s under the auspices of CENTO, was being markedly enhanced during the late 1970s by a more modern air defense radar network. In late 1977 the United States agreed to sell Iran seven Boeing 707 Airborne Warning and Control System

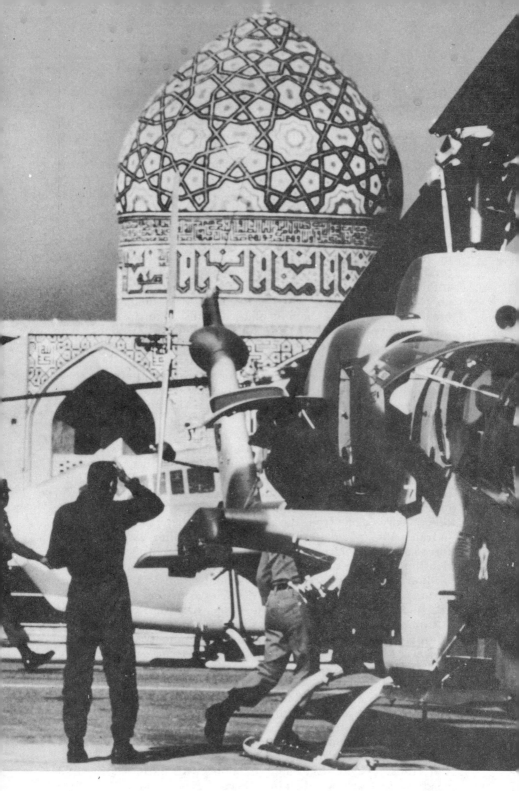

Imperial Iranian Armed Forces helicopter on the alert

(AWACS) aircraft to complement its improved ground radar system. These extremely sophisticated craft have a unique capability of detecting objects beneath them. The air force's three SAM battalions were additionally being reinforced by eight battalions of improved Hawks, a huge project involving over 1,800 missiles.

The air force's primary maintenance facility was located at Mehrabad Air Base. The nearby Iran Aircraft Industries provided main overhaul back up for the maintenance unit; aircraft design and production capabilities were planned.

Source and Quality of Manpower

The armed forces experienced spectacular increases in manpower during the mid-1970s. From just under 200,000 in 1972, total armed forces personnel increased to some 350,000 by 1977. Informed sources projected that by 1980 this number would probably rise to more than 400,000 because of the manpower needs created by the large amount of technically sophisticated equipment being purchased. In addition to active-duty personnel, some 300,000 ex-servicemen were subject to recall to duty, though in 1977 there were no organized reserve units.

The majority of army personnel were conscripts; in the air force and navy, some 90 percent were volunteers. The Military College was the largest single source of commissioned officers in the 1970s, although a large number of air force and naval officers had attended academies or participated in cadet programs in the United States, Great Britain, or Italy. Class differences have traditionally been well defined: commissioned officers emanated from upper-class families, career noncommissioned and warrant officers from the urban middle class, and conscripts from lower class backgrounds. By the 1970s an increasing segment of the officer corps came from the educated middle class.

Iran's 1977 population of more than 34 million gave the armed forces a large pool from which to fill its manpower needs. Of about 8 million males between the ages of fifteen and forty-nine, nearly 5 million were considered physically and mentally fit for military service should the need arise. Each year some 350,000 men reached conscription age, but less than half were called.

Compulsory conscription laws have been in effect since 1925. All males must register at age nineteen; draftees are chosen in a yearly lottery and begin their military service at age twenty-one. The total period of service is twenty-five years; after two years of active military service, draftees spend six years in standby military service, then eight years in first-stage reserve and nine years in second-stage reserve. Those not conscripted in three successive drafts are exempted permanently. Temporary or permanent exemptions are provided for the physically disabled, hardship cases, convicted felons, students, and certain professionals. In times of war, those previously exempted, along with those who have already served, can be called into service. Draft evaders are subject to arrest, trial before a military court, and imprisonment.

A consistent weakness of the armed forces has been the high rate of illiteracy among conscripts and volunteers. In 1977 over half of all armed forces personnel were illiterate. This problem reflected widespread illiteracy and the fact that many better educated Iranians were able to obtain exemptions or, if conscripted, served in one of the noncombat corps rather than the regular army. A considerable number of conscripts, moreover, were from tribal areas where Farsi, the national language, was not spoken (see Ethnic Groups and Languages, ch. 5).

To combat this problem, the armed forces have conducted extensive literacy training programs with the goal of providing each soldier with basic skills. Outside observers note, however, that this announced goal is often not achieved and that much effort is put into combatting the problem by encouraging literate conscripts and volunteers to serve beyond their two-year tour of duty.

Nevertheless this perennial weakness of the armed forces became far more serious with the policy of the 1970s of purchasing modern equipment, vastly increasing the requirement for highly trained personnel for maintenance and operation. One foreign observer noted in 1977 that "Iranian instructors, mostly recruited from ill-educated (if not illiterate) troops, are in no way able to keep pace with the extent and tempo of arms deliveries."

This manpower problem was most acute within the largely conscript ground forces, though all three services reported difficulties in recruiting technical personnel. The air force, though it had been most successful in developing training facilities for support personnel, also had the greatest requirement for technically trained manpower; its needs were estimated at 20,000 in 1976 and were expected to double within five years. In 1976 the air force was thought to be 7,000 short of this requirement for technicians, and foreign military and civilian advisers, particularly from the United States but also including a significant number of Pakistani technicians, supplied the skilled manpower needed for the operation, maintenance, and logistical functions associated with the new equipment. A United States Senate Staff report written in that year projected that it would be well into the 1980s before the more sophisticated air force weapons would be fully operational without direct support from American personnel (see Foreign Influence, this ch.). This report concluded that Iran's ability to meet its new manpower needs will be a major test of the success of the modernization program of the armed forces.

Pay, Rank Structure, and Retirement

Salaries and benefits of armed forces personnel are fixed by public law and approved by the shah and the Majlis. Salaries have increased regularly in an effort to satisfy and retain personnel. This effort was hampered during the mid-1970s, however, by a high inflation rate and rapidly rising civilian salaries, particularly for skilled technicians, which the armed forces often had difficulty in matching.

Basic salaries were quite low. A bill sent to the Majlis in 1974 set the monthly salary of a volunteer soldier, for example, at the equivalent of US$114, a third lieutenant at US$182, and a full general at US$1,083. The addition of allowances for cost of living, hardship assignment, technical skill, and a yearly bonus, however, can augment basic salaries considerably. Paid annual leave is accrued at the rate of one month a year for officers and noncommissioned officers, fifteen days a year for conscripts and volunteers.

Benefits included a limited amount of family housing and access to commissaries. Senior grade officers were extended special benefits including sizable cash bonuses and privileges to import such luxury goods as automobiles without paying customs duties. With such bonuses the senior most officers were among the best paid citizens of Iran. Nevertheless the pay of lower ranking officers was steadily declining in comparison to civilian salaries during the 1970s, creating significant recruitment and morale problems by 1977.

The rank structure is conventional, with the exception of the addition of the rank of third lieutenant in the army and air force for those commissioned out of the high school military training program. The authorized strength of the officer corps is fixed at 10 percent of armed forces strength, although it regularly exceeds that proportion.

Promotion of officers is based on minimum time in each grade, occupation of a military position commensurate with rank, and performance. The shah personally approves all promotions above the rank of major and reviews the lists of lesser ranks. Noncommissioned officers and privates are promoted on the basis of efficiency and length of service. Opportunities for movement from enlisted or noncommissioned ranks to officer status, however, are slight. In 1975 the minimum length of service was shortened for several ranks, thus making promotions faster for both commissioned and noncommissioned officers.

Regular officers with more than twenty years' service may request retirement; it is mandatory for those who have served at least twenty years and have reached specified ages for each grade. Noncommissioned officers with at least twenty years of service are retired at age forty-eight. Those officers who have served thirty years and have been passed over for promotion three times may be retired at the discretion of the Ministry of War. Retired monthly pay is computed at the rate of one-thirteenth of the last regular active-duty pay multiplied by the number of years of service, though not to exceed the last monthly active-duty pay. Pensions in the amount of two-thirds of retirement pay are granted to heirs of deceased retired officers.

Training

The army conducts basic training for its newly inducted conscripts at six replacement training centers. After this thirteen-week session, selected new soldiers are assigned to one of four service schools for additional specialized training in artillery, armored, infantry, or combat support capacities. Draftees unable to read and write Farsi spend four hours a week in basic literacy training throughout the two-year period of conscription. During the final three months of service, a large number of conscripts participate in the army's vocational training program. Taught by army sergeants and designed to facilitate the soldiers' return to civilian life, these courses range from welding, carpentry, and plumbing to tailoring, leathercraft, and shoe repair.

In-country training for naval personnel is conducted at Bandar Pahlavi, where sailors, specialists, and noncommissioned officers receive basic seamanship and speciality training. The air force conducts combat crew training at Vahdati Air Base and in 1977 was in the process of establishing various technical training centers for its volunteers throughout the country.

Military training is also conducted at high schools and colleges; students are paid salaries, and time spent in these programs counts toward their active-duty obligation. If successful in passing the military academic requirements, high school graduates can be commissioned third lieutenants and college graduates, second lieutenants.

The Military College trains officers who are commissioned before entering the regular service. The three-year course includes classroom and field training. All applicants for Military College must be high school graduates and must have a character reference from a general officer attesting to the reputation of the candidate and his family. The Military College provides instruction for all three services. Air force and naval academies were planned, but during the 1970s air force officers received speciality training in the United States, and navy officers went either to the United States or Great Britain.

Basic and advanced staff training were conducted at the Army Staff College and at the War Academy. Although expanding, these facilities were insufficient to meet the needs of the armed forces, and a large number of officers, particularly from the navy and air force, also received command and staff training in West European countries or the United States. Partly to combat the dependence on foreign sources for advanced officer training, Iran established the National Defense University in 1968. Amalgamating high command, joint staff, and management training, the university trained and provided a forum for senior officers to discuss such issues as national and international security, defense strategy, the role of the armed forces in Iranian society, and resource management.

An increasingly important component of armed forces training in the 1970s was in the form of short-term technical training in the logistical, maintenance, and operational aspects of Iran's rapidly expanding equipment inventory. Conducted both in Iran and abroad, technical instruction on new equipment was provided by personnel from the country of its origin (see Foreign Influence, this ch.).

Uniforms and Insignia

Uniforms are locally manufactured, and most officers and non-commissioned officers prefer to accept the uniform allowance and have their uniforms tailored. Regular service uniforms for officers are similar to those of United States military personnel: a short jacket with brass buttons, trousers without cuffs, low-cut shoes, a leather belt, and either garrison or field cap. For the ground forces, service uniforms are olive drab in winter and desert brown in summer; for the air force, they are dark blue in winter, light blue in summer; and for the navy, they are blue in winter and white in summer. The national symbol of the golden lion with the sun rising over its back is used on buttons, cap insignia, belt buckles, and other parts of the uniform.

Navy enlisted men wear the conventional navy-blue jumpers with wide flap collar, neckerchief, and cap without bill. There is a full complement of specialized and functional uniforms, including those for Military College students, horse cavalry, ski patrol, and for parades and ceremonies.

Rank insignia for commissioned officers are rather elaborate, uniformly gold for all three services and on shoulder boards that are dark green for the army, blue for the air force, and black for the navy. Rank insignia for warrant officers and enlisted men are identical for the army and air force—gold on a light green background (see fig. 14). The army and navy also use insignia or badges to identify an individual's branch or specific work assignment.

Decorations and Awards

The government makes liberal use of decorations and awards. Although the majority are exclusively for Iranian military personnel, four may also be awarded to civilians and to foreigners. Medals are awarded on the basis of status, outstanding service to Iran, performance in a specific field, or participation in important national events. Most awards are given in several classes, depending on the rank of the recipient. Except for sashes and neck decorations, ribbons denoting the decorations are worn above the left breast pocket (see table 22, Appendix A).

Decorations and awards are given with the approval of the shah, but not all are personally awarded by him. Several decorations are accompanied by monetary awards.

Military Justice

Military personnel are subject to the rules of military justice from their first contact with the armed forces. Students taking military subjects in high school or college come under the authority of military law and may be punished by the armed forces for violations committed while engaged in military training. An individual who evades or attempts to evade conscription will, on apprehension, be tried before a military court along with those

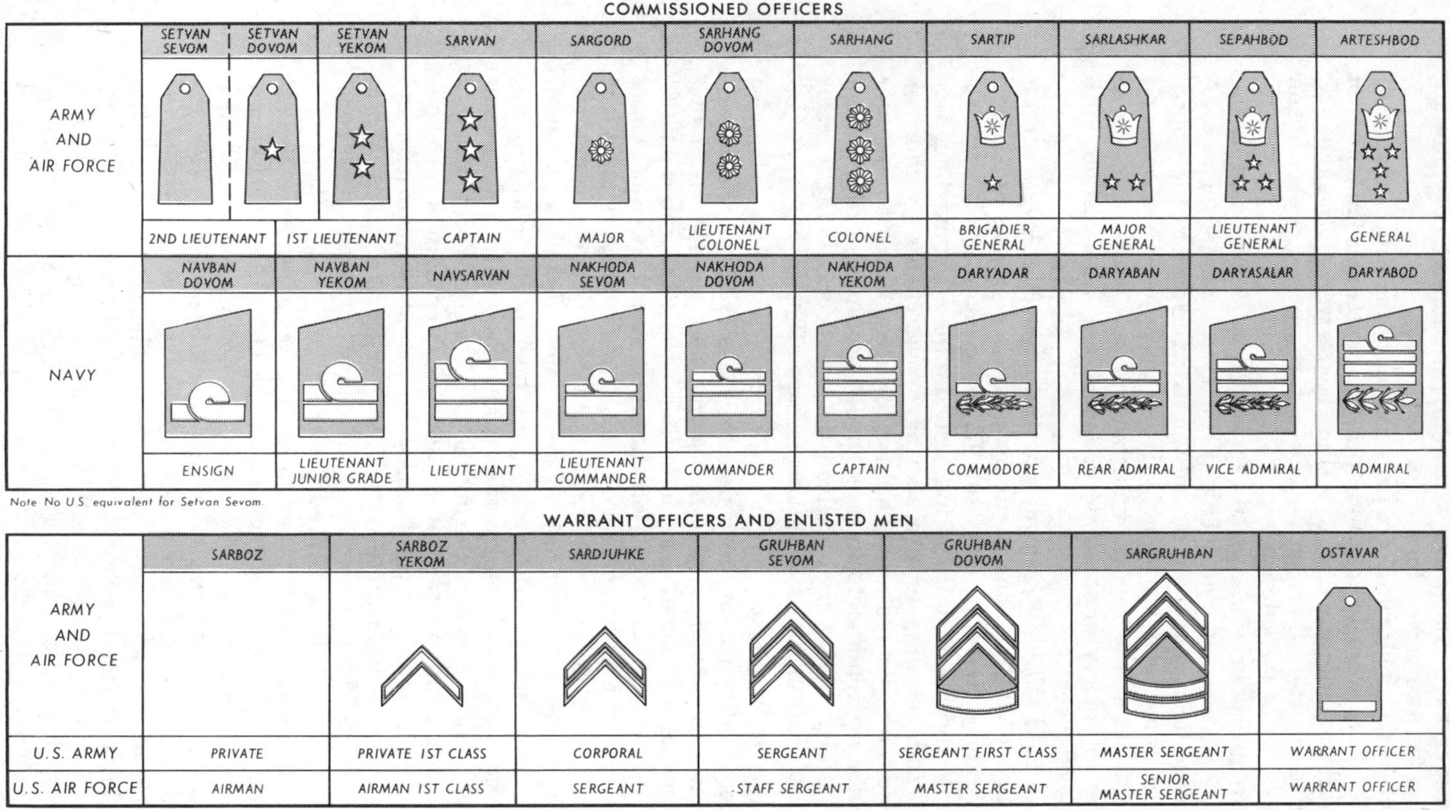

COMMISSIONED OFFICERS

	SETVAN SEVOM	SETVAN DOVOM	SETVAN YEKOM	SARVAN	SARGORD	SARHANG DOVOM	SARHANG	SARTIP	SARLASHKAR	SEPAHBOD	ARTESHBOD
ARMY AND AIR FORCE		2ND LIEUTENANT	1ST LIEUTENANT	CAPTAIN	MAJOR	LIEUTENANT COLONEL	COLONEL	BRIGADIER GENERAL	MAJOR GENERAL	LIEUTENANT GENERAL	GENERAL
	NAVBAN DOVOM		NAVBAN YEKOM	NAVSARVAN	NAKHODA SEVOM	NAKHODA DOVOM	NAKHODA YEKOM	DARYADAR	DARYABAN	DARYASALAR	DARYABOD
NAVY	ENSIGN		LIEUTENANT JUNIOR GRADE	LIEUTENANT	LIEUTENANT COMMANDER	COMMANDER	CAPTAIN	COMMODORE	REAR ADMIRAL	VICE ADMIRAL	ADMIRAL

Note: No U.S. equivalent for Setvan Sevom.

WARRANT OFFICERS AND ENLISTED MEN

	SARBOZ	SARBOZ YEKOM	SARDJUHKE	GRUHBAN SEVOM	GRUHBAN DOVOM	SARGRUHBAN	OSTAVAR
U.S. ARMY	PRIVATE	PRIVATE 1ST CLASS	CORPORAL	SERGEANT	SERGEANT FIRST CLASS	MASTER SERGEANT	WARRANT OFFICER
U.S. AIR FORCE	AIRMAN	AIRMAN 1ST CLASS	SERGEANT	STAFF SERGEANT	MASTER SERGEANT	SENIOR MASTER SERGEANT	WARRANT OFFICER

Figure 14. Insignia of Rank, Iranian Armed Forces and United States Equivalents

413

who might have conspired with him, whether or not they are members of the armed forces.

Military tribunals consist of primary courts and courts of appeal. In 1968 there were twenty-nine primary courts and ten courts of appeal throughout the country. These courts were permanent and attended by either three or five active-duty officers, depending on the severity of the offense.

Court procedures and penal regulations were governed by the Military Justice and Penal Law of 1938, as amended. The complaining officer sends a fully substantiated report to the appropriate tribunal, which may hold trial or make judgment based on the contents of the report. Punishments vary from demotion or transfer to fines or imprisonment; appeals may be heard for more serious offenses.

Since the 1950s military courts have also played an ever-increasing role in trying civilians accused of a variety of crimes considered detrimental to state security. In 1977 these included all terrorist-related activities, counterfeiting, armed robbery, smuggling, sabotage, and hoarding or profiteering by merchants. Authorities justified the expanded role of military justice as necessary in order to render swift judgment in cases involving state security, though many foreign observers criticized the practice as being a major source of human rights violations (see ch. 12).

Foreign Influence

Foreign influence on the armed forces has invariably been massive and vital, though both the source and the nature of that influence have changed over time. Before the 1920s and the unification of the armed forces, foreign officers from Sweden, Great Britain, and Russia commanded various Iranian military units (see Historical Background, this ch.). Reza Shah made a concerted effort to minimize direct foreign involvement though Swedish officers continued to hold command positions in the gendarmerie, and large numbers of Iranian officers attended military academies in France and Germany. During the years before World War II, a particularly strong German influence was accepted in a conscious attempt to counter the traditional influence of Great Britain and Russia (by that time the Soviet Union) in Iranian affairs. World War II led to the introduction of new kinds of foreign influence, particularly that of the United States.

United States military programs in Iran began modestly in 1943 with the establishment of a small United States Military Mission to the Imperial Iranian Gendarmerie (known as GENMISH), which limited advisory activities to noncombatant branches. In 1947 the United States established a more comprehensive mission to the Ministry of War and the Iranian army, called the United States Army Mission Headquarters (ARMISH), to enhance the efficiency of Iran's military forces. Shortly thereafter, many Iranian officers began training the United States. The United States began its grant military assistance program to Iran in 1950, and a Military

Assistance Advisory Group (MAAG) was established for its administration. In 1962 the two United States military missions were consolidated into a single organization, ARMISH-MAAG, which remained active in Iran in 1977. Since 1973 the United States has also provided military support in the form of Technical Assistance Field Teams (TAFTs), which provide short-term in-country instruction to Iranian personnel on specific equipment purchased from the United States. The small GENMISH program was terminated in 1976.

The United States provided over US$1.4 billion in military assistance to Iran between 1947 and 1969, primarily in the form of grant aid before 1965 and of foreign military sales credits during the late 1960s. After 1969 it was determined that Iran could finance its own defense needs, and the financial assistance programs were terminated. Since that time, Iran has paid cash for its arms acquisitions and has paid the bulk of the expenses for United States military assistance: in 1976 70 percent of the cost of the 209-man ARMISH-MAAG and 100 percent of the 868-man TAFTs were absorbed by the government of Iran (by 1977 Iran paid 97 percent of the cost of ARMISH-MAAG, and TAFT personnel had been reduced to less than 500). Even so, in 1976 the United States military mission in Iran was by far the largest in the world in terms of personnel. In that year, United States Department of Defense personnel, including those assigned to the American Embassy, totaled over 1,400.

United States military ties with Iran also stem from its observer status within CENTO and from a 1959 executive agreement with Iran, which, although not a formal treaty commitment, provides that "In case of aggression against Iran, the . . . United States . . . will take such appropriate action, including the use of armed forces, as may be mutually agreed upon . . ." During the mid-1970s, however, these relationships became less significant than the growing government-to-government Foreign Military Sales program. Arms transfers increased dramatically after the 1973 oil price hike, and as of late 1977, despite mounting opposition within the United States Congress to the dollar arms trade with Iran, no definite steps had been taken within either country to slow their pace. From FY 1972 through FY 1976, American arms sales to Iran totaled some US$10.4 billion, and informed sources projected that from FY 1977 through FY 1981 sales would total between US$10 and US$15 billion.

During the mid-1970s a great majority of United States Department of Defense personnel in Iran were either administering the foreign military sales program or training Iranians to use new equipment. Training in the operation and maintenance of new equipment was also provided by an estimated 3,000 American civilians on contract from some fifty private firms involved in arms sales to Iran. This number was expected to rise to between 8,500 and 18,000 by 1980 as more highly sophisticated military hardware was delivered to Iran.

The presence of such large numbers of American advisers had a vast influence on the Iranian armed forces. One indicator of this fact was that, during the 1970s, English became the basic language for most skilled military operations in Iran, and all officers received at least some English-language training. The preponderance of American weapons also made a large portion of the Iranian armed forces, at least in the short run, dependent on the United States for logistics and support systems for spare parts and for advisers for weapons operation and maintenance. The extent of this dependence was suggested in the 1976 Senate Staff report, which concluded that "it is unlikely that Iran could engage in major combat operations [with its more sophisticated weaponry] during the next five to ten years . . . without sustained U. S. support."

Other countries engaged in less intensive arms sales programs. By far the largest arms supplier after the United States was Great Britain, which provided some US$3.5 billion worth of arms between 1972 and 1976, primarily to the Iranian ground forces. Other suppliers in the 1970s included the Soviet Union, West Germany, France, and Italy. Arms sales contracts with each of these countries (except the Soviet Union whose sales, as of 1977, consisted of less sophisticated armored personnel carriers, and artillery and missile systems) included provisions for operations and maintenance training of Iranian personnel. The shah has pointed out that these alternative sources of arms are available should the United States refuse to continue to be Iran's major arms supplier, and during his November 1977 trip to France the shah indicated a desire to buy large quantities of arms from France and other countries because of recent delays in the supply of United States armaments.

The vast arms trade with Iran had a secondary effect of making Iran itself a foreign influence as a source of arms. During the 1970s, as Iran acquired the most modern weapons, it transferred part of its older matériel to third countries, including Jordan, Pakistan, Ethiopia, and Morocco.

A more traditional source of foreign influence stems from the foreign training of officer personnel. Here, again, the United States predominated, though Great Britain also played a significant role. Between 1950 and 1974, over 11,000 Iranian officers, including all pilots, were trained in the United States. In 1977 there were about 2,200 Iranian military personnel, mostly from the air force, training at Lackland Air Force Base in Texas and at other United States military installations. Iranian naval officers, once trained in Italy, were trained in either the United States or Great Britain during the 1970s. In this as in other areas, the reduction of such a vast foreign influence was a major goal of the Iranian armed forces. Yet in 1977 the ongoing upgrading of Iran's military establishment continued to rely heavily on foreign sources of modern information and technology.

* * *

The United States Senate Staff report entitled "U. S. Military Sales to Iran" is an essential document. Although its primary focus is on United States military programs in Iran, it also provides considerable information on internal aspects of Iran's armed forces. R. D. M. Furlong's "Iran: A Power to be Reckoned With" is a detailed account of Iran's military build up focusing particularly on the acquisition and manufacture of weapons systems. The best source of current data on the size, budget, and equipment inventory of the armed forces is the yearly *The Military Balance,* published by the International Institute of Strategic Studies. Historical background material is presented most completely in J. C. Hurewitz' *Middle East Politics: The Military Dimension.* (For further information see Bibliography.)

Appendix A

Table 1. Highlights of the Iranian Press

Estimated Total Press Circulation, 1976

	Tehran	Provinces	Total
Daily newspapers	700,000	20,000	720,000
Weekly magazines	550,000	0[1]	550,000
Monthly magazines	500,000	20,000	520,000
Almanacs	100,000	0[1]	100,000

Major Daily Newspapers of Tehran, 1976

Newspaper	Orientation	Estimated Circulation
Kayhan	Political and social	300,000
Ettelaat	-do-	200,000
Rastakhiz	Iran National Resurgence Party organ	100,000
Ayandegan	Political, social, and economic	40,000
Kayhan International (English language)	General government news	15,000
Peigham-e Emruz	Political and social	6,000
Tehran Journal (English language)	Political	6,000
Bourse	Economic	6,000

Major Weekly and Monthly Magazines of Tehran, 1976

Magazine	Character	Estimated Circulation
Zan-e Ruz	Women's weekly	150,000
Ettelaat Banovan	-do-	100,000
Tasmasha	Radio and television weekly	60,000
Ettelaat Haftegi	General weekly	50,000
Rastakhiz Javanan	Youth weekly of Iran National Resurgence Party	50,000
Rastakhiz Rusta	Farmers' monthly of Iran National Resurgence Party	200,000
Rastakhiz Kargaran	Workers' monthly of Iran National Resurgence Party	150,000
Khandaniha	Political	30,000

Table 1 *(continued)*

Number of Printing Presses and Employees, 1972 and 1976[2]

	Printing Presses		Employees	
	1972	1976	1972	1976
Tehran	106	120	3,061	3,200
Provinces	26	30	434	500
TOTAL	132	150	3,495	3,700

[1]Inconsequential.
[2]Estimated.

Source: Based on information from *Iran Almanac and Book of Facts, 1976,* (15th ed.), Tehran, pp. 118–123.

Table 2. Population Growth, Selected Years 1900–76
(number in millions; growth in percent)

Year	Total Population		Urban Population		Rural Population	
	Number	Growth	Number	Growth	Number	Growth
Enumerated Data						
1956	19.0	. . .	6.0	. . .	13.0	. . .
1966	25.3	2.9	10.0	5.1	15.3	1.3
1976*	33.5	. . .	16.3	. . .	17.2	. . .
Estimated and Corrected Data						
1900	10.1	. . .	2.3	. . .	7.8	. . .
1926	11.9	0.1	2.5	0.1	9.4	0.1
1934	13.3	1.5	2.8	1.5	10.5	1.5
1940	14.5	1.5	3.2	2.3	11.3	1.3
1956	20.4	2.2	6.3	4.4	14.1	1.4
1966	27.1	2.9	10.6	5.3	16.5	1.7

. . .means not applicable.
*Preliminary data.

Table 3. Average Expenditure by a Rural Household During a Thirty-Day Period, 1965 and 1970
(in rials)*

	1965	1970
Food and Tobacco	2,517.9	2,791.1
Nonfood Items		
Housing	377.8	240.9
Household operation	68.0	293.6
Household effects	130.0	128.6
Clothing	367.1	396.5
Personal care and health	154.4	227.5
Transportation	76.3	101.7
Education and study	18.0	12.6
Recreation	9.8	14.8
Gifts	48.8	54.1
Other	0.4	17.8
Total Nonfood Items	1,250.6	1,388.1
TOTAL	3,768.5	4,179.2

*For value of the rial—see Glossary

Source: Based on information from G.W. Irwin, *Roads and Redistribution: Social Cost and Benefits of Labor Intensive Road Construction in Iran,* Geneva, 1975, table 37.

Table 4. Growth of School Enrollments, 1963 and 1973

	Thousands of Students		Percent	
	1963	1973	Annual Growth	Overall Growth
Kindergarten	13	24	6	84
Primary	1,719	3,424	7	99
Secondary				
General	327	995	17	380
Technical	12	66	19	450
Higher	24	83	16	350
Literacy program	2,900	8,250	15	184

Source: Based on information from Kenneth Watson, "The Shah's White Revolution: Education and Reform in Iran," *Comparative Education,* 12, No. 1, March 1976, table 1.

Table 5. Number of University Students, School Year 1974–75

	Number			
	Total	Junior College	Under-graduate	Post-graduate
University of Isfahan	4,123	. . .	3,171	952
Pahlavi University (Shiraz)	4,890	355	2,379	2,156
Azarbaijan University (Tabriz)	7,250	. . .	6,018	1,232
Tehran University	17,379	773	9,829	6,777
Jondi-Shapour University (Ahvaz)	3,142	. . .	2,651	491
Aryamehr University of Technology	2,899	. . .	2,825	74
Ferdowsi University (Meshed)	4,513	60	3,610	843
National University of Iran	6,896	136	5,344	1,416
Teachers Training University	3,828	. . .	3,735	93
TOTAL	54,920	1,324	39,562	14,034

. . .means not applicable.

Source: Based on information from Iran, Press and Information Office, "The Development of Education in Iran," *Profile on Iran,* July 1976, Tehran, p. 31.

Table 6. GDP and GNP, Selected Fiscal Years 1959–76[1,2]
(in billions of rials at current prices)[3]

Sector	1959	1974	1975	1976
Agriculture	85	303	334	430
Oil	47	1,442	1,376	1,741
Industry (mining, water, and power)	32	338	413	524
Construction	13	98	208	415
Services				
Transportation and communication	28	99	132	151
Banking and insurance	6	137	202	266
Trade	23	159	201	253
Public services	23	277	346	468
Other	29	217	266	332
Total Services	109	889	1,147	1,470
GDP (factor costs)	286	3,070	3,478	4,580
Net indirect taxes	18	89	112	110
GDP (market prices)	304	3,159	3,590	4,690
Net factor income	−20	−10	−15	−5
GDP (market prices)	284	3,149	3,575	4,685

[1] GDP—gross domestic product; GNP—gross national product.
[2] Data are for fiscal years (FY), which end in March.
[3] For value of the rial—see Glossary.

Source: Based on information from Bank Markazi Iran, *Annual Report and Balance Sheet, 2535*, Tehran, 1977, p. 99 (and earlier Bank Markazi Iran reports).

Table 7. Composition of Imports,
Selected Fiscal Years 1971-75[1, 2]
(in millions of United States dollars)

Commodities	1971	1973	1974	1975
Food and Beverages				
Cereals	104	113	461	560
Sugar	11	76	157	537
Other	59	143	247	484
Total Food and Beverages	174	332	865	1,581
Fats and Oils	45	61	240	291
Chemicals				
Pharmaceuticals	50	97	149	208
Plastics	18	79	130	174
Other	96	180	370	453
Total Chemicals	164	356	649	835
Basic Manufactures				
Iron and steel	300	583	1,155	1,845
Yarns and textiles	128	321	487	501
Other	264	444	738	1,192
Total Basic Manufactures	692	1,348	2,380	3,538
Machinery and Equipment				
Machinery	439	804	1,137	2,539
Electrical	256	311	409	801
Transport	171	288	563	1,633
Total Machinery and Equipment	866	1,403	2,109	4,973
Other	120	237	371	478
TOTAL IMPORTS	2,061	3,737	6,614	11,696

[1] Some imports excluded from trade statistics—primarily defense equipment.
[2] Data are for fiscal years (FY), which end in March.

Source: Based on information from Nicholas Cumming-Bruce, *Iran: A MEED Special Report*, London, February 1977, p. 30.

Table 8. Composition of Non-Oil and Gas Exports, Selected Fiscal Years 1970–74[1]
(in millions of United States dollars)[2]

Non-Oil Exports	1970	1972	1973	1974
Traditional Commodities				
Carpets	54	90	107	118
Cotton	57	79	148	84
Fruits (fresh and dried)	35	58	93	71
Hides	14	28	29	28
Mineral ores	20	20	24	32
Caviar	5	8	8	7
Other	42	54	114	75
Total Traditional Commodities	227	337	523	415
New Industrial Products				
Soaps and detergents	8	15	6	12
Shoes	7	13	11	7
Vegetable oils	3	7	6	4
Clothes and knitwear	14	36	29	44
Chemicals	5	15	15	22
Vehicles	2	2	12	22
Other	12	15	25	51
Total New Industrial Products	51	103	104	162
TOTAL	278	440	627	577

[1] Data are for fiscal years (FY), which end in March.
[2] Converted from SDRs (special drawing rights) at the following rates: one SDR equaled US$1.00 in 1970, US$1.086 in 1972, US$1.192 in 1973, and US$1.203 in 1974.

Source: Based on information from Bank Markazi Iran data as published in *Iranian-American Economic Survey, 1976/2535*, October 1976, p. 69.

Table 9. Balance of Payments, Fiscal Years 1974–76[1]

	1974	1975	1976
Current Receipts			
Oil and gas[2]	21,014	20,034	24,179
Other exports	582	592	518
Services	1,714	2,466	3,279
Total Current Receipts	23,310	23,092	27,976
Current Payments			
Imports	−9,299	−15,362	−16,147
Services and transfers[2,3]	−2,218	−3,370	−4,419
Total Current Payments	−11,517	−18,732	−20,566
Current Account Balance	11,793	4,360	7,410
Capital Movements			
Private Sector			
Direct investments—oil	−1,534	−180	−2,488
Other direct investments in Iran	445	661	617
Other private capital	−210	−898	−989
Total Private Sector	−1,299	−417	−2,860
Government Capital			
Loan repayments	−1,313	−729	−711
Public borrowing	257	300	560
Aid and investment abroad (net)	−2,388	−2,941	−1,273
Other	−13	−2	0
Total Government Capital	−3,457	−3,372	−1,424
Banking Sector	58	318	331
Balance Capital Account	−4,698	−3,471	−3,953
Balancing Items			
Changes in foreign assets (−=increase)	−5,184	207	−2,784
Errors and omissions	−1,911	−1,096	−673

[1] Data are for fiscal years (FY), which end in March.
[2] Foreign oil companies treated as nonresidents; export earnings include imputed service payments to oil companies.
[3] Unrequited transfers were negligible.

Source: Based on information from data published by Bank Markazi Iran, *Annual Report and Balance Sheet, 2535*, Tehran, 1977, pp. 108–11.

Table 10. Summary of Government Budget, Fiscal Years 1972–76[1,2]
(in billions of rials)[3]

	1972	1973	1974[4]	1975[4]	1976[4]
Revenues					
Oil	178	311	1,205	1,247	1,329
Direct taxes	35	47	65	144	177
Indirect taxes	60	78	86	119	154
Other taxes	4	6	7	8	11
Nontax[5]	25	22	31	64	73
Total Revenues	302	464	1,394	1,582	1,744
Expenditures					
Current	227	317	728	929	1,060
Development	132	161	349	527	629
Other	0	0	176	112	102
Total Expenditures	359	478	1,253	1,568	1,791
Surplus (−Deficit)	−57	−14	141	14	−47
Financing Deficits					
Domestic sources	46	59	−7	−10	23
Foreign sources					
Borrowing	11	−2	−51	−14	9
Aid and investments abroad	0	−1	−161	−167	−99
Other	0	−42	78	177	114

[1] Central government operations; excludes government profit and nonprofit agencies.
[2] Data are for fiscal years (FY), which end in March.
[3] For value of the rial—see Glossary.
[4] Subject to revision in final accounting.
[5] Revenue and dividends from some government operations including income from foreign investments.

Source: Based on information from Bank Markazi Iran, *Annual Report and Balance Sheet*, 2535, Tehran, 1977, pp. 103–107.

Iran: A Country Study

Table 11. Fifth Development Plan (FY 1973–78) Investments
(in billions of rials)[1]

Sector	Projected[2]			Actual FY 1973–75 Expenditures by Public Sector[4]
	Public Sector	Private Sector[3]	Total	
Agriculture and natural resources	177	132	309	80
Water resources	162	4	166	65
Electricity	310	0	310	n.a.
Manufacturing	277	503	780	168
Oil	536	88	624	n.a.
Gas	120	48	168	n.a.
Mining	62	4	66	40
Transportation	402	90	492	n.a.
Post and telecommunications	91	0	91	n.a.
Housing	240	685	925	110
Education	127	5	132	n.a.
Urban development	74	0	74	n.a.
Rural development	60	0	60	n.a.
Other	481	21	502	n.a.
TOTAL	3,119	1,580	4,699	1,037

n.a.—not available.
[1] For value of the rial—see Glossary.
[2] 1974 revised targets.
[3] Includes government credits to private sector.
[4] Data are for fiscal years (FY), which end in March.

Source: Based on planned expenditures from *Financial Times*, London, *Survey of Iran*, July 28, 1975, p. 14. Total actual expenditures FY1973–75 from Bank Markazi Iran, *Annual Report and Balance Sheet 2535*, Tehran, 1977, p. 103. Data for actual budget expenditures FY1973–75 for individual sectors from various sources reporting on elements of plan activity.

Table 12. Crude Production and Oil Revenues, 1955–75

Year	Average Barrels per Day (in thousands)	Oil Receipts (in millions of United States dollars)
1955	329.2	90.2
1956	538.8	150.9
1957	721.8	212.8
1958	825.8	247.2
1959	927.3	262.4
1960	1,052.9	285.0
1961	1,178.3	291.2
1962	1,314.2	343.2
1963	1,465.8	380.0
1964	1,690.1	482.2
1965	1,885.4	514.1
1966	2,113.3	608.2
1967	2,596.6	751.6
1968	2,847.6	853.4
1969	3,374.9	922.8
1970	3,828.6	1,109.3
1971	4,539.6	1,851.1
1972	5,024.1	2,396.0
1973	5,861.1	4,399.2
1974	6,021.7	21,443.2
1975	5,300.0	20,000.0*

*Estimated

Source: Based on information from Iran, Press and Information Office, *Profile on Iran*, May 1976, p. 3.

Table 13. Natural Gas Production, 1974 and 1975
(in millions of cubic feet per day)

	1974	1975
Khuzestan oil fields	4,490.8	4,025.5
National Iranian Oil Company and affiliated oil companies	347.5	367.3
Other	125.3	127.2
TOTAL	4,963.6	4,520.0

Source: Based on information from Iran, Press and Information Office, *Profile on Iran*, Washington, May 1976, p. 11.

Table 14. Consumption and Export of Natural Gas, 1974 and 1975
(in millions of cubic feet per day)

	1974	Planned 1975
Domestic consumption	184	217
National Iranian Gas Company internal use	93	105
Shahpour petrochemical	125	120
Kharg petrochemical	146	148
Abadan refinery	96	92
Oil fields consumption	509	486
Export to Soviet Union	879	925
TOTAL	2,032	2,093

Source: Based on information from Iran, Press and Information Office, *Profile on Iran* (as originally published in National Iranian Gas Company Reports), Washington, May 1976, p. 12.

Table 15. Gas Consumption Projections, 1975, 1977, and 1982
(in millions of cubic feet per day)

	1975	Planned 1977	1982
Oil Fields and Abadan Refinery[1]	578.0	650.0	750.0
Internal Consumption[2]			
Domestic	3.1	9.5	52.2
Industries	106.8	190.6	944.2
Electricity generation	106.8	255.6	756.7
National Iranian Gas Company use	105.0	105.0	105.0
Export to the Soviet Union	925.0	965.0	965.0
TOTAL	1,824.7	2,175.7	3,573.1

[1] Excludes requirement of gas injection in oil fields.
[2] Excludes petrochemical feedstock.

Source: Based on information from Iran, Press and Information Office, *Profile on Iran* (as originally published in National Iranian Gas Company Reports), Washington, May 1976, p. 13.

Table 16. Production of Various Manufactured Goods, Selected Fiscal Years 1969–77[1]

Product	Unit	1969	1973	1975	Planned 1977
Cement	million tons	2	3	5	20
Fertilizer	thousand tons	66	436	440	1,700
Knitwear	-do-	n.a.	12	44	60
Motor vehicles	thousand units	35	77	99	500
Paint	thousand tons	14	22	33	n.a.
Refined sugar	-do-	485	697	720	1,000
Refrigerators	thousand units	174	257	340	250
Steel	thousand tons	106	246	1,000	10,000
Telephones	thousand sets	87	113	114	240
Television sets	-do-	73	219	325	720
Textiles	million meters[2]	455	520	546	850
Tires	thousand tons	10	24	30	n.a.
Vegetable oil	-do-	146	183	247	n.a.

n.a.—not available
[1] Data are for fiscal years (FY), which end in March.
[2] One meter is equal to 39.37 inches.

Table 17. Production of Major Agricultural Crops, Selected Fiscal Years 1969–77[1]

(in thousands of tons)

Commodity	1969	1972	1975	1977[2]
Wheat	4,400	3,700	4,700	5,000
Sugar beets	3,410	3,980	4,300	5,250
Barley	1,160	900	863	1,100
Rice	960	1,050	1,313	1,400
Cotton (unginned)	545	444	715	425
Oilseeds	10	46	79	89
Green tea	81	65	96	88
Sugarcane	n.a.	n.a.	1,100	800
Dates	n.a.	n.a.	378	346

n.a.—not available.
[1] Data are for fiscal years (FY), which end in March.
[2] Preliminary estimates.

Source: Based on information from *Iran Economic News*, 3, No. 8, August 1977, p. 6; and *Iran Economic News*, 3, No. 9, September 1977, p. 8.

Table 18. *Police Statistics on Incidence of Crime,*
Selected Fiscal Years 1968, 1970, and 1973*

Crime or Offense	1968	1970	1973
Going on strike	4	9	6
Plotting, rioting, and unlawful crowding	21	8	8
Fire and destruction	1,775	1,807	2,113
Calumny	3,521	3,488	6,428
Family dispute and offenses against children	19,647	21,698	19,611
Embezzlement	57	60	168
Land dispute	4,625	5,296	5,746
Distribution of prohibited printed matter	12	27	37
Forcibly detained	2,862	2,408	2,122
Encroachment upon individuals' rights by government officials	55	53	45
Disobedience and insolence to officials while accomplishing duties	1,199	1,271	1,241
Forgery	199	373	397
Offenses against property	26	19	63
Drawing knives	1,578	1,561	2,190
Drawing bad checks	8,867	10,161	9,911
Dealing in stolen goods	186	210	214
Kidnapping	319	69	81
Bribery	42	36	30
Driving without a license	27,627	43,339	22,706
Abortion	105	56	51
Armed robbery	52	39	85
Counterfeiting coins	76	16	53
Helping culprits to escape from prison or concealing them	19	7	22
Smuggling	7,194	4,726	3,061
Gambling	1,221	1,231	1,414
Fraud, trickery, and breach of trust	3,743	3,611	3,844
High treason and following communist doctrine	34	2	0
Poisoning	1,043	1,626	1,581
Causing trouble to women	2,972	3,318	3,744
Defaming government officials	123	107	51
Unlawful entry	102	101	110
Sexual crimes	1,427	1,231	1,158
Other	78,396	70,133	54,140
TOTAL	169,129	178,097	142,431

*Data are for fiscal years (FY), which end in March.

Source: Based on information from *Iran Almanac and Book of Facts 1976.* (15th ed.), Tehran, 1976, p. 104.

Table 19. Imperial Iranian Ground Forces, Major Weapons Systems, 1977

Type and Description	Inventory[1]	On Order[2]
Tanks (medium)		
Chieftain	760	1,220
M–47/48	400	0
M–60A1	460	0
Tanks (light)		
Scorpion	250	110
Armored personnel carriers		
M–113 and BTR–50/60	2,000	0
VC1 BMP–1	0	n.a.
Guns and howitzers (including self-propelled)		
75mm, 105mm, 130mm, 155mm,		
175mm and 203mm	650	0
Recoilless rifles (106mm)	n.a.	0
Rocket launchers (M–21)	64	0
Antiaircraft guns (including self-propelled)		
23mm, 35mm, 40mm, 57mm, and		
85mm	650	0
ZSU–23/4	0	n.a.
Antitank guided weapons		
ENTAC, SS–11, SS–12, and TOW,		
Dragon	n.a.	0
ASU–85	0	n.a.
Fixed-wing aircraft		
Cessna 185	45	0
Cessna 0–2A	10	0
Cessna 310	6	0
Shrike commander	5	0
F–27	3	0
Helicopters		
AH–1J	202	0
Bell 214–A	293	0
Huskie	20	0
AB–205A	93	0
CH–47C	90	0

n.a.—not available.
[1] Exact quantities may vary slightly.
[2] Represents confirmed orders as of November 1976.

Source: Based on information from International Institute for Strategic Studies, *Military Balance, 1976–1977*, London, 1976; International Institute for Strategic Studies, *Military Balance, 1977–1978*, London, 1977; and Stockholm International Peace Research Institute, *World Armaments and Disarmament, SIPRI Yearbook 1977*, Cambridge, 1977.

Table 20. *Imperial Iranian Navy, Sea and Air Vessels, 1977*

Type and Description	Inventory	On Order
Destroyers		
With surface-to-air missiles	3	0
Spruance-class DD963	0	4
Submarines (Tang-class)	0	3
Frigates (with surface-to-surface and		
surface-to-air missiles)	4	0
Fast patrol boats (with		
surface-to-surface missiles)	0	12
Patrol boats	25	0
Corvettes	4	0
Minesweepers	5	0
Landing ships and craft	4	2
Logistical support ships	2	0
Hovercraft		
SRN–6	8	0
Wellington BH–7	6	0
Helicopters		
AB–205A	5	0
AB–206A	14	0
AB–212	6	0
SH3D	20	0
S–65A	6	0
RH–53D	6	0

Source: Based on information from International Institute for Strategic Studies, *Military Balance, 1976–1977*, London, 1976; and International Institute for Strategic Studies, *Military Balance, 1977–1978*, London, 1977.

Table 21. Imperial Iranian Air Force, Aircraft and Missile Systems, 1977

Type and Description	Inventory[1]	On Order[2]
Fighter-bombers (with air-to-air and air-to-surface missiles)		
F–4E Phantom	141	36
F–4D	32	0
Fighters		
F–5E	141	0
F–5F	28	0
F–14A Tomcat with Phoenix missiles	60	20
F–16	0	160
Reconnaissance		
RF–4E	16	0
P–3 (Maritime)	6	0
F–5A	12	0
Transports		
C–130 E/H	57	0
F–27	23	2
Aero Commander 690	3	0
Falcon 20	4	0
Boeing 747	6	2
Tankers		
Boeing 707	12	0
Boeing 747	3	0
Trainers		
Bonanza F–33 A/C	30	19
T–33	9	0
F–5B/F	18	0
Helicopters		
Huskie	10	0
AB–205	6	0
AB–206A	4	0
AB–212	5	0
CH–47C	2	0
Super Frelon	16	0
Bell 214C	17	26
AS–61A	0	2
Surface-to-air missiles		
Rapier	n.a.	n.a.
Tigercat	n.a.	0
Improved HAWK	650	1,200
HAWK	n.a.	0
SAM–7/9	0	n.a.
Airborne warning and control ships (AWACS)		
Boeing 707	0	7

n.a.—not available.
[1] Exact quantities may vary slightly.
[2] Represents confirmed orders as of October 1977.

Source: Based on information from International Institute for Strategic Studies, *Military Balance, 1976–1977*, London, 1976; International Institute for Strategic Studies, *Military Balance, 1977–1978*, London, 1977; and Stockholm International Peace Research Institute, *World Armaments and Disarmament, SIPRI Yearbook 1977*, Cambridge, 1977.

Table 22. Awards and Decorations

Decoration	Recipient	Basis of Award
Order of Pahlavi	Reigning monarchs, heirs apparent, and foreign heads of state	Status
Order of Taj .... (Order of the Crown)	High-ranking officers and government officials (national and foreign)	Outstanding service to Iran
Order of Homayun	Officers and government officials (national and foreign)	Outstanding service and devotion to duty
Order of Zolfaghar ...... (Order of the Conqueror)	Officers and enlisted men	Extraordinary gallantry in battle
Order of Sepah .... (Order of the Army)	Officers	Performance of duties in a superior fashion; exceptional initiative
Order of Liyaghat .... (Order of Merit)	Officers and medical personnel	Excellent service in army branches, educational institutions, or medical service
Medal of Eftekhar .... (Medal of Honor)	Military personnel (national and foreign)	Outstanding service and meritorious deeds
Order of Danesh .... (Order of Knowledge)	Officers and cadets	Scholarship
Order of Rastahiz	Military personnel	Active support of the shah in the 1953 coup d'etat
Order of 28th Amordad	-do-	Loyalty to the crown
Askari Medal .... (Military Medal)	Officers and enlisted men	Outstanding service in combat
Khedmat Medal .... (Service Medal)	Military personnel	Faithful service (ten to thirty years)
Science Medal	Officers	Contribution to military doctrine; honor graduates from Staff College
Sapah Varzash Medal ... (Sports Service Medal)	Military personnel	Sports promotion
Razi Medal .... (Health Medal)	Medical personnel	Exceptional performance
Parachute Medal	Air force personnel	Safe parachute descent from disabled aircraft

Summary of Developments in the International Oil Industry Affecting Iran's Oil Revenues

THE ERA OF cheap energy ended in the early 1970s when Iran and other members of the Organization of Petroleum Exporting Countries (OPEC) took control of pricing from the international oil companies. Petroleum-exporting nations tremendously increased their revenues, and the sudden change shocked most of the world.

One factor contributing to the sharp change in the price of energy was the steeply rising world demand caused by the mechanization of so many activities during the previous 100 years. One estimate indicated that the fuel and power consumed by an average American amounted to the energy equivalent of 200 full-time servants. Between 1962 and 1971 the estimated world demand for energy increased at an annual rate of 4.8 percent, a rate that would result in a doubling of demand every fifteen years. Energy requirements were accelerating so rapidly that observers predicted critical energy shortages in the twenty-first century and the exhaustion of known oil deposits relatively soon. World oil production was expected to peak about 1990 and decline thereafter. The primary energy sources—coal, oil, and natural gas—were being depleted at an astonishing rate.

Accompanying the growth in energy demand was a radical shift in the source of energy. When the world's first oil well began producing in 1859, men and animals supplied much of the world's power needs, supplemented by waterwheels, windmills, and steam generated by burning coal and wood. Coal powered an early part of the industrial revolution; in 1910, for example, coal supplied 90 percent of American commercial energy requirements. Coal still made up over half the world's commercial sources of energy in 1960, but oil was rapidly displacing it as the world's primary fuel.

Petroleum was used long before the Christian era. Noah reportedly waterproofed his ark with bitumen, an asphalt of Asia Minor used in ancient times in mud bricks and mortar. Early man also used oil for medicinal purposes and as fuel for lamps. Until modern times petroleum was collected from natural seepage. Not until 1859, when a drilling rig was set up on Oil Creek near Titusville, Pennsylvania, was oil sought commercially.

The oil industry grew rapidly after the first well came in. Within a decade Russia, Romania, Canada, Italy, and the United States were producing oil. Several more countries began producing soon afterward, and oil was discovered in Iran in 1908.

During the late nineteenth century petroleum was used primarily as a lubricant and as lamp fuel. In 1900 about 58 percent of petroleum consumption in the United States, the largest producer and consumer of oil, was in the form of kerosine for heaters and lamps; most of the rest was used as fuel oil for heating and in power plants.

Development of the internal-combustion engine vastly expanded the demand for petroleum products. World War I and World War II greatly accelerated engine development. Improvements in petroleum refining accompanied diversification and refinement of engines. Research added to the uses for petroleum products: a whole new field of petrochemicals emerged, producing dyes, fertilizers, and other products and increasing the demand for crude oil.

Petroleum was cleaner, more convenient, and cheaper than other fuels. In addition it was the unique fuel for internal-combustion engines, feedstock for petrochemicals, and base for lubricants. As a result the market for oil grew much more rapidly than the total demand for energy. World consumption (excluding communist countries) went from 1 million barrels (see Glossary) per day in 1915 to more than 5 million barrels per day in 1940 and about 48 million barrels per day in 1976. Between 1962 and 1971 world consumption of petroleum increased at an annual rate of 7 percent, a doubling of consumption in ten years. Of the energy consumed in 1970 by noncommunist countries, a little more than one-half came from oil. Coal accounted for nearly one-fourth, natural gas supplied about one-fifth, and nuclear power provided less than 0.5 percent; hydropower contributed the remainder.

Another factor contributing to the sharp rise in the price of energy was the growing international trade in petroleum products. The Soviet Union surpassed the United States as the largest producer of crude oil in 1974 as a result of the declining output of American fields (4 percent a year) that set in at the end of the 1960s. Both countries, however, consumed most of their own production. The Soviet Union began exporting relatively small amounts of petroleum in the 1950s, and the United States began importing increasing quantities of oil to meet consumption needs some years before. The main stimulus for the international petroleum trade came from the rapid economic growth and increased oil consumption in Western Europe and Japan after World War II. These countries lacked significant crude oil deposits and required large and increasing imports to satisfy growing consumption needs. Between 1962 and 1971 the petroleum imports of Western Europe more than doubled, and Japan's increased more than fourfold. Petroleum became the most important commodity in value in international trade, and by the mid-1970s petroleum products accounted for more than one-half of all seaborne commerce.

Geologists have determined the outlines of a large basin extending from the Taurus Mountains in southeast Turkey to the Arabian Sea in the south and underlying western Iran, eastern Saudi Arabia, Iraq, and most of the Persian Gulf. In 1976 this basin held 55 percent of the world's proven reserves (see fig. 15). The development of these Middle Eastern fields after World War

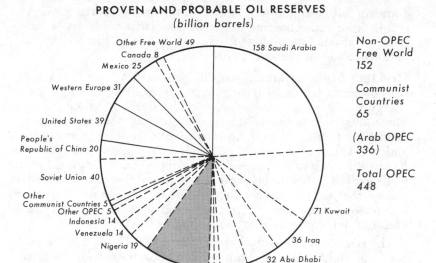

PROVEN AND PROBABLE OIL RESERVES
(billion barrels)

Other Free World 49
Canada 8
Mexico 25
Western Europe 31
United States 39
People's Republic of China 20
Soviet Union 40
Other Communist Countries 5
Other OPEC 5
Indonesia 14
Venezuela 14
Nigeria 19
Iran 60
Qatar 7
7 Algeria
25 Libya
32 Abu Dhabi
36 Iraq
71 Kuwait
158 Saudi Arabia

Non-OPEC Free World 152

Communist Countries 65

(Arab OPEC 336)

Total OPEC 448

TOTAL 665

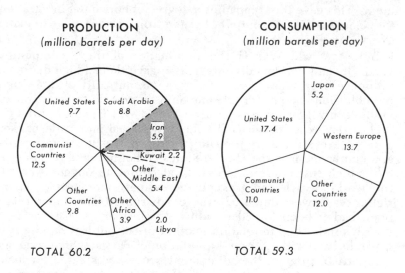

PRODUCTION
(million barrels per day)

United States 9.7
Saudi Arabia 8.8
Iran 5.9
Kuwait 2.2
Other Middle East 5.4
Communist Countries 12.5
Other Countries 9.8
Other Africa 3.9
2.0 Libya

TOTAL 60.2

CONSUMPTION
(million barrels per day)

Japan 5.2
United States 17.4
Western Europe 13.7
Communist Countries 11.0
Other Countries 12.0

TOTAL 59.3

Note—OPEC—Organization of Petroleum Exporting Countries; production includes natural gas liquids.

Figure 15. World Oil, 1975

II made them the world's most important crude oil source, supplying about 37 percent of world production in 1976. Crude oil production costs have been low because pressure in these prolific fields is generally high; transportation costs have been low because the fields are relatively close to water routes. The countries owning these reserves have relatively small populations, little domestic oil consumption, and an interest in exporting oil. As a result these states became the most important exporters of petroleum products, supplying nearly two-thirds of the oil in international trade in the mid-1970s.

Structure of the International Oil Industry

Another factor contributing to the sharp rise in the price of energy was the changing structure of the international oil industry. The industry is divided into several distinct phases—exploring, producing crude oil, refining into usable products, transporting, and marketing—and each phase requires costly investments. Even with modern techniques, for example, only 10 percent of the wells drilled in new fields produce oil or gas, and only 2 percent of the wells are significant producers. The industry as first developed consisted of a few very large companies vertically integrating all phases from exploration to marketing.

The petroleum industry before World War II was dominated by seven or eight major oil companies. Five of these were American; the others were European. These major companies held most of the foreign concession agreements for exploration and development. This gave the companies a degree of horizontal integration; they could adjust the output of crude from various areas to match overall marketing needs.

Before World War II the dominance of these companies, vertically and horizontally integrated, gave them a high degree of influence over supply and price through mutuality of interests if not collusion. The major oil companies were able to exert considerable control for some years after World War II; output from the prolific, low-cost Persian Gulf fields was phased into world markets without excessive disruption to pricing, petroleum investments, and employment in the United States and output and revenues in other high-cost crude oil areas. Coal mining throughout most of the world, which had become increasingly more costly as the richer seams were depleted, was less disrupted than it might have been had it been forced to adjust to cheaper oil. The price of energy diminished in relation to other prices but less rapidly than it would have with quicker exploitation of Persian Gulf crude and competitive pricing; the adjustment process was eased for many countries but at the cost of windfall profits to the oil companies.

By the 1950s the dominance of the major oil companies was gradually diminishing. The booming oil business encouraged the entrance of smaller oil companies. Some, such as the Getty Oil Company, were private firms; others, such as the French and Italian national petroleum companies, were state-owned businesses. The smaller companies won concessions in oil-producing countries by offering the host governments more favorable terms than those of the major oil companies. The Soviet Union also began to export oil over which the major companies had no control. These developments occurred within the broader framework of the bipolar relations between the leading communist and noncommunist countries. A group of developing countries, calling themselves the third world, were asserting more control over their own destiny and natural resources at the insistence of domestic nationalistic groups. Diminishing dominance by the major oil companies meant an increasing inability to match petroleum supplies to consumption needs. By the end of the 1950s a growing supply of oil started to push prices downward. The downward pressure on petroleum prices was favored by the consumer, but it reduced revenues for the oil-producing states.

Oil Pricing

Oil pricing is a vast and controversial subject complicated by the vertical integration of much of the industry and the secretiveness of the companies involved. Price can simply match supply and demand, or it can incorporate political decisions to achieve some possibly noneconomic goal. The United States, though an avowed advocate of free enterprise and free trade, had long interfered in the pricing of some commodities—as in price supports for major agricultural crops—and has regulated phases of the domestic oil and gas industry for particular goals that to a degree affected international prices of petroleum. Other oil-producing countries have also sought to exert various controls over their petroleum resources with the result that oil pricing and trade have reflected forces other than just supply and demand.

The major international oil companies are largely housed in the United States and have domestic fields, refineries, and outlets. There have been many United States congressional investigations of the oil companies, and their operations in foreign countries have been watched, threatened, and in some instances taken over by the host government. Contrary to their popular image the oil companies have not been free agents concerned only with maximizing profits. This is not to say, however, that they have not wielded considerable domestic as well as international power, done unsavory things, or secured huge profits.

Early in the 1900s the United States was the world's major oil exporter, and international crude oil pricing by the major oil companies was based on the United States price plus transportation costs. This was a base-point pricing system in which the price to the buyer was equivalent to the price of oil shipped to him from the Gulf of Mexico, regardless of actual source. There were other oil-exporting countries at the time, but the oil companies' price was the same to India, for example, even if the oil was shipped from Iran, with transportation costs substantially less than from the Gulf of Mexico. This system worked when there were only a few oil companies with mutual interests; it protected their investments in the United States and other areas and provided a high return for developing fields, such as those in the Persian Gulf region. How much the oil company kept and how much the government owning the field received depended on the concession agreement, but there was not a downward pressure on the price of crude oil produced in the new foreign fields in the Caribbean and Middle East.

Between 1945 and 1950 the increased supply of crude from foreign fields, the emergence of independent oil companies, and United States pressure applied through its help in rebuilding postwar Europe brought about major modification of the single base-point price system. The major oil companies set crude oil prices in conjunction with transportation costs from actual point of shipment to establish a series of equalization points—points where the landed price of Middle East oil was the same as crude from the Gulf of Mexico and Venezuela. The equalization point was first southern Europe, then London, and eventually New York. The shifting of the equalization point northward and westward increased transportation costs, thereby requiring lower quotations for Middle East crude. When the equalization point was New York, Middle East oil had a competitive advantage in European markets formerly held by United States, Mexican, and Venezuelan crude.

The oil companies were caught in conflicting squeezes. The cost of producing oil in the Middle East was a fraction of that in Venezuela, which in turn was substantially less than that in the United States. If prices were based on cost of production, Middle East crude would have forced other countries out of the market. The oil companies, American politicians, and American businesses did not want this. In fact Morris A. Adelman, in his authoritative study *The World Petroleum Market,* concluded that an effective coalition in the United States limited imports of foreign oil for the large United States market for at least ten years before official import quotas were established in 1959. The oil companies would have profited from more imports, and the Middle Eastern oil-producing countries would have been happy, at least for a while, if the companies had taken more oil, because their revenues would have gone up. However, the Venezuelans and other relatively high-cost producers did not want to be forced out of crude production. The oil companies faced a no-win situation. Each producing country wanted to remain in the oil business and earn more money but did not want to suffer competition from cheap suppliers or have the price of its oil go down. The dominance of the major companies over the industry reduced for all producers the pain of adjustment to the large supply of low-cost Middle East crude entering the market.

From about 1950 to the early 1970s there was a system of posted prices for each country—prices at which oil companies would sell crude oil to anybody. Transportation costs were not included. Because anybody generally meant independent oil companies that the major oil companies did not want to encourage, posted prices were higher than the actual price at which the bulk of crude oil sales took place. Moreover a short-term oversupply of crude developed in the late 1950s as newly discovered fields began to produce, causing a downward pressure on crude oil prices. By the 1960s, if not earlier, the posted price became only a reference point for calculating the taxes and royalty payments due oil-producing states under the concession agreements.

Economists have had difficulty in analyzing the pricing system because of inadequate data to establish what actual market prices were; perhaps four-fifths of crude oil sales were bookkeeping transactions within integrated companies. There is widespread agreement, however, that actual market prices of crude oil had a substantial downward trend between 1950 and 1970, although posted prices remained fixed for prolonged periods.

The posted price per barrel of Saudi Arabian light (34 degrees on the American Petroleum Institute (API) gravity scale) marker crude oil was US$2.05 in June 1948, US$1.70 in November 1950, US$2.08 in June 1958, US$1.80 in August 1960, and US$2.18 in February 1971. The marker price is the basic price for a typical regional crude—in this case Arabian light used for the Persian Gulf—from which regional prices are derived. The posted prices of Iranian light crude were very close to Saudi prices (see ch. 10).

Although the major oil companies exerted considerable influence on crude oil prices, the oil industry was not a closed system, and market forces had an impact. Before 1973 crude oil was priced largely in the context of supply and demand; after 1973 crude oil pricing took into consideration the costs of other energy sources and the long-term supply of petroleum. The frame of reference for pricing decisions was vastly broader and less favorable to consumers than the one that had previously prevailed.

Organization of Petroleum Exporting Countries

The sheer size and integrated nature of the major international oil companies afforded them considerable advantages when negotiating concession agreements with countries having known or probable deposits. Moreover many of the concession agreements were arranged with developing countries generally lacking in sophistication and usually hard pressed for funds. The governments of these countries often failed to appreciate the value of their resources and were frequently so desperate for funds that they lacked bargaining power even if they understood the value of their oil. The oil states of the Persian Gulf region were certainly in this position when the original concession agreements were let before World War II.

Efforts by oil-producing countries to exercise control over their resources without causing excessive domestic economic and financial disruption were difficult because of the pressures the oil companies brought to bear. Mexico nationalized its oil industry in 1938, but it was a costly and prolonged experience. When Iran nationalized its oil industry in 1951, the oil companies refused to buy or transport the oil, causing a severe financial and political crisis in the country for some years (see ch. 10).

OPEC was more than a decade in gestation. Part of the initial impetus came from Venezuela, which in 1943 began to press the international oil companies for more control over and a better return on its oil resources. Conscious of Mexico's difficult experience, Venezuela established contacts with Persian Gulf oil states in an attempt to develop coordinated efforts among oil exporters. Some analysts have interpreted the rapid development of the Persian Gulf oil fields after World War II by the major oil companies as both a means of forcing Venezuela to temper its demands and an expansion of an alternative source of oil should the Venezuelan government's demands become unreasonable. Other observers stressed the low cost and other advantages inherent in Persian Gulf oil as a natural cause for development of Middle East fields.

The Middle East countries recognized the usefulness of concerted action to protect their interests. Many of the countries, however, were desperately in need of revenues and independently pushed the oil companies to take more of their oil to increase their income. Not until the oil companies unilaterally cut the posted price in the spring of 1959 to reflect the glut of oil on the market and the growing discounts that they had been giving on posted prices did a movement begin toward joint action. In response to the price cuts the League of Arab States (Arab League) sponsored the first Arab oil conference in the summer of 1959; Venezuela and Iran attended as observers.

As a result of the contacts developed during the 1959 conference, Saudi Arabia and Venezuela issued a joint statement in May 1960 urging all oil-producing countries to adopt common policies to safeguard their economic interests. In August 1960 the oil companies further cut the posted prices of Middle East crude oil. The price reduction lopped US$30 million from Saudi Arabia's estimated income for the year and thus severely hampered efforts to balance the budget and execute development programs. When the Saudi Arabian minister of petroleum attended an emergency meeting of authorities from oil-exporting states in Baghdad after the price reduction, he argued vigorously and successfully for the founding of OPEC.

OPEC was formed in September 1960 by Iran, Iraq, Kuwait, Saudi Arabia, and Venezuela to develop some bargaining power among oil-exporting countries vis-à-vis the international oil companies. Other countries joined subsequently. By 1977 Algeria, Ecuador, Gabon, Indonesia, Libya, Nigeria, Qatar, and the United Arab Emirates (UAE) were members, and applications for membership from other oil-producing countries were under consideration.

The foundation document of the organization noted the dependence of its members on revenue from oil exports, the wasting nature of the petroleum resources, and the interdependence of all countries. The first objectives of OPEC were to restore crude oil prices to the 1958 level and to stabilize prices through mutual cooperation with the oil companies. OPEC acknowledged the need for oil prices that balanced the interests of producing and consuming nations and provided a fair return on investments of the oil companies. The founding members agreed to stick together against efforts by the oil companies to woo any member country or apply sanctions against one that was following a unanimous decision of OPEC.

OPEC policy is officially set almost entirely at its semiannual or more frequent conferences of high-level representatives from each member government. Unanimously adopted resolutions of these conferences become oil policy for the member governments. In 1975 OPEC countries controlled about 70 percent of the world's crude oil reserves, over 50 percent of world oil production, and more than 80 percent of petroleum exports; OPEC resolutions therefore had considerable impact.

Conferences are supported by a full-time staff, including a secretariat, an extensive petroleum library, a legal department versed in petroleum matters, and a technical department that follows technical developments in the oil industry. OPEC selected Vienna as its headquarters site. An economic commission was established in 1964 with liaison to the top levels of the oil departments of the member governments. The economic commission collects data, including apparently very good petroleum statistics, and prepares studies. In early 1977 the studies were not available to the public but appeared to have been the basis for many of OPEC's resolutions since 1970.

OPEC was unsuccessful during the 1960s in restoring crude oil prices to the level preceding the cuts of 1959 and 1960, but it won half the battle in that the oil companies did not make further cuts. OPEC also fostered negotiations with the oil companies to increase the revenues of the oil-exporting states. The negotiations concerned methods of calculating and increasing royalty payments and taxes due the host government that raised the costs of producing crude oil. The added costs at least partly explained the absence of further price cuts in a situation tending toward oversupply in the international crude oil markets.

The payments due host governments were spelled out in the concession agreements granted the oil companies. The more important concessions had been granted before World War II, when the host governments had little bargaining power. As a result the financial return to the host governments was usually quite low. Venezuela started a major and important adjustment in concession agreements in 1943 by legislating a 50-percent tax on the net income earned by oil companies in the country, and it became effective in 1947. A similar arrangement was discussed in Iran in 1948 but not put into effect until establishment of the consortium in 1954 (see ch. 10). The so-called fifty-fifty profit sharing was negotiated by Saudi Arabia with the Arabian American Oil Company (Aramco) in 1950, and it had become standard in the

Persian Gulf by 1952. Profit-sharing arrangements substantially increased oil revenues for host governments. OPEC helped refine the calculations of taxes and royalties to the advantage of the host governments during the 1960s. OPEC also helped the oil-exporting governments negotiate considerably better terms in concession agreements granted after its founding.

The June 1967 War between Israel and several Arab states started a chain of events that led to a transformation in the world energy market. The war closed the Suez Canal, and several Arab oil states embargoed oil exports briefly. The canal remained closed until June 1975. The transportation problems of the much longer haul around Africa to Europe were partly offset by the use of new supertankers and by the increasing oil production in Africa, particularly in Algeria and Libya, which were close to southern Europe. Dependence on North African oil became even greater in 1970 as a result of civil war in Nigeria and disruption of operations of the pipeline from Saudi Arabia to the Mediterranean coast in Lebanon. The new military regime in Libya seized the opportunity of its enhanced position to cut back crude oil production and to secure higher posted prices and tax rates from the oil companies under the threat of cessation of exports if their demands were not met. An independent oil company, Occidental, agreed to the much more favorable terms for Libya, and other oil companies acceded to Libyan demands in September 1970.

Meanwhile in a July 1970 speech, the Algerian representative to OPEC requested that other members seize control of pricing their internationally traded crude oil. OPEC followed with a unanimous resolution in December 1970 calling for substantial revisions and increases in crude oil pricing. Negotiations were held in Tehran in February 1971 for the Persian Gulf region. The posted price of Persian Gulf oil was raised by more than one-third, provision was made for yearly price increases of about 5 percent a year until 1975 to compensate for inflation, and the tax rate was raised to 55 percent. Libya negotiated an agreement in April 1971 whereby it won a substantially larger increase in the posted price plus an increase of the tax rate to 55 percent. Algeria pressed for an increase in crude oil prices above that won by the Persian Gulf but less than that won by Libya. Venezuela legislated rather than negotiated price and tax increases in March 1971.

These assorted actions effectively transferred control over crude oil prices from the oil companies to the producing states. When the United States dollar was devalued in 1971, a clause in the Persian Gulf and Libyan agreements was invoked for new negotiations. An 8.5-percent increase in posted prices was arrived at in Geneva in January 1972 to compensate for the devaluation, and further negotiations took place again after another devaluation in 1973.

OPEC members had long discussed having a hand in oil operations, but the oil companies made only token gestures. Discussion switched to taking control of the oil industries in their countries, and it was evident that some members would eventually act. Action came suddenly. Algeria and Libya seized properties of some concessionaires in 1971, and Iraq nationalized some of its fields in 1972. In January 1972 Arab OPEC members from the Persian Gulf region began negotiations with the oil companies for a gradual takeover of company operations through participation. Participation—essentially buying part ownership of the operating company—was far less drastic than nationalization, and it had the particular advantage that the services, technical skills, and marketing chains of the oil companies were retained during the takeover. Participation avoided a problem faced by nearly all of the Arab oil states on the Persian Gulf—an acute shortage of highly trained personnel capable of managing their oil fields.

The Saudi oil minister, Shaykh Ahmad Zaki Yamani, led OPEC participation negotiations during several months of hard bargaining in 1972. The result was an immediate 25-percent participation in ownership by the oil states with 51-percent participation by 1983 through annual 5-percent increments starting in 1979. Individual Persian Gulf oil states negotiated actual arrangements, such as compensation to the oil companies for the equity they yielded, as well as the process of phasing the country into marketing so that the companies could continue to meet their sales contracts. Some of the arrangements were not completed until 1974, but they were backdated to January 1, 1973.

The Kuwait National Assembly upset the schedule for a gradual increase in ownership when it refused to ratify the 25-percent participation agreement. Some members demanded 100-percent Kuwaiti ownership. Kuwait's negotiators arranged for 60-percent participation in 1974, effective January 1. Most other OPEC members also negotiated 60-percent ownership effective in 1974. In early 1975 the Kuwait government announced its intention to buy 100-percent ownership in the main producing company, and negotiations were completed in December but backdated to March 1975. Saudi Arabia negotiated 100-percent participation in Aramco in early 1976, although final arrangements were not completed by early 1978. Other gulf oil states were negotiating full ownership in early 1978.

The October 1973 War between Israel and Arab states created further disarray in oil markets. A selective embargo and phased cutback in crude production was imposed by several Arab countries. Iran, however, increased rather than cut back oil exports. No oil-consuming country was seriously hurt by the embargo, because the oil companies juggled supplies to keep oil flowing to all countries, but all consumers felt the threat and the supply pinch. Bidding for oil from Iran reportedly reached US$17 a barrel.

OPEC, and particularly the six member states in the gulf region, took the opportunity to raise the price of crude oil almost twelve times in 1973 and then raised it by more than 100 percent at the beginning of 1974. The posted price for Arabian marker crude, on which other gulf prices were based, was US$5.12 a barrel in

449

October 1973; the price became US$11.25 effective January 1, 1974. The posted price remained a reference price for assessing taxes and royalty payments. The actual selling price of crude was 93 percent of the posted price, or US$10.46 per barrel. A 10-percent increase decreed by OPEC in September 1975 raised Arabian marker crude to US$12.38 posted price and US$11.51 actual price per barrel. OPEC justified the more than fourfold increase in prices of crude between 1971 and 1975 as necessary to approximate the true cost of energy, compensate the oil producers adequately for depletion of their limited resources, and make up for the long period when oil prices were kept low while prices for manufactured goods continuously increased.

Several times during 1974 the Arab states of the Persian Gulf also increased the royalty rates on each barrel of oil produced and the tax rates on foreign oil companies. The purpose was to diminish the wide differential between the costs to the oil companies of equity oil and oil bought back from the host governments. Equity oil was much cheaper than buy-back oil. As a result of a meeting in Abu Dhabi the UAE, Qatar, and Saudi Arabia increased the royalty rate to 20 percent and the tax rate on foreign oil companies to 85 percent while dropping the posted price for Arabian marker crude by US$0.40 per barrel effective November 1, 1974. The changes raised the cost of equity oil close to the price of buy-back oil and resulted in an average return to the governments of just over US$10 per barrel. In a December 1974 meeting OPEC members agreed to move toward such a unitary price system. OPEC members and most other oil-producing countries adopted the same royalty and tax rates, which were still in effect in early 1978.

The impact of all these changes on oil revenues of the producing countries was tremendous. Saudi Arabia illustrated the situation for the oil states on the Persian Gulf. Saudi revenues per barrel increased from US$0.22 in 1948 to US$0.89 in 1970. By 1973 they had reached US$1.56 per barrel, and in 1974 they were above US$10.10 per barrel. By the beginning of 1976 revenues were US$11.15 per barrel because of the OPEC price increase in October 1975. Iran's oil revenues increased from US$4.4 billion in 1973 to US$21.4 billion in 1974.

After 1973 OPEC members had control of crude oil pricing and a large degree of control over production. The members had not given OPEC authority to allocate production among producers, however, and OPEC had no formal means of matching supply to demand. This need arose immediately; world oil consumption declined in 1974 and declined further in 1975 because of a recession in the industrialized countries and conservation measures by all oil-consuming nations. Strains were apparent among OPEC members because of lower production and declining revenues.

In early 1978 OPEC remained a loose confederation of diverse nations that had united to combat the power of the international oil companies. Its diversity had been its salvation so far in the difficult task of controlling supply to maintain price. There were two main groups within OPEC. The first was made up of oil exporters with large reserves and small populations, such as Saudi Arabia, the UAE, and Kuwait. This group might be called the low-price group, because they were earning more oil revenues than they could profitably invest. Immediate higher prices were not very attractive because they would probably intensify development by industrialized countries of new technology and energy sources. The countries' interest was in a moderate price and a slow rate of exploitation so that their reserves would continue to finance their economic development long into the future.

The second group might be called the high-price advocates. It was made up of such countries as Iran and Indonesia, which had relatively small oil reserves, large populations, and economic potentials other than oil. Because their reserves would not last long, they wanted to maximize current earnings on their limited reserves through high prices. They would then invest the earnings primarily in their own country to develop other resources and industries for self-sustaining growth. Some of these countries, Iran for one, had pushed for substantially higher oil prices since 1973 than those adopted by OPEC members.

In 1974 and 1975 OPEC members maintained their united front and even increased export prices in the face of reduced demand for crude oil by importing countries. Several countries cut back crude production to avoid an oversupply that might lead to price cutting by members pressed for funds. Saudi Arabia, Kuwait, and other Arab gulf states shouldered much of the burden of lower crude production and revenues to avoid pressure on OPEC prices in the years from 1973 through 1976.

Saudi Arabia's huge reserves and production potential make it pivotal in OPEC discussions and provide nearly veto power in most OPEC decisions. Saudi officials advocated only a 5-percent price increase in September 1975, but they reluctantly accepted a 10-percent increase as a compromise between their position and that of members such as Iran, which wanted a 20- to 25-percent increase. The Saudis clearly indicated opposition to further increases in the immediate future, however.

The OPEC meeting in Qatar in December 1976 produced a major test between members advocating higher prices and those favoring lower prices. Iran sought a 15-percent price increase, and others wanted an even larger increase. Saudi Arabia indicated a willingness to accept a 5-percent increase at most. In an attempted compromise a 10-percent price increase for marker crude effective January 1, 1977, and a further 5-percent increase effective July 1, 1977, were proposed with the implicit understanding that the July increase could be altered if circumstances warranted. Eleven of the thirteen members voted for the compromise and put it into effect at the beginning of 1977 even though the decision was not unanimous. On January 1, 1977, Iran's posted price increased from US$11.62 to

US$12.81 per barrel for light crude (34-degree API).

Saudi Arabia and the UAE increased posted prices for marker crude by only 5 percent, effective January 1, 1977 (from US$11.51 to US$12.09 per barrel for Arabian light 34-degree API). Moreover Saudi officials said that they would increase production to full capacity (nearly 12 million barrels per day) if needed to minimize the impact of the larger price increase by most OPEC members. Saudi officials justified breaking with OPEC's price unanimity because the larger price increase would, in their judgment, threaten the weak economic recovery in progress in industrialized countries at the beginning of 1977 and perhaps undermine political institutions in Italy, Great Britain, and France.

During early 1977 OPEC's two-tiered pricing system caused problems. Saudi Arabia's crude oil production and sales increased, for example, while Iran's declined. Some observers viewed the two-tiered pricing system as largely a test of strength between the two countries. Saudi Arabia was the apparent winner because the 5-percent price increase scheduled for July was not put into effect. At the December 1977 OPEC meeting in Venezuela, Iran and Saudi Arabia were successful in arranging for a continuation of the OPEC price freeze lasting until late 1978. Moreover a surplus of available crude oil on the world market during the second half of 1977 led to price discounts by several OPEC countries including Iran. By late 1977 the two-tiered pricing system had largely disappeared.

Another source of tension existed among OPEC members in late 1977 although it had also been present in 1975 and 1976. OPEC pricing procedures had allowed individual members to determine the application of OPEC price changes to the premiums and discounts on each country's crude, which varied because of sulfur content, gravity, shipping costs, and other factors. Members including Iran often resorted to adjustments of premiums and discounts when they found it difficult to market the quantity of oil planned. Some of the price discounts provoked charges of undercutting from other members particularly during the period of oversupply of crude during the latter part of 1977. The issue of premiums and discounts had received increasing attention at OPEC meetings, but a satisfactory resolution had not been achieved by late 1977.

Outside analysts differed about OPEC's future. Some thought that the centrifugal forces were too great and would lead to its dissolution as had happened to other cartels. Other observers believed that the members would manage to avoid a rupture that would be costly to all. This latter view gained adherents when the open split and two-tiered pricing system gradually resolved itself in 1977.

Organization of Arab Petroleum Exporting Countries

The Organization of Arab Petroleum Exporting Countries (OAPEC) was formed in 1968, largely on the initiative of Saudi Arabia, to provide a supplemental organization for the major Arab oil exporters. Saudi Arabia, Kuwait, and Libya were the founding members. Membership was originally limited to Arab states whose "principal and basic source of national income" was oil. The OAPEC constitution was subsequently amended to permit Egypt and Algeria to join. By 1977 Bahrain, Iraq, Qatar, Syria, and the UAE had joined, bringing the membership to ten countries.

OAPEC has two functions. One is to develop cooperation and promote Arab interests, as in the fund of US$80 million established in 1975 for Arab oil-importing states experiencing foreign exchange difficulties. The second function is to promote joint ventures among interested members in various phases of the oil business. The organization was a juridical entity that could participate in commercial ventures. By early 1977 OAPEC had formed the Arab Maritime Petroleum Transport Company; the Arab Shipbuilding and Repair Company, its first project a dry dock in Bahrain; and the Arab Petroleum Investments Company to finance petrochemical plants in the Arab world. OAPEC representatives decided in 1975 to set up an Arab energy institute to study alternative energy sources and the best use of oil and to establish a petroleum services company in Libya to study downstream (see Glossary) investments. OAPEC was also working on the question of a single Arab currency.

*   *   *

The literature on the oil industry in general and on specific areas is quite large, rapidly growing, and often polemical. Morris A. Adelman's *The World Petroleum Market* is a basic study of the industry, though somewhat overtaken by events since 1973. Leonard Mosley's *Power Play* presents a readable account of the intrigues and issues in the initial concessions granted by the oil states of the Persian Gulf regions. Michael Field's *A Hundred Million Dollars a Day,* Neil H. Jacoby's *Multinational Oil,* and Anthony Sampson's *The Seven Sisters: The Great Oil Companies and the World They Made* are among the many studies easily available in the mid-1970s. OPEC's *Annual Statistical Bulletin* provides a considerable amount of data, and most OPEC members publish statistical yearbooks. (For further information see Bibliography.)

Bibliography

A

Abolfathi, Farid, and Leo Hazelwood. "How Iran Spends Its Oil Revenue: Utilization of Capital in a Major Oil Exporting Country with Rapidly Diminishing Reserves." (Paper presented at the 1970 Annual Meeting of Midwest Political Science Association, April 29–May 1, 1976.) Chicago; 1976.

————. *Medium Term Ability of the Oil Producing Countries to Absorb Real Goods and Services.* (Report prepared for the U.S. Department of State.) Arlington: March 1976.

————. *Medium Term Ability of the Oil Producing Countries to Acquire Energy-Related Technologies.* (Report prepared for the U.S. Department of State.) Arlington: November 1976.

Abrahamian, Ervand. "Communism and Communalism in Iran: The Tudeh and the Firqah-i Dimukrat" *International Journal of Middle East Studies* [London], 1, No. 4, October 1970, 291–316.

————. "Oriental Despotism: The Case of Qajar Iran," *International Journal of Middle East Studies* [London], 5, No. 1, January 1974, 3–31.

Adelman, Morris A. "The Political Economy of World Oil." (Paper presented at the Annual Meeting of the American Economic Association.) New York: December 1973.

————. "Politics, Economics, and World Oil," *American Economic Review*, 64, No. 2, May 1974, 58–67.

————. *The World Petroleum Market.* Baltimore: Johns Hopkins University Press, 1972.

Admanov, L. and L. Teploy. "CENTO: After the Tehran Session," *International Affairs* [Moscow], No. 6, June 1969, 81–83.

Ahanchian, Amir H. "Foreign Capital Investment, Development, and Dependency: A Study of a Multinational Corporation in Iran." (Paper presented at 1977 Meeting of International Studies Association, St. Louis, Missouri. March 16–20, 1977.)

Algar, Hamid. *Mirza Malkum Khan.* Berkeley: University of California Press, 1973.

————. *Religion and State in Iran Seventeen Eighty-five to Nineteen Six: The Role of the Ulama in the Qajar Period.* Berkeley: University of California Press, 1969.

Amnesty International. *Iran.* (Briefing Paper, No. 7.) London: X, 1976.

Amuzegar, Jahangir. *Iran: An Economic Profile.* Washington: The Middle East Institute, 1977.

Amuzegar, Jahangir, and M. Ali Fekrat. *Iran: Economic Development under Dualistic Conditions.* Chicago: University of Chicago Press, 1971.

Annual Statistical Bulletin, 1974. Vienna: OPEC, June 1975.

Arasteh, A. Reza in collaboration with Josephine Arasteh. *Man and Society in Iran.* Leiden, Netherlands. E.J. Brill, 1970.

Arberry, Arthur J. *Shiraz, Persian City of Saints and Poets.*

Norman: University of Oklahoma Press, 1960.

Avery, Peter. "The Many Faces of Iran's Foreign Policy," *New Middle East* [London], No. 47, August 1972, 17–19.

B

Bagley, F.R.C. "A Bright Future After Oil: Dams and Agro-Industry in Khuzistan," *Middle East Journal*, 30, No. 1, Winter 1976, 25–35.

Bakhtiar, Lelah. *Sufi, Expressions of the Mystic Quest*. New York: Avon Books, 1976.

Balance of Payments Yearbook. Vol. 28. Washington: International Monetary Fund, 1977.

Baldwin, Gordon B. "The Legal System of Iran," *International Lawyer*, 7, No. 2, April 1973, 493–504.

Balfour, Paul H.G. "Recent Developments in the Persian Gulf," *Royal Central Asian Journal* [London], LVI, Part I, February 1969, 12–19.

Banani, Amin. *The Modernization of Iran, 1921–1941*. Stanford: Stanford University Press, 1961.

Bank Markazi Iran. *Annual Report and Balance Sheet, 2535*. Tehran: Bank Markazi Iran, 1977.

Baraheni, Reza. "The Shah's Executioner," *Index on Censorship* [London], 5, No. 1, Spring 1976, 13–20.

_____. "Terror in Iran," *New York Review of Books*, 23, No. 17, October 28, 1976, 21–25.

Barth, Fredrik. *Nomads of South Persia*. London: Oslo University Press, 1961.

Beaumont, Peter. "Water Resource Development in Iran," *Geographical Journal* [London], 140, 3, October 1974, 419–431.

Becker, Abraham S. "Oil and the Persian Gulf in Soviet Policy in the 1970s." (Rand Corporation Memo No. P–4743.) Santa Monica: Rand Corporation, December 1971. (mimeo.).

Bedore, James and Louis Turner. "Saudi and Iranian Petrochemicals and Oil Refining," *International Affairs* [London], 53, No. 4, October 1977, 572–586.

Beeman, William O. "Status, Style and Strategy in Iranian Interaction." *Anthropological Linguistics*, 18, October 1976, 305–22.

_____. "What is (Iranian) National Character? A Sociolinguistic Approach." *Iranian Studies*, Winter 1976, 22–48.

Bharier, Julian. "The Growth of Towns and Villages in Iran, 1900–66," *Middle Eastern Studies* [London], 8, No. 1, January 1972, 51–61.

Bhattacharya, Anindya D. "Financial Realities Behind Oil Power in Iran," *Foreign Service Journal*, August 1976, p. 9, 10, and 28.

Bill, James A. "Modernization and Reform from Above: The Case of Iran," *Journal of Politics*, 32, No. 1, February 1970, 19–40.

_____. "The Plasticity of Informal Politics: The Case of Iran," *Middle East Journal*, 27, No. 2, Spring 1973, 131–151.

Bill, James Alban. "Iran: Is the Shah Pushing It Too Fast?" *Christian Science Monitor*, November 9, 1977, 16–17.

_____. *The Politics of Iran: Groups, Classes and Modernization.* Columbus, Ohio: Charles E. Merrill Publishing, 1972.

Binder, Leonard. "Iranian Nationalism." Pages 224–230 in Benjamin Rivlin and Joseph Szyliowicz (eds.), *The Contemporary Middle East.* New York: Random House, 1965

Black-Michaud, Jacob. "An Ethnographic and Ecological Survey of Luristan, Western Persia: Modernization in a Nomadic Pastoral Society." *Middle Eastern Studies* [London], 10, 2, May 1974, 210–228.

Blanchet, Jean Pierre. *Rapport d'information fait au monde la formiccion des affaires sociales (1) a la suite d'une mission d'information chargée d'étudier les problems sanitares et sociaux se pasend en Inde, en Indonesie et en Iran.* Paris: Senate Commission des affaires sociales, No. 153, Seconde Session, Ordinaire de 1973–74.

Blandy, Richard, and Mahyar Nashat. "The Education Corps in Iran: A Survey of Its Social and Economic Aspects," *International Labour Review* [Geneva], 93, No. 5, May 1966.

Borshchevsky, Yu. E., and Yu. E. Bregel. "The Preparation of a Bio-Bibliographical Survey of Persian Literature," *International Journal of Middle East Studies* [London], 3, No. 2, April 1972, 169–186.

Branigan, William. "Tehran Sensitive about Renown of Its Secret Police," *Washington Post*, September 4, 1976, A7.

Bromberger, Christian and Jean-Pierre Digard. "Pourquoi, comment des cartes ethnographique de l'Iran." *Objets et Mondes* [Paris], 15, 1, 1975, 7–24.

Buell, Floyd Clarence. "Communism in Iran." Unpublished Master's thesis. Washington: School of Public and International Affairs, George Washington University, 1968.

Burrell, R.M. "Iranian Foreign Policy During the Last Decade," *Asian Affairs* [London], 61, February 1974, 7–15.

Burrell, R.M. and Alvin J. Cottrell. *Iran, Afghanistan, Pakistan: Tensions and Dilemmas.* (The Washington Papers Series.) Beverly Hills: Sage Publications, 1974.

Butler, William J. "Civil and Political Rights in Iran," *World Issue* [London], 1, No. 1, October–November 1976, 20–22.

Butler, William J., and Georges Levasseur. *Human Rights and the Legal System in Iran: Two Reports by William J. Butler, Esq., and Professor George Levasseur.* Geneva: International Commission of Jurists, March 1976.

C

Campbell, John C. "Oil Power in the Middle East." *Foreign Affairs*, 56, No. 1, October 1977, 89–110.

Carey, Jane Perry Clark, and Andrew Galbraith Carey. "Iranian Agriculture and its Development," *International Journal of Middle East Studies*, [London], 7, No. 3, July 1976, 359–382.

Chubin, Shahram and Sepehr Zabih. *The Foreign Relations of Iran: A Developing State in a Zone of Great-Power Conflict.*

Berkeley: University of California Press, 1974.

Citibank in Iran. *Investment Guide.* Tehran, 1976.

Clark, B.D. "Changing Population Patterns." Pages 68–96 in J.I. Clarke and W.B. Fisher (eds.), *Populations of the Middle East and North Africa: A Geographical Approach.* New York: Africana Publishing, 1972.

_____. "Iran: Changing Population Patterns." Pages 83–111 in Jamshid A, Momeni. *The Population of Iran: A Selection of Readings.* East-West Population Institute, The East-West Center, Honolulu, Hawaii and the Pahlavi University, Shiraz, Iran, 1977.

Cobban, Helena. "Shah Strives to Revitalize Iran Politics." *Christian Science Monitor,* September 20, 1977, 26.

Connell, John. "Economic Changes in an Iranian Village," *Middle East Journal* [London], 28, No. 3, Summer 1974.

Cooley, John K. "Iran feels impact of Carter human-rights messages," *Christian Science Monitor,* March 3, 1977, 6.

_____. "New-found unity on Persian Gulf," *Christian Science Monitor,* April 28, 1975, 3.

_____. "Saudis, Iranians try to soothe troubled waters," *Christian Science Monitor,* March 9, 1977, 12.

_____. "Shah's New Team Watched for Continued Rights Gains," *Christian Science Monitor,* August 24, 1977, 6.

Cottrell, Alvin J. "Iran, The Arabs and the Persian Gulf," *Orbis,* XVII, No. 3, Fall 1973, 978–988.

_____. "Iran and the Central Treaty Organization." Pages 68–83 in the Royal United Services Institute for Defense Studies (ed.), *R.U.S.I. and Brassey's Defense Yearbook 1976–77.* Boulder, Colorado: Westview Press, 1976.

_____. *Iran: Diplomacy in a Regional and Global Context.* Washington: American Enterprise Institute for Public Policy Research, 1975, 1–21.

_____. "A New Persian Hegemony," *Interplay,* 3, No. 12, September 1970, 9–15.

Cottrell, Alvin J. and R.M. Burrell (eds.). *The Indian Ocean: Its Political, Economic, and Military Importance.* New York: Praeger, 1972.

Croizat, Victor J. "Imperial Iranian Gendarmerie," *Marine Corps Gazette,* October 1975, 28–31.

Crowe, Kenneth C. "The Shah's American Baby." (The Alicia Patterson Foundation in KCC–10) June 4, 1976.

Cumming-Bruce, Nicholas. "Iran: Government Changes Signify Move to Pragmatism." *Middle East Economic Digest* [London], August 12, 1977, 5–6.

_____. *Iran: A MEED Special Report* [London], February 1977.

D

Davidson, Harutiun. "The Application of Some Basic Psychological Theories in the Iranian Cultural Context," *International Social Science Journal,* 25, No. 4, 1973, 532–546.

Defense and Foreign Affairs Handbook 1976–77. Washington: Gregory R. Copley, 1976.

Demographic Yearbook, 1976. New York: Statistical Office. Department of Economic and Social Affairs, United Nations, 1976.

Denman, D.R. *The King's Vista: A Land Reform Which Has Changed the Face of Persia.* The Keep, Berkhamstead, Hertsfordshire: Graphic Publications, 1973.

Duchesne-Guillemin, Jacques. *Religion of Ancient Iran.* Bombay: Tata Press, 1973.

E

"Education: Scattered Brains, But Iran Is Out to Harness Them," *To the Point, International* [Antwerp], 4, No. 1, January 10, 1977, 49.

Elahi, Cyrus. "Stability: What is it? A Note on Iran." (Prepared for delivery at the Sixth Annual Conference of the Middle East Studies Association of North America, State University of New York at Binghamton.) November 2–4, 1972.

Elwell-Sutton, L.P. *Modern Iran.* New York: Gordon Press, 1976.

_____. "Political Parties in Iran," *Middle East Journal*, 3, No. 1, January 1949, 45–62.

English, Paul Ward. "Selections from City and Village in Iran," Pages 308–343 in Louise E. Sweet (ed.). *Peoples and Cultures of the Middle East, Volume 2: Life in the Cities, Towns and Countryside.* New York: The Natural History Press, 1970.

F

Fallaci, Oriana. "An Oriana Fallaci Interview: The Shah of Iran." *The New Republic*, December 1, 1973, 16–21.

Farman-Farmaian, Sattareh. "Women and decision making: with special reference to Iran and other developing countries." *Labour and Society* [Geneva], 1, 2, April 1976, 25–32.

Farmayan, Hafez F. "Observations on Sources for the Study of Nineteenth and Twentieth Century Iranian History," *International Journal of Middle East Studies* [London], 5, No. 1, January 1974, 32–49.

_____. *The Foreign Policy of Iran: A Historical Analysis.* Salt Lake City: University of Utah, 1971.

Faroughy, Ahmad. "Repression and Iran," *Index on Censorship* [London], 3, No. 4, Winter 1974, 9–18.

Farvar, Mohammed Taghi and Catherine Razavi Farvar. "The lessons of Lorestan," *Ceres* [Rome], 9, 2, April 1976, 44–47.

Fazel, G. Reza. "Social and Political Status of Women among Pastoral Nomads: The Boyr Ahmad of Southwest Iran." *Anthropological Quarterly*, 50, 2, April 1977, 77–87.

Feili, Omran Yahya, and Arlene R. Fromchuck. "The Kurdish Struggle for Independence," *Middle East Review*, IX, No. 1, Fall 1976, 47–59.

Fesharaki, Fereidun. *Development of the Iranian Oil Industry: International and Domestic Aspects.* (Praeger Special Studies in International Economics and Development.) New York:

Praeger, February 1976.

Firoozi, Ferydoon. "The Iranian Budgets: 1964–1970." *International Journal of Middle East Studies* [London], 5, 3, June 1974, 328–343.

Freeman, S. David. *Energy: The New Era.* New York: Vintage Books, 1974.

Freivalds, John. "Farm Corporations in Iran: An Alternative to Traditional Agriculture," *Middle East Journal*, 26, No. 2, Spring 1972, 185–194.

Frejka, Tomas. *The Future of Population Growth: A Population Council Book.* New York: John Wiley and Sons, 1973.

Frye, Richard N. *The Golden Age of Persia.* London: Weidenfeld and Nicolson, 1975.

_____. *Iran.* London: George Allen, 1954.

Frye, Richard Nelson (ed.). *The Cambridge History of Iran. Vol. IV.* Cambridge: Cambridge University Press, 1975.

Furlong, R.D.M. "Iran—A Power to be Reckoned With," *International Defense Review* [Geneva], 6, No. 6, December 1973, 719–729.

G

Garrod, Oliver. "The Qashqai Tribes of Fars." *Royal Central Asian Journal* [London], XXXIII, 1946, 293–306.

Garthwaite, Gene R. "The Bakhtiyari Ilkhani: An Illusion of Unity," *International Journal of Middle East Studies* [London], 8, No. 2, April 1977, 145–160.

_____. "The Bakhtiyari Khans: The Government of Iran and the British, 1846–1915," *International Journal of Middle East Studies* [London], 3, No. 1, January 1972, 24–44.

_____. "The Bakhtiyari in the Twentieth Century." (Prepared for delivery at the Sixth Annual Conference of the Middle East Studies Association of North America, State University of New York at Binghamton.) November 2–4, 1972.

Gates, David F. and Irving Heymont. "An Exploratory Study of the Role of the Armed Forces in Education: Iran, Israel, Peru, and Turkey." (Research Paper.) McLean, Virginia: Research Analysis Corporation, 1967.

Geographic and Drafting Institute. *Atlas of Iran: White Revolution Proceeds and Progresses.* Tehran.

Ghadiri, Bagher. "Aperćus Sur la Réforme Agraire en Iran." *Revue d'Economique Politique* [Paris], 85, No. 1, January–February 1975, 133–36.

Goodman, Raymond W., et al. "Iran," Pages 67–78 in *A Compendium of European Theater Terrorist Groups.* (A research study submitted to the faculty of the Air University.) Maxwell Air Force Base, Alabama: United States Air University, May 1976.

Graham, Robert. "Iran: Political Switch," *Financial Times* [London], July 28, 1977, 13.

_____. "Iran: Time for Tighter Belts," *Financial Times* [London],

July 25, 1977, 11.

_____. "Moscow steps up pressure against the Shah," *Financial Times* [London], November 23, 1976, 7.

_____. "A Most Troublesome Experiment: The Failure of Large Scale Commercial Farming in Iran," *Financial Times* [London], October 21, 1976, 6.

Guha, Sunil. "The Contribution of Non-farm Activities to Rural Employment Promotion: Experience in Iran, India, and Syria," *International Labour Review* [Geneva], 109, No. 1, January 1974, 235–250.

Gulick, Margaret E. and John Gulick. "Migrant and Native Married Women in the Iranian City of Isfahan." *Anthropological Quarterly*, 49, 1, January 1976, 53–61.

Gurfinkel, Mariano. "As Oil Prices Rise," *IMF Survey*, October 13, 1975, 297–305.

H

Hamby, Gavin. "Attitudes and Aspirations of the Contemporary Iranian Intellectual." *Royal Central Asian Journal* [London], LI, 57, April 1964, 127–140.

Hammeed, Kamal A. and Margaret N. Bennett. "Iran's Future Economy," *Middle East Journal*, 29, 4, Autumn 1975, 418–32.

Hammond World Atlas. Maplewood, New Jersey: Hammond Incorporated, 1971.

Hatami, Aziz. *Iran*. Tehran: General Department of Publications and Broadcasting, 1963.

Hendershot, Clarence. *Politics, Polemics and Pedagogs*. New York: Vantage Press, 1975.

Hess, Gary R. "The Iranian Crisis of 1944–46 and the Cold War," *Political Science Quarterly*, 89, No. 1, March 1974, 117–146.

Historical Atlas of the Muslim Peoples. Amsterdam: Djambatan, 1957.

Hitti, Philip K. *Islam, A Way of Life*. Minneapolis: University of Minnesota Press, 1970.

Hodgson, Marshall G.S. "How Did the Early Shia Become Sectarian," *Journal of the American Oriental Society*, 75, No. 1, January–March 1955, 1–13.

_____. *The Venture of Islam*. 3 vols. Chicago: University of Chicago Press, 1974.

Hout, Jean-Louis. *Persia I*. Cleveland: World Publishing Company, 1965.

"Human Rights in the World: Iran," *Review of the International Commission of Jurists* [Geneva], No. 8, June 1972, 5–10.

Hurewitz, J.C. *Middle East Politics: The Military Dimension*. New York: Praeger, 1969.

I

International Institute for Strategic Studies. *The Middle East and the International System, Pt. II: Security and the Energy Crisis*. (Adelphi Papers No. 115.) London: 1975.

_____. *The Military Balance, 1976–1977*. London: 1976.

————. *The Military Balance, 1977–1978.* London: 1977.
International Labour Office. *Report to Government of Iran on Labour Statistics.* Geneva: 1970.
International Planned Parenthood Federation. *Islam and Family Planning: A Faithful Translation of the International Islamic Conference Held in Rabat (Morocco),* I and II, December 1971. Beirut: International Planned Parenthood Federation, Middle East and North Africa Region, 1974.
"Interview with the Shah of Iran (with CBS news correspondent Mike Wallace)." (Transcript of "60 Minutes," VI, No. 9, March 19, 1974, produced by CBS News, New York.)
"Interview with the Shah of Iran (with CBS news correspondent Mike Wallace)." (Transcript of "60 Minutes," IX, No.6, October 24, 1976, produced by CBS News, New York.)
Iran. Embassy in Washington. "Banking in Iran." *Profile on Iran,* II, 4, April 1977, 4–36.
————. "Iran and the United Nations," *Profile on Iran,* September 1976, 1–59.
————. *Profile on Iran.* June, July, and August 1975.
————. *Profile on Iran.* April and May 1976.
Iran. Central Bureau of the Budget, Plan Organization. *The Budget for the Year 1351 (21 March 1972–20 March 1973).* Tehran: 1972.
Iran. Ministry of Economic Affairs and Finance. Customs Department. *Foreign Trade Statistics of Iran* (Annual) March 21, 1976 through March 21, 1977 and other years. Tehran: 1977.
Iran. Ministry of Information. "Anti-illiteracy Campaign in Iran," *Iran Facts and Figures* [Tehran], No. 11, December 1969.
————. *Her Imperial Majesty Farah Pahlavi, Shahbanou of Iran.* Tehran: January 1968.
————. "Iranian Workers After the White Revolution," *Iran Facts and Figures* [Tehran], No. 11, December 1969, n.p.
————. *Persepolis and Naghshe Rustam.* Tehran: Offset Press, 1966.
————. *Revolution in Iran's Agricultural System.* (Iran Facts and Figures Series, No. 16.) Tehran: February 1970.
————. *Transformation of Iranian Villages.* (Iran Facts and Figures, No. 5.) Tehran: September 1969.
Iran. Press and Information Office. "Agricultural Growth and Development in Iran." *Profile on Iran,* Tehran: January 1976, 1–40.
————. "Caviar: The Black Pearl of the Caspian Sea," *Profile on Iran,* Tehran: August 1976, 4–18.
————. "The Development of Education in Iran," *Profile on Iran,* Tehran: July 1976.
————. "Land Reform in Iran: A Perspective of Revolutionary Change," *Profile on Iran,* Tehran: October 1975, 3–30.
————. "Language of Iran," *Profile on Iran,* Tehran: February 1976, 3–33.

_____. "Tehran: The Capital of Iran," *Profile on Iran*, November 1975, entire issue.

Iran Almanac and Book of Facts, 1967. (6th ed.) Tehran: The Echo of Iran, 1967.

Iran Almanac and Book of Facts, 1969. (8th ed.) Tehran: The Echo of Iran, 1969.

Iran Almanac and Book of Facts, 1970. (9th ed.) Tehran: The Echo of Iran, 1970.

Iran Almanac and Book of Facts, 1971. (10th ed.) Tehran: The Echo of Iran, 1971.

Iran Almanac and Book of Facts, 1972. (11th ed.) Tehran: The Echo of Iran, 1972.·

Iran Almanac and Book of Facts, 1973. (12th ed.) Tehran: The Echo of Iran, 1973.

Iran Almanac and Book of Facts, 1974. (13th ed.) Tehran: The Echo of Iran, 1974.

Iran Almanac and Book of Facts, 1975. (14th ed.) Tehran: The Echo of Iran, 1975.

Iran Almanac and Book of Facts, 1976. (15th ed.) Tehran: The Echo of Iran, 1976.

Iran Almanac and Book of Facts, 1977. (16th ed.) Tehran: The Echo of Iran, 1977.

Iran Economic News. 3, No. 8, August 1977.

Iran Economic News. 3, No. 9, September 1977.

"Iran: Foreign Policy—Worry about U.S. Arms Cutbacks dominate Shah's diplomacy." *Middle East Economic Digest* [London], February 1977, 28–29.

"Iran: Trying So Much So Fast," *To The Point, International* [Antwerp], January 12, 1976, 6–9.

Iranian-American Economic Survey 1976/2535. New York: Manhattan Publishing, October 1976.

Irwin, G.W. *Roads and Redistribution: Special Cost and Benefits of Labour Intensive Road Construction in Iran.* Geneva: International Labour Organization, 1975.

Issawi, Charles. "The Tabriz—Trabzon Trade, 1830–1900: Rise and Decline of a Route," *International Journal of Middle East Studies* [London], 1, No. 1, June 1970, 18–27.

Ivanov, M.S. "Contemporary National Processes in Iran," *Central Asian Review* [London], XVI, No. 3, 1968, 223–228.

J

Jakubiak, Henry E. and M. Taher Dajani. "Oil Income and Financial Policies in Iran and Saudi Arabia." *Finance and Development*, 13, 4, December 1976, 12–15 and 42.

Joseph, Ralph. "Iran: Mounting Campaign Against Guerrillas," *Middle East* [London], No. 23, September 1976, 18–20.

Joyner, Christopher C. "The Petrodollar Phenomenon and Changing International Economic Relations," *World Affairs*, 138, No. 2, Fall 1975, 152–176.

K

Kappeler, Dietrich. "Iran: Transition and Hegemony," *Swiss Review of World Affairs* [Zurich], XXVII, 7 October 1977, 8–12, 21, 23, 25.

Katouzian, M.A. "Land Reform in Iran: A Case Study in the Political Economy of Social Engineering," *Journal of Peasant Studies* [London], 1, No. 2, January 1974, 220–39.

Kazemi, Farhad and Ervand Abrahamian. "The Non-Revolutionary Peasantry of Modern Iran." (U.S. Department of State, Office of External Research, Foreign Affairs Research Paper, No. FAR 26403.) Washington.

Keddie, Nikki R. "Iranian Politics, 1900–05: Background to Revolution, III," *Middle Eastern Studies* [London], 5, No. 3, October 1969, 234–250.

_____. "The Iranian Power Structure and Social Change 1800–1969: An Overview." *International Journal of Middle East Studies* [London], 2, No. 1, January 1971, 3–20.

_____. "Stratification, Social Control, and Capitalism in Iranian Villages: Before and After Land Reform." Pages 364–402 in Richard Antoun and Iliya Harik (eds.), *Rural Politics and Social Change in the Middle East*. Bloomington: Indiana University Press, 1972.

Kennedy, Edward M. "The Persian Gulf: Arms Race or Arms Control?" *Foreign Affairs*, 54, No. 1, October 1975, 14–35.

Khatibi, Nosratallah. "Land Reform in Iran and Its Role in Rural Development," *Land Reform, Land Settlement, and Cooperatives* [Rome], No. 2, 1972, 61–68.

Kiannejad, Hamid. "Poles of Spatial Discrimination in Promoting Development in Iran." Nagoya, Japan: United Nations, Center for Regional Development, April 1976.

Kinnane, Derek. "Iran: Bringing Literacy and Work Skills Together," *Panorama*, No. 49, 1971 (Fourth Quarter), 17–25.

Kirk, R.L. et al. "Genes and People in the Caspian Littoral: A Population Genetic Study in Northern Iran," *American Journal of Physical Anthropology*, 46, No. 3, May 1977, 377–390.

"Kissinger Looking at SAVAK Spies," *Iran Times*, VI, No. 33, November 5, 1976, I.

Kowsar, Mehdi. "Temporary or Contemporary?" *Ekistics* [Athens], 43, 256, March 1977, 144–148.

Kritzeck, James. *Modern Islamic Literature from 1800 to the Present*. New York: Holt, Rinehart, and Winston, 1970.

Kudsi-Zadeh, A. Albert. "Iranian Politics in the late Qajar Period: A Review," *Middle Eastern Studies* [London], 5, No. 3, October 1969, 251–256.

Kurtzig, Michael E. "U.S. Farm Exports to Iran Rebound," *Foreign Agriculture*, October 31, 1977, 204.

L

Lambton, Ann K.S. "Islamic Society in Persia." Pages 74–101 in Louise E. Sweet (ed.), *Peoples and Cultures of the Middle East,*

Vol. I: Depth and Diversity. New York: The Natural History Press, 1970.

————. "Land Reform and the Rural Cooperative Societies." Pages 5–43 in Ehsan Yar-Shater (ed.), *Iran Faces the Seventies.* New York: Praeger Publications, 1971.

————. *The Persian Dialects.* Hertford, England: Stephen Austin and Sons, 1938.

————. *The Persian Land Reform 1926–66.* New York: Oxford University Press, 1969.

Langer, Frederic. "Iran: Oil Money and the Ambitions of a Nation." (U.S. Department of State, Office of External Research, Foreign Affairs Research Paper, No. FAR 25573.) Washington: March 1975.

Law and Judicial Systems of Nations. Washington: World Peace Through Law Center, 1968.

Lenczowski, George. "The Communist Movement in Iran," *Middle East Journal,* 1, No. 1, January 1947, 29–45.

Levy, Reuben. *An Introduction to Persian Literature.* New York: Columbia University Press, 1969.

————. "Persia and the Arabs." Pages 69–93 in Stewart J. Robinson, (ed.), *The Traditional Near East.* Englewood Cliffs: Prentice-Hall, 1966.

————. *The Persian Language.* London: Hutchinson House, 1951.

Lifscultz, Lawrence. "Pakistan: Festering Dilemma for Bhutto," *Far Eastern Economic Review* [Hong Kong], 92, No. 22, May 28, 1976, 32–38.

Looney, Robert E. *The Economic Development of Iran: A Recent Survey with Projections to 1981.* New York: Praeger, 1973.

————. "Income Distribution Policies and Economic Growth in Semi-Industrialized Countries: A Comparative Study of Iran, Mexico, Brazil, and South Korea," *Journal of Economic Literature,* 14, No. 4, December 1976, 1313–1317.

M

McDonald, Patrick J. "The Iranian Military Build-up." (A research study submitted to the faculty of The Air Command and Staff College, Air University.) Maxwell Air Force Base, Alabama: United States Air University, May 1974.

McLachan, Keith, and Ghorban Narsi. "Oil Production, Revenues, and Economic Development." *Quarterly Economic Review* (Special No. 18.) London: The Economist Intelligence Unit Limited, 1975.

McLaughlin, Gerald T. "The Poppy is Not an Ordinary Flower: A Survey of Drug Policy in Iran," *Fordham Law Review,* XLIV, No. 4, March 1976, 701–772.

Mace, John. *Modern Persian.* New York: David McKay, 1974.

Magnus, Ralph H. "Middle East Oil," *Current History,* 68, No. 402, February 1975, 49–53.

Majidi, Abdol-Majid. "Iran 1980–85: Problems and Challenges of Development." *The World Today* [London], 33, 7, July 1977,

267–74.

Manzoor, Cyrus. "University Reform in Iran: Problems and Prospects," *Bulletin of the UNESCO Regional Office in Asia* [Bangkok], Supplement to Vol. III, No. 1, September 1972, 23–26.

Martell, Robert J. *Review of the "White Revolution" in Iran.* (Paper presented at the Seventeenth Session: Senior Seminar in Foreign Policy, Department of State, Washington D.C., 1974–1975.

Mauroy, H. de. "Les minorities sub-musselmanes dans la population iranienne." *Revue de Geographie de Lyon* [Lyon, France], 48, 2, 1973, 165–206.

Mehryar, A.H. "Relative Effect of Father's Education and 'Psychoticism' on Some Measures of Aptitude in Iran." *Perceptual and Motor Skills*, 44, 1977, 464–466.

Meier, Fritz. "The Mystic Path, the Sufi Tradition." Pages 117–140 in Bernard Lewis (ed.), *Islam and the Arab World.* New York: Alfred A. Knopf and American Heritage, 1976.

Meier, Richard L. "Teheran: A New World City." (Institute of Urban and Regional Development. Working Paper, No. 249.) Berkeley: University of California, November 1974.

——. "Update on Tehran and Its Environment." (Working Paper No. 273.) Berkeley: University of California, Institute of Urban and Regional Development, July 1976. (mimeo.)

Meister, Jurg. "Iran's Naval Buildup," *Swiss Review of World Affairs* [Zurich], XXIII, No. 4, July 1973.

Merchant, N.M., and Elaine L. Mura. "Environment and Sanitation: A Universal Priority," *Journal of Environmental Health*, 39, No. 1, July/August 1976, 58–60.

The Middle East and North Africa 1975–76. (22d ed.). London: Europa Publications, 1975.

Miller, William Green. "Political Organization in Iran from Dowreh to Political Party," *Middle East Journal*, 23, 2, Spring 1969, 159–176.

Mirvahabi, Farin. "The Status of Women in Iran," *Journal of Family Law*, 14, 3, Louisville: University of Louisville School of Law, 1975, 383–404.

Mobasser, Mohsen H. "National Police of Iran," *International Police Academy Review*, 2, No. 1, January 1968, 1–3, 12–13.

Mohammadi-Nejad, Hassan. "The Iranian Parliamentary Elections of 1975." *International Journal of Middle East Studies* [London], 8, No. 1, January 1977, 103–116.

Mohseni, Manouchehr. "Sociological Research in Iran," *International Social Science Journal*, XXVIII, No. 2, 1976, 337–90.

Momeni, Djamchid. "Husband-wife Age Differentials in Shiraz, Iran," *Social Biology*, 23, 4, Winter 1976, 341.

Momeni, Djamchid A. "Polygyny in Iran," *Journal of Marriage and the Family*, 37, 2, May 1975, 453–456.

Momeni, Jamshid A. (ed.). *The Population of Iran: A Selection of*

Readings. East-West Population Institute, The East-West Center, Honolulu, Hawaii and Pahlavi University, Shiraz, Iran, 1977.

Moorey, Peter Roser Stuart. *Ancient Iran.* Oxford: Ashmolean Museum, 1975.

Morgan, Theodore H. "Why Oil Prices Go Up: OPEC Wants Them," *Foreign Policy,* 25, Winter 1976–77, 58–77.

Mosley, Leonard. *Power Play.* New York: Random House, 1973.

Mottahedeh, Roy P. "The Shu'ubiyah Controversy and the Social History of Early Islamic Iran," *International Journal of Middle East Studies,* [London], 7, No. 2, April 1976, 161–182.

N

Naini, Ahmad. "The Fifth Development Plan," *Intereconomies* [Hamburg], No. 8, August 1975, 253–255.

Nasr, Isam R., Hasan S. Karmi, and Mahmud Y. Zayid. *Islam and Family Planning.* 2 Vols. Beirut, Lebanon: International Planned Parenthood Federation, 1974.

Nasr, Seyyed Hossein. *Islamic Philosophy in Contemporary Persia: A Survey of Activity During the Past 2 Decades.* Salt Lake City, Middle East Center, University of Utah, 1972.

_____. "Ithna Ashari Shiism and Iranian Islam." Pages 96–118 in A.J. Arberry (ed.), *Religion in the Middle East Vol. 2, Islam.* Cambridge: Cambridge University Press, 1969.

O

"The Oil Crisis in Perspective," *Daedalus,* 104, No. 4, Fall 1975.

Oppenheim, V. H. "Why Oil Prices Go Up: The Past; We Pushed Them," *Foreign Policy,* 25, Winter, 1976–77, 24–57.

Oren, Stephen. "The Assyrians of the Middle East," *Middle East Review* IX, No. 1, Fall 1976, 36–40.

P

Pace, Eric. "Corruption and Mistrust of Officials Continuing to Plague Iranian Government," *New York Times,* February 22, 1976, 16.

_____. "Shah Courts Popular Support: New Party System Aims at Broader Citizen's Role," *New York Times,* May 13, 1975, 4.

Pahlavi, Mohammad Reza. *Mission for My Country.* New York: McGraw-Hill, 1961.

_____. *The White Revolution of Iran.* Tehran: The Imperial Pahlavi Library, August 1967.

Paydarfar, Ali A. "The Modernization Process and Household Size: A Provincial Comparison for Iran," *Journal of Marriage and the Family,* 37, 2, May 1975, 446–452.

_____. *Social Change in a Southern Province in Iran.* Chapel Hill: University of North Carolina at Chapel Hill, 1974.

Pfau, Richard. "The Legal Status of American Forces in Iran." *Middle East Journal,* 28, No. 2, Spring 1974, 141–154.

Philipp, Mangal Bayat. "The Concepts of Religion and Government in the Thought of Marza Aqa Khan Kirmani. A Nineteenth

Century Persian Revolutionary," *International Journal of Middle East Studies* [London], 5, No. 4, September 1974, 381–400.

Psacharopoulos, George, and Gareth Williams. "Public Sector Earnings and Educational Plannings," *International Labour Review* [Geneva], 108, No. 1, July 1973, 43–57.

R

Rahman, Fazlur. *Islam*. New York: Doubleday, 1968.

Ramazani, Rouhollah K. *Foreign Policy of Iran, 1943–1974*. Charlottesville: University of Virginia Press, 1975.

――――. "Iran and the United States: An Experiment in Enduring Friendship," *Middle East Journal*, XXX, No. 3, Summer 1976, 322–350.

――――. "Iran's Changing Foreign Policy," *Middle East Journal*, XXIV, No. 4, Autumn 1970, 421–438.

――――. "Iran's Search for Regional Cooperation," *Middle East Journal*, XXX, No. 2, Spring 1976, 173–186.

――――. "Iran's White Revolution: A Study in Political Development," *International Journal of Middle East Studies* [London], 5, No. 2, April 1974, 124–139.

――――. *The Persian Gulf: Iran's Role*. Charlottesville: University of Virginia Press, 1972.

Rand, Christopher T. *Making Democracy Safe for Oil*. Boston: Atlantic-Little, Brown, 1975.

Razi, Gholam Hossein. "The Press and Political Institutions of Iran," *Middle East Journal*, XXII, No. 4, Autumn 1968, 463–474.

Reppa, Robert B., Sr. *Israel and Iran: Bilateral Relationship and Effect on the Indian Ocean Basin*. New York: Praeger, 1974.

The Revolution of the Shah and The People. London: Transorient Books, 1967.

Rischer, Gunter. "The Shah's Wider Share Ownership Programme," *Euromoney*, [London], January 1976, 35–42.

Roosevelt, Archie Jr. "The Kurdish Republic of Mahabad," *Middle East Journal*, I, No. 3, July 1947, 247–269.

Rosignoli, Guido. *Ribbons of Orders, Decorations and Medals*. New York: Acro Publishing Company, 1977.

Rosman, Abraham and Paula G. Rubel. "Nomad-Sedentary Interethnic Relations in Iran and Afghanistan," *International Journal of Middle East Studies*, [London] 7, No. 4, October 1976, 545–570.

Ross, Jay. "Iran Switches Economic Priorities, Plans Slower Industrial Development." *Washington Post*, August 20, 1977, 12.

Rotblat, H. "Social Organization and Development in an Iranian Provincial Bazaar," *Economic Development and Cultural Change*. 23, 2, January 1975, 292–305.

Rouleau, Eric. "The Shah's Dream of Glory," *Atlas World Press Review*, 24, No. 1, January 1977, 16–19.

Rypka, Jan. *History of Iranian Literature.* Dordrecht, Holland: D. Reidel, 1968.

S

Safai, Hossein. "Les Causes de Divorce en Droit Iranien Depuis La Réforme de 1967." *Revue Internationale de Droit Comparé,* [Paris], No. 1, January-March 1973, 69–79.

_____. "La Garde des Enfants en Droit Musulman Chiite et dans la Législation Iranienne." *Revue Internationale de Droit Comparé* [Paris], No. 3, July–September 1972, 551–562.

Sale, Richard T. "Arms Quarrels Strains U.S.-Iranian Ties," *Washington Post,* May 13, 1977, 1, 12.

_____. "The Shah's Americans," *Washington Post,* May 12, 1977, 1, 10.

_____. "Shah's Vision of Progress Clashes with Iran Reality." *Washington Post,* May 8, 1977, 14.

Sami, Ali. *Persepolis.* (Trans., R. Sharp.) Shiraz, Iran: Musavi Printing Office, Spring 1967.

Sampson, Anthony. *The Seven Sisters: The Great Oil Companies and the World They Made.* New York: Viking Press, 1975.

Saney, Parviz. *Law and Population Growth in Iran.* (Law and Monograph Series, No. 21.) Medford, Massachusetts: Fletcher School of Law and Diplomacy, 1974.

Sanghvi, Ramesh. *Aryamehr: The Shah of Iran—A Political Biography.* London: Transorient Books, 1968.

Sanghvi, Ramesh, Clifford German, and David Missen (eds.). *The Revolution of the Shah and the People.* London: Transorient Books, 1967.

Santone, Karl L. "Iran: Power in the Persian Gulf?" Unpublished research study. Maxwell Air Force Base, 1974.

"SAVAK." (Transcript of "60 Minutes," IX, No. 24, March 6, 1977, produced by CBS News, New York.)

Savory, Roger. "Land of the Lion and the Sun." Pages 245–272 in Bernard Lewis (ed.), *Islam and the Arab World.* New York: Alfred A. Knopf and American Heritage, 1976.

_____. "The Principle of Homeostasis Considered in Relation to Political Events in Iran in the 1960s," *International Journal of Middle East Studies* [London], 3, No. 3, July 1972, 282–302.

Schulz, Ann T. "Iran's New Industrial State." *Current History,* 72, 423, January 1977, 15–18 and 38.

Schuon, Frithjof. *Understanding Islam.* (The Penguin Metaphysical Library Series). Baltimore: Penguin Books, 1972.

Scuka, Dario. *"O.P.E.C., Background, Review and Analysis."* (Library of Congress, Congressional Service, HD 9560 Middle East, 74–189E.) Washington: Library of Congress, October 24, 1974.

Sedghi, Hamideh. "Women in Iran." Pages 219–228 in Lynne B. Iglitzin and Ruth Ross (eds.), *Women in the World—a Comparative Study.* Santa Barbara, California: Clio Press, 1976.

Shahanshah. "Shahanshah: Iran will make it, Iranian-style," *Kayhan Weekly International Edition* [Tehran], December 11, 1976, 4–5.

Shapiro, W. "Arming the Shah: Arms for the Rule," *Washington Monthly*, 6, No. 12, February 1975, 28–32.

Shapurian, Reza and Peter F. Merenda. "Iranian Students' Perceptions of Hovayda and the Ideal Self." *Perceptual and Motor Skills*, 43, No. 1, August 1976, 40–42.

Shirin, Tahir-Kheli. "Iran and Pakistan: Cooperation in an Area of Conflict," *Asian Survey*, XVII, No. 5, May 1977, 474–490.

Shojar, Donald A. "Western Influence on the Development of Modern Iranian Literature." (Paper presented at the Conference on Near Eastern Society in Literature, May 1976.) Princeton: Princeton University, May 1976.)

Singer, A. "Tribal Migrations on the Irano-Afghan Border," *Asian Affairs* [London], 60, No. 2, 1973, 160–165.

Smart, Ian. "Future Political Patterns in the Middle East." *The World Today* [London], XXXII, No. 7, July 1976, 243–250.

_____. "Oil, the Super-Power and the Middle East," *International Affairs* [London], 53, No. 1, January 1977, 17–35.

Smolansky, O.M. "Moscow and the Persian Gulf: An Analysis of Soviet Ambitions and Potential." *Orbis*, XIV, No. 1, Spring 1970, 92–108.

Spooner, Brian. "Continuity and Change in Rural Iran: The Eastern Deserts." Pages 1–19 in Peter J. Chelkowski (ed.), *Iran: Continuity and Change*. New York: The Center for Near Eastern Studies and the Center for International Studies, New York University, 1971.

The Statesman's Year-book, 1976–77. (Ed., John Paxton.) New York: St. Martin's Press, 1976.

Statistical Yearbook, 1974. (26th ed.). New York: Statistical Office, Department of Economic and Social Affairs, United Nations, 1975.

Stevens, Roger. *The Land of the Great Sophy*. London: Methuen, 1962.

Stockholm International Peace Research Institute. *World Armaments and Disarmament, SIPRI Yearbook 1977*. Cambridge: The MIT Press, 1977.

"A Survey of Iran," *The Economist*, [London], August 28, 1976.

Sykes, Percy. *A History of Persia*. 2 vols. London: Macmillan, 1963.

Syzliowicz, Joseph S. *Education and Modernization in the Middle East*. Ithaca: Cornell University Press, 1973.

T

Tabatabai, Allamah Sayyid Muhammad Husayn. *Shiite Islam*. Albany: State University of New York Press, 1975.

Tahtinen, Dale R. *Arms in the Persian Gulf*. Washington: American Enterprise Institute for Public Policy Research, 1974.

Talbot-Rice, David. *Islamic Art*. New York: Praeger, 1965.

Text of His Imperial Majesty the Shahanshah Aryamehr's Order for the Formation of Iran National Resurgence Party. Tehran: Ministry of Information and Tourism, March 1975.

Thurgood, Liz. "Iranian Police Tighten Screws," *Manchester Guardian* [Manchester], January 9, 1977.

"Torture as Policy: The Network of Evil," *Time*, August 16, 1976, 31–34.

Treadway, Roye, Robert W. Gillespie, and Mehdi Loghmani. "The Model Family Planning Project in Isfahan, Iran," *Studies in Family Planning*, 7, 11, March 1976, 308–321.

U

United Nations Educational, Scientific and Cultural Organization. *World Guide to Higher Education*. Paris: UNESCO Press, 1976.

_____. *World Survey of Education, IV: Higher Education*. Paris: UNESCO Press, 1966.

_____. *World Survey of Education, V: Policy, Legislation and Administration*. Paris: UNESCO Press, 1971.

U.S. Agency for International Development. Bureau for Population and Humanitarian Assistance. Office of Population. *United States Aid to Developing Countries*. Washington: GPO, 1974.

U.S. Central Intelligence Agency. *National Basic Intelligence Factbook*. Washington: GPO, 1977.

_____. *Research Aid, Handbook of Economic Statistics, 1975*. McLean: August 1975.

_____. *Research Aid, Handbook of Economic Statistics, 1976*. McLean: September 1976.

_____. *Research Aid, Handbook of Economic Statistics, 1977*. McLean: September 1977.

U.S. Congress. 92nd, 2nd Session. House of Representatives. Committee on Foreign Affairs. Subcommittee on the Near East. *U.S. Interests in and Policy Toward the Persian Gulf*. Washington: GPO, 1972.

U.S. Congress. 93rd, 1st Session. House of Representatives. Committee on Foreign Affairs on the Near East and South Asia. *New Perspectives on the Persian Gulf*. Washington: GPO, 1973.

U.S. Congress, 93rd, 2nd Session. House of Representatives. Committee on Foreign Affairs. Subcommittee on the Near East and South Asia. *The Persian Gulf, 1974: Money, Politics, Arms, and Power*. Washington, GPO, 1974.

_____. Senate. Committee on Foreign Relations. Subcommittee on Multinational Corporations. *Multinational Corporations and United States Foreign Policy, Hearings, February 20 and 21, March 27 and 28, 1974*. Washington: GPO, 1974.

U.S. Congress. 94th, 1st Session. House of Representatives. Committee on International Relations. *United States Arms Sales to the Persian Gulf*. Washington: GPO, 1975.

U.S. Congress. 94th, 2d Session. House of Representatives.
Committee on International Relations. Subcommittee on International Organization. *Human Rights in Iran.* Washington:
GPO, August 3–September 1976.
———. House of Representatives. Committee on International
Relations. Subcommittee on International Organizations.
*Human Rights and U.S. Policy: Argentina, Haiti, Indonesia,
Iran, Peru, and the Philippines.* Washington: GPO, December
31, 1976.
———. House of Representatives. Committee on International
Relations. Subcommittee on International Organizations.
Human Rights in Iran (Hearings, August 3 and September 8,
1976). Washington: GPO, September 1976.
———. Senate. Committee on Foreign Relations. Subcommittee
on Foreign Assistance. *U.S. Military Sales to Iran.* Washington:
GPO, July 1976.
U.S. Department of Commerce. Office of Technical Services.
Joint Publications Research Service—JPRS (Washington).
The following items are from the JPRS series:
Translations on Iran.
"Background of Alsthom Contract Case Reviewed." *Iran
Political Digest,* 11 September 1977. (JPRS 69946, October
12, 1977, 42–49.
"Nation's 1976–77 Budget Detailed, Compared with Past
Two Years." *Ettelaat,* 3 February 1976. (JPRS No. 66955,
March 12, 1976, 1–44.)
"Role of Agriculture in Independence National Policy." *Iran
Political Digest,* 18 September 1977. (JPRS: 69946, October
12, 1977, 50–57.)
Translations on Near East.
"Civil Service Act Amended," *Kayhan,* Tehran, December 2,
1972. (JPRS: 58038, No. 888, January 23, 1973.)
"Drive to Decentralize," *Kayhan International,* Tehran,
August 31, 1974. (JPRS: 63076, No. 1237, September 27,
1974.)
"Public in Despair with Judicial System," *Khandaniha,*
Tehran, May 7, 1974. (JPRS: 62168, No. 1173, June 5,
1974.)
Translations on Near East and North Africa.
"Branches of the Two Wings Being Formed in the Majlis,"
Kayhan, Tehran, July 12, 1975. (JPRS 65991, No. 1429,
October 23, l975.)
"Civil Service Codes to be Amended," *Ettelaat,* Tehran,
February 24, 1975. (JPRS: 64928, No. 1359, June 5, 1975.
Ganji, Manuchehr. "Power Must be Distributed Throughout
the Country," *Ettelaat,* Tehran, May 10, 1976. (JPRS:
76445, No. 1525, June 14, 1976.)
"Law on Formation of Sharestan and Provincial Councils is
Modified," *Ettelaat,* Tehran, June 25, 1975. (JPRS: 65482,

No. 1396, August 18, 1975.)

"People Urged to Take Part in Elections," *Ettelaat*, Tehran, May 6, 1975. (JPRS: 65033, No. 1366, June 18, 1975.)

"Prime Minister, at a Meeting of Rural Cooperative Employees, States: Decentralization Policy Can Be One of Most Important Factors in Iran's Progress," *Restakhiz*, Tehran, February 15, 1976. (JPRS: 67144, No. 1501, April 15, 1976.)

"Prime Minister's Reception Honoring Candidates Who Did Not Make It to the Majlis: Hoveyda, The Wings Do Not Mean Blocs or Parliamentary Majorities and Minorities: Final Decision on Viewpoints of Wings Belongs to the Party," *Kayhan*, Tehran, July 23, 1975. (JPRS: 65969, No. 1428, October 21, 1975.)

U.S. Department of Health, Education and Welfare. *Social Security Programs Throughout the World, 1973*. Washington: December 1973.

U.S. Department of State. *Country Reports on Human Rights Practices*. (Report submitted to the Committee on International Relations, U.S. House of Representatives, and Committee on Foreign Relations, U.S. Senate, February 3, 1978.) Washington: GPO, December 1978.

U.S. Department of State. Bureau of Intelligence and Research. *World Strength of the Communist Party Organizations, 1973*. Washington: GPO, 1974.

U.S. Department of State. Bureau of Public Affairs. Office of Media Services. *Background Notes: Iran*. (Department of State publication No. 7760.) Washington: GPO, December 1976.

U.S. Embassy in Tehran. *Iran: Agricultural Situation*. Tehran, February 7, 1976. (mimeo.).

V

van der Molen, Gerben. "Economic Impacts of Education and Personnel Management: Case Studies from Industrial Sector in Iran and Surinam," *Economic Development and Change*, No. 7, 1976, 45–65.

Varlet, Henri and Jessik Mammoumian. "Education for Tribal Populations in Iran," *Prospects: A Quarterly Review of Education*, 5, No. 2, 1975, 37–47.

Vielle, Paul. "Un mariage en Iran." *Revue francaise de Sociologie* [Paris], VII, 1, Janviers–Mars, 1966, 48–57.

Vielle, Paul and Morteza Kotobi. "Familles et Unions de Familles en Iran." *Cahiers Internationaux de Sociologie* [Paris], XIII, 41, 1966, 93–104.

Vreeland, Herbert H. (ed.). *Iran*. New Haven: Human Relations Area Files, 1957.

W

Watson, Kenneth. "The Shah's White Revolution: Education and Reform in Iran," *Comparative Education*, 12, No. 1, March

1976, n.p.

Weinbaum, Marvin G. "Iran Finds a Party System: The Institutionalization of Iran Novin," *Middle East Journal*, 27, No. 4, Autumn 1973.

Whitley, Andrew. "Flexible View on Foreign Affairs," *Financial Times* [London], July 25, 1977, 13.

Wilber, Donald N. *Iran Past and Present* (7th ed.). Princeton: Princeton University Press, 1975.

_____. *Riza Shah Pahlavi: The Resurrection and Reconstruction of Iran, 1878–1944*. Hicksville: Exposition Press, 1975.

Wilson, Barbara A. "Target Environment and Situation Analysis-Iran." Washington: Center for Research in Social Systems, Cultural Information Analysis Center, The American University, May 1967.

Woodward, Bob. "IBEX: Deadly Symbol of U.S. Arms Sales Problems," *Washington Post*, January 2, 1977, A1, A17.

World Debt Tables. Vol. I and II. (Ec–167–77) Washington: International Bank for Reconstruction and Development, September 2, 1977.

World Debt Tables—Supplements (Ec–167/77S4.) Washington: International Bank for Reconstruction and Development, September 7, 1977.

World Health Organization. *Fifth Report on the World Health Situation, 1969–72*. (Official Reports No. 225). Geneva: 1975.

The World of Learning, 1975–76. London: Europa Publications, 1975.

Wright, Sir Denis. "Iran: Ancient Land of Great Potential," *Optima* [Johannesburg, South Africa], 23, No. 2, June 1973, 105–112.

Wrobel, Brian. "Human Rights in Iran." (Amnesty International Report. Testimony to the Subcommittee on International Organizations of the Committee on International Relations of the U. S. House of Representatives, February 28, 1978.) (mimeo.).

Y

Yager, Joseph A., and Eleanor B. Steinberg. *Energy and U. S. Foreign Policy*. Cambridge: Ballinger Publishing, 1974.

Yar-Shater, Ehsan (ed.). *Iran Faces the Seventies*. New York: Praeger, 1971.

Year Book of Labour Statistics, 1976 (36th ed.). Geneva: International Labour Office, 1976.

Yost, Charles W. "U. S. and Iran: Repairing Rifts," *Christian Science Monitor*, June 3, 1976, 27.

Z

Zabih, Sepher. *The Communist Movement in Iran*. Berkeley: University of California Press, 1966.

_____. "Iran Today." *Current History*, 66, 390, February 1974, 66–69, 87.

_____. "Iran's International Posture: De Facto Nonalignment

within a Pro-Western Alliance." *Middle East Journal*, XXIV, No. 3, Summer 1970, 302–318.

Zand, S. "OPEC: Birth, Growth, Achievements." (Paper presented at the Seminar on International Oil, April 14, 1975.) Washington: The American University, 1975. (mimeo.).

Zonis, Marvin. *The Political Elite of Iran*. Princeton: Princeton University Press, 1971.

(Various issues of the following periodicals were also used in the preparation of this book: *Arab Report and Record* [London], January 1975–January 1977; *The Asian Recorder* [New Delhi], June 1970–October 1977; *Christian Science Monitor* [Boston], June 1970–December 1977; *Financial Times* [London], January 1975–November 1977; *Foreign Broadcast Information Service* [Washington], January 1974–December 1977; *IMF International Financial Statistics* [Washington], 1970–November 1977; *Iran Economic News* [Washington], January 1975–November 1977; *Kayhan International* [Tehran], January 1975–August 1977; *Keesing's Contemporary Archives* [London], January 1971–October 1977; *Middle East Economic Digest* [London], January 1974–November 1977; *New York Times*, June 1970–December 1977; *Profile on Iran* [Tehran], January 1975–August 1977; and *Washington Post*, June 1970–December 1977.)

Glossary

barrels per day—Production of crude oil and petroleum products is frequently measured in barrels per day, often abbreviated bpd or bd. A barrel is a volume measure of forty-two United States gallons. Conversion of barrels to metric tons depends on the density of the specific product. About 7.3 barrels of average crude oil weigh one metric ton. Heavy crude would be about seven per metric ton. Light products, such as gasoline and kerosine, would average close to eight barrels per metric ton.

downstream—The oil industry views the production, processing, transportation, and sale of petoleum products as a flow process starting at the wellhead. Downstream includes any stage between the point of reference and the sale of products to the consumer. Upstream is the converse and includes exploration and drilling of wells.

fifth plan—Iran's development plans have been of varying length and had various names, some of which appeared incorrect in their English translations (e.g., the Fifth Five Year National Development Plan, 1973–78). The plans and their dates were: First Development Plan—September 21, 1948, to September 20, 1955; Second Development Plan—September 21, 1955, to September 20, 1962; Third Development Plan—September 21, 1962, to March 20, 1968; Fourth Development Plan—March 21, 1968, to March 20, 1973; and Fifth Development Plan—March 21, 1973, to March 20, 1978.

fiscal year (FY)—Corresponds to the Iranian calendar year, which begins March 21 and ends March 20 (see fig. A).

hadith—Tradition based on the precedent of Muhammad's words and deeds that serves as one of the sources of Islamic law (sharia).

hijra (pl., *hujar*)—Literally, to migrate, to sever relations, to leave one's tribe. Throughout the Muslim world hijra refers to the migration of Muhammad and his followers to Medina. In this sense the word has come into European languages as Hegira and is usually and somewhat misleadingly translated as flight.

imam—A word used in several senses. In general use it means the leader of congregational prayers; as such it implies no ordination or special spiritual powers beyond sufficient education to carry out this function. It is also used figuratively by many Sunni (*q.v.*) Muslims to mean the leader of the Islamic community. Among Shiites (*q.v.*) the word takes on many complex and controversial meanings; in general, however, it indicates that particular descendant of the House of Ali who is believed to have been God's designated repository of the spiritual authority inherent in that line. The identity of this individual and the means of ascertaining his identity have been the major issues causing divisions among Shiites.

Islamic clergy—The religious leaders of Shiite Islam, which group

477

includes numerous mullahs, who in general possess only rudimentary religious education; *mujtahids,* a relatively small body of religious scholars; and a few *ayatollahs,* the most learned and revered of the *mujtahids.*

jihad—The struggle to establish the law of God on earth, often interpreted to mean holy war.

kadkhuda—Literally, "little god"; traditionally the landlord's agent and/or the village headman in rural society; also used as the name for leaders of tribal clans.

kalantar—Leader of a subtribe; also used as the name for the head of a guild.

mujtahid—See Islamic clergy.

rial—The Iranian currency unit composed of 100 dinars. Ten rials equal one toman. In 1957 the par value of the rial was established with the International Monetary Fund (IMF) at 75.75 rials per US$1. This par value remained in effect until 1973 although the rial value changed vis-à-vis other currencies. In September 1972 the rial par value in terms of special drawing rights (SDRs), the IMF market basket of currencies, was depreciated with IMF concurrence to 82.2425 rials per 1 SDR and the gold content of the rial established at 0.0108055 gram. This par value with the SDR remained in effect in 1977 although the market rate of the rial/SDR varied a little from year to year. In February 1975 the rial was pegged to the SDR instead of the US dollar. Since 1972 the rial/dollar exchange rate varied. It was 68.88 rials per US$1 in 1973, 67.62 rials per US$1 in 1974, 67.64 rials per US$1 in 1975, 70.22 rials per US$1 in 1976, and 70.62 rials per US$1 through September 1977.

In January 1974 the central bank authorized two exchange markets—the commercial or official and the noncommercial or free market. The markets were structured in a manner to bring the official and free market exchange rates together. Between June 1974 and late 1977 the free market exchange rate was identical to the official rate. The combination of the two markets and some other changes made the rial largely free of exchange restrictions. The central bank quoted only an official rate for the US dollar but published daily rates for fourteen other currencies (to facilitate circulation of fees and duties) based on the London market rate against the dollar.

rud—Farsi word for river.

shaykh—Leader or chief. Word of Arabic origin used to mean either a political or a learned religious leader. Also used as an honorific.

Shiite (or Shia)—A member of the smaller of the two great divisions of Islam. The Shiites supported the claims of Ali and his line to presumptive right to the caliphate and leadership of the world Muslim community, and on this issue they divided from the Sunni *(q.v.)* in the first great schism of Islam. Later schisms have produced further divisions among the Shiites.

Sunni—The larger of the two great divisions of Islam. The Sunnis who rejected the claim of Ali's line believe that they are the true followers of the Sunna, the guide to proper behavior composed of the Quran and the hadith *(q.v.)*.

waqf (pl., *awqaf*)—In Muslim law a permanent endowment or trust, usually of real estate, in which the proceeds are spent for purposes designated by the benefactor. Usually devoted to public or private charitable purposes.

weights and measures—Iran officially employs the metric system, but an earlier indigenous system remains in use in the bazaars and rural markets. Common units in relation to metric units are: Weights: one *seer* equals seventy-five grams; one *charak* equals 750 grams; four *charak* equal one *man,* which equals three kilograms; 100 *man* equal one *kharvar,* which equals 300 kilograms. Measures: one *zar* equals 100 centimeters; 6,000 *zar* equal one *farsakh;* one *farsakh* equals, approximately, six kilometers, although sometimes used to equal ten kilometers.

White Revolution--As promulgated by the shah in January 1963 (as the White Revolution of the Shah and the People), consisted of six reform measures, the most important of which provided for land reform. By 1977 thirteen other measures had been added and the program had become known as the Shah-People Revolution.

Index

police. *See* gendarmerie; National Police
political offenses: 192, 201–202, 207, 208, 382
political parties (*see also* specific names): xvi, 54, 55, 56, 59, 64, 208–213; communist-inspired, 363
polygyny: 176
population: xvi, 70–74, 422
ports: xxviii, 12, 252, 253, 278, 301, 323
Portuguese: 43
prestige: foreign affairs ministry, 227; foreign university degrees, 102; landowners, 164; military officers, 205, 391, 392, 396, 397; teachers, 105
Price, Harold: 364
prices: 86, 87, 278; controlled, 258, 266, 272
primary schools: 95, 96, 97, 98, 423
prisons: 374, 383–384
private schools: 102
Protestants: 135
provinces: xvii, 192, 194

Qaboos, Sultan: 400
Qadikolahi tribe: 148
Qajar: dynasty, xiii, 19, 45–48, 72, 151, 390; family, 156, 184
qanat system: 13, 25, 48, 333
Qarepakhs: 151
Qashqai tribes: xvi, 57, 72, 148, 149, 150–151, 363
Qatar: 229, 236, 446, 450, 453
Qazvin: 76, 302, 354
Qeshm Island: 43, 306
Qom: 143, 302, 366
Qom madrasah: 126, 127, 129
Qsar prison: 383
Qumsari dialect: 140
Quran: 115, 117, 120, 123, 141
Quraysh tribe: 115

Rabii, Amir Hossein: 406
radar network: 406, 408
radio and television: 5, 88, 253; communist stations, 232, 362; gendarmerie network, 369
railroads: xviii, xxviii, 252, 265, 310
rainfall: xv, 11, 12, 331
Rasht: 194, 302
Rastakhiz Party. *See* Iran National Resurgence Party
Razmara, Ali: 59

recreation: 87–88
Red Cross: 89, 384
Red Lion and Sun Society: 89, 92
religion: xvi, 33, 34, 35, 109–136
religious law (shariah): 109, 173, 174, 190
research: 96, 98
Reuter, Paul Julius von: 48, 254, 286
Reza Cyrus, Prince: 65, 186
Reza Khan (*see also* Pahlavi, Reza Shah): 52, 53, 371, 390, 391
Reza Radmanesh: 363
Reza Shah. *See* Pahlavi, Reza Shah
Reza Shah Kabir Dam: 312
Rezaiyeh: 194, 402
rice: 346–348, 433
riots and rebellion: 204–205, 366, 367, 396; terrorist groups, 361, 363, 364
roads and highways: xviii, xxviii, 25, 234, 252, 289
Roman Catholics: 135, 154
Roman influence: 30, 31, 113
Roosevelt, Franklin D.: 56
rugs and carpets: 259, 283, 309, 316, 347, 355, 427
rural areas: 69, 76, 84, 89, 165–170, 423; diet, 82; education, 96, 98, 104; gendarmerie, 368; health, 92, 93
Russia (*see also* Soviet Union): influence on Iran, xiii, 19, 44, 45, 46, 48, 49, 50, 51, 150, 231, 414; language, 143, 144; tea from, 349

Sadat, Mohammad Anwar as–: 239
Sadozai tribe: 148
Safavi, Nabab: 361
Safavid dynasty: 40–44, 109, 116
Saffarid dynasty: 37
Safi al Din: 41
Safid Rud Dam: 347
Samanid dynasty: 37
Sanandaj: 194, 402
Sandipour, Reza: 364
Saravan tribe: 148
Sari: 194
Sasani tribe: 148
Sassanian Empire: xi, 3, 19, 30–33, 36, 112, 114, 115, 116; language, 140
satrapy system: 24
Saudi Arabia: 63, 229, 236, 237, 260; oil, 297, 445, 446, 447, 450, 451, 452, 453
SAVAK. *See* National Intelligence and Security Organization
Savory, Roger: 122

Published Country Studies
(Area Handbook Series)

550-65	Afghanistan		550-21	India
550-98	Albania		550-154	Indian Ocean
550-44	Algeria			Territories
550-59	Angola		550-39	Indonesia
550-73	Argentina		550-68	Iran
550-169	Australia		550-31	Iraq
550-176	Austria		550-25	Israel
550-175	Bangladesh		550-182	Italy
550-170	Belgium		550-69	Ivory Coast
550-66	Bolivia		550-177	Jamaica
550-20	Brazil		550-30	Japan
550-168	Bulgaria		550-34	Jordan
550-61	Burma		550-56	Kenya
550-83	Burundi		550-50	Khmer Republic
550-166	Cameroon			(Cambodia)
550-96	Ceylon		550-81	Korea, North
550-159	Chad		550-41	Korea, Republic of
550-77	Chile		550-58	Laos
550-60	China, People's		550-24	Lebanon
	Republic of		550-38	Liberia
550-63	China, Republic of		550-85	Libya
550-26	Colombia			
550-67	Congo, Democratic		550-163	Malagasy Republic
	Republic of (Zaire)		550-172	Malawi
550-91	Congo, People's		550-45	Malaysia
	Republic of		550-161	Mauritania
550-90	Costa Rica		550-79	Mexico
550-152	Cuba		550-76	Mongolia
550-22	Cyprus		550-49	Morocco
550-158	Czechoslovakia		550-64	Mozambique
550-54	Dominican Republic		550-35	Nepal, Bhutan and
550-52	Ecuador			Sikkim
550-43	Egypt		550-88	Nicaragua
550-150	El Salvador		550-157	Nigeria
550-28	Ethiopia		550-94	Oceania
550-167	Finland		550-48	Pakistan
550-29	Germany		550-46	Panama
550-155	Germany, East		550-156	Paraguay
550-173	Germany, Federal		550-92	Peripheral States of
	Republic of			the Arabian
550-153	Ghana			Peninsula
550-87	Greece		550-85	Persian Gulf States
550-78	Guatemala		550-42	Peru
550-174	Guinea		550-72	Philippines
550-82	Guyana		550-162	Poland
550-164	Haiti		550-181	Portugal
550-151	Honduras		550-160	Romania
550-165	Hungary		550-84	Rwanda

550-51	Saudi Arabia	550-53	Thailand
550-70	Senegal	550-178	Trinidad and Tobago
550-180	Sierra Leone	550-89	Tunisia, Republic of
550-184	Singapore	550-80	Turkey
550-86	Somalia		
550-93	South Africa, Republic of	550-74	Uganda
		550-97	Uruguay
550-171	Southern Rhodesia	550-71	Venezuela
550-95	Soviet Union	550-57	Vietnam, North
550-179	Spain	550-55	Vietnam, South
550-27	Sudan, Democratic Republic of	550-183	Yemens, The
550-47	Syria	550-99	Yugoslavia
550-62	Tanzania	550-75	Zambia

☆ U.S. GOVERNMENT PRINTING OFFICE : 1978 O—280-990